Contents

Contributors

Editors

Boping Yuan

Sally K. Church

Appendices

Sarah Waldram

Yicheng Wu

Proprietary terms

Introduction

The *Oxford Beginner's Chinese Dictionary* represents a major departure from traditional bilingual dictionaries on several fronts. It has been specially designed for beginners and is not simply a scaled-down version of a larger dictionary. It approaches the specific needs of the English-speaking learner of Chinese from a very different angle.

It looks different

The dictionary page is refreshingly uncluttered, with streamlined typeface and symbols providing a consistent structure for the information both in English and Chinese. Subdivisions of text are clearly indicated using bullet points and Arabic numerals. The move from one language to the other is explicitly indicated in **=** signs. Points of basic grammar are reinforced using the **!** signs, and informal or colloquial usage is marked ✖ for Chinese.

It provides essential information in a new way

Every effort has been made to approach the foreign language from the point of view of the beginner who may be unfamiliar with the conventions of the more traditional bilingual dictionary.

The only abbreviations you will find are those which are entirely self-explanatory as headwords in the wordlist. Parts of speech and grammatical terms are all given in full, with a glossary providing explanations and examples of different parts of speech in use. More complex grammatical issues are dealt with in short notes at appropriate points in the text or in the more detailed boxed grammar notes. All Chinese headwords and examples are presented in both *pinyin* (the Chinese phonetic system) and Chinese characters to make the dictionary more user-friendly for beginners. Only simplified characters are used.

Sets of words which behave in a similar way are treated in a consistent manner and the user is encouraged to cross-refer to different parts of the dictionary, for example, to the boxed usage note on *Age* and the boxed note on *Be*, to learn the correct expressions.

The language used in examples and in sense indicators (or signposts to the correct translation) is carefully screened and reflects current English and Chinese as it is based on up-to-date corpus information.

British and American varieties of English are covered and clearly labelled on the English-Chinese side, while users on both sides of the Atlantic will recognize the appropriate English-language equivalent for items in the Chinese-English part of the dictionary.

The two sides of the dictionary have distinct functions

Each side of the dictionary is shaped by its specific function. The Chinese-English side is designed to capitalize on what English speakers know about their language, hence the more streamlined presentation of English-language information. The *Oxford Beginner's Chinese Dictionary* provides generous coverage of those aspects of Chinese which are less easy to decode for English speakers.

The English-Chinese side is longer, providing the user of the foreign language with maximum guidance in the form of detailed coverage of essential grammar, clear signposts to the correct translation for a particular context, and lots of examples.

The *Oxford Beginner's Chinese Dictionary* is unique as an accessible and user-friendly introduction to the Chinese language. It has been designed to deal with the perennial problems of language learning and language teaching in a radically different way.

How to use the dictionary

The English into Chinese side

The English into Chinese side of the dictionary attempts to give full guidance on how to write and speak correctly in Chinese. Plenty of examples are given to demonstrate not only the translation of words into Chinese but also hints about their usage in Chinese sentences. You will find additional information on grammatical points, such as the use of words in certain contexts, in the grammatical notes that occur within the entries on certain words. These notes are designed to help you produce correct Chinese in areas where mistakes are frequently made. Information about alternative pronunciations is also given in these notes.

If you are unable to translate an English word into Chinese because you cannot find it in the wordlist, try to use another word with the same or a similar sense, or choose another form of wording which will enable you to find what you're looking for. For instance, if you want to translate the adjective *complex* but cannot find it in the dictionary, you could try *complicated* as an alternative, which gives *fùzá* 复杂 as the Chinese equivalent.

A very useful feature of this dictionary is the boxed usage notes which cover sets of related words based on topics such as *games and sports*, *days of the week*, and *nationalities*. At the entry for *fireman*, you'll see a number which refers you to the page containing a boxed note dealing with *shops, trades, and professions*. (See **The structure of English-Chinese entries** for an illustration.) The information there is relevant for all other words of this kind in the dictionary.

The Chinese into English side

The Chinese into English side of the dictionary is organized alphabetically by *pinyin* spelling. If you already know the *pinyin* romanization for a word, you can go straight to the Chinese-English side and look it up alphabetically. Words that have the same *pinyin* spelling but different tones are arranged according to tone, with the first tone first, followed by the second, third, fourth, and neutral tones. (See the section on **Tones in Mandarin Chinese** for information on tones.) Thus *fán* will come before *fǎn*, and *bǎ* will come before *bà*. Words beginning with the same character are grouped together to give a sense of the semantic range of that character. Words that begin with different characters having the same romanization and tone are arranged according to the number of strokes in the character, with the smaller number first. Thus *jiān* 尖 comes before *jiān* 肩 because the former has six strokes and the latter eight strokes. If words or compounds begin with the same character, romanization, and tone, they are arranged alphabetically according to the first letter of the second syllable or word in *pinyin*. For example, *miànqián* comes before *miàntiáor*.

In the cases of *yi* 一 (*one*) and *bu* 不 (*not*), where the tone of the character changes depending on the character that follows it (see the subsection on **Tone Changes** in the section on **Tones in Mandarin Chinese**), all words and compounds beginning with the character in question are listed together, regardless of tone, and are arranged alphabetically by the *pinyin* romanization of the second character in the word or compound. For instance, *bùguǎn* 不管 is listed before *búyào* 不要 because *g* comes before *y* in the alphabet, even though *bu* in the first has a fourth tone and *bu* in the second has a second tone.

If you have only the Chinese character but do not know how it is pronounced, or spelled in *pinyin*, you can use the **Radical Index** and the **Character Index** in the **Index** section to find the pronunciation.

How to use the Index

The **Index** is divided into the **Radical Index** and the **Character Index**. The **Character Index** lists every character that is either a headword or the first character of a headword in the dictionary. It lists them by radical and provides their *pinyin* romanization, which is the key to finding them in the Chinese-English side.

To find a character in the **Character Index**, you need first to identify the radical under which the character is categorized. The **Radical Index** provides a list of radicals and their numbers in order of their appearance in the **Character Index**. These radicals are listed according to the number of strokes used to write them, with the smallest number of strokes coming first. When you have identified the most likely radical of a character, note its radical number in the **Radical Index**, and use this number to find the radical in the **Character Index**. Because it is sometimes difficult to figure out which radical is used to categorize any given character, the **Character Index** lists some characters under more than one radical for your convenience. For example, the character 胃 is listed both under the 田 radical and the 月 radical in the **Character Index**.

The **Character Index** lists each radical by number, followed by all the characters categorized under that radical. The characters under each radical are listed according to the number of strokes beyond those needed to write the radical portion of the character. For instance, supposing you are looking for the character 树 in the **Index**. You guess that it is probably listed under the radical (木), which is often called the *tree radical*. This radical is Number 81 in the **Radical Index**. To find the pronunciation of 树, first find where radical 81 is in the **Character Index**. You will see all the characters having this radical listed below it. The *tree radical* has four strokes. Now count the number of strokes that remain after you have written those four strokes. The answer is five. If you look down the list of characters to the subsection entitled "Five Strokes", you will see that the character 树 is listed within that group. The listing tells you that the character is pronounced *shù*; now you can look up *shù* in the Chinese-English side.

By following this procedure, you should be able to find any character you are looking for, providing that it is in the dictionary as a headword or the first character of a headword. If you have trouble finding a character in the **Character Index**, first check above or below in the list under that radical, in case your stroke count was incorrect. It is best to write the character down as you count, being sure to write it using the proper strokes and stroke order. (See the section on **Basic Rules for Writing Chinese Characters** for advice on correct stroke order.) If you still cannot find it, the character is probably listed under a different radical, and you will need to start again from the beginning of the process described above, looking under a different radical. Beginners sometimes find this process frustrating, but if you keep trying, it will become easier.

Each Chinese character corresponds to a syllable in *pinyin*, but a Chinese word can consist of more than one character. There is no obvious way to distinguish word boundaries in a written text unless one knows what the characters and words mean. Because only headwords and first characters of headwords are indexed in this dictionary, the absence of a character from the **Index** does not mean that it is not in the dictionary. It could be the second or third character in a word or expression, whose first character is in the **Character Index**. If the character you are looking for happens to be such a second, third, or fourth character, you may not find it in the **Index**. In that case you must look back at your text to see if it might be the latter part of a word beginning with a different character. For instance, if you find the character *bì* 壁 in your text, and try to look it up in the dictionary, you will not find it in the **Index** or under *bì* in the Chinese into English side. However, after looking again at your text you may find that it occurs after the character *gé* 隔, as the second character of the word *gébì* 隔壁 (= next door). You can then try looking up *gébì* 隔壁 under g in the dictionary. Sometimes the **Character Index** gives you more than one pronunciation. It is best to check all the different pronunciations until you learn which one is used for the meaning of the character you are looking for.

Tones in Mandarin Chinese

Chinese is a tonal language. In Mandarin Chinese, there are four tones, indicated respectively by the tone marks ¯, ˊ, ˇ and ˋ.

Tone	Tone mark	Description	Example
First tone	¯	high, level pitch	tī 踢 = kick
Second tone	ˊ	starting high and rising	tí 提 = lift
Third tone	ˇ	falling first, then rising	tǐ 体 = body
Fourth tone	ˋ	starting high and falling	tì 替 = replace

As can be seen from the fourth column above, the tone is marked above the vowel in the romanized syllable. It is marked only in the *pinyin* romanization, not in the characters. Some words have unstressed syllables. These are toneless, and are not given tone marks. For example, in *wǒmen* 我们 (= we, us), the syllable *men* is toneless and therefore has no tone mark on it. This type of syllable is often called a neutral tone syllable.

Tone Changes

Sometimes the tone of a syllable or a word changes according to the tone of the syllable that follows it.

1. The negative adverb *bù* 不 (=not)

Normally, the negative adverb *bù* 不 is pronounced in the fourth tone:

wǒ **bù** tīng yīnyuè 我不听音乐 = *I don't listen to music*
wǒ **bù** xué Zhōngwén 我不学中文 = *I don't study Chinese*
wǒ **bù** mǎi Zhōngwén shū 我不买中文书 = *I don't buy Chinese books*

However, when it is followed by a fourth-tone syllable, its tone changes to the second tone.

wǒ **bú** shì Zhōngguórén 我不是中国人 = *I'm not Chinese*

2. The numeral *yī* 一 (=one)

When read in isolation, in counting, or in reading numbers, the numeral *yī* 一 is pronounced in the first tone.

yī, èr, sān, sì ... 一, 二, 三, 四 ... = *1, 2, 3, 4 ...*
yījiǔjiǔbā 一九九八 = *1998*

However, when the numeral *yī* 一 precedes a first-, second-, or third-tone syllable, its tone changes to the fourth tone.

yìzhāng zhǐ 一张纸 = *a piece of paper*
yìpán cídài 一盘磁带 = *a tape*
yìběn shū 一本书 = *a book*

When it is followed by a fourth-tone syllable, its tone changes to the second tone.

yíliàng qìchē 一辆汽车 = *a car*

3. A third-tone syllable preceding another third-tone syllable

When a third-tone syllable precedes another third tone, it is pronounced in the second tone even though the tone mark remains the same.

wǔběn shū 五本书 = *five books*
nǐ hǎo! 你好 = *hello!*
hǎohǎo xuéxí 好好学习 = *study well*

The structure of Chinese-English entries

headword ······ **bǎohù** 保护

numbers indicating grammatical categories

1 *verb*

= protect, safeguard

2 *noun*

= protection

translations clearly indicated by =

Chinese characters

pinyin ······ **běibiān** 北边 *noun* ······ part of speech

= the North, the north side, on the north

explanatory note ······ **!** *This term can also be used to refer to the northern border or what is north of the border.*

example of its use ······ **Měiguó de běibiān shì Jiānádà** 美国的北边是加拿大 = north of the United States of America is Canada

cross-reference to headword ······ **shàngmian** 上面 ▶ **shàngbian** 上边

Shèngdàn(jié) 圣诞(节) *noun* ······ optional use

= Christmas (Day)

yánjiū 研究

bullet points indicating a separate sense of the headword

1 *verb*

- = study, do research
- (*for problems, suggestions, applications*) = consider, discuss

2 *noun*

= research, study

compounds presented at end of entry

yánjiūhuì 研究会 = research association

yánjiūshēng 研究生 = research student, postgraduate student

yánjiūsuǒ 研究所 = research institute

yuán 员 *noun*

indicator which spells out the sense of the headword ······ (*a professional in an occupation or member of a party, etc.*) = member, personnel, staff

example indicating generative structure ······ [**dǎng** | **hǎi** | **chuīshì** | **shòuhuò**] **yuán** [党 | 海 | 炊事 | 售货] 员 = [party member | seaman | cook | shop clerk]

zhāng 张 *measure word* ▶ **157** ······ page number cross-reference to a usage section

(*for flat things such as paper, paintings, tables, etc.*)

The structure of English-Chinese entries

headword · **cool** *adjective* · *pinyin*

- (*fresh, not hot*) = liáng 凉, liángkuai 凉快 · Chinese character
  a cool drink = yíge lěngyǐn 一个冷饮
  it's much cooler today = jīntiān liángkuai duō le 今天凉快多了 · translations clearly indicated by =
- (*calm*) = lěngjìng 冷静
- (*fashionable*) = kù 酷✖ · symbol drawing attention to register

bullet points indicating separate senses of the headword

dance
numbers indicating grammatical categories
1 *verb*
= tiàowǔ 跳舞
2 *noun*
a dance = yíge wǔdǎo 一个舞蹈 · numeral plus measure word

director *noun*
- (*of a film or play*) = dǎoyǎn 导演
  a director = yíge dǎoyǎn 一个导演
- a director (*of a research institute or department*) = yíge suǒzhǎng 一个所长, yíge zhǔrèn 一个主任
  (*of a factory*) = yíge chǎngzhǎng 一个厂长
  (*of a company*) = yíge zǒngcái 一个总裁, yígè zhǔrèn 一个主任

indicators which spell out the different senses of the headword

except *preposition* · part of speech made clear
= chúle... (yǐwài) 除了... (以外)
indicator of optional use

fireman *noun* ▶ 344 · page number cross-reference to a usage note
a fireman = yíge xiāofáng duìyuán 一个消防队员

fire station *noun*
a fire station = yíge xiāofángzhàn 一个消防站

separate entries for compounds

kick *verb*
= tī 踢
to kick someone = tī mǒurén 踢某人

kick off
(*in a football match*) = kāiqiú 开球

kick out
to kick someone out = jiěgù mǒurén 解雇某人

phrasal verbs presented in independent blocks

plenty *pronoun*
example indicating generative structure · to have plenty of [time | money | friends...]
= yǒu hěn duō [shíjiān | qián | péngyou...] 有很多[时间 | 钱 | 朋友...]

population *noun*
a population = rénkǒu 人口

information on correct grammatical usage ·
! *Note that* rénkǒu 人口 *is uncountable and does not have a measure word.*

Glossary of grammatical terms

This section explains the basic terms that are used in this dictionary to help you to find the information that you need.

Adjective An adjective is used to add extra information to a noun – *an **experienced** worker, a **beautiful** girl, a **black** cat*. In Chinese: *yíge **yǒu jīngyàn de** gōngrén* 一个有经验的工人, *yíge **piàoliang de** gūniang* 一个漂亮的姑娘, *yìzhī **hēi** māo* 一只黑猫. As can be seen in the examples above, the Chinese adjective is often followed by ***de*** 的 when used to modify a noun. In some Chinese grammar books, some Chinese adjectives are called stative verbs, because the adjective indicates the state of the subject, and the Chinese equivalent of the verb *be* is not used. For more information, see the boxed note on **Be** on page 182.

> *he <u>is</u> **tired*** = tā__**lèi** le 他__累了
> *these students <u>are</u> very **intelligent*** = zhèxiē xuésheng __ hěn **cōngming** 这些学生__很聪明

Adverb An adverb is used to add extra information to a verb, an adjective, or another adverb – *to walk **slowly**, **extremely** satisfied, **quite** frequently*. In Chinese: ***hěn màndе*** *zǒu* 很慢地走, ***fēicháng*** *mǎnyì* 非常满意, ***xiāngdāng*** *pínfán* 相当频繁. When used to modify a verb, the Chinese adverb is often followed by ***de*** 地.

Auxiliary verb An auxiliary verb is a verb, such as *be*, *do*, *have*, which is used to form a particular tense or grammatical function of another verb, or to form an interrogative, negative, or imperative sentence. Here are some English examples: *it **is** raining; **did** you see him?; she **didn't** come; he **has** left; **don't** go!*.

Comparative The comparative, as its name indicates, is the form of the adjective or adverb which enables us to compare two or more nouns or pronouns. In English, this is usually done by putting *more*, *less*, or *as* before the appropriate adjective or adverb, or by changing the base form to the comparative form ending in *-er*. Chinese adjectives and adverbs do not have comparative forms. The comparison is usually indicated by ***bǐ*** 比, the Chinese equivalent of ***than***, as can be seen in the following examples:

> *my mother is **more** patient (**than** my father)* = wǒ māma (**bǐ** wǒ bàba) nàixīn 我妈妈(比我爸爸)耐心
> *he has **less** money (**than** I have)* = tāde qián (**bǐ** wǒde) shǎo 他的钱(比我的)少
> *Tom is tall**er** (**than** his father)* = Tāngmǔ (**bǐ** tā bàba) gāo 汤姆(比他爸爸)高
> *he walked **more** slowly (**than** my mother)* = tā (**bǐ** wǒ māma) zǒu de màn 他(比我妈妈)走得慢
> *he is **as** tired **as** I am* = tā **hé** wǒ **yíyàng** lèi 他和我一样累

Note that when the comparison is implied, that is, when ***bǐ*** 比 (= *than*) is not used, the Chinese adjective has a sense of comparison by itself, as in the example below.

> A: *Of you two, who is **older**?* = nǐmen liǎ rén shéi **dà**? 你们俩人谁大?
> B: *I'm **older*** = wǒ **dà** 我大
> C: *Yes. I'm **younger*** = duì, wǒ **xiǎo** 对，我小

If the sentence describes the state or condition of the subject, and no comparison is implied, it is necessary to add the adverb ***hěn*** 很 (= *very*) before the adjective, as in the example below. Otherwise, the sentence has a sense of comparison.

> *she is tall* = tā **hěn** gāo 她很高

Conditional A conditional sentence is one in which the statement contained in the main clause can only be fulfilled if the condition stated in the subordinate clause is also fulfilled. This condition is usually introduced by *if* in English and *rúguǒ* 如果 in Chinese.

> *If it is fine tomorrow, we'll go to the seaside* = rúguǒ míngtiān tiānqì hǎo, wǒmen jiù qù hǎibiān 如果明天天气好，我们就去海边
> *I would go travelling if I had lots of money* = rúguǒ wǒ yǒu hěn duō qián, wǒ jiù qù lǚxíng 如果我有很多钱，我就去旅行

Conjunction A conjunction can be either (i) a word like *and* or *but* which is used to join words or simple sentences together, or (ii) a word like *when, although, if, where*, which is used to form a complex sentence. Note that *and* is not translated into Chinese when it joins two simple sentences or two verbal phrases. See the following examples:

(i) *Britain* **and** *China* = Yīngguó **hé** Zhōngguó 英国和中国
he is tired **but** *happy* = tā hěn lèi **dànshì** hěn gāoxìng 他很累但是很高兴
I went to Beijing **and** *she went to Shanghai* = wǒ qùle Běijīng, ___ tā qùle Shànghǎi 我去了北京, ___她去了上海
she went to the shop **and** *bought some apples* = tā qù shāngdiàn ___mǎile yìxiē píngguǒ 她去商店___买了一些苹果

(ii) *he has agreed to help me* **even though** *he is busy* = **suīrán** tā hěn máng, dàn tā tóngyì bāngzhù wǒ 虽然他很忙, 但他同意帮助我
when *I was about to go out, the telephone rang* = wǒ zhèngyào chūqù **de shíhou**, diànhuà líng xiǎng le 我正要出去的时候, 电话铃响了

Determiner A determiner is used before a noun in order to identify more precisely what is being referred to. Here are some examples:

the *book* = **zhè**běn shū 这本书
my *book* = **wǒde** shū 我的书
that *book* = **nà**běn shū 那本书
these *books* = **zhèxiē** shū 这些书
some *books* = **yìxiē** shū 一些书

Note that the English determiner *a* is usually translated into Chinese as a numeral plus an appropriate nominal measure word:

a *book* = **yìběn** shū 一本书

Exclamation An exclamation is a word or phrase conveying a reaction such as surprise, shock, disapproval, indignation, amusement, etc. In both English and Chinese, it is usually followed by an exclamation mark.

Excellent! = Hǎo jí le! 好极了!
What nice weather! = Duōme hǎo de tiānqì a! 多么好的天气啊!

Imperative An imperative sentence is used to indicate an order, command, prohibition, suggestion, etc.

come here quickly = kuài lái 快来
don't go out = bié chūqu 别出去
let's go = zánmen zǒu ba 咱们走吧

Infinitive The infinitive is a form of the verb which has no indication of person or tense. In English, it is often preceded by *to*, as in *to walk, to run, to read, to receive*. In Chinese, there is no word like *to* or any change of form to indicate the infinitive.

Measure word ▶ **Nominal measure word, Verbal measure word**

Nominal measure word In Chinese, a numeral cannot quantify a noun by itself. It has to be accompanied by the measure word that is appropriate for the noun that is being used. Each noun has a specific measure word or set of measure words that can be used with it. There is often a link between the measure word and the shape of the object. In expressions of quantification, the numeral comes first, followed by the measure word and the noun. When the determiner *this* or *that* is used, an appropriate measure word is also required. As can be seen in the examples below, we have put the numeral/determiner and the measure word together as one word in *pinyin* to correspond to the numeral or the determiner in English. Note that some nominal measure words can also be used as verbal measure words. (For a list of common nominal measure words and examples of their use, see the section on **Measure Words** on page 157)

a computer = yì**tái** jìsuànjī 一台计算机
four dictionaries = sì**běn** cídiǎn 四本词典
this student = zhè**ge** xuésheng 这个学生
that river = nà**tiáo** hé 那条河

Noun A noun is used to identify a person, an animal, an object, an idea, or an emotion. It can also be the name of an individual, a company, or an institution.

student = xuésheng 学生
dog = gǒu 狗
table = zhuōzi 桌子
plan = jìhuà 计划
happiness = xìngfú 幸福

Peter = Bǐdé 彼得
America = Měiguó 美国

Number A number, as a part of speech, refers to numerical figures, such as *five*, *twenty*, *thousand*, etc., or words indicating quantity. As a grammatical concept, it refers to the state of being either singular or plural. Nouns in English usually change to their plural forms by adding *-s* to the end: *a table*, *two tables*. Chinese nouns usually do not change to form singular and plural.

a table = yìzhāng zhuōzi 一张桌子
*two table**s*** = liǎngzhāng zhuōzi 两张桌子

Occasionally, *-men* -们 can be attached to the end of a noun to mark the plural form, but it is optional and applies only to nouns referring to animate entities:

*student**s*** = xuésheng(**men**) 学生(们)
*worker**s*** = gōngrén(**men**) 工人(们)

Object The object of a sentence is the word or group of words which is immediately affected by the action indicated by the verb. In the following English sentence, the word *child* is the subject, *broke* is the verb and ***a cup*** is the object. Similarly, in the Chinese translation, *zhège háizi* 这个孩子 is the subject, *dǎpòle* 打破了 is the verb and ***yíge chábēi*** 一个茶杯 is the object.

the child broke a cup = zhège háizi dǎpòle yíge chábēi 这个孩子打破了一个茶杯

There may be two kinds of object in a sentence, a direct object and an indirect object. In the example above, *a cup* and *yíge chábēi* 一个茶杯 are strictly direct objects. However, in the following English sentence, *he* is the subject, *gave* is the verb, *the child* is the indirect object and *a cup* is the direct object. Similarly, in the Chinese translation, *tā* 他 is the subject, *gěile* 给了 is the verb, *zhège háizi* 这个孩子 is the indirect object and *yíge chábēi* 一个茶杯 is the direct object. In general terms, the indirect object indicates the person or thing which 'benefits' from the action of the verb upon the direct object.

he gave the child a cup = tā gěile zhège háizi yíge chábēi 他给了这个孩子一个茶杯

Phrasal verb A phrasal verb is a verb combined with a preposition or an adverb and having a particular meaning. For example, *to **run away***, meaning to flee, and *to **see to** something*, meaning to ensure that something is done, are phrasal verbs. If you look up *to run away* for example, you will see that the phrasal verbs beginning with the word *run* are listed after all the other meanings of the word *run*, in alphabetical order of the following adverb or preposition.

Pinyin Designed in the People's Republic of China during the mid-1950s, *pinyin* is a phonetic system of the Chinese language. It adopts the roman alphabet to represent phonemic sounds in Mandarin Chinese. In this dictionary, all Chinese headwords, translations, and examples are given first in *pinyin* and then in Chinese characters.

Preposition A preposition is a word, such as *under*, *beside*, *across*, *in*, which is usually followed by a noun in English. In Chinese, the preposition often consists of two parts, such as *zài ... xiàmian* 在 ... 下面 (= *under*), and the noun is placed between them, as in the examples below.

***under** the table* = **zài** zhuōzi **xiàmian** 在桌子下面
***beside** the road* = **zài** lù **pángbiān** 在路旁边
***in** the garden* = **zài** huāyuán **lǐ** 在花园里

Most preposition +noun groups indicate movement

*he ran **towards the house*** = tā **cháo nàzuò fángzi** pǎoqù 他朝那座房子跑去

position

*your books are **on the table*** = nǐde shū **zài zhuōzi shang** 你的书在桌子上

or time

*I'll be there **at 4 o'clock*** = wǒ **sì diǎnzhōng** huì dào nàr 我四点钟会到那儿

Pronoun A pronoun is used instead of a noun in order to avoid repeating it unnecessarily. There are the personal pronouns *I*, *you*, *he*, *she*, *it*, *we*, *you* (plural), *they*; the possessive pronouns *mine*, *yours*, *his*, *hers*, *its*, *ours*, *yours* (plural), *theirs*; the interrogative pronouns used in questions *who*, *which*, *what*; the demonstrative pronouns *this*, *that, these, those*; the relative pronouns used in relative clauses *who, which, whose*; and the reflexive pronouns *myself, yourself, himself, herself, itself, ourselves, yourselves, themselves*. To find the Chinese equivalents of these pronouns, please look them up in the English-Chinese side of the dictionary.

Reflexive pronoun ▶ Pronoun

Relative pronoun ▶ Pronoun

Subject The subject of a sentence is often the word or group of words which performs the action indicated by the verb. In the sentence *John laughed*, *John* is the subject of the verb *laughed*. Of course, the verb doesn't necessarily express an action as such. For example, in the sentence *John is tall*, *John* is the subject of the verb *is*. In the Chinese sentence *Yuēhàn xiào le* 约翰笑了, *Yuēhàn* 约翰 is similarly the subject of the verb *xiào le* 笑了, and in the sentence *Yuēhàn hěn gāo* 约翰很高, *Yuēhàn* 约翰 is the subject of *hěn gāo* 很高.

Superlative The superlative is the form of the adjective or adverb which is used to express the highest or lowest degree. In English, the adjective or adverb is usually preceded by *most* or *least*. Some adjectives and adverbs (usually of one syllable) have their own form: *best, worst, biggest, smallest, fastest, slowest*, etc. In Chinese, the superlative is formed by putting *zuì* 最 before the adjective or adverb.

> ***most** important* = **zuì** zhòngyào 最重要
> ***least** important* = **zuì bú** zhòngyào 最不重要
> ***most** carefully* = **zuì** zǐxì 最仔细
> ***least** carefully* = **zuì bù** zǐxì 最不仔细
> *small**est*** = **zuì** xiǎo 最小

Tense The tense of a verb expresses whether the action takes place in the past, present, or future. Unlike English verbs, Chinese verbs do not have any particular form to express tense; the time of the action is usually indicated by the adverb or in the context.

Present tense

> *he is telephoning his friends* = tā zài gěi tāde péngyou dǎ diànhuà 他在给他的朋友打电话

Past tense

> *I didn't go* = wǒ méi qù 我没去

Future tense

> *they will come tomorrow* = tāmen míngtiān lái 他们明天来

Tone Please see the section on **Tones in Mandarin Chinese** on page vii.

Verb The verb propels the sentence along, telling us what is happening. Note these examples:

> *Paul bought a new car* = Bǎoluó mǎile yíliàng xīn chē 保罗买了一辆新车
> *The flood caused a lot of damage* = shuǐzāi zàochéngle hěn dàde sǔnhài 水灾造成了很大的损害

Sometimes, of course, the verb doesn't describe an action, but rather a state of affairs:

> *He has a problem* = tā yǒu yígè wèntí 他有一个问题
> *The damage appears quite serious* = sǔnhài kànlái xiāngdāng yánzhòng 损害看来相当严重
> *I am ill* = wǒ bìng le 我病了

Note that the verb *am* in the sentence *I am ill* is not translated into Chinese. For more information and examples of this type of sentence, see the boxed note on **Be** on page 182. See also the entry on **Adjective** in the glossary above.

Verbal measure word Verbal measure words are generally used to indicate the number of times an action or state occurs. As in the case of nominal measure words, the numeral and verbal measure word are spelled together as one *pinyin* word in this dictionary. The numeral + measure word unit is preceded by the verb and is usually followed by the object, if there is one (i.e. if the verb is transitive). For a list of common verbal measure words and examples of their use, see the section on **Measure words** on page 157.

> *I've been to Hong Kong twice* = wǒ qùguo liǎng**cì** Xiānggǎng 我去过两次香港
> *he nodded his head several times* = tā diǎnle jǐ**xià** tóu 他点了几下头

Index

1. Radical Index

One stroke

1 丶
2 一
3 丨
4 丿
5 乙 (乛 ㇆ 乚)

Two strokes

6 亠
7 冫
8 冖
9 讠
10 二
11 十
12 厂
13 匚
14 卜 (⺊)
15 刂
16 冂
17 八 (丷)
18 人 (入)
19 亻
20 勹
⺈ (see 刀)
21 儿
22 几
23 厶
24 又 (ヌ)
25 廴
26 卩 (㔾)
27 阝 (on the left)
28 阝 (on the right)
29 凵
30 刀 (⺈)
31 力
㔾 (see 卩)

Three strokes

32 氵
33 忄
34 宀
35 丬
36 广
37 门
38 辶
39 工
40 土
41 士
42 艹
43 大
44 廾 (underneath)
45 尢
46 寸
47 弋
48 扌
49 小 (⺌)
50 口
51 囗
52 巾
53 山
54 彳
55 彡
56 夕
57 夂
58 犭
59 饣
60 彐 (⺕)
61 尸
62 己 (巳)
63 弓
64 屮
65 女
66 幺
67 子 (孑)
68 纟
69 马
70 巛

Four strokes

71 灬
72 斗
73 文
74 方
75 火
76 心
77 户
78 礻
79 王
80 韦
81 木
82 犬
83 歹
84 车
85 戈
86 比
87 瓦
88 止
89 攴
90 日
91 曰 (⺜)
92 贝
93 见
94 父
95 牛 (牜 ⺧)
96 手
97 毛
98 气
99 攵
100 片
101 斤
102 爪 (爫)
103 月 (⺝)
104 欠
105 风
106 殳
107 肀
108 水 (氺)

Five strokes

109 母
110 穴
111 立
112 疒
113 衤
114 示
115 石
116 龙
117 业
118 目
119 田
120 罒
121 皿
122 钅
123 矢
124 禾
125 白
126 瓜
127 鸟
128 用
氺 (see 水)
129 矛
⺻ (see 艮)
130 疋
131 皮

Six strokes

132 衣
133 羊 (⺶ ⺷)
134 米
135 耒
136 老
137 耳
138 臣
139 西 (覀)
140 页
141 虍
142 虫
143 缶
144 舌
145 竹 (⺮)
146 臼
147 自
148 血
149 舟
150 羽
151 艮 (⺻)
152 糸

Seven strokes

153 辛
154 言
155 麦
156 走
157 赤
158 豆
159 酉
160 辰
161 豕
162 卤
163 里
164 足 (⻊)
165 豸

2. Character Index

Aa

ā 阿 *prefix*
(*informal name prefix especially in Yangtze delta region*)
ā Q 阿Q = Ah Q

Ālābó 阿拉伯 *noun*
= Arabia

āyí 阿姨 *noun*
- (*child's word for a woman of his or her mother's generation*) = auntie
- (*child's word for a child-minder*) = nanny, baby-sitter

ā 啊
1 *exclamation*
(*to express surprise*) = Oh! Ah!
ā, nǐ lái le! 啊，你来了! = Ah, here you are!
2 *particle*
(*placed at the end of a sentence to express admiration, warning, or request*)
duō hǎo de tiānr ā! 多好的天儿啊! = what a beautiful day!
bié chídào a! 别迟到啊! = don't be late!
nǐ kuài lái a! 你快来啊! = come here quickly!

āi 哎 *exclamation*
(*to express surprise or discontent*)
āi, nǐ bǎ qián fàng zài nǎlǐ le? 哎，你把钱放在哪里了? = but where did you put the money?

āiyā 哎呀 *exclamation*
(*expressing surprise*) = My goodness!
āiyā, wǒde qiánbāo diū le! 哎呀，我的钱包丢了! = Oh dear, I've lost my wallet!

āi 挨 *verb* ▶ *See also* **ái** 挨.
- (*get close to, be next to or near to*)
  tā jiā āizhe xuéxiào 他家挨着学校 = his house is next to the school
- (*in sequence, by turns*)
  shénme shíhou néng āidào wǒ? 什么时候能挨到我? = when can it be my turn?

ái 挨 *verb* ▶ *See also* **āi** 挨.
= suffer, endure
ái mà 挨骂 = get a scolding
ái dǎ 挨打 = get a beating, come under attack

ái 癌 *noun*
= cancer
áizhèng 癌症 = cancer

ǎi 矮 *adjective*
- (*in stature*) = short
- (*of inanimate objects*) = low

ài 爱 *verb*
- (*if the object is a person*) = love, be fond of
  wǒ ài nǐ 我爱你 = I love you
- (*if the object is an activity*) = like, love
  wǒ ài tīng nàge gùshi 我爱听那个故事 = I like to hear that story

Ài'ěrlán 爱尔兰 *noun*
= Ireland

àihào 爱好
1 *verb*
= be keen on
àihào dǎ wǎngqiú 爱好打网球 = be keen on tennis
2 *noun*
= hobby
qí mǎ shì tāde àihào 骑马是她的爱好 = horse-riding is her hobby

> **!** *Note that* **hào** 好 *in this essentially verbal usage is fourth tone.*

àihù 爱护 *verb*
= cherish, treasure, protect
àihù zìjǐ de shēntǐ 爱护自己的身体 = take good care of one's own health

àiqíng 爱情 *noun*
(*between lovers*) = love, affection

àiren 爱人 *noun*
= husband or wife, lover, spouse
wǒde àiren shì lǎoshī 我的爱人是老师 = my wife/husband is a teacher

àixi 爱惜 *verb*
= cherish, treasure, use sparingly

ān 安
1 *adjective*
= peaceful, secure, content
xīnlǐ bù ān 心里不安 = feel worried
2 *verb*
- = install
- = settle down
  ān jiā 安家 = settle a family down in a place

āndìng 安定
1 *verb*
- (*for a family, system, etc.*) = settle down in peace
  xíngshì yǐjīng āndìngxiàlai le 形势已经安定下来了 = the situation has calmed down
- = stabilize

2 *adjective*
= settled, stable, secure
yíge āndìng de shèhuì huánjìng 一个安定的社会环境 = a stable social environment

ānjìng 安静 *adjective*
= peaceful, quiet
qǐng ānjìng! 请安静! = please be quiet!

ānpái 安排
1 *verb*
= arrange, plan, fix up
ānpái shísù 安排食宿 = arrange room and board
2 *noun*
= arrangements

ānquán 安全
1 *adjective*
= safe, secure
zhèlǐ bù ānquán 这里不安全 = this place is not safe
ānquándài 安全带 = safety belt
2 *noun*
= safety, security
bǎohù tāmende ānquán 保护他们的安全 = preserve their safety

ānwèi 安慰
1 *verb*
= comfort, console
2 *noun*
= comfort, reassurance

ānxīn 安心 *verb*
= feel at ease, be relieved
shǐ tā ānxīn 使她安心 = make her feel at ease

ānzhuāng 安装 *verb*
= install
ānzhuāng jìsuànjī 安装计算机 = have a computer installed

àn 按
1 *preposition*
= according to, by
qǐng nǐ àn wǒ shuō de zuò 请你按我说的做 = please do it the way I told you
àn yuè suàn 按月算 = calculate by the month
2 *verb*
- = press, push down
  ànxià diànniǔ 按下电钮 = press down the button
- = restrain, control
  tā àn bú zhù zìjǐ de fènnù 他按不住自己的愤怒 = he cannot restrain his anger

ànshí 按时 *adverb*
= on time, on schedule
huǒchē huì ànshí dào ma? 火车会按时到吗? = will the train arrive on time?

ànzhào 按照 *preposition*
= according to, based on
ànzhào tāmende àihào, wǒ gěi tāmen měige rén mǎile yíjiàn lǐwù 按照他们的爱好, 我给他们每个人买了一件礼物 = I bought each of them a present according to their hobbies

àn 岸 *noun*
= bank, shore, coast
[**hǎi** | **hú** | **hé**] **àn** [海 | 湖 | 河] 岸 = [seashore | lake shore | river bank]
shàng àn 上岸 = go ashore

àn 暗 *adjective*
- = dark, dim, dull
  nàjiān wūzi hěn àn 那间屋子很暗 = that room is very dark
- = hidden, secret
  wǒmen zài àn chù guānchá dírén de xíngdòng 我们在暗处观察敌人的行动 = we were observing the enemy's actions from a hidden position

āngzāng 肮脏 *adjective*
= dirty, filthy

Àolínpǐkè Yùndònghuì 奥林匹克运动会 *noun*
= the Olympic Games

Àodàlìyà 澳大利亚 *noun*
= Australia

àohuǐ 懊悔 *adjective*
= regret, feel remorse, repent

àonǎo 懊恼 *adjective*
= annoyed, upset, vexed

àomàn 傲慢 *verb*
= arrogant, haughty

Bb

bā 八 *number*
= eight

bāyuè 八月 *noun*
= August

bá 拔 *verb*
- = pull, pull out, uproot
  bá yá 拔牙 = extract a tooth or have a tooth extracted
- (*for people of talent*) = choose, select
  xuǎnbá 选拔 = select from a number of candidates
- = capture, seize

bǎ 把
1 *measure word* ▶ **157**
- (*for objects with a handle or with something a person can hold*)
- (*for things that can be grouped in bunches or bundles*) = bunch, bundle
- = handful

2 *preposition*

> **!** *As a preposition,* **bǎ** 把 *acts as a structural device that brings the object from the post-verbal position to the pre-verbal position. The object of the preposition* **bǎ** 把 *is also the object of the verb.*

wǒ xiǎng bǎ tā mài le 我想把它卖了 = I want to sell it
háizimen bǎ táng dōu chīwán le 孩子们把糖都吃完了 = the children ate all the sweets
xiān bǎ liànxí zuòwán 先把练习作完 = finish the exercises first
tā bǎ wǒ qìhuài le 他把我气坏了 = he made me very angry
bǎ quán jiā jiàoqǐlai 把全家叫起来 = awaken the whole family

bàba 爸爸 *noun*
= father, dad, papa

ba 吧 *particle*
- (*used to make a mild imperative sentence*)
  zámen zǒu ba 咱们走吧 = let's go
  gěi wǒ shū ba 给我书吧 = give me the book
  gěi nǐ ba 给你吧 = here, you take it
  chī bǐnggān ba? 吃饼干吧? = how about having a biscuit?
  bié gàosu tā ba 别告诉他吧 = better not tell him
- (*used to imply agreement*)
  jiù zhèyàng ba 就这样吧 = OK, let's leave it like that
- (*used to imply a degree of certainty*)
  tā jīntiān lái ba? 他今天来吧? = he is coming today, isn't he?
- (*to express unwillingness, reluctance, or hesitation*)
  nǐ quèshí xiǎng mǎi, nà nǐ jiù qù mǎi ba 你确实想买, 那你就去买吧 = if you really want to buy it, go and buy it then

bái 白
1 *adjective*
- = white
- = pure, plain, blank
  báifàn 白饭 = plain rice
  kòngbái 空白 = blank
  báihuà 白话 = vernacular Chinese, modern Chinese

2 *adverb*
- = in vain, to no effect
  bái pǎo yítàng 白跑一趟 = make a trip for nothing
  bái fèi jìn 白费劲 = waste one's effort
- = free of charge
  bái sòng 白送 = give as a gift
- **qīngbái** 清白 = clean, pure

báicài 白菜 *noun*
= Chinese cabbage

báitiān 白天 *noun*
= daytime, day

bǎi 百 *number*
= hundred, unit of a hundred

bǎi 摆 *verb*
- = put, place, arrange
- = sway, wave
  xiàng mǒurén bǎi shǒu 向某人摆手 = wave one's hand at someone

bài 败 *verb*
- = be defeated in a battle or contest
  tāmen bài de hěn cǎn 他们败得很惨 = they suffered a heavy defeat
- (*of an enemy or opponent*) = defeat
  dǎbài 打败 = defeat
- = spoil, ruin
  bàihuài míngyù 败坏名誉 = to spoil one's reputation
- = wither

bān 班
1 *noun*
- = class
  èrniánjí yǒu sānge bān 二年级有三个班 = there are three classes in second grade
- = shift, duty
  shàng bān 上班 = go to work
  [**zǎo** | **zhōng** | **yè**] **bān** [早 | 中 | 夜] 班 = [morning | afternoon | night] shift
- = squad

2 *measure word* ▶ **157**
(*for scheduled services of public transportation*)

bānzhǎng 班长 *noun*
= head of a class, squad, or team

bān 搬 *verb*
- = take away, move, remove
- = move house
  tā bānzǒu le 他搬走了 = he moved away

bǎn 板 *noun*
= board, plank, plate

bàn 办 *verb*
- = handle, manage, attend to
  méiyǒu qián, zěnme bàn? 没有钱，怎么办？ = what will we do if we have no money?
  zhèjiàn shì tā bàn bù wán 这件事他办不完 = he can't finish this
- = set up, run
  bàn xuéxiào 办学校 = run a school
  bàn gōngsī 办公司 = set up a company
- = hold, have
  bàn yícì zuòwén bǐsài 办一次作文比赛 = hold a writing competition
  bàn zhǎnlǎnhuì 办展览会 = hold an exhibition

bànfǎ 办法 *noun*
= way, method, way to handle a problem

bàngōng 办公 *verb*
= handle official business

bàngōngshì 办公室 *noun*
= office

bànshì 办事 *verb*
= handle affairs, handle a matter, work

bàn 半 *adjective*
- = half
  bànge píngguǒ 半个苹果 = half an apple
  yígebàn yuè 一个半月 = one and a half months
- = partly, about half
  tā chīle yíbàn jiù zǒu le 他吃了一半就走了 = he ate about half his meal and then left

bàndǎotǐ 半导体 *noun*
= semi-conductor, transistor

bàntiān 半天 *noun*
- = half a day
- = for a long time, quite a while
  tā yǐjīng shuōle bàntiān le 他已经说了半天了 = he has already been talking for a long time

bànyè 半夜 *noun*
- = midnight, in the middle of the night
- = half a night
  qián bànyè 前半夜 = first half of the night
  hòu bànyè 后半夜 = second half of the night

bāng 帮 *verb*
= help, assist
wǒ kěyǐ bāng nǐ 我可以帮你 = I can help you

bāngmáng 帮忙, **bāng...máng** 帮... 忙 *verb*
= help, lend a hand, do a favour
tā bú yuànyì bāngmáng 他不愿意帮忙 = he is not willing to help
tā xǐhuān bāng biérén de máng 她喜欢帮别人的忙 = she likes to help other people

bāngzhù 帮助 *verb*
= help, assist
wǒ yuànyì bāngzhù nǐ 我愿意帮助你 = I am willing to help you

bǎngyàng 榜样 *noun*
= good example, model
wèi dàjiā zuòchū yíge bǎngyàng 为大家作出一个榜样 = set an example for everyone

bàngwǎn 傍晚 *noun*
= at dusk, toward evening or nightfall

bāo 包
1 *noun*
- = parcel, package, bundle
- = bag

2 *measure word* ▶ **157**
= package, packet, bundle

3 *verb*
- = wrap with paper, cloth, or some other material

bǎ dōngxi bāoqǐlai 把东西包起来 = wrap things up
bāo jiǎozi 包饺子 = make *jiaozi* (Chinese dumplings)
- = assure, guarantee
bāo nǐ gāoxìng 包你高兴 = You'll be happy, I assure you
- = hire, charter
bāo yíliàng chūzūchē 包一辆出租车 = hire a taxi
bāojī 包机 = a chartered plane

bāokuò 包括 *verb*
= include, consist of, comprise

bāozi 包子 *noun*
= steamed stuffed bun

báo 薄 *adjective*
- = thin, slight, insubstantial
- (*how a person is treated*) = coldly, shabbily
dài tā bù báo 待他不薄 = treat him generously

bǎo 饱 *adjective*
- (*to describe a person after eating*) = full, replete
wǒ chībǎo le 我吃饱了 = I have eaten my fill
- (*to describe a thing*) = full, plump

bǎoguì 宝贵 *adjective*
= valuable, precious

bǎo 保 *verb*
- = protect, defend, safeguard
- = keep, maintain, preserve
bǎo xiān 保鲜 = keep something fresh
- = guarantee, ensure
bǎo zhì bǎo liàng 保质保量 = ensure both quality and quantity

bǎochí 保持 *verb*
= keep, maintain
bǎochí ānjìng 保持安静 = keep quiet

bǎocún 保存 *verb*
= preserve, conserve, keep
bǎocún de hěn wánzhěng 保存得很完整 = be well preserved, be intact

bǎohù 保护
1 *verb*
= protect, safeguard
2 *noun*
= protection

bǎohùrén 保护人 *noun*
= guardian

bǎoliú 保留 *verb*
- = retain, keep
réngjiù bǎoliú yǐqián de tàidu 仍旧保留以前的态度 = still retain one's former attitude
- = hold or keep back, reserve
bǎoliú (...de) quánlì 保留(...的)权利 = reserve the right (to...)

bǎoshǒu 保守 *adjective*
= conservative

bǎowèi 保卫 *verb*
= defend, protect, safeguard

bǎoxiǎn 保险 *noun*
= insurance

bǎozhèng 保证
1 *verb*
= pledge, guarantee, assure
bǎozhèng fù kuǎn 保证付款 = pledge or guarantee to pay
2 *noun*
= guarantee

bào 抱 *verb*
- = embrace, enfold, carry in the arms
- (*when referring to a child*) = adopt
- = cherish, harbour
tā duì zhèjiàn shì bào hěn dà de xīwàng 他对这件事抱很大的希望 = he has a lot of hope for that matter

bàoqiàn 抱歉
1 *adjective*
= sorry
hěn bàoqiàn 很抱歉 = I'm sorry
2 *verb*
= apologize

bào 报 *noun*
- = newspaper
[rì | wǎn | zǎo] bào [日 | 晚 | 早] 报 = [daily | evening | morning] paper
- = periodical, journal
yuèbào 月报 = monthly journal
zhōubào 周报 = weekly
- = bulletin, report
jǐngbào 警报 = alarm, warning
xǐbào 喜报 = good news

bàochóu 报仇 *noun*
= revenge

bàodào 报到 *verb*
= report for work, check in, register

bàodào 报道, bàodǎo 报导
1 *verb*
= report or cover the news

2 *noun*
= news reporting, story
guānyú dìzhèn de bàodào 关于地震的报道 = reports about the earthquake

bàogào 报告
1 *verb*
= report, make known
yīnggāi xiàng jīnglǐ bàogào 应该向经理报告 = should report it to the manager
2 *noun*
= report, speech, lecture
zuò bàogào 做报告 = make a speech

bàomíng 报名 *verb*
= register, sign up

bàozhǐ 报纸 *noun*
= newspaper, newsprint

bēi 杯 *noun*
- = cup, glass, tumbler
yìbēi chá 一杯茶 = a cup of tea
- (*as a prize*) = cup, trophy
Shìjiè Bēi 世界杯 = the World Cup

bēizi 杯子 *noun*
= cup, glass, mug

bēi 背 *verb*
- = carry on one's back
- = bear, shoulder
tā bēizhe chénzhòng de jīngshén fùdān 他背着沉重的精神负担 = he has a heavy load on his mind

bēitòng 悲痛 *adjective*
= grieved, feeling melancholy

bēi 碑 *noun*
= large stone tablet or stele used for commemorative purposes
jìniàn bēi 纪念碑 = commemorative monument
mùbēi 墓碑 = tombstone

běi 北 *noun*
= north
Huāběi 华北 = North China
Běijí 北极 = North Pole

běibiān 北边 *noun*
= the North, the north side, on the north

> **!** *This term can also be used to refer either to the northern border or what is north of the border.*

Měiguó de běibiān shì Jiānádà 美国的北边是加拿大 = north of the United States of America is Canada

běibù 北部 *noun*
= the north, northern section or part
Sūgélán zài Yīngguó de běibù 苏格兰在英国的北部 = Scotland is in the north of Britain

běifāng 北方 *noun*
- = the north
- = the northern part of China, the area north of the Yangtze River

Běijīng 北京 *noun*
= Beijing, the capital of China
Běijīng kǎoyā 北京烤鸭 = Peking duck

bèi 背 *noun*
= the back of the body, the back of an object
zài mǎ bèi shàng 在马背上 = on the back of the horse

bèihòu 背后 *noun*
- = behind, at the back, to the rear
tā duǒ zài mǔqīn bèihòu 他躲在母亲背后 = he hid behind his mother
- = behind someone's back
tā cháng zài rénjiā de bèihòu luàn shuō 她常在人家的背后乱说 = she often gossips behind people's backs

bèimiàn 背面 *noun*
= reverse side
xiàngpiàn de bèimiàn 相片的背面 = the back of the photograph

bèi 倍 *noun*
= times, -fold
shíbèi 十倍 = ten times
X bǐ Y zhòng shíjǐbèi X比Y重十几倍 = X is more than ten times heavier than Y

bèi 被 *preposition*
= by

> **!** *The preposition* **bèi 被** *is used in a passive sentence and usually marks the agent in a passive construction.*

wǒ de háizi bèi tā dǎ le 我的孩子被他打了 = my child was hit by him
tā zuìjìn bèi cítuì le 他最近被辞退了 = he was recently discharged from his job

bèizi 被子 *noun*
= quilt, duvet

běn 本
1 *noun*
= edition of a book

Yīngwén běn 英文本 = English edition

2 *measure word* ▶ 157
(*for things that are bound, such as books, magazines, etc.*)

3 *adjective*
- = one's own, oneself, personally
  wǒ běnshēn bù zhīdào 我本身不知道 = I personally don't know
  tā běnrén méiyǒu qù 他本人没有去 = he didn't go himself
- = this, current, present
  běn xiào 本校 = our school
  běn nián 本年 = this year
- (*when referring to a place*) = native
  běndì rén 本地人 = a native of this place

4 *adverb*
= originally
wǒ běn xiǎng qù, kěshì hòulái méi qù 我本想去, 可是后来没去 = originally I wanted to go, but in the end I didn't go

běnlái 本来
1 *adverb*
= originally, at first
wǒ běnlái xiǎng zài cānguǎn chīfàn, kěshì tài wǎn le 我本来想在餐馆吃饭, 可是太晚了 = I originally wanted to eat at a restaurant, but it was too late
2 *adjective*
= original
wǒ běnlái de xiǎngfǎ 我本来的想法 = my original idea

běnlǐng 本领 *noun*
= skill, ability, capability

běnshi 本事 *noun*
= ability

běnzhì 本质 *noun*
= essence, true nature

běnzi 本子 *noun*
= notebook, exercise book

bèn 笨 *adjective*
- (*of a person's mental ability*) = slow, stupid, dull
- (*of a person's physical ability*) = clumsy, awkward
  tiáowǔ wǒ xué bú huì; wǒ tài bèn! 跳舞我学不会; 我太笨! = I can't learn how to dance; I'm too clumsy!

bī 逼 *verb*
- = force, compel, press
- = press for, extort
  bī gòng 逼供 = extort a confession
  bīsǐ 逼死 = hound to death
  bī zū 逼租 = press for payment of rent
- = press on towards, press up to, close in on
  bījìn 逼近 = draw close to, press hard upon (*as an army to a city*)

bízi 鼻子 *noun*
= nose

bǐ 比
1 *preposition*
- = compared with, than
  tā bǐ wǒ gāo 他比我高 = he is taller than I am
  nǐ fùqīn bǐ nǐ mǔqīn dà jǐ suì? 你父亲比你母亲大几岁? = how many years older than your mother is your father?
- (*comparison over time*)
  tā yìtiān bǐ yìtiān jiēshi 他一天比一天结实 = he gets stronger every day
- (*indicating a score of a match or game*)
  wǔ bǐ sān 五比三 = five to three

2 *verb*
= compare, emulate
bǎ hóng de gēn lán de bǐyibǐ 把红的跟蓝的比一比 = make a comparison between the red one and the blue one

3 **bǐfāng (shuō)** 比方(说)
= for example, such as

4 **bǐrú (shuō)** 比如(说)
= for example, such as

bǐjiào 比较
1 *adverb*
= quite, relatively, rather
wǒ bǐjiào xǐhuān dú shū 我比较喜欢读书 = I rather enjoy reading
2 *verb*
= compare, contrast
bǐjiào liǎngjiàn yīfu de zhìliàng 比较两件衣服的质量 = compare the qualities of the two items of clothing

bǐlì 比例 *noun*
= ratio, proportion
nán-nǚ xìngbié bǐlì 男女性别比例 = the ratio of males to females

bǐsài 比赛
1 *verb*
= compete
gēn Yīnggélán duì bǐsài 跟英格兰队比赛 = have a match against the English team
2 *noun*
= match, competition

bǐ 笔
1 *noun*
• = pen, brush
• = stroke, touch of the brush
zhège zì de bǐhuà 这个字的笔划 = the strokes that make up this Chinese character
zhège zì de dìyībǐ 这个字的第一笔 = the first stroke of the character
2 *measure word* ▶ 157
• (*for sums of money*)
• (*for deals in business or trade*)

bǐjì 笔记 *noun*
= notes
bǐjìběn 笔记本 = notebook

bìrán 必然 *adjective*
= inevitable, certain
yíge bìrán de guīlǜ 一个必然的规律 = an inexorable law

bìxū 必须 *verb*
= must, have to
nǐ bìxū lái 你必须来 = you must come

bìyào 必要 *adjective*
= necessary

bìyè 毕业 *verb*
= graduate, finish school

bì 闭 *verb*
= shut, close
bìshàng yǎnjīng 闭上眼睛 = close one's eyes
bì zuǐ! 闭嘴! = hold your tongue!, shut up!

bì 避 *verb*
• = avoid, stay away from, hide
bì fēng yǔ 避风雨 = get out of the wind and rain
bìnàn 避难 = run away from trouble, escape calamity, seek asylum
• = prevent, keep away, repel
bìyùn 避孕 = contraception

bìmiǎn 避免 *verb*
= avoid, refrain from, avert

biān 边 *noun*
• = side
[**nà** | **zhè** | **běi** | **shàng** | **xià**] **biān** [那 | 这 | 北 | 上 | 下] 边 = [over there | over here | the north | above | below]
• = frontier, border
biānjiāng 边疆 = border
biānjiè 边界 = border
• = limit, edge
shùlín biān 树林边 = the edge of a forest
• = close by
zhàn zài chuāng biān 站在窗边 = stand by the window

biān...biān... 边...边... *conjunction*

> **!** Biān 边 *is used before two different verbs to indicate simultaneous actions. It is sometimes expressed as* yìbiān...yìbiān... 一边... 一边....

(yì) biān chī (yì) biān tán (一)边吃(一)边谈 = eat and talk at the same time
yìbiān tīng yīnyuè yìbiān kàn shū 一边听音乐一边看书 = read while listening to music

biān 编 *verb*
• = edit, arrange in order, compile
biān cídiǎn 编词典 = edit or compile a dictionary
• = weave, plait

biǎn 扁 *adjective*
= flat
lúntāi biǎn le 轮胎扁了 = the tyre has become flat

biàn 变 *verb*
• = change, become different
xiànzài Zhōngguó biàn le 现在中国变了 = China has changed now
• = transform, change, turn
biàn huàishì wéi hǎoshi 变坏事为好事 = turn a bad thing into a good thing

biànchéng 变成 *verb*
= change into
bǎ hēi zì biànchéng hóng zì 把黑字变成红字 = turn the black characters into red ones

biànhuà 变化
1 *verb*
= change, vary
2 *noun*
= change

biàn 便 ▶ *See also* **pián** 便.
1 *adverb*
= then
tiān yí liàng tā biàn shàngbān qù le 天一亮她便上班去了 = she left for work as soon as it was light
2 *adjective*
= convenient
biànlì 便利 = convenient

biàntiáo 便条 *noun*
= an informal note

biàn 遍
1 *measure word* ▶ 157
(*to indicate the number of times an action or state occurs*) = time

> **!** *Note that* **biàn** 遍 *is different from* **cì** 次 *in that it emphasizes the whole process from the beginning to the end.*

2 *adverb*
= everywhere, all over
yóu biàn quán shìjiè 游遍全世界 = travel all over the world

biāodiǎn 标点 *noun*
= punctuation
biāodiǎn fúhào 标点符号 = punctuation mark

biāozhǔn 标准
1 *noun*
= standard
biāozhǔnhuà 标准化 = standardization
2 *adjective*
= standard
nǐde Zhōngguó huà hěn biāozhǔn 你的中国话很标准 = your Chinese is very good

biǎo 表 *noun*
- = table, form, list
  shíjiānbiǎo 时间表 = timetable, schedule
  shēnqǐngbiǎo 申请表 = application form
- = meter, gauge
- = watch
  shǒubiǎo 手表 = wrist watch
- = the relationship between children with two common grandparents but without sharing the same paternal grandfather
  biǎogē 表哥 = elder male cousin
  biǎodì 表弟 = younger male cousin
  biǎojiě 表姐 = elder female cousin
  biǎomèi 表妹 = younger female cousin

biǎodá 表达 *verb*
(*thoughts and feelings, ideas*) = express

biǎomiàn 表面 *noun*
= surface, face, outside appearance

biǎomíng 表明 *verb*
= make known, make clear, state clearly

biǎoshì 表示
1 *verb*
= show, express, indicate
2 *noun*
= gesture, manifestation

biǎoxiàn 表现
1 *verb*
- = show, display, manifest
- = show off
  tā xǐhuān biǎoxiàn zìjǐ 他喜欢表现自己 = he likes to show off
- = behave

2 *noun*
- = expression, manifestation
- = behaviour

biǎoyǎn 表演
1 *verb*
= perform, act, play
2 *noun*
= performance

biǎoyáng 表扬 *verb*
= praise

bié 别
1 *adverb*
(*negative imperative*) = not
bié [**qù** | **zǒu** | **chī**] 别 [去 | 走 | 吃] = don't [go | leave | eat]
wǒ ràng tā bié lái 我让他别来 = I told him not to come
2 *adjective*
= other, another
bié chù 别处 = elsewhere, another place
nǐ hái yào bié de (dōngxi) ma? 你还要别的(东西)吗? = do you want anything else?

biéren 别人 *noun*
= others, other people
biéren dōu shuō yǒu yìsi 别人都说有意思 = other people all say it's interesting

bīnguǎn 宾馆 *noun*
= hotel, guesthouse

bīng 冰 *noun*
= ice

bīngqiú 冰球 *noun*
= ice hockey

bīng 兵 *noun*
= soldier, troops

bǐnggān 饼干 *noun*
= biscuit, cracker, cookie

bìng 并
1 *adverb*
(*used before a negative for emphasis*)
= actually, in reality, in fact
tā bìng méi qù 他并没去 = he actually didn't go
2 *conjunction*
= and, also

bìngqiě 并且 *conjunction*
• = and

> **!** *Often used in a pattern with* **búdàn** 不但 *to mean* **not only...but also....**

tā búdàn hěn cōngming bìngqiě hěn hǎokàn 他不但很聪明并且很好看 = he is not only intelligent but also very handsome
• = moreover, besides

bìng 病
1 *verb*
= be ill, become ill
tā bìng le 他病了 = he is ill
2 *noun*
= disease, ailment
tā yǒu bìng 他有病 = he has an illness
tā shēng bìng le 他生病了 = he has become ill
kàn bìng 看病 = examine someone who is ill, be examined by a doctor

bìngfáng 病房 *noun*
= hospital ward, hospital room

bìngjūn 病菌 *noun*
= bacteria, germs

bìngrén 病人 *noun*
= ill person, patient

bōli 玻璃 *noun*
= glass
bōli bēi 玻璃杯 = a glass

bófù 伯父, **bóbo** 伯伯 *noun*
= father's elder brother, uncle

bómǔ 伯母 *noun*
= aunt, wife of father's elder brother

bówùguǎn 博物馆 *noun*
= museum

bózi 脖子 *noun*
= neck

bǔ 补 *verb*
• = mend, patch, repair
• = fill, supply, make up for
bǔ kòngquē 补空缺 = fill a vacancy
• = nourish
bǔ shēntǐ 补身体 = build up health
bǔ xuě 补血 = enrich the blood

bǔchōng 补充
1 *verb*
= replenish, supplement
2 *adjective*
= supplementary
bǔchōng cáiliào 补充材料 = supplementary materials

bǔkè 补课 *verb*
= make up for a missed lesson
gěi xuésheng bǔkè 给学生补课 = give tutorials to students who have missed classes

bǔxí 补习 *verb*
= take lessons after school or work
bǔxíbān 补习班 = special class for supplementary learning

bǔ 捕 *verb*
= catch, seize, arrest

bú 不, **bù** 不

> **!** *As is true of* **yi** 一, *the tone on* **bu** 不 *changes depending on the tone of the word that follows it. It is pronounced* **bù** *before words in first, second, and third tone, but* **bú** *before the fourth tone. Because the tone changes for* **bu** 不 *do not indicate any difference in meaning, but only of pronunciation, combinations beginning with* **bu** 不 *are listed in alphabetical order below, regardless of tone.*

adverb
• (*used to form a negative*) = no, not
wǒ bù kěn qù 我不肯去 = I'm not willing to go
• (*used to indicate negative potentiality*)
tā bā diǎn yǐqián zuò bù wán zuòyè 他八点以前做不完作业 = he won't be able to finish his homework by 8 o'clock

búbì 不必 *verb*
= need not, be unnecessary
wǒmen jīntiān búbì shàngkè 我们今天不必上课 = we don't have to attend class today

búcuò 不错 *adjective*
• = correct, right
nǐde jìsuàn yìdiǎnr dōu búcuò 你的计算一点儿都不错 = your calculations were completely correct
• (*to indicate that what has been said is right*)
búcuò, tā míngtiān yào lái 不错，他明天要来 = yes, he will come tomorrow
• (*colloquial*) = not bad, pretty good
tāde zuòwén búcuò 他的作文不错 = his essay was pretty good

búdà 不大 *adverb*
• = not very, not too
jiàqián búdà piányi 价钱不大便宜 = the prices are not very cheap
• = not often
tā wǎnshang búdà niànshū 他晚上不大念书 = he doesn't study in the evening very often

búdàn 不但 *conjunction*

> ! *Usually used in a sentence pattern with* érqiě 而且 *or* bìngqiě 并且 *in the form* búdàn... érqiě/bìngqiě 不但... 而且/并且... *to mean* not only...but also....

= not only
tā búdàn yǎnjīng bù hǎo, érqiě jìxìng yě bù kěkào 他不但眼睛不好，而且记性也不可靠 = not only is his eyesight bad but his memory is also unreliable

bùdébù 不得不 *verb*
= have no choice or option but to, cannot but, have to
tā bùdébú qù 他不得不去 = he has to go

bùdéliǎo 不得了
1 *adjective*
= extremely serious, important, extreme
zhè bú shì shénme bùdéliǎo de wèntí 这不是什么不得了的问题 = this is not such a desperate matter
2 *adverb*
(*used after* **de** 得 *as a complement*) = extremely, exceedingly
tā gāoxìng dé bùdéliǎo 她高兴得不得了 = she is overjoyed

búduàn 不断 *adverb*
= unceasingly, continuously, in an uninterrupted fashion
búduàn de késou 不断地咳嗽 = cough continuously

bù gǎn dāng 不敢当

> ! *This is a polite expression in reply to a compliment.*

= thank you! you're flattering me! I don't deserve it

bùguǎn 不管 *conjunction*
= no matter what or how
bùguǎn dào shénme dìfang qù dōu xíng 不管到什么地方去都行 = it doesn't matter where we go, it will be fine with me

búguò 不过
1 *conjunction*
= but, however
dàxiǎo kěyǐ, búguò yánsè bù xíng 大小可以，不过颜色不行 = the size is fine, but the colour won't do
2 *adverb*
= only, merely
tā búguò shì ge háizi 他不过是个孩子 = he's only a child
3 *superlative emphatic*
zài [hǎo | jiǎndān | xìngyùn] búguò le 再[好 | 简单 | 幸运]不过了 = couldn't be [better | simpler | luckier]

bù hǎoyìsi 不好意思 *adjective*
= feel embarrassed, be ill at ease, find embarrassing

bùjǐn 不仅
• = not only
zhè bùjǐn shì tāzìjǐ de kànfǎ 这不仅是他自己的看法 = this is not only his personal view
• **bùjǐn rúcǐ** 不仅如此 = not only that, moreover

bùjiǔ 不久 *adverb*
• = soon, before long
nǐmen bùjiǔ jiù yào bìyè le 你们不久就要毕业了 = soon you will graduate
• = not long after, soon after
xiàle kè bùjiǔ jiù kāishǐ xiàyǔ le 下了课不久就开始下雨了 = not long after class ended it began to rain

búlùn 不论 *conjunction*
= no matter what, it doesn't matter

búlùn nǐ zuò shénme shì, dōu yào zuò hǎo 不论你做什么事, 都要做好 = it doesn't matter what you do, you must do it well

bùpíng 不平 *adjective*
- = indignant, resentful
- = unjust

bùrán 不然 *conjunction*
= or else, otherwise, if not
nǐ děi fùxí shēngcí, bùrán huì dōu wàng le 你得复习生词, 不然会都忘了 = you must revise the new words or else you'll forget them all

bùrú 不如 *verb*
- (*before a noun*) = not as...as, not measure up to, compare unfavourably with
  wǒ Hànyǔ shuō de bùrú tā liúlì 我汉语说得不如她流利 = my spoken Chinese is not as fluent as hers
- (*before a clause*) = had better
  nǐ bùrú jīntiān niànshū 你不如今天念书 = you had better study today

bùshǎo 不少 *adjective*
= quite a bit, quite a few
bùshǎo qián 不少钱 = quite a large amount of money

bùtóng 不同 *adjective*
= different, distinct

bùxíng 不行 *verb*
- = it's out of the question, it's not allowed
- = be no good, won't work

búxìng 不幸
1 *adjective*
= unfortunate, unlucky, sad
2 *noun*
= misfortune

bù xǔ 不许 *verb*
- = not allow
  wǒde mǔqīn bù xǔ wǒ chū mén 我的母亲不许我出门 = my mother doesn't allow me to leave the house
- = must not, be forbidden
  nǐ bù xǔ chōu yān 你不许抽烟 = you mustn't smoke

bú yào 不要 *verb*
= don't
bú yào nàyàng wúlǐ 不要那样无礼 = don't be so rude

bú yàojǐn 不要紧
1 *adjective*
- = not important
- = not serious
  wǒde shāng bú yàojǐn 我的伤不要紧 = my injury is not serious

2 **búyàojǐn** 不要紧
= it doesn't matter

bùyídìng 不一定 *adverb*
= not necessarily
wǒ bùyídìng néng qù 我不一定能去 = I won't necessarily be able to go

bú yòng 不用 *verb*
= need not
bú yòng jǐnzhāng 不用紧张 = you needn't be nervous

bù 布 *noun*
= cloth, cotton cloth

bùzhì 布置 *verb*
- = fix up, arrange, decorate
  bùzhì bàngōngshì 布置办公室 = decorate the office
- = assign, arrange
  bùzhì zuòyè 布置作业 = assign homework

bù 步 *noun*
- = step, pace
- = stage, step, procedure
- = condition, situation, state
  nǐ zěnme luòdào zhè yíbù? 你怎么落到这一步? = how could you get yourself into such a situation?

bù 部
1 *noun*
- = part, area, section
  xī bù 西部 = the western part
- = unit, ministry, department
  wàijiāo bù 外交部 = Ministry of Foreign Affairs
  biānjí bù 编辑部 = editorial board or office

2 *measure word* ▶ 157
(*for novels, films, etc.*)

bùduì 部队 *noun*
- = army
- = troops, unit in a military force

bùfen 部分 *noun*
= part, section, portion
dìyī bùfen 第一部分 = Part One

bùmén 部门 *noun*
= department or branch in a government, company, etc.

bùzhǎng 部长 *noun*
= minister, head of a department
wàijiāo bù bùzhǎng 外交部部长 = Minister of Foreign Affairs

Cc

cā 擦 *verb*
- = wipe, clean
- (*spread on*)
  zài liǎn shang cā yóu 在脸上擦油 = put cream on one's face

cāi 猜 *verb*
= guess, conjecture, speculate

cāixiǎng 猜想 *verb*
= suppose, guess, suspect

cái 才
1 *noun*
= ability, talent, gift
2 *adverb*
- = just
  diànyǐng cái kāishǐ 电影才开始 = the film has just started
- = so late
  nǐ zěnme cái lái 你怎么才来 = why are you so late?
- = only
  tā cái shísān suì 他才十三岁 = he is only 13 years old
- = then and only then
  wǒmen děi děng tā huílái yǐhòu, cái néng zǒu 我们得等他回来以后, 才能走 = we have to wait until he comes back; then we can go

cáinéng 才能 *noun*
= ability, talent

cáizǐ 才子 *noun*
= talented scholar

cáiliào 材料 *noun*
= material, data

cáichǎn 财产 *noun*
= property

cáifù 财富 *noun*
= wealth

cáizhèng 财政 *noun*
= finance

cáifeng 裁缝 *noun*
= tailor, dressmaker

cáipàn 裁判 *noun*
= referee, umpire, judge

cǎi 采 *verb*
= pick, gather

cǎifǎng 采访 *verb*
(*by a news reporter*) = gather material, cover news, interview

cǎigòu 采购 *verb*
= purchase, buy

cǎiqǔ 采取 *verb*
= adopt, take
cǎiqǔ jǐnjí cuòshī 采取紧急措施 = take emergency steps

cǎiyòng 采用 *verb*
= adopt for use, use
cǎiyòng xīn jìshù 采用新技术 = adopt new techniques

cǎisè 彩色 *noun*
= colour, multicolour
cǎisè diànshì 彩色电视 = colour television

cǎi 踩 *verb*
= step on

cài 菜 *noun*
- = vegetable
- (*food in general*) = food
  mǎi cài 买菜 = shop for food
- = dish, course

càidān 菜单 *noun*
= menu

cānguān 参观 *verb*
= visit, look around

cānjiā 参加 *verb*
- = join, take part in
- = attend
  cānjiā huìyì 参加会议 = attend meetings

cānkǎo 参考
1 *verb*
= consult, refer to
2 *noun*
cānkǎo shū 参考书 = reference book

cānmóu 参谋
1 *noun*
= adviser, staff officer
cānmóu zhǎng 参谋长 = chief of staff
2 *verb*
= give advice

cān 餐 *noun*
= food, meal
[Xī | Zhōng | wǔ | yě] **cān** [西 | 中 | 午 | 野] 餐 = [Western food | Chinese food | lunch | picnic]

cānchē 餐车 *noun*
= dining car, restaurant car

cāntīng 餐厅 *noun*
= dining room, dining hall

cánfèi 残废 *adjective*
= disabled, physically handicapped

cánkù 残酷 *adjective*
= cruel, ruthless, brutal

cánkuì 惭愧 *adjective*
= feel ashamed

căn 惨 *adjective*
= miserable, pitiful, tragic

cànlàn 灿烂 *adjective*
= magnificent, splendid, bright

cāngkù 仓库 *noun*
= warehouse, storehouse

cāngbái 苍白 *adjective*
= pale

cāngying 苍蝇 *noun*
= fly

cāng 舱 *noun*
= cabin
kècāng 客舱 = passenger cabin
huòcāng 货舱 = a (ship's) hold

cáng 藏 *verb*
= hide, store, put by

cāochăng 操场 *noun*
= playground, sports ground, drill ground

căo 草 *noun*
= grass, straw

căodì 草地 *noun*
= grassland, meadow, lawn

căoyuán 草原 *noun*
= steppe, grasslands, prairie

cè 册 *measure word* ▶ 157
- (*for books or volumes of books*) = volume, book
- (*for copies of books*) = copy

cèsuŏ 厕所 *noun*
= lavatory, toilet, loo

cèyàn 测验
1 *verb*
= test
2 *noun*
= test

cèlüè 策略 *noun*
= tactics, strategy

céng 层
1 *measure word* ▶ 157
- = storey, floor
- (*for a layer, coat, sheet*)

2 *noun*
= floor
wŏde fángjiān zài sāncéng 我的房间在三层 = my room is on the third floor

> **!** *Note that Chinese is similar to US usage where the 1st floor is the ground floor, whereas in British English the storey above the ground floor is called the 1st floor.*

céng 曾 *adverb*
= once, formerly, sometime ago
tā céng zuòguo zhèzhŏng gōngzuò 他曾做过这种工作 = he did this kind of work once before

céngjīng 曾经 *adverb*
= once, formerly
tāmen céngjīng shì hăo péngyou 他们曾经是好朋友 = they were once good friends

chāzi 叉子 *noun*
= fork

chā 插 *verb*
- = stick in, insert
- = interpolate; insert

tā bànjù huà yě chā bú jìnqu 他半句话也插不进去 = he couldn't get a word in edgeways

chá 茶 *noun*
= tea

chábēi 茶杯 *noun*
= teacup

chádiăn 茶点 *noun*
= tea and snacks, tea and biscuits

cháguăn 茶馆 *noun*
= teahouse

cháhú 茶壶 *noun*
= teapot

cháyè 茶叶 *noun*
= tea leaves

chá 查 *verb*
- = check, examine, inspect
- = look into, investigate, find out
- = look up, consult

chá zìdiăn 查字典 = consult a dictionary

chà 差
1 *verb*
= differ from, fall short of
chà de yuǎn 差得远 = differ substantially
2 *adjective*
= wanting, short of
hái chà liǎng kuài qián 还差两块钱 = still two yuan short
chà wǔ fēn qī diǎn 差五分七点 = five minutes to seven

chàbuduō 差不多 *adjective*
- = almost, nearly
tā líkāi chàbuduō liǎng nián le 他离开差不多两年了 = he's been gone nearly two years now
- = about the same, similar

chàdiǎnr 差点儿 *adverb*
= almost, nearly, on the verge of
tā chàdiǎnr shībài 她差点儿失败 = she very nearly failed

chāi 拆 *verb*
- = take apart, tear open
- = pull down, demolish
- = unravel
bǎ yíjiàn jiù máoyī chāi le 把一件旧毛衣拆了 = unravel an old jumper

chǎnliàng 产量 *noun*
= output, yield

chǎnpǐn 产品 *noun*
= product, produce

chǎnshēng 产生 *verb*
- = produce, engender, bring about
- = emerge, come into being

cháng 长 *adjective*
= long

Chángchéng 长城 *noun*
= the Great Wall

chángchù 长处 *noun*
= good qualities, strong points

chángdù 长度 *noun*
= length

Chángjiāng 长江 *noun*
= Yangtze River, Yangtse River

chángjiǔ 长久 *adjective*
= long-lasting, long-term

chángqī 长期 *noun*
= a long period of time, long-term

chángtú 长途 *noun*
= long-distance
chángtú diànhuà 长途电话 = long-distance telephone call

cháng 尝 *verb*
= taste, try the flavour of

cháng 常, **chángcháng** 常常
adverb
= frequently, often

chǎng 场
1 *measure word* ▶ 157
- (*for the whole process of being ill*)
- (*for a natural disturbance, war, disaster, etc.*)
- (*for a show, performance, game, or debate*)
- (*to indicate the occasion on which a state or an action occurs*)

2 *noun*
- = site, spot, place where people gather
- (*for ballgames*) = court, field, ground
[lánqiú | páiqiú | zúqiú | wǎngqiú] chǎng [篮球 | 排球 | 足球 | 网球] 场 = [basketball court | volleyball court | football field | tennis court]
- = stage
dēng chǎng 登场 = come on stage

chàng 唱 *verb*
= sing

chànggē 唱歌 *verb*
= sing songs

chāo 抄 *verb*
- = copy, transcribe
- = plagiarize

chāoxiě 抄写 *verb*
= make a clear copy

chāo 超 *verb*
= exceed, surpass, overtake

chāoguò 超过 *verb*
= outstrip, surpass, exceed

chāojí shìchǎng 超级市场
noun
= supermarket

cháo 朝
1 *preposition*
= facing, towards
cháo Lúndūn kāi 朝伦敦开 = drive towards London
2 *verb*
= face, towards
zhè fángzi cháo nán 这房子朝南 = this house faces south

3 *noun*
= dynasty or period
Hàn cháo 汉朝 = the Han Dynasty

Cháoxiān 朝鲜 *noun*
= North Korea

cháo 巢 *noun*
= nest

chǎo 吵
1 *verb*
= quarrel, wrangle, squabble
wèi yìxiē xiǎoshì chǎojià 为一些小事吵架 = bicker over small matters
2 *adjective*
= noisy

chǎojià 吵架 *verb*
= quarrel, have an argument

chǎonào 吵闹 *verb*
= make a fuss, make trouble

chǎozuǐ 吵嘴 *verb*
= quarrel, bicker

chǎo 炒 *verb*
= stir-fry

chē 车 *noun*
= vehicle, car, bus

chēdài 车带 *noun*
= tyre on a car or bicycle

chējiān 车间 *noun*
= workshop

chēpiào 车票 *noun*
= bus ticket, train ticket

chēzhàn 车站 *noun*
= station, stop

chèdǐ 彻底 *adjective*
= thorough

chén 沉
1 *verb*
= sink, sink down, lower
2 *adjective*
- **shuì de hěn chén 睡得很沉** = sleep soundly, sleep deeply
- = heavy

chénmò 沉默 *adjective*
- = reticent, uncommunicative
- = silent

chénzhòng 沉重 *adjective*
= heavy

chénliè 陈列 *verb*
= display, exhibit

chènshān 衬衫 *noun*
= shirt

chènyī 衬衣 *noun*
= underclothes, shirt

chèn 趁 *verb*
= take advantage of, avail oneself of
chèn zhège jīhuì xiūxi yíxià 趁这个机会休息一下 = take this opportunity to have a rest

chēng 称 *verb*
- = name, call
  wǒmen dōu chēng tā shūshu 我们都称他叔叔 = we all call him Uncle
- = weigh
- = state, say

chēngzàn 称赞 *verb*
= praise, acclaim, commend

chéng 成 *verb*
- = become, change to, develop into
  tā chéngle yíge dàifu 他成了一个大夫 = he became a doctor
- = accomplish, succeed
  zhèbǐ jiāoyì méi chéng 这笔交易没成 = the deal did not succeed

chéngfèn 成分(成份) *noun*
- = composition, component part, ingredient
- = one's class status or family background

chénggōng 成功
1 *verb*
= succeed
2 *noun*
= success

chéngguǒ 成果 *noun*
= accomplishment, achievement

chéngjì 成绩 *noun*
= achievement, success

chéngjiā 成家 *verb*
(*referring to a man*) = get married

chéngjiù 成就 *noun*
= achievement, accomplishment, attainment

chénglì 成立 *verb*
= set up, found, establish

chéngnián 成年 *verb*
= grow up, come of age

chéngrén 成人 *noun*
= adult

chéngshú 成熟
1 *verb*
= ripen, mature

2 *adjective*
= ripe, mature

chéngwéi 成为 *verb*
= become, change to, develop into

chéngzhǎng 成长 *verb*
= grow up

chéngkěn 诚恳 *adjective*
= sincere

chéngshí 诚实 *adjective*
= honest

chéng 城 *noun*
- = city, town
- = city wall, wall

chéngshì 城市 *noun*
= town, city

chéngzhèn 城镇 *noun*
= cities and towns, town

chéngrèn 承认 *verb*
- = admit, acknowledge, recognize
- = give diplomatic recognition to, recognize

chéngshòu 承受 *verb*
= bear, endure

chéng 乘 *verb*
- = ride
  chéng [huǒchē | fēijī | gōnggòng qìchē] lǚxíng 乘 [火车 | 飞机 | 公共汽车] 旅行 = travel by [train | plane | bus]
- = take advantage of
- (*in mathematical operations*) = multiply
  wǔ chéng sān děngyú shíwǔ 五乘三等于十五 = five times three equals fifteen

chéngwùyuán 乘务员 *noun*
= train attendant, conductor, ticket collector

chéngdù 程度 *noun*
= level, degree, extent

chī 吃 *verb*
= eat

chīcù 吃醋 *adjective*
= be jealous

chījīng 吃惊 *verb*
= be startled, be shocked, be amazed
dà chī yì jīng 大吃一惊 = be greatly surprised

chídào 迟到 *verb*
= be late

chǐ 尺 *noun*
(*unit of length, 1|3 metre*) = *chi*

chǐzi 尺子 *noun*
(*to measure length*) = ruler

chǐcùn 尺寸 *noun*
= size, measurement, dimension

chìdào 赤道 *noun*
= equator

chìbǎng 翅膀 *noun*
= wing

chōngfèn 充分 *adjective*
= full, ample, abundant

chōngmǎn 充满 *verb*
= be full of, be brimming with

chōngzhíkǎ 充值卡 *noun*
= top-up card

chōngzú 充足 *adjective*
= adequate, ample, abundant

chōng 冲 *verb*
- = pour boiling water on
  chōng chá 冲茶 = make tea
- = rinse, flush, wash away
  chōng cèsuǒ 冲厕所 = flush the toilet
- = charge, rush, dash
  chōng jìn fángzi 冲进房子 = rush into the house
- (*for film*) = develop

chōngtū 冲突 *noun*
= conflict, clash

chóngzi 虫子 *noun*
= insect, worm

chóng 重 *adverb* ▶ See also **zhòng** 重.
= over again
chóng fǎng Yīngguó 重访英国 = revisit the U.K.

chóngdié 重叠 *verb*
= overlap, pile on top of one another

chóngfù 重复 *verb*
= repeat, duplicate

chóngxīn 重新 *adverb*
= again, anew, afresh

chónggāo 崇高 *adjective*
= lofty, high

chǒng'ài 宠爱 *verb*
= dote on, make a pet of someone

chōu 抽 *verb*
- = take out (*from in between*)

cóng shūjià shang chōuchū yìběn shū 从书架上抽出一本书 = take a book from the shelf
- (*cigarette, pipe*) = smoke
- (*water*) = draw

chōu shuǐ 抽水 = draw water (*from a well, etc.*)
- = lash, whip, thrash

chōuxiàng 抽象 *adjective*
= abstract

chōuyān 抽烟 *verb*
= smoke (a cigarette or a pipe)

chóu 愁 *verb*
= worry, be anxious
bié chóu 别愁 = don't worry

chǒu 丑 *adjective*
= ugly, disgraceful

chòu 臭 *adjective*
= smelly, stinking, foul
chòu jīdàn 臭鸡蛋 = rotten egg
chòu dòufu 臭豆腐 = fermented beancurd

chū 出 *verb*
- = go or come out
- = issue, put forth
- = produce, turn out, publish

chū xīn shū 出新书 = publish new books
- = arise, happen, occur

chū shìgù 出事故 = there was an accident
- = exceed, go beyond

bù chū sān nián 不出三年 = within three years
- = vent

chū qì 出气 = vent one's spleen, express one's anger

chūbǎn 出版 *verb*
= publish

chūbǎnshè 出版社 *noun*
= publishing company, publishing house

chūfā 出发 *verb*
- = set out, start off
- = start, proceed

chūfādiǎn 出发点 *noun*
= starting point, point of departure

chūguó 出国 *verb*
= go abroad, leave the country

chūkǒu 出口
1 *verb*
= export
2 *noun*
- = export
- = exit

chūlai 出来 *verb*
- = come out
- (*after a verb to indicate movement in an outward direction or a completed action*)

bǎ qián náchūlai 把钱拿出来 = take out the money
xiāngpiàn xǐchūlai le 相片洗出来了 = the photographs have been developed
tā xiǎngchūlaile yíge hǎo bànfǎ 他想出来了一个好办法 = he thought of a good solution

chūlù 出路 *noun*
= a way out, a solution to a problem

chūmíng 出名 *adjective*
= famous, well-known

chūqu 出去 *verb*
- = go out, get out
- (*after a verb to indicate movement in an outward direction*)

cóng wūlǐ pǎochūqu 从屋里跑出去 = run out from the room

chūsè 出色 *adjective*
= excellent, outstanding, remarkable

chūshēng 出生 *verb*
= be born

chūxí 出席 *verb*
(*when speaking of a meeting, banquet, etc.*) = attend, be present

chūxiàn 出现 *verb*
= appear, emerge, come to light

chūyuàn 出院 *verb*
= leave hospital, be discharged from hospital after recovery

chūzū qìchē 出租汽车 *noun*
= taxi

chū 初
1 *adjective*
- = early

chū [dōng | chūn | xià | qiū] 初 [冬 | 春 | 夏 | 秋] = early [winter | spring | summer | autumn]
- = elementary, rudimentary

chūzhōng 初中
(*abbreviation of* chūjí zhōngxué 初级中学) = junior middle school, junior high school

- (*used to enumerate days of the lunar month up to ten*)
  chū [yī | èr | sān | sì...] 初 [一 | 二 | 三 | 四...] = the [first | second | third | fourth...] day of a lunar month

2 *noun*
= beginning
[zhège yuè | míngnián | shàngge shìjì] chū [这个月 | 明年 | 上个世纪] 初 = the beginning of [this month | next year | the last century]

chūbù 初步 *adjective*
= initial, preliminary, tentative

chūjí 初级 *adjective*
= elementary, primary

chú 除 *verb*
- = get rid of, do away with, remove
  chúdiào [huài xíguàn | jiù sīxiǎng] 除掉 [坏习惯 | 旧思想] = get rid of [bad habits | old ways of thinking]
- = divide
  sān chú liú dé èr 三除六得二 = six divided by three equals two

chúfēi 除非 *conjunction*

> **!** *When* **chúfēi 除非** *is used, it is often necessary to use* **fǒuzé 否则** *or* **bùrán 不然** *at the beginning of the main clause to indicate the necessary consequence of the clause introduced by* **chúfēi 除非**.

= only if, unless
chúfēi tiānqì bù hǎo, fǒuzé wǒmen míngtiān qù hǎibiān wánr 除非天气不好, 否则我们明天去海边玩儿 = we'll go to the seashore tomorrow unless the weather isn't good

chúle ... (yǐwài) 除了...(以外) *preposition*

> **!** *Note that the use of* **yǐwài 以外** *is optional.*

- (*used with* **dōu 都** *or* **yě 也**) = except
  chúle tā (yǐwài), biéren dōu bú huì chàng zhèshǒu gē 除了她(以外), 别人都不会唱这首歌 = no one can sing this song except her
- (*used with* **hái 还**) = apart from, besides, in addition to...
  tā chúle kànshū yǐwài, hái xiězuò 她除了看书以外, 还写作 = in addition to reading she also does some writing

chúfáng 厨房 *noun*
= kitchen

chǔ 处 *verb*
- = deal with, handle
  chǔ shì 处事 = handle affairs, manage matters
- = be in a certain position (*literal or figurative*)
  chǔyú 处于 (*literal or figurative*) = to be located in a place or position
  tā chǔyú bú lì dìwèi 他处于不利地位 = he is in a disadvantageous position

chǔfèn 处分
1 *noun*
= disciplinary action, punishment
2 *verb*
= take disciplinary action against, punish

chǔlǐ 处理
1 *verb*
- = handle, deal with, dispose of
  chǔlǐ jiāwù 处理家务 = do household chores
- **chǔlǐ jiàgé 处理价格** = reduced price, bargain price
  chǔlǐpǐn 处理品 = goods sold at reduced or sale prices

2 *noun*
= handling, treatment, disposal

chù 处 *noun*
- = place
  tíngchēchù 停车处 = car park, parking lot
- = point, feature
  gòngtóng zhī chù 共同之处 = common feature
- = department, office
  mìshūchù 秘书处 = secretariat

chuān 穿 *verb*
- = wear, put on, be dressed in
- = pierce through, penetrate
  chuāntòu 穿透 = penetrate
- = pass through, cross
  chuānguò mǎlù 穿过马路 = cross the road
  chuānshang 穿上 = put on
  chuānshang nǐde dàyī 穿上你的大衣 = put on your coat

chuán 传 *verb*
- = pass, pass on
- (*for news, rumours, etc.*) = spread, transmit

C

- = hand down
- (*for heat, electricity, etc.*) = transmit, conduct

chuánbō 传播 *verb*
= propagate, disseminate, spread

chuánrǎn 传染 *verb*
= infect, catch
wǒ bǎ gǎnmào chuánrǎngěile tā 我把感冒传染给了他 = he caught my cold

chuánshuō 传说 *noun*
= rumour, legend

chuántǒng 传统 *noun*
= tradition, conventions

chuánzhēn 传真 *noun*
= facsimile, fax

chuán 船 *noun*
= boat, ship

chuāng(hu) 窗(户) *noun*
= window

chuáng 床
1 *noun*
= bed
shàng chuáng shuìjiào 上床睡觉 = go to bed, get into bed
2 *measure word* ▶ 157
(*for quilt, blanket, sheet*)

chuángdān 床单 *noun*
= (bed) sheet

chuǎng 闯 *verb*
= rush, force one's way in or out

chuàng 创 *verb*
= initiate, achieve for the first time, innovate
chuàng jìlù 创记录 = set a record

chuàngzào 创造
1 *verb*
= create, produce, bring about
2 *noun*
= creation

chuàngzuò 创作
1 *verb*
(*works of art or literature*) = create, write, produce
2 *noun*
= literary or artistic creation

chuī 吹 *verb*
- = blow, exhale

chuī yìkǒu qì 吹一口气 = blow out a puff of air
- (*wind instruments*) = play

chuī dízi 吹笛子 = play the flute
- (*colloquial*) = brag, boast
- (*colloquial, referring to a relationship*) = break off, break up, fall through

tāmen liǎ chuī le 他们俩吹了 = they have broken up
chuīmiè 吹灭 = blow out
bǎ làzhú chuīmiè 把蜡烛吹灭 = blow out the candle

chuīniú 吹牛 *verb*
= brag, boast

chuīxū 吹嘘 *verb*
= brag, boast

chūn 春 *noun*
(*the season*) = spring
chūnjì 春季 = spring season

Chūnjié 春节 *noun*
= Spring Festival, the Chinese New Year

chūntiān 春天 *noun*
= spring, springtime

chúncuì 纯粹 *adjective*
= pure, simple

chún 唇 *noun*
= lip

cí 词 *noun*
- = word, term
- = speech, statement

kāimùcí 开幕词 = opening speech

cídiǎn 词典 *noun*
= dictionary, lexicon

cíhuì 词汇 *noun*
= vocabulary

cízhí 辞职 *verb*
= leave or quit a job, resign

cídài 磁带 *noun*
= (magnetic) tape

cǐ 此 *determiner*
= this
cǐ [chù | rén] 此[处 | 人] = this [place | person]

cǐwài 此外 *adverb*
= besides, moreover, in addition

cì 次 *measure word* ▶ 157
- (*for events such as examinations, accidents, experiments, etc.*)
- (*to indicate the number of times an action or state occurs*) = time

cì 刺
1 *verb*
- = prick, stab
- = irritate, criticize

2 *noun*
= thorn

cìshā 刺杀 *verb*
= assassinate

cōngmáng 匆忙 *adverb*
= hurriedly, hastily

cōngming 聪明 *adjective*
= intelligent, bright, clever

cóng 从 *preposition*
(*used to indicate the starting point*) = from
cóng Běijīng chūfā 从北京出发 = start off from Beijing
cóng lǐlùnshang jiǎng 从理论上讲 = theoretically speaking

cóng bù/méi 从不/没 *adverb*
= never
wǒ cóng bù hē jiǔ 我从不喝酒 = I never drink wine
wǒ cóng méi qùguo Yìdàlì 我从没去过意大利 = I've never been to Italy

cóngcǐ 从此 *adverb*
= from now on, henceforth

cóng...dào... 从...到... *preposition*
= from...to...
cóng zǎoshàng jiǔ diǎn dào wǎnshàng bā diǎn 从早上九点到晚上八点 = from 9:00 am to 8:00 pm

cóng'ér 从而 *conjunction*
= thus, and then, and then proceed to

cónglái 从来 *adverb*
= always, all along

> **!** *Note that* cónglái 从来 *normally precedes the negative word* bù 不 *or* méi 没.

wǒ cónglái méi jiànguo tā 我从来没见过他 = I have never seen him before
tā cónglái bù hē jiǔ 他从来不喝酒 = he never drinks wine

cóng...qǐ 从...起 *preposition*
= from...on, from...forward
cóng xiànzài qǐ... 从现在起... = from now on...

cóngqián 从前 *adverb*
= before, in the past, formerly

cóngshì 从事 *verb*
= go in for, be engaged in

còuqiǎo 凑巧 *adverb*
= luckily, by coincidence

còuhe 凑合 *verb*
- = gather together, get together
  tāmen měige zhōumò dōu còuhe zài yìqǐ hē chá liáotiān 他们每个周末都凑合在一起喝茶聊天 = every weekend they get together for tea and have a chat
- = make do
  tā yìzhí zài còuhezhe yòng nàtái jiù jìsuànjī 他一直在凑合着用那台旧计算机 = he has been making do with that old computer all along
- = do in a pinch, be OK, be not too bad
  'nàbù Měiguó diànyǐng zěnmeyàng?'—'hái còuhe' '那部美国电影怎么样?'—'还凑合' = 'how was that American film?'—'it wasn't too bad'

cū 粗 *adjective*
- = thick
- = careless, negligent

cūxīn 粗心 *adjective*
= careless, thoughtless

cùjìn 促进 *verb*
= promote, advance, accelerate

cù 醋 *noun*
- = vinegar
- (*in love affairs*) = jealousy

cuī 催 *verb*
= hurry, urge, speed up

cūn 村 *noun*
= village

cūnzhuāng 村庄 *noun*
= village

cūnzi 村子 *noun*
= village

cún 存 *verb*
- = store, keep, preserve
- = place something for safe keeping, deposit
  bǎ qián cún zài yínháng lǐ 把钱存在银行里 = save money in a bank
- = exist, live, survive

cúnfàng 存放 *verb*
= leave in someone's care

cúnkuǎn 存款 *noun*
= deposit account, bank savings

cúnzài 存在 *verb*
= exist

C

cùn 寸 *noun* (*a unit of length, 1/30 metre*) = *cun*

cuòshī 措施 *noun*
= measure, step, suitable action

cuò 错
1 *adjective*
= wrong, mistaken, erroneous
cuò zì 错字 = wrong Chinese character
2 *noun*
= mistake, error, fault
zhè búshì nǐde cuò 这不是你的错 = it's not your fault
2 *adverb*
= by mistake, in the wrong way
zuòcuò le 做错了 = made a mistake
zuòcuòle chē 坐错了车 = took the wrong bus

cuòguò 错过 *verb*
= miss, let slip
bié cuòguò zhège hǎo jīhuì 别错过这个好机会 = don't miss this good opportunity

cuòwù 错误 *noun*
= mistake, error

Dd

dā 搭 *verb*
- = put up, put together, construct
  dā yíge xiǎo péng 搭一个小棚 = put up a shed/arbour
- = join up with, establish contact
  dā huǒ 搭伙 = join a group
  dāshang guānxi 搭上关系 = establish contact
- (*a ship, train, plane, etc.*) = go by, go aboard
  dā [**chuán** | **huǒchē** | **chē**] 搭 [船 | 火车 | 车] = go by [ship | train | car]

dāying 答应 *verb*
- = respond, reply
  méi rén dāying 没人答应 = no one answered
- = agree, promise
  tā dāying qù 他答应去 = he agreed to go

dádào 达到 *verb*
= attain, reach
dádào mùdì 达到目的 = attain a goal

dá 答 *verb*
= answer, reciprocate

dá'àn 答案 *noun*
= answer, solution

dáfù 答复 *verb*
(*in a formal way*) = reply, answer

dájuàn 答卷 *noun*
= answer booklet, answer sheet

dǎ 打 *verb*
- = hit, strike, beat
  dǎ rén 打人 = hit a person
- = fight, make (war)
- (*when talking about an object*) = break, smash, destroy
  dǎpò jìngzi 打破镜子 = break a mirror
  (*when talking about prejudice, tradition, record, relationship, etc.*)
  dǎpò [**piānjiàn** | **jiù chuántǒng** | **jìlù**] 打破 [偏见 | 旧传统 | 纪录] = [dispel a prejudice | break an old tradition | break a record]
- (*for games played with the hands, some musical instruments*) = play
  dǎ qiú 打球 = play a (ball) game
  dǎ tàijíquán 打太极拳 = practice taiji boxing
  dǎ pái 打牌 = play cards
  dǎ gǔ 打鼓 = play a drum/drums
- = type on a typewriter, use a keyboard on a computer
  dǎzì 打字 = type, typing
- = send, dispatch
  dǎ [**diànbào** | **diànhuà**] 打 [电报 | 电话] = [send a telegram | make a phone call]
- (*other uses*)
  dǎ chái 打柴 = gather firewood
  dǎ gōng 打工 = do odd jobs
  dǎ liè 打猎 = go hunting
  dǎ máoyī 打毛衣 = knit a sweater
  dǎ qì 打气 (*for tyres*) = inflate with air
  (*for people*) = encourage, boost morale
  dǎ qiāng 打枪 = fire a gun
  dǎ shuǐ 打水 = fetch water
  dǎ yóu 打油 = buy oil
  dǎ yú 打渔 = catch fish

dǎbài 打败 *verb*
= defeat

dǎbàn 打扮 *verb*
= dress up, deck out, make up

dǎdǎo 打倒 *verb*
= down with..., overthrow

dǎjī 打击 *verb*
= attack, hit, strike

dǎjià 打架 *verb*
= fight, come to blows

dǎkāi 打开 *verb*
= open (something)

dǎ pēntì 打喷嚏 *verb*
= sneeze

dǎrǎo 打扰 *verb*
= bother, disturb, trouble

dǎsǎo 打扫 *verb*
(*when referring to housework*) = clean, sweep

dǎsuàn 打算
1 *verb*
= intend to, plan to
2 *noun*
= intention, plan

dǎting 打听 *verb*
= ask about, inquire about

dǎyìnjī 打印机 *noun*
= printer

dǎzhàng 打仗 *verb*
= fight, make war

dǎ zhāohu 打招呼 *verb*
= greet politely, make a sign of greeting politely

dǎzhēn 打针 *verb*
= inject, give or have an injection

dǎzì 打字 *verb*
= type, word-process, key in

dà 大
1 *adjective*
- = big, large, major
- = heavy, strong
  fēng hěn dà 风很大 = the wind is strong
- (*when referring to sound*) = loud
- (*when referring to age*) = old, elder
  háizi duō dà le? 孩子多大了? = how old is the child?
  dà jiě 大姐 = elder sister

2 *adverb*
- (*to a great extent, to an extreme*)
  dà nào 大闹 = create a major disturbance
- (*after a negative*) = not very, not often
  bú dà hǎo 不大好 = not very good
  bú dà huì 不大会 = cannot (do something) very well

dàdǎn 大胆 *adjective*
= bold, daring, audacious

dàduōshù 大多数 *noun*
= the great majority

dàgài 大概
1 *adjective*
= general, approximate
yíge dàgài de yìnxiàng 一个大概的印象 = a general impression
2 *adverb*
= probably

dàhuì 大会 *noun*
= large meeting, plenary session

dàhuǒr 大伙儿 *pronoun*
= we all, you all, everyone
zhè shì wǒmen dàhuǒr de yìjiàn 这是我们大伙儿的意见 = this is the view that we all take

dàjiā 大家 *pronoun*
(*often used with* dōu 都 *when it's the subject of a sentence*) = everybody, everyone
dàjiā dōu xǐhuān tā 大家都喜欢他 = everyone likes him

dàjiē 大街 *noun*
= main road, boulevard, avenue

dàliàng 大量
1 *adjective*
= large amount of, a great quantity of
dàliàng de liángshi 大量的粮食 = a large quantity of food
2 *adverb*
= in large numbers, by a great quantity
dàliàng xuējiǎn jīngfèi 大量消减经费 = reduce expenses by a large amount

dàlù 大陆 *noun*
= mainland, continent

dàmǐ 大米 *noun*
= uncooked white rice

dàpī 大批 *adjective*
= large quantity/number of
yí dàpī xuésheng 一大批学生 = a large group of students

dàren 大人 *noun*
= adult, grown-up

dàshēng 大声 *adverb*
= loudly
dàshēng jiào 大声叫 = call out in a loud voice

D

dàshǐ 大使 *noun*
= ambassador

dàshǐguǎn 大使馆 *noun*
= embassy

dàtǐshàng 大体上 *adverb*
= for the most part, generally, more or less

dàxiǎo 大小 *noun*
= size

dàxíng 大型 *adjective*
= large-scaled, large-sized, large
dàxíng fādòngjī 大型发动机 = large-sized motor

dàxué 大学 *noun*
= university, college
shàng dàxué 上大学 = attend university

dàyī 大衣 *noun*
= coat, overcoat

dàyuē 大约 *adverb*
= approximately, about
dàyuē yào yíge xiǎoshí 大约要一个小时 = it will take about one hour

dāi 呆
1 *adjective*
- = slow-witted, dull
- (*with fear or amazement*) = blank, wooden
tā zhàn zài nàr fā dāi 他站在那儿发呆 = he stood there staring blankly

2 *verb* = stay
dāi zài jiālǐ 呆在家里 = stay at home

dāi 待 *verb* ▶ *See also* **dài** 待.
= stay

dàifu 大夫 *noun*
= doctor, physician

dài 代
1 *noun*
- = historical period
Táng dài 唐代 = the Tang Dynasty
- = generation
xīn yídài 新一代 = a new generation

2 *verb*
- = on behalf of
qǐng dài wǒ wènhòu tā 请代我问候他 = please give him my greetings
- = acting
dài zǒnglǐ 代总理 = acting premier

dàibiǎo 代表
1 *noun*
= representative

2 *verb*
= represent

dàijià 代价 *noun*
= cost, price to pay for

dàitì 代替 *verb*
= stand in place of, substitute

dài 带
1 *noun*
- = belt, ribbon
- = tyre
- = region, area
zài Huánghé yídài 在黄河一带 = in the region of the Yellow River

2 *verb*
- = take, bring along, bring
kěyǐ dài háizi qù ma? 可以带孩子去吗? = can we take children with us?
- = have with, attached, included
yíkuài dài rìlì de shǒubiǎo 一块带日历的手表 = a date watch, a calendar watch
- (*when talking about children*) = look after, bring up
tāde zǔmǔ bǎ tā dài dà 他的祖母把他带大 = his grandmother raised him

dài 待 *verb* ▶ *See also* **dāi** 待.
- = treat, deal with
- = wait for, await
dài dào míngtiān 待到明天 = wait until tomorrow

dài 袋 *noun*
= bag, sack
yídài tǔdòu 一袋土豆 = a sack of potatoes

dài 戴 *verb*
(*on the head, neck, or wrist*) = put on, wear

dānrèn 担任 *verb*
= assume the responsibility for, hold the position of

dānxīn 担心 *verb*
= worry about, be concerned that

dān 单
1 *adjective*
- = single, of one unit, simple
dānrén chuáng 单人床 = single bed
- (*referring to numbers*) = odd
dān shù 单数 = odd number

2 *adverb*
- = singly, separately
bǎ zhèběn shū dān fàng 把这本书单放 = keep this book in a separate place

3 *noun*
- (*for a bed*) = sheet
- = bill, list
  dānzi 单子 = list

dāncí 单词 *noun*
(*as a linguistic unit*) = word

dāndiào 单调 *adjective*
= monotonous, dull, drab

dāndú 单独 *adjective*
= alone

dānwèi 单位 *noun*
- = unit of measurement
- = organizational unit
  gōngzuò dānwèi 工作单位 = work unit

dǎnliàng 胆量 *noun*
= courage

dàn 但 *conjunction* ▶ *See also* **búdàn** 不但.
= but, yet, nevertheless

dànshì 但是 *conjunction*
= but, however, yet

dànyuàn 但愿 *verb*
= I wish, if only

dànzi 担子 *noun*
= load, burden, task

dànshēng 诞生 *verb*
= be born, emerge, come into being

dàn 淡 *adjective*
- = lacking salt
  tā zuò de cài tài dàn 他做的菜太淡 = the dishes he cooks are not salty enough
  dàn shuǐ hú 淡水湖 = freshwater lake
- = tasteless, insipid, weak
  zhèbēi chá tài dàn 这杯茶太淡 = this cup of tea is too weak
- (*in colour*) = light
  dàn lǜ 淡绿 = pale green
- = slack, poor
  dànjì 淡季 = low season, slack season

dàn 蛋 *noun*
= egg
dànbái 蛋白 = egg white, protein
dànhuáng 蛋黄 = egg yolk

dàngāo 蛋糕 *noun*
= cake

dāng 当 ▶ *See also* **dàng** 当.
1 *verb*
= act in the role of, undertake/occupy the position of
dāng lǎoshī 当老师 = be a teacher, work as a teacher

2 *preposition*
- (*when referring to a certain time or place*) = when, at, whilst
  dāng...de shíhòu 当...的时候 = when..., at the time...
  dāng wǒ dào de shíhòu, tā yǐjīng zǒu le 当我到的时候，他已经走了 = when I arrived, he had already left

dāngchǎng 当场 *adverb*
= on the spot, there and then, red-handed

dāngdài 当代 *noun*
= contemporary, the present age

dāngdì 当地 *adjective*
= local
dāngdì shíjiān 当地时间 = local time

dāngjīn 当今 *adverb*
= now, at present, nowadays

dāngnián 当年 *adverb* ▶ *See also* **dàngnián** 当年.
= in those years

dāngqián 当前
1 *adjective*
= present, current
2 *adverb*
= at present

dāngrán 当然 *adverb*
= of course, naturally

dāngshí 当时 *adverb*
= at that time

dāngxīn 当心 *verb*
= be careful, look out

dǎng 挡 *verb*
= stand in the way of, bar, block
dǎngzhù dàolù 挡住道路 = bar the way

dǎng 党 *noun*
= political party

dǎngyuán 党员 *noun*
= party member

dàng 当 *verb* ▶ *See also* **dāng** 当.
- = treat as, regard as
- = equal to
- = think that, take it to be that

dàngnián 当年 *adverb* ▶ *See also* **dāngnián** 当年.
= in the same year, that very year

dàngzuò 当做 *verb*
= consider as, take as

dāo 刀 *noun*
= knife, sword, razor

dāozi 刀子 *noun*
= knife, penknife

dǎo 岛 *noun*
= island

dǎo 倒 *verb* ▶ *See also* **dào** 倒.
- = fall, fall down
  tā dǎo zài dì shang le 他倒在地上了
  = he fell down to the ground
- = collapse, be overthrown, close down
- = go bankrupt
- = change, exchange
  dǎo chē 倒车 = change a train/bus

dǎobì 倒闭 *verb*
= close down, go bankrupt

dǎoméi 倒霉 *adjective*
= unlucky, have bad luck

dào 到
1 *verb*
- = arrive, reach
- = go to

> **!** *Often used with* qù 去 *or* lái 来 *in the pattern* dào...qù 到... 去 *or* dào...lái 到... 来.

dào Lúndūn qù 到伦敦去 = go to London
dào Běijīng lái 到北京来 = come to Beijing

2 *verb*
(*used after other verbs to indicate successful attainment*)
[**mǎi** | **zhǎo** | **bàn**] **dào** [买 | 找 | 办] 到 = manage to [buy | find | accomplish] something
(*used with the negative* **bù** 不 *to indicate impossible attainment*)
[**kàn** | **tīng** | **zuò**] **bú dào** [看 | 听 | 做] 不到 = be unable to [see | hear | do] something
(*used with the negative* **méi** 没 *to indicate unsuccessful attainment*)
tā méi mǎidào 他没买到 = he was unable to buy it

3 *preposition*
= until, to, towards
yì tiān dào wǎn 一天到晚 = from morning to night
huì yìzhí kāi dào bā diǎnzhōng 会一直开到八点钟 = the meeting lasted until 8 o'clock

dàochù 到处 *adverb*
= in all places, everywhere

dàodá 到达 *verb*
= arrive, reach

dàodǐ 到底 *adverb*
- = after all, really
- = in the end, at last, finally
- = to the end, to the finish

dào 倒 ▶ *See also* **dǎo** 倒.
1 *verb*
- = pour, pour out, dump
- = reverse, go backwards
  dào chē 倒车 = reverse the car

2 *adverb*
- = back, in the opposite direction
- = upside down
  guàdào le 挂倒了 = hang upside down
- (*for emphasis*) = indeed, after all, on the contrary
  dào shì 倒是 (*used in a question to find out the fact of a matter*) = (really)...or not?
  nǐ dào shì qù bú qù? 你倒是去不去? = are you really going or not?

dào 道
1 *noun*
- = road, way, path
- = way, method

2 *adjective*
= Taoist, Daoist

3 *verb*
= speak, say, or tell

4 *measure word* ▶ **157**
- (*for orders issued by an authority, questions on an examination*)
- (*for things in the shape of a line*)
- (*for courses in a meal*)

dàodé 道德 *noun*
= morality, ethical code, ethics

Dàojiào 道教 *noun*
= Taoism, Daoism

dàolǐ 道理 *noun*
- = teaching, doctrine, principle
- = reason, sense
  yǒu dàolǐ 有道理 = make sense, be reasonable

dàolù 道路 *noun*
= way, road, course

dàoqiàn 道歉 *verb*
= apologize

de 的 *particle*

> **!** *The particle* **de** 的 *is often used to transform a word, phrase, or clause to modify a noun or noun phrase. It can also be used to transform an adjective into a noun or a verb phrase into a noun phrase.*

- = of
  xuéxiào de guīdìng 学校的规定 = the rules of the school
- (*to indicate possession*)
  wǒ māma de shū 我妈妈的书 = my mother's book
- (*after an adjective to modify a noun*)
  měilì de gūniang 美丽的姑娘 = a beautiful girl
- (*after a clause to make it modify a noun*)
  tā mǎi de shū 他买的书 = the books he bought
- (*after an adjective to transform it into a noun*)
  hóng de shì wǒde 红的是我的 = the red one is mine
- (*after a verb phrase to transform it into a noun phrase*)
  tā shuō de bù hǎotīng 他说的不好听 = what he said was not pleasant
- (*in the* **shì...de 是...的** *construction for emphasis*)
  wǒ shì zuótiān dào de 我是昨天到的 = I arrived yesterday

de 得 *particle*
- (*used between two verbs to indicate possibility*)

> **!** *Note that the first verb indicates the action, while the second indicates a possible result or attainment.*

bān de dòng 搬得动 = be able to move it
zuò de dào 做得到 = be able to do it

> **!** *In expressions like these, the possibility is negated by the use of* **bu 不** *in place of* **de 得**, *thus the expressions* **bān bú dòng 搬不动**, **zuò bú dào 做不到** *mean* **be unable to move** *and* **be unable to do.**

- (*used between a verb and an adjective or a clause to indicate degree or extent*)
  pǎo de kuài 跑得快 = run fast
  bìng de hěn lìhai 病得很厉害 = be very ill
  lèi de tóu tòng 累得头痛 = be tired to the point of having a headache
- (*used in a negative form to advise someone strongly against doing something*)
  [shuō | gān | chī] bù dé [说 | 干 | 吃] 不得 = mustn't/can't [say | do | eat] (something)

dé 得 *verb*
- = get, have, obtain
- (*when used with* **bu 不**)
  bù dé 不得 = disallow, prohibit

dédào 得到 *verb*
= obtain, receive, gain

dézuì 得罪 *verb*
= offend

de 地 *particle* ▶ *See also* **dì 地**.
(*used after an adjective to form an adverb, equivalent to* **-ly** *in English*)
cōngmáng de jìnlai 匆忙地进来 = rush in hurriedly

Déguó 德国 *noun*
= Germany

Déwén 德文 *noun*
= German language (usually written)

Déyǔ 德语 *noun*
= German language (usually spoken)

děi 得 *verb*
- = have to, must
  xuésheng děi niànshū 学生得念书 = students have to study
- = require
  mǎi zhèběn shū děi duōshǎo qián? 买这本书得多少钱? = how much money will I need to buy this book?

dēng 灯 *noun*
= lamp, light
diǎn dēng 点灯 = light a lamp

dēng 登 *verb*
- (*for a bus, train, or other vehicle*) = mount, ascend, board
- = land, alight
  dēng lù 登陆 = land on shore, disembark
- = publish, print
  dēng bào 登报 = print in a newspaper

dēngjì 登记 *verb*
= register

děng 等
1 *verb*
= wait, await
2 *noun*
= grade, class
3 *pronoun*
(*used at the end of an enumeration*) = etc., and so on
děngděng 等等 = and so on, etc.
děngdeng 等等 = wait a moment

D

děngdài 等待 *verb*
= wait, wait for

děnghòu 等侯 *verb*
= wait, wait for

děngyú 等于 *verb*
- = be equal to, be equivalent to
- = be the same as, amount to, be tantamount to

dèng(zi) 凳(子) *noun*
= stool, bench

dī 低
1 *adjective*
= low
2 *verb*
= lower
dī tóu 低头 = bow one's head

dī 滴 *measure word* ▶ **157**
= drop

díquè 的确 *adverb*
= indeed, really

dírén 敌人 *noun*
= enemy

dǐxia 底下 *preposition*
= under, below, beneath
zhuōzi dǐxia 桌子底下 = under the table

dì 地 *noun* ▶ *See also* **de** 地.
- = the ground, floor
- = earth, soil
- = place, location

dìbù 地步 *noun*
- = situation, condition
- = extent, point

dìdài 地带 *noun*
= area, region

dìdiǎn 地点 *noun*
= place, location

dìfang 地方 *noun*
= place

dìfāng 地方 *adjective*
= local

dìlǐ 地理 *noun*
= geography

dìmiàn 地面 *noun*
= ground, the earth's surface

dìqiú 地球 *noun*
= the earth, the globe

dìqū 地区 *noun*
= district, area

dìtiě 地铁 *noun*
= underground, subway, tube

dìtú 地图 *noun*
= map

dìwèi 地位 *noun*
= status, social position

dìxià 地下 *noun*
= underground

dìxiàshì 地下室 *noun*
= basement, cellar

dìzhèn 地震 *noun*
= earthquake

dìzhǐ 地址 *noun*
= address

dìzhǔ 地主 *noun*
= landlord

dìdi 弟弟 *noun*
= younger brother

dì 递 *verb*
= hand over, pass

dì 第 *particle*
(*used to indicate ordinal numbers*)
dìyī cì 第一次 = first time
dìyī míng 第一名 = number one, champion, winner
dì'èr tiān 第二天 = the next day
dìjǐ kè? 第几课? = which lesson?

diāndǎo 颠倒
1 *verb*
= reverse, invert, turn upside down
2 *adjective*
= muddled, confused, upside down

diǎn 点
1 *noun*
- = dot, drop, speck
- (*in decimals*) = point
  sān diǎn liù 三点六 = three point six
- (*used in time expressions, referring to hours on the clock*) = o'clock
  sān diǎn zhōng 三点钟 = 3 o'clock
- (*when talking about abstract ideas*) = point
  xiàmian liǎng diǎn 下面两点 = the following two points, the two points below

2 *measure word* ▶ **157**
(*for suggestions, requirements, ideas, opinions*)
3 *verb*
- = touch slightly
- = mark, punctuate
- = tick off on a list, check

- = choose
  diǎn cài 点菜 = select dishes from a menu
- (*as fire or flame*) = light

4 *adverb*
- = a little, slightly
  [**hǎo** | **dà** | **xiǎo**] **diǎnr** [好 | 大 | 小] 点儿
  = a little [better | bigger | smaller]

diǎn míng 点名 *verb*
= take a roll call, mention by name

diǎn tóu 点头 *verb*
= nod the head

diǎnxin 点心 *noun*
= light refreshments, pastry, snacks

diàn 电
1 *noun*
= electricity
2 *adjective*
= electric

diànbào 电报 *noun*
= telegram, cable

diànbīngxiāng 电冰箱 *noun*
= refrigerator, fridge

diànchē 电车 *noun*
= trolley, street car, tram

diàndēng 电灯 *noun*
= electric light

diànfēngshàn 电风扇, **diànshàn** 电扇 *noun*
= electric fan

diànhuà 电话 *noun*
= telephone

diànhuà zhōngxīn 电话中心 *noun*
= call centre, call center

diànnǎo 电脑 *noun*
= computer

diànshì 电视 *noun*
= television, TV

diànshìtái 电视台 *noun*
= television station

diàntái 电台 *noun*
= radio station

diàntī 电梯 *noun*
= lift, elevator, escalator

diànyǐng 电影 *noun*
= film, movie

diànyǐngyuàn 电影院 *noun*
= cinema, movie theatre

diànzǐ 电子
1 *noun*
= electron
2 *adjective*
= electronic

diànzǐ yóujiàn 电子邮件 *noun*
= e-mail

diàn 店 *noun*
- = store, shop
- = inn, hotel

diào 吊 *verb*
= pull up by a rope, hang, suspend

diào 钓 *verb*
= fish, angle
diào yú 钓鱼 = to fish

diào 调 ▸ *See also* **tiáo** 调.
1 *noun*
= melody, tune
2 *verb*
- (*when talking about troops or personnel*) = transfer, move, send
- = change direction, turn, exchange

diàochá 调查
1 *verb*
= investigate
2 *noun*
= investigation

diào 掉 *verb*
- = fall down, drop, come off
- (*used after such verbs as* **shī** 失, **qù** 去, **mài** 卖, **táo** 逃, **wàng** 忘, **miè** 灭, **rēng** 扔, *and* **cā** 擦 *to indicate loss, end of supply*)
  shīdiào 失掉 = lose
  qùdiào 去掉 = get rid of
  màidiào 卖掉 = sell off, sell out
- = lose, be missing
- = turn, turn round
  diàoguò tóu lai 掉过头来 = turn the head round
- = change, exchange
  diàohuàn 掉换 = exchange

diē 跌 *verb*
- = fall down
- (*of prices*) = fall

dǐng 顶
1 *noun*
= top, summit
2 *adjective*
- = topmost, extreme
  dǐng tóu 顶头 = furthest end, top

3 *adverb*
- = very, extremely, most
  dǐng hǎo 顶好 = the best, the greatest

4 *verb*
- = carry on the head
- = push the head against
- = go against

D

5 *measure word* ▶ 157
(*for hats, caps, or things with a top*)

dìng 定
1 *adverb*
= definitely, certainly
2 *adjective*
= stable, calm
3 *verb*
= decide, fix, settle

dìng qī 定期
1 *verb*
= set a date
2 *adverb*
= regularly

dìng 订 *verb*
- = make an agreement, cement a relationship
  dìnghūn 订婚 = become engaged
  dìng hétong 订合同 = make a contract
- = subscribe to, order, book
  dìng zázhì 订杂志 = order a magazine
  dìng fángjiān 订房间 = book a room

diū 丢 *verb*
- = lose
  tā diūle yíjiàn dōngxi 他丢了一件东西 = he lost something
- = throw, cast, toss
- = put or lay aside

dōng 东 *noun*
= east
dōng [bian | bù | fāng | miàn] 东[边 | 部 | 方 | 面] = eastern [side | part | direction | side]

dōngběi 东北 *noun*
= northeast, Manchuria, the three provinces of Heilongjiang, Jilin, and Liaoning

dōngfāng 东方 *noun*
- = east
- = the Orient

dōngnán 东南 *noun*
= southeast

dōngxi 东西 *noun* = thing, things
mǎi dōngxi 买东西 = go shopping, buy things

dōng 冬 *noun*
= winter
dōngtiān 冬天 = winter

dǒng 懂 *verb*
= understand

dǒngdé 懂得 *verb*
= understand, know

dǒngháng 懂行 *verb*
= know a business, be experienced in a profession

dǒngshì 懂事 *adjective*
= sensible, wise

dòng 动 *verb*
- = move
- = start action
- = stir, arouse
- = use

dòngjing 动静 *noun*
- = stirring noises, sound of people speaking or moving about
- = movement, activity

dònglì 动力 *noun*
- = power
- = driving force, motive, impetus

dòngrén 动人 *adjective*
= moving, touching

dòngshēn 动身 *verb*
= embark on a journey, set off

dòngshǒu 动手 *verb*
- = start, make a move to
- = raise a hand to fight or hit
- = touch
  qǐng wù dòngshǒu! 请勿动手! = please don't touch!

dòngwù 动物 *noun*
= animal

dòngwùyuán 动物园 *noun*
= zoo

dòngyuán 动员 *verb*
= mobilize

dòngzuò 动作 *noun*
= action, movement

dòng 冻 *verb*
= freeze
dòngsǐ 冻死 = freeze to death

dòng 洞 *noun*
= hole, cave

dòng 栋 *measure word* ▶ 157
(*for buildings*)

dōu 都

> **!** *Can also be pronounced* dū 都 *with a different meaning.*

adverb

- = all, both
  tāmen dōu hěn hǎo 他们都很好 = they are all well
  dōu shì wèile zhuàn qián 都是为了赚钱 = it's all to make money
- (*when used with a negative*)

> **!** *Note that* bù 不 *before* dōu 都 *means* not all do *or* some don't; *while* dōu 都 *before* bù 不 *means* none do.

  tāmen dōu bú huì chànggē 他们都不会唱歌 = none of them can sing well
  tāmen bù dōu huì chànggē 他们不都会唱歌 = they can't all sing well
- (*when used with the interrogative* shénme 什么 what) = everything
  nǐ shénme dōu huì 你什么都会 = you can do everything
  (*when used with the interrogative* shénme 什么 *and a negative*) = nothing, not anything
  tā shénme dōu méi zuò 他什么都没做 = he hasn't done anything
- (*when used with the interrogative* shéi 谁 who) = everyone
  shéi dōu zhīdào 谁都知道 = everyone knows
  (*when used with the interrogative* shéi 谁 *and a negative*) = no one
  shéi dōu bù chuān zhèzhǒng yīfu 谁都不穿这种衣服 = no one wears clothing like this
- (*in the pattern* lián...dōu... 连... 都...) = even

> **!** *Note that in practice when the first element of this pattern is omitted, the word* dōu 都 *alone retains the sense of the pattern and means* even.

  lián zhège wèntí tā dōu bù dǒng 连这个问题他都不懂 = he can't even understand this kind of question
  tā yīfu dōu méi xǐ 他衣服都没洗 = he didn't even wash his clothes
- = already

dòuzhēng 斗争
1 *verb*
= struggle, fight, strive
2 *noun*
= struggle, combat

dòufu 豆腐 *noun*
= beancurd, tofu

dòu 逗
1 *verb*
= tease
2 *adjective*
= funny

dòuliú 逗留 *verb*
= stay (for a short time), stop over

dúlì 独立
1 *verb*
= be independent, become independent
zhège guójiā dúlì le 这个国家独立了 = this country became independent
2 *noun*
= independence
3 *adjective*
= independent
nàge háizi hěn dúlì 那个孩子很独立 = that child is very independent

dúshēn 独身 *adjective*
= single, unmarried

dúshēngnǚ 独生女 *noun*
= only daughter

dúshēngzǐ 独生子 *noun*
= only son

dúzì 独自 *adjective*
= alone, by oneself

dú 读 *verb*
- = read
- = read aloud
- = study (at school, college, or university)
  dú dàxué 读大学 = study at university

dúshū 读书 *verb*
- = study, read books
- = attend school

dúzhě 读者 *noun*
= reader

dǔ 堵
1 *verb*
= obstruct, block up
2 *measure word* ▶ 157
(*for walls*)

dùzi 肚子 *noun*
= stomach, belly

dù 度
1 *noun*
- (*unit or measurement for angles, temperature, etc.*) = degree

D

língxià sān (shèshi)dù 零下三(摄氏)度 = 3 degrees below zero centigrade
sānshíèr huáshidù 三十二华氏度 = 32 degrees Fahrenheit
• = occasion, time
2 *verb*
= spend, pass

dù(guò) 度(过) *verb*
= spend, pass

dù 渡 *verb*
• (*when talking about a body of water*) = cross over
dù [hé | hǎi] 渡[河 | 海] = cross [a river | an ocean]
• (*a difficulty, or a period of time*) = go through
dùguò kùnnan shíqī 渡过困难时期 = go through a difficult time

duān 端
1 *noun*
(*of a long, narrow object*) = end, end point
2 *verb*
= hold something level with the hand(s)

Duānwǔjié 端午节 *noun*
= Dragon Boat Festival

> **!** *It falls on the fifth day of the fifth month of the lunar calendar.*

duǎn 短
1 *adjective*
(*in length*) = short
2 *noun*
= weak point, fault

duǎnchù 短处 *noun*
= shortcoming

duǎnqī 短期 *noun*
= short-term

duǎnxìn 短信 *noun*
= text message

duàn 段 *measure word* ▶ 157
• (*for lengths of road, cable, etc.*) = section, segment
• (*for periods of time*) = period, length
• (*for units of writing, articles, speeches, etc.*) = piece, paragraph

duàn 断 *verb*
= break, cut off

duàndìng 断定 *verb*
= conclude, decide, judge

duànduàn xùxù 断断续续
adverb
= intermittently, on-and-off

duànliàn 锻炼 *verb*
= do physical training, take exercise, improve one's physical fitness

duī 堆
1 *verb*
= heap up, pile up
2 *noun*
= pile, stack, heap
yìduī dōngxi 一堆东西 = a pile of things

duì 队 *noun*
• = team, group
• = a queue/line of people

duìwu 队伍 *noun*
= troops, ranks

duìyuán 队员 *noun*
= member of a team

duìzhǎng 队长 *noun*
= captain of a team, team leader

duì 对
1 *adjective*
= correct, accurate, right
2 *preposition*
• (*introducing a target, aim*) = to, towards, with
duì wǒ shēngqì 对我生气 = angry with me
• = regarding, about, on
duì zhèjiàn shì de kànfǎ 对这件事的看法 = views on this matter
• (*in sports*) = against
Sūgélán duì Yīnggélán 苏格兰对英格兰 = Scotland vs. England
3 *verb*
• = treat, deal with
• = face
chuānghu duìzhe huāyuán 窗户对着花园 = the window faces the garden
4 *measure word* ▶ 157
= pair, couple
duì wǒ lái shuō 对我来说 = in my view, as far as I'm concerned

duìbǐ 对比
1 *verb*
= contrast, compare
2 *noun*
• = comparison, contrast
• = ratio, correlation

duìbuqǐ 对不起 *verb*
- = let someone down, act unworthily toward
  nǐ yǒu shénme duìbuqǐ tā de shì ma? 你有什么对不起他的事吗? = did you let him down in some way?
- = sorry, I'm sorry, excuse me

duìdài 对待 *verb*
= treat, handle, deal with

duìfāng 对方 *noun*
(*in negotiations, games, competitions*) = the other party, opposite side

duìfu 对付 *verb*
- = deal with, cope with
- = serve for the time being, make do

duìhuà 对话 *noun*
= dialogue

duìmiàn 对面 *preposition*
= opposite

duìxiàng 对象 *noun*
- = goal, objective
- = boyfriend, girlfriend, partner

duìyú 对于 *preposition*
= with regard to

dūn 吨 *noun*
(*a unit of weight*) = ton

dūn 蹲 *verb*
= squat

dùn 顿 *measure word* ▶ 157
- (*for meals*)
- (*for actions that take place in single sessions*)

duō 多
1 *adjective*
- = many, much, more
- = more than
  wǔshí duō yuán 五十多元 = over fifty yuan (*between fifty and sixty*)
- = extra, additional
  duōle sān yīngbàng 多了三英镑 = three pounds extra

2 *adverb*
- (*to indicate degree or extent in comparison*) = much, a great deal
  jīntiān tiānqi hǎo duō le 今天天气好多了 = the weather is a lot better today
- (*in questions asking for a number, degree, age, etc.*)
  duō dà [niánlíng | suìshù] 多大 [年龄 | 岁数]? = how old?
  duō dà de [fángjiān | xié]? 多大的 [房间 | 鞋]? = [how big a room? | what size shoes?]
- (*in comparisons, after a verb, expressing a large extent*) = much, a lot
  [hǎo | nán | kěxiào] de duō [好 | 难 | 可笑] 得多 = much [better | harder | funnier]

duō(me) 多(么) *adverb*
- (*to exclaim about the high degree to which an action is done*) = such...! what a...!
  nǐ fùmǔ duō(me) ài nǐ a! 你父母多(么)爱你啊! = your parents love you so much!
- (*to exclaim or ask about the extent of a quality*)
  duō(me) kě'ài de háizi! 多(么)可爱的孩子! = what a lovable child!

duōshǎo 多少 *determiner*
- (*as an interrogative*) = how many? how much?
  duōshǎo [rén | tiān | běn shū | gōnglǐ] 多少 [人 | 天 | 本书 | 公里] = how many [people | days | books | kilometres]
- (*to indicate an uncertain amount*) = how many, how much
  wǒ bù xiǎng zhīdào tā yǒu duōshǎo qián 我不想知道他有多少钱 = I don't want to know how much money he has

duōshù 多数 *noun*
= majority, most

duōyú 多余 *adjective*
= extra, excess, surplus

duó 夺 *verb*
- = rob, snatch, seize by force
- = strive for, win

duóqǔ 夺取 *verb*
= seize by force

duǒ 朵 *measure word* ▶ 157
(*for flowers, clouds*)

duǒ 躲 *verb*
= hide oneself away from, avoid, dodge

Ee

Éguó 俄国 *noun*
= Russia

Éwén 俄文 *noun*
= Russian language (usually written)

Éyǔ 俄语 *noun*
= Russian language (usually spoken)

é 鹅 *noun*
= goose

è 饿
1 *adjective*
= hungry
wǒ è le 我饿了 = I'm hungry
2 *verb*
= starve
èsǐ 饿死 = starve to death

értóng 儿童 *noun*
= children

érzi 儿子 *noun*
= son

ér 而 *conjunction*
- (*connecting two adjectives, two verbs, etc.*) = and
  cóngming ér yǒnggǎn 聪明而勇敢 = intelligent and brave
- (*connecting an affirmative clause with a negative clause*) = but, yet, while
  tā zhǐ xiǎng zìjǐ, ér bù xiǎng biéren 他只想自己，而不想别人 = he thinks only of himself and not of others
- (*connecting an adverb of manner with a verb*)
  qiāoqiāo ér qù 悄悄而去 = depart quietly
- (*connecting the cause of an action with the action itself*) = because of, on the grounds of
  tā yīnwèi gōngzuò ér fàngqì xiū jià 他因为工作而放弃休假 = he gave up his holidays because of his work
  bú shì...ér shì... 不是...而是... = not...but...
  wǒ bú shì Měiguórén ér shì Jiānádàrén 我不是美国人而是加拿大人 = I am not an American but a Canadian

érqiě 而且 *conjunction*
= and also, moreover, in addition
búdàn...érqiě... 不但...而且... = not only...but also...
tā búdàn lèi érqiě bù shūfu 他不但累而且不舒服 = he's not only tired but also unwell

ěrduo 耳朵 *noun*
= ear

èr 二 *number*
= two

> **!** *Note that when used with a measure word,* **èr** 二 *usually changes to* **liǎng** 两.

▶ *See also* **liǎng** 两.

èryuè 二月 *noun*
= February

Ff

fā 发 *verb* ▶ *See also* **fà** 发.
- = send out, issue
  fā hěn duō xìn 发很多信 = send out a lot of letters
- = start, grow, develop
  fā yá 发芽 = put out shoots
- = get into a state, become
  fā [jí | nù | hóng] 发 [急 | 怒 | 红] = [become agitated | get angry | turn red]
- = break out in, have a sensation of
  fā [má | yǎng] 发 [麻 | 痒] = get [pins and needles | itchy]

fābiǎo 发表 *verb*
- = publish, issue
- = express, state

fācái 发财 *verb*
= get rich, make lots of money

fāchū 发出 *verb*
- = send out, issue
  fāchū tōngzhī 发出通知 = send out notification
- = give off, give out, give rise to
  fāchū guāngliàng 发出光亮 = emit light

fādá 发达 *adjective*
= prosperous, flourishing, developed

fādòng 发动 *verb*
- = launch, start
- = mobilize

fādòngjī 发动机 *noun*
= engine, motor

fādǒu 发抖 *verb*
= shiver, tremble

fā duǎnxìn 发短信 *verb*
= send a text message

fāhuī 发挥 *verb*
- = bring into play, give free rein to
  fāhuī tāde cáinéng 发挥他的才能 = give full play to his talents
- (*when talking about an idea, a theme, etc.*) = develop, expand on, elaborate
  bǎ zhège tímù zài fāhuī yíxià 把这个题目再发挥一下 = develop this topic further

fā huǒ 发火 *verb*
- = catch fire
- = become angry, lose one's temper

fāmíng 发明
1 *verb*
= invent
2 *noun*
= invention

fāshāo 发烧 *verb*
= have or run a fever

fāshēng 发生 *verb*
= occur, happen, take place

fāxiàn 发现
1 *verb*
= discover, find
2 *noun*
= discovery

fāyán 发言 *verb*
= speak, make a speech/statement

fāyáng 发扬 *verb*
= develop, expand, carry on

fāyīn 发音
1 *verb*
= pronounce
2 *noun*
= pronunciation

fāzhǎn 发展
1 *verb*
= develop, expand
2 *noun*
= development

fá 罚 *verb*
= punish, penalize

fákuǎn 罚款 *verb*
= fine, make someone pay a penalty

fǎ 法 *noun*
= law, method

Fǎguó 法国 *noun*
= France
Fǎguórén 法国人 = French people, Frenchman, Frenchwoman

fǎlǜ 法律 *noun*
= law

fǎtíng 法庭 *noun*
= court of law

Fǎwén 法文 *noun*
= French language (usually written)

Fǎyǔ 法语 *noun*
= French language (usually spoken)

fǎyuàn 法院 *noun*
= court of law

fǎzi 法子 *noun*
= way, method

fà 发 *noun* ▶ *See also* **fā** 发.
= hair

fānqié 番茄 *noun*
= tomato

fān 翻 *verb*
- (*when talking about sheets, pages in a book*) = flip, thumb through
- = turn, turn over
- = translate
- = cross, get over
  fānguò nàzuò shān 翻过那座山 = cross that mountain
- = rummage, search
  tā zài fān wǒde shūbāo 他在翻我的书包 = he is searching my book bag
- = multiply
  fān yìfān 翻一番 = double, increase two-fold

fānyì 翻译
1 *verb*
= translate, interpret
2 *noun*
- = translator, interpreter
- = translation

fán (shì) 凡(是) *adverb*
= every, all

> **!** *The term* fán shì 凡是 *is used at the beginning of a sentence and followed by a noun or noun-clause to mean* whatever *or* whoever. *The subject of the sentence, thus defined, is usually followed by* dōu 都.

E F

fán (shì) tā mǎi de dōu hěn piàoliang 凡(是)她买的都很漂亮 = everything she buys is attractive

fán 烦
1 *adjective*
• = irritated, annoyed, vexed
• = tired of
2 *verb*
= trouble, bother

fánnǎo 烦恼 *adjective*
= worried, vexed

fánróng 繁荣
1 *adjective*
= prosperous
2 *verb*
= make prosperous
3 *noun*
= prosperity

fǎndòng 反动 *adjective*
= reactionary

fǎnduì 反对 *verb*
= oppose, object, combat

fǎnfù 反复 *adverb*
= again and again, over and over

fǎnkàng 反抗 *verb*
= resist, oppose, react against

fǎnmiàn 反面 *noun*
• = reverse side, wrong side
• = negative side, opposite side

fǎnyìng 反映
1 *verb*
• = reflect, mirror
• = report, make known, express
xiàng lǐngdǎo fǎnyìng 向领导反映 = make something known to one's superiors
2 *noun*
= reflection

fǎnyìng 反应
1 *verb*
= react
2 *noun*
= reaction

fǎnzhèng 反正 *adverb*
= in any case, anyway

fǎnhuí 返回 *verb*
= return, go back

fàn 犯 *verb*
• (*when talking about the law, rules*) = offend, violate
• (*when talking about a mistake, a crime, etc.*) = commit
fàn cuòwu 犯错误 = make a mistake
• (*when talking about an old illness*) = have another attack of

fàn 饭 *noun*
= cooked rice, food, a meal

fàndiàn 饭店 *noun*
= hotel, restaurant

fànguǎn 饭馆 *noun*
= restaurant

fàntíng 饭厅 *noun*
= dining hall, dining room

fànwéi 范围 *noun*
= scope, sphere, jurisdiction

fāng 方
1 *noun*
• = direction
[dōng | nán | xī | běi] fāng [东 | 南 | 西 | 北] 方 = the [east | south | west | north]
• = side, party
dān fāng 单方 = one side, unilateral
2 *adjective*
= square
fāngkuàizì 方块字 = Chinese characters

fāng'àn 方案 *noun*
= plan, scheme

fāngbiàn 方便
1 *adjective*
= convenient
2 *verb*
= to go to the lavatory

fāngfǎ 方法 *noun*
= way, method

fāngmiàn 方面 *noun*
= aspect, respect, side
yì fāngmiàn...yì fāngmiàn... 一方面... 一方面... = on the one hand...on the other hand...

fāngshì 方式 *noun*
= method, style, formula

fāngxiàng 方向 *noun*
= direction

fāngyán 方言 *noun*
= dialect

fāngzhēn 方针 *noun*
= policy, guiding principle

fáng 防 *verb*
= prevent, guard against, defend against

fángzhǐ 防止 *verb*
= prevent

fángdōng 房东 *noun*
= landlord

fángjiān 房间 *noun*
= room

fángzi 房子 *noun*
= house, building, room

fángzū 房租 *noun*
= rent

fǎngwèn 访问
1 *verb*
= visit, call on
2 *noun*
= visit

fǎngfú 仿佛
1 *verb*
= seem as if
2 *adverb*
= apparently, seemingly

fǎngzhī 纺织 *noun*
= spinning, weaving textiles

fàng 放 *verb*
- = put down, place
- = let go, release (*physically*)
  bié fàng tā 别放他 = don't release him
  (*emotionally or psychologically*)
  fàngshēng dà kū 放声大哭 = burst into tears
- (*when talking about something that explodes or fires*) = let off, fire, shoot
  fàng [**pào** | **qiāng** | **yānhuo**] 放 [炮 | 枪 | 烟火] = [fire a cannon | shoot a gun | let off fireworks]
- = tend, herd
  fàng [**niú** | **yáng**] 放 [牛 | 羊] = pasture [cows | sheep]
- = readjust slightly
  dǎnzi fàng dà diǎnr 胆子放大点儿 = be a bit braver
- (*film, recording, etc.*) = show, play

fàngdà 放大 *verb*
= enlarge, magnify

fàngjià 放假 *verb*
= go on holiday/vacation, have a day off

fàngqì 放弃 *verb*
= give up, abandon, forego

fàngsōng 放松 *verb*
= relax, loosen

fàngxīn 放心 *verb*
= feel relieved, set one's mind at rest, be at ease
fàngxīn bù xià 放心不下 = can't relax, feel anxious

fàngxué 放学 *verb*
= let out of school, classes are over

fēi 飞 *verb*
= fly

fēijī 飞机 *noun*
= aircraft, aeroplane, airplane

fēixíng 飞行 *noun*
= flight, flying

fēi...bùkě 非… 不可 *verb*
- (*emphatic*) = must, have to
  fēi qù bùkě 非去不可 = must go
- = will inevitably, will be bound to
  tā fēi chídào bùkě 他非迟到不可 = he will definitely be late
- = insist on

fēicháng 非常 *adverb*
= very, extremely, unusually

Fēizhōu 非洲 *noun*
= Africa

féi 肥 *adjective*
- = fat
- (*when talking about clothes*) = loose, large
- (*of soil*) = fertile, rich

féizào 肥皂 *noun*
= soap

fèi 废 *adjective*
= useless, waste, discarded

fèi 肺 *noun*
= lungs

fèi 费
1 *verb*
= expend, consume, waste
fèi shíjiān 费时间 = be time-consuming, take a long time
2 *noun*
= fee, fees

fèiyòng 费用 *noun*
= expense, expenses, cost

fēn 分
1 *verb*
- = separate, divide
- = distinguish
  bù fēn hǎo huài 不分好坏 = not to distinguish the good from the bad
- = divide, share, receive a share of
  fēndào yífèn jiǎngjīn 分到一份奖金 = get a share of the prize money
- = distribute
  bǎ zhèxiē dōngxi fēn gěi biéren 把这些东西分给别人 = distribute these things to others

2 *adjective*
(*describing an organization*) = branch, sub-
fēn gōngsī 分公司 = a branch company
3 *noun*
- (*of a dollar*) = cent
(*of Chinese currency, RMB*) = fen
(*of an hour*) = minute
- (*to represent a point or mark*) = point, mark
dé qī fēn 得七分 = get seven points
...fēn zhī... ...分之... (*to represent a fraction or parts of the whole*)
sān fēn zhī èr 三分之二 = two thirds

fēnbié 分别
1 *verb*
- = part, leave each other, say good-bye to each other
- = separate, distinguish, differentiate

2 *adverb*
- = differently
- = separately, respectively

fēnkāi 分开 *verb*
= separate, part

fēnpèi 分配 *verb*
= assign, distribute

fēnshǒu 分手 *verb*
= part company, separate, say good-bye

fēnshù 分数 *noun*
= mark, grade

fēnxī 分析
1 *verb*
= analyze
2 *noun*
= analysis

fēnfù 吩咐 *verb*
= tell, order, instruct

fēnfēn 纷纷 *adverb*
- = in quick succession, one right after another
- = in profusion and confusion

fénmù 坟墓 *noun*
= grave, tomb

fěnbǐ 粉笔 *noun*
= chalk

fěnhóng 粉红 *noun*
= pink

fèn 份 *measure word* ▶ 157
- = portion, share
- (*for copies of newspapers, magazines, or manuscripts*)

fèndòu 奋斗 *verb*
= struggle/strive toward a goal

fènnù 愤怒
1 *adjective*
= angry
2 *noun*
= anger, indignation

fēngfù 丰富
1 *adjective*
= plentiful, abundant
2 *verb*
= enrich

fēngshōu 丰收 *noun*
= good harvest, bumper harvest

fēng 风 *noun*
- = wind, breeze, storm
- = custom, practice, habit

fēnggé 风格 *noun*
= style

fēngjǐng 风景 *noun*
= scenery, landscape, view

fēnglì 风力 *noun*
= wind power, force of the wind

fēngshui 风水 *noun*
= geomancy

fēngsú 风俗 *noun*
= social customs

fēng 封
1 *measure word* ▶ 157
(*for letters, telegrams*)
2 *verb*
= seal, close

fēngjiàn 封建 *adjective*
= feudal

fēng 疯 *adjective*
= mentally unbalanced, mad, crazy

fēng 蜂 *noun*
= bee, wasp

fēngmì 蜂蜜 *noun*
= honey

féng 逢 *verb*
= meet, come upon, chance upon
féng nián guò jié 逢年过节 = on New Year's Day or other festivals

fěngcì 讽刺 *verb*
= satirize

Fójiào 佛教 *noun*
= Buddhism

fǒurèn 否认 *verb*
= deny

fǒudìng 否定 *verb*
= deny, negate, decide in the negative

fǒuzé 否则 *conjunction*
= if not, or else, otherwise

fūfù 夫妇 *noun*
= husband and wife, Mr. and Mrs.

fūqī 夫妻 *noun*
= husband and wife

fūren 夫人 *noun*
= Mrs., Madam, wife
Zhōu Fūren 周夫人 = Mrs. Zhou

fú 扶 *verb*
- = support with the hand
  fúzhe lǎorén zhànqǐlai 扶着老人站起来 = help the elderly person stand up
- = place one's hands on somebody/something for support
  tā fúzhe qiáng zǒu 她扶着墙走 = she walked along holding the wall for support

fúcóng 服从 *verb*
= obey, be subordinate to

fúwù 服务
1 *verb*
= serve, provide service to
2 *noun*
= service

fúwùyuán 服务员 *noun*
= attendant, steward, waiter

fúzhuāng 服装 *noun*
= costume, outfit, uniform

fú 浮 *verb*
= float, drift

fúhé 符合 *verb*
= conform to, fit, coincide
fúhé tāde àihào 符合他的爱好 = suit his hobby

fú 幅 *measure word* ▶ 157
(*for paintings, works of calligraphy*)

fǔdǎo 辅导 *verb*
= advise/coach in studies, give tutorials to

fú 福 *noun*
= good fortune, blessing, happiness

fǔbài 腐败 *adjective*
= rotten, decayed, corrupt

fùmǔ 父母 *noun*
= parents

fùqin 父亲 *noun*
= father

fù 付 *verb*
= pay
fù [fángzū | shuì | lìxī] 付 [房租 | 税 | 利息] = pay [the rent | taxes | interest]

fùnǚ 妇女 *noun*
= woman

fùdān 负担
1 *noun*
= burden, load
2 *verb*
= bear (a burden), shoulder (a burden)

fùzé 负责
1 *verb*
= be responsible for, be in charge of
2 *adjective*
- = responsible
- = conscientious

fùjiàn 附件 *noun*
= attachment

fùjìn 附近
1 *adjective*
= nearby, close
2 *adverb*
= closely, nearby, in the vicinity of

fù 服 *measure word* ▶ 157
(*for doses of Chinese medicine*)

fùyìn 复印 *verb*
= photocopy, duplicate

fùxí 复习 *verb*
= review, revise

fùzá 复杂 *adjective*
= complicated, complex

fù 副
1 *measure word* ▶ 157
- (*for things that come in pairs or sets*)
  = set, pair
- (*for facial expressions*)

2 *adjective*
- = deputy, assistant, vice-
  fù xiàozhǎng 副校长 = vice-principal
- = subsidiary, secondary
  fù zuòyòng 副作用 = side-effect

fù 富 *adjective*
= wealthy, rich

F

Gg

gāi 该
1 *verb*
- = should, ought to
  wǒ gāi zǒu le 我该走了 = I must leave now, I have to go
- = be one's turn to do something
  gāi wǒ le 该我了 = it's my turn

2 *determiner*
= this, that, the above-mentioned
gāi xuéxiào 该学校 = that school

gǎi 改 *verb*
- = change, transform
- = alter, correct
  gǎi zuòyè 改作业 = correct students' homework

gǎibiàn 改变
1 *verb*
= change, alter, transform
2 *noun*
= change

gǎigé 改革
1 *verb*
= reform
2 *noun*
= reform

gǎijìn 改进
1 *verb*
= improve, make better
2 *noun*
= improvement

gǎiliáng 改良 *verb*
= change for the better, improve, reform

gǎishàn 改善
1 *verb*
= improve, better
2 *noun*
= improvement

gǎizào 改造
1 *verb*
= transform, reform, remould
2 *noun*
= transformation, reform

gǎizhèng 改正 *verb*
= correct, amend, put right

gài 盖 *verb*
- = build, construct
- = cover
- = apply, affix with
  gài zhāng 盖章 = apply a chop/seal

gàizi 盖子 *noun*
= cover, lid

gàikuò 概括
1 *verb*
= summarise, generalise
2 *noun*
= summary

gàiniàn 概念 *noun*
= concept, notion, idea

gān 干 *adjective* ▶ *See also* **gàn**.
- = dry
- (*taken into nominal kinship*)
  gān érzi 干儿子 = nominally adopted son

gānbēi 干杯 *verb*
(*when drinking a toast*) = "Bottoms up!"

gāncuì 干脆
1 *adjective*
= straightforward, frank, clear-cut
2 *adverb*
= simply, just

gānjìng 干净 *adjective*
= clean

gānshè 干涉
1 *verb*
= interfere with
2 *noun*
= interference

gānzào 干燥 *adjective*
= dry, arid

gān 杆 *noun*
= pole, post, stake

gān 肝 *noun*
= liver

gǎn 赶 *verb*
- (*an animal, an enemy*) = drive, drive away
  bǎ tā gǎnzǒu 把他赶走 = chase him away
- = catch up
- = hurry, rush
  gǎn huí jiā 赶回家 = hurry home
- = catch
  gǎn chē 赶车 = catch the bus

gǎnjǐn 赶紧 *adverb*
= speedily, at once, hurriedly

gănkuài 赶快 *adverb*
= in a hurry, hurriedly, at once

gănshàng 赶上 *verb*
= catch up with

găn 敢
1 *verb*
= dare, venture, be certain
2 *adjective*
= bold, daring

găndào 感到 *verb*
= feel, sense

găndòng 感动
1 *verb*
(*referring to the emotions*) = move, be moved, touch
2 *adjective*
= moving, touching

Găn'ēnjié 感恩节 *noun*
= Thanksgiving, Thanksgiving Day

gănjī 感激 *verb*
= feel grateful, be thankful

gănjué 感觉
1 *verb*
= sense, feel, perceive
2 *noun*
= perception, feeling

gănmào 感冒
1 *verb*
= catch cold, have a cold
2 *noun*
= cold, flu

gănqíng 感情 *noun*
• = feelings, emotions, sentiments
• = affection

gănxiăng 感想 *noun*
= impressions, feelings

gănxiè 感谢
1 *noun*
= thanks, gratitude
2 *verb*
= thank, be grateful

găn xìngqù 感兴趣 *verb*
= be interested in

> **!** *The preposition* duì 对 *is used to introduce the object of interest expressed by* in *in English, and the prepositional phrase comes before the verb.*

wǒ duì yǔyán găn xìngqù 我对语言感兴趣 = I am interested in languages

gàn 干 *verb* ▶ *See also* **gān**.
= do, work
nǐ xiăng gàn shénme? 你想干什么?
= what do you want to do?
gànmá? 干吗?
• = why? why on earth?
nǐ gànmá măi zhèběn shū? 你干吗买这本书? = why on earth did you buy this book?
• **nǐ gànmá? 你干吗?** = what are you doing?

gànbù 干部 *noun*
= cadre, government official

gàn huó(r) 干活(儿) *verb*
= work, work on a job, do some work

gāng 刚 *adverb*
• (*referring to something that is happening or about to happen*) = just this minute, just now, just about to
tā gāng yào zǒu 他刚要走 = he is just about to leave
• (*referring to something that has just happened*) = only a short time ago, just
tā gāng zǒu 他刚走 = he has just left
• (*when talking about suitability*) = exactly
zhèshuāng xié gāng hăo 这双鞋刚好 = this pair of shoes fits perfectly
• (*when talking about quantity*) = just, no more than
gāng shíbā suì 刚十八岁 = just eighteen years old

gāngcái 刚才 *adverb*
= just now, just a few minutes ago

gānggāng 刚刚 *adverb*
• = just now, just a few minutes ago
• = just, only, exactly

gāng 钢 *noun*
= steel

gāngbǐ 钢笔 *noun*
= fountain pen

gāngqín 钢琴 *noun*
= piano

găng 港 *noun*
= port, harbour

găngkǒu 港口 *noun*
= port, harbour

G

gāo 高
1 *adjective*
- = tall, high
- = advanced, superior
  gāojí 高级 = high level

2 *adverb*
= in a high/loud voice, loudly
gāo hǎn 高喊 = shout at the top of one's voice

gāodà 高大 *adjective*
= tall and big

gāoděng 高等 *adjective*
= high level, advanced
gāoděng jiàoyù 高等教育 = higher education

gāodù 高度
1 *noun*
= altitude, height
2 *adverb*
= highly, to a high degree

gāosù gōnglù 高速公路 *noun*
= motorway

gāoxìng 高兴 *adjective*
= happy, pleased, in high spirits

gāoyuán 高原 *noun*
= plateau, highland

gāozhōng 高中 *noun*
(*abbreviation of* **gāojí zhōngxué** 高级中学) = senior middle school, senior high school

gǎo 搞 *verb*
- (*work, a task, etc.*) = do, work
  gǎo gōngzuò 搞工作 = do work
- = set up, establish, arrange
- = be involved in

gào 告 *verb*
- = tell, inform, notify
- = accuse, sue
  gào mǒurén 告某人 = sue someone

gàobié 告别 *verb*
= take leave of, say good-bye to

gàojiè 告诫 *verb*
= warn, admonish

gàosu 告诉 *verb*
= tell, inform, let know

gēge 哥哥 *noun*
= elder brother

gēbo 胳膊 *noun*
= arm

gē 搁 *verb*
- = place, put down
  gēxia 搁下 = put down
- = put aside, put to one side, shelve
  gē zài yìbiān 搁在一边 = put aside

gē 割 *verb*
= cut, cut down, lop off

gē 歌 *noun*
= song

gējù 歌剧 *noun*
= opera

gēqǔ 歌曲 *noun*
= song

gémìng 革命
1 *verb*
= revolt, carry out a revolution
2 *noun*
= revolution

géwài 格外 *adverb*
= especially, all the more

gé 隔
1 *verb*
- = divide, separate, partition
- = be separated by

2 *adverb*
- (*when talking about an interval of time*) = later, afterwards, every other
  gé yìtiān zài lái 隔一天再来 = come back a day later
  gé yìtiān dǎ yícì diànhuà 隔一天打一次电话 = phone every other day
- (*when talking about a physical distance*) = apart, at a distance of
  gé yìtiáo mǎlù 隔一条马路 = one street apart
  géchéng... 隔成... = separate into, partition into
  bǎ yīge wūzi géchéng liǎngjiān 把一个屋子隔成两间 = partition one room into two

gébì 隔壁 *noun*
= next door

gè 个 *measure word* ▶ **157**

> **!** *This is the most common measure word. It can take the place of many nominal measure words, and is handy to use if one does not know the measure word that is specific to a particular noun. It usually has a neutral tone, but has a fourth tone when stressed.*

gèbié 个别 *adjective*
- = individual
- = very few, rare

gèrén 个人
1 *noun*
- = oneself, one's own
  zhè shì wǒ gèrén de yìjiàn 这是我个人的意见 = this is my personal view
- (*as an abstract concept*) = the individual

2 *adjective*
= individual, private
gèrén zhǔyì 个人主义 = individualism

gètǐ 个体 *adjective*
= individual, self-, private

gèzi 个子 *noun*
= height, stature, build

gè 各 *determiner*
= each, every
gè chù 各处 = every place, everywhere

gèzhǒng 各种 *pronoun*
= every kind, all kinds
gèzhǒng bù tóng... 各种不同... = all kinds of..., different kinds of...
gèzhǒng bù tóng de shuǐguǒ 各种不同的水果 = all kinds of fruit

gèzì 各自 *determiner*
= each, respective

gěi 给

> **!** *Can also be pronounced* jǐ 给 *with a different meaning.*

1 *verb*
- = give
  tā gěi wǒ yìběn shū 他给我一本书 = he gave me a book
- (*used with* jiào 叫, ràng 让, *or* bǎ 把 *before the main verb for emphasis*)
  tāmen bǎ tā gěi dǎ le 他们把他给打了 = they gave him a beating

2 *preposition*
- (*when handing over or transferring something to someone*) = to, with, for
  [**jiāo** | **sòng** | **jièshao**] **gěi tā** [交 | 送 | 介绍] 给他 = [hand over | give | introduce] to him
- (*when doing something for someone*) = for, on behalf of, for the benefit of
  gěi tā [**zuòfàn** | **mǎi shū** | **shōushi wūzi**] 给她 [做饭 | 买书 | 收拾屋子] = [cook | buy books | clean his room] for him
- (*when introducing the recipient of an action, often translated as* let, allow)
  gěi wǒ kànkan 给我看看 = let me have a look
  wǒ gěi nǐ kàn yíjiàn dōngxi 我给你看一件东西 = let me show you something
- (*indicating the passive voice*) = by
  wǒde shū gěi xiǎotōu tóuzǒu lé 我的书给小偷偷走了 = my book was stolen by a thief
  gěi...kàn 给... 看 = show (to someone)
  qǐng nǐ bǎ nàshuāng xié gěi wǒ kànkan 请你把那双鞋给我看看 = please show me that pair of shoes

gēn 根
1 *measure word* ▶ **157**
(*for long, thin objects*)

2 *noun*
- (*of a plant or tree*) = root
- (*of a structure*) = foot, base, basis
- = cause, origin, source

gēnběn 根本
1 *noun*
= root, foundation, base

2 *adjective*
= basic, fundamental, essential

3 *adverb*
- = radically, thoroughly
  tā méiyǒu gēnběn gǎibiàn tāde tàidù 他没有根本改变他的态度 = his attitude hasn't radically changed
- (*in the negative*) = at all, simply
  wǒ gēnběn bù zhīdào 我根本不知道 = I have no idea

gēnjù 根据
1 *preposition*
= on the basis of, according to, in the light of
gēnjù tā shuō de huà... 根据他说的话... = according to what he said...

2 *noun*
= basis, grounds
nǐ yǒu shénme gēnjù shuō zhèzhǒng huà? 你有什么根据说这种话? = on what basis do you say this?

3 *verb*
= base on

G

gēn 跟
1 *preposition*
• = together with, with
wǒ gēn nǐ yìqǐ qù 我跟你一起去 = I'll go with you
• = to, towards
gēn tā shuōhuà 跟她说话 = speak to her
• (*with certain verbs*) = from
gēn tā jiè shū 跟他借书 = borrow books from him
wǒ gēn tǎ xué Zhōngwén 我跟他学中文 = I am learning Chinese from him
2 *conjunction*
• (*when connecting two nouns or noun phrases*) = and, with
wǒ gēn tā shì tóngshì 我跟他是同事 = he and I are colleagues
3 *verb*
= follow, accompany
qǐng gēnzhe wǒ shuō 请跟着我说 = please say after me

gēnqián 跟前 *noun*
= in front of, near

gēngdì 耕地
1 *verb*
= plough, till
2 *noun*
= cultivated land, arable land

gèng 更 *adverb*
= still more, even more
gèng [**hǎo** | **dà** | **yǒuqù**] 更 [好 | 大 | 有趣] = even [better | bigger | more interesting]

gèngjiā 更加 *adverb*
= still more, even more
gèngjiā kěpà 更加可怕 = even more frightening

gōngchǎng 工厂 *noun*
= factory, plant

gōngchéng 工程 *noun*
• (*as a field of study or work*) = engineering
• = project, engineering project, construction work
gōngchéngshī 工程师 = engineer

gōngfu 工夫 *noun*
• = free time, leisure time
wǒ méi yǒu gōngfu 我没有工夫 = I don't have time
• = work, effort
huāle hěn dà de gōngfu 花了很大的工夫 = put in a lot of effort
• = ability, skill

gōnghuì 工会 *noun*
= labour union, trade union

gōngjù 工具 *noun*
= tool, instrument

gōngrén 工人 *noun*
= worker, workman

gōngyè 工业
1 *noun*
= industry
2 *adjective*
= industrial
gōngyèhuà 工业化 = industrialization

gōngyìpǐn 工艺品 *noun*
= handicraft item

gōngzī 工资 *noun*
= wages, salary

gōngzuò 工作
1 *verb*
= work
2 *noun*
= work, job, employment

gōngān 公安 *noun*
= public security
gōngānjú 公安局 = public security bureau

gōngbù 公布 *verb*
= make public, announce

gōngfèi 公费 *adjective*
= at public/state expense, publicly funded
gōngfèi lǚxíng 公费旅行 = travel at state expense

gōngchǐ 公尺 *noun*
= metre

gōngfēn 公分 *noun*
= centimetre

gōnggòng 公共 *adjective*
= public, common, communal

gōnggòng qìchē 公共汽车 *noun*
= bus
gōnggòng qìchē zhàn 公共汽车站 = bus stop

gōngjīn 公斤 *noun*
= kilogram

gōngkāi 公开
1 *adjective*
= open, public, open to the public
2 *verb*
= make public

gōnglǐ 公里 *noun*
= kilometre

gōnglù 公路 *noun*
= highway

gōngmín 公民 *noun*
= citizen

gōngpíng 公平 *adjective*
= fair, just, reasonable

gōngshè 公社 *noun*
= commune

gōngsī 公司 *noun*
= corporation, company, firm

gōngyòng 公用 *adjective*
= public
gōngyòng diànhuà 公用电话 = public telephone

gōngyuán 公园 *noun*
= park

gōngyuán 公元 *noun*
= A.D., the Christian era; or C.E., the Common Era
gōngyuánqián 公元前 = B.C., before Christ, or B.C.E., Before Common Era

gōngfu 功夫 *noun*
= martial arts, kung-fu, skill

gōngkè 功课 *noun*
= schoolwork, homework, assignment

gōngláo 功劳 *noun*
= contribution, credit, service

gōngjī 攻击 *verb*
= attack, assault

gōng 供 *verb*
= supply, provide, support
gōng de qǐ 供得起 = be able to support financially

gōngjǐ 供给 *verb*
= supply, provide, furnish

gōngyìng 供应 *verb*
= supply

gǒnggù 巩固
1 *adjective*
(*of a foundation, organization, ambition*) = strong, firm, solid
2 *verb*
= consolidate, strengthen

gòng 共 *adverb*
• = together
gòngshì 共事 = work together
• = in all, altogether
zhège bān gòng yǒu èrshímíng xuésheng 这个班共有二十名学生 = in all there are twenty students in this class

Gòngchǎndǎng 共产党 *noun*
= the Communist Party

gòngchǎn zhǔyì 共产主义
noun
= communism

gònghéguó 共和国 *noun*
= republic

gòngtóng 共同
1 *adjective*
= common
2 *adverb*
= together, jointly

gòngxiàn 贡献
1 *verb*
= contribute, dedicate, devote
2 *noun*
= contribution

gǒu 狗 *noun*
= dog

gòuchéng 构成 *verb*
= constitute, make up

gòuzào 构造 *noun*
= construction, structure

gòuwù 购物 *verb*
= shop, go shopping

gòu 够
1 *adjective*
= enough, sufficient, adequate
2 *adverb*
= rather, quite
gòu lèi 够累 = rather tired
3 *verb*
(*when referring to a certain standard, etc.*) = attain, reach, be up to
tā [gòu dé shàng | gòu bú shàng] hǎo xuésheng 他[够得上 | 够不上]好学生 = he [is | is not] good enough to be a good student

gūlì 孤立 *adjective*
= isolated

G

gūjì 估计
1 *verb*
= estimate, appraise, reckon
2 *noun*
= estimate, appraisal

gūniang 姑娘 *noun*
= girl, young girl

gūgu 姑姑 *noun*
= aunt, father's sister

gútou 骨头 *noun*
= bone
gútou jiàzi 骨头架子 = skeleton

gǔ 古 *adjective*
= ancient, old, old-fashioned

gǔwén 古文 *noun*
= ancient Chinese, classical Chinese

gǔdài 古代 *noun*
= ancient times, antiquity

gǔdiǎn 古典 *adjective*
= classical

gǔjì 古迹 *noun*
= historic site, place of historic interest

gǔlǎo 古老 *adjective*
= ancient, age-old

gǔ 鼓 *noun*
= drum

gǔchuī 鼓吹
1 *verb*
= advocate
2 *noun*
= advocacy

gǔdòng 鼓动 *verb*
= incite, instigate, agitate

gǔlì 鼓励
1 *verb*
= encourage, urge
2 *noun*
= encouragement

gǔwǔ 鼓舞
1 *verb*
= encourage, inspire, hearten
2 *noun*
= inspiration, encouragement

gǔzhǎng 鼓掌
1 *verb*
= applaud, clap one's hands
2 *noun*
= applause

gùshi 故事 *noun*
= story, tale

gùxiāng 故乡 *noun*
= home town, native place

gùyì 故意 *adverb*
= intentionally, deliberately, purposely

gù 顾 *verb*
- = turn round to look at
- = take care of, look after, manage
- = pay attention to, attend to, take into consideration

gùkè 顾客 *noun*
= customer, client

guā 瓜 *noun*
= melon, gourd

guā 刮 *verb*
- = scrape
  guā húzi 刮胡子 = shave
- (*as the wind*) = blow

guà 挂 *verb*
- (*when speaking of a painting, poster, etc.*) = hang up, suspend
  qiáng shang guàzhe yìzhāng huà 墙上挂着一张画 = a picture is hanging on the wall
- = ring, phone, call
  gěi mǒurén guà diànhuà 给某人挂电话 = phone someone
- = be concerned about
  guà zài xīn shang 挂在心上 = keep in mind
- = register
- = hang up a receiver
  guàshang 挂上 (*when speaking of a telephone*) = hang up

guàhào 挂号
1 *verb*
(*at a hospital, at a doctor's office, etc.*)
= register, take a number
2 *adjective*
= registered
guàhàoxìn 挂号信 = registered letter

guǎi 拐 *verb*
- (*when speaking of walking, riding, cycling, driving, etc.*) = turn
  wàng zuǒ guǎi 往左拐 = turn to the left
- = limp

guài 怪
1 *adjective*
= strange, odd, peculiar

2 *verb*
= blame

guàibude 怪不得 *conjunction*
= no wonder, so that's why

guān 关 *verb*
- = close, shut, lock
- = turn off, shut off
- (*as a business, school or factory*) = close down
- = concern, involve

zhè bù guān nǐde shì 这不关你的事 = it's none of your business, this doesn't concern you
guāndiào 关掉 = close, shut, turn off
guānshang 关上 = close, turn off
bǎ mén guānshang 把门关上 = close the door

guānjiàn 关键 *noun*
(*when talking about issues, problems, matters*) = key, crux

guānhuái 关怀 *verb*
= show loving care for, show solicitude to

guānmén 关门 *verb*
- = close a door
- (*when speaking of a shop, store, or business*) = close, shut

guānxi 关系
1 *noun*
- = relationship, connection, tie
- = bearing, relevance, consequence

méi(yǒu) guānxi 没(有)关系 = it doesn't matter, don't worry, never mind
- (*explaining a cause or reason*)

yóuyú shēntǐ de guānxi, tā jīntiān méiyǒu lái 由于身体的关系, 他今天没有来 = because of his health, he didn't come today

2 *verb*
= concern, affect, involve
zhè guānxidào rénmín de shēnghuó 这关系到人民的生活 = this concerns the life of the people

guānxīn 关心
1 *verb*
= concern oneself with, pay great attention to
2 *noun*
= concern, care

guānyú 关于 *preposition*
= about, concerning, with respect to
guānyú jīngjì de wèntí 关于经济的问题 = the economic problem

guānzhào 关照 *verb*
= look after, keep an eye on

guānchá 观察
2 *verb*
= observe, examine
2 *noun*
= observation

guāndiǎn 观点 *noun*
= point of view, standpoint, viewpoint

guānkàn 观看 *verb*
= watch, view

guānniàn 观念 *noun*
= concept

guānzhòng 观众 *noun*
= audience, spectator, viewer

guān 官 *noun*
- = government official, officer
- = government

guǎn 管
1 *verb*
- = run, manage, be in charge of

zhèjiàn shì shéi lái guǎn? 这件事谁来管? = who will take care of this matter?
- = mind, attend to, bother about

bié guǎn wǒ 别管我 = don't concern yourself about me

2 *noun*
= pipe, tube

guǎnlǐ 管理
1 *verb*
= manage, run
2 *noun*
= management

guǎnzi 管子 *noun*
= tube, pipe

guànjūn 冠军 *noun*
= champion

guànchè 贯彻 *verb*
= implement thoroughly, carry out, put into effect

guàntou 罐头 *noun*
= tin, can

guāng 光
1 *noun*
- = light, ray
- = brightness, shine, lustre
- = glory, honour

G

2 *adjective*
- = smooth, shiny
- = bare, naked
  guāngzhe tóu 光着头 = be bareheaded
- = used up
  shuǐguǒ màiguāng le 水果卖光了 = the fruit is completely sold out

3 *adverb* = solely, merely, alone
guāng shuō bù néng jiějué wèntí 光说不能解决问题 = we cannot solve the problem solely by talking

guānghuī 光辉
1 *noun*
= splendour, brilliance, glory
2 *adjective*
= splendid, brilliant, glorious

guāngmíng 光明
1 *adjective*
- = bright, promising
- = open, above-board

2 *noun*
= light

guāngróng 光荣
1 *adjective*
= glorious, honourable
2 *noun*
= glory, honour, credit

guāngxiàn 光线 *noun*
= light, ray

guǎngbō 广播
1 *verb*
(*on radio or television*) = broadcast
2 *noun*
= broadcast
guǎngbō diàntái 广播电台 = broadcasting station
guǎngbōyuán 广播员 = announcer, broadcaster

guǎngchǎng 广场 *noun*
= public square

guǎngdà 广大 *adjective*
- = vast, broad, extensive
- = numerous

guǎngfàn 广泛 *adjective*
= wide-ranging, widespread, extensive

guǎnggào 广告 *noun*
= advertisement
guǎnggào pái 广告牌 = hoarding

guǎngkuò 广阔 *adjective*
= vast, wide, broad

guàng 逛 *verb*
= stroll, roam
guàng shāngdiàn 逛商店 = go window shopping

guī 归 *verb*
- = go back to, return, give back to
- = turn over to..., be for...to handle, be up to...
  zhèjiàn shì guī tā chǔlǐ 这件事归他处理 = this matter is for him to handle

guīdìng 规定
1 *verb*
= regulate, prescribe, stipulate
2 *noun*
= rule, regulation

guīlǜ 规律 *noun*
= law (of nature), regular pattern

guīmó 规模 *noun*
= scale, scope, magnitude
dà guīmó 大规模 = large-scale

guīzé 规则 *noun*
= rule, regulation

guǐ 鬼 *noun*
- = devil, ghost
- (*suffix used in some terms of criticism or abuse*) [**lǎn** | **jiǔ**] **guǐ** [懒 | 酒] 鬼 = [lazy bones | drunkard]

guì 贵 *adjective*
- = expensive, costly
- = precious, valuable
- = noble, honoured
  guì bīn 贵宾 = honoured guest
- (*polite word*) = your
  nín guìxìng? 您贵姓? = your surname please?

guì 跪 *verb*
= kneel

gǔn 滚 *verb*
- (*for round things*) = roll
- (*abusive command*)
  gǔnchūqù! 滚出去! = get out of here! shove off!
  gǔnkāi! 滚开! = shove off! scram!

gùnzi 棍子 *noun*
= rod, stick

guō 锅 *noun*
= pot, pan, cooker

guó 国 *noun*
= country, nation, state

guófáng 国防 *noun*
= national defence

guójí 国籍 *noun*
= nationality

guójì 国际 *adjective*
= international

guójiā 国家 *noun*
= country, nation, state

guómín 国民 *adjective*
= national
Guómíndǎng 国民党 = Nationalist Party, Kuomintang (KMT)

guóqí 国旗 *noun*
= national flag

guóqìng 国庆 *noun*
= National Day
Guóqìng Jié 国庆节 = National Day

guówáng 国王 *noun*
= king

guóyíng 国营 *adjective*
= state-operated, state-run

guóyǔ 国语 *noun*
(*used primarily in Taiwan*) = Mandarin Chinese

guǒrán 果然 *adverb*
= indeed, sure enough, as expected

guò 过
1 *verb*
- = cross, pass, pass over
  guò [**jiē** | **hé** | **qiáo**] 过 [街 | 河 | 桥] = cross a [street | river | bridge]
- (*a series of things, a process*) = go through
- (*when talking about time, a holiday, a special day, etc.*) = spend, celebrate
  guò rìzi 过日子 = spend one's days
  guò shēngri 过生日 = celebrate one's birthday
- = exceed, go beyond
- (*used after a verb to indicate a result*) = past, through, over
  [**tiào** | **fēi** | **zǒu**] **guò** [跳 | 飞 | 走]过 = [jump over | fly over | walk past]
- (*used after a verb to indicate completion of an action*) = finished, over
  chīguò fàn yǐhòu 吃过饭以后 = after eating
- (*used after* **de** 得 *to indicate potentiality*) = be better than, surpass, get the better of
  [**shuō** | **pǎo** | **dǎ**] **de guò** [说 | 跑 | 打]得过 = out [argue | run | fight]

2 *adverb*
- = exceedingly, excessively, too
  guò [**dà** | **duō** | **gāo**] 过 [大 | 多 | 高] = exceedingly [big | many | tall]
- = over, around, over to the other side

3 *preposition*
= after, over
guò yìhuǐr zài lái 过一会儿再来 = come back in a little while

guo 过 *particle*
(*after a verb to indicate or emphasize past experience*) = have (ever), have (never)
nǐ qùguo Zhōngguó ma? 你去过中国吗? = have you ever been to China?

> **!** *To express this idea in the negative,* **méi (yǒu)** 没(有), *rather than* **bù** 不, *is used before the main verb.*

tā méi shàngguo xué 他没上过学 = he has never attended school

guòchéng 过程 *noun*
= process, course

guòfèn 过分 *adjective*
= excessive

guòlai 过来 *verb*
- = come over, come here
  qǐng nǐ guòlai ba 请你过来吧 = please come over here
- (*after a verb to indicate a direction towards the speaker*)
  bǎ shū náguòlai 把书拿过来 = bring the book over (to me)
- (*after a verb to indicate returning to a normal state*)
  xǐngguòlai 醒过来 = wake up, regain consciousness

guò nián 过年 *verb*
= celebrate the New Year, spend the New Year

guòqù 过去
1 *noun*
= the past
2 *adjective*
= former, previous

guòqu 过去 *verb*
- = go through, get through
  qǐng ràng wǒ guòqu 请让我过去 = please let me get through

G

- (*after a verb to indicate a direction away from the speaker*)
  zǒuguòqu 走过去 = walk over (there)
- (*after a verb to indicate changing from a normal state*)
  tā hūnguòqu le 他昏过去了 = he's lost his consciousness
- (*after a verb to indicate success or attainment*)
  tā hùnguòqu le 他混过去了 = he got through by cheating

hāhā 哈哈 *exclamation*
- (*to express laughter*) = ha ha!
- (*to express satisfaction*) = Aha!

hái 还 *adverb* ▶ *See also* **huán** 还.
- = still, yet
- (*when making comparisons*) = even more, still more
  tā bǐ wǒ hái gāo 他比我还高 = he is even taller than I am
- = also, too, in addition
- = rather, fairly
- (*for emphasis*)
  zhè hái bù róngyì! 这还不容易! = this couldn't be easier!, this is very easy!
- (*indicating something unexpected*)
  wǒ hái zhēn wàngle tāde míngzi 我还真忘了他的名字 = I really have forgotten his name
  hái...ne 还... 呢 = still, yet
  (*continuing, in suspense*) **wǒ hái méiyǒu chī fàn ne** 我还没有吃饭呢 = I still haven't eaten

háishì 还是
1 *adverb*
- = still, all the same, nevertheless
- = ought to, had better
  nǐ háishì bú qù ba 你还是不去吧 = you'd better not go

2 *conjunction*
= or

háizi 孩子 *noun*
= child, children, son or daughter

hǎi 海 *noun*
= sea, ocean

hǎi'àn 海岸 *noun*
= coast, seashore

hǎibiān 海边 *noun*
= seashore, beach

hǎiguān 海关 *noun*
= customs house, customs

hǎijūn 海军 *noun*
= navy

hǎiwài 海外 *adverb*
= overseas, abroad

hǎixiá 海峡 *noun*
= strait

hǎiyáng 海洋 *noun*
= seas and oceans, ocean

hài 害
1 *noun*
- = evil, harm, calamity
- = disadvantage, damage, injury

2 *verb*
- = harm, impair, cause trouble to
- = kill, murder
- = suffer from (an illness or disease), become ill
  hài bìng 害病 = become ill

hàichu 害处 *noun*
= harm

hàipà 害怕 *verb*
= fear, be afraid

hán 含 *verb*
- = hold in the mouth
- = contain

hánjià 寒假 *noun*
= winter holiday, winter vacation

hánlěng 寒冷 *adjective*
= bitterly cold

Hánguó 韩国 *noun*
= South Korea

hǎn 喊 *verb*
= shout, call, yell

Hànyǔ 汉语 *noun*
= Chinese language

Hànzì 汉字 *noun*
= Chinese characters

Hànzú 汉族 *noun*
= Han nationality

hàn 汗 *noun*
= sweat, perspiration
chū hàn 出汗 = sweat, perspire

háng 行 ▶ *See also* **xíng** 行.
1 *noun*
- = line, row
- = trade, profession, line of business
  nǐ xǐhuan zhè yì háng ma? 你喜欢这一行吗? = do you like this profession?

2 *measure word* ▶ **157**
(*for things that form a line*)

hángkōng 航空 *noun*
= aviation, aeronautics
hángkōngxìn 航空信 = airmail letter

háobù 毫不 *adverb*
= not in the least, not at all, not the slightest

háowú 毫无 *adverb*
= without the slightest

hǎo 好 ▶ *See also* **hào** 好.
1 *adjective*
- = good, fine, alright
- = in good health, well
- (*in comparisons*) = better

2 *adverb*
- = well
- = easy to
  kuàizi hǎo yòng 筷子好用 = chopsticks are easy to use
- = good to (taste, smell, etc.)
  hǎo [**chī** | **hē**] 好[吃 | 喝] = good [to eat | to drink]
- (*emphatic*)
  = how...! so...! very...!
  hǎo lěng de tiānqì! 好冷的天气! = how cold the weather is!
- (*when used after a verb to indicate completion*) = done, finished, ready
  wǒ zuòhǎo le 我做好了 = I have finished doing it

3 *conjunction*
= so as to, so that
jīntiān xiàwǔ wǒ yào bǎ zuòyè zuòwàn, wǎnshàng hǎo qù kàn diànyǐng 今天我要把作业做完,晚上好去看电影 = this afternoon I want to finish all my homework so that I can go to the cinema this evening

hǎochī 好吃 *adjective*
= good to eat, tasty, delicious

hǎochu 好处 *noun*
- = good point, benefit, advantage
- = profit, gain

hǎohǎor (de) 好好儿(地) *adverb*
= properly, carefully, thoroughly
nǐmén yào hǎohǎor de yánjiū yíxià 你们要好好儿地研究一下 = you should research this thoroughly

hǎo jiǔ 好久 *adverb*
= for a long time, a long time since
hǎo jiǔ bú jiàn 好久不见 = haven't seen you for a long time, 'long time no see'

hǎokàn 好看 *adjective*
- = good-looking, nice-looking, attractive
- (*as a book, movie, etc.*) = interesting

hǎotīng 好听 *adjective*
= pleasing to the ear, pleasant to listen to

hǎo róngyì 好容易, **hǎo bu róngyì** 好不容易 *adverb*
= with difficulty, with great effort

hǎowánr 好玩儿 *adjective*
= interesting, amusing, fun

hǎoxiàng 好象 *verb*
= seem as if, seem as though, be like

hǎoxiē 好些 *adjective*
= quite a few, a good many of, a great deal of

hào 号 *noun*
- = mark, sign, signal
- (*of size, house, room, telephone*) = number
- = day, date
  jīntiān shísān hào 今天十三号 = today is the 13th
- = horn, bugle, bugle call

hàomǎ 号码 *noun*
= number

hàozhào 号召
1 *verb*
= call, appeal to, attract
2 *noun*
= call, appeal

hào 好 *verb* ▶ *See also* **hǎo** 好.
- = like, love, be fond of
  hào xué 好学 = like studying, be eager to learn
- = be apt to, be liable to, have a tendency to
  hào shēngqì 好生气 = apt to lose one's temper

H

hē 喝 *verb*
- = drink
- = drink liquor, drink an alcoholic beverage

hēzuì 喝醉 = get drunk

hé 合
1 *verb*
- = come together, join, combine
- (*as eyes, etc.*) = close, shut

bǎ yǎnjīng héqǐlai 把眼睛合起来 = close your eyes
- = agree, suit, accord with
- = be equal to, add up to, be equivalent to

yì yīngbàng hé shísān kuài Rénmínbì 一英镑合十三块人民币 = one pound sterling is equal to thirteen *yuan* in Renminbi

2 *adjective*
= suitable

3 *adverb*
= jointly, together with others

hé bàn 合办 = run jointly

héfǎ 合法 *adjective*
= legal

hésuàn 合算 *adjective*
= worthwhile

hélǐ 合理 *adjective*
= reasonable, rational

héshì 合适 *adjective*
= suitable, fitting, appropriate

hétong 合同 *noun*
= contract, agreement

hézuò 合作
1 *verb*
= co-operate, collaborate, work together

2 *noun*
= co-operation, collaboration

hé 和
1 *conjunction*
(*connects parallel expressions*) = and, together with

2 *preposition*
- = with

wǒ hé nǐ yíkuàir qù 我和你一块儿去 = I'll go with you
- (*denoting relations, comparison, etc.*)

tā hé wǒ yíyàng gāo 他和我一样高 = he is as tall as I am

hépíng 和平 *noun*
= peace

héqì 和气 *adjective*
= polite, kind, gentle

hé 河 *noun*
= river

hébì 何必 *adverb*
= what need...? why bother...?, there is no need to...

hékuàng 何况 *conjunction*
= let alone, not to speak of

zhège wèntí lián lǎoshī dōu bù dǒng, hékuàng wǒmen xuésheng ne 这个问题连老师都不懂, 何况我们学生呢 = even the teacher cannot understand this problem, let alone we students

hé 盒 *noun*
= box, case

yìhé cháyè 一盒茶叶 = a box of tea

hézi 盒子 *noun*
= box, case

hēi 黑 *adjective*
- = black

hēisè 黑色 = black in colour
- (*when talking about weather*) = dark

tiān hēi le 天黑了 = it's getting dark

hēi'àn 黑暗
1 *adjective*
= black, dark

hēi'àn de yímiàn 黑暗的一面 = the dark side

2 *noun*
= darkness

hēibǎn 黑板 *noun*
= chalk board, blackboard

hēi 嘿 *exclamation*
= hey!

hénjī 痕迹 *noun*
= trace, track, mark

hěn 很 *adverb*
= very, quite, very much

hèn 恨
1 *verb*
= hate

2 *noun*
= hate, hatred, regret

héng 横 *adjective*
= horizontal, across, sideways

hóng 红 *adjective*
= red

hóng chá 红茶 *noun*
= black tea

hónglǜdēng 红绿灯 *noun*
= traffic lights

hóngqí 红旗 *noun*
= red flag/banner

hóngshuǐ 洪水 *noun*
= flood

hóuzi 猴子 *noun*
= monkey

hòu 后
1 *adverb*
= later
2 *adjective*
= rear, back, the latter
3 *preposition*
= after, behind
wǔfàn hòu 午饭后 = after lunch
4 *conjunction*
= after

hòubian 后边 *noun*
= back, rear

hòudài 后代 *noun*
= descendant, later generations

hòuguǒ 后果 *noun*
= result, consequence

hòuhuǐ 后悔 *verb*
= regret, feel regretful

hòulái 后来 *adverb*
= later on, afterwards

hòumén 后门 *noun*
= back door (literally and figuratively)

hòumian 后面, **hòutou** 后头
adverb
- = at the back, in the rear, behind
- = later

hòunián 后年 *noun*
= the year after next

hòutiān 后天 *noun*
= the day after tomorrow

hòu 厚 *adjective*
- = thick
- = deep, profound
- = large, substantial, generous

hū 呼 *verb*
- = call, call out, shout
- = exhale, breathe out

hūxī 呼吸
1 *verb*
= breathe
2 *noun*
= breath, breathing, respiration

hūrán 忽然 *adverb*
= suddenly, all of a sudden

hūshì 忽视 *verb*
= ignore, overlook

húluàn 胡乱 *adverb*
= blindly, confusedly, recklessly

húshuō 胡说
1 *verb*
= talk nonsense
2 *noun*
= nonsense
húshuō bādào 胡说八道 = total nonsense, utter rubbish

hútòng 胡同 *noun*
= lane, alley

húzi 胡子 *noun*
= beard, moustache

hú 壶 *noun*
= kettle, pot
yìhú kāfēi 一壶咖啡 = a pot of coffee

hú 湖 *noun*
= lake

hútu 糊涂, **húlihútu** 糊里糊涂
adjective
= confused, muddle-headed

hù 户
1 *noun*
= door
2 *measure word* ▶ 157
(*for households*)

hùxiāng 互相 *adverb*
= mutual, mutually

hùlǐyuán 护理员 *noun*
= carer

hùshi 护士 *noun*
(*medical*) = nurse

hùzhào 护照 *noun*
= passport

huā 花
1 *noun*
= flower, blossom, bloom
2 *adjective*
= multicoloured, variegated
3 *verb*
(*of money, time, etc.*) = spend, expend
huā [qián | shíjiān] 花 [钱 | 时间] = [spend money | take time]

huāfèi 花费 *noun*
= expenditure, expenses

huāyuán 花园 *noun*
= flower garden, garden

huáqiáo 华侨 *noun*
= overseas Chinese

huárén 华人 *noun*
= Chinese person with a non-Chinese nationality

huá 划 *verb* ▶ *See also* **huà** 划.
• (*a boat, etc.*) = paddle, row
• = make a scratch/cut, be scratched/cut

huá 滑 *adjective*
• = slippery, slick, smooth
• = cunning, crafty

huábīng 滑冰 *verb*
= skate, ice skate

huáxuě 滑雪 *verb*
= ski

huà 化 *verb*
• = transform, change, turn into
• = melt, dissolve
• (*after an adjective or noun to form a verb*) = -ise or -ize
xiàndàihuà 现代化 = modernization

huàxué 化学 *noun*
= chemistry
huàxué chéngfèn 化学成分 = chemical composition
huàxué fǎnyìng 化学反应 = chemical reaction

huà 划 ▶ *See also* **huá** 划.
1 *verb*
• (*a boundary between regions, classes, etc.*) = delineate, draw (a line)
• = appropriate, assign, transfer
2 *noun*
(*when speaking of a Chinese character*) = stroke

huà 画 *verb*
= paint, draw
huà huàr 画画儿 = draw/paint a picture

huà(r) 画(儿) *noun*
= drawing, painting, picture

huàbào 画报 *noun*
= pictorial, illustrated magazine/newspaper

huà 话 *noun*
= speech, language, words

huàjù 话剧 *noun*
= play, modern drama

huái 怀
1 *noun*
= arms, heart, bosom
2 *verb*
= cherish, harbour (feelings)

huáiniàn 怀念 *verb*
= miss, cherish the memory of, think of

huáiyí 怀疑 *verb*
= doubt, suspect

huáiyùn 怀孕 *verb*
= be pregnant, get pregnant

huài 坏
1 *adjective*
• = bad
• = broken, ruined
• (*as food or other perishables*) = spoiled
2 *verb*
= go bad, become spoiled, get out of order
mǐfàn huài le 米饭坏了 = the rice has gone bad
3 *adverb*
(*when used after an adjective, showing an extreme extent*) [lèi | kě | qì] huài le [累 | 渴 | 气] 坏了 = terribly [tired | thirsty | angry]

huàichu 坏处 *noun*
= harm, fault, disadvantage

huānlè 欢乐 *adjective*
= happy, merry

huānsòng 欢送 *verb*
= send off
huānsònghuì 欢送会 = farewell party, send-off

huānxǐ 欢喜
1 *adjective*
= happy, delighted
2 *verb*
= like, be fond of, delight in

huānyíng 欢迎 *verb*
= welcome, greet

huán 还 *verb* ▶ *See also* **hái** 还.
= go/come back, return, repay
qǐng nǐ bǎ qián huán gěi tā 请你把钱还给他 = please return the money to him

huán 环 *noun*
= ring, hoop, link

huánjìng 环境 *noun*
= environment, surroundings, circumstances

huǎnmàn 缓慢 *adjective*
= slow, sluggish

huànxiǎng 幻想 *noun*
= fantasy, illusion

huànxǐng 唤醒 *verb*
= awaken (someone), wake (someone) up

huànqǐ 唤起 *verb*
= call, arouse

huàn 换 *verb*
= exchange, trade
huàn yíjù huà shuō 换一句话说 = to put it another way, in other words

huàn 患 *verb*
(*when talking about an illness, etc.*) = contract, suffer from

huāng 荒 *adjective*
- = waste
- = barren, deserted, uncultivated

huāng(zhāng) 慌(张) *adjective*
= flurried, flustered, confused

huángdì 皇帝 *noun*
= emperor

huáng 黄 *adjective*
= yellow

huángguā 黄瓜 *noun*
= cucumber

Huánghé 黄河 *noun*
= Yellow River

huánghūn 黄昏 *noun*
= dusk

huángyóu 黄油 *noun*
= butter

huǎng(huà) 谎(话) *noun*
= lie, falsehood
shuō huǎng 说谎 = tell a lie

huī 灰
1 *adjective*
= grey
2 *noun*
= ash, dust

huīchén 灰尘 *noun*
= dust, dirt

huī 挥 *verb*
= wield, wave

huīfù 恢复
1 *verb*
= recover, restore, re-establish
2 *noun*
= recovery, restoration

huí 回
1 *verb*
- = return, go back
- = answer, reply, reciprocate
- = turn round

2 *measure word* ▶ 157
(*for times, occurrences*)

huídá 回答
1 *verb*
= answer, reply
2 *noun*
= answer, response

Huíjiào 回教 *noun*
= Islam

huílai 回来 *verb*
- = come back, return
- (*when used after a verb to indicate action coming back toward the speaker*)

bǎ yàoshi jiāohuílai 把钥匙交回来 = hand back the key

huíqu 回去 *verb*
- = go back, return
- (*when used after a verb to indicate action going back to the place of origin*)

bǎ shū huánhuíqu 把书还回去 = return the book

huítóu 回头
1 *verb*
- = turn the head round
- = repent, change one's ways

2 *adverb*
= later
wǒ huítóu qù kàn tā 我回头去看她 = I'll go and see her later

huíxiǎng 回想 *verb*
= think back, recollect, recall

huíxìn 回信
1 *verb*
= reply to a letter, write in reply
2 *noun*
= letter of reply

H

huíyì 回忆
1 *verb*
= recall, recollect
2 *noun*
= reminiscence, recollection

huǐ 毁 *verb*
= destroy, ruin

huì 汇
1 *verb*
- = remit
- = converge, gather together, collect

2 *noun*
= compilation, collection

huì 会

> **!** *Can also be pronounced* **kuài** 会 *with a different meaning.*

1 *verb*
- = know how to, be able to, can
  huì yòng jìsuànjī 会用计算机 = know how to use a computer
- = be likely to, be going to, be sure to
  huì bú huì xià yǔ? 会不会下雨? = is it going to rain?
- = be accomplished in, be good at
  tā huì hěn duō zhǒng wàiyǔ 他会很多种外语 = he can speak many foreign languages
- (*when used after a verb to indicate accomplishment*) = acquire, master, command
  tā xuéhuìle zhège jìshù 他学会了这个技术 = he has mastered the technique
- (*to express future tense*) = will, shall
  kǒngpà nǐ huì tài lèi le 恐怕你会太累了 = I'm afraid you'll be too tired
- = get together, meet, assemble

2 *noun*
- = meeting, conference, party
- = association, society, union

huìchǎng 会场 *noun*
= meeting place, conference centre, assembly hall

huìhuà 会话
1 *verb*
= to engage in a conversation/dialogue
2 *noun*
= conversation, dialogue

huìjiàn 会见
1 *verb*
= meet with
2 *noun*
= a meeting

huìkè 会客 *verb*
= receive a visitor/guest
huìkè shíjiān 会客时间 = visiting hours
huìkèshì 会客室 = reception room

huìtán 会谈
1 *verb*
= hold negotiations, talk, discuss
2 *noun*
= negotiation, discussion, talk

huìyì 会议 *noun*
= meeting, conference

húnshēn 浑身 *adverb*
= from head to toe, the whole body

hūnmí 昏迷
1 *verb*
= faint, lose consciousness, be in a coma
2 *noun*
= coma

hūnlǐ 婚礼 *noun*
= wedding ceremony, wedding

hūnyīn 婚姻 *noun*
= marriage

hùn 混 *verb*
- = confuse, mix up
- = pass for, pass off as
  tā hùnjìnle huìchǎng 他混进了会场 = he conned his way into the conference hall
- = live aimlessly, muddle along, drift along
  tā zài Xiānggǎng hùnle yì nián 他在香港混了一年 = he idled away a year in Hong Kong
- = get along with
  wǒ gēn tā hùn de búcuò 我跟他混得不错 = I get along with him rather well

hùnluàn 混乱 *noun*
= chaos, disorder, confusion

huó 活
1 *verb*
= live, be alive
2 *adjective*
= alive, lively

huór 活儿 *noun*
- = work
  gàn huór 干活儿 = to work
- = product

huódòng 活动
1 *noun*
= activity, event
2 *verb*
= move about, get exercise
3 *adjective*
= loose, movable, mobile

huópo 活泼 *adjective*
= lively, vivid

huóyuè 活跃
1 *verb*
= invigorate, animate
2 *adjective*
= lively, active, dynamic

huǒ 火 *noun*
- = fire
- = anger, temper
- = firepower, firearms, ammunition

huǒchái 火柴 *noun*
= match

huǒchē 火车 *noun*
= train
huǒchēzhàn 火车站 = railway station

huǒjī 火鸡 *noun*
= turkey

huǒjiàn 火箭 *noun*
= rocket

huǒyào 火药 *noun*
= gunpowder

huǒ 伙 *measure word* ▶ **157**

> **!** *This measure word usually has a negative connotation.*

(*for groups or bands of people*)

huǒbàn 伙伴 *noun*
= partner, companion

huǒshí 伙食 *noun*
= meals, food, board

huò(zhě) 或(者)
1 *conjunction*
= or, either...or...
huòzhě zuò huǒchē qù, huòzhě zuò qìchē qù, dōu kěyǐ 或者坐火车去，或者坐汽车去，都可以 = we can go either by train or by car
2 *adverb*
= maybe, perhaps, probably

huò 货 *noun*
= goods, products, commodities

huòbì 货币 *noun*
= money, currency

huòwù 货物 *noun*
= goods, products, merchandise

huò(dé) 获(得) *verb*
- = obtain, acquire, gain
- = win, achieve
- = reap, harvest

huò 祸 *noun*
= misfortune, disaster

Jj

jīhū 几乎 *adverb*
= almost, nearly

jī 击 *verb*
(*using a mouse*) = click

jīchǎng 机场 *noun*
= airport

jīguān 机关 *noun*
= organization, agency

jīhuì 机会 *noun*
= opportunity

jīqì 机器 *noun*
= machine
jīqì rén 机器人 = robot

jīxiè 机械
1 *noun*
= machinery, mechanism, engine
2 *adjective*
= mechanical

jī 鸡 *noun*
= chicken

jīdàn 鸡蛋 *noun*
(*of a chicken*) = egg

> **!** *Note that in Chinese the kind of egg has to be specified;* **jīdàn** 鸡蛋 *is not used for the egg of any animal other than a chicken.*

jījí 积极 *adjective*
- = positive, affirmative, optimistic
- = active, energetic, vigorous

jījíxìng 积极性 *noun*
= positive attitude, zeal, enthusiasm

jīlěi 积累 *verb*
= accumulate, build up

jīběn 基本 *adjective*
= basic, fundamental, essential

jīchǔ 基础
1 *noun*
= foundation, basis
2 *adjective*
= basic, elementary

jīdòng 激动 *adjective*
- = moving, exciting
- = excited, moved

jīliè 激烈 *adjective*
= heated, intense, sharp

jí 及 *conjunction*
(*used between nouns or noun phrases; the noun after* jí 及 *is often less important than the one before it*) = and, and including

jígé 及格 *verb*
(*when speaking of a test or examination*) = pass, reach an acceptable standard

jíshí 及时 *adjective*
1 *adjective*
= timely
2 *adverb*
- = on time
- = right away, promptly, without delay

jí 级 *noun*
- = grade, rank, quality
- (*in school*) = year, class, grade

jí 极 *adverb*
= extremely, exceedingly, to the highest degree
...jí le ..极了 (*follows an adjective when indicating an extreme degree*) = extremely
hǎochī jí le 好吃极了 = extremely delicious

jíqí 极其 *adverb*
= extremely, exceptionally

jí 即 *verb*
- (*equivalent to* jiùshì 就是) = be, be exactly, be none other than
- = that is, i.e.

jíjiāng 即将 *adverb*
= will, going to, about to

jíshǐ 即使, **jíbiàn** 即便
conjunction
= even if, even though, even

jí 急 *adjective*
- = anxious, worried, uneasy
- = in a hurry
- = angry, annoyed, impatient
- (*as a wind, a storm, or water in a river*) = violent, strong, fast
- = urgent, pressing

jímáng 急忙 *adverb*
= in a hurry, hurriedly, hastily

jí 集
1 *verb*
= collect, gather, assemble
2 *noun*
- = collection, anthology
- = volume, part
- = market, fair

gǎn jí 赶集 = go to market

jíhé 集合 *verb*
= gather together

jítǐ 集体
1 *noun*
= collective
2 *adjective*
= collective

jízhōng 集中
1 *verb*
- = concentrate, amass, put together
- = centralize

2 *adjective*
= concentrated, centralized

jǐ 几 *determiner*
- (*when unstressed*) = a few, several

> **!** *Note that when used with numerals, the meaning of* jǐ 几 *changes depending on whether it comes before or after the numeral. The phrase* jǐ shí bù 几十步 *means* several tens of steps, *i.e., 20, 30, 40, etc. (sometimes translated as* dozens *or* scores, *while the phrase* shíjǐ bù 十几步 *means* more than 10 steps, *that is, over 10 but under 20.*

- (*when stressed*) = how many?

xiànzài jǐ diǎn le? 现在几点了? = what time is it now?

jǐ 己 *noun*
= oneself, one's own

jǐ 挤
1 *verb*
• = crowd, press, squeeze
• = push, jostle
• (*by squeezing an animal's udder*) = milk
2 *adjective*
= crowded

jìhuà 计划
1 *noun*
= plan, project
2 *verb*
= plan, arrange, map out
jìhuà shēngyù 计划生育 = family planning, birth control

jìsuàn 计算
1 *verb*
= compute, calculate
2 *noun*
= calculation

jìsuànjī 计算机 *noun*
= computer

jì 记 *verb*
• = remember, keep in mind
• = record, note, jot down

jìde 记得 *verb*
= remember

jìlù 记录
1 *verb*
= record, take notes, keep minutes
2 *noun*
• (*of meetings, etc.*) = minutes, notes, record
• (*in athletics, etc.*) = record

jìyì 记忆
1 *verb*
= remember, recall
2 *noun*
= memory, memories

jìzhě 记者 *noun*
= reporter, journalist

jìzhu 记住 *verb*
= remember, keep in mind, learn by heart

jìlǜ 纪律 *noun*
= discipline

jìniàn 纪念
1 *verb*
= commemorate, observe
2 *noun*
• = souvenir, memento, keepsake
yíge jìniànpǐn 一个纪念品 = a souvenir
• = commemoration, memorial, anniversary

jìshù 技术 *noun*
= technique, skill

jìshùyuán 技术员 *noun*
= technician

jì(jié) 季(节) *noun*
= season

jì 既 *conjunction*
= since, now that
jì...yě/yòu... 既...也/又... = both...and..., as well as
zhège rén jì nǔlì, yòu cóngming 这个人既努力又聪明 = this person is both hardworking and intelligent

jìrán 既然 *conjunction*
= since, now that, as

jìxù 继续 *verb*
= continue, carry on

jì 寄 *verb*
= send, post, mail

jiā 加 *verb*
• (*as a mathematical function*) = add, plus
• = increase, raise

jiāgōng 加工 *verb*
(*of raw materials*) = process into a finished product

Jiānádà 加拿大 *noun*
= Canada

jiāqiáng 加强 *verb*
= strengthen, reinforce

jiāyǐ 加以
1 *verb*
= add more, apply additionally
2 *conjunction*
= in addition, moreover

jiā 夹
1 *verb*
• = pinch, squeeze, compress
• (*with chopsticks, pincers, etc.*) = pick up, hold
• = place between, insert between
• = mix, mingle
2 *noun*
• = tweezers, pincers, pliers
• = fastener, clip
• = folder

jiā 家
1 *noun*
- = home, family, household
- (*when it follows a subject or field*) = a specialist, a professional
  kēxuéjiā 科学家 = scientist
- = school of thought

2 *measure word* ▶ **157**
(*for families, enterprises, restaurants, hotels, etc.*)

jiājù 家具 *noun*
= furniture

jiātíng 家庭 *noun*
= family, home

jiāxiāng 家乡 *noun*
= home town, native place

jiǎ 假 *adjective* ▶ *See also* **jià** 假.
= false, artificial, fake

jiàgé 价格 *noun*
= price, charge

jiàqian 价钱 *noun*
= price, charge

jiàzhí 价值 *noun*
= value, worth, cost

jià 架
1 *measure word* ▶ **157**
(*for aeroplanes, pianos, cameras, etc.*)
2 *noun*
- = stand, rack, shelf
- = structure, scaffold

3 *verb*
- = erect, put up
- = support, help

jià 假 *noun* ▶ *See also* **jiǎ** 假.
= holiday, vacation, leave of absence

jiàtiáo 假条 *noun*
- = leave permit, permit to take leave, doctor's certificate
- = application for leave

jiān 尖
1 *adjective*
- = sharp, pointed
- = sharp in sound, shrill
- (*of the senses*) = keen, acute
  [**ěrduo** | **bízi**] **jiān** [耳朵 | 鼻子] 尖 = have an acute sense of [hearing | smell]

2 *noun*
= sharp tip/point, hook

jiānruì 尖锐 *adjective*
- (*of objects*) = sharp, pointed
- (*of perception, analysis, thought, etc.*) = penetrating, incisive, sharp
- (*of sound*) = shrill, piercing
- (*of activity, struggle, opposition*) = intense, acute

jiānchí 坚持
1 *verb*
= hold firmly to, persist in, insist
2 *adjective*
= persistent, insistent

jiāndìng 坚定 *adjective*
= firm, resolute, determined

jiānjué 坚决
1 *adjective*
= resolute, decided, determined
2 *adverb*
= decidedly, determinedly

jiānqiáng 坚强 *adjective*
= strong, solid

jiān 间
1 *measure word* ▶ **157**
(*for rooms*)
2 *noun*
= room
3 *preposition*
= between, amongst

jiān 肩 *noun*
= shoulder

jiānjù 艰巨 *adjective*
= extremely difficult

jiānkǔ 艰苦
1 *adjective*
= hard, difficult, tough
2 *noun*
= hardship, difficulty

jiǎnchá 检查
1 *verb*
= inspect, examine
2 *noun*
= inspection, examination

jiǎndān 简单 *adjective*
= simple, easy, uncomplicated

jiǎn 拣 *verb*
= choose, pick out, select

jiǎn 捡 *verb*
= pick up, gather

jiǎn 剪 *verb*
(*with scissors*) = cut, clip, cut off

jiǎn 减 *verb*
- = subtract, minus, take away
- = decrease, reduce, cut

jiǎnqīng 减轻 *verb*
= lighten, reduce, mitigate

jiǎnshǎo 减少 *verb*
= diminish, reduce, decrease

jiàn 见 *verb*
- = see, catch sight of
- = meet
- = call on, visit, have an interview with
- = appear, manifest, be evident
- (*used as a suffix to certain verbs to indicate successful perception by the senses*)
  [kàn | tīng | wén] jiàn [看 | 听 | 闻] 见 = [see | hear | smell]

jiànmiàn 见面 *verb*
= meet (face to face), see

jiàn 件 *measure word* ▶ **157**
(*for luggage, clothes, furniture, matters, etc.*)

jiàn 建 *verb*
- = build, construct
- = establish, found, create

jiànlì 建立
1 *verb*
= establish, set up, create
2 *noun*
= establishment

jiànshè 建设
1 *verb*
= build up, construct
2 *noun*
= construction

jiànyì 建议
1 *verb*
= suggest, recommend, give advice
2 *noun*
= suggestion, recommendation, proposal

jiànzhù 建筑
1 *noun*
- = building, structure
- = architecture

2 *verb*
= build, construct

jiànkāng 健康
1 *adjective*
= healthy, vigorous, robust
2 *noun*
= health

jiànjiàn 渐渐 *adverb*
= gradually, step by step

jiàn 箭 *noun*
= arrow

jiāng 江 *noun*
- = river
- = the Changjiang (Yangtze) River
  Jiāng nán 江南 = south of the Yangtze River

jiāng 将
1 *adverb*
- = about to, going to
  jiāng kāishǐ 将开始 = about to begin
- (*when indicating future tense*) = will, shall, be going to

2 *preposition*
(*used to introduce a verbal phrase by placing the object before the verb; functions like* bǎ 把)
jiāng tāde xíngli ná huí jiā 将他的行李拿回家 = take his luggage back home

jiānglái 将来
1 *noun*
= future
2 *adverb*
= in the future

jiāngyào 将要 *verb*
= will, be going to, be about to
jiāngyào shàngkè de shíhou... 将要上课的时候... = when the lesson is about to start...

jiǎng 讲 *verb*
- = say, tell, remark
- = talk, discuss, negotiate
- = explain, interpret
- = pay attention to, be particular about

jiǎnghuà 讲话 *verb*
= talk, speak, converse

jiǎngzuò 讲座 *noun*
= lecture

jiǎng 奖
1 *noun*
= prize, award
2 *verb*
= praise, commend, reward

jiǎngxuéjīn 奖学金 *noun*
= scholarship

jiàng 降 *verb*
- = descend, fall, drop
- = lower, reduce, cut down

jiàngdī 降低 *verb*
= lower, drop, reduce

jiàngluò 降落 *verb*
(*when talking about an aeroplane*) = descend, land

jiàngyóu 酱油 *noun*
= soy sauce, soya sauce

jiāo 交 *verb*
- = hand in, hand over, give up
- = meet, join, come into contact with
- = befriend, associate with
  jiāo péngyou 交朋友 = make friends

jiāohuàn 交换
1 *verb*
= exchange, swap, interchange
2 *noun*
= exchange, interchange, swap

jiāojì 交际
1 *noun*
= social interaction, communication
2 *verb*
= be socially active, interact with people

jiāoliú 交流
1 *verb*
= exchange, interchange
2 *noun*
= exchange, interchange

jiāotán 交谈 *verb*
= converse, have a chat

jiāotōng 交通 *noun*
- = communications, transportation
- = traffic

jiāoqū 郊区 *noun*
= suburban district, suburbs

jiāo'ào 骄傲
1 *adjective*
= proud, arrogant, haughty
wǒ wèi nǐ jiāo'ào 我为你骄傲 = I'm proud of you
2 *noun*
= pride, conceit

jiāo 教

> **!** *Can also be pronounced* jiào *with a different meaning.*

verb
= teach, train, instruct
jiāoshū 教书 = teach

jiǎo 角 *noun*
- (*a unit of Chinese money*)
  yì jiǎo qián 一角钱 = ten *fen*, 1/10 of a *yuan*
- = corner
- (*in geometry*) = angle
- (*of an animal*) = horn, antler

jiǎozi 饺子 *noun*
= boiled dumpling filled with meat and vegetable

jiǎo 脚 *noun*
- (*part of the body*) = foot
- (*of an object, mountain, structure, etc.*) = base, foot, leg

jiào 叫
1 *verb*
- = call out, cry out, shout
- (*as a taxi*) = summon, order, hire
- = name, call, address as
  tā jiào wǒ lǎoshī 他叫我老师 = he calls me 'Teacher'
- = be named, be called
  tā jiào shénme míngzi? 她叫什么名字? = what is her name?
- = tell, order
- = let, allow, permit
  tā bú jiào wǒ kàn tāde shū 她不叫我看她的书 = she won't let me read her book

2 *noun*
(*of a bird or animal*) = call, cry
[**gǒu** | **niǎo**] **jiào** [狗 | 鸟] 叫 = [dog's bark | bird's call]
3 *preposition*
(*when used to introduce the agent in a passive construction*) = by
tā jiào lǎoshī pīpíngle yídùn 他叫老师批评了一顿 = he was given a reprimand by the teacher

jiàozuò 叫做, **jiàozuò** 叫作
verb
(*when giving the name or term for something*) = be called, be known as
zhè jiàozuò làngfèi 这叫做浪费 = this is called being wasteful

jiàocái 教材 *noun*
(*textbooks, etc.*) = teaching materials

jiàoliàn 教练 *noun*
(*in sports, etc.*) = coach, instructor

jiàoshī 教师 *noun*
= teacher

jiàoshì 教室 *noun*
= classroom

jiàoshòu 教授 *noun*
= professor

jiàoxué 教学
1 *verb*
= teach
2 *noun*
= teaching

jiàoxùn 教训
1 *verb*
- = teach (someone a lesson), lecture (someone for wrongdoing)
- = reproach, reprimand, chide

2 *noun*
= lesson, teaching, moral
cóng shìgù zhōng xīqǔ jiàoxùn 从事故中吸取教训 = learn a lesson from the accident

jiàoyù 教育
1 *verb*
= teach, educate, inculcate
2 *noun*
= education

jiàoyuán 教员 *noun*
= teacher, instructor

jiào 较
1 *verb*
= compare
2 *adverb*
= comparatively, relatively, relatively
3 *preposition*
= compared with, than

jiēduàn 阶段 *noun*
(*of development*) = stage, phase

jiējí 阶级 *noun*
= (social) class

jiēshi 结实 *adjective*
- (*when talking about objects*) = strong, durable, solid
- (*of people*) = sturdy, tough, strong

jiē 接 *verb*
- (*when referring to guests or visitors*) = meet, receive, welcome, pick up
- (*when speaking of a letter, a ball, etc.*) = receive, take hold of, catch
- (*for the telephone, etc.*) = answer, accept, take over
- = connect, join, unite

jiēchù 接触
1 *verb*
= touch, come into contact with, meet up with
2 *noun*
= contact

jiēdài 接待
1 *verb*
(*when referring to guests or visitors*) = receive, host, admit
2 *noun*
= reception

jiēdào 接到 *verb*
= receive

jiējiàn 接见 *verb*
(*when referring to guests or visitors*) = receive, meet

jiējìn 接近
1 *verb*
= approximate, come close to, approach
2 *adjective*
= close to, near to, on intimate terms with

J

jiēshòu 接受 *verb*
= receive, take, accept

jiēzhe 接着
1 *verb*
= follow, carry on, catch
2 *adverb*
= right afterwards, following

jiē 街 *noun*
- = road, street, thoroughfare
- = downtown, shopping district

jiēdào 街道 *noun*
= road, street

jié 节
1 *noun*
- (*of an object*) = segment, section, division
- = sequence of events, proceedings, programme
- = festival, holiday

2 *verb*
= save, economize
3 *measure word* ▶ 157
- (*for sections of things*) = section, length, segment
- (*for torch batteries, railway carriages, class periods at school*)

jiémù 节目 *noun*
(*of a performance, or on radio or TV*) = programme, item on a programme

jiérì 节日 *noun*
= festival day, holiday

jiéshěng 节省
1 *verb*
= save, economize
2 *adjective*
= economical, thrifty, frugal

jiéyuē 节约
1 *verb*
= economize, save
2 *noun*
= austerity

jiégòu 结构 *noun*
= structure, construction, composition

jiéguǒ 结果
1 *noun*
= result, outcome
2 *adverb*
= consequently, finally, as a result

jiéhé 结合
1 *verb*
• = join together, unite, marry
• = combine, integrate
2 *noun*
= unity, combination

jiéhūn 结婚
1 *verb*
= marry, get married
2 *noun*
= marriage

jiélùn 结论 *noun*
• (*of an argument or statement*) = conclusion
• (*of a law case*) = conclusion, verdict

jiéshù 结束 *verb*
= finish, conclude, wind up

jiějie 姐姐 *noun*
= elder sister

jiěmèi 姐妹 *noun*
= sisters

jiě 解 *verb*
• = loosen, untie, unfasten
• = free, relieve, put an end to
• = dispel, dissolve, be dissolved
• = understand, comprehend, realize
• = solve, explain, interpret

jiědá 解答 *verb*
= answer, explain, solve

jiěfàng 解放
1 *verb*
= liberate, set free, emancipate
2 *noun*
= liberation, emancipation

jiějué 解决 *verb*
• = settle, solve, resolve
• = dispose of, finish off
tā bǎ nàxiē shēng fàn quán jiějué le 他把那些剩饭全解决了 = he finished all the food that was left over

jiěshì 解释
1 *verb*
= explain, clarify, interpret
2 *noun*
= explanation, interpretation

jièshào 介绍 *verb*
= introduce, present, recommend
wǒ gěi nǐ jièshào jièshào 我给你介绍介绍 = let me introduce you

jiè 届 *measure word* ▶ 157
• (*for regular sessions, conferences, sports tournaments, terms of office, etc.*)
• (*for students graduating in the same year*) = year, class, grade

jiè 界 *noun*
• = boundary
• = world, circle
[zìrán | xuéshù | shāngyè] jiè [自然 | 学术 | 商业] 界
[natural world | academic circles | business circles]

jiè 借 *verb*
• = borrow
gēn tā jiè qián 跟他借钱 = borrow money from him
• = lend
wǒ bǎ wǒde cídiǎn jiè gěi tā 我把我的词典借给他 = I lent my dictionary to him
• = use, make use of, take advantage of

jīn 斤 *noun*
(*a unit in the Chinese weight system*) = 1/2 kilogram

jīnnián 今年 *noun*
= this year, the current year

jīnhòu 今后 *adverb*
= from now on, in the future, hereafter

jīntiān 今天 *noun*
• = today
• = nowadays, the present

jīn 金
1 *noun*
= gold

2 *adjective*
= golden

jīnshǔ 金属 *noun*
= metal, metal product

jǐn(jǐn) 仅(仅) *adverb*
- = only, merely, just
- = barely, scarcely

jǐn 尽 *adverb* ▶ *See also* **jìn** 尽.
= to the greatest extent, to the utmost, furthest
jǐn [zǎo | dōngbian | shàngmian] 尽[早 | 东边 | 上面] = [as soon as possible | the easternmost | the highest]

jǐnguǎn 尽管
1 *adverb*
= freely, with no hesitation, without restriction
2 *conjunction*
= in spite of, even though, even if
jǐnguǎn...dōu/yě/hái... 尽管...都 / 也 / 还... = although...still, in spite of...still
jǐnguǎn tā shēntǐ bù hǎo, kě hái jìxù gōngzuò 尽管她身体不好, 可还继续工作 = in spite of her ill health, she still continues to work

jǐnliàng 尽量**, jìnliàng** 尽量
adverb
= to the fullest extent, as much as possible, to one's utmost

jǐn 紧
1 *adjective*
- = tight, taut, tense
- = urgent, important, pressing
- = near, close

2 *adverb*
= tightly, closely

jǐnjí 紧急 *adjective*
= urgent, pressing, critical

jǐnzhāng 紧张 *adjective*
- (*of a person*) = tense, nervous, intense
- (*of a situation or supply*) = critical, tight, short

jìn 进 *verb*
- = enter, go into, come into
- = advance, move forward, go ahead
- (*used after a verb to indicate inward direction*) = into, in

zǒujìn shāngdiàn 走进商店 = walk into the store

jìnbù 进步
1 *noun*
= progress, advancement, improvement
2 *verb*
= advance, make progress, improve
3 *adjective*
= progressive

jìngōng 进攻
1 *verb*
= attack, assault
2 *noun*
= assault, offensive, attack

jìnhuà 进化 *verb*
= evolve, develop

jìnkǒu 进口
1 *verb*
(*as goods, products, etc.*) = import
2 *noun*
= import

jìnlai 进来 *verb*
(*when indicating a movement toward the speaker*) = enter, come in
zǒujìnlai 走进来 = walk in

jìnqu 进去 *verb*
(*when indicating a movement away from the speaker*) = enter, go in
zǒujìnqu 走进去 = walk in

jìnrù 进入 *verb*
- = enter, go into, penetrate
- = be admitted to

jìnxíng 进行 *verb*
- = proceed, go ahead, carry on
- = undertake, engage in

jìnxiū 进修
1 *verb*
= receive further training, pursue further studies
2 *noun*
= further training

jìnyíbù 进一步
1 *verb*
= go a step further
2 *adverb*
= further
3 *adjective*
= better

jìn 近 *adjective*
- (*in place or time*) = near, nearby, close
- = intimate, closely related

J

jìnlái 近来 *adverb*
= recently, of late, lately

jìn 尽 ▶ *See also* **jǐn** 尽.
1 *verb*
- = exhaust, use up, come to an end
- = do one's utmost, try one's best, live up to

2 *adverb*
= exhaustively, exclusively, to the highest degree

jìn 劲 *noun*
- (*physical*) = strength, energy, force
- (*mental or spiritual*) = vigour, drive, spirit
- = air, manner, expression
  kàn tā nà jǐnzhāng jìnr 看他那紧张劲儿 = notice how nervous he is
- = interest, relish, gusto
  xué shùxué zhēn méi jìnr 学数学真没劲儿 = I don't have any interest in studying mathematics

jìnzhǐ 禁止 *verb*
= forbid, prohibit, ban

jīngjù 京剧, **jīngxì** 京戏 *noun*
= Peking opera

jīng 经 *verb*
- (*when talking about a place or an experience*) = go through, pass through, via
- = manage, deal in
- = stand, endure
  tā jīng bù qǐ zhèzhǒng dǎjī 她经不起这种打击 = she can't stand this kind of blow

jīngcháng 经常 *adverb*
= frequently, often, regularly

jīngguò 经过
1 *verb*
(*when talking about a place or experience*) = pass by, pass through, go through

2 *preposition*
- = as a result of, after, through
- = by means of

3 *noun*
= process, course

jīngjì 经济 *noun*
- = economy, economics
- = financial condition, income

jīnglǐ 经理 *noun*
= manager, director

jīnglì 经历
1 *verb*
= experience, undergo

2 *noun*
= experience, past career

jīngyàn 经验 *noun*
= experience

jīngqí 惊奇 *adjective*
= surprised, amazed

jīngrén 惊人 *adjective*
= astonishing, amazing, alarming

jīngyà 惊讶 *adjective*
= surprised, amazed, astonished

jīngcǎi 精彩 *adjective*
= brilliant, splendid, wonderful

jīnglì 精力 *noun*
= energy, vitality, vigour

jīngshén 精神
1 *noun*
- = mind, consciousness
- = gist, essence, spirit

2 *adjective*
= spiritual, mental

jīngshen 精神
1 *noun*
= vigour, vitality, drive

2 *adjective*
= vigorous, lively, spirited

jǐng 井 *noun*
= well

jǐngsè 景色 *noun*
= scenery, landscape, scene

jǐngchá 警察 *noun*
= police, police officer, policeman

jǐnggào 警告 *verb*
= warn, caution, admonish

jìngsài 竞赛
1 *verb*
= compete, race

2 *noun*
= competition, race, contest

jìngzhēng 竞争
1 *verb*
= compete

2 *noun*
= competition

jìng'ài 敬爱 *adjective*
= respectful, honourable, esteemed

jìnglǐ 敬礼 *verb*
- = salute, give a salute
- = give a greeting
- (*when closing a letter respectfully*)
  cǐ zhì jìnglǐ 此致敬礼 = with best wishes

jìng 静 *adjective*
= quiet, peaceful, still

jìngzi 镜子 *noun*
- = mirror
  zhào jìngzi 照镜子 = look at one's reflection in the mirror
- = lens, glass, spectacles
  fàngdà jìng 放大镜 = magnifying glass, magnifier

jiūzhèng 纠正
1 *verb*
= correct (a mistake), put right
2 *noun*
= correction

jiūjìng 究竟 *adverb*
- = after all, in the end
- = actually, exactly

jiǔ 九 *number*
= nine

jiǔyuè 九月 *noun*
= September

jiǔ 久 *adverb*
= for a long time, long since

jiǔ 酒 *noun*
= wine, liquor, alcoholic drink

jiù 旧 *adjective*
- = old, used
- = former, past
- = old-fashioned, outdated

jiù 救 *verb*
= save, rescue, help

jiù 就
1 *adverb*
- = soon, immediately, right away
- (*sooner or earlier than expected*) = already, as early as, as soon as
  tā zuótiān jiù lái le 他昨天就来了 = he arrived yesterday
- = as soon as, right after
  tā chīle fàn jiù zǒu le 他吃了饭就走了 = he left as soon as he had eaten
- = only, just, alone
- = precisely

2 *conjunction*
- (*when used in a complex sentence with the second clause introduced by* **yě** 也) = even if, even though
  nǐ jiù bù qǐng wǒ, wǒ yě huì lái 你就不请我, 我也会来 = even if you don't invite me, I'll still come
- (*when introducing a subsequent action*) = then
  zhǐyào nǐ yuànyì, wǒ jiù gēn nǐ yìqǐ qù 只要你愿意, 我就跟你一起去 = I'll go with you if you wish
- (*when used between two identical words or phrases to indicate that one is making a concession*) = what's done is done, nothing can be done about it
  tā bù lái jiù bù lái ba, fǎnzhèng wǒmen bù néng qiángpò tā lái 他不来就不来吧, 反正我们不能强迫他来 = if he doesn't come, he doesn't come; anyway, we cannot force him to come
- (*when used with* **běnlái** 本来, *to mean all along, from the start*)
  tā běnlái jiù bù xiǎng xué Déyǔ 他本来就不想学德语 = he never wanted to study German

3 *preposition*
= according to, with regard to

jiùshì 就是
1 *adverb*
- = precisely
- (*used with* **le** 了 *at the end of a sentence to indicate an affirmative and positive sense*) = just
  bié dānxīn nǐde gōngzuò, huí jiā hǎohǎo xiūxi jiùshì le 别担心你的工作, 回家好好休息就是了 = don't worry about your work, just go home and get a good rest

2 *conjunction*
- (*when used in the sense of* **either...or...**) = or
  búshì...jiùshì... 不是...就是... = either...or...
  tā búshì zài túshūguǎn jiùshì zài shítáng 他不是在图书馆就是在食堂 = he is either in the library or in the dining hall
- = even if, even
  jiùshì...yě 就是... 也 = even..., even if....

J

jiùshì tā qù, wǒ yě bú qù 就是他去, 我也不去 = I won't go even if he goes

jiùjiu 舅舅 *noun*
= mother's brother, uncle

jūzhù 居住 *verb*
= live, reside, dwell

júzhǎng 局长 *noun*
(*of an office, bureau, department, etc.*) = head, director, chairperson

júzi 橘子 *noun*
= orange, tangerine
júzi shuǐ/zhī 橘子水/汁 = orange juice

jǔ 举 *verb*
- = raise, lift, hold up
- (*an example, etc.*) = cite, enumerate
  jǔ yíge lìzi 举一个例子 = cite as an example

jǔbàn 举办 *verb*
(*when talking about an exhibition, competition, etc*) = hold, run

jǔxíng 举行 *verb*
(*when talking about a meeting, ceremony, discussion, etc*) = hold, conduct

jù 句
1 *noun*
= sentence, line of verse
2 *measure word* ▶ 157
(*for lines, sentences, units of speech, poetry, etc.*)

jùzi 句子 *noun*
(*when talking about language*) = sentence

jùdà 巨大 *adjective*
= great, enormous, huge

jùjué 拒绝
1 *verb*
= refuse, reject, turn down
2 *noun*
= refusal

jùbèi 具备 *verb*
(*when speaking of necessary conditions, qualifications, or requirements*) = have, possess

jùtǐ 具体 *adjective*
= concrete, specific, particular

jùyǒu 具有 *verb*
= have, possess, be equipped with

jùlèbù 俱乐部 *noun*
= club

jù 剧 *noun*
= drama, play, opera

jùchǎng 剧场 *noun*
= theatre

jù 据
1 *verb*
= occupy, seize
2 *preposition*
= according to
jùshuō 据说 = it is said, they say, I hear

jùlí 距离
1 *noun*
= distance, gap, separation
2 *preposition*
= apart/away from, at a distance from
wǒ jiā jùlí Běijīng sānshí gōnglǐ 我家距离北京三十公里 = my house is thirty kilometres from Beijing

juǎn 卷
1 *verb*
- = roll up
  juǎnqǐlai 卷起来 = roll up
- = sweep off, carry along

2 *noun*
= roll, scroll

jué 决 *adverb*
(*used before a negative word*) = definitely, certainly
wǒ jué bù tóngyì 我决不同意 = under no circumstances will I agree

juédìng 决定
1 *verb*
= decide, make up one's mind
2 *noun*
= decision, resolution

juéxīn 决心
1 *noun*
= determination, resolution, decision
2 *verb*
= determine, be determined

juéde 觉得 *verb*
= feel, think

juéwù 觉悟
1 *verb*
= become aware of, become awakened, realize

2 *noun*
= consciousness, awareness, understanding

juéduì 绝对
1 *adjective*
= absolute
2 *adverb*
= absolutely, definitely

jūn 军 *noun*
(*an armed force as a whole*) = the army, the military

jūnduì 军队 *noun*
= army, armed force

jūnshì 军事
1 *noun*
= military affairs, military matters
2 *adjective*
= military

kāfēi 咖啡 *noun*
= coffee
kāfēi guǎn 咖啡馆 = café

kǎchē 卡车 *noun*
= lorry, truck

kāi 开 *verb*
- = open
- (*a vehicle or engine*) = operate, start, run
  kāi chē 开车 = drive a car
- (*a business, shop, store*) = open, be in business
- (*a business, shop, store, factory*) = set up, establish, run
- (*as a ship, vehicle, or troops on a journey or expedition*) = set off, start away
- (*land, waterway, etc.*) = open up, develop, reclaim
- (*flowers, trees, etc.*) = blossom, bloom
- (*a switch, engine, heat*) = turn on
- (*as a restriction, ban, etc.*) = remove, lift, allow
- (*meeting, exhibition, performance, school, class*) = hold, begin, start
- (*setting out in detail*) = write, list, itemize
  kāi yàofāng 开药方 = write a prescription
- (*for water*) = boil
  shuǐ kāi le 水开了 = the water is boiling
- (*after a verb to indicate outward movement, getting out of the way, etc.*) = away, off, out
  [**chuánkāi** | **zoǔkaī** | **duǒkaī**] [传开 | 走开 | 躲开] = [spread around | get out of the way | step aside]

kāifàng 开放
1 *verb*
- = open to the public, allow public use
- = be open
  duì wài kāifàng 对外开放 = be open to the outside

2 *adjective* = liberal, open

kāihuì 开会 *verb*
= hold a meeting

kāiguān 开关 *noun*
= switch

kāikè 开课 *verb*
- (*an academic course or class*) = give a course, teach
- (*referring to a school or university term*) = begin, start

kāimíng 开明 *adjective*
= liberal, enlightened, progressive

kāimù 开幕 *verb*
- = raise the curtain, begin the show
- = open, inaugurate

kāipì 开辟 *noun*
(*a country, route, road, source of revenue, etc.*) = open up, develop, utilize

kāishǐ 开始
1 *verb*
= begin, start, commence
2 *noun*
= beginning, start, outset

kāitóu 开头 *noun*
= beginning, opening

kāi wánxiào 开玩笑 *verb*
= make fun of, crack a joke
gēn tā kāi wánxiào 跟他开玩笑 = make fun of him

kāixīn 开心 *verb*
= feel happy

kāixué 开学 *verb*
= open/begin/start school

kāiyǎn 开演 *verb*
= begin/start a performance, raise the curtain

kāizhǎn 开展 *verb*
= develop, carry out, launch

kān 看 *verb* ▶ *See also* **kàn** 看.
= look after, take care of
kān háizi 看孩子 = look after a child

kǎn 砍 *verb*
= chop, cut, cut down

kàn 看 *verb* ▶ *See also* **kān** 看.
- = look, look at, watch
- (*silently*) = read
- = think, consider, regard as
  wǒ kàn tā tài shoù le 我看她太瘦了 = I think she's too thin
- = visit, call on
- (*in changeable circumstances*) = depend on
  yào kàn tā máng bù máng 要看他忙不忙 = that depends on whether he's busy or not
- (*after a verb, especially when used in reduplicated form*) = just...and see, try...and see
  shìshì kàn 试试看 = try and see (how it is, etc.)
  wènwèn kàn 问问看 = ask and see (what the person says, etc.)

kànbìng 看病 *verb*
- (*when talking about a patient seeing a doctor*) = see the doctor, have an examination
- (*when talking about a doctor seeing a patient*) = see, examine, treat

kànbuqǐ 看不起 *verb*
= look down on, scorn, despise
tā kànbuqǐ wǒ 他看不起我 = he looks down on me

kànchéng 看成 *verb*
= treat as, regard as, consider as

kàndài 看待 *verb*
= regard, treat

kàndào 看到 *verb*
= catch sight of, see, notice

kànfǎ 看法 *noun*
= viewpoint, view, way of thinking

kànjiàn 看见 *verb*
- (*implying perception as well as looking*) = see
  wǒ zuìjìn méi kànjiàn tā 我最近没看见他 = I haven't seen him recently

> **!** *When used to negate the verb,* bù 不 *comes between the two syllables of this word.*

  wǒ kàn bú jiàn nǐ 我看不见你 = I can't see you
- (*when used in the negative, taking on a passive sense*) = (dis)appear, become (in)visible
  húrán tā kàn bú jiàn le 忽然他看不见了 = he suddenly disappeared

kàn(qǐ)lai 看(起)来, **kàn yàngzi** 看样子 *verb*
= it looks as if, it seems that, it appears that
[kànlai | kàn yàngzi] yào xiàyǔ [看来 | 看样子] 要下雨 = it looks like rain

kāngkǎi 慷慨 *adjective*
= generous, vehement

káng 扛 *verb*
= carry on the shoulder/shoulders

kàngyì 抗议
1 *verb*
= protest
2 *noun*
= protest

kǎo 考 *verb*
- = examine, give/take an examination/test
- = investigate
  kǎoshang 考上 (*to attain entry to a school or university*) = to pass entrance exams
  kǎoshang dàxué 考上大学 = pass the entrance examination to enter university

kǎolǜ 考虑 *verb*
= consider, weigh, think over

kǎoshì 考试
1 *verb*
= take/give an examination
2 *noun*
= examination, test

kǎoyàn 考验 *noun*
= test, trial

kǎo 烤 *verb*
= roast, bake
kǎohuǒ 烤火 = warm oneself next to a fire

kào 靠
1 *verb*
- = lean on, lean against
- = depend upon, rely on
- (*a person or a livelihood for a living*) = depend on
  tā kào mài jìsuànjī shēnghuó 他靠卖计算机生活 = he relies on selling computers for a living
- = approach, get near to

2 *preposition*
= near, towards, along
kào běibù yǒu hěnduō shān 靠北部有很多山 = there are many mountains towards the north

kē 科 *noun*
- = area/branch of study
  wénkē 文科 = the humanities
  lǐkē 理科 = the sciences
- = administrative unit, section, department

kējì 科技 *noun*
(*abbreviation of* **kēxué jìshù** 科学技术) = science and technology

kēxué 科学 *noun*
= science

kēxuéjiā 科学家 *noun*
= scientist

kēxuéyuàn 科学院 *noun*
= academy of sciences

kēyán 科研 *noun*
(*abbreviation of* **kēxué yánjiū** 科学研究) = scientific research

kēzhǎng 科长 *noun*
= section chief

kē 棵 *measure word* ▶ 157
(*for trees, plants*)

kē 颗 *measure word* ▶ 157
- (*for small, round things such as pearls, teeth, and hearts; also for things that appear small such as stars, satellites and planets*)
- (*for bullets, bombs, etc.*)

késou 咳嗽 *verb*
= cough

kě 可
1 *verb*
- = may, can, be permitted
- = approve

2 *adverb*
(*for emphasis*) = indeed, certainly, surely
kě bié wàng le 可别忘了 = mind you, don't forget it

3 *conjunction*
= but, yet, however

kě'ài 可爱 *adjective*
- = lovely, beloved
- = lovable, cute

kěkào 可靠 *adjective*
= reliable, trustworthy, dependable

kělián 可怜
1 *adjective*
- = meagre, inadequate, pitiable
- = poor, helpless, pitiful

2 *verb*
= have pity on, feel sorry for, be merciful to
wǒ hěn kělián tā 我很可怜他 = I feel very sorry for him

kěnéng 可能
1 *adjective*
= possible, probable
zhè shì kěnéng de 这是可能的 = this is possible

2 *verb*
= may, might
tā kěnéng yào qù 他可能要去 = he may want to go

3 *noun*
= possibility
méiyǒu kěnéng 没有可能 = there is no possibility

kěnéngxìng 可能性 *noun*
= possibility

kěpà 可怕 *adjective*
= frightful, terrible, dreadful

kěshì 可是 *conjunction*
= but, yet, however

kěxī 可惜 *noun*
= pity
shízài tài kěxī le 实在太可惜了 = it's really such a shame

kěxiào 可笑 *adjective*
= laughable, funny

kěyǐ 可以
1 *verb*
= may, can, may be permitted to
nǐ yě kěyǐ cānjiā 你也可以参加 = you too can take part in it

2 *adjective*
= fine, OK, not bad

wǒmen de shēnghuó hái kěyǐ 我们的生活还可以 = our life is pretty good

kě 渴 *adjective*
= thirsty

kè 克 *noun*
(*unit of weight*) = gram

kèfú 克服 *verb*
(*as a difficulty, hardship, inconvenience*) = overcome, surmount, conquer

kè 刻
1 *noun*
= quarter of an hour
2 *verb*
= carve, engrave, inscribe

kèkǔ 刻苦 *adjective*
- = hard-working, willing to endure hardships
- = frugal, austere

kèguān 客观 *adjective*
= objective

kèqi 客气 *adjective*
- = polite, courteous, standing on ceremony
- = unassuming, modest, humble

kèren 客人 *noun*
= guest, visitor

kètīng 客厅 *noun*
= living room

kè 课 *noun*
- (*in school or university*) = class
  [shàng | xià] kè [上 | 下] 课 = [start | finish] class
- = course, subject
- = lesson
  Dìyī kè 第一课 = Lesson One

kèběn 课本 *noun*
= textbook

kèchéng 课程 *noun*
= course of study, curriculum
kèchéng biǎo 课程表 = school timetable, lecture list

kètáng 课堂 *noun*
= classroom

kètí 课题 *noun*
= question for study, research project

kèwén 课文 *noun*
(*of a lesson or in a book*) = text

kěn 肯 *verb*
= be willing to, consent to

kěndìng 肯定
1 *verb*
= affirm, confirm
2 *adjective*
= affirmative, positive, certain

kōng 空
1 *adjective*
= empty, vacant
2 *adverb*
= in vain
3 *noun*
= air, sky, space

kōngjiān 空间 *noun*
- = empty space
- (*beyond the earth's orbit*) = space

kōngjūn 空军 *noun*
= airforce

kōngtiáo 空调 *noun*
(*abbreviation of* **kōngqì tiáojié qì 空气调节器**) = air conditioner

kōngqì 空气 *noun*
- = air, atmosphere
- (*in a figurative sense: social, political, aesthetic, etc.*) = atmosphere
  jīntiān xuéxiào de kōngqì hěn jǐnzhāng 今天学校的空气很紧张 = there is a tense atmosphere at school today

kōngqián 空前
1 *adjective*
= unprecedented
2 *adverb*
= in an unprecedented fashion

kōngzhōng 空中 *noun*
= in the sky, in the air
kōngzhōng xiǎojiě 空中小姐 = air hostess

kǒng 孔
1 *noun*
= opening, hole, empty space
2 *adjective*
= Confucian

Kǒngzǐ 孔子 *noun*
= Confucius

kǒngpà 恐怕
1 *adverb*
= probably, perhaps
2 *verb*
= be afraid that, think that

kǒngpà tā bù lái le 恐怕他不来了 = I'm afraid he's not coming

kòngr 空儿 *noun*
- = empty space, vacant space
- = leisure, spare time
  wǒ méiyǒu kòngr 我没有空儿 = I don't have time

kòngzhì 控制
1 *verb*
= control, dominate
2 *noun*
= control, hold

kǒu 口
1 *noun*
- = mouth
- (*of a river, building, etc.*) = opening, entrance
- = cut, wound, tear

2 *measure word* ▶ 157
- (*for the number of people in a family or village*)
- (*for spoken languages, used with the verb "speak" and with the number one, yì* 一)

kǒudài 口袋 *noun*
= pocket, bag, sack

kǒuhào 口号 *noun*
= slogan

kǒuqì 口气 *noun*
= tone, note, implication

kǒutóu 口头 *adjective*
= oral

kǒuyīn 口音 *noun*
= accent

kǒuyǔ 口语 *noun*
= spoken language

kòu 扣
1 *verb*
- = button, fasten
- = deduct, reduce
- (*for a criminal*) = detain, arrest

2 *noun*
= button
kòuzi 扣子 = button
kòushang 扣上 = button up

kū 哭 *verb*
= cry, weep

kǔ 苦
1 *adjective*
- (*in taste*) = bitter
- (*in life*) = bitter, difficult, painful

2 *adverb*
= painstakingly, earnestly, at one's utmost
3 *noun*
= hardship, suffering, misery
4 *verb*
= cause (someone) suffering

kǔnán 苦难 *noun*
= hardship, misery, suffering

kùzi 裤子 *noun*
= trousers

kuājiǎng 夸奖 *verb*
= praise, commend

kuāzhāng 夸张 *verb*
= exaggerate, overstate

kuǎ 垮 *verb*
= collapse, fall

kuà 跨 *verb*
- = step astride, step across, take a step
- (*when talking about a horse or other animal for riding*) = mount
- = transcend, go beyond, go over
  kuà dìqū 跨地区 = transregional

kuài 块
1 *noun*
- = piece, lump, cube
  bīng kuài 冰块 = ice cubes
- (*units of money*) = dollar, *yuan*
  liùbái kuài qián 六百块钱 = six hundred *yuan*

2 *measure word* ▶ 157
- (*for things that come in chunks or solid pieces*)
- (*for things that are shaped like sheets*)
- (*for slices, sections, divisions, etc.*)

kuài 快
1 *adjective*
- = fast, quick
- (*of a knife*) = keen, sharp
  zhèbǎ jiǎnzi hěn kuài 这把剪子很快 = this pair of scissors is very sharp
- (*when used with a negative*) = pleased, happy, joyful
  xīn zhōng bú kuài 心中不快 = heavy-hearted

2 *adverb*
- = almost, soon, about to
  tā kuài yào bìyè le 她快要毕业了 = she will graduate soon
- = quickly

kuài huílai 快回来 = come back quickly

3 *verb*

= hurry

kuài diǎnr! 快点儿! = hurry up!

kuàihuo 快活 *adjective*

= happy, cheerful

kuàilè 快乐

1 *adjective*

= happy, joyful

2 *noun*

= happiness, joy

kuàizi 筷子 *noun*

= chopsticks

kuān 宽 *adjective*

- = wide, broad
- = generous, broad-minded, liberal

kuāndài 宽带 *noun*

= broadband

kuǎn 款 *noun*

= fund, funds, money

kuáng 狂 *adjective*

= mad, deranged, crazy

kuàngqiě 况且 *adverb*

= moreover, besides

kuàng 矿 *noun*

- = ore/mineral deposit
- = mine, excavation

kǔn 捆

1 *verb*

= tie into a bundle, bind up, tie up

2 *noun*

= bundle

kùn 困

1 *adjective*

- = sleepy
- = in difficulty, stranded, hard-pressed

2 *verb*

= surround

kùnnan 困难

1 *noun*

= difficulty, quandary, hardship

2 *adjective*

= difficult, hard to cope with

kuòdà 扩大

1 *verb*

= enlarge, expand, spread out

2 *noun*

= expansion

Ll

lā 拉 *verb*

- = pull, drag
- = haul, transport by vehicle
- (*certain musical instruments*) = play
  lā [xiǎotíqín | shǒufēngqín] 拉[小提琴 | 手风琴] = play the [violin | accordion]
- = extend, extenuate, draw out
- = implicate, drag in
- lā guānxi 拉关系 = use one's influence/connections
- lā dùzi 拉肚子 = have diarrhoea

lākāi 拉开

- = pull open
- = space out, widen

lāshang 拉上 (*curtains, etc.*) = close

lājī 垃圾 *noun*

= rubbish, garbage, trash

lājī yóujiàn 垃圾邮件 *noun*

= spam

la 啦 *particle*

(*a fusion of* le 了 *and* a 啊, *which incorporates the function of* le 了 *while denoting exclamation or interrogation*)

tā yǐjīng dāying la! 他已经答应啦! = he has already agreed!

lǎba 喇叭 *noun*

- = horn or similar instrument
- = loudspeaker

là 辣 *adjective*

= hot, spicy, peppery

làjiāo 辣椒 *noun*

= hot pepper, chili pepper

làzhú 蜡烛 *noun*

= candle

lái 来

1 *verb*

- = come, arrive
- = do
  ràng wǒ lái 让我来 = let me do it
- = bring
  zài lái yìwǎn fàn 再来一碗饭 = bring another bowl of rice
- (*when following a verb to indicate direction of action*)

qǐng nǐ guòlai 请你过来 = please come over here

- (*when following* **dé 得** *or* **bù 不** *to indicate possibility*)

  chī [**de** | **bù**] **lái 吃** [**得** | **不**] **来** = [it is | it is not] to (someone's) taste

> **!** *The word* **lái 来** *regularly follows certain verbs as a complement, such as* **qǐ 起** *in* **qǐlai 起来**, **chū 出** *in* **chūlai 出来**, **guò 过** *in* **guòlai 过来**, *and so forth. For these expressions, see the verbs that precede* **lái 来**. *In other instances it follows a verb as a directional complement, as in* **shànglai 上来** come up, *and* **xiàlai 下来**, come down.

2 *preposition*

(*with time expressions*) = since, for, during

sān nián (yǐ)lái 三年(以)来 = during the past three years

3 *adverb*

- (*following a numeral that acts as an adjective*) = about, approximately, over

  shí lái ge 十来个 = over ten

- (*when preceding the main verb, to indicate purpose*) = to, in order to

láibují 来不及 *verb*
= be unable to do in time, lack sufficient time for

láidejí 来得及 *verb*
= be able to do in time, have enough time for

láihuí 来回

1 *adverb*
= back and forth, to and fro

2 *noun*
= return journey, round trip

láiwǎng 来往

1 *verb*
= come and go

2 *noun*
= contacts, dealings

láixìn 来信 *noun*
= your letter, a letter from...

lái zì 来自 *verb*
= come from, originate from

lán 拦 *verb*
= hinder, obstruct, block

lán 蓝 *adjective*
= blue

lánqiú 篮球 *noun*
= basketball

lǎn 懒 *adjective*

- = lazy, idle, indolent
- = sluggish, drowsy

làn 烂 *adjective*

- (*of fruit, a wound, etc.*) = rotten, over-ripe, festering
- (*of clothes, cloth*) = ragged, worn-out
- (*of meat, stew, etc.*) = well-done, thoroughly cooked

láng 狼 *noun*
= wolf

lǎngdú 朗读 *verb*
= read aloud

làng 浪 *noun*
= wave

làngfèi 浪费

1 *verb*
= waste, squander

2 *adjective*
= extravagant, wasteful

3 *noun*
= extravagance, waste

làngmàn 浪漫 *adjective*
= romantic

lāo 捞 *verb*
= trawl, dredge, drag for (fish, etc.)

láodòng 劳动 *verb*
= work, labour, toil

láojià 劳驾 *verb*
(*polite expression*) = excuse me...? may I trouble you...? would you mind...?

lǎo 老

1 *adjective*

- = old, elderly, aged
- = long-term, of long standing

  lǎo péngyou 老朋友 = an old friend

- = old-fashioned, outdated
- (*of meat*) = tough
- (*of vegetation*) = overgrown
- (*prefix before ordinal numbers to differentiate between children of a family*)

  lǎo [**dà** | **èr...**] **老** [**大** | **二...**] = [eldest | second eldest...]

- (*courteous or affectionate prefix to a name, title, or relationship*) lǎo [Zhāng | xiānsheng | dàgē] 老[张 | 先生 | 大哥] = [my pal Zhang | Sir | dear elder brother]

2 *adverb*

= always, ever, keep on

tā lǎo zhème shuō 他老这么说 = he always says this

lǎoshì 老是

- = always, ever, keep on
- (*with a negative*) = hardly ever, rarely, seldom

tā lǎoshì bú niànshū 他老是不念书 = he hardly ever studies

lǎobǎixìng 老百姓 *noun*

= common people, ordinary people

lǎobǎn 老板 *noun*

= boss, employer, shopkeeper

lǎodàmā 老大妈, **dàmā** 大妈 *noun*

(*respectful address for an older woman*) = Madam, granny, aunty

lǎodàniáng 老大娘 *noun*

(*respectful address for an older woman*) = Madam, granny, aunty

lǎodàye 老大爷, **dàye** 大爷 *noun*

(*respectful address for an older man*) = Sir, grandpa

lǎohǔ 老虎 *noun*

= tiger

lǎojiā 老家 *noun*

= hometown, old home

lǎoshī 老师 *noun*

= teacher

lǎoshi 老实

1 *adjective*

- = honest, frank, trustworthy
- = well-behaved
- = simple-minded, naive

2 *adverb*

= honestly, truthfully

lǎoshǔ 老鼠 *noun*

= mouse, rat

lǎotàitai 老太太 *noun*

(*term of respect for an elderly woman*) = Madam, old lady

lǎotóur 老头儿 *noun*

(*rude word for an old man*) = old man

lè 乐

> **!** *Can also be pronounced* **yuè** *with a different meaning.*

adjective

= happy, joyful

lèguān 乐观

1 *adjective*

= optimistic, positive

2 *noun*

= optimism

lèqù 乐趣 *noun*

= pleasure, joy

le 了 *particle* ▶ *See also* **liǎo** 了.

- (*indicating a past event*)

tā shàngge xīngqī qù le 他上个星期去了 = he went last week

- (*indicating a completed action*)

tā zǒu le 他走了 = he has gone

- (*indicating a change of situation or state*)

tā bìng le 他病了 = he's been taken ill

'huǒchē láile méiyǒu?'—'méi lái' '火车来了没有?'—'没来' = 'has the train come?'—'no, it hasn't'

> **!** *Note that* **le** 了 *is usually negated with* **méi** 没, *rather than with* **bù** 不.

- (*used with* **bù** 不 *to mean* **no longer, not any more**)

wǒ bù xiě le 我不写了 = I'm not writing (it) any more

- (*used with* **búyào** 不要 *or* **bié** 别 *to stop someone from doing something*)

búyào jiǎng le 不要讲了 = stop talking about it, don't talk about it any more

léi 雷 *noun*

= thunder

léiyǔ 雷雨 = thunderstorm

lèi 泪 *noun*

= tear, tears, teardrop

lèi 类

1 *noun*

= category, sort, type

2 *measure word* ▶ **157**

= kind of, sort of

lèisì 类似

1 *verb*

= resemble, be similar to, be like

2 *adjective*
= similar, like

lèi 累 *adjective*
= tired, fatigued, weary

lěng 冷 *adjective*
= cold

lěngjìng 冷静 *adjective*
= calm, sober, clear-headed

lěngyǐn 冷饮 *noun*
= cold drink

límǐ 厘米 *noun*
= centimetre

lí 离
1 *verb*
= leave, part, separate from
2 *preposition*
= from, off, away from
xuéxiào lí zhèr sān yīnglǐ lù 学校离这儿三英里路 = the school is three miles from here

líhūn 离婚 *verb*
= divorce, be divorced

líkāi 离开 *verb*
= depart, leave, separate

lí 梨 *noun*
= pear

lǐ 礼 *noun*
- = ceremony, ritual
- = propriety, courtesy, manners
- = gift, present

lǐbài 礼拜 *noun*
- = week
- (*used for the days of the week*)
lǐbài [**yī** | **èr** | **sān**...] 礼拜[一 | 二 | 三...] = [Monday | Tuesday | Wednesday...]

lǐbàitiān 礼拜天, **lǐbàirì** 礼拜日 *noun*
= Sunday

lǐmào 礼貌
1 *noun*
= courtesy, politeness, manners
2 *adjective*
= polite, courteous

lǐtáng 礼堂 *noun*
= assembly hall, auditorium

lǐwù 礼物 *noun*
= present, gift

lǐ 里
1 *noun*
(*unit of length, 1/2 kilometre*) = Chinese mile, *li*
2 *preposition*
= in, inside, among
wū lǐ 屋里 = in the room

lǐbian 里边, **lǐmiàn** 里面
1 *preposition*
= inside, in, within
wūzi lǐbian yǒu sānge rén 屋子里边有三个人 = there are three people in the room
2 *noun*
= inside, within
tā zài lǐbian 他在里边 = he is inside

lǐtou 里头 (*informal, colloquial*)
▶ **lǐbian** 里边

lǐfà 理发 *verb*
= have a haircut, have one's hair cut/styled

lǐjiě 理解
1 *verb*
= understand, comprehend
2 *noun*
= understanding, comprehension

lǐkē 理科 *noun*
(*a branch of learning*) = science, natural sciences

lǐlùn 理论 *noun*
= theory, theoretical idea

lǐxiǎng 理想 *noun*
= ideal, dream

lǐyóu 理由 *noun*
= reason, argument

lìshǐ 历史 *noun*
= history, record of the past

lì 力 *noun*
= strength, power, force

lìliang 力量 *noun*
= strength, force, power

lìqi 力气 *noun*
= physical strength, effort, energy

lì 立 *verb*
- = stand
- = establish, set up, erect

lìchǎng 立场 *noun*
= standpoint, position, point of view

lìfāng 立方 *noun*
- = cube
- = cubic metre
sān lìfāng shāzi 三立方沙子 = three cubic metres of sand

L

lìjí 立即 *adverb*
= immediately, right away

lìkè 立刻 *adverb*
= immediately, right away

lìhai 利害, 厉害 *adjective*
- (*when talking about the weather, etc.*) = severe, extreme
  zhèr de tiānqì rè de lìhai 这儿的天气热得利害 = the weather here is extremely hot
- (*as a teacher or disciplinarian*) = formidable, strict

lìxī 利息 *noun*
(*when talking about finance*) = interest

lìyì 利益 *noun*
= interest, benefit

lìyòng 利用 *verb*
= utilize, make use of, take advantage of

lì 例 *noun*
= example, case, instance
lìrú 例如 = for example, for instance, such as

lìwài 例外 *noun*
= exception

lìzi 例子 *noun*
= example, instance

lì 粒 *measure word* ▶ 157
(*for small, round things, such as peas, peanuts, bullets, or grains*)

liǎ 俩 *number* (*colloquial*)
- = two
- = some, several

lián 连
1 *verb*
= connect, link, join
2 *adverb*
- = in succession, one after the other
- = even, including
  lián...dōu/yě... 连...都/也... = even...
  lián tā dōu bù zhīdào 连他都不知道 = even he doesn't know

liánjiē 连接 *verb*
= join, link

liánmáng 连忙 *adverb*
= promptly, at once

liánxù 连续 *adverb*
= continuously, successively, one after the other

liánxùjù 连续剧 (*on TV or radio*) = a serial, a series

liánhé 联合 *verb*
= unite, join together, ally

Liánhéguó 联合国 *noun*
= the United Nations

liánhuān 联欢
1 *verb*
= have a get-together/party
2 *noun*
= social get-together

liánxì 联系
1 *verb*
= connect, make connections with, link
2 *noun*
= connection, link

liǎn 脸 *noun*
- = face
- = self-respect, honour
  diū liǎn 丢脸 = lose face

liàn 练 *verb*
= train, practise, drill

liànxí 练习
1 *verb*
= practise, exercise
2 *noun*
= practise, drill
liànxíbù/běn 练习簿/本 = exercise book

liàn'ài 恋爱 *noun*
= love, love affair

liánghǎo 良好 *adjective*
= good, well

liáng 凉 ▶ *See also* **liàng** 凉.
1 *adjective*
- = cool, cold
- = discouraged, disappointed

2 *noun*
= cold, flu
zháo liáng 着凉 = catch cold

liángkuai 凉快 *adjective*
= cool, pleasantly cool

liáng 量 *verb* ▶ *See also* **liàng** 量.
(*for length, weight, distance, etc.*) = measure

liángshi 粮食 *noun*
= food, provisions, grain

liǎng 两
1 *number*

! *Note that* liǎng 两 *is like* èr 二 *but tends to be used in combination with measure words and nouns to specify two of something.*

= two

liǎngzhāng zhǐ 两张纸 = two sheets of paper

2 *determiner*

! *Note that* liǎng 两 *in this sense is usually unstressed.*

= a few, some, a couple of

shuō liǎng jù 说两句 = speak a few words

3 *pronoun*

= both

4 *noun*

(*traditional unit of weight equivalent to 1.33 English ounces or 0.05 kilo*)

yì liǎng jiǔ 一两酒 = an ounce of liquor

liàng 亮

1 *adjective*

= bright, light, shiny

2 *verb*

= get light, be light, be switched on

liàng 凉 *verb* ▶ *See also* **liáng 凉**.

= cool, allow to cool

liàng 晾 *verb*

= dry in the air/sun

liàng 辆 *measure word* ▶ 157

(*for vehicles*)

liàng 量 *noun* ▶ *See also* **liáng 量**.

= amount, quantity, capacity

liáo 聊 *verb*

= chat idly

wǒ xiǎng gēn nǐ liáoliáo 我想跟你聊聊 = I'd like to have a chat with you

liáotiān 聊天 *verb*

= chat to pass the time of day

liǎo 了 *verb* ▶ *See also* **le 了**.

! *Can also be pronounced* liào *with a different meaning.*

- = finish, end

wǒ shénme shíhou néng liǎole zhèjiàn shì? 我什么时候能了了这件事? = when will I be able to finish this task?

- (*after* dé 得 *or* bù 不 *to indicate the possibility or impossibility of accomplishing or finishing something*)

zhège bēibāo zhuāng [de | bu] liǎo zhèxiē dōngxi 这个背包装[得|不]了这些东西 = this backpack [can | cannot] hold these things

liǎobuqǐ 了不起 *adjective*

= extraordinary, astounding, amazing

liǎojiě 了解

1 *verb*

- = understand, comprehend, know
- = find out, inquire

liǎojiě yíxià zhèr de shēnghuó 了解一下这儿的生活 = find out about the life here

2 *noun*

= understanding, knowledge

liè 列

1 *verb*

= list, arrange in order, enumerate

2 *measure word* ▶ 157

(*for trains*)

lièchē 列车 *noun*

= train

lièchēyuán 列车员 = train attendant

línjū 邻居 *noun*

= neighbour

lín 临

1 *verb*

- = face, overlook
- (*when talking about problems, decisions*) = face, confront

2 *adverb*

= on the point of, upon coming to...

lín zǒu 临走 = about to depart

línshí 临时

1 *adjective*

= temporary, provisional, last-minute

2 *adverb*

= at the time, at the last moment, when the time comes

tā línshí juédìng bú qù Běijīng le 他临时决定不去北京了 = he made a last-minute decision not to go to Beijing

línyù 淋浴 *noun*

= shower

línghún 灵魂 *noun*

= spirit, soul, mind

L

línghuó 灵活 *adjective*
- (*referring to mental capacities, etc.*) = quick-witted, resourceful, agile
- (*when describing actions, movements, etc.*) = nimble, quick
- (*when talking about the quality of material objects*) = flexible, elastic

líng 铃 *noun*
= bell, small bell

líng 零 *number*
= zero, nought

língqián 零钱 *noun*
= small change, pocket money

líng 龄 *noun*
- = age, years
- = length of time, duration

lǐng 领
1 *verb*
- = lead, command, usher
- (*as a prize, award, pension, etc.*) = receive, draw, get

2 *noun*
= neck, collar

lǐngdǎo 领导
1 *verb*
= lead, be a leader
2 *noun*
= leadership, guidance

lǐngdài 领带 *noun*
= tie, necktie

lǐnghuì 领会 *verb*
= understand, comprehend

lǐngtǔ 领土 *noun*
= territory

lǐngxiù 领袖 *noun*
= leader, chief

lìng 另
1 *adjective*
= another, other
lìng yì fāngmiàn... 另一方面... = another aspect..., on the other hand...
2 *adverb*
= separately, another
lìng zhǎo yíge fāngfǎ 另找一个方法 = look for another method

lìngwài 另外
1 *adjective*
= separate, other, another
lìngwài yíge rén 另外一个人 = another person
2 *adverb*
= separately, besides, in addition
lìngwài xiě yíge jùzi 另外写一个句子 = write another sentence

liú 留 *verb*
- = keep, preserve, save
- = stay, remain, linger
- = allow to stay, ask to stay, detain
  wǒ xiǎng liú nǐ zài wǒ jiā zhù jǐ tiān 我想留你在我家住几天 = I would like you to stay at my house for a few days
- = leave, leave behind
  bǎ shūbāo liú zài jiā lǐ 把书包留在家里 = leave the satchel at home

liúniàn 留念
1 *verb*
= accept/keep as a souvenir
2 *noun*
= souvenir, keepsake

liúxué 留学 *verb*
= study abroad
liúxuéshēng 留学生 = student studying abroad

liú 流
1 *verb*
= flow
2 *noun*
- = flow, stream, current
  [**hé** | **diàn** | **qì**] **liú** [河 | 电 | 气] 流 = [river | electric current | air current]
- = class, grade

liúchuán 流传 *verb*
= spread, circulate, pass down

liúlì 流利 *adjective*
= fluent, smooth

liúmáng 流氓 *noun*
= hooligan, gangster, rogue

liúxíng 流行 *adjective*
= popular, fashionable, prevalent

liù 六 *number*
= six

liùyuè 六月 *noun*
= June

lóng 龙 *noun*
= dragon

lóng 聋 *adjective*
= deaf, hearing impaired

lóu 楼 *noun*
- (*of more than one story*) = building, tower

- = storey, floor

  yì lóu 一楼 = ground floor (*British English*), first floor (*US English*)
  lóushàng 楼上 = upstairs
  lóuxià 楼下 = downstairs

lóutī 楼梯 *noun*
= stairs, stairway

lòu 漏 *verb*
- = leak, flow/drip out
- = disclose, divulge
- = leave out, omit, be missing

lòu 露 ▶**lù** 露

lǔyā 卤鸭 *noun*
= pot-stewed duck

lùdì 陆地 *noun*
= dry land, land

lùxù 陆续 *adverb*
= in succession, one after another

lù 录 *verb*
(*on tape*) = record, copy

lùxiàng 录像
1 *verb*
= make a video recording, record on videotape
2 *noun*
= video recording
lùxiàngdài 录像带 = video tape
lùxiàngjī 录像机 = video cassette recorder, VCR

lùyīn 录音
1 *verb*
= make a sound recording, tape-record, tape
2 *noun*
= sound recording, audio-tape
lùyīndài 录音带 = magnetic tape, tape
lùyīnjī 录音机 = tape recorder

lù 鹿 *noun*
= deer

lù 路 *noun*
- = road, path, route
- = journey, distance
- = way, means
- (*referring to the number of a bus route, etc.*) = route

  yāo líng sì lù (qìchē) 104路(汽车) = No. 104 (bus)

lùguò 路过 *verb*
= pass by/through (a place)

lùkǒu 路口 *noun*
= crossing, intersection

lùshang 路上 *adverb*
= on the way, on the road

lùxiàn 路线 *noun*
= route, line, approach

lù 露 *verb*
= show, reveal, betray

lùtiān 露天 *noun*
= in the open air, open-air, outdoors

lǚguǎn 旅馆 *noun*
= hotel

lǚkè 旅客 *noun*
= traveller, passenger, hotel guest

lǚtú 旅途 *noun*
= journey, trip, route

lǚxíng 旅行 *verb*
= travel, journey, trip
lǚxíngshè 旅行社 = travel service, travel agency

lǚyóu 旅游 *verb*
= tour, travel

lǜshī 律师 *noun*
= solicitor, barrister, lawyer

lǜ 绿 *adjective*
= green

luàn 乱
1 *adjective*
= in a mess, in confusion, in turmoil
2 *adverb*
= in a disorderly manner, recklessly

luànqībāzāo 乱七八糟 *adjective*
= in a mess, in a muddle, in confusion

lüè 略
1 *verb*
= omit, leave out
2 *adverb*
= slightly, a little, briefly

lúnchuán 轮船 *noun*
= steamer, steamship, steamboat

lùnwén 论文 *noun*
= thesis, dissertation, treatise

Lúndūn 伦敦 *noun*
= London

luóbo 萝卜 *noun*
= turnip, radish

luò 落 *verb*
- = fall, drop, come down
- = lower

L

bǎ liánzi luòxiàlai 把帘子落下来 = lower the blinds
- (*referring to the sun or moon*) = set, go down
  tàiyáng luò shān le 太阳落山了 = the sun has set
- = lag behind, fall behind, decline
- = leave behind, result in

luòhòu 落后
1 *adjective*
= backward, behind the times
2 *verb*
= fall behind, be backward

Mm

mā 妈 *noun*
= mother
māma 妈妈 = mother, mum

máfan 麻烦
1 *verb*
= trouble, bother
máfan nǐ le 麻烦你了 = sorry to have troubled you
2 *adjective*
= troublesome, bothersome, annoying
3 *noun*
= trouble, bother

mǎ 马 *noun*
= horse

mǎhu 马虎 *adjective*
= careless, casual, in a sloppy manner

mǎkè 马克 *noun*
(*unit of German currency*)
= mark

mǎlù 马路 *noun*
= street, avenue

mǎmǎhūhū 马马虎虎 *adjective*
- = so-so
- = careless, casual

mǎshàng 马上 *adverb*
= immediately, at once
wǒ mǎshàng jiù lái 我马上就来 = I'll be right there

mǎtou 码头 *noun*
= dock, pier, wharf

mà 骂 *verb*
= curse, swear, scold

ma 吗 *particle*
(*used to turn a declarative sentence into a question*)
shì nǐ ma? 是你吗? = is it you?

ma 嘛 *particle*
- (*used to show that something is obvious*)
  zhè shì wǒde ma! 这是我的嘛! = obviously this is mine!
- (*used to mark a pause*)
  zhège wèntí ma, wǒ lái jiějué 这个问题嘛，我来解决 = as for this question, let me solve it

mái 埋 *verb*
= bury, hide in the ground

mǎi 买 *verb*
= buy, purchase
mǎi dōngxi 买东西 = go shopping, buy things

> **!** *Note that in expressions denoting buying something for someone, the English word* for *is rendered as* gěi 给.

nǐ gěi tā mǎi shū ma? 你给她买书吗? = do you buy books for her?
mǎi de qǐ 买得起 = able to afford

mǎimai 买卖 *noun*
= business, trade
zuò mǎimai 做买卖 = do business, engage in a trade

mài 迈 *verb*
= take a step, stride
màiguò 迈过 = step over

mài(zi) 麦(子) *noun*
= wheat

mài 卖 *verb*
= sell, sell for
nàtái diànshìjī mài duōshǎo qián? 那台电视机卖多少钱? = how much is the TV selling for?
mài gěi... 卖给... = sell to
nǐ bǎ jìsuànjī mài gěi shéi? 你把计算机卖给谁? = to whom are you selling the computer?
mài [de | bù] **chū(qu)** 卖[得 | 不]出(去) = [able to | unable to] sell (well)

mántou 馒头 *noun*
= steamed bun, steamed bread

mǎn 满
1 *adjective*
- = full, filled
- = whole, entire
  mǎn tiān xīngxing 满天星星 = the sky is filled with stars
- = satisfied, content, satisfactory

2 *adverb*
= quite, rather
mǎn shūfu 满舒服 = quite comfortable
3 *verb*
= reach, reach the limit of
tā hái bù mǎn shíbā suì 他还不满十八岁 = he still hasn't reached the age of 18

mǎnyì 满意
1 *adjective*
= satisfied, pleased
2 *verb*
= be pleased, be satisfied

mǎnzú 满足
1 *verb*
- = be content, be satisfied
- = fulfill, satisfy, meet

2 *adjective*
= satisfied, content

màn 慢
1 *adjective*
= slow
2 *adverb*
= slowly

máng 忙 *adjective*
= busy, occupied, bustling
nǐ máng shénme? 你忙什么? = what are you so busy doing? what are you doing?
diànhuà xiànlù hěn máng 电话线路很忙 = the telephone lines are busy
máng bú guòlái 忙不过来 (*referring to too much work*) = unable to manage
mángzhe... 忙着... = be busy doing...
mángzhe xiě zuòwén 忙着写作文 = busy writing an essay

māo 猫 *noun*
= cat
xiǎomāo 小猫 = kitten

máo 毛 *noun*
- (*a unit of Chinese money*) = ten *fen*, 1/10 of a *yuan*
  wǔ máo qián 五毛钱 = five *mao*
- = hair on the body, fur
- = feather, down
- = wool

máobǐ 毛笔 *noun*
= writing brush

máobìng 毛病 *noun*
- = trouble, defect
  zhèliàng qìchē chángcháng chū máobìng 这辆汽车常常出毛病 = this car often breaks down
- = illness
- = fault, shortcoming, bad habit

máojīn 毛巾 *noun*
= towel

máoyī 毛衣 *noun*
= jumper, sweater

máodùn 矛盾
1 *noun*
= contradiction, inconsistency
2 *adjective*
= contradictory, inconsistent

mào 冒 *verb*
- = risk, brave, take risks
  mào [xuě | yǔ | sǐ] 冒[雪 | 雨 | 死] = [brave the rain | brave the snow | risk death]
- = falsify, feign
  mào [míng | pái] 冒[名 | 牌] = falsify [a name | a brand]
- = emit, give off, spew forth
  mào [qì | yān | hàn] 冒[气 | 烟 | 汗] = [be steaming | emit smoke | sweat]

màoyì 贸易 *noun*
= trade, commerce, economic exchange

màozi 帽子 *noun*
= hat, cap

mào 貌 *noun*
= appearance, looks

méi 没
1 *adverb*
(*when negating a completed action, an ongoing action, or a past experience*) = not
wǒ méi qù 我没去 = I didn't go
tā méi zài kàn diànshì 他没在看电视 = he was not watching TV
wǒ méi qùguo Běijīng 我没去过北京 = I have never been to Beijing
2 *verb*
(*short for* **méi yǒu** 没有) = not have, there is not

méicuò 没错 = it's right, you're right
méi fǎzi 没法子 = no way, it can't be helped
méi guānxi 没关系 = it doesn't matter, it's alright, don't worry
méi shénme 没什么 = it's nothing, it doesn't matter, never mind
méishìr 没事儿
- = it's alright, it's not important, it doesn't matter
- = be free, have nothing pressing to do

wǒ méi shì, kěyǐ bāng nǐ 我没事，可以帮你 = I'm free; I can help you
méixiǎngdào... 没想到... = unexpectedly, I never imagined..., I was surprised that...
méi yìsi 没意思 = dull, uninteresting, boring
méi yòng 没用 = useless, of no use
méi (yǒu) le 没(有)了 = be gone, be used up, have disappeared

méiyǒu 没有 *adverb*
- (*when negating a completed action*) = haven't, hasn't, didn't

tā hái méiyǒu shuìzháo 他还没有睡着 = he hasn't fallen asleep yet
- (*when negating a past experience*) = haven't...before, hasn't...before, hasn't ever...

nǐ méiyǒu jiànguo tā 你没有见过他 = you haven't met him before
- = less than

qián méiyǒu sāntiān jiù huāwán le 钱没有三天就花完了 = the money was spent in less than three days
méiyǒu...yǐqián 没有...以前 = before...
tā méiyǒu jiéhūn yǐqián hěn jìmò 他没有结婚以前很寂寞 = he was very lonely before he got married

méi 煤 *noun*
= coal

méiqì 煤气 *noun*
= gas, coal gas

měi 每 *determiner*
= every, each
měi cì 每次 = every time
měi...dōu... 每...都... = every..., each...
měi yíge háizi dōu xǐhuan chī táng 每一个孩子都喜欢吃糖 = every child likes to eat sweets

měi 美
1 *adjective*
- = pretty, beautiful
- = high-quality, good, happy

2 *noun*
- = beauty, perfection
- (*short for* **Měiguó** 美国) = America

[**Běi** | **Nán**] **Měizhōu** [北 | 南] 美洲 = [North | South] America

Měiguó 美国 *noun*
= the United States of America, USA
Měiguórén 美国人 = an American, a person from the USA

měihǎo 美好 *adjective*
= good, desirable, bright

měilì 美丽 *adjective*
= beautiful

měishù 美术 *noun*
= art, fine arts

měishùguǎn 美术馆 *noun*
= art gallery

měiyuán 美元, **měijīn** 美金 *noun*
= American dollar

mèimei 妹妹 *noun*
= younger sister

mēn 闷 ▶ *See also* **mèn** 闷.
adjective
= stuffy, close

mén 门
1 *noun*
- = door, gate, entrance
- = family, house

2 *measure word* ▶ **157**
(*for academic courses, subjects or disciplines*)

ménkǒu 门口 *noun*
= doorway, gateway, entrance

mèn 闷 *adjective* ▶ *See also* **mēn** 闷.
= bored, depressed

men 们 *particle*
(*used to make plural forms of personal pronouns or nouns referring to animate entities*)
[**wǒmen** | **nǐmen** | **tāmen**] [我们 | 你们 | 他们] = [we | you | they]
[**xuéshengmen** | **háizimen** | **péngyoumen**] [学生们 | 孩子们 | 朋友们] = [students | children | friends]

mèng 梦 *noun*
= dream
zuò mèng 做梦 = have a dream

mí 迷
1 *verb*
- = be confused, be lost
- = be fascinated by

2 *noun*
= fan, enthusiast
wǎngqiú mí 网球迷 = tennis fan

míxìn 迷信 *noun*
= superstition

míyǔ 谜语 *noun*
= riddle, conundrum

mǐ 米 *noun*
- = husked rice, uncooked rice, grain
- = metre

mǐfàn 米饭 *noun*
= cooked rice

mìmì 秘密
1 *noun*
= secret
2 *adjective*
= secret, confidential
3 *adverb*
= secretly

mìshū 秘书 *noun*
= secretary, clerk

mì 密
1 *adjective*
- = dense, thick, close
- = intimate, close, secret

2 *adverb*
= secretly, intimately

mìmǎ 密码 *noun*
- = code
- = PIN

mìqiè 密切
1 *adjective*
(*of relationships*) = close, intimate
2 *adverb*
= carefully, closely, attentively

mì 蜜 *noun*
= honey

mìfēng 蜜蜂 *noun*
= bee, honeybee

miánhua 棉花 *noun*
= cotton

miányī 棉衣 *noun*
= cotton-padded jacket or clothes

miǎnbùliǎo 免不了 *adjective*
= unavoidable

miǎndé 免得 *conjunction*
= so that...not..., so as not to, so as to avoid
miǎndé shēngbìng 免得生病 = so as to avoid getting sick

miǎnqiǎng 勉强
1 *adverb*
- = reluctantly, grudgingly
  tā miǎnqiǎng dāyingle wǒ 他勉强答应了我 = he promised me reluctantly
- = barely enough, narrowly
  tā miǎnqiǎng tōngguòle kǎoshì 他勉强通过了考试 = he narrowly passed the examination

2 *adjective*
= unconvincing, far-fetched
tāde jiěshì hěn miǎnqiǎng 他的解释很勉强 = his explanation is quite unconvincing
3 *verb*
- = force (someone to do something)
  bié miǎnqiǎng tā 别勉强她 = don't force her
- = do with difficulty
  bìngrén miǎnqiǎng chīle diǎnr fàn 病人勉强吃了点儿饭 = the patient has managed to eat some food

miàn 面
1 *noun*
- = face
- = surface, top side, outside
- = side, dimension, aspect
- = wheat flour, flour, powder

2 *verb*
= face
3 *adverb*
= personally, directly
4 *measure word* ▶ 157
(*for flat, smooth objects, such as mirrors, flags, etc.*)

miànbāo 面包 *noun*
= bread

miànduì 面对 *verb*
= face, confront

miànfěn 面粉 *noun*
= flour, wheat flour

miànji 面积 *noun*
= area, surface area

M

miànmào 面貌 *noun*
- (*of people*) = facial features, looks, appearance
- (*of things*) = appearance, look

miànqián 面前 *adverb*
= in front of (someone), to one's face
bié zài lǎoshī miànqián shuō zhèzhǒng huà 别在老师面前说这种话 = don't say such things in front of the teacher

miàntiáor 面条儿 *noun*
= noodles

miáoshù 描述 *verb*
= describe

miáoxiě 描写 *verb*
= describe, depict, delineate

miǎo 秒 *noun*
= second, 1/60 of a minute
yì miǎozhōng 一秒钟 = one second

miào 妙 *adjective*
- = miraculous, wonderful, excellent
- = ingenious, clever, skilled

miào 庙 *noun*
= temple

miè 灭 *verb*
- (*as a light, fire, etc.*) = extinguish, put out, go out
- (*by killing*) = exterminate, obliterate, wipe out

míngē 民歌 *noun*
= folk song

mínjiān 民间 *adjective*
= of the common people, popular, folk

mínzhǔ 民主
1 *noun*
= democracy
2 *adjective*
= democratic

mínzú 民族 *noun*
= race, tribe, nation
shǎoshù mínzú 少数民族 = minority nationality, ethnic group

míng 名
1 *noun*
- = name
- = fame, reputation
- = pretext, surface meaning

yǐ...wéi míng 以... 为名 = in the name of..., under the pretext of...
2 *adjective*
= famous, well-known
3 *measure word* ▶ **157**
(*for persons with professional or prominent social identities*)

míngshèng 名胜 *noun*
= famous site, place of interest, scenic spot

míngzi 名字 *noun*
= name, given name, first name

míngbai 明白
1 *adjective*
- = clear, obvious, plain
- = frank, explicit, unequivocal
- = sensible, reasonable

2 *verb*
= understand, realize, know

míngliàng 明亮 *adjective*
- = bright, well-lit, shining
- (*of understanding*) = clear

míngnián 明年 *noun*
= next year

míngquè 明确
1 *adjective*
= clear, definite
2 *verb*
= clarify, specify

míngtiān 明天 *noun*
= tomorrow

míngxiǎn 明显 *adjective*
= obvious, clear, evident

míngxīng 明星 *noun*
= famous person, star

mìng 命 *noun*
- = life
- = lot, fate, destiny
- = order, command

mìnglìng 命令
1 *noun*
= command, order
2 *verb*
= command, order

mìngyùn 命运 *noun*
= destiny, fate

mō 摸 *verb*
- = touch gently, feel, stroke
- = grope for, feel for

- = search for, try to find out, figure out

mófàn 模范 *noun*

> **!** *The word* mó *is sometimes pronounced* mú *with a different meaning.*

= model, fine example

mófǎng 模仿
1 *verb*
= copy, imitate, model after
2 *noun*
= copy, imitation, model

móxíng 模型 *noun*
= model, pattern

mótuōchē 摩托车 *noun*
= motorbike, motorcycle, motor bicycle

mó 磨 *verb*
- = rub, wear down, wear away
- = sharpen, polish, grind
  mó dāo 磨刀 = sharpen a knife
- = waste time, wile away time
  mó shíjiān 磨时间 = kill time
- = torment, bother, put through the grind

mǒ 抹 *verb*
- = apply, smear, put on
- = wipe, erase

mòshēng 陌生 *adjective*
= strange, unfamiliar
mòshēng rén 陌生人 = stranger

mò 墨
1 *noun*
= ink, ink stick
2 *adjective*
= black, dark

mòshuǐ 墨水 *noun*
= ink

mǒu 某 *determiner*
= certain, some
mǒurén 某人 = a certain person, someone
mǒumǒu... 某某... = such-and-such..., so-and-so

múyàng 模样 *noun*

> **!** *The word* mú *is sometimes pronounced* mó *with a different meaning.*

= appearance, shape, look

mǔ 母
1 *noun*
- = mother
- = aunt, elder female relative
  [zǔmǔ | gūmǔ | jiùmǔ] [祖母 | 姑母 | 舅母] = [grandmother | aunt (father's sister) | aunt (mother's brother's wife)]

2 *adjective*
(*of a species*) = female
[mǔláng | mǔxiàng | mǔmāo] [母狼 | 母象 | 母猫] = female [wolf | elephant | cat]

mǔqīn 母亲 *noun*
= mother

mǔ 亩 *noun*
(*unit for measuring land area*) = 0.0667 hectares, 1/6 of an acre

mù 木
1 *noun*
- = tree, timber
- = wood

2 *adjective*
- = wooden, made out of wood
- (*of body or mind*) = numb, insensitive, dull

mùtou 木头 *noun*
= wood, log, timber

mùbiāo 目标 *noun*
= goal, aim, target

mùdì 目的 *noun*
= aim, objective, purpose

mùqián 目前 *adverb*
= currently, at present, at this moment

mùmín 牧民 *noun*
= herdsman

mù 墓 *noun*
= grave, tomb, mausoleum

mù 幕 *noun*
- = curtain, screen
- (*of a dramatic performance*) = act

Nn

ná 拿
1 *verb*
- (*in one's hands*) = take, take hold of, carry
- (*with* **qù** 去 *and* **lái** 来 *to mean* **take** *and* **bring** *respectively*)
  náqù 拿去 = take (it) away
  nálái 拿来 = bring here
- = take...as/for
  tā méi ná wǒ dāng kèrén 他没拿我当客人 = he didn't treat me as a guest

2 *preposition*
= with
ná kuàizi chī 拿筷子吃 = eat with chopsticks
ná...láishuō 拿... 来说 = speaking of..., take... as an example
ná...zuò... 拿... 做... = take...as...
tā ná wǒ zuò xiǎo háizi kàn 他拿我做小孩子看 = he treats me like a child

nǎ 哪
1 *determiner*
- = which? what?
  nǐ yào nǎkuài biǎo? 你要哪块表? = which watch would you like?
- (*used with* **dōu** 都) = any, whatever, whichever
  nǐ yào nǎkuài biǎo dōu kěyǐ 你要哪块表都可以 = you can have any watch you want

2 *adverb*
(*used in a rhetorical question*) = how is it possible that...?
wǒ nǎ zhīdào tāde míngzi? 我哪知道他的名字? = how could I know his name?

nǎge 哪个 *determiner*
= which? which one?
nǎge rén? 哪个人? = which person?

nǎli 哪里, **nǎr** 哪儿
1 *adverb*
- (*in a question*) = where?
  nǐde chē zài nǎli? 你的车在哪里? = where is your car?
- (*with* **dōu** 都 *in a statement*) = anywhere, wherever, everywhere
  fàng zài nǎli dōu kěyǐ 放在哪里都可以 = you can put it anywhere

2 *adverb*
(*used to form a rhetorical question*) = how can it be that...?
wǒ nǎli mǎi de qǐ qìchē? 我哪里买得起汽车? = how could I possibly afford to buy a car?
nǎli = you're welcome, don't mention it
'xièxiè nǐ de bāngzhù.'—'nǎli, nǎli' '谢谢你的帮助.'—'哪里, 哪里' = 'thanks for your help.'—'don't mention it.'

nǎpà 哪怕 *conjunction*
= even, even if, no matter how
nǎpà...yě... 哪怕... 也... = even if, even though
nǎpà nǐ bù tóngyì, wǒ yě yào qù 哪怕你不同意, 我也要去 = I'll still go even if you don't agree

nǎxiē 哪些
1 *pronoun*
(*plural form*) = which? which ones? what?
nǎxiē shì xīn de? 哪些是新的? = which ones are new?

2 *determiner*
= which
nǎxiē shū shì nǐde? 哪些书是你的? = which books are yours?

nà 那
1 *pronoun*
= that
nà shì tāde shū 那是他的书 = that is his book

2 *determiner*
(*before a number plus a measure word*) = that, those
nà sānzhāng zhuōzi dōu hěn guì 那三张桌子都很贵 = those three tables are all very expensive

3 *conjunction*
= then, in that case
nà wǒ yě yào mǎi yíge 那我也要买一个 = in that case I want to buy one too

nà biān 那边 *adverb*
= that side, over there

nàge 那个 *determiner*
= that
nàge wèntí 那个问题 = that problem

nàli 那里, **nàr** 那儿 *adverb*
= there, that place, over there

nàme 那么 *adverb*
- = in that way, like that, so
  nǐ wèishénme nàme zuò? 你为什么那么做? = why do you do it like that?
- = in that case, then
  nàme zánmen yíkuàir qù ba 那么咱们一块儿去吧 = then let's go together

nàxiē 那些
1 *pronoun*
(*plural form*) = those, that quantity of
2 *determiner*
= those

nàyàng 那样 *adverb*
= like that, so, in that way
nǐ bié nàyàng zuò 你别那样做 = don't do it that way

na 哪 *particle*
(*when expressing appreciation or confirmation, or when giving advice or encouragement*)
kuài lái na! 快来哪! = hurry up!

nǎi 奶 *noun*
= milk

nǎinai 奶奶 *noun*
= paternal grandmother

nàifán 耐烦 *adjective*
= patient

nàixīn 耐心
1 *adjective*
= patient
2 *adverb*
= patiently
3 *noun*
= patience

nàiyòng 耐用 *adjective*
= enduring, durable, capable of withstanding heavy use

nán 男 *adjective*
(*refers to humans only*) = man, male

nánháizi 男孩子 *noun*
= boy

nánpéngyou 男朋友 *noun*
= boyfriend

nánrén 男人 *noun*
= man, husband

nán 南
1 *noun*
= south
2 *adjective*
= south, southern

nánbian 南边 *noun*
= the south, south side

nánbù 南部 *noun*
= southern part

nánfāng 南方 *noun*
- (*as a direction*) = south
- = southern part of the country

nánjí 南极 *noun*
= South Pole, Antarctic

nán miàn 南面 ▸ **nán bian** 南边

nán 难 *adjective*
- = difficult, hard
- (*when it precedes a verb*) = bad, unpleasant
  nán [chī | tīng] 难 [吃 | 听] = [bad tasting | unpleasant to the ear]

nándào 难道 *adverb*
(*in rhetorical questions that end with the particle* ma 吗) = could it be that...? you don't mean to say that...? is it really true that...?
nándào nǐ lián yí kuài qián yě méi yǒu ma? 难道你连一块钱也没有吗? = do you mean to say you don't even have one *yuan*?

> ! *Note that the speaker doubts or questions the statement that occurs within this pattern.*

nánguài 难怪 *conjunction*
= no wonder that

nánguò 难过
1 *adjective*
= sad, aggrieved
2 *verb*
= have a hard time

nánkàn 难看 *adjective*
- = ugly, unpleasant to look at, disgraceful looking
- = unhealthy, pale
- = embarrassing, shameful

nánmiǎn 难免
1 *adjective*
= difficult to avoid
2 *adverb*
= inevitably

nánshòu 难受 *adjective*
- = unbearable, hard to stand
- = uncomfortable, unwell
- = unhappy, distressed, miserable

N

nǎodai 脑袋 *noun*
(*part of the body*) = head

nǎojīn 脑筋 *noun*
= brain, mind

nǎozi 脑子 *noun*
- (*part of the body*) = brain
- (*mental capacity*) = brains, mind, intelligence

nào 闹
1 *verb*
- = make a disturbance, make a noise, cause trouble
- = suffer bad effects from, be troubled by, undergo
  nào jīhuāng 闹饥荒 = suffer from famine
- (*when talking about something disruptive or troublesome*) = cause to happen, do, undertake
  nǐ bǎ zhè shì nào fùzá le 你把这事闹复杂了 = you made this matter complicated
- (*when speaking of emotions like anger or resentment*) = give vent to
  nào qíngxù 闹情绪 = be moody

2 *adjective*
= noisy, loud

nàozhōng 闹钟 *noun*
= alarm clock

ne 呢 *particle*
- (*for questions on a subject under consideration*)
  'nǐ hǎo ma?'—'hǎo, nǐ ne?' '你好吗?'—'好, 你呢?' = 'how are you?'—'fine, and you?'
- (*to indicate continued action*)
  tā zài nàr zuòzhe ne 他在那儿坐着呢 = he is sitting there
- (*to indicate emphasis or suspense*)
  hái yǒu shí fēnzhōng ne 还有十分钟呢 = there are still ten minutes left
- (*to introduce a topic*) = as for, with regard to
  zhège wèntí ne, wǒmen kěyǐ yǐhòu zài tǎolùn 这个问题呢, 我们可以以后再讨论 = as for this problem, we can talk about it later
- = where?
  wǒde gāngbǐ ne? 我的钢笔呢? = where is my pen?

nèi 内
1 *preposition*
(*when referring to time, place, scope or limits*) = within, in, inside
yì liǎng tiān nèi 一两天内 = within one or two days

2 *adjective*
= inner, internal

nèibù 内部 *adjective*
= internal, interior, on the inside

> **!** *This term sometimes refers to something that is* for officials only, *meaning that it is* restricted *or* exclusive.

nèibù wénjiàn 内部文件 = restricted document

nèikē 内科 *noun*
(*department of*) = internal medicine

nèiróng 内容 *noun*
= content, contents, the inner part

néng 能
1 *verb*
= can, be able to
tā néng shuō wǔzhǒng wàiyǔ 他能说五种外语 = he can speak five foreign languages

2 *noun*
- = ability, capability, skill
- (*in science*) = energy

nénggàn 能干 *adjective*
= capable, able, competent

nénggòu 能够 *verb*
= can, be able to, be capable of

nénglì 能力 *noun*
= capability, potentiality, ability

néngyuán 能源 *noun*
(*in the power industry*) = energy source, energy

ní 泥 *noun*
- = mud, clay, mire
- = puréed/mashed vegetable/fruit

nǐ 你 *pronoun*
(*singular*) = you

nǐmen 你们 *pronoun*
(*plural*) = you

nián 年 *noun*
- = year
- = New Year
- = person's age
- = every year, annual, yearly

niándài 年代 *noun*
- = era, period, age
- = decade
  qīshí niándài 七十年代 = the seventies

niánjí 年级 *noun*
(*in school or university*) = year, form, grade

niánjì 年纪, **niánlíng** 年龄 *noun*
(*when speaking of a person*) = age

niánqīng 年轻, **niánqīng** 年青 *adjective*
= young

nián 粘 ▶ **zhān** 粘

niàn 念 *verb*
- (*a course or subject*) = study
- = read, read aloud

niànshū 念书 *verb*
= study, read books

niáng 娘 *noun*
= mother, ma, mum

niǎo 鸟 *noun*
= bird

nín 您 *pronoun*
(*polite form of* nǐ 你) = you

nìngkě 宁可, **nìngkěn** 宁肯, **nìngyuàn** 宁愿 *adverb*
= would rather, better

niú 牛 *noun*
= ox, cow, cattle

niúnǎi 牛奶 *noun*
= cow's milk

niúròu 牛肉 *noun*
= beef

niǔ 扭 *verb*
- = turn, rotate, turn round
- = twist, wrench, sprain
- = grapple, wrestle
- = swing back and forth, sway from side to side

Niǔyuē 纽约 *noun*
= New York

nóng 农 *noun*
= farming, agriculture

nóngchǎng 农场 *noun*
= farm

nóngcūn 农村 *noun*
= village, rural area, countryside

nónglì 农历 *noun*
= traditional Chinese lunar calendar

nóngmín 农民 *noun*
= farmer, farming population, peasant

nóngyè 农业 *noun*
= agriculture, farming

nóng 浓 *adjective*
- (*when talking about tea, smoke, colour, atmosphere, fog, etc.*) = dense, concentrated, thick
  nóng chá 浓茶 = strong tea
- (*when speaking of degree or extent*) = great, rich, strong

nòng 弄 *verb*
- = do, make, cause
  nòng [**huài** | **cuò** | **qīngchu**] 弄 [坏 | 错 | 清楚] = [ruin | make a mistake | clear up]
- = handle, manage
- = obtain, get hold of
  zhèzhǒng yào hěn nán nòngdào 这种药很难弄到 = this type of medicine is very difficult to obtain
- = play with, fiddle with, do for amusement

nǔlì 努力
1 *verb*
= work hard, make a strenuous effort, exert oneself
2 *adjective*
= hardworking, studious, diligent
3 *adverb*
= studiously, diligently

nù 怒
1 *adjective*
= angry, furious, indignant
2 *noun*
= anger, passion, rage

nǚ 女 *adjective*
= female, woman

nǚ'ér 女儿 *noun*
= daughter, girl

nǚháizi 女孩子 *noun*
= girl

nǚpéngyou 女朋友 *noun*
= girlfriend

nǚrén 女人 *noun*
(*less polite than* nǚshì 女士) = woman

nǚshì 女士 *noun*
(*polite form of address or reference*) = lady, miss

nuǎn 暖
1 *adjective*
= warm, genial
2 *verb*
= warm up, make warm

nuǎnhuo 暖和
1 *adjective*
= warm, comfortably warm
2 *verb*
= warm up, make warm

nuǎnqì 暖气 *noun*
= warm air, heating, central heating

ó 哦 *exclamation*
(*connoting a sense of doubt:* really? *or* is that really so?) = Oh!

ò 哦 *exclamation*
(*showing understanding or realization*) = Oh!

ōuyuán 欧元 *noun*
= euro

Ōuzhōu 欧洲 *noun*
= Europe

ǒurán 偶然 *adverb*
= by chance, accidentally

Pp

pá 爬 *verb*
- = crawl, creep
- = climb

pà 怕 *verb*
- = fear, be afraid
- = be worried/concerned about
- (*especially when anticipating a negative reaction*) = think, suppose

wǒ pà tā bú huì lái 我怕他不会来 = I'm afraid he won't come

pāi 拍 *verb*
- = beat, clap, tap
- = take, send, shoot

pāi [zhào | diànyǐng | diànbào] 拍[照 | 电影 | 电报] = [take a picture | make a film | send a telegram]

pāi(zi) 拍(子) *noun*
(*used in some games*) = raquet, bat

pái 排
1 *noun*
= row, line
2 *measure word* ▶ **157**
(*for things grouped or set in rows*) = row
3 *verb*
- = set in a row, line up, arrange in order
- (*for drama performances, etc.*) = rehearse

páiduì 排队 *verb*
= queue (up), line up, form a line

páiqiú 排球 *noun*
= volleyball

pái 牌 *noun*
- = sign, signboard
- = trademark, brand
- = cards, dominoes

dǎ pái 打牌 = play cards

pài 派
1 *verb*
= send, dispatch, appoint
2 *noun*
- = school of thought, sect
- = clique, group, faction

pán 盘
1 *noun*
- = plate, dish, tray
- (*used in some games*) = board

qípán 棋盘 = chessboard

2 *measure word* ▶ **157**
- (*for flat things*)
- (*for board games*)

pánzi 盘子 *noun*
= dish, plate, tray

pànduàn 判断
1 *verb*
= decide, judge, assess
2 *noun*
= judgement, assessment, decision

pàn(wàng) 盼(望) *verb*
= hope for, yearn for

páng 旁
1 *noun*
• = side
lù páng 路旁 = roadside
• (*part of a Chinese character*) = radical
2 *adjective*
• = side, on the side
• = other, else

pángbiān 旁边
1 *noun*
= side, nearby position
2 *adverb*
= beside, alongside, nearby

pàng 胖 *adjective*
= fat, obese

pāoqì 抛弃 *verb*
= abandon, forsake, discard

pǎo 跑 *verb*
• = run, run away, escape
• = do errands, run around busily
• (*after a verb, indicating quick movement away*)
gǎnpǎo le 赶跑了 = drive away

pǎobù 跑步
1 *verb*
= run, jog
2 *noun*
= jogging, running

pào 炮 *noun*
= artillery, cannon

péi(tóng) 陪(同) *verb*
= accompany, be in the accompany of, keep company with

péiyǎng 培养 *verb*
= train, foster, develop

péiyù 培育 *verb*
= cultivate, nurture, breed

péi 赔 *verb*
• = lose money, sustain a financial loss
• = reimburse, compensate, indemnify

pèi 配 *verb*
• = deserve, be worthy of, be qualified
• = fit
• = match
• = blend, mix, compound
• (*when talking about animals*) = mate

pèihé 配合 *verb*
= co-ordinate, co-operate

pēn 喷 *verb*
= gush, spurt, spray

pén 盆 *noun*
= basin, pot, tub

péngyou 朋友 *noun*
= friend

pěng 捧 *verb*
• = carry in the hands
• = flatter, praise excessively

pèng 碰 *verb*
• = touch, knock against, collide
• = encounter, meet, run into
• = try one's luck

pèngjiàn 碰见 *verb*
= encounter, meet unexpectedly, run into

pèngqiǎo 碰巧 *adverb*
= coincidentally, by chance, happen to

pī 批
1 *measure word* ▶ 157
(*for people or goods*) = group, batch, lot
2 *verb*
• (*written work, etc.*) = correct, mark
• = criticise

pīpàn 批判
1 *verb*
= criticise
2 *noun*
= critique, criticism

pīpíng 批评
1 *verb*
= criticise
2 *noun*
= comment, criticism

pīzhǔn 批准 *verb*
= approve, grant (a request), ratify

pī 披 *verb*
= wear over the shoulders, wrap round

pí 皮 *noun*
• = skin, hide, leather
• = bark, peel, outer covering

píbāo 皮包 *noun*
= leather handbag, briefcase, portfolio

pífū 皮肤 *noun*
= skin

píjuàn 疲倦 *adjective*
= tired, fatigued, weary

píláo 疲劳 *adjective*
= tired, exhausted

píjiǔ 啤酒 *noun*
= beer

píqi 脾气 *noun*
= temperament, disposition
fā píqi 发脾气 = get angry, lose one's temper

pǐ 匹 *measure word* ▶ 157
(*for horses, mules*)

pìrú 譬如 *adverb*
= for example, for instance, such as

piān 偏 ▶ *See also* **piānpiān** 偏偏.
1 *adverb*
(*contrary to expectation*) = deliberately, insistently, stubbornly
nǐ piān yào gēn tā láiwǎng 你偏要跟他来往 = you insist on having dealings with him
2 *adjective*
- = slanted, inclined, leaning
- = favouring one side, partial, biased

piānjiàn 偏见 *noun*
= prejudice, bias

piānpiān 偏偏 *adverb*
- = deliberately, stubbornly, insistently
- (*contrary to expectation*)

yǒu yíjiàn hěn jǐnjí de shìqing yào tā zuò, piānpiān tā bìng le 有一件很紧急的事情要他做, 偏偏他病了 = there is a very urgent matter for him to deal with, but he has unexpectedly fallen ill

piān 篇 *measure word* ▶ 157
(*for papers, articles, written versions of a speech*)

piányi 便宜

> **!** *Note that in other uses* **pián** 便 *is pronounced* **biàn**.

1 *adjective*
= cheap, inexpensive
2 *noun*
= advantages, gain

piàn 片 *measure word* ▶ 157
- (*for flat, thin things or things in slices*)
- (*for expanses or stretches of ocean, desert, mist, fog, etc.*)
- (*for atmospheres, moods, etc.*)

piànmiàn 片面 *adjective*
= partial, incomplete, one-sided

piàn 骗 *verb*
= cheat, swindle, deceive

piāo 漂 *verb*
(*when talking about something in the water*) = float, drift

piāo 飘 *verb*
= float in the air, be borne by the wind

piāoyáng 飘扬 *verb*
(*when talking about something in the wind*) = fly, flutter, wave

piào 票 *noun*
= ticket, ballot

piàoliang 漂亮 *adjective*
= pretty, good-looking, beautiful

pīnmìng 拼命
1 *verb*
= give one's all, risk one's life
2 *adverb*
= to the death, with all one's effort

pīnyīn 拼音 *noun*
- = Chinese phonetic alphabet
- = combined sounds in syllables

pínkǔ 贫苦 *adjective*
= poor, poverty-stricken

pínqióng 贫穷 *adjective*
= poor, impoverished

pǐndé 品德 *noun*
= moral character, morality

pǐngé 品格 *noun*
- (*when talking about a person*) = character, morality
- (*when talking about literary or artistic works*) = quality, style

pǐnzhì 品质 *noun*
= character, quality

pǐnzhǒng 品种 *noun*
= breed, strain, variety

pīngpāngqiú 乒乓球 *noun*
= table tennis, ping-pong

píng 平
1 *adjective*
- = flat, level, equal
- = ordinary, average, common
- = peaceful, calm, balanced
- = fair, objective, impartial

2 *verb*
- = even out, level, make even
- = pacify, bring peace to, calm down
- (*in a game, match, race, etc.*) = draw, tie

píng'ān 平安
1 *adjective*
= peaceful
2 *noun*
= peace

píngcháng 平常
1 *adjective*
= ordinary, usual, common
2 *adverb*
= ordinarily, usually

píngděng 平等
1 *adjective*
= equal
2 *noun*
= equality

píngfán 平凡 *adjective*
= ordinary, common

píngfāng 平方 *noun*
(*in measuring area*) = square
yì píngfāng gōnglǐ 一平方公里 = a square kilometre

píngjìng 平静 *adjective*
= quiet, peaceful, calm

píngjūn 平均
1 *adjective*
= average, mean
2 *adverb*
= equally

píngshí 平时 *adverb*
= ordinarily, usually, normally

píngyuán 平原 *noun*
= plain, flatlands

pínglùn 评论
1 *verb*
= comment on, discuss
2 *noun*
= commentary, comment, review

píngguǒ 苹果 *noun*
= apple

píng 凭 *verb*
- = go by, take as the basis, base on
- = rely on, depend on

píng(zi) 瓶(子) *noun*
= bottle, jar, vase

pō 坡 *noun*
= slope, incline, bank

pòqiè 迫切
1 *adjective*
= urgent, pressing
2 *adverb*
= urgently

pò 破
1 *verb*
= break, cut, destroy
2 *adjective*
- = broken, damaged, in ruins
- = torn, worn-out

pòhuài 破坏 *verb*
= break, destroy, spoil

pū 扑 *verb*
- = rush toward, assault, pounce on
- = devote all one's energies to
tā zhěngtiān pū zài xuéxí shang 他整天扑在学习上 = he devotes all his time to his studies

pū 铺 *verb*
- = spread out, extend, unfold
- = spread over, cover
- = pave, lay
pū [chuáng | lù | tiěguǐ] 铺[床 | 路 | 铁轨] = [make the bed | pave a road | lay a railway track]

pǔshí 朴实 *adjective*
- = simple, plain
- = down-to-earth, sincere and honest, guileless

pǔsù 朴素 *adjective*
= simple, plain

pǔbiàn 普遍 *adjective*
= general, common, universal

pǔtōng 普通 *adjective*
= general, common

pǔtōnghuà 普通话 *noun*
= common spoken Chinese, Mandarin

Q

Qq

qī 七 *number*
= seven

qīyuè 七月 *noun*
= July

qī 期
1 *noun*
- = period of time, date, term
- = due date, deadline, scheduled time
dào qī 到期 = be due
- (*of a project, etc.*) = stage, phase

2 *measure word* ▶ 157
(*for issues of periodicals, magazines, journals, etc.*) = issue

qīdài 期待 *verb*
= hope, expect, look forward to

qījiān 期间 *noun*
= period of time, course of time

qīwàng 期望
1 *verb*
= hope, anticipate, expect
2 *noun*
= hope, anticipation, expectation

qīpiàn 欺骗 *verb*
= cheat, deceive

qīzi 妻子 *noun*
= wife

qí 齐
1 *adjective*
- = neat, tidy, in good order
- = complete, ready
- = similar, alike
- = together

2 *adverb*
= together, simultaneously, in unison

qícì 其次 *adverb*
(*in order or importance*) = next, secondly, secondarily

qíshí 其实 *adverb*
= in fact, actually

qítā 其他
1 *pronoun*
= the others
2 *adjective*
= other, else

qíyú 其余 *noun*
= the rest, the remaining

qízhōng 其中 *adverb*
(*a group or situation*) = in which, among whom

qíguài 奇怪 *adjective*
= strange, peculiar, surprising

qíjī 奇迹 *noun*
= miracle, wonder

qí 骑 *verb*
(*a horse or cycle*) = ride
qí chē 骑车 = ride a bicycle

qí 棋 *noun*
= chess, board game

qízi 旗子 *noun*
= flag, banner

qǐqiú 乞求 *verb*
= beg, supplicate

qǐtú 企图
1 *verb*
= try, seek, attempt
2 *noun*
= try, attempt

qǐyè 企业 *noun*
= enterprise, business

qǐfā 启发
1 *verb*
= inspire, stimulate, open the mind
2 *noun*
= inspiration, stimulation

qǐ 起 *verb*
- = rise, get up, arise
- = raise, grow
- = begin, start
- (*after another verb, to indicate upward movement*) = up
  [**ná** | **tí**] **qǐ** [拿 | 提] 起 = [take | lift] up
- (*after another verb, to indicate the beginning of an action*) = start, begin
  cóng tóu shuō qǐ 从头说起 = tell it from the beginning
- (*after another verb that is followed by* **de** 得 *or* **bu** 不, *to mean* can *or* cannot *attain a certain standard*)
  mǎi [**de** | **bù**] **qǐ** 买 [得 | 不] 起 = [can | cannot] afford

qǐchuáng 起床 *verb*
= get up, get out of bed

qǐdiǎn 起点 *noun*
= starting point

qǐfēi 起飞 *verb*
= take off (as an airplane)

qǐlai 起来 *verb*
- = get up, rise, get out of bed
- = stand up
- (*in opposition, rebellion, etc.*) = arise, rise up, stand up against
- (*after a verb, to indicate upward direction*) = raise, lift
- (*after a verb, indicate the beginning of an action*) = start, begin
- (*after a verb, to indicate an accomplishment*)
  xiǎngqǐlai... 想起来... = think of..., remember...
- (*after a verb, to indicate one's impression in the midst of an activity*)
  tīngqǐlai... 听起来... = it sounds...
  kànqǐlai... 看起来... = it looks...

qì 气
1 *verb*
- = become angry, become enraged, fume
- = make angry, anger, enrage

2 *noun*
- = air, gas, fumes
- = breath

  chuī yìkǒu qì 吹一口气 = blow out a puff of air
- = smell, odour

qìfēn 气氛 *noun*
= atmosphere, ambience

qìhòu 气候 *noun*
- = climate, weather
- = situation, atmosphere

qìwēn 气温 *noun*
= air temperature

qìxiàng 气象 *noun*
= weather, climatic/atmospheric phenomena

qì 汽 *noun*
= steam, vapour

qìchē 汽车 *noun*
- = car, automobile, vehicle
- = bus

  qìchēzhàn 汽车站 = bus station, bus stop

qìshuǐ 汽水
= carbonated drink, soft drink, pop

qìyóu 汽油 *noun*
= petrol, gasoline

qì 器 *noun*
= implement, utensil, instrument, machine
yuèqì 乐器 = musical instrument

qiàdàng 恰当 *adjective*
= appropriate, suitable, fitting

qiàhǎo 恰好 *adverb*
= it so happened that, luckily
qiàhǎo tā yě zài nàr 恰好她也在那儿 = it just so happened that she was there too

qiān 千 *number*
- = thousand
- = a large number of

qiānwàn 千万
1 *adverb*
(*in a warning*) = please do...at all costs
qiānwàn yào jìzhù! 千万要记住! = please do remember!
2 *number*
= ten million, millions upon millions

qiān 牵 *verb*
= lead by the hand, pull

qiānbǐ 铅笔 *noun*
= pencil

qiānxū 谦虚 *adjective*
= modest, self-effacing

qiāndìng 签订 *verb*
(*as an agreement, etc.*) = sign, put one's signature on

qiānmíng 签名 *verb*
= sign name, autograph

qiānzì 签字 *verb*
= sign, affix signature

qián 前
1 *noun*
= front, the front, ahead
2 *adjective*
- = preceding, former
- = front, first, top

3 *adverb*
= forward, ahead, ago
4 *preposition*
- = in front of, ahead of
- (*sometimes preceded by* **yǐ** 以) = before

qiánbian 前边**, qiántou** 前头 *adverb*
= in front, ahead

qiánjìn 前进 *verb*
= advance, go forward, move ahead

qiánmian 前面 *adverb*
- = in front, ahead
- (*referring to something mentioned before*) = above, the above, preceding

qiánnián 前年 *noun*
= the year before last, two years ago

qiántiān 前天 *noun*
= the day before yesterday

qiántú 前途 *noun*
= the future, future prospects, the road ahead

qiánxī 前夕 *noun*
= eve

qián 钱 *noun*
- = money
- = coins
- (*when talking about cost*) = money, cost

píngguǒ duōshǎo qián? 苹果多少钱? = how much are the apples?
táng yì máo qián 糖一毛钱 = the sweets cost 10 cents

qiánbāo 钱包 *noun*
= purse, wallet

qiǎn 浅 *adjective*
- = shallow
- = superficial, not profound
- = elementary, simple, easy
- (*of colour*) = light
  qiǎn lǜ 浅绿 = light green

qiàn 欠 *verb*
- (*debt, gratitude, etc.*) = owe
- = need, be short of, lacking

qiāng 枪 *noun*
= gun, rifle, pistol

qiáng 强 *adjective*
- = strong, powerful
- = better

qiángdà 强大 *adjective*
= strong, powerful

qiángdào 强盗 *noun*
= robber, bandit

qiángdiào 强调
1 *verb*
= emphasise, stress
2 *noun*
= emphasis, stress

qiángdù 强度 *noun*
= degree of strength, degree of intensity

qiángliè 强烈 *adjective*
= strong, intense, fervent

qiángpò 强迫 *verb*
= compel, coerce, force

qiáng 墙 *noun*
= wall

qiǎng 抢 *verb*
- = rob, snatch, loot
- = vie for
- (*in an emergency*) = rush, seize the moment
  qiǎng gòu shípǐn 抢购食品 = rush to buy food

qiāoqiāo 悄悄 *adverb*
= silently, quietly, stealthily

qiāo 敲 *verb*
- (*a door, etc.*) = knock, tap
- (*a drum, gong, etc.*) = beat, strike

qiáo(liáng) 桥(梁) *noun*
= bridge

qiáo 瞧 *verb*
= see, look at
qiáo [de | bù] qǐ 瞧[得 | 不] 起 = look [up to | down on]

qiǎo 巧
1 *adjective*
- = skilful, clever, ingenious
- = artful, cunning, deceiving
- = by coincidence, fortuitous, lucky

2 *adverb*
- = cleverly
- = fortuitously, coincidentally

qiǎomiào 巧妙 *adjective*
(*of methods, skills, etc.*) = brilliant, ingenious, clever

qiē 切 *verb*
(*as meat, fruit, vegetables, etc.*) = cut, slice

qīnluè 侵略
1 *verb*
= invade, encroach
2 *noun*
= invasion, aggression

qīn 亲
1 *noun*
- = parent
- = blood relation, next of kin, relative
- = marriage, match

2 *adjective*
= close, intimate, dear
3 *adverb*
= in person, oneself
4 *verb*
= kiss

qīn'ài 亲爱 *adjective*
= dear, darling, beloved

qīnjìn 亲近 *verb*
= be close to, be on intimate terms with

qīnmì 亲密 *adjective*
= close, intimate

qīnqi 亲戚 *noun*
= relative(s), relation(s), kin

qīnqiè 亲切 *adjective*
= warm, kind, cordial

qīnrè 亲热 *adjective*
= affectionate, intimate, warmhearted

qīnzì 亲自 *adverb*
= in person, personally, oneself

qín 琴 *noun*
(*general name for stringed musical instruments*)
xiǎotíqín 小提琴 = violin

qínliúgǎn 禽流感 *noun*
= bird flu

qīng 青 *adjective*
= blue, green

qīngnián 青年 *noun*
= youth, young person

qīngshàonián 青少年 *noun*
= teenager, youngster

qīng 轻
1 *adjective*
• (*in weight or importance*) = light
• (*in degree or age*) = small
• (*when talking about one's work or job*) = easy
2 *adverb*
= lightly, softly, gently

qīngsōng 轻松 *adjective*
= light, relaxed

qīngxiàng 倾向
1 *noun*
= tendency, trend, inclination
2 *verb*
= be inclined to, prefer

qīng 清
1 *adjective*
= clear, distinct
2 *verb*
(*an account, etc.*) = clear up, settle

qīngchu 清楚
1 *adjective*
= clear, distinct
2 *verb*
= understand, know

qīngjié 清洁 *adjective*
= clean

qīngjìng 清静 *adjective*
= quiet, peaceful, undisturbed

qíngjié 情节 *noun*
• (*when talking about literature*) = plot
qíngjié jǐncòu 情节紧凑 = a tightly constructed plot
• = circumstances

qíngjǐng 情景 *noun*
• = scene, sight
• = situation, circumstances

qíngkuàng 情况 *noun*
= situation, condition, circumstance

qíngxing 情形 *noun*
= situation, condition, circumstance

qíngxù 情绪 *noun*
= state of mind, mood, morale

qíng 晴 *adjective*
(*referring to the sky or weather*) = clear, fair, fine

qínglǎng 晴朗 *adjective*
= fine, sunny

qǐng 请 *verb*
• (*word used in polite requests*) = please
qǐng [zuò | jìn | chīfàn] 请 [坐 | 进 | 吃饭] = please [sit down | come in | start eating]
• = invite, ask, request

qǐngjià 请假 *verb*
= ask for time off

qǐngjiào 请教 *verb*
= ask for advice, consult

qǐngkè 请客 *verb*
= invite someone to dinner, treat, entertain guests

qǐngqiú 请求
1 *verb*
= ask, request
2 *noun*
= request

qǐngwèn 请问 *verb*
(*polite way of asking a question*) = may I ask...,

qìnghè 庆贺 *verb*
= congratulate, celebrate

qìngzhù 庆祝
1 *verb*
= celebrate
2 *noun*
= celebration

qióng 穷 *adjective*
= poor, impoverished

qiū(tiān) 秋(天) *noun*
= autumn, fall

qiú 求 *verb*
= seek, request, strive for

qiú 球 *noun*
• = ball, game played with a ball
• = sphere, globe, earth

qiúchǎng 球场 *noun*
= playing field, court, diamond

qiúmí 球迷 *noun*
(*someone fond of games played with a ball*) = fan
zúqiúmí 足球迷 = football fan

qū 区 *noun*
- = area, region, zone
- = district, precinct, administrative division

qūbié 区别
1 *noun*
= difference
2 *verb*
= discriminate, distinguish

qūfēn 区分 *verb*
= differentiate, distinguish

qūshì 趋势 *noun*
= trend, tendency

qūxiàng 趋向
1 *noun*
= trend, tendency, direction
2 *verb*
= tend to, incline to

qú 渠 *noun*
= drain, ditch, channel

qǔzi 曲子 *noun*
= song, tune, melody

qǔ 取 *verb*
- = take, fetch, obtain
- (*money from a bank, etc.*) = withdraw, draw out, take out
- (*as a candidate*) = accept, admit, select
- (*as a course of action*) = aim for, choose

qǔdé 取得 *verb*
= obtain, achieve, gain

qǔxiāo 取消 *verb*
= cancel, abolish, call off

qù 去 *verb*
- = go
- = leave, depart
- (*after a verb, indicating action directed away from the speaker*) = (move) away
  náqu 拿去 = take away
- (*expressing purpose or reason for an action*) = to, in order to
  ná yìdiǎnr qián qù mǎi dōngxi 拿一点儿钱去买东西 = take some money and go shopping
- = remove, get rid of, discard

qùshì 去世 *verb*
= die, pass away

qùnián 去年 *noun*
= last year

qùwèi 趣味 *noun*
- = interest, delight
- = taste, liking, preference

quān 圈
1 *noun*
- = circle, ring
- = enclosure

2 *verb*
= enclose, fence in, encircle

quán 全
1 *adjective*
- = whole, entire
- = complete

2 *adverb*
= completely, entirely, all

quánbù 全部
1 *adjective*
= whole, complete, all
2 *adverb*
= wholly, completely

quánmiàn 全面 *adjective*
= overall, all-round, comprehensive

quántǐ 全体
1 *noun*
= as a whole, whole body/group
2 *adjective*
= all, entire, whole

quán 权 *noun*
- = right
- = power, authority

quánlì 权力 *noun*
= power, authority

quán 泉 *noun*
= spring
wēnquán 温泉 = hot spring

quán(tou) 拳(头) *noun*
= fist

quán 鬈 *adjective*
(*when describing hair*) = curly, wavy

quàn 劝 *verb*
= persuade, advise, urge

quàngào 劝告 *verb*
= advise, urge, exhort

quē 缺 *verb*
= lack, be short of

quēdiǎn 缺点 *noun*
= defect, shortcoming, deficiency

quēfá 缺乏
1 *verb*
= lack, be short of
2 *noun*
= lack, deficiency

quēshǎo 缺少 *verb*
= lack, be short of

què 却 *conjunction*
= however, but, yet

quèdìng 确定
1 *verb*
= settle on, determine, fix
2 *adjective*
= settled, definite, sure

quèshí 确实
1 *adjective*
= certain, true, reliable
2 *adverb*
= certainly, really, indeed

qúnzi 裙子 *noun*
= skirt

qún 群
1 *measure word* ▶ **157**
(*for a group of, many*) = group, herd, flock
2 *noun*
= group, crowd, herd

qúnzhòng 群众 *noun*
= the masses, the public
qúnzhòng yùndong 群众运动 = mass movement

rán'ér 然而 *conjunction*
= but, however, nevertheless

ránhòu 然后 *adverb*
= thereafter, afterwards, subsequently

ránshāo 燃烧 *verb*
= burn

rǎn 染 *verb*
- = dye
- (*when talking about a disease, etc.*) = contract, become infected with
- (*when talking about a bad habit, etc.*) = acquire

rǎng 嚷 *verb*
= yell, shout

ràng 让
1 *verb*
- = let, allow, permit
  ràng tā qù ba 让她去吧 = let her go
- = make, cause
  zhèjiàn shì ràng tā hěn gāoxìng 这件事让她很高兴 = this matter made her very happy
- = yield, give way, concede
  ràng zuò 让座 = give up one's seat

2 *preposition*
(*when used to introduce the agent in a passive construction*) = by
tā zuò de cài ràng gǒu chī le 他做的菜让狗吃了 = the food he made was eaten by the dog

ràngbù 让步 *verb*
= make concessions

ráo 饶 *verb*
= forgive, pardon

rǎoluàn 扰乱 *verb*
= disturb, create confusion, harass

rào 绕 *verb*
- = move around, encircle, coil
  rào dìqiú yì zhōu 绕地球一周 = go round the world once
- = bypass, go round
  ràoguo zhàng'ài 绕过障碍 = bypass an obstacle

rě 惹 *verb*
- = provoke, annoy, tease
- (*when talking about trouble, nuisance, attention, etc.*) = stir up, incite, attract

rè 热
1 *adjective*
(*of weather, temperature, etc.*) = hot
2 *verb*
= heat up, warm up
3 *noun*
- = heat
- = temperature, fever
  fā rè 发热 = have a high temperature
- = rush, craze
  [**chūguó** | **jīng shāng** | **wǎngqiú**] **rè** [出国 | 经商 | 网球] 热 = a craze for [going abroad | business | tennis]

rè'ài 热爱 *verb*
= love, feel warm affection for

rèliè 热烈 *adjective*
= enthusiastic, passionate, fervent

rènao 热闹
1 *adjective*
= bustling, lively, boisterous
2 *verb*
= liven up, have a jolly time
3 *noun*
= excitement, fun

rèqíng 热情
1 *adjective*
= warm-hearted, enthusiastic, zealous
2 *noun*
= passionate feelings, love, ardour

rèxīn 热心 *adjective*
= earnest, warm-hearted, enthusiastic

rén 人 *noun*
- = person, people, humanity
- = others, other people

tā duì rén bú kèqi 他对人不客气 = he is impolite to others
rénrén 人人 = everyone, everybody

réncái 人才 *noun*
= talent, talented person

réngōng 人工
1 *adjective*
= artificial, man-made
2 *noun*
- = manual work
- = labour

nàr de réngōng hěn guì 那儿的人工很贵 = labour there is very expensive

rénjiā 人家 *noun*
= household, family

rénjia 人家 *pronoun*
- = others, other people
- (*when referring indirectly to a certain person or people*) = 'they', someone

nǐ yàoshì xiǎng qǐng tā chī fàn, nǐ zuìhǎo zǎo diǎn gàosu rénjia 你要是想请他吃饭，你最好早点告诉人家 = if you want to invite him to a meal, you had better tell him ahead of time
- (*when referring indirectly to the speaker*) = someone, one

wǒ cuò le, rénjia xiàng nǐ dàoqiàn hái bù xíng ma? 我错了，人家向你道歉还不行吗？= I was wrong and I apologize to you; won't that do?

rénkǒu 人口 *noun*
- = population
- = family members, number of family members

rénlèi 人类 *noun*
= humankind, humanity
rénlèixué 人类学 = anthropology

rénmen 人们 *noun*
= people, men

rénmín 人民 *noun*
= people, the people

Rénmínbì 人民币 *noun*
(*official currency of the People's Republic of China*) = Renminbi (RMB)

rénquán 人权 *noun*
= human rights

rénshēng 人生 *noun*
= life, human life

rénwù 人物 *noun*
- = personage, figure
- (*in a literary work*) = character

rényuán 人员 *noun*
= staff members, personnel

rénzào 人造 *adjective*
= man-made, artificial

rěn 忍 *verb*
= endure, tolerate, be patient

rěnnài 忍耐 *verb*
= be patient, endure, restrain oneself

rěnshòu 忍受 *verb*
= bear, endure

rěnxīn 忍心 *verb*
= be hard-hearted, be callous

rèn 认 *verb*
- (*when speaking of a person, object, etc.*) = recognize, know, identify
- (*when speaking of a fact, fault, problem, etc.*) = admit, acknowledge, recognize

rèn...zuò... 认...作... = regard...as..., take...for...

rènde 认得 *verb*
= be acquainted with, know, recognize

rènshi 认识
1 *verb*

- (*when speaking of a person*) = be acquainted with, know, recognize
- (*when speaking of a fact, reason, error, etc.*) = realize, understand

2 *noun*
= understanding, knowledge

rènwéi 认为 *verb*
= consider that, think that, take it that

rènzhēn 认真 *adjective*
= serious, earnest, conscientious

rèn 任 *verb*
- = appoint, assign, be responsible for
- = let, allow

rèn(píng) 任(凭) = no matter (who, what, how)
rènpíng tā zěnme hǎnjiào, méi yǒu rén lǐ tā 任凭他怎么喊叫, 没有人理他 = no matter how much he shouted, no one paid attention to him

rènhé 任何 *determiner*
= any, whatever
tā bú rènshì rènhé rén 她不认识任何人 = she doesn't know anyone

rènmìng 任命 *verb*
= employ, appoint

rènwu 任务 *noun*
= assigned duty, task, responsibility

rēng 扔 *verb*
= throw, throw away, cast aside

réngjiù 仍旧 *adverb*
= as before, still, yet

réng(rán) 仍(然) *adverb*
= still, yet, as before

rì 日 *noun*
- = sun
- = day, daytime
- (*in general*) = time
- = every day, day by day

rìbào 日报 *noun*
= daily paper, daily

Rìběn 日本 *noun*
= Japan

rìcháng 日常 *adjective*
= daily, day to day, everyday

rìchéng 日程 *noun*
= daily schedule, agenda, programme

rìchū 日出 *noun*
= sunrise

rìjì 日记 *noun*
= diary

rìlì 日历 *noun*
= calendar

rìluò 日落 *noun*
= sunset

rìqī 日期 *noun*
= date

Rìwén 日文 *noun*
= Japanese language (usually written)

rìyì 日益 *adverb*
= increasingly, day by day

rìyòngpǐn 日用品 *noun*
= daily necessities, basic commodities

Rìyǔ 日语 *noun*
= Japanese language (usually spoken)

rìyuán 日元 *noun*
= Japanese yen

rìzi 日子
- = day, date
- = a period of time, days
- = way of life, livelihood

róng 容 *verb*
- = allow, let, permit
- = tolerate
- = hold, contain

róngnà 容纳 *verb*
= hold, have the capacity of

róngrěn 容忍 *verb*
= tolerate, put up with

róngxǔ 容许 *verb*
= allow, permit

róngyì 容易 *adjective*
- = easy
- = likely, apt

xiàtiān niúnǎi hěn róngyì huài 夏天牛奶很容易坏 = in the summer milk goes bad easily

ròu 肉 *noun*
- (*of an animal*) = meat, flesh
- (*of a person*) = muscle, flesh
- (*of fruit or vegetable*) = pulp, flesh

rú 如
1 *verb*
- = be like, be as, be similar to
- (*when used with a negative*) ▶ *See also* **bùrú** 不如.

2 *preposition*
= in accordance with, according to
3 *conjunction*
= if, supposing
rú xiàyǔ, wǒmen jiù bú qù le 如下雨, 我们就不去了 = if it rains, we just won't go
4 rú 如 = such as, for example
Běijīng yǒu hěn duō míngshèng, rú Chángchéng, Gùgōng, děngděng 北京有很多名胜, 如长城, 故宫, 等等 = Beijing has many famous places, such as the Great Wall, the Forbidden City, etc.

rúcǐ 如此 *adverb*
= so, such, in this way

rúguǒ 如果 *conjunction*
= if, supposing that, in case

rúhé 如何 *adverb*
(*in a question or a statement*) = how, what
nǐde kǎoshì rúhé? 你的考试如何? = how was your examination?
tā bù zhīdào rúhé wánchéng zhèxiàng rènwu 他不知道如何完成这项任务 = he doesn't know how to finish this task

rújīn 如今 *adverb*
= these days, nowadays, at the present time

rúyì 如意 *adjective*
= ideal, as one wishes

rù 入 *verb*
- = enter, come in, go in
- = join, be admitted to, become a member of

ruǎn 软 *adjective*
- = soft, gentle, flexible
- (*when referring to physical weakness*) = weak, feeble
- (*when speaking about a person*) = easily moved/influenced

ruògān 若干 *determiner*
= a certain number of, several

ruòshì 若是 *conjunction*
= if

ruò 弱 *adjective*
- = weak, feeble
- = inferior, not up to standard

ruòdiǎn 弱点 *noun*
= weakness, weak point

Ss

sā 撒 *verb*
= let go, let out, cast

sǎ 洒 *verb*
= sprinkle, spill, spray

sài 赛
1 *verb*
- = compete, race
- = rival, overtake, surpass

2 *noun*
= competition, race, match

sān 三 *number*
= three

sānyuè 三月 *noun*
= March

sǎn 伞 *noun*
= umbrella, parasol, sunshade

sànbù 散步 *verb*
= take a stroll, go for a walk

sǎngzi 嗓子 *noun*
= throat, larynx, voice

sǎo 扫 *verb*
= sweep, clean

sǎozi 嫂子 *noun*
= sister-in-law, elder brother's wife

sàozhou 扫帚 *noun*
= broom

sè 色 *noun*
- = colour, look, quality
- = expression, countenance
- = sex, physical attraction, sexual passion

sēnlín 森林 *noun*
= forest

shā 杀 *verb*
- = kill, put to death
- = weaken, reduce

shāfā 沙发 *noun*
= sofa

shāmò 沙漠 *noun*
= desert

shāzi 沙子 *noun*
- = sand, grains of sand
- = small grains, pellets, grit

shǎ 傻 *adjective*
= foolish, stupid, silly

shài 晒 *verb*
- (*when speaking about the sun*) = shine upon
- (*when speaking about people*) = sunbathe, dry in the sun

shài tàiyáng 晒太阳 = sunbathe

shān 山 *noun*
= mountain, hill

shānmài 山脉 *noun*
= mountain range

shānqū 山区 *noun*
= mountainous region

shǎn 闪 *verb*
- = evade, dodge, duck
- (*as a light, lightning, inspiration, etc.*) = flash

dǎ shǎn 打闪 = lightning flashes

shànyú 善于 *verb*
= be good at

shāng 伤
1 *verb*
(*physically, emotionally, etc.*) = wound, injure, hurt
2 *noun*
= wound, harm, injury

shāngxīn 伤心 *adjective*
= sad, broken-hearted

shāngchǎng 商场 *noun*
= market

shāngdiàn 商店 *noun*
= shop, store

shāngliang 商量 *verb*
= talk over, consult, discuss

shāngpǐn 商品 *noun*
= goods, commodities, merchandise

shāngyè 商业 *noun*
= commerce, business, trade

shàng 上
1 *verb*
- = go up, ascend

shàng lóu 上楼 = go upstairs
- (*when talking about getting on or into a vehicle, mode of transport, stage or platform*) = mount, board, get on

shàng [gōnggòng qìchē | chuán | fēijī] 上[公共汽车 | 船 | 飞机] = board [the bus | the boat | the plane]
- = go, come

2 *adverb*
- (*after a verb to indicate an upward direction or accomplishment*) = up

[guān | dēng | chuān] shang [关 | 登 | 穿] 上 = [close up | climb up to, reach | put on]
- (*to indicate the beginning and continuity of an action*)

tāmen zhùshangle xīn fángzi 他们住上了新房子 = they now live in a new house

3 *adjective*
- = up, upper, high
- (*in grade or quality*) = first, top
- = first, preceding, previous

shàng...qù 上... 去 = go...
nǐ shàng nǎr qù? 你上那儿去? = where are you going?
shàng... [qù | lái] 上... [去 | 来] = [go | come]
wǒ shàng xuéxiào qù 我上学校去 = I am going to the school

shàngbān 上班 *verb*
= go to the office, start work

shàngbian 上边
1 *noun*
= top, above, higher parts
- = the top of, the surface of
- = the higher authorities, the higher-ups
- = aspect, respect, regard

tā bú yòng zài zhè shàngbian huā hěn duō shíjiān 他不用在这上边花很多时间 = he does not need to spend much time on this

2 *adjective*
= above-mentioned, aforesaid, foregoing

shàngdàng 上当 *verb*
= be swindled, be taken in, fall into a trap

Shàngdì 上帝 *noun*
= God

Shànghǎi 上海 *noun*
= Shanghai city

shàngjí 上级 *noun*
- = upper grade, higher level
- = higher authority

shàngkè 上课 *verb*
- = go to class, attend a lecture
- = teach a class

shànglai 上来 *verb*
- = come up
- (*after a verb to indicate a direction up and toward the speaker*) = ...up
  náshànglai 拿上来 = bring up
- (*after a verb to indicate accomplishment*)
  tā dá bú shànglai zhège wèntí 他答不上来这个问题 = he is unable to answer this question

shàngmian 上面 ▸**shàngbian** 上边

shàngqu 上去 *verb*
- = go up
- (*after a verb to indicate a direction up and away from the speaker*) = up
  náshàngqu 拿上去 = take up

shàngtou 上头 ▸**shàngbian** 上边

shàngwǔ 上午 *noun*
= morning, a.m., forenoon

shàngxué 上学 *verb*
= attend school, go to school

shàngyī 上衣 *noun*
= outer garment (worn on the upper half of the body), jacket

shāo 烧
1 *verb*
- = burn
- = heat, cook
- = bake, stew, roast
- = have a temperature, have a fever

2 *noun*
= temperature, fever

shāo 稍, **shāowēi** 稍微 *adverb*
= a little, somewhat, slightly

sháozi 勺子 *noun*
= spoon, ladle

shǎo 少

> **!** *Can also be pronounced* **shào** *with a different meaning.*

1 *adjective*
- = few, little, scarce
- (*in comparisons*) = less

2 *adverb*
= seldom, hardly ever, scarcely ever

3 *verb*
- = be short of, lack, be missing
- (*used in imperative sentences*) = stop, quit, reduce
  nǐ shǎo guǎn xiánshì 你少管闲事 = stop meddling in other people's affairs

shǎoshù 少数 *noun*
= minority
shǎoshù mínzú 少数民族 = ethnic minority, minority peoples

shàonián 少年 *noun*
- (*a time of life*) = youth
- (*a person*) = youth, young person

shétou 舌头 *noun*
= tongue

shé 蛇 *noun*
= snake, serpent

shèbèi 设备 *noun*
= equipment

shèjì 设计
1 *verb*
= design, plan, draw up plans

2 *noun*
= design, plan, project

shèhuì 社会 *noun*
= society, community

shè 射 *verb*
- = shoot
- = emit, radiate, send out

sheí 谁 *pronoun*

> **!** *Also pronounced* **shuí**.

- = who?
  nǐ shì shéi? 你是谁? = who are you?
- = anybody
  yǒu shéi yuànyì qù? 有谁愿意去? = would anyone like to go?
- (*used with* **dōu** 都) = everybody
  shéi dōu xǐhuan kàn shū 谁都喜欢看书 = everybody likes to read books
- (*used with* **dōu** 都 *in the negative*) = nobody
  shéi dōu méi qián 谁都没钱 = nobody has any money

shēn 伸 *verb*
= stretch, extend

shēn 身 *noun*
- = body
- = life
- = oneself, personally, itself

shēnbiān 身边
1 *noun*
= one's side, one's person

2 *adverb*
= at/by one's side, at hand, nearby

shēntǐ 身体 *noun*
- = body
- = health

shēn 深
1 *adjective*
- (*of water, thought, etc.*) = deep, profound
- (*of understanding, etc.*) = thorough, penetrating
- (*of friendships, relationships, etc.*) = close, intimate
- (*of forests, mysteries, etc.*) = hidden, inaccessible, obscure
- (*of colours*) = dark, deep
- (*of night, season, etc.*) = late

2 *adverb*
= profoundly, greatly, deeply

shēnhòu 深厚 *adjective*
(*of friendships, foundations, etc.*) = deep, profound, solid

shēnkè 深刻 *adjective*
(*of impressions, etc.*) = deep, profound

shēnrù 深入
1 *verb*
= penetrate deeply into, go deeply into
2 *adjective*
= deep, thorough, penetrating

shénme 什么
1 *pronoun*
- = what? what kind of?
nǐ xué shénme? 你学什么? = what do you study?
- = something
wǒ xiǎng jìn chéng mǎi diǎnr shénme 我想进城买点儿什么 = I want to go into town to buy something
- (*when it comes before* dōu 都) = everything
tā shénme dōu chī 她什么都吃 = she eats everything
- (*when used in the negative before* yě 也 *or* dōu 都) = nothing, not anything
tā shénme yě bù zhīdào 他什么也不知道 = he doesn't know anything
- (*when enumerating things*) = etc., ...and what not
shénme yīfu a, shípǐn a, wánjù a, nàge shāngdiàn dōu mài 什么衣服啊, 食品啊, 玩具啊, 那个商店都卖 = that shop sells clothes, food, toys, and what not

2 *exclamation*
- (*to indicate surprise or displeasure*) = what?

3 *determiner*
= what
xiànzài shì shénme shíhòu? 现在是什么时候? = what time is it (now)?
...shénme...shénme ...什么...什么 = whatever
nǐ yào shénme jiù mǎi shénme 你要什么就买什么 = buy whatever you want

shénmede 什么的 *pronoun*
= and so forth, etc.

shén 神
1 *noun*
- = spirit, god, deity
- = spirit, mind
- = expression, look

2 *adjective*
= spiritual, supernatural, magical

shénjīng 神经 *noun*
(*of the body*) = nerve

shènzhì(yú) 甚至(于) *adverb*
= even, so much so that, so far as to

shēng 升
1 *verb*
- = rise, ascend, move upward
- (*in position or rank*) = promote

2 *noun*
(*unit for measuring liquids*) = litre

shēng 生
1 *verb*
- = be born, give birth to, give rise to
- = grow
- = become

2 *adjective*
- = living, alive, live
- = unripe, green, raw
- = unprocessed, unrefined
- = unfamiliar, strange

3 *noun*
- = life, existence
- = living, livelihood
- = lifetime

shēngchǎn 生产
1 *verb*
- = produce, make, manufacture
- = give birth

2 *noun*
= production

shēngcí 生词 *noun*
= new word, new vocabulary

shēngdòng 生动 *adjective*
= moving, vivid, lively

shēnghuó 生活
1 *noun*
- = life
- = living, livelihood

2 *verb*
= live

shēngmìng 生命 *noun*
(*biological existence*) = life

shēngri 生日 *noun*
= birthday

shēngqì 生气 *adjective*
= angry

shēngwù 生物 *noun*
= living beings, organisms
shēngwùxué 生物学 = biology

shēngyi 生意 *noun*
= business, trade
zuò shēngyi 做生意 = do business

shēngzhǎng 生长 *verb*
- = grow, develop
- = grow up, be brought up

shēng 声
1 *noun*
- = voice, sound
- (*as in the linguistic tone of a Chinese word*) = tone

sìshēng 四声 = the four tones of Chinese

2 *measure word* ▶ 157
(*for counting cries, shouts, or other utterances*)

shēngdiào 声调 *noun*
- (*of words, sentences, speaking*) = tone, intonation
- (*of a Chinese character*) = tone
- = melody

shēngyīn 声音 *noun*
= sound, voice, noise

shéngzi 绳子 *noun*
= cord, string, rope

shěng 省
1 *noun*
= province
2 *verb*
- (*when talking about time or money*) = economize, save, spare
- = omit, leave out

Shèngdàn(jié) 圣诞(节) *noun*
= Christmas (Day)

shèng 胜
1 *noun*
= victory, success
2 *verb*
- = conquer, win, defeat
- = excel, surpass, be better than

shènglì 胜利
1 *verb*
= be victorious, be successful, win
2 *noun*
= victory
3 *adverb*
= victoriously, successfully

shèngxia 剩下 *verb*
- = remain, be left over, have...left over
- = leave behind

shèngxia(lai) 剩下(来) = remain, be left over

shībài 失败
1 *verb*
= fail, be defeated
2 *noun*
= failure, defeat

shīqù 失去 *verb*
(*when talking about objects, opportunities, friends, etc.*) = lose

shīwàng 失望
1 *adjective*
= disappointed
2 *verb*
= lose hope, lose confidence

shīyè 失业
1 *verb*
= be unemployed, lose one's job
2 *noun*
= unemployment

shīfu 师傅 *noun*
- = master worker, teacher, instructor
- = a polite term of address to people who have skill or specialized knowledge

shī 诗 *noun*
= poetry, poem, verse
shīrén 诗人 = poet

shīzi 狮子 *noun*
= lion

shīgōng 施工 *verb*
= be under construction, engage in construction

shī 湿 *adjective*
= damp, humid, wet

shīrùn 湿润 *adjective*
= humid, moist

shí 十 *number*
= ten, tens, multiples of ten

shíyuè 十月 *noun*
= October

shí'èr 十二 *number*
= twelve

shí'èryuè 十二月 *noun*
= December

shífēn 十分 *adverb*
= completely, fully, utterly

shíyī 十一 *number*
= eleven

shíyīyuè 十一月 *noun*
= November

shízì lùkǒu 十字路口 *noun*
= crossroads

shí 石, **shítou** 石头 *noun*
= rock, stone, pebble

shíyóu 石油 *noun*
= petroleum, oil

shídài 时代 *noun*
= time, period, age

shíhou 时候
1 *noun*
- = time, length of time
- (*when speaking of time on the clock*) = time, moment in time, point in time
  tā shì shénme shíhòu zǒu de? 他是什么时候走的? = what time did he leave?

2 *conjunction* **...de shíhòu** ...的时候 = when..., during..., while...
dāng...shíhòu 当... 时候 = when..., while...

shíjiān 时间 *noun*
- (*as an abstract concept*) = time
- (*a set period of time*) = time, duration
- (*point of time*) = time
  nǐ shénme shíjiān dào de? 你什么时间到的? = what time did you arrive?
- = time zone
  Běijīng shíjiān 北京时间 = Beijing time
  shíjiānbiǎo 时间表 = timetable, schedule

shíkè 时刻
1 *noun*
= time, hour
2 *adverb*
= every moment, constantly, always

shíqī 时期 *noun*
= time period

shíjì 实际
1 *noun*
= reality, fact
2 *adjective*
= realistic, practical
shíjìshang 实际上 = actually, in fact, in reality

shíjiàn 实践
1 *verb*
= put into practice, carry out
2 *noun*
= practice

shíshì 实事 *noun*
= fact, facts
shíshì qiúshì 实事求是 = seek truth from facts, be realistic

shíxiàn 实现 *verb*
(*as a hope, dream, plan*) = realise, come true, actualise

shíxíng 实行 *verb*
= implement, put into practice, carry out

shíyàn 实验
1 *verb*
= experiment
2 *noun*
= experiment
shíyànshì 实验室 = laboratory

shíyòng 实用 *adjective*
= practical, functional, applied

shízài 实在
1 *adjective*
= true, real, honest
2 *adverb*
= actually, really

shí 拾 *verb*
= pick up, gather, collect

shípǐn 食品 *noun*
= food, provisions

S

shítáng 食堂 *noun*
= dining hall, cafeteria

shíwù 食物 *noun*
= food

shǐ 使 *verb*
- = use, employ, apply
- = enable, cause, make

shǐyòng 使用
1 *verb*
= utilise, make use of, apply
2 *noun*
= use, deployment

shǐzhōng 始终 *adverb*
= from beginning to end, all along

shìjì 世纪 *noun*
= century

shìjiè 世界 *noun*
= world

shì 市 *noun*
- = municipality, city
- = market, fair
- (*pertaining to the Chinese system of weights and measures*)
  yí shìjīn 一市斤 = 1/2 kilo

shìchǎng 市场 *noun*
= market, bazaar

shìyàng 式样 *noun*
= style, type, model

shì 事 *noun*
- = affair, matter, event
- = trouble, accident
- = work, job
  zuòshì 做事 = work at a job

shìgù 事故 *noun*
= accident

shìjiàn 事件 *noun*
= incident, event

shìqing 事情 *noun*
= thing, matter, affair

shìshí 事实 *noun*
= reality, fact
shìshíshang 事实上 = in fact, as a matter of fact, in reality

shìwù 事务 *noun*
- = affairs, matters
- = work, routine, duties

shìwù 事物 *noun*
= thing, object, matter

shìxiān 事先 *adverb*
= prior to, in advance, beforehand

shìyè 事业 *noun*
- = profession, career, cause
- = enterprise, undertaking

shì 试
1 *verb*
= try, try out, test
2 *noun*
= test, examination
shìshi kàn 试试看 = try and see

shìjuàn 试卷 *noun*
= examination paper, answer booklet, script

shìyàn 试验
1 *verb*
= test, experiment
2 *noun*
= experiment, test, trial

shì 是
1 *verb*
- (*the verb* to be) = am, is, are
- = certainly, indeed
  wǒ shì méi qù 我是没去 = I certainly did not go

2 *adjective*
- = right, correct
- (*used to answer the affirmative*) = yes, right
  shì, nǐ shuō de duì 是, 你说得对 = yes, what you said is correct

3 (*used in certain patterns*)
- **bú shì...ér shì...** 不是… 而是… = it's not...but....
- **yào bú shì...jiù shì...** 要不是…就是… = if it's not..., it's...
  shì...de 是… 的
- (*for emphasis*)
  tā shì hěn yònggōng de 她是很用功的 = she studies hard
- (*when giving the details about someone or something, its origin, manufacture, provenence, etc.*)
  zhèliàng qìchē shì Rìběn zào de 这辆汽车是日本造的 = this car was made in Japan
  shì bú shì? 是不是? = is it?
  shì...háishì... 是… 还是… = ...or..., whether...or...
  nǐ shì zǒulù lái de, háishì qí chē lái de? 你是走路来的, 还是骑车来的? = did you walk or come by bicycle?

...shì..., kěshì... ...是..., 可是...
(*here* shì 是 *is used in a clause of concession*) = yes, it is..., but..., although..., yet...
zhèbù diànyǐng hǎo shì hǎo, kěshì tài cháng le 这部电影好是好, 可是太长了 = although this movie is good, it's too long

shìdàng 适当 *adjective*
= suitable, appropriate, proper

shìhé 适合 *verb*
= fit, suit, be appropriate

shìyìng 适应 *verb*
= adapt, suit, fit

shìyòng 适用 *adjective*
= suitable, applicable, appropriate

shì 室 *noun*
= room

shōu 收 *verb*
- = receive, accept
- = collect, gather, harvest

shōuhuílai 收回来 = recover, get back
shōuqǐlai 收起来 = put away

shōuhuò 收获
1 *verb*
= harvest, gather in the crops, reap
2 *noun*
(*of hard work, study, etc.*) = results

shōurù 收入
1 *verb*
= receive, take in
2 *noun*
= income, revenue

shōushi 收拾 *verb*
- = put in order, straighten up, tidy
- = repair, fix, mend

shōuyīnjī 收音机 *noun*
= radio

shóu 熟 ▶ **shú** 熟

shǒu 手
1 *noun*
= hand
2 *adverb*
= by hand

shǒubiǎo 手表 *noun*
= watch, wristwatch

shǒuduàn 手段 *noun*
= method, means

shǒugōng 手工
1 *noun*
= handicraft, handiwork
2 *adjective*
= manual, handmade
3 *adverb*
= by hand

shǒujī 手机 *noun*
= mobile phone, cell phone

shǒujī zhìnéngkǎ 手机智能卡 *noun*
= SIM card

shǒujuàn 手绢 *noun*
= handkerchief

shǒushù 手术 *noun*
= surgical operation

shǒutào 手套 *noun*
= gloves

shǒutí diànnǎo 手提电脑 *noun*
= laptop

shǒuxù 手续 *noun*
= procedures, formalities, process

shǒuzhǐ 手指 *noun*
= finger
shǒuzhǐjia 手指甲 = fingernail

shǒu 首
1 *noun*
- (*part of the body*) = head
- (*a person*) = leader, chief, head

2 *measure word* ▶ **157** (*for poems, music*)
3 *adjective*
= first, beginning, most important

shǒudū 首都 *noun*
(*of a country*) = capital

shǒuxiān 首先 *adverb*
= first, in the first place, above all

shòu 受 *verb*
- = receive, accept
- = suffer, be subjected to
- = stand, endure, bear
- (*used to express the passive voice*) = receive, be subject to

shòuhuòyuán 售货员 *noun*
= shop assistant

shòupiàoyuán 售票员 *noun*
- (*on a bus*) = conductor
- (*at a train station*) = clerk
- (*at a cinema or theatre*) = clerk

shòu 瘦 *adjective*
- (*of people*) = thin, emaciated
- (*of clothing*) = tight

shū 书 *noun*
- = book
- = letter

shūbāo 书包 *noun*
= satchel, book bag, school bag

shūdiàn 书店 *noun*
= bookshop, bookstore

shūfǎ 书法 *noun*
= calligraphy

shūjì 书记 *noun*
(*of a political party or a political organization*) = secretary

shūjià 书架 *noun*
= bookcase, bookshelf

shūzhuō 书桌 *noun*
= desk

shūshu 叔叔 *noun*
- = uncle, father's younger brother
- (*a man in one's father's generation*) = uncle

shūfu 舒服 *adjective*
= comfortable, feeling well

shūshì 舒适 *adjective*
= comfortable, cosy

shū 输 *verb*
- = transport, transmit, convey
- (*when speaking about a game, a gamble*) = lose, be defeated

shūcài 蔬菜 *noun*
= vegetables

shú 熟

> **!** *Can also be pronounced* shóu.

1 *adjective*
- (*of fruit, etc.*) = ripe, mature
- (*of food*) = cooked, done, processed
- (*of people*) = familiar, well-acquainted
- (*in a subject, a type of work, etc.*) = skilled, trained, experienced

2 *adverb*
(*of sleep*) = deeply, soundly
shúrén 熟人 = acquaintance

shúliàn 熟练 *adjective*
= expert, adept, proficient

shúxī 熟悉 *verb*
= know well, be familiar with

shǔjià 暑假 *noun*
= summer holidays, summer vacation

shǔyú 属于 *verb*
- = belong to, pertain to, be part of

shǔ 数 *verb* ▶ *See also* **shù** 数.
- = count, enumerate, list
- = count as, be counted as
shǔ de shàng 数得上 = qualify, count, be counted
shǔ bù qīng 数不清 = countless

shǔ 鼠 *noun*
= mouse, rat

shǔbiāo 鼠标 *noun*
= (computer) mouse

shù 束 *measure word* ▶ **157**
= bunch

shù 树
1 *noun*
= tree
2 *verb*
= establish, set up

shùlín 树林 *noun*
= woods

shù 数 ▶ *See also* **shǔ** 数.
1 *noun*
= number, figure
2 *determiner*
= several, a few

shùliàng 数量 *noun*
= number, quantity, amount

shùmǎ 数码
1 *noun*
= numeral, number
2 *adjective*
= digital

shùxué 数学 *noun*
= mathematics

shùzì 数字
1 *noun*
= number, figure, digit
2 *adjective*
= digital

shuā 刷 *verb*
- = brush, scrub
- = paint, whitewash, paste up

shuāi 摔 *verb*
- = fall, stumble
- = break, smash
  shuāiduàn 摔断 = break
- = throw down, cast

shuǎi 甩 *verb*
- = swing, move back and forth
- = fling, cast away, throw

shuài 率, **shuàilǐng** 率领 *verb*
= lead, head, command

shuāng 双
1 *measure word* ▶ **157**
(*for things that come in twos, such as shoes, socks, chopsticks, etc.*) = pair

2 *adjective*
- = double, twin, dual
  shuāng shǒu 双手 = both hands
- (*when talking about numbers*) = even
  shuāng shù 双数 = even numbers

shuāngfāng 双方 *noun*
= both sides

shuí 谁 ▸ **shéi 谁**

shuǐ 水 *noun*
= water, juice, liquid

shuǐdào 水稻 *noun*
= rice grown in a paddy field

shuǐguǒ 水果 *noun*
= fruit, fresh fruit

shuǐní 水泥 *noun*
= cement

shuǐpíng 水平 *noun*
= standard, level

shuì 睡 *verb*
= sleep
shuìzháo 睡着 = go to sleep, fall asleep, be sleeping

shuìjiào 睡觉 *verb*
= sleep

shùn 顺
1 *preposition*
= along, in the direction of
2 *verb*
- = obey, submit to
- = follow, accord with, go with

3 *adjective*
- = favourable, successful
- = smooth, fluent
  shùnzhe 顺着 = along, following

shùnbiàn 顺便 *adverb*
= along the way, in passing

shùnlì 顺利
1 *adjective*
= smooth, successful, with no obstacles
2 *adverb*
= smoothly, successfully, well

shuō 说 *verb*
- = say, speak, talk
- = explain
- = scold, rebuke

shuōmíng 说明
1 *verb*
= make clear, explain
2 *noun*
= instructions, explanation, directions
shuōmíngshū 说明书 = directions, instructions, synopsis

sījī 司机 *noun*
= driver, chauffeur

sī 丝 *noun*
- = silk
- = fine thread
- = slight amount, trace

sī 私
1 *adjective*
- = private, secret, confidential
- = selfish
- = illegal, underhanded

2 *adverb*
= privately, confidentially, secretly

sīrén 私人 *adjective*
= private, personal

sīxiǎng 思想 *noun*
= thought, philosophy, ideas

sī 撕 *verb*
= tear, rip, shred

sǐ 死
1 *verb*
= die, pass away
2 *adjective*
- = dead
- = stagnant, inflexible

3 *adverb*
- (*when it comes before a verb*) = to the death
  sǐ shǒu 死守 = defend to the death
- (*when it comes after a verb*) = die of, to death
  [**dòng** | **yān** | **è**] **sǐ** [**冻** | **淹** | **饿**] **死** = [freeze | drown | starve] to death
- (*when it comes after an adjective*) = extremely
  [**lè** | **qì** | **lèi**] **sǐ le** [**乐** | **气** | **累**] **死了** = extremely [happy | angry | tired]

sì 四 *number*
= four

sìyuè 四月 *noun*
= April

sìhū 似乎
1 *adverb*
= seemingly, apparently
2 *verb*
= seem, appear, seem to be
sìhū tài wǎn le 似乎太晚了 = it seems too late

S

sōng 松
1 *noun*
= pine tree, fir tree
2 *adjective*
= loose, lax, slack
3 *verb*
= relax, loosen, slacken

sòng 送 *verb*
- (*as a gift*) = give, present
sòng gěi tā yíjiàn lǐwù 送给她一件礼物 = give her a present
- = deliver, take, bring
- = see off, accompany

sòngxíng 送行 *verb*
= see off, wish someone a safe journey

sōu 艘 *measure word* ▶ 157
(*for ships*)

Sūgélán 苏格兰 *noun*
= Scotland

sùjìng 肃静 *adjective*
= solemn and silent

sùchéng xiàngjī 速成相机 *noun*
= speed camera

sùdù 速度 *noun*
= speed, velocity

sùshè 宿舍 *noun*
= dormitory

sùliào 塑料 *noun*
= plastic, plastics

suān 酸
1 *adjective*
- = sour tasting
- = sad, distressed, sorrowful
- (*muscles, back, etc.*) = sore, aching

2 *noun*
= acid

suàn 算 *verb*
- = figure, count, calculate
- = include, count in
- = be counted as, be considered as
tā suàn shì wǒmen de hǎo péngyou 他算是我们的好朋友 = he can be considered our good friend
- = carry weight, count
suànshang 算上 = count in, include
suànle 算了 = forget it, let it be, let's drop the matter

suīrán 虽然 *conjunction*
= although, though
suīrán...kěshì/dànshì... 虽然...可是/但是... = although..., (still, yet)...

suí 随
1 *preposition*
= along with
tā suí(zhe) wēndù ér biànhuà 它随(着)温度而变化 = it varies with the temperature
2 *verb*
- = follow, go along with
- (*whatever one wishes or finds convenient*)
mǎi bù mǎi suí nǐ 买不买随你 = it's up to you whether you buy it or not

suíbiàn 随便
1 *adjective*
- = casual, informal, random
- = careless, thoughtless, cursory

2 *adverb*
- = as one pleases, freely
- = carelessly, randomly

3 *conjunction*
= no matter whether, whatever, in whatever way

suíshí 随时 *adverb*
= at any time

suì 岁 *noun*
= year of age, year old
tāde érzi wǔ suì 他的儿子五岁 = his son is five years old

suì 碎
1 *adjective*
= broken, shattered, fragmentary
2 *verb*
= break, break in pieces, smash to bits

sūnnǚ 孙女 *noun*
= granddaughter

sūnzi 孙子 *noun*
= grandson

sǔnshī 损失
1 *verb*
= lose, damage, harm
2 *noun*
= loss, damage

suō 缩 *verb*
- (*in size*) = shrink, reduce, contract
- (*in movement*) = shrink back, withdraw

suǒ 所
1 *measure word* ▶ 157
(*for buildings, houses, schools, etc.*)

2 *noun*
- = place, site, station
- = office, bureau, institute

3 *particle*
- (*used with* **wéi** 为 *or* **bèi** 被 *to indicate the passive voice*)
  bèi dàjiā suǒ chēngzàn 被大家所称赞 = be praised by everyone
- (*when it precedes a verb*) = what, whatever
  wǒ suǒ [**shuō de** | **xǐhuan de** | **zuò de**] 我所[说的 | 喜欢的 | 做的] = [what I said | what I like | what I do/did]

suǒwèi 所谓 *adjective*
= so-called, what is called

suǒyǐ 所以 *conjunction*
- = therefore, thus, as a result
  tā bìng le, suǒyǐ méi lái 他病了, 所以没来 = he is ill, so he didn't come
- (*when giving a cause or reason*) = the reason why...
  tā zhī suǒyǐ shēngbìng shì yīnwèi nàtiān chūqu méi chuān dàyī 他之所以生病是因为那天出去没穿大衣 = the reason why he became ill is that he went out that day without a coat

suǒyǒu 所有
1 *determiner*
= all
2 *noun*
= possession

Tt

tā 他 *pronoun*
- = he, him
- = another, other, some other
  tārén 他人 = other people

tāmen 他们 *pronoun*
= they, them

tā 它 *pronoun*
(*neuter, for animals and things*) = it

tāmen 它们 *pronoun*
(*neuter, for animals and things*) = they, them

tā 她 *pronoun*
= she, her

tāmen 她们 *pronoun*
(*when referring to females*) = they

tǎ 塔 *noun*
= pagoda, tower

tà 踏 *verb*
= step on, tread, set foot on

tái 台
1 *noun*
- = terrace, raised platform, stage
- = stand, support
- = broadcasting station

2 *measure word* ▶ 157
(*for stage performances, machines, equipment, etc.*)

táifēng 台风 *noun*
= typhoon

Táiwān 台湾 *noun*
= Taiwan

tái 抬 *verb*
= lift, raise, carry

tài 太 *adverb*
- = too, excessively
- = extremely
- (*in the negative*) = (not) very
  bú tài gāo 不太高 = not very tall

tàijíquán 太极拳 *noun*
= Taijiquan, traditional Chinese shadow boxing

tàikōng 太空 *noun*
= outer space

Tàipíngyáng 太平洋 *noun*
= the Pacific Ocean

tàitai 太太 *noun*
- = married woman, wife
- = Mrs., Madam

tàiyáng 太阳 *noun*
= sun, sunshine, sunlight

tàidu 态度 *noun*
= attitude, manner, bearing

tān 摊 *noun*
(*for selling things*) = stand, booth, stall

tán 谈 *verb*
= talk, discuss, chat

tánhuà 谈话
1 *verb*
= talk, chat, carry on a conversation
2 *noun*
= conversation, discussion

tánlùn 谈论 *verb*
= talk about, discuss

tánpàn 谈判
1 *verb*
= negotiate, talk, discuss
2 *noun*
= negotiation, talk

tán 弹 *verb*

> **!** *Can also be pronounced* **dàn** 弹 *with a different meaning.*

- = shoot, send forth
- (*as fingers, ashes off a cigarette, etc.*) = flick, flip, snap
- (*a stringed instrument, piano, etc.*) = play, pluck

tǎnzi 毯子 *noun*
= rug, carpet, blanket

tànqì 叹气 *verb*
= sigh

tàn 探 *verb*
- = search out, seek, explore
- = visit, pay a call on

tāng 汤 *noun*
= soup, broth

táng 堂
1 *noun*
= hall
2 *measure word* ▶ **157**
(*for classes or periods at school or university*) = period, class

táng 糖 *noun*
= sugar, sweets, candy

tǎng 躺 *verb*
= lie, recline, be lying

tàng 烫
1 *verb*
- = scald, burn
- (*clothes*) = iron
- (*using heat on the hair*) = curl, set, perm
- = heat up, warm

2 *adjective*
= hot to the touch, scalding

tàng 趟 *measure word* ▶ **157**
- (*for scheduled services of public transportation*)
- (*for trips, journeys, visits, etc.*) = time, trip

tāo 掏 *verb*
(*with the hand as from a pocket*) = take out, fish out, extract

táo 逃 *verb*
= escape, run away, evade

táo(zi) 桃(子) *noun*
= peach

tǎolùn 讨论
1 *verb*
= discuss, debate, talk over
2 *noun*
= discussion, debate

tǎoyàn 讨厌
1 *adjective*
- = disgusting, objectionable
- = troublesome, annoying, a nuisance

2 *verb*
= dislike, be disgusted with

tào 套
1 *measure word* ▶ **157**
(*for sets of books, clothing, tools, furniture, etc.*) = set, suit, suite
2 *noun*
= cover, sheath, case

tè 特 *adverb*
= specially, particularly, exceptionally

tèbié 特别
1 *adjective*
= special, distinctive, unique
2 *adverb*
= especially, specially

tècǐ 特此 *adverb*
= hereby

tèdiǎn 特点 *noun*
= special characteristic, special feature

tèsè 特色 *noun*
= unique feature

tèshū 特殊 *adjective*
= special, particular, exceptional

téng 疼 *verb*
- = ache, hurt, be painful
- = love, be fond of, have affection for

tī 踢 *verb*
- = kick
- (*when talking about football or other games requiring kicking*) = play

tí 提 *verb*
- = lift, raise, carry
- (*when talking about a subject*) = bring up, mention

- (*when talking about money in a bank*) = draw out, take out, withdraw
- (*when talking about a suggestion, an objection, etc.*) = put forward, bring up, raise

tíchàng 提倡 *verb*
= advocate, promote

tíchū 提出 *verb*
= put forward, raise, advance

tígāo 提高 *verb*
- = raise, elevate, increase
- = enhance, improve

tígōng 提供 *verb*
= offer, make available to, provide

tíqián 提前
1 *verb*
(*when speaking of an appointment or deadline*) = bring forward, advance, change to an earlier time/date
2 *adverb*
= in advance, ahead of time, beforehand

tíxǐng 提醒 *verb*
= remind, warn

tíyì 提议
1 *verb*
= propose, suggest
2 *noun*
= proposal, suggestion, motion

tí 题
1 *noun*
= subject, topic, title
2 *verb*
(*on a poem, painting, fan, etc.*) = inscribe

tímù 题目 *noun*
(*of a lecture, discussion, essay, etc.*) = subject, title, topic

tǐhuì 体会
1 *verb*
= sense, realize, understand
2 *noun*
= sense, feeling, understanding

tǐjī 体积 *noun*
= bulk, physical volume

tǐxì 体系 *noun*
= system

tǐyàn 体验 *verb*
= learn through practice/experience

tǐyù 体育 *noun*
= sports, physical education, training

tǐyùchǎng 体育场 *noun*
= stadium, arena

tǐyùguǎn 体育馆 *noun*
= gymnasium, gym

tì 替
1 *verb*
= substitute for, take the place of, replace
2 *preposition*
= for, on behalf of

tiān 天 *noun*
- = sky, heaven
- = God, Heaven
- = weather
- = day
- = season
- = nature, world of nature

tiāntiān 天天 = every day

Tiān'ānmén 天安门 *noun*
= Tian An Men, the Gate of Heavenly Peace

tiāncái 天才 *noun*
= talent, gift, genius

Tiānjīn 天津 *noun*
= Tianjin (City)

tiānkōng 天空 *noun*
= the sky, the heavens

tiānqì 天气 *noun*
= weather

tiānrán 天然 *adjective*
= natural

tiānxià 天下
1 *noun*
= all under heaven, the whole world, the whole of China
2 *adverb*
= everywhere under heaven, all over the world, all over China

tiānzhēn 天真 *adjective*
= innocent, naive, pure

tiān 添 *verb*
= add, supplement with, replenish

tián 田 *noun*
= farm, field

tiányě 田野 *noun*
= field, open country

tián 甜 *adjective*
- (*in flavour, love, dreams, music*) = sweet
- (*when referring to sleep*) = sound

tián 填 *verb*
(*a hole, a blank space*) = fill up, fill in

tiāo 挑 *verb*

> ! *Can also be pronounced* tiǎo *with a different meaning.*

- = choose, select
- (*with a pole on the shoulders*) = carry
  tiāo shuǐ 挑水 = carry water
- (*as heavy responsibilities*) = shoulder, carry

tiáo 条
1 *measure word* ▶ **157**
- (*for long, narrow things*)
- (*for items of news, laws, ideas, views*)
- (*for limbs of the human body*)
- (*for human lives*)
  four lives = sìtiáo rénmìng 四条人命

2 *noun*
- = strip, slip
- = slip of paper, short note, message
- (*in a treaty, constitution, law, contract, or other written document*) = item, clause, article

tiáojiàn 条件 *noun*
- (*of an agreement*) = condition, term, stipulation
- = requirement, qualification, condition

tiáoyuē 条约 *noun*
= treaty, agreement, pact

tiáo 调 *verb* ▶ *See also* **diào** 调.
= mix, adjust, mediate

tiáopí 调皮 *adjective*
= naughty, mischievous, unruly

tiáozhěng 调整
1 *verb*
= adjust, reorganize, revise
2 *noun*
= adjustment, revision

tiǎozhàn 挑战

> ! *The character* tiǎo 挑 *can also be pronounced* tiāo *with a different meaning.*

1 *verb*
= challenge, challenge to a contest, challenge to battle
2 *noun*
= challenge

tiào 跳 *verb*
- = jump, hop, leap
- (*as a heart, etc.*) = beat
- = skip, skip over, miss out

tiàowǔ 跳舞 *verb*
= dance

tiē 贴 *verb*
- = paste, stick on
- = stay next to, nestle close to

tiě 铁 *noun*
= iron

tiělù 铁路, **tiědào** 铁道 *noun*
= railway, railroad

tīng 厅 *noun*
- = hall
- = office, department

tīng 听 *verb*
- = listen to, hear
- = obey, heed
- = allow, let

tīnghuà 听话 *adjective*
= obedient

tīngjian 听见 *verb*
= hear, perceive by hearing

tīngjiǎng 听讲 *verb*
= listen to a talk, attend a lecture

tīngshuō 听说 *verb*
= hear, it is said, hear it said that

tīngxiě 听写
1 *verb*
= dictate
2 *noun*
= dictation

tíng 停 *verb*
- = stop, cease, halt
- = stay, stop over
- (*of cars*) = park
- (*of ships*) = anchor, lie at anchor

tíngzhǐ 停止 *verb*
= stop, cease

tǐng 挺 *adverb*
= rather, quite, very

tōng 通
1 *verb*
- = go through, pass through
- = communicate with, get through

wǒ cháng hé tā tōngxìn 我常和他通信 = I often communicate with him by letter
- = lead to, go to

2 *adjective*
- = open, passable
- (*of writing, arguments*) = logical, coherent, grammatical

3 *noun*
= authority, expert
Zhōngguó tōng 中国通 = China expert, old China hand

tōngcháng 通常
1 *adverb*
= usually, normally, generally
2 *adjective*
= usual, normal, general

tōngguò 通过
1 *preposition*
= by means of, by way of, via
2 *verb*
- = pass through
- (*by voting*) = pass, carry, adopt

tōngxùn 通讯 *noun*
- = communication
- = news report, news despatch, newsletter

tōngzhī 通知
1 *verb*
= notify, inform
2 *noun*
= notice, notification

tóng 同
1 *adjective*
= same, identical, similar
2 *adverb*
= together, in the same way
3 *preposition*
= with

tóngbàn 同伴 *noun*
= companion

tóngqíng 同情
1 *verb*
= sympathize with, be sympathetic toward, share feelings with
2 *noun*
= sympathy, compassion

tóngshí 同时 *adverb*
- = at the same time, simultaneously, meanwhile
- = moreover, besides

tóngshì 同事 *noun*
= colleague, fellow worker

tóngwū 同屋 *noun*
= roommate

tóngxué 同学 *noun*
= classmate, schoolmate, fellow student

tóngyàng 同样
1 *adjective*
= same, alike, similar
2 *adverb*
= in the same way, equally

tóngyì 同意 *verb*
= agree

tóngzhì 同志 *noun*
= comrade

tóng 铜 *noun*
= copper, bronze, brass

tóngnián 童年 *noun*
= childhood

tǒngjì 统计
1 *noun*
= statistics
2 *verb*
= count, add up

tǒngyī 统一
1 *verb*
= unify, unite
2 *adjective*
= unified

tǒngzhì 统治 *verb*
= control, rule, govern

tǒng 桶 *noun*
= bucket, barrel, keg

tòng 痛
1 *verb*
= hurt, ache, pain
2 *noun*
= pain, sorrow
3 *adverb*
- = thoroughly, extremely, deeply
- (*when speaking of unpleasant actions*) = severely, bitterly

tòngkǔ 痛苦
1 *adjective*
= bitter, painful
2 *noun*
= suffering, agony, pain

tòngkuai 痛快
1 *adjective*
- = happy, delighted, refreshed
- = frank, outspoken, forthright

2 *adverb*
- = frankly, outspokenly
- = to one's heart's content, with abandon, to one's great satisfaction

tōu 偷
1 *verb*
= steal, attack
2 *adverb*
= stealthily, secretly, illegally

tōutōu 偷偷 *adverb*
= stealthily, secretly, on the sly

tóu 头
1 *noun*
- = head
- = top, beginning
- = terminus, end
- = chief, head

2 *measure word* ▶ 157
- (*for certain animals*)
- (*for garlic bulbs*)

3 *adjective*
= first, leading, the first

tóufa 头发 *noun*
(*on a person's head*) = hair

tóunǎo 头脑 *noun*
= brains, mind

tóu 投 *verb*
- = throw in/at, put in, drop
- (*when voting*) = cast
- (*when talking about suicide, in a river, sea, etc.*) = throw oneself into

tóurù 投入 *verb*
= throw into, put into

tóuxiáng 投降 *verb*
= surrender, capitulate

tóuzī 投资
1 *verb*
= invest
2 *noun*
= investment

tòu 透
1 *verb*
= penetrate, pass through, seep through
2 *adjective*
= thorough, complete
3 *adverb*
= fully, thoroughly, completely

tūchū 突出
1 *verb*
= stress, highlight, give prominence to
2 *adjective*
- = protruding, projecting
- = prominent, outstanding

3 *adverb*
= conspicuously

tūjī 突击
1 *verb*
- = attack suddenly, assault, take by surprise
- = attack a job to get it done, go all out to finish a task

2 *noun*
= attack, sudden attack

tūrán 突然
1 *adjective*
= sudden, abrupt, unexpected
2 *adverb*
= suddenly, abruptly

tú 图
1 *noun*
- = picture, map, diagram
- = plan, scheme

2 *verb*
= seek, pursue

túshūguǎn 图书馆 *noun*
= library

tú 涂 *verb*
- = smear, spread on, apply
- = scribble, scrawl, disfigure by marking
- = delete, blot out, cross out

tǔ 土
1 *noun*
- = earth, soil, dust
- = land, territory, ground

2 *adjective*
- = local, native, locally produced
- = earthen, made of earth
- = rustic, crude, unenlightened

tǔdì 土地 *noun*
= land, territory

tǔdòu 土豆 *noun*
= potato

tǔ 吐 *verb* ▶ *See also* **tù** 吐.
- = spit, spit out
- (*as in releasing one's emotions*) = speak out, pour out, say

tù 吐 *verb* ▶ *See also* **tǔ** 吐.
= vomit, disgorge, regurgitate

tùzi 兔子 *noun*
= rabbit, hare

tuán 团
1 *noun*
- = group of people, organization
- = lump, round mass

2 *measure word* ▶ 157
(*for certain round things*)
3 *verb*
= unite, round up

tuánjié 团结
1 *verb*
= unite, band together, rally
2 *noun*
= unity

tuántǐ 团体 *noun*
= organization, group, team

tuányuán 团圆 *noun*
(*of a family*) = reunion

tuī 推 *verb*
- = push, shove
- = push forward, promote, advance
- = promote, elect, recommend
- (*as a responsibility*) = decline, refuse, shirk
- = put off, postpone

tuīchí 推迟 *verb*
= put off, postpone, defer

tuīdòng 推动 *verb*
= prod, promote, push forward

tuīguǎng 推广 *verb*
- = spread, extend
- = promote, popularise

tuījiàn 推荐
1 *verb*
= recommend
2 *noun*
= recommendation

tuǐ 腿 *noun*
= leg, thigh

tuì 退 *verb*
- = retreat, withdraw, step back
- = return, give back
- = decline, recede, subside
- = resign, quit, retire
- = cancel, break off, quit

tuìbù 退步
1 *verb*
= regress, slip back, fall behind
2 *noun*
= retrogression

tuìxiū 退休 *verb*
= retire (from work)

tuō 托
1 *verb*
- (*on the palm of one's hand*) = support from underneath, hold up, hold
- = entrust, rely on
- = make excuses, give as a pretext

2 *noun*
= tray, stand

tuō'érsuǒ 托儿所 *noun*
= nursery, child-care centre

tuō 拖 *verb*
- = pull, haul, drag
- = procrastinate, delay

tuō 脱 *verb*
- (*when talking about clothes, shoes, etc.*) = take off, remove, cast off
- (*when talking about difficult situations, danger, etc.*) = free oneself from, get away from, escape from

tuōlí 脱离 *verb*
- = leave, break away from, escape from
- = separate from, divorce, break off

tuǒdàng 妥当
1 *adjective*
= proper, appropriate
2 *adverb*
= properly, appropriately

wā 挖 *verb*
= dig, excavate

wàzi 袜子 *noun*
= socks

wāi 歪 *adjective*
- = crooked, askew, awry
- = devious, dishonest, immoral

wài 外
1 *noun*
- = out, outside
- = foreign country/countries

duì wài màoyì 对外贸易 = foreign trade
2 *adjective*
- = outside, other
- = foreign, external

- (*referring to relatives of one's mother, sister, or daughter*)
  wài zǔfù 外祖父 = maternal grandfather

3 *preposition*
= out of, outside, beyond

wàibian 外边 *noun*
= outside, out

wàidì 外地 *noun*
(*beyond one's home area or place of residence*) = outside area, external region, other parts of the country

wàiguó 外国 *noun*
= foreign country
wàiguórén 外国人 = foreigner

wàihuì 外汇 *noun*
= foreign currency, foreign exchange

wàijiāo 外交 *noun*
= foreign affairs, diplomacy
Wàijiāobù 外交部 = Ministry of Foreign Affairs

wàikē 外科 *noun*
= surgical department

wàimian 外面 ▶ **wàibian** 外边

wàitou 外头 ▶ **wàibian** 外边

wàiwén 外文 *noun*
(*referring primarily to a written language*) = foreign language

wàiyǔ 外语 *noun*
(*referring primarily to a spoken language*) = foreign language

wān 弯
1 *verb*
= bend, flex
2 *noun*
= bend, curve, corner
guǎi wānr 拐弯儿 = go round a bend, turn a corner
3 *adjective*
= bent, curved, crooked

wán 完 *verb*
- = finish, complete
- (*after a verb to indicate completing an action*) = finish..., use up, run out of
  wǒ chīwán le 我吃完了 = I've finished eating

wánchéng 完成 *verb*
= complete, finish, accomplish

wánquán 完全
1 *adjective*
= complete, whole
2 *adverb*
= completely, fully

wánzhěng 完整
1 *adjective*
= complete, perfect, whole
2 *noun*
= wholeness, integrity

wánjù 玩具 *noun*
= toy, plaything

wánr 玩儿 *verb*
- = play, play with, have fun
- (*for sports and other recreational activities*) = play, engage in

wánxiào 玩笑 *noun*
= joke, jest
(gēn mǒurén) kāi wánxiào (跟某人) 开玩笑 = play a joke (on someone)

wǎn 晚
1 *adjective*
= late, late in the day, late in life
2 *adverb*
= late
3 *noun*
= evening, night

wǎnfàn 晚饭 *noun*
= supper, dinner

wǎnhuì 晚会 *noun*
= evening party, soirée

wǎnshang 晚上 *noun*
= evening, night, night time

wǎn 碗 *noun*
= bowl

wàn 万 *number*
- = ten thousand
- = a very great number

wànsuì 万岁 *verb*
= long live...!

wànyī 万一
1 *conjunction*
= just in case, if by any chance
2 *noun*
= contingency, eventuality

wǎng 网 *noun*
= net, web, network

wǎngqiú 网球 *noun*
- = tennis
- = tennis ball

wǎng 往 ▶ *See also* **wàng** 往.
1 *verb*
= go

2 *adjective*
= past, previous
3 *preposition*
= towards, in the direction of

wǎngwǎng 往往 *adverb*
= often, frequently

wàng 忘, **wàngjì** 忘记 *verb*
= forget

wàng 往 *preposition* ▶ *See also* **wǎng** 往.
= to, towards, in the direction of

wàng 望 *verb*
- = look up, gaze
- = hope, expect

Wēi'ěrshì 威尔士 *noun*
= Wales

wēihài 危害
1 *verb*
= endanger, harm, damage
2 *noun*
= danger, harm

wēijī 危机 *noun*
= crisis

wēixiǎn 危险
1 *adjective*
= dangerous, critical
2 *noun*
= danger

wēixiào 微笑
1 *verb*
= smile (slightly)
2 *noun*
= (slight) smile

wéi 为 ▶ *See also* **wèi** 为.
1 *verb*
- = be, equal
- = do, act
- = act as, serve as

2 *preposition*
(*used with* **suǒ** 所 *in passive sentences*) = by
wéi rénmín suǒ hèn 为人民所恨 = be hated by the people

wéinán 为难
1 *adjective*
= embarrassed, awkward
2 *verb*
= make things difficult for

wéifǎn 违反 *verb*
= violate, go against

wéi 围 *verb*
= surround, enclose

wéijīn 围巾 *noun*
= scarf

wéirào 围绕 *verb*
= surround, circulate, revolve around

wéiyī 唯一, **wéiyī** 惟一 *adjective*
= only, sole

wéihù 维护 *verb*
= protect, guard, defend

wěidà 伟大 *adjective*
= great, remarkable

wěi 尾 *noun*
= tail, end

wěiba 尾巴 *noun*

> **!** *This word is sometimes pronounced* **yǐba**.

= tail

wěiyuán 委员 *noun*
= committee member

wèishēng 卫生
1 *adjective*
= clean, good for health, hygienic
2 *noun*
= sanitation, health, hygiene

wèixīng 卫星 *noun*
= satellite

wèi 为 *preposition* ▶ *See also* **wéi** 为.
- (*indicating who will benefit*) = for, on account of, for the sake of
  wèi tā mǔqīn mǎi yào 为她母亲买药 = buy medicine for her mother
- (*indicating the reason or purpose for an action*) = for the sake of, out of concern for, in order to
  wèi shěng qián 为省钱 = in order to save money
  wèi...ér... 为...而... = ...for the sake of...
  wèi hépíng ér fèndòu 为和平而奋斗 = struggle for peace

wèile 为了 *preposition*
= for the sake of, in order to

wèishénme 为什么 *adverb*
= why, for what reason

wèi 未 *adverb*
= not, not yet

wèilái 未来 *noun*
= future, time to come

wèi 位 *measure word* ▶ 157
(*a polite measure word for people*)

wèiyú 位于 *verb*
= be situated in, be located in, lie in

wèizhi 位置 *noun*
= position, place, post

wèizi 位子 *noun*
= seat, place

wèi(dao) 味(道) *noun*
= flavour, taste

wèi 胃 *noun*
= stomach

wèi 喂
1 *verb*
(*when talking about a person or animal*) = feed, give food to
2 *exclamation*
(*as a greeting or to attract attention*) = hello!, hey!

wēndù 温度 *noun*
= temperature

wēnnuǎn 温暖 *adjective*
= warm

wénhuà 文化 *noun*
- = civilisation, culture
- = education, schooling, literacy

wénjiàn 文件 *noun*
= document, paper

wénkē 文科 *noun*
(*a branch of learning*) = liberal arts

wénmíng 文明
1 *noun*
= civilisation, culture, enlightenment
2 *adjective*
= enlightened, civilised

wénwù 文物 *noun*
= relic, antique

wénxué 文学 *noun*
= literature
wénxuéjiā 文学家 = writer of literary works

wényì 文艺 *noun*
= literature and the arts, art and literature

wénzhāng 文章 *noun*
= essay, article, literary composition

wénzì 文字 *noun*
= written language, characters, script

wén 闻 *verb*
- = hear
- = smell

wénmíng 闻名 *adjective*
= well-known, famous, renowned

wénzi 蚊子 *noun*
= mosquito

wěn 稳 *adjective*
= stable, steady, sure

wěndìng 稳定
1 *adjective*
= firm, stable
2 *verb*
= stabilize

wèn 问 *verb*
= ask, inquire, question

wènhǎo 问好 *verb*
= send one's regards to, ask after
xiàng tāmen wènhǎo 向他们问好 = send my regards to them

wènhòu 问候 *verb*
= send one's respects to, extend greetings to

wèntí 问题 *noun*
- = question, problem, issue
- = trouble, mishap
  tāde qìchē chū wèntí le 他的汽车出问题了 = he had trouble with his car
- = examination question

wǒ 我 *pronoun*
= I, me, self

wǒmen 我们 *pronoun*
= we, us

wòpù 卧铺 *noun*
= sleeping compartment, berth

wòshì 卧室 *noun*
= bedroom

wò 握 *verb*
= grasp, hold fast to

wòshǒu 握手 *verb*
= shake hands, clasp hands

wūrǎn 污染
1 *verb*
= pollute, contaminate
2 *noun*
= pollution

wū 屋 *noun*
= house, room

wūzi 屋子 *noun*
= room

wú 无
1 *verb*
= have not, there is not
2 *noun*
= nothing, void
3 *adjective*
= no
4 *adverb*
= not

wúliáo 无聊 *adjective*
- = boring
- = bored
- = silly, stupid, senseless

wúlùn 无论 *conjunction*
= no matter what/how, regardless, whether (or not)
wúlùn rúhé 无论如何 = whatever happens, in any case

wúshù 无数 *adjective*
= countless, innumerable

wúsuǒwèi 无所谓
1 *adjective*
= indifferent
2 *verb*
- = be indifferent, not matter
- = cannot be taken as, cannot be designated as

wúxiàn 无限
1 *adjective*
= infinite, boundless, unlimited
2 *adverb*
= infinitely, without bounds

wǔ 五 *number*
= five

wǔyuè 五月 *noun*
= May

wǔfàn 午饭 *noun*
= lunch, midday meal

wǔqì 武器 *noun*
= weapon, armament, arms

wǔshù 武术 *noun*
= martial arts

wǔ 舞, **wǔdǎo** 舞蹈 *noun*
= dance

wǔtái 舞台 *noun*
= stage, arena

wù 勿 *adverb*
(*when indicating prohibition*) = not, don't

wù 物 *noun*
= thing, matter

wùjià 物价 *noun*
= price

wùlǐ 物理 *noun*
= physics

wùzhì 物质
1 *noun*
= matter, material, substance
2 *adjective*
(*of resources, etc.*) = physical, material

wùhuì 误会
1 *verb*
= misunderstand
2 *noun*
= misunderstanding

wù 雾 *noun*
= fog, mist

xī 西
1 *noun*
= west
2 *adjective*
= west, western

Xībānyá 西班牙 *noun*
= Spain
Xībānyárén 西班牙人 = Spaniard
Xībānyáwén 西班牙文, **Xībānyáyǔ** 西班牙语 (*the language*) = Spanish

xīběi 西北
1 *noun*
= northwest
2 *adjective*
= northwest, northwestern

xībian 西边 *noun*
= western side

xīcān 西餐 *noun*
= Western food

xīfāng 西方 *noun*
1 *noun*
• (*a direction*) = the west
• (*part of the world*) = the West
2 *adjective*
= western

xīfú 西服 *noun*
= Western-style clothes

xīguā 西瓜 *noun*
= watermelon

xīhóngshì 西红柿 *noun*
= tomato

xīnán 西南 *noun*
1 *noun*
= southwest
2 *adjective*
= southwestern

xīmian 西面 ▶ **xībian** 西边

xīzhuāng 西装 ▶ **xīfú** 西服

Xīzàng 西藏 *noun*
= Tibet

xī 吸 *verb*
• = inhale, breathe
• = attract, absorb

xīshōu 吸收 *verb*
• = absorb, take in, assimilate
• = recruit, enrol, admit

xīyān 吸烟 *verb*
= smoke cigarettes, smoke

xīyǐn 吸引 *verb*
= attract, draw

xīwàng 希望
1 *verb*
= hope, wish
2 *noun*
= hope, expectation

xīshēng 牺牲 *verb*
= sacrifice

xíguàn 习惯
1 *noun*
= habit, custom
2 *verb*
= be accustomed to, get used to

xǐ 洗 *verb*
= wash, clean

xǐyījī 洗衣机 *noun*
= washing machine

xǐzǎo 洗澡 *verb*
= have a bath/shower

xǐ 喜
1 *adjective*
= happy, pleased, delighted
2 *noun*
= happiness, happy event

xǐhuan 喜欢 *verb*
= be pleased with, like, prefer
tā xǐhuan kàn shū 他喜欢看书 = he likes to read

xì 戏 *noun*
= play, opera, drama

xìjù 戏剧 *noun*
= play, drama

xì 系 *noun*
= department in a university/college, faculty

xìtǒng 系统 *noun*
= system

xì 细 *adjective*
1 *adjective*
• = fine, thin, delicate
• = careful, meticulous, detailed
2 *adverb*
= attentively, carefully, in detail

xìjūn 细菌 *noun*
= bacteria, germs

xìxīn 细心
1 *adjective*
= attentive, careful, meticulous
2 *adverb*
= attentively, with concentration

xiā 虾 *noun*
= shrimp
duìxiā 对虾 = prawn

xiā 瞎 *adjective*
= blind

xià 下
1 *verb*
• = descend, go down from, get off
• (*when referring to weather*) = fall
xià [yǔ | xuě | báozi] le 下[雨 | 雪 | 雹子]了 = it is [raining | snowing | hailing]
• (*as an order*) = issue, give, proclaim
• (*in making or sending down a decision*) = decide, determine
xià [juéxīn | jiélùn | dìngyì] 下[决心 | 结论 | 定义] = [make up one's mind | draw a conclusion | give a definition]

- (*when speaking of animals or eggs*) = give birth to, lay

2 *adverb*
- (*after a verb to indicate downward movement*) = down
  zuòxia 坐下 = sit down
- (*after a verb to indicate having space for something*)
  zhèlǐ fàng bú xia 这里放不下 = there's no room to put (it) here
- (*after a verb to indicate completion or result*)
  dìngxia kāihuì de shíjiān 定下开会的时间 = fix a time for the meeting

3 *adjective*
- = next
  xiàge yuè 下个月 = next month
- = lower, inferior

4 *preposition*
= under, below
chuáng xià 床下 = under the bed

5 *measure word* ▶ 157
(*for brief actions*) = time

xiàbān 下班 *verb*
= go off duty, get out of work

xiàbian 下边
1 *noun*
= the bottom, below
2 *adjective*
= next, following
3 *preposition*
= below, under, underneath

xiàkè 下课 *verb*
= class is over, dismiss class

xiàlai 下来 *verb*
- = come down
- (*after a verb to indicate downward movement*)
  tiàoxiàlai 跳下来 = jump down
- (*after a verb to indicate movement away*)
  bǎ yǎnjìng zhāixiàlai 把眼镜摘下来 = take off your glasses
- (*after a verb to indicate completion or result of an action*)
  wǒ bǎ nǐde dìzhǐ jìxiàlai le 我把你的地址记下来了 = I noted down your address

xiàmian 下面 ▶ **xiàbian** 下边

xiàqu 下去 *verb*
- = go down, descend
- (*when referring to the future*) = continue, go on
- (*used after a verb to express the continuation of an action*)
  shuōxiàqu 说下去 = keep on speaking

xiàtou 下头 ▶ **xiàbian** 下边

xiàwǔ 下午 *noun*
= afternoon, p.m.

xià 吓 *verb*
- = frighten, scare
- = be frightened
- = intimidate, threaten

xiàtiān 夏天 *noun*
= summer, summer season

xiān 先 *adverb*
= first, before, in advance
xiān...zài... 先...再... = first...and then...
xiān chīfàn zài xiūxi 先吃饭再休息 = first eat, then rest
xiān...cái... 先...才... = not...until..., must first...before...
nǐ děi xiān gěi wǒ jiěshì yíxià, wǒ cái néng qù bàn 你得先给我解释一下, 我才能去办 = I can't do it until you explain it to me

xiānhòu 先后
1 *noun*
= order of precedence, priority
2 *adverb*
= successively, one after another

xiānjìn 先进 *adjective*
(*as in techniques, experience, etc.*) = advanced

xiānsheng 先生 *noun*
- = Mr.
- = husband
- (*courteous address to scholars, elders*) = sir

xiānwéi 纤维 *noun*
= fibre, fibrous tissue

xiān 掀 *verb*
(*as a cover, etc.*) = raise, lift

xiān 鲜 *adjective*
- (*as in food or air*) = fresh
- = tasty, delicious
- = bright, colourful

xiānhuā 鲜花 *noun*
= fresh flowers

xián 闲
1 *adjective*
- (*as a person, a room, etc.*) = idle, unoccupied, free
- (*when referring to time*) = free, leisure

2 *adverb*
= leisurely, freely

xiǎnde 显得 *verb*
= appear, seem

xiǎnrán 显然
1 *adjective*
= obvious, clear
2 *adverb*
= obviously, evidently, clearly

xiǎnshì 显示 *verb*
= display, show, manifest

xiǎnzhù 显著 *adjective*
= distinct, prominent, marked

xiàn 县 *noun*
= district, county

xiàndài 现代
1 *noun*
= contemporary era, modern age
2 *adjective*
= modern, contemporary

xiàndàihuà 现代化
1 *adjective*
= modernized
2 *noun*
= modernization

xiànshí 现实
1 *noun*
= reality
2 *adjective*
= practical, realistic
xiànshí zhǔyì 现实主义 = realism

xiànxiàng 现象 *noun*
= phenomenon

xiànzài 现在
1 *noun*
= present, now
2 *adverb*
= now, at present, currently

xiànzhì 限制
1 *verb*
= control, restrict, limit
2 *noun*
= control, restriction, limit

xiàn 线 *noun*
- = thread, string, wire
- = line

xiànmù 羡慕 *verb*
- = admire
- = envy

xiàn 献 *verb*
- = offer up, present
- = donate, dedicate

xiāng 乡 *noun*
- = country, countryside, village
- = native place, home

xiāngxia 乡下 *noun*
= country, countryside, village

xiāng 相 *adverb*

> **!** *Can also be pronounced* xiàng *with a different meaning.*

= mutually, reciprocally, each other

xiāngdāng 相当
1 *adjective*
= suitable, appropriate
2 *adverb*
= fairly, quite, rather

xiāngfǎn 相反
1 *adjective*
= opposite, contrary
2 *adverb*
= on the contrary

xiānghù 相互
1 *adjective*
= mutual, reciprocal
2 *adverb*
= mutually, each other

xiāngsì 相似
1 *adjective*
= similar to, like
2 *verb*
= resemble, be alike

xiāngtóng 相同 *adjective*
= alike, the same, similar

xiāngxìn 相信 *verb*
= believe, believe in, trust

xiāng 香
1 *adjective*
- (*of flowers, etc.*) = fragrant, scented, pleasant smelling
- (*of food*) = delicious, appetizing

2 *noun*
- = fragrance, aroma
- = perfume, incense, joss stick

xiāngcháng 香肠 *noun*
= sausage

Xiānggǎng 香港 *noun*
= Hong Kong

xiāngjiāo 香蕉 *noun*
= banana

xiāngzào 香皂 *noun*
= perfumed soap, toilet soap

xiāngzi 箱子 *noun*
= trunk, box, case

xiángxì 详细
1 *adjective*
= careful, meticulous, in detail
2 *adverb*
= carefully, thoroughly, meticulously

xiǎngshòu 享受
1 *verb*
= enjoy
2 *noun*
= enjoyment

xiǎng 响
1 *adjective*
(*as a sound or noise*) = loud, noisy
2 *verb*
= make a sound
3 *noun*
= sound, noise

xiǎngyìng 响应
1 *verb*
= respond, answer
2 *noun*
= response, answer

xiǎng 想 *verb*
• = think, consider, ponder
• = think about, miss, long for
• = want to, intend to, plan to

xiǎngfa 想法 *noun*
= viewpoint, opinion, way of thinking

xiǎngniàn 想念 *verb*
= remember, long for, miss

xiǎngxiàng 想象
1 *verb*
= imagine
2 *noun*
= imagination

xiàng 向
1 *preposition*
= towards, facing
2 *verb*
• = face
• = incline towards, side with
3 *noun*
= direction, trend

xiàng 巷 *noun*
= lane, alley

xiàngpiàn 相片 *noun*
= photograph, picture

xiàng 项 *measure word* ▶ 157
• (*for work, projects, tasks, requirements, etc.*)
• (*for decisions or announcements*)

xiàngmù 项目 *noun*
= item, project

xiàng 象
1 *noun*
= elephant
2 *verb*
= be like, look as if

xiàngzhēng 象征
1 *noun*
= symbol, emblem
2 *verb*
= symbolize, signify, stand for

xiàng 像
1 *verb*
= be like, resemble, look like
2 *adjective*
= similar, alike
3 *noun*
= portrait, picture, image
xiàng...yíyàng/yìbān 像...一样/一般 = resemble..., be like...

xiàngpí 橡皮 *noun*
= rubber, eraser

xiāofèi 消费 *verb*
= consume
xiāofèipǐn 消费品 = consumer goods

xiāohuà 消化
1 *verb*
= digest
2 *noun*
= digestion

xiāomiè 消灭 *verb*
= wipe out, extinguish, destroy

xiāoshī 消失 *verb*
= vanish, disappear

xiāoxi 消息 *noun*
= news, information

xiǎo 小 *adjective*
• = small, little
• = young
• = unimportant, trifling

xiǎochī 小吃 *noun*
= snack, refreshments

xiǎoháir 小孩儿 *noun*
= child, children

xiǎohuǒzi 小伙子 *noun*
= young man, lad

xiǎojie 小姐 *noun*
= young lady, Miss, daughter

xiǎomài 小麦 *noun*
= wheat

xiǎomàibù 小卖部 *noun*
= small shop, snack bar

xiǎopéngyǒu 小朋友 *noun*
= child, children

xiǎoqì 小气 *adjective*
= mean, stingy, petty

xiǎoshí 小时 *noun*
= hour

xiǎoshuō 小说 *noun*
= fiction, short story, novel

xiǎotōu 小偷 *noun*
= petty thief, sneak thief, pilferer

xiǎoxīn 小心
1 *adjective*
= careful, cautious
2 *verb*
= be careful, look out, take care

xiǎoxué 小学 *noun*
= elementary/primary school

xiǎozǔ 小组 *noun*
= group

xiǎode 晓得 *verb*
= know

xiàoyuán 校园 *noun*
= school yard, campus

xiàozhǎng 校长 *noun*
(*of a school, college, or university*) = headmaster, principal, president

xiào 笑 *verb*
• = smile, laugh
• = laugh at, make fun of, ridicule

xiàohua 笑话
1 *noun*
= joke, funny story
2 *verb*
= laugh at, ridicule, make fun of

xiàoguǒ 效果 *noun*
= effect, result

xiàolǜ 效率 *noun*
= efficiency

xiē 些
1 *determiner*
= some, a few
ná xiē shuǐguǒ lái 拿些水果来 = bring some fruit
2 *adverb*
= a little, a bit

xiē 歇 *verb*
= rest, have a rest

xiéhuì 协会 *noun*
= association, society

xié 斜 *adjective*
= slanting, inclined, askew

xié 鞋 *noun*
= shoes
xiézi 鞋子 = shoes

xiě 写 *verb*
= write, compose

xiězuò 写作 *noun*
= writing

xiě 血 ▸ **xuè** 血

xièxie 谢谢 *verb*
= thank you, thanks

xīn 心 *noun*
• = heart
• = mind, feeling
• = middle, centre

xīndé 心得 *noun*
= insight, understanding

xīnqíng 心情 *noun*
= feelings, mood, state of mind

xīnzàng 心脏 *noun*
(*the organ in the body*) = heart
xīnzàng bìng 心脏病 = heart disease

xīnkǔ 辛苦
1 *adjective*
= laborious, hard, hard-working
2 *adverb*
= with great difficulty and effort, laboriously
3 *verb*
= work very hard, undergo many hardships, take trouble
4 *noun*
= hardship, laborious work

xīnshǎng 欣赏 *verb*
= enjoy, appreciate

xīn 新
1 *adjective*
• = new, fresh, recent
• = up-to-date, modern

2 *adverb*
= newly, recently, freshly

xīnláng 新郎 *noun*
= bridegroom

xīnnián 新年 *noun*
= New Year

xīnniáng 新娘 *noun*
= bride

xīnwén 新闻 *verb*
= news
xīnwénjiè 新闻界 = the press

xīnxiān 新鲜 *adjective*
= fresh, new

xìn 信
1 *noun*
- = letter, mail, correspondence
- = message, information

2 *verb*
= believe, believe in

xìnfēng 信封 *noun*
= envelope

xìnrèn 信任
1 *noun*
= trust, confidence
2 *verb*
= trust, have confidence in

xìnxī 信息 *noun*
= information, news, message

xìnxīn 信心 *noun*
= confidence, faith

xīngfèn 兴奋 *adjective*
= excited

xīngqī 星期 *noun*
= week
xīngqī [yī | èr | sān | sì | wǔ | liù] 星期 [一 | 二 | 三 | 四 | 五 | 六] = [Monday | Tuesday | Wednesday | Thursday | Friday | Saturday]

xīngqīrì 星期日, **xīngqītiān** 星期天 *noun*
= Sunday

xīngxīng 星星 *noun*
= star

xíng 行

> **!** *Can also be pronounced* **háng** *with a different meaning.*

1 *verb*
- = go, walk, travel
- = do, carry out, practise

2 *adjective*
- = satisfactory, all right, OK
  zhèyàng zuò xíng bù xíng? 这样做行不行? = is it all right to do (it) this way?
- = capable, proficient, competent

3 *noun*
- = trip, journey
- = conduct, behaviour, actions

xíngdòng 行动
1 *verb*
= move, act, take action
2 *noun*
= movement, physical movement, action

xíngli 行李 *noun*
= luggage, baggage

xíngrén 行人 *noun*
= pedestrian

xíngshǐ 行驶 *verb*
(*when talking about buses, trains, ships, etc.*) = travel, go, run

xíngwéi 行为 *noun*
= behaviour, action, conduct

xíngchéng 形成 *verb*
- = take shape, take form, form into
- = develop, evolve, form

xíngróng 形容 *verb*
= describe

xíngshì 形式 *noun*
= form

xíngshì 形势 *noun*
- = situation, circumstances
- = terrain, lie of the land

xíngxiàng 形象 *noun*
= form, appearance, image

xíngzhuàng 形状 *noun*
= shape, form, appearance

xǐng 醒 *verb*
- = wake up, awaken, be awakened
- = regain consciousness, sober up

xìngqù 兴趣 *noun*
= interest, interest in
tā duì lìshǐ yǒu/gǎn xìngqù 她对历史有/感兴趣 = she is interested in history

xìngfú 幸福
1 *adjective*
= happy
2 *noun*
= happiness, well-being

xìnghǎo 幸好 ▶ **xìngkuī** 幸亏

xìngkuī 幸亏 *adverb*
= fortunately, luckily

xìngyùn 幸运
1 *adjective*
= fortunate, lucky
2 *noun*
= good luck, good fortune

xìng 性 *noun*
- = quality, nature, character
- (*used at the end of many words to make them nouns*)
  = -ity, -ness
  kěnéngxìng 可能性 = probability
  chuàngzàoxìng 创造性 = creativity
- = sex, gender
  [**nán** | **nǚ**] **xìng** [男 | 女] 性 = the [male | female] sex

xìngbié 性别 *noun*
= sex, gender

xìnggé 性格 *noun*
= personality, character, temperament

xìngzhì 性质 *noun*
= quality, nature

xìng 姓
1 *verb*
= be surnamed
tā xìng Zhào 他姓赵 = his surname is Zhao
2 *noun*
= surname, family name

xìngmíng 姓名 *noun*
= surname and given name, full name

xiōngdì 兄弟 *noun*
= brothers
xiōngdì jiěmèi 兄弟姐妹 = brothers and sisters, siblings

xiōng 胸 *noun*
= chest, thorax, breast

xióng 雄 *adjective*
- (*when referring to animals*) = male
- (*in reference to humans*) = strong, powerful, virile

xióngwěi 雄伟 *adjective*
= magnificent, imposing, grand

xióng 熊 *noun*
= bear

xióngmāo 熊猫 *noun*
= panda

xiūxi 休息 *verb*
= rest, take a rest

xiū 修 *verb*
- = repair, mend, maintain
- = build, construct
- = study, cultivate a knowledge of

xiūgǎi 修改
1 *verb*
= correct, revise, amend
2 *noun*
= revision, modification

xiūlǐ 修理 *verb*
= repair, mend

xiù(zi) 袖(子) *noun*
= sleeve

xūxīn 虚心
1 *adjective*
= humble, modest
2 *adverb*
= humbly, with humility

xūyào 需要
1 *verb*
= need, require
2 *noun*
= need, demand

xǔ 许 *verb*
- = allow, permit, give consent
- = promise, pledge

xǔduō 许多 *determiner*
= a lot of, many, much

xùshù 叙述 *verb*
= narrate, recount

xuānbù 宣布
1 *verb*
= declare, proclaim
2 *noun*
= declaration, proclamation

xuānchuán 宣传
1 *verb*
= propagate, propagandize
2 *noun*
= propaganda, dissemination

xuǎn 选
1 *verb*
- = choose, select
- = elect

2 *noun*
= selection, election

xuǎnjǔ 选举
1 *verb*
= elect, vote

2 *noun*
= election
xuǎnjǔ quán 选举权 = the right to vote

xuǎnzé 选择
1 *verb*
= choose, pick out, select
2 *noun*
= selection, choice

xué 学
1 *verb*
- = study, learn
- = imitate

2 *noun*
- = school, institution of learning, level of schooling
  [**xiǎo** | **zhōng** | **dà**] **xué** [小 | 中 | 大] 学 = [primary or elementary school | secondary or high school | college or university]
- (*added to fields of study, similar to the English ending* **-ology**) = study of, field of
  [**wén** | **shù** | **rénlèi**] **xué** [文 | 数 | 人类] 学 = [literature | mathematics | anthropology]
- = learning, knowledge

xuéfèi 学费 *noun*
= school fees, tuition

xuéqī 学期 *noun*
= term, semester

xuésheng 学生 *noun*
= student, pupil

xuéshù 学术
1 *noun*
= learning, scholarship, academic research
2 *adjective*
= academic, learned
xuéshùjiè 学术界 = academic circles

xuéwen 学问 *noun*
= scholarship, learning

xuéxí 学习 *verb*
= study, learn

xuéxiào 学校 *noun*
= school

xuéyuàn 学院 *noun*
= academic institution, college, institute

xuézhě 学者 *noun*
= scholar, learned person

xuě 雪 *noun*
= snow
xià xuě le 下雪了 = it's snowing

xuěhuā 雪花 *noun*
= snowflake

xuè 血 *noun*

> **!** *Can also be pronounced* **xiě**.

= blood

xuèyè 血液 *noun*
= blood

xúnzhǎo 寻找 *verb*
= look for, seek, search for

xúnwèn 询问 *verb*
= inquire, ask about

xùnliàn 训练 *verb*
= instruct, train, drill

xùnsù 迅速
1 *adjective*
= fast, rapid
2 *adverb*
= fast, rapidly, at high speed

yā 压
1 *verb*
- = press down, apply pressure, crush
- (*when speaking of emotions, disorder, rebellion, etc.*) = control, suppress

2 *noun*
= pressure

yālì 压力 *noun*
= pressure

yāpò 压迫
1 *verb*
= oppress, repress, constrict
2 *noun*
= oppression, repression

yā 呀 *exclamation*

> **!** *Can also be pronounced* **ya** 呀 *in a neutral tone with a different meaning.*

(*indicating surprise*) = ah! oh!

yā(zi) 鸭(子) *noun*
= duck

yá 牙 *noun*
= tooth, teeth

yáshuā 牙刷 *noun*
= toothbrush

Yàzhōu 亚洲 *noun*
= Asia

yān 烟 *noun*
- = smoke
- = cigarette, tobacco

yángé 严格
1 *adjective*
= stern, strict, rigorous
2 *adverb*
= strictly, rigidly

yánsù 严肃 *adjective*
= solemn, serious, earnest

yánzhòng 严重 *adjective*
(*when talking about a situation, a condition, health, etc.*) = serious, grave, critical

yáncháng 延长
1 *verb*
= extend, prolong, lengthen
2 *noun*
= prolongation, extension

yán 沿 *preposition*
= along, alongside

yánjiū 研究
1 *verb*
- = study, do research
- (*for problems, suggestions, applications*) = consider, discuss

2 *noun*
= research, study
yánjiūhuì 研究会 = research association
yánjiūshēng 研究生 = research student, postgraduate student
yánjiūsuǒ 研究所 = research institute
yánjiūyuán 研究员 = research fellow
yánjiūyuàn 研究院 = research institute, academy

yán 盐 *noun*
= salt

yánsè 颜色 *noun*
= colour

yǎn 眼 *noun*
- = eye
- = hole, opening

yǎnjing 眼睛 *noun*
= eye, eyes

yǎnjìng 眼镜 *noun*
= glasses, spectacles

yǎnlèi 眼泪 *noun*
= tears

yǎnqián 眼前 *adverb*
- = in front of one's eyes, before one's eyes
- = at the present moment, momentarily

yǎn 演 *verb*
(*when speaking of a play, film, show*)
= perform, act, show

yǎnchū 演出
1 *verb*
(*when talking about a play, film, show*)
= perform, show, put on
2 *noun*
= performance, production

yǎnyuán 演员 *noun*
= actor, actress, performer

yàn 咽 *verb*
= swallow

yànhuì 宴会 *noun*
= banquet, feast

yáng 羊 *noun*
= sheep, goat

yángròu 羊肉 *noun*
= mutton, lamb

yángguāng 阳光 *noun*
= sunlight, sunshine

yǎng 仰 *verb*
- = look up, face upward
- = look up to, admire, respect

yǎng 养
1 *verb*
- (*as dependents*) = nurture, support, provide for
- (*as animals, flowers, etc.*) = raise, keep, grow
- = give birth to

2 *adjective*
(*as a foster parent, etc.*) = foster

yàng 样
1 *measure word* ▶ **157**
(*for things in general*) = kind, sort, type
2 *noun*
- = way, manner
- = form, appearance, shape
- = pattern, model, sample

yàngzi 样子 *noun*
- = form, appearance, shape
- = pattern, sample, model
- (*describing how something or someone looks*)
  tā xiàng shì bìngle de yàngzi 她象是病了的样子 = she has the appearance of being ill
- = manner, air

yāoqiú 要求

> ! *The word* yāo 要 *can also be pronounced* yào *with a different meaning.*

1 *verb*
= demand, request, ask for
2 *noun*
= demand, request, need

yāo 腰 *noun*
- (*of a person or a garment*) = waist
- (*of a person*) = back, small of the back

yāoqǐng 邀请
1 *verb*
(*formal word*) = invite
2 *noun*
= invitation

yáo 摇 *verb*
- = shake, wag, wave
- = sway back and forth, rock
- (*when talking about a boat*) = row
- (*when talking about a bell*) = ring

yǎo 咬 *verb*
= bite, snap at

yào 药 *noun*
= medicine, drug, certain chemicals

yào 要
1 *verb*
- = want, wish, desire
- = need, must
- (*when talking about an amount of time*) = need, take
  dào Lúndūn qù yào yíge xiǎoshí 到伦敦去要一个小时 = it takes an hour to get to London
- = demand, request
- = beg
- = need to, must, should
  nǐ yào xiǎoxīn 你要小心 = you must be careful
- (*when talking about what one expects will happen*) = will, be going to
  tiān kuài yào hēi le 天快要黑了 = it's going to get dark soon

2 *conjunction*
- (*short for* yàoshi 要是) = if
  nǐ yào bú qù, tā huì hěn shīwàng 你要不去，她会很失望 = if you don't go, she'll be very disappointed

3 *adjective*
= important

yàobu(rán) 要不(然) *conjunction*
= if not, or else, otherwise

yàobushi 要不是 *conjunction*
= if it were not for, but for

yàojǐn 要紧 *adjective*
- = important
- (*as an illness*) = critical, serious

yàoshi 要是 *conjunction*
= if, suppose, in case
yàoshi...jiù...(le) 要是…就…(了) = if...then...
yàoshi kāichē qù jiù kěyǐ fāngbiàn yìxiē 要是开车去就可以方便一些 = if you drive it is slightly more convenient

yàoshi 钥匙 *adverb*
(*to a lock*) = key

yéye 爷爷 *noun*
- = paternal grandfather, grandpa
- (*a polite and respectful way of addressing an old man, used by children*) = grandpa

yě 也 *adverb*
- = also, too
- (*indicating concession*) = still
  nǐ gěi wǒ qián, wǒ yě bú qù 你给我钱，我也不去 = I won't go even if you give me money
  yě bù 也不 = not either, neither
  tā bú huì tán qín, yě bú huì chànggē 他不会弹琴，也不会唱歌 = he can neither play the piano nor sing

yěxǔ 也许 *adverb*
= maybe, perhaps, possibly

yěcān 野餐 *noun*
= picnic

yèwù 业务 *noun*
= business affairs, professional work

yèyú 业余
1 *adjective*
- = extracurricular, done outside business hours
  yèyú huódòng 业余活动 = extracurricular activities
- = amateur

2 *adverb*
= in one's spare time

yèzi 叶子 *noun*
(*of a plant*) = leaf, leaves

yè 页 *noun*
(*in a book*) = page, leaf

yè 夜 *noun*
= night, evening

yèli 夜里 *adverb*
= at night, during the night, in the night

yèwǎn 夜晚 *noun*
= night, evening

yī 一

> **!** *The tone on* yi 一 *changes, depending on the tone of the word that follows it. It is pronounced* yì *before words in first, second, and third tone, but* yí *before the fourth tone. When used to count numbers,* yi 一 *has the first tone. Because the tone changes for* yi 一 *do not indicate any difference in meaning, but only in pronunciation, combinations beginning with* yi 一 *are listed in alphabetical order below, regardless of tone.* ▶ **vii**

1 *number*
= one
2 *determiner*
- = a, an
- = each, per

3 *adjective*
- = single, alone, only one
- = the same, together
- = whole, all, throughout

yí yè 一夜 = the whole night
4 *adverb*
(*indicating a brief action or one taken lightly*) = briefly
qǐng nǐ kàn yí kàn 请你看一看 = please take a look
5 *conjunction*
- = once
- = as soon as

tā yí kàn jiù xiào le 他一看就笑了 = he laughed as soon as he saw it
yī...jiù... 一...就... = as soon as
yī...yě... 一...也... (*used with the negative particle* bù 不 *or* méi 没) = (not) slightly, (not) at all
tā yíge Hànzì yě bú rènshi 他一个汉字也不认识 = he doesn't know a single Chinese character

yìbān 一般
1 *adjective*
- = alike, the same, just as
- = general, common, ordinary
- = so so

2 *adverb*
- = the same as, similarly
  tā hé tā gēge yìbān gāo 她和她哥哥一般高 = she is as tall as her elder brother
- = generally, in general, ordinarily

yíbàn 一半 *noun*
= half, one-half

yíbèizi 一辈子
1 *adverb*
= throughout one's life, all one's life
2 *noun*
= lifetime

yìbiān 一边 *noun*
= one side
yìbiān...yìbiān... 一边...一边... (*indicating two simultaneous actions*) = at the same time, simultaneously
háizimen yìbiān zǒulù, yìbiān chànggē 孩子们一边走路，一边唱歌 = the children are singing while they are walking

yídào 一道 *adverb*
= together, side by side, alongside

yìdiǎnr 一点儿
1 *adverb*
= a bit, a little
wǒ yìdiǎnr dōu bù zhīdào 我一点儿都不知道 = I have not the faintest idea
2 *pronoun*
= a little
zhǐ shèngxia zhème yìdiǎnr, gòu yòng ma? 只剩下这么一点儿，够用吗？ = there's so little left, is it enough for the present purposes?
3 *determiner*
= a little, some
yìdiǎnr fàn 一点儿饭 = a little rice

yídìng 一定
1 *adjective*
- = certain, given, particular
- = fixed, definite, specified
- = proper, fair, due

2 *adverb*
= certainly, definitely, surely

yì fāngmiàn 一方面 *noun*
= one side

yì fāngmiàn... (lìng) yì fāngmiàn... 一方面...(另)一方面... *adverb*
= on the one hand...on the other hand...; for one thing...for another...

yígòng 一共 *adverb*
= altogether, in all, in total

yíhuìr 一会儿 *adverb*
= in a moment, for a little while, shortly
yíhuìr...yíhuìr... 一会儿... 一会儿... = one moment..., the next...

yíkuàir 一块儿 *adverb*
= together

yílù 一路 *adverb*
= all the way, on the journey
yílù píng'ān 一路平安 = have a pleasant journey, have a good trip
yílù shùnfēng 一路顺风 = have a pleasant journey, have a good trip

yìqí 一齐 *adverb*
= together, at the same time, sumultaneously

yìqǐ 一起 *adverb*
= together, in the same place

yíqiè 一切
1 *determiner*
= all, every, whole
2 *pronoun*
= all, everything, the whole thing

yìshēng 一生 *noun*
= all one's life, one's whole life

yìshí 一时 *adverb*
- = for a period of time
- = for the moment, for a short while, temporarily
- = by chance, accidentally, it just so happened that

yìshí...yìshí... 一时... 一时... = now... now..., ...one moment and...the next

yìtóng 一同 *adverb*
= together, at the same time and place

yì tiān dào wǎn 一天到晚 *adverb*
= all day long, from morning till night, from dawn to dusk

yíxià(r) 一下(儿) *adverb*
- (*indicating short duration*) = once, a bit, for a short while
- (*indicating a sudden change*) = all at once, all of a sudden, suddenly

yíxiàzi 一下子 *adverb*
= suddenly, all at once

yìxiē 一些 *determiner*
= some, a few, a little

yíyàng 一样
1 *adjective*
= alike, the same, similar
2 *adverb*
= equally, similarly

yīyuè 一月 *noun*
= January

yìzhí 一直 *adverb*
- = continuously, consistently, all the time
- = straight, straight on

yìzhí méi...guo 一直没... 过 = have never...

yízhì 一致
1 *adjective*
= consistent, the same, identical
2 *adverb*
= consistently, unanimously

yīfu 衣服 *noun*
= clothes, clothing, dress

yīguì 衣柜 *noun*
= wardrobe

yīkào 依靠
1 *verb*
= depend upon, rely on
2 *noun*
= dependence, support

yīrán 依然 *adverb*
= still, as before

yīzhào 依照 *preposition*
= in accordance with, in the light of

yīshēng 医生 *noun*
= doctor, physician

yīwùshì 医务室, **yīwùsuǒ** 医务所 *noun*
= clinic

yīxué 医学 *noun*
(*as a field of study*) = medicine

yīyuàn 医院 *noun*
= hospital

yíqì 仪器 *noun*
(*usually for scientific use*) = apparatus, equipment, instrument

yí 姨 *noun*
= aunt on one's mother's side, mother's sister

yí 移 *verb*
- = change position, move, shift
- = change, alter

yídòng 移动 *verb*
= move, shift

yíhàn 遗憾
1 *verb*
= regret
2 *noun*
= regret, pity

yíwèn 疑问 *noun*
= question, doubt, query

yǐ(jīng) 已(经) *adverb*
= already

yǐ 以
1 *preposition*
- = according to
- (*indicating implement, instrument, etc.*) = with, using

2 *adverb*
(*indicating purpose*) = in order to, so as to
3 *verb*
- = use, take
- = take, consider
yǐ...wéi... 以…为…= take...as..., consider...as...

yǐbiàn 以便 *conjunction*
= in order that, so that, in order to

yǐhòu 以后
1 *preposition*
= after
2 *adverb*
= later, hereafter, afterwards
3 *conjunction*
= after

yǐjí 以及 *conjunction*
= and, as well as, along with

yǐlái 以来 *preposition*
- (*sometimes the time-word or cut-off point is preceded by* **zì** 自 *or* **zìcóng** 自从, *meaning* **from**) = since, after, until now
- (*when it follows a quantity of time*) = during the past..., in the past..., for the past...
jǐ qiān nián yǐlái 几千年以来 = for several thousand years

yǐnèi 以内 *preposition*
= within, less than

yǐqián 以前
1 *preposition*
= before, prior to
2 *adverb*
= previously, formerly, ago
3 *conjunction*
= before

yǐshàng 以上
1 *preposition*
= over, above
2 *adverb*
= above

yǐwài 以外 *preposition*
- = outside, beyond
- (*when used in the pattern* **chú(le)...yǐwài, ...dōu...** 除(了)…以外, …都…) = except, except for
chú(le) tā yǐwài, wǒmen dōu bú huì zuò 除了他以外, 我们都不会做 = none of us can do it except him
- (*when used in the pattern* **chú(le)...yǐwài, ...hái...** 除(了)…以外, …还…) = besides, apart from, in addition to
chú(le) Běijīng yǐwài, wǒmen hái qùle Shànghǎi 除了北京以外, 我们还去了上海 = apart from Beijing, we also went to Shanghai

yǐwéi 以为 *verb*
- = think, regard, consider
- = thought, used to think

> **!** *Note that in this use,* **yǐwéi** 以为 *means that one originally thought something was true, but later found it to be false.*

yǐxià 以下
1 *preposition*
= below, under
2 *adverb*
= below

yǐzhì 以致 *conjunction*
(*when indicating an unpleasant consequence*) = so that, with the result that, consequently

yǐzi 椅子 *noun*
= chair

yì 亿 *number*
= hundred million, 100,000,000
shíyì 十亿 = one billion

yìshù 艺术
1 *noun*
- = art
- = skill, technique, craft

2 *adjective*
= artistic, in good taste
yìshùpǐn 艺术品 = work of art
yìshùjiā 艺术家 = artist

yìlùn 议论
1 *verb*
= discuss, comment, talk
2 *noun*
= opinion, discussion, comment

yìcháng 异常
1 *adjective*
= unusual, abnormal, exceptional
2 *adverb*
= unusually, exceedingly, extremely

yìjiàn 意见 *noun*
= idea, opinion, view

yìsi 意思 *noun*
- = meaning, idea, theme
- = opinion, wish, desire
- = interest, fun

yǒu yìsi 有意思 = interesting, enjoyable

yìwài 意外
1 *adjective*
= unexpected, unforeseen, surprising
2 *noun*
= accident, mishap, unexpected development

yìwèizhe 意味着 *verb*
= signify, mean, imply

yìyì 意义 *noun*
= significance, meaning

yìzhì 意志 *noun*
= will, volition, will power

yīncǐ 因此 *adverb*
= therefore, for this reason

yīn'ér 因而 *adverb*
= because of this, thus, as a result

yīnsù 因素 *noun*
= element, factor

yīnwèi 因为 *conjunction*
= because, since, as

yīn 阴 *adjective*
= cloudy, overcast, shady

yīnyuè 音乐 *noun*
= music
yīnyuèhuì 音乐会 = concert

yín 银 *noun*
(*the metal or the colour*) = silver

yínháng 银行 *noun*
= bank

yǐnqǐ 引起 *verb*
= cause, give rise to, bring about

yǐnliào 饮料 *noun*
= drink, beverage

yìn 印
1 *verb*
= print, engrave, replicate
2 *noun*
- = imprint, print, mark
- = stamp, chop, seal

yìnshuā 印刷 *verb*
= print

yìnxiàng 印象 *noun*
= impression

yīngbàng 英镑 *noun*
= British pound

Yīnggélán 英格兰 *noun*
= England

Yīngguó 英国 *noun*
= Britain, the United Kingdom

Yīngwén 英文 *noun*
= English language (usually written)

yīngxióng 英雄
1 *noun*
= hero, heroine
2 *adjective*
= heroic

yīngyǒng 英勇 *adjective*
= heroic, brave, valiant

Yīngyǔ 英语 *noun*
= English language (usually spoken)

yīng(dāng) 应(当) *verb*

> **!** *The word* yīng 应 *can also be pronounced* yìng *with a different meaning.*

= should, ought to

yīnggāi 应该 *verb*
= should, ought to

yīng'ér 婴儿 *noun*
= baby, infant

yíngjiē 迎接 *verb*
= welcome, greet, meet

Y

yíngyǎng 营养 *noun*
= nutrition, nourishment

yíngyè 营业 *verb*
= do business

yíng 赢 *verb*
= gain, win, beat

yǐngdié 影碟 *noun*
= DVD

yǐngdié bōfàngjī 影碟播放机 *noun*
= DVD player

yǐngxiǎng 影响
1 *verb*
= influence, affect
shòu...yǐngxiǎng 受... 影响 = be influenced by...
2 *noun*
= influence

yǐngzi 影子 *noun*
= shadow, reflection

yìngyòng 应用

> **!** *The word* yìng 应 *can also be pronounced* yīng *with a different meaning.*

1 *verb*
= apply, use, make use of
2 *adjective*
= applied
3 *noun*
= use, application

yìng 硬
1 *adjective*
= hard, stiff, tough
2 *adverb*
= by force, stubbornly

yōngbào 拥抱 *verb*
= hug, embrace

yōnghù 拥护 *verb*
= support, endorse

yōngjǐ 拥挤
1 *verb*
= crowd, push
2 *adjective*
= crowded, packed

yǒngyuǎn 永远 *adverb*
= always, forever

yǒnggǎn 勇敢 *adjective*
= brave, daring, courageous

yǒngqì 勇气 *noun*
= bravery, courage

yòng 用
1 *verb*
= use, employ, apply
2 *preposition*
= with, using
3 *noun*
= use, usefulness
[**yǒu** | **méi**] **yòng** [有 | 没] 用 = [useful | useless]
yòng bu zháo 用不着 = no need to, have no use

yòngchu 用处 *noun*
= use, application

yònggōng 用功 *adjective*
= diligent, studious, hard-working

yònglì 用力
1 *verb*
= exert one's strength
2 *adverb*
= with all one's strength

yōudiǎn 优点 *noun*
= good point, strong point, merit

yōuliáng 优良 *adjective*
= fine, good

yōuměi 优美 *adjective*
= beautiful, graceful, exquisite

yōuxiù 优秀 *adjective*
= outstanding, excellent

yōujiǔ 悠久 *adjective*
= long, long-standing

yóuqí 尤其 *adverb*
= especially
yóuqí shì 尤其是 = especially

yóu 由
1 *preposition*
= from, by, through
2 *verb*
• = follow, obey
• = let, allow

yóuyú 由于 *preposition*
= because of, due to the fact that

yóudìyuán 邮递员 *noun*
= postman, postwoman

yóujú 邮局 *noun*
= post office

yóupiào 邮票 *noun*
= postage stamp

yóuyù 犹豫
1 *verb*
= hesitate
2 *adjective*
= hesitant, undecided

3 *noun*
= hesitation

yóu 油 *noun*
= oil, fat, grease

yóuqī 油漆 *noun*
= paint

yóukè 游客 ▸ **yóurén** 游人

yóulǎn 游览 *verb*
= tour, visit, go sightseeing

yóurén 游人 *noun*
= tourist, sightseer, excursionist

yóuxì 游戏 *noun*
(*for recreation and amusement*) = game

yóuyǒng 游泳
1 *verb*
= swim
2 *noun*
= swimming

yóuyǒngchí 游泳池 *noun*
= swimming pool

yǒuhǎo 友好 *adjective*
= friendly

yǒuyì 友谊 *noun*
= friendship

yǒu 有
1 *verb*
- = have, possess
- = there is, there are, exist
- (*when making an estimate of age, height, weight, degree, distance, etc.*) = be about as much as
  tā yǒu nǐ nàme gāo 她有你那么高 = she is about your height
- (*used with a noun to make an adjective*) = having..., with...
  yǒu yì 有意 = intentional
- = have a good deal of, have much
  yǒu xuéwèn 有学问 = learned, knowledgeable
- = take place, happen, occur
  nàr yǒu hěn dà de biànhuà 那儿有很大的变化 = great changes have taken place there

2 *determiner*
= some
yǒu rén 有人 = some, some people

yǒude 有的
1 *determiner*
= some
yǒude rén 有的人 = some people
2 *pronoun*
= some, some people
yǒude...yǒude... 有的..., 有的... = some..., others...
yǒude xǐhuan kāfēi, yǒude xǐhuan chá 有的喜欢咖啡, 有的喜欢茶 = some like coffee, others like tea

yǒu(de) shíhòu 有(的)时候 *adverb*
= sometimes, at times

yǒudeshì 有的是 *verb*
= have plenty of, there's no lack of
yǒudeshì shíjiān 有的是时间 = there's plenty of time

yǒu diǎn(r) 有点(儿)
1 *verb*
= there is a little/some, have a little/some
2 *adverb*
= somewhat, a little, a bit

yǒuguān 有关
1 *verb*
= be related to, have something to do with, concern
2 *adjective*
= relevant, concerned

yǒulì 有利 *adjective*
= beneficial, advantageous

yǒulì 有力 *adjective*
= strong, powerful, energetic

yǒumíng 有名 *adjective*
= famous, well-known

yǒuqù 有趣 *adjective*
= interesting, amusing, fascinating

yǒu shí(hòu) 有时(候)
▸ **yǒu(de) shíhòu** 有(的)时候

yǒuxiàn 有限 *adjective*
= limited

yǒuxiào 有效 *adjective*
= effective, efficient, valid

yǒuxiē 有些
1 *pronoun*
= some, a few, several
2 *determiner*
= some, a few, several

yǒu yìdiǎn(r) 有一点(儿)
▸ **yǒu diǎn(r)** 有点(儿)

yǒu yìsi 有意思 *adjective*
= interesting, enjoyable, meaningful

yǒu yòng 有用 *adjective*
= useful

yòu 又 *adverb*
- = also, in addition
- = again
- = however

  wǒ xiǎng gěi tā xiě xìn, kě yòu bù zhīdào tāde dìzhǐ 我想给她写信, 可又不知道她的地址 = I want to write her a letter but I don't know her address

  yòu...yòu... 又... 又... = both...and..., on the one hand... on the other...

yòu 右
1 *noun*
- = right, the right-hand side, the right
- (*when speaking of politics*) = right-wing

2 *adjective*
  = right, right-hand

yòubian 右边 *noun*
  = right-hand side, right side

yòu'ér 幼儿 *noun*
  = child, infant
  yòu'éryuán 幼儿园 = pre-school, nursery school, kindergarten

yú 于 *preposition*
- = in, on, at
- = from, by
- = to, than

yúshì 于是 *adverb*
  = consequently, thus, as a result

yú 鱼 *noun*
  = fish

yúlè 娱乐 *noun*
  = entertainment, amusement, recreation

yúkuài 愉快 *adjective*
  = happy, pleased, joyful

yǔ 与
1 *preposition*
  = with, to, for
2 *conjunction*
  = and

yǔmáoqiú 羽毛球 *noun*
- = badminton
- = shuttlecock

yǔ 雨 *noun*
  = rain

yǔsǎn 雨伞 *noun*
  = umbrella

yǔyī 雨衣 *noun*
  = raincoat

yǔdiào 语调 *noun*
  = intonation, sentence intonation

yǔfǎ 语法 *noun*
  = grammar

yǔqì 语气 *noun*
  = tone, tone of voice, manner of speaking

yǔyán 语言 *noun*
  = language

yǔyīn 语音 *noun*
  = pronunciation

yǔyīn yóujiàn 语音邮件 *noun*
  = voicemail

yùmǐ 玉米 *noun*
  = maize, corn

yùshì 浴室 *noun*
  = bathroom, shower room

yùbào 预报
1 *noun*
  = forecast
2 *verb*
  = forecast

yùbèi 预备 *verb*
  = prepare, get ready

yùfáng 预防 *verb*
  = prevent, take precautions against

yùxí 预习 *verb*
  (*usually referring to an academic lesson*) = prepare

yù 遇, **yùdào** 遇到 *verb*
  = meet, encounter

yùjiàn 遇见 *verb*
  = meet, meet by chance

yùwàng 欲望 *noun*
  = desire, wish, lust

yuán 元 *noun*
  = dollar, *yuan*

Yuándàn 元旦 *noun*
  = New Year's Day

yuánxiāo 元宵 *noun*
  = sweet dumplings made of glutinous rice flour
  Yuánxiāojié 元宵节 = Lantern Festival (the 15th of the first month in the lunar year)

yuán 员 *noun*
  (*of a profession, party, or other organisation*) = member, personnel

[dǎng | hǎi | chuīshì | shòuhuò] **yuán** [党 | 海 | 炊事 | 售货] 员 = [party member | sailor | cook | shop assistant]

yuánlái 原来
1 *adjective*
= original, former, previous
2 *adverb*
- = it turns out that, as a matter of fact
- = originally, in the first place

yuánliàng 原谅 *verb*
= forgive, excuse, pardon

yuánliào 原料 *noun*
= raw material, source material

yuányīn 原因 *noun*
= cause, reason

yuánzé 原则 *noun*
= principle
yuánzé shang 原则上 = in principle

yuán 圆
1 *adjective*
- = round, circular

2 *noun*
- = circle
- (*a unit of Chinese money*) = *yuan*

yuánzhūbǐ 圆珠笔 *noun*
= biro, ball-point pen

yuán 园 *noun*
= garden, park

yuǎn 远 *adjective*
= far away, distant, remote

yuàn 院 *noun*
- = courtyard, compound
- (*public facility*)
[yī | diànyǐng | bówù] **yuàn** [医 | 电影 | 博物] 院 = [hospital | cinema | museum]

yuànzhǎng 院长 *noun*
(*of an academy or organization*) = director, president, chairman

yuànzi 院子 *noun*
= court, yard, compound

yuànwàng 愿望 *noun*
= hope, wish

yuàn(yì) 愿(意) *verb*
- = wish, would like, want
- = be willing, be ready

yuē 约
1 *verb*
- = make an appointment, arrange a meeting, set a time to meet

2 *adverb*
= about, approximately
3 *noun*
- = agreement, contract, treaty
- = appointment, date

yuēhuì 约会 *noun*
= engagement, appointment, meeting

yuè 月 *noun*
- = moon
- = month

yuèliang 月亮 *noun*
= moon, moonlight

yuèqiú 月球 *noun*
(*as an astronomical body*) = moon

yuèqì 乐器 *noun*
= musical instrument

yuèdú 阅读 *verb*
= read

yuèlǎnshì 阅览室 *noun*
= reading room

yuè...yuè... 越... 越... *adverb*
= the more...the more...
xuéxí yuè nǔlì, chéngjī yuè hǎo 学习越努力, 成绩越好 = the harder one studies the better one's marks

yuèlái yuè... 越来越... *adverb*
= getting more and more..., becoming more and more...
tiānqì yuèlái yuè rè 天气越来越热 = the weather is getting hotter

yún 云 *noun*
= cloud

yǔnxǔ 允许 *verb*
= allow, permit, give permission to

yùn 运
1 *verb*
= transport, ship
2 *noun*
= luck, fate

yùndòng 运动
1 *verb*
= move, exercise, engage in sports
2 *noun*
- = movement, motion
- = sports, athletics, exercise
- (*social or political*) = movement, campaign

yùndònghuì 运动会 *noun*
= sports meet, athletic contest, games

yùndòngyuán 运动员 *noun*
= athlete

yùnqi 运气 *noun*
= fortune, luck

yùnshū 运输
1 *verb*
= transport, move, ship
2 *noun*
= transport, transportation, conveyance

yùnyòng 运用 *verb*
= utilize, wield, apply

Zz

zá 杂 *adjective*
= miscellaneous, mixed, varied

zájì 杂技 *noun*
= acrobatics

zázhì 杂志 *noun*
= magazine

zá 砸 *verb*
- = break, smash
- = pound, tamp

zāi 灾 *noun*
= disaster, calamity, misfortune

zāihài 灾害 *noun*
= disaster, calamity

zāinàn 灾难 *noun*
= disaster, calamity, suffering

zāi 栽 *verb*
= plant, grow

zài 再 *adverb*
- = again, once more, further
- = even, still
- (*when predicting what will happen if an action continues*) = still, continue, keep ...-ing (any) longer
  nǐ zài hēxiàqu huì hēzuì de 你再喝下去会喝醉的 = you will get drunk if you continue to drink any longer
- (*when preceded by a negative, to indicate that an action will not continue*) = (no) longer, (never) again
  wǒ bú zài shuō le 我不再说了 = I won't ever say it again
- (*when one actions follows another*) = after, then, only after
  xǐle zǎo zài qù shuìjiào 洗了澡再去睡觉 = go to bed after you've had your bath

zàijiàn 再见 *verb*
= good-bye, see you again

zàisān 再三 *adverb*
= over and over again

zàishuō 再说
1 *adverb*
= furthermore, in addition, besides
2 *verb*
= postpone until some time later

zài 在
1 *preposition*
= in, at, on
2 *verb*
- = exist, be alive, be present
- = depend on, be conditional on

3 *adverb*
= just in the midst of, in the process of doing something
tā zài mǎi cài 他在买菜 = he is shopping for food
zài...shang 在...上
- (*referring to a place*) = at, above, on top of
- (*rhetorically*) = in
  zài yuánzé shang 在原则上 = in principle

zài...xià 在...下
- (*referring to physical location*) = under, underneath
- (*referring to help, leadership, etc.*) = with, under
  zài tāde bāngzhù xià 在她的帮助下 = with her help

zài...hòu 在...后 = after
zài...lǐ 在...里 = inside
zài...nèi 在...内 = within, among, in
zài...qián 在...前 = before
zài...shí 在...时 = when
zài...wài 在...外 = out of, outside
zài...yídài 在...一带 = in the region of
zài...zhōngjiān 在...中间 = between

zàihu 在乎 *verb*
(*usually used in a negative sentence*)
= care about , mind, take seriously

zàixiàn 在线 *adjective*
= online

zàiyú 在于 *verb*
- = lie in, consist in, rest with
- = be determined by, depend on

zán(men) 咱(们) *pronoun*
(*used to include only the speaker and those directly spoken to*) = we, the two of us, you and I

zǎn 攒 *verb*
= save, accumulate, hoard

zànshí 暂时
1 *adjective*
= temporary, transient
2 *adverb*
= temporarily, for the time being

zànchéng 赞成 *verb*
= agree, agree with, approve

zànměi 赞美 *verb*
= praise, sing the praises of, eulogize

zànyáng 赞扬 *verb*
= praise, speak highly of, commend

zāng 脏 *adjective*

> **!** *This word is pronounced* zàng *when it means* viscera, organs, *as in* xīnzàng 心脏.

= dirty, filthy

zāodào 遭到 *verb*
(*usually referring to something unpleasant*) = meet with, encounter, suffer

zāoshòu 遭受 *verb*
= suffer, be subjected to

zāogāo 糟糕
1 *adjective*
= terrible, disastrous, unfortunate
2 *exclamation*
= too bad, bad luck

zǎo 早
1 *adjective*
= early
2 *adverb*
• = early
• = in advance, beforehand
• = a long time ago
3 *noun*
= morning
nǐ zǎo! 你早! = good morning!
zǎo jiù 早就 = a long while ago
zǎo yǐ 早已 = long ago, for a long time

zǎochén 早晨 *noun*
= morning, early morning

zǎofàn 早饭 *noun*
= breakfast

zǎoshang 早上 *noun*
= morning, early morning

zào 造 *verb*
• = make, create, manufacture
• = build, establish

zàojù 造句 *verb*
= make up sentences

zé 则
1 *conjunction*
(*when talking about cause, effect, or condition*) = then
2 *noun*
= rule, regulation

zébèi 责备 *verb*
= blame, reproach, reprove

zérèn 责任 *noun*
= responsibility, duty

zěnme 怎么 *adverb*
• (*in the interrogative*) = how, in what way, why
• (*in the positive*) = however, whatever
zěnme zuò dōu kěyǐ 怎么做都可以 = any way you do it is fine
• (*in the negative to indicate inadequacy*) = (not) very
bù zěnme hǎo 不怎么好 = not very good
zěnme le? 怎么了? = what? what's the matter?
zěnme huí shì? 怎么回事? = how come? how did this happen? what happened?

zěnmeyàng 怎么样 *adverb*
• (*in the interrogative*) = how, how about
• (*colloquial greeting*) = how are you? how's everything? how's it going?
• (*in the negative*) = (not) very good/well
nàbù diànyǐng bù zěnmeyàng 那部电影不怎么样 = that film is not very good

zěnyàng 怎样 *adverb*
= how, in what way

zēngjiā 增加
1 *verb*
= increase, add
2 *noun*
= increase

zēngzhǎng 增长 *verb*
= increase, grow, become larger

zhā 扎 *verb*
= pierce, prick, stick into

zhá 炸 *verb* ▶ *See also* **zhà** 炸.
= deep-fry, fry in deep fat/oil

zhà 炸 *verb* ▶ *See also* **zhá** 炸.
- = explode, burst
- = blow up, bomb, blast

zhāi 摘 *verb*
- (*for flowers, fruit, etc.*) = pick, pluck
- (*for hats, glasses, etc.*) = take off, remove

zhǎi 窄 *adjective*
= narrow, tight

zhān 粘
1 *verb*
= stick, paste, glue
2 *adjective*
= sticky

zhǎnchū 展出 *verb*
= show, put on display, exhibit

zhǎnkāi 展开 *verb*
= develop, unfold, open up

zhǎnlǎn 展览
1 *verb*
= exhibit, show, put on display
2 *noun*
= exhibition, display
zhǎnlǎnguǎn 展览馆 = exhibition centre, exhibition hall
zhǎnlǎnhuì 展览会 = exhibition
zhǎnlǎnpǐn 展览品 = item on display, exhibit

zhǎnxīn 崭新 *adjective*
= brand-new, completely new

zhàn 占 *verb*
- = occupy, seize
- = constitute, make up, hold

zhàndòu 战斗
1 *verb*
= fight, struggle
2 *noun*
= fight, struggle

zhànshèng 战胜 *verb*
= defeat, win in battle/war, overcome

zhànshi 战士 *noun*
= soldier, warrior, fighter

zhànzhēng 战争 *noun*
= war, warfare

zhàn 站
1 *verb*
= stand
2 *noun*
= station, depot, stop

zhǎn 盏 *measure word* ▶ **157**
(*for lamps*)

zhāng 张
1 *measure word* ▶ **157**
(*for flat things such as paper, paintings, tables, etc.*)
2 *verb*
= open, stretch, extend

zhāng 章 *noun*
- = chapter, section
- = rules, regulations
- = stamp, seal

zhǎng 长 ▶ *See also* **cháng** 长.
1 *verb*
- = grow, develop, form
- = gain, acquire
- = increase

2 *noun*
(*often used as a suffix*) = head, chairman, director
[**suǒ** | **shì** | **xiào**] **zhǎng** [所 | 市 | 校] 长 = [director of an institute | mayor | principal]

zhǎng 涨 *verb*
(*of water-level, prices, etc.*) = rise, go up

zhǎngwò 掌握 *verb*
= grasp, control, master

zhàng 丈 *noun*
(*measure of length*) = 3.3 metres, 10 Chinese feet

zhàngfu 丈夫 *noun*
= husband

zhāodài 招待 *verb*
(*of guests, visitors, etc.*) = entertain, receive, serve

zhāodàihuì 招待会 *noun*
= reception, welcoming party

zhāohu 招呼 *verb*
- = call, notify, tell
- = hail, greet, say hello to

xiàng/gēn mǒurén dǎ zhāohu 向/跟某人打招呼 = say hello to someone

zháojí 着急 *adjective*
= worried, anxious

zháo 着 *verb* ▶ *See also* **zhe** 着.
- = touch
- (*when speaking of an illness*) = catch, be affected by
  zháoliáng 着凉 = catch cold
- = burn
  zháohuǒ 着火 = catch fire
- (*after a verb to indicate accomplishment or result*)
  [**zhǎo** | **diǎn** | **shuì**] **zháo** [找 | 点 | 睡] 着 = [find | succeed in lighting | fall asleep]

zhǎo 找 *verb*
= look for, seek
- = give change, return a balance
  tā zhǎo wǒ wǔ kuài qián 他找我五块钱 = he gave me five dollars change
  zhǎodào 找到 = find
  zhǎozháo 找着 = find

zhàokāi 召开 *verb*
(*when talking about a conference, meeting, etc.*) = hold, convene

zhào 照
1 *verb*
- = shine on, put a light on, illuminate
- = reflect, look at one's reflection
- = take (a photograph)

2 *preposition*
- = according to
- = towards

zhàocháng 照常 *adverb*
= as usual, as normally done

zhàogu 照顾 *verb*
- = take care of, look after, attend to
- = take into account, consider

zhàokàn 照看 *verb*
- = take care of, look after, attend to
- = keep an eye on

zhàoliào 照料 *verb*
= care for, look after, attend to

zhàopiàn 照片 *noun*
= photograph, picture

zhàoxiàng 照相 *verb*
= take a picture or photograph, have a photograph taken

zhàoxiàngjī 照相机 *noun*
= camera

zhé 折 *verb*
= bend, fold

zhéxué 哲学 *noun*
= philosophy
  zhéxuéjiā 哲学家 = philosopher, specialist in philosophy

zhè 这
1 *pronoun*
= this
2 *determiner*
= this

zhèbiān 这边 *adverb*
= this side, over here

zhège 这个
1 *pronoun*
= this, this one
2 *determiner*
= this

zhèr 这儿, **zhèlǐ** 这里 *adverb*
= here

zhème 这么 *adverb*
- = by this means, in this way, like this
- = to this degree, so, such

zhèxiē 这些
1 *pronoun*
= these
2 *determiner*
= these

zhèyàng 这样 *adverb*
= in this way, like this, so

zhe 着 *particle* ▶ *See also* **zháo** 着.
(*indicating a continuous state or action, often translated by the present participle* [-ing] *in English*)
  [**zǒu** | **tīng** | **chàng**] **zhe** [走 | 听 | 唱] 着 = [walking | listening | singing]

zhēn 真
1 *adjective*
= real, genuine, true
2 *adverb*
= really, truly

zhēnlǐ 真理 *noun*
(*as an abstract concept*) = truth

zhēnshí 真实 *adjective*
= true, real, factual

zhēnzhèng 真正 *adjective*
= genuine, true

zhēn 针 *noun*
- = needle, pin
- = stitch
- (*as for medical treatment*) = injection

zhēnduì 针对 *verb*
- = point exactly against, be directed against, be aimed at

= in view of, in the light of, in accordance with

zhěntou 枕头 *noun*
= pillow

zhèn 阵 *measure word* ▶ **157**
(*for events or states of short duration*)

zhèn 镇 *noun*
= town

zhēngyuè 正月 *noun*

> ! *The character* **zhēng** 正 *is also pronounced* **zhèng** *with a different meaning.*

= first month of the lunar year

zhēng 争 *verb*
- = fight over, compete
- = argue about, dispute

zhēnglùn 争论
1 *verb*
= debate, argue
2 *noun*
= argument, debate

zhēngqǔ 争取 *verb*
- = strive for, gain by fighting, win
- = win over, persuade

zhēngqiú 征求 *verb*
(*as opinions, advice, etc.*) = consult, solicit, seek

zhēng 睁 *verb*
(*used for the eyes*) = open

zhěng 整 *adjective*
- = whole, entire, complete
- (*when talking about the time*) = sharp, exact

bā diǎn zhěng 八点整 = eight o'clock sharp

zhěnggè 整个 *adjective*
= whole, entire

zhěnglǐ 整理 *verb*
= tidy up, put in order, arrange

zhěngqí 整齐 *adjective*
= in good order, neat, tidy

zhèng 正

> ! *Can also be pronounced* **zhēng** *with a different meaning.*

1 *adjective*
- = right, straight, upright
- = right side up, right side out
- = chief, main
- (*of time*) = punctual, exact, precise

2 *adverb*
- = precisely, exactly
- (*indicating that an action is in progress*) = right in the midst of, just now

tā zhèng xiězhe nàfēng xìn 他正写着那封信 = he is just writing that letter

zhèngcháng 正常 *adjective*
= normal

zhèngdāng 正当 *conjunction*
= just when, just at the time when

zhèngdàng 正当 *adjective*
= proper, appropriate, legitimate

zhènghǎo 正好
1 *adjective*
(*in time, quantity, etc.*) = just right
2 *adverb*
- (*referring to time, quantity, etc.*) = just right
- = happen to, chance to, as it happens

zhèngqiǎo 正巧 *adverb*
- = it so happens, as it happens, happen to
- = just in time, just at the right time, in the nick of time

zhèngquè 正确 *adjective*
= correct, right

zhèngshì 正式
1 *adjective*
= formal, regular, official
2 *adverb*
= formally

zhèngyào 正要 *adverb*
= about to, on the point of

zhèngzài 正在 *adverb*
(*indicating an ongoing action or condition*) = in the midst of

wǒ zhèngzài kàn tā xiě de shū 我正在看她写的书 = I am just now reading the book she wrote

zhèngmíng 证明
1 *verb*
= certify, prove
2 *noun*
= proof, documentation, certificate

zhèngcè 政策 *noun*
= policy

zhèngdǎng 政党 *noun*
= political party

zhèngfǔ 政府 *noun*
= government

zhèngquán 政权 *noun*
= political power, state political power, regime

zhèngzhì 政治 *noun*
= politics, political affairs
zhèngzhìjiā 政治家 = politician, statesman

zhèng 挣 *verb*
= earn, make

...zhīhòu ...之后 *preposition*
= after..., behind...

...zhījiān ...之间 *preposition*
= between..., among...

...zhīqián ...之前 *preposition*
= before..., prior to..., in front of...

...zhīshàng ...之上 *preposition*
= above..., on top of...

...zhīxià ...之下 *preposition*
= below..., under...

...zhīzhōng ...之中 *preposition*
= amid..., among..., within...

zhī 支 *measure word* ▶ **157**
• (*for stick-like things*)
• (*for music, songs, or teams*)

zhīchí 支持
1 *verb*
= support
2 *noun*
= support

zhīyuán 支援
1 *verb*
= support, aid, assist
2 *noun*
= support, aid, assistance

zhī 只 *measure word* ▶ **157**
▶ *See also* **zhǐ** 只.
• (*one of a pair*)
• (*for some animals*)
• (*for boats*)

zhīdao 知道 *verb*
= know, know how, know that

zhīshi 知识 *noun*
= knowledge

zhī 织 *verb*
= weave, spin, knit

zhī 枝
1 *noun*
(*of a tree or other plant*) = branch
2 *measure word* ▶ **157**
(*for stick-like things*)

zhíxíng 执行 *verb*
= carry out, execute, implement

zhí 直
1 *adjective*
• (*as a line, road, etc.*) = straight
• (*in expressing opinions, etc.*) = straightforward, frank
2 *adverb*
• = directly, straight
• = in a straightforward manner, frankly

zhídào 直到 *preposition*
= until, up to

zhíjiē 直接
1 *adjective*
= direct, straightforward, straight
2 *adverb*
= directly, straightforwardly, frankly

zhíde 值得 *verb*
= be worthwhile, be worth

zhígōng 职工 *noun*
= workers, staff

zhíyè 职业 *noun*
= profession, occupation

zhíyuán 职员 *noun*
= office worker, member of staff

zhíwù 植物 *noun*
= plant, vegetation, flora

zhǐ 止
1 *verb*
= stop
2 *noun*
= end, terminus
dào xīngqīliù wéizhǐ 到星期六为止 = up to Saturday, until Saturday
3 *adverb*
= only
bù zhǐ yícì 不止一次 = not just once

zhǐ 只 *adverb* ▶ *See also* **zhī** 只.
= only, merely

zhǐhǎo 只好 *adverb*
= have to, can only, the only thing to do is
yīnwèi tā bú zài, suǒyǐ wǒ zhǐhǎo huí jiā 因为他不在，所以我只好回家 = since he's not in, I have to go home

Z

zhǐshì 只是
1 *adverb*
= just, only
2 *conjunction*
= but, however

zhǐyào 只要 *conjunction*
= so long as, provided
zhǐyào yǒu hǎo diànyǐng, wǒ jiù qǐng nǐ qù kàn 只要有好电影, 我就请你去看 = as long as there's a good film showing, I'll invite you to see it

zhǐyǒu 只有
1 *adverb*
= only
2 *conjunction*
= only, only if, unless
zhǐyǒu...cái... 只有... 才... = only...can...
zhǐyǒu nǔlì xuéxí, cái néng xuéhuì 只有努力学习, 才能学会 = you can master (it) only if you study hard

zhǐ 纸 *noun*
= paper

zhǐ 指
1 *verb*
= point at, point to, point toward
2 *noun*
= finger

zhǐchū 指出 *verb*
= point out, indicate

zhǐdǎo 指导
1 *verb*
= guide, direct
2 *noun*
= direction, guidance, advice
zhǐdǎo lǎoshī 指导老师 = supervisor, advisor

zhǐhuī 指挥
1 *verb*
(*for an army, an orchestra, etc.*) = direct, command, conduct
2 *noun*
(*of an orchestra*) = conductor

zhǐshì 指示
1 *noun*
= instructions, directive
2 *verb*
- = point out, indicate
- = instruct, direct

zhì 至 *preposition*
= to, until

zhìjīn 至今 *adverb*
= until now, so far, up to now

zhìshǎo 至少 *adverb*
= at least

zhìyú 至于 *preposition*
= as for, as to
bú zhìyú 不至于 = wouldn't go so far as to

zhìliàng 质量 *noun*
= quality

zhì 治 *verb*
- = rule, govern, manage
- (*water, emotions, etc.*) = harness, control
- = heal, cure, treat

zhìliǎo 治疗
1 *noun*
= medical treatment
2 *verb*
= cure, treat

zhìdìng 制定 *verb*
(*as a plan, policy, law, etc.*) = draft, draw up, formulate

zhìdìng 制订 *verb*
(*as a scheme, a solution, etc.*) = work out, come up with, formulate

zhìdù 制度 *noun*
= system

zhìzào 制造 *verb*
- = manufacture, make, create
- (*as a lie, a rumour, etc.*) = make up, fabricate, invent

zhìxù 秩序 *noun*
= order, sequence

zhōng 中
1 *noun*
- = middle, centre
- (*short for* Zhōngguó 中国) = China

2 *preposition*
= in, in the midst of, among
3 *adjective*
- = middle, mid-
- = medium, intermediate
- = Chinese

Zhōngshì 中式 = Chinese style

Zhōngcān 中餐 *noun*
= Chinese food

Zhōngguó 中国 *noun*
= China

Zhōngguóhuà 中国话 *noun*
= Chinese (spoken) language

Zhōngguórén 中国人 *noun*
= Chinese person, Chinese people

Zhōnghuá Mínguó 中华民国 *noun*
= the Republic of China

Zhōnghuá Rénmín Gònghéguó 中华人民共和国 *noun*
= the People's Republic of China

zhōngjiān 中间
1 *noun*
= middle, centre
2 *preposition*
= amongst, between, in the middle of

Zhōngqiūjié 中秋节 *noun*
= Mid-autumn Festival, Moon Festival (15th of the 8th lunar month)

Zhōngwén 中文 *noun*
= Chinese language (usually written)

zhōngwǔ 中午 *noun*
= noon, midday

zhōngxīn 中心 *noun*
= centre, heart, core

zhōngxué 中学 *noun*
= middle school, secondary school, high school

zhōngyāng 中央 *noun*
= centre, middle

Zhōngyào 中药 *noun*
(*as a drug or remedy*) = traditional Chinese medicine

Zhōngyī 中医 *noun*
(*as a field or department*) = traditional Chinese medicine

zhōngyú 终于 *adverb*
= in the end, at last, finally

zhōng 钟 *noun*
- = bell
- = clock
- (*for telling time*)
wǔ diǎn zhōng 五点钟 = five o'clock
wǔ fēn zhōng 五分钟 = five minutes

zhōngbiǎo 钟表 *noun*
= clock, clocks and watches

zhōngtóu 钟头 *noun*
= hour

zhǒng 种 ▶ *See also* **zhòng** 种.
1 *noun*
- = seed
- = breed, species, ethnic group

2 *measure word* **▶ 157**
= kind, type, sort

zhǒnglèi 种类 *noun*
= kind, type, sort

zhǒngzi 种子 *noun*
= seed

zhòng 种 *verb* ▶ *See also* **zhǒng** 种.
= plant, sow, cultivate

zhòng 重 ▶ *See also* **chóng** 重.
1 *adjective*
- = heavy
- = important, weighty, serious

2 *noun*
= weight

zhòngdà 重大 *adjective*
= great, weighty, important

zhòngdiǎn 重点 *noun*
= point of emphasis, main point

zhòngliàng 重量 *noun*
= weight

zhòngshì 重视 *verb*
= regard as important, take seriously, value

zhòngyào 重要 *adjective*
= important, significant

zhōu 周 *noun*
- = all around, circumference, circuit
- = week

zhōudào 周到 *adjective*
= thoughtful, considerate

zhōumò 周末 *noun*
= weekend

zhōuwéi 周围 *noun*
= circumference, surroundings, environment

zhū 猪 *noun*
= pig, hog

zhūròu 猪肉 *noun*
= pork

zhúzi 竹子 *noun*
= bamboo

zhúbù 逐步 *adverb*
= gradually, step by step

zhújiàn 逐渐 *adverb*
= gradually, bit by bit

zhŭdòng 主动
1 *noun*
= initiative
2 *verb*
= hold/take the initiative

zhŭguān 主观 *adjective*
= subjective

zhŭrén 主人 *noun*
- = owner
- = host, hostess

zhŭrèn 主任 *noun*
= director, chairperson

zhŭxí 主席 *noun*
= chairperson, chair, chairman

zhŭyào 主要 *adjective*
= main, principal, chief

zhŭyì 主义 *noun*
= doctrine, -ism

zhŭyì 主意 *noun*
= idea, plan, decision

zhŭzhāng 主张
1 *verb*
= propose, suggest, advocate
2 *noun*
= proposal, suggestion

zhŭ 煮 *verb*
= boil, cook

zhù 住 *verb*
- = live, reside, stay
- (*after certain verbs to indicate coming to a halt or grasping hold*)
[zhuā | zhàn | jì] zhù [抓 | 站 | 记] 住 = [hold on to | stop | remember]

zhùsù jiā zăocān 住宿加早餐
noun
= bed and breakfast

zhùyuàn 住院 *verb*
= be in hospital, be hospitalized

zhùyì 注意 *verb*
= pay attention to, take notice of

zhù 祝 *verb*
= wish, extend wishes

zhùhè 祝贺 *verb*
= congratulate

zhùmíng 著名 *adjective*
= famous, prominent, well-known

zhùzuò 著作 *noun*
= writings, works

zhuā 抓 *verb*
- = grasp, seize
- = catch, arrest
- = scratch

zhuājĭn 抓紧 *verb*
= grasp firmly, pay close attention to, make the best use of

zhuānjiā 专家 *noun*
= specialist, expert

zhuānmén 专门 *adjective*
= specialized, special

zhuānxīn 专心
1 *adjective*
= attentive, with undivided attention, with concentration
2 *adverb*
= attentively

zhuānyè 专业 *noun*
= specialty, specialized field/profession

zhuān 砖 *noun*
= brick

zhuăn 转 *verb* ▶ *See also* **zhuàn** 转.
- = turn, change, shift
- (*when speaking of a message, phone call, etc.*) = transfer, pass on, forward

zhuănbiàn 转变 *verb*
= turn, change, transform

zhuăngào 转告 *verb*
(*as a message*) = forward, pass on

zhuàn 转 *verb* ▶ *See also* **zhuăn** 转.
- = turn, revolve, rotate
- = walk around, stroll

zhuàn 赚 *verb*
(*when talking about money or profit*) = make, gain, earn

zhuāngjia 庄稼 *noun*
= crop, crops

zhuāngyán 庄严 *adjective*
= dignified, solemn, stately

zhuāng 装
1 *verb*
- = install, fit, put in
- = pack, load
- = pretend, disguise, play a part
2 *noun*
= clothing, outfit, dress

zhuàngkuàng 状况 *noun*
= state of affairs, situation

zhuàngtài 状态 *noun*
= condition, appearance, state of affairs

zhuàng 撞 *verb*
= bump/knock against, bump into, collide

zhuī 追 *verb*
= follow, pursue, chase

zhuīqiú 追求 *verb*
- = seek, go after, pursue
- = court, woo

zhǔn 准
1 *adjective*
= accurate
2 *adverb*
= accurately, certainly
3 *verb*
= permit, allow

zhǔnbèi 准备
1 *verb*
- = prepare, get ready for, prepare to
- = plan, intend

2 *noun*
= preparation

zhǔnquè 准确 *adjective*
= accurate, precise, exact

zhǔnshí 准时 *adjective*
= on time, punctual

zhuō 捉 *verb*
= seize, arrest, catch hold of

zhuōzi 桌子 *noun*
= table, desk

zīliào 资料 *noun*
= information, data

zīyuán 资源 *noun*
= resources, natural resources

zǐnǚ 子女 *noun*
= sons and daughters, children

zǐxì 仔细
1 *adjective*
= careful of detail, meticulous, attentive
2 *adverb*
= in detail, meticulously, carefully

zǐ 紫 *adjective*
= purple

zì 自
1 *pronoun*
= oneself, one's own
2 *preposition*
= from, since
3 *conjunction*
= since

zìcóng 自从
1 *preposition*
= since, from
2 *conjunction*
= since
zìcóng...yǐhòu 自从... 以后 = from... (that time) on, ever since...
zìcóng...yǐlái 自从... 以来 = ever since...

zìdòng 自动
1 *adjective*
= automatic, voluntary, self-motivated
2 *adverb*
= automatically, voluntarily, on one's own initiative

zìfèi 自费 *adjective*
= at one's own expense, self-funded

zìjǐ 自己 *pronoun*
= self, oneself

zìjué 自觉
1 *adjective*
- = conscious, aware
- = conscientious

2 *adverb*
- = consciously
- = conscientiously

zìláishuǐ 自来水 *noun*
= running water, tap water

zìrán 自然
1 *noun*
= nature, the natural world
2 *adjective*
= natural
3 *adverb*
- = of course
- = naturally

zìsī 自私 *adjective*
= selfish

zìwǒ 自我 *pronoun*
= self, self-, oneself

zìxíngchē 自行车 *noun*
= bicycle, bike

zìxué 自学 *verb*
= self-study, study by oneself, teach oneself

zìyóu 自由
1 *noun*
= freedom, liberty

2 *adjective*
= free, unrestrained

zìyuàn 自愿 *adjective*
= voluntary, of one's own accord

zì 字 *noun*
= word, written character

zìdiǎn 字典 *noun*
= dictionary

zìmǔ 字母 *noun*
= letters of an alphabet, letter

zōngjiào 宗教 *noun*
= religion

zōnghé 综合
1 *verb*
= synthesize, summarize
2 *adjective*
= comprehensive, overall

zǒng 总
1 *adverb*
- = always, in every case, all the time
- = eventually, sooner or later, inevitably
- = in any event, anyway, after all

2 *adjective*
- = general, total
- = chief, main, master

zǒngjié 总结
1 *verb*
= sum up, summarize
2 *noun*
= summary, report

zǒnglǐ 总理 *noun*
= prime minister, premier

zǒngshì 总是 *adverb*
= always, in every case, all the time

zǒngtǒng 总统 *verb*
(*of a republic*) = president

zǒu 走 *verb*
- = walk, go
- = depart, leave
- (*for something mechanical*) = work, tick, go

zǒudào 走道 *noun*
= path, walkway

zǒu hòumén 走后门 *verb*
- = get in by the back door
- = do business or other things by means of backdoor dealings

zǒuláng 走廊 *noun*
= corridor, passage, passageway

zǒulù 走路 *verb*
= walk

zū 租 *verb*
- = rent, hire, charter
- = rent out, let out, lease

zúqiú 足球 *noun*
= football, soccer

zǔzhǐ 阻止 *verb*
= prevent, stop

zǔ 组 *noun*
= group

zǔzhī 组织
1 *verb*
= organize
2 *noun*
= organisation

zǔfù 祖父 *noun*
= grandfather on the father's side

zǔguó 祖国 *noun*
= one's native country, motherland, fatherland

zǔmǔ 祖母 *noun*
= grandmother on the father's side

zǔxiān 祖先 *noun*
= ancestors, forefathers

zuān 钻 *verb*
= drill, bore, enter

zuānyán 钻研 *verb*
= study intensively

zuǐ 嘴 *noun*
= mouth

zuì 最 *adverb*
(*indicating the superlative*) = most, the most

zuìchū 最初
1 *adjective*
= first, initial
2 *adverb*
= at first, in the beginning, initially

zuìhǎo 最好
1 *adjective*
= best
2 *adverb*
= had better

zuìhòu 最后
1 *adjective*
= final, ultimate, last
2 *adverb*
= at last, finally, eventually

zuìjìn 最近
1 *adjective*
- (*in the recent past*) = last, recent
- (*in the near future*) = next, coming

2 *adverb*
- (*in the recent past*) = lately, recently
- (*in the near future*) = soon, in the near future, coming

zuì 罪 *noun*
- = crime, guilt
- = suffering, pain, hardship
  shòu zuì 受罪 = have a hard time, endure suffering, be in pain

zuì 醉 *adjective*
= drunk, intoxicated, inebriated

zūnjìng 尊敬
1 *verb*
= respect, honour, esteem
2 *adjective*
= honourable, distinguished

zūnzhòng 尊重 *verb*
= respect, esteem

zūnshǒu 遵守 *verb*
= comply with, observe, abide by

zuótiān 昨天 *noun*
= yesterday

zuǒ 左
1 *noun*
- = left, left-hand side, the left
- (*when speaking of politics*) = left-wing

2 *adjective*
= left, left-hand

zuǒbian 左边 *noun*
= left-hand side, left side

zuǒyòu 左右 *adverb*
(*after an expression of quantity*) = approximately, about, more or less

zuò 作 *verb*
- = do, make
  zuò bàogào 作报告 = make a report
- = create, write, compose
  zuò qǔ 作曲 = compose a piece of music
- = act as, be, become
- = regard as, treat as
  tā bǎ wǒ dāngzuò qīnshēng nǚ'ér 她把我当作亲生女儿 = she treats me like her own daughter

zuòjiā 作家 *noun*
= writer

zuòpǐn 作品 *noun*
= literary/artistic work

zuòwéi 作为
1 *verb*
- = serve as, function as, use as
- = regard as

2 *preposition*
= as, being
3 *noun*
- = conduct, action, deed
- = achievement, accomplishment

zuòwén 作文 *noun*
= composition, essay

zuòyè 作业 *noun*
= school assignment

zuòyòng 作用 *noun*
- = purpose, function, role
  qǐ hěn dà de zuòyòng 起很大的作用 = perform an important function
- = action, effect

zuòzhě 作者 *noun*
= author, writer

zuò 坐 *verb*
- = sit
- = ride on, go by, travel by
  zuò [**gōnggòng qìchē** | **huǒchē** | **fēijī**] 坐[公共汽车 | 火车 | 飞机] = travel by [bus | train | plane]

zuò 座
1 *measure word* ▶ **157**
(*for mountains, buildings, structures, etc.*)
2 *noun*
= seat, place to sit

zuòtán 座谈
1 *verb*
= discuss
2 *noun*
= discussion
zuòtánhuì 座谈会 = discussion, symposium, forum

zuòwèi 座位 *noun*
= seat, place to sit

zuò 做 *verb*
- = do, be engaged in
  zuò shìyàn 做试验 = do experiments
- = make, create, manufacture
  zuò yīfu 做衣服 = make clothes
- = cook, prepare (food)
  zuò cài 做菜 = cook a meal, prepare a meal

- = be, act as, take on the role of
  tā kuài zuò māma le 她快做妈妈了 = she is about to become a mother
- (*when talking about posts, positions, professions, etc.*) = work as, be, become
  tā zuòle sān nián xì zhǔrèn le 他做了三年系主任了 = he has been chairperson of the department for three years
- = serve as, be used as
  zhège fángjiān kěyǐ zuò wǒde shūfáng 这个房间可以做我的书房 = this room can serve as my study

zuòfǎ 做法 *noun*
= way of doing things, method, practice

zuòkè 做客 *verb*
= be a guest

zuòmèng 做梦 *verb*
= dream, have a dream

Basic Chinese measure words

Nominal Measure Words

In Chinese, a numeral cannot quantify a noun by itself. It has to be accompanied by the measure word that is appropriate for the noun that is being used. Each noun has a specific measure word or set of measure words that can be used with it. There is often a link between the measure word and the shape of the object. In expressions of quantification, the numeral comes first, followed by the measure word and the noun. Below is a list of commonly used nominal measure words, along with descriptions of the types of nouns for which they are used, translations (if appropriate), and some examples of their uses. A list of verbal measure words follows this list. Some nominal measure words can also be used as verbal measure words, and these are cross-referenced below.

bǎ 把
- (*for objects with a handle or with something a person can hold*)
  three [**brushes** | **knives** | **keys** | **umbrellas** | **chairs...**] = sānbǎ [shuāzi | dāo | yàoshi | yǔsǎn | yǐzi...] 三把 [刷子 | 刀 | 钥匙 | 雨伞 | 椅子...]
- (*for things that can be grouped in bunches or bundles*) = bunch, bundle
  a bunch of flowers = yìbǎ✖ huā 一把✖花
  a bundle of chopsticks = yìbǎ kuàizi 一把筷子
- = handful
  a handful of [**sand** | **rice** | **beans...**] = yìbǎ [shāzi | dàmǐ | dòuzi...] 一把 [沙子 | 大米 | 豆子...]

bān 班
(*for scheduled services of public transportation*)
this train service to London = qù Lúndūn de zhèbān huǒche
the next flight to Beijing = qù Běijīng de xià yìbān fēijī 去北京的下一班飞机

bāo 包
= package, packet, bundle
a packet of cigarettes = yìbāo xiāngyān 一包香烟
two packages of sweets = liǎngbāo táng 两包糖
this bundle of clothes = zhèbāo yīfu 这包衣服

běn 本
(*for things that are bound, such as books, magazines, etc.*)
five books = wǔběn shū 五本书

bǐ 笔
- (*for sums of money*)
  that sum of money = nàbǐ qián 那笔钱
- (*for deals in business or trade*)
  this deal = zhèbǐ jiāoyì 这笔交易

biàn 遍 ▶ *See the list of Verbal Measure Words below.*

bù 部
(*for novels, films, etc.*)
three [**novels** | **films**] = sān bù [xiǎoshuō | diànyǐng] 三部 [小说 | 电影]

cè 册
- (*for books or volumes of books*) = volume, book
  this novel has two volumes = zhèbù xiǎoshuō yǒu liǎng cè 这部小说有两册
- (*for copies of books*) = copy
  shí wàn cè shū 十万册书 = 100,000 books

céng 层
- = storey, floor
  a five-storey building = yīzuò wǔ céng dàlóu 一座五层大楼
- (*for a layer, coat, sheet*)
  a coat of paint = yī céng yóuqī 一层油漆
  a thin sheet of ice = yī céng báo bīng 一层薄冰

✖less formal

chǎng 场 ▶ *See also the list of Verbal Measure Words below.*
- (*for the whole process of being ill*)
  an illness = yī chǎng bìng 一场病
- (*for a natural disturbance, war, disaster, etc.*)
  a rain shower, a cloudburst = yī chǎng yǔ 一场雨
- (*for a show, performance, game, or debate*)
  [**the showing of a film** | **a performance of Peking opera** | **a debate**] = yī chǎng [diànyǐng | jīngjù | biànlùn] 一场[电影 | 京剧 | 辩论]
  two [**football matches** | **basketball games**] = liǎng chǎng [zúqiú bǐsài | lánqiú bǐsài] 两场[足球比赛 | 篮球比赛]

chuáng 床
(*for quilts, blankets, sheets*)
three [**quilts** | **blankets** | **sheets**] = sān chuáng [bèizi | tǎnzi | chuángdān] 三床[被子 | 毯子 | 床单]

cì 次 ▶ *See also the list of Verbal Measure Words below.*
(*for events such as examinations, accidents, experiments, etc.*)
two [**examinations** | **accidents** | **experiments...**] = liǎngcì [kǎoshì | shìgù | shíyàn...] 两次[考试 | 事故 | 实验...]

dào 道
- (*for orders issued by an authority, questions on an examination*)
  an [**order** | **arithmetic question**] = yídào [mìnglìng | suànshù tí] 一道[命令 | 算术题]
- (*for things in the shape of a line*)
  a [**crack** | **ray of light** | **wrinkle**] = yídào [lièfèng | guāngxiàn | zhòuwén] 一道[裂缝 | 光线 | 皱纹]
- (*for courses in a meal*)
  a three-course lunch = yǒu sān dào cài de wǔfàn 有三道菜的午饭

dī 滴
= drop
six drops of blood = liùdī xuè 六滴血

diǎn 点
(*for suggestions, requirements, ideas, opinions*)
two [**suggestions** | **requirements** | **ideas**] = liǎng diǎn [jiànyì | yāoqiú | yìjiàn] 两点[建议 | 要求 | 意见]

dǐng 顶
(*for hats, caps, or things with a top*)
a [**hat** | **tent**] = yīdǐng [màozi | zhàngpeng] 一顶[帽子 | 帐篷]

dòng 栋
(*for buildings*)
ten buildings = shídòng lóufáng 十栋楼房

dǔ 堵
(*for walls*)
a wall = yìdǔ qiáng 一堵墙

duàn 段
- (*for lengths of road, cable, etc.*) = section, segment
  a section of highway = yíduàn gōnglù 一段公路
- (*for periods of time*) = period, length
  that period of history = nà yíduàn lìshǐ 那一段历史
- (*for units of writing, articles, speeches, etc.*) = piece, passage, paragraph
  a piece of music = yíduàn yīnyuè 一段音乐

duì 对
= pair, couple
a (married) couple = yíduì fūqī 一对夫妻
a pair of vases = yíduì huāpíng 一对花瓶

dùn 顿 ▶ *See also the list of Verbal Measure Words below.*
(*for meals*)
three meals every day = měitiān sāndùn fàn 每天三顿饭

duǒ 朵
(*for flowers, clouds*)
a few [**flowers** | **clouds**] = jǐduǒ [huā | yún] 几朵[花 | 云]

fèn 份
- = portion, share
  a portion of food = yífèn fàn 一份饭
  a gift = yífèn lǐwù 一份礼物
- (*for copies of newspapers, magazines, or manuscripts*)
  two documents = liǎngfèn wénjiàn 两份文件

fēng 封
(*for letters, telegrams*)
eight letters = bāfēng xìn 八封信

fú 幅
(*for paintings, works of calligraphy, maps*)
a landscape painting = yìfú shānshuǐhuà 一幅山水画

fù 服
(*for doses of Chinese medicine*)
four doses of Chinese medicine = sìfù zhōngyào 四服中药

fù 副
- (*for things that come in pairs or sets*) = set, pair
  a set of chess = yífù xiàngqí 一副象棋
  a pair of [**gloves** | **glasses...**] = yífù [shǒutào | yǎnjìng...] 一副 [手套 | 眼镜...]
- (*for facial expressions*)
  a [**smiling face** | **serious expression**] = yífù [xiàoliǎn | yánsù de biǎoqíng] 一副 [笑脸 | 严肃的表情]

gè 个

> **!** *This is the most common measure word. It can take the place of many nominal measure words, and is handy to use if one does not know the measure word that is specific to a particular noun. It usually has a neutral tone, but has a fourth tone when stressed.*

a [**person** | **problem** | **month** | **school...**] = yíge [rén | wèntí | yuè | xuéxiào...] 一个 [人 | 问题 | 月 | 学校...]

gēn 根
(*for long, thin objects*)
a [**rope** | **needle** | **pillar** | **sausage...**] = yìgēn [shéngzi | zhēn | zhùzi | xiāngcháng...] 一根 [绳子 | 针 | 柱子 | 香肠...]

háng 行
(*for things that form a line*)
two lines of Chinese characters = liǎng háng Hànzì 两行汉字

hù 户
(*for households*)
five Chinese households = wǔ hù Zhōngguórén 五户中国人

huí 回 ▶ *See the list of Verbal Measure Words below.*

huǒ 伙

> **!** *This measure word usually has a negative connotation.*

(*for groups or bands of people*)
a gang of [**people** | **robbers** | **hooligans...**] = yì huǒ [rén | qiángdào | liúmáng...] 一伙 [人 | 强盗 | 流氓...]

jiā 家
(*for families, enterprises, restaurants, hotels, etc.*)
twelve [**families** | **factories** | **banks** | **shops...**] = shí'er jiā [rénjiā | gōngchǎng | yínháng | shāngdiàn...] 十二家 [人家 | 工厂 | 银行 | 商店...]

jià 架
(*for aeroplanes, pianos, cameras, etc.*)
six [**aeroplanes** | **cameras**] = liù jià [fēijī | zhàoxiàngjī] 六架 [飞机 | 照相机]

jiān 间
(*for rooms*)
a(n) [**room** | **office** | **kitchen**] = yì jiān [wūzi | bàngōngshì | chúfáng] 一间 [屋子 | 办公室 | 厨房]

jiàn 件
(*for luggage, clothes, furniture, matters, etc.*)
a [**piece of luggage** | **shirt** | **matter**] = yí jiàn [xíngli | chènshān | shì] 一件 [行李 | 衬衫 | 事]

jié 节
- (*for sections of things*) = section, length, segment
  a section of bamboo = yì jié zhúzi 一节竹子
- (*for torch batteries, railway carriages, class periods at school*)
  four [**carriages** | **batteries** | **periods**] = sì jié [chēxiāng | diànchí | kè] 四节 [车厢 | 电池 | 课]

jiè 届
- (*for regular sessions, conferences, sports tournaments, terms of office, etc.*)
  the tenth [**session of the UN General Assembly** | **Agriculture Conference** | **presidency**] = dì-shí jiè [Liánhéguó Dàhuì | Nóngyè Huìyì | zǒngtǒng] 第十届 [联合国大会 | 农业会议 | 总统]
- (*for students graduating in the same year*) = year, class, grade
  the fourth graduating class = dì-sì jiè bìyèbān 第四届毕业班

jù 句
(*for lines, sentences, units of speech, poetry, etc.*)

a [sentence | line of a poem] = yī jù [huà | shī] 一句 [话 | 诗]

kē 棵

(*for trees, plants*)

a [tree | grass | daffodil] = yì kē [shù | cǎo | shuǐxiānhuā] 一棵 [树 | 草 | 水仙花]

kē 颗

- (*for small, round things such as pearls, teeth and hearts; also for things that appear small such as stars, satellites and planets*)

  a [pearl | bean | satellite] = yìkē [zhūzi | dòuzi | wèixīng] 一颗 [珠子 | 豆子 | 卫星]
- (*for bullets, bombs, etc.*)

  a [bullet | bomb] = yìkē [zǐdàn | zhàdàn] 一颗 [子弹 | 炸弹]

kǒu 口

- (*for the number of people in a family or village*)

  eight people = bākǒu rén 八口人
- (*for spoken languages, used with the verb "speak" and with the number* one, yì 一)

  to speak Beijing dialect = shuō yìkǒu Běijīng huà 说一口北京话

kuài 块

- (*for things that come in chunks or solid pieces*)

  three [soaps | sweets | stones] = sānkuài [féizào | táng | shítou] 三块 [肥皂 | 糖 | 石头]
- (*for things that are shaped like sheets*)

  five [table cloths | wooden boards | handkerchiefs] = wǔkuài [zhuōbù | mùbǎn | shǒujuàn] 五块 [桌布 | 木板 | 手绢]
- (*for slices, sections, divisions, etc.*)

  four pieces of [cake | cloth | land] = sìkuài [dàngāo | bù | dì] 四块 [蛋糕 | 布 | 地]

lèi 类

= kind of, sort of

zhèlèi dōngxi 这类东西 = this type of thing, this kind of thing

lì 粒

(*for very small, round things, such as peas, peanuts, bullets, or grains*)

a grain of [rice | sand] = yílì [mǐ | shāzi] 一粒 [米 | 沙子]

three pills/tablets = sānlì yào 三粒药

liàng 辆

(*for vehicles*)

ten [cars | bikes | lorries] = shíliàng [qìchē | zìxíngchē | kǎchē] 十辆 [汽车 | 自行车 | 卡车]

liè 列

(*for trains*)

a train = yíliè huǒchē 一列火车

mén 门

(*for academic courses, subjects or disciplines*)

a [course | science | speciality] = yìmén [kèchéng | kēxué | zhuānyè] 一门 [课程 | 科学 | 专业]

miàn 面

(*for flat, smooth objects, such as mirrors, flags, etc.*)

a [red flag | mirror] = yímiàn [hóngqí | jìngzi] 一面 [红旗 | 镜子]

míng 名

(*for persons with professional or prominent social identities*)

seven [students | doctors | soldiers | workers] = qīmíng [xuésheng | yīshēng | shìbīng | gōngrén] 七名 [学生 | 医生 | 士兵 | 工人]

pái 排

(*for things grouped or set in rows*) = row

a row of [seats | trees | houses] = yìpái [zuòwèi | shù | fángzi] 一排 [座位 | 树 | 房子]

pán 盘

- (*for flat things*)

  a video tape = yìpán lùxiàngdài 一盘录像带
- (*for board games*)

  a game of chess = yìpán qí 一盘棋

pī 批

(*for people or goods*) = group, batch, lot

a group of people = yì pī rén 一批人

two batches of goods = liǎng pī huòwù 两批货物

pǐ 匹

(*for horses, mules*)

three [horses | mules] = sān pǐ [mǎ | luózi] 三匹 [马 | 骡子]

piān 篇

(*for papers, articles, written versions of a speech*)

an [essay | diary | editorial] = yī piān [lùnwén | rìjì | shèlùn] 一篇 [论文 | 日记 | 社论]

piàn 片

- (*for flat, thin things or things in slices*)
  three slices of bread = sān piàn miànbāo 三片面包
  two [tablets | biscuits] = liǎng piàn [yàopiàn | bǐnggān] 两片 [药片 | 饼干]
- (*for expanses or stretches of ocean, desert, mist, fog, etc.*)
  a stretch of sandy beach = yī piàn shātān 一片沙滩
- (*for atmospheres, moods, etc.*)
  a scene of great joy = yī piàn huānlè 一片欢乐

qī 期

(*for issues of periodicals, magazines, journals, etc.*)
the first issue of that magazine = nàběn zázhì de dì yī qī 那本杂志的第一期

qún 群

(*for a group, crowd, herd, or flock*) = group, crowd, flock
a crowd of football fans = yī qún zúqiúmí 一群足球迷
a flock of birds = yī qún niǎo 一群鸟

shēng 声 ▶ *See the list of Verbal Measure Words below.*

shǒu 首

(*for songs, poems, music*)
six [songs | poems] = liù shǒu [gē | shī] 六首 [歌 | 诗]

shù 束

= bunch
a bunch of flowers = yī shù huā 一束花

shuāng 双

(*for things that come in twos, such as shoes, socks, chopsticks, etc.*) = pair
a pair of [shoes | socks | eyes] = yī shuāng [xié | wàzi | yǎnjīng] 一双 [鞋 | 袜子 | 眼睛]

sōu 艘

(*for ships*)
three [ships | oil tankers | warships] = sān sōu [chuán | yóulún | jūnjiàn] 三艘 [船 | 油轮 | 军舰]

suǒ 所

(*for buildings, houses, schools, etc.*)
two [hospitals | schools | houses] = liǎng suǒ [yīyuàn | xuéxiào | fángzi] 两所 [医院 | 学校 | 房子]

tái 台

(*for stage performances, machines, equipment, etc.*)
nine [TV sets | washing machines | computers] = jiǔ tái [diànshìjī | xǐyījī | jìsuànjī] 九台 [电视机 | 洗衣机 | 计算机]
a theatrical performance = yī tái xì 一台戏

táng 堂

(*for classes or periods at school or university*) = period, class
four periods = sì táng kè 四堂课

tàng 趟 ▶ *See also the list of Verbal Measure Words below.*

(*for scheduled services of public transportation*)
the next train service to Beijing = qù Běijīng de xià yī tàng huǒchē 去北京的下一趟火车

tào 套

(*for sets of books, clothing, tools, furniture, etc.*) = set, suit, suite
a set of [stamps | regulations | textbooks] = yī tào [yóupiào | guīzé | kèběn] 一套 [邮票 | 规则 | 课本]

tiáo 条

- (*for long, narrow things*)
  a [towel | boat | pair of trousers | skirt | river | road | street | snake | fish | dog] = yī tiáo [máojīn | chuán | kùzi | qúnzi | hé | lù | jiē | shé | yú | gǒu] 一条 [毛巾 | 船 | 裤子 | 裙子 | 河 | 路 | 街 | 蛇 | 鱼 | 狗]
- (*for items of news, laws, ideas, views*)
  three [news items | laws | ideas] = sān tiáo [xiāoxi | fǎlǜ | yìjiàn] 三条 [消息 | 法律 | 意见]
- (*for limbs of the human body*)
  two [legs | arms] = liǎng tiáo [tuǐ | gēbo] 两条 [腿 | 胳膊]
- (*for human lives*)
  four lives = sì tiáo rénmìng 四条人命

tóu 头

- (*for certain animals*)
  five [cows | pigs | sheep | elephants | lions...] = wǔtóu [niú | zhū | yáng | xiàng | shīzi…] 五头 [牛 | 猪 | 羊 | 象 | 狮子…]
- (*for garlic bulbs*)
  a bulb of garlic = yī tóu suàn 一头蒜

tuán 团
(*for certain round things*)
a ball of wool = yītuán máoxiàn 一团毛线

wèi 位
(*a polite measure word for people*)
a [gentleman | lady | teacher | professor...] = yī wèi [xiānsheng | nǚshì | lǎoshī | jiàoshòu...] 一位 [先生 | 女士 | 老师 | 教授...]

xià 下 ▶ *See the list of Verbal Measure Words below.*

xiàng 项
- (*for work, projects, tasks, requirements, etc.*)
  a [piece of work | project] = yíxiàng [gōngzuò | gōngchéng] 一项 [工作 | 工程]
- (*for decisions or announcements*)
  a(n) [decision | announcement] = yī xiàng [juédìng | shēngmíng] 一项 [决定 | 声明]

yàng 样
(*for things in general*) = kind, sort, type
three types of tool = sān yàng gōngjù 三样工具

zhǎn 盏
(*for lamps*)
a lamp = yī zhǎn dēng 一盏灯

zhāng 张
(*for flat things such as paper, paintings, tables, maps, etc.*)
a [sheet of paper | newspaper | table | bed | picture | ticket | postage stamp] = yìzhāng [zhǐ | bào | zhuōzi | chuáng | huà | piào | yóupiào] 一张 [纸 | 报 | 桌子 | 床 | 画 | 票 | 邮票]

zhèn 阵
(*for events or states of short duration*)
a [downpour of rain | gust of wind | fit of coughing] = yízhèn [dà yǔ | fēng | késou] 一阵 [大雨 | 风 | 咳嗽]

zhī 支
- (*for stick-like things*)
  a [pen | chopstick | candle | flute] = yìzhī [bǐ | kuàizi | làzhú | dízi] 一支 [笔 | 筷子 | 蜡烛 | 笛子]
- (*for music, songs, or teams*)
  a piece of music = yìzhī qǔzi 一支曲子

zhī 只
- (*one of a pair*)
  a(n) [shoe | eye | ear | hand | foot] = yìzhī [xié | yǎnjīng | ěrduo | shǒu | jiǎo] 一只 [鞋 | 眼睛 | 耳朵 | 手 | 脚]
- (*for some animals*)
  a [chicken | sheep | monkey | bird | cat | crab] = yìzhī [jī | yáng | hóuzi | niǎo | māo | pángxiè] 一只 [鸡 | 羊 | 猴子 | 鸟 | 猫 | 螃蟹]
- (*for boats*)
  a small boat = yìzhī xiǎo chuán 一只小船

zhī 枝
(*for stick-like things*) ▶ *See* **zhī 支** *above.*
a rifle = yìzhī bùqiāng 一枝步枪
a long-stemmed rose = yìzhī méiguìhuā 一枝玫瑰花

zhǒng 种
= kind, type, sort
two kinds of [people | plants | clothes | dictionaries] = liǎngzhǒng [rén | zhíwù | yīfu | zìdiǎn] 两种 [人 | 植物 | 衣服 | 字典]

zuò 座
(*for mountains, buildings, structures, etc.*)
a [mountain | bridge | building | palace | cinema] = yízuò [shān | qiáo | lóu | gōngdiàn | diànyǐngyuàn] 一座 [山 | 桥 | 楼 | 宫殿 | 电影院]

Verbal Measure Words

Below is a short list of commonly used verbal measure words. These are generally used to indicate the number of times an action or a state occurs. The numeral and measure word are preceded by the verb and are usually followed by the object if there is one (i.e. if the verb is transitive). Some verbal measure words, such as *shēng* 声 and *xià* 下, imply that the action involved is short and brief. Please note that some verbal measure words can also be used as nominal measure words and therefore also occur in the list of Nominal Measure Words above.

biàn 遍
(*to indicate the number of times an action or state occurs*) = time

> ! *Note that* biàn 遍 *is different from* cì 次 *in that it emphasizes the whole process from the beginning to the end.*

I've read that book twice = nàběn shū wǒ kànle liǎngbiàn 那本书我看了两遍

chǎng 场 ▶ *See also the list of Nominal Measure Words above.*
(*to indicate the occasion on which a state or an action occurs*)
last month she was sick = shàngge yuè tā bìngle yìchǎng 上个月她病了一场
I went back to my room and had a cry = wǒ huídào wǒde fángjiān kūle yìchǎng 我回到我的房间哭了一场

cì 次 ▶ *See also the list of Nominal Measure Words above.*
(*to indicate the number of times an action or state occurs*)
= time
he came three times = tā láile sāncì 他来了三次

dùn 顿 ▶ *See also the list of Nominal Measure Words above.*
(*for actions that take place in single sessions*)
he received [**some criticism** | **a reprimand** | **a beating**] = tā bèi [pīpíngle | màle | dǎle] yídùn 他被[批评了|骂了|打了]一顿

huí 回
(*for times, occurrences*)

> ! *Note that* huí 回 *is colloquial and informal.*

I'd like to try two more times = wǒ yào zài shì liǎnghuí 我要再试两回

shēng 声
(*for counting cries, shouts, or other utterances*)
she called me twice = tā hǎnle wǒ liǎngshēng 她喊了我两声
give me a shout before you go = nǐ zǒu yǐqián hǎn wǒ yìshēng 你走以前喊我一声

tàng 趟 ▶ *See also the list of Nominal Measure Words above.*
(*for trips, journeys, visits, etc.*) = time, trip
last month I made three trips to Beijing = shàngge yuè wǒ qùle sāntàng Běijīng 上个月我去了三趟北京
she came to my room twice yesterday = zuótiān tā dào wǒ fángjiān láile liǎngtàng 昨天她到我房间来了两趟

xià 下
(*for brief actions*) = time
I knocked at the door three times = wǒ qiàole sānxià mén 我敲了三下门
he nodded his head several times = tā diǎnle jǐxià tóu 他点了几下头

Basic Rules for writing Chinese characters

Basic strokes

1. The horizontal stroke is written from left to right.

2. The vertical stroke is written from the top downward.

3. The downward stroke to the left is written from top-right to bottom-left.

4. The downward stroke to the right is written from top-left to bottom-right.

5. The dot is usually written from the top to the bottom-right. Sometimes it is written from the top to the bottom-left.

6. The stroke with a hook: the hook is written by lifting the pen quickly as you approach the end of the hook.

7. The upward stroke to the right is written from bottom-left to top-right.

8. The horizontal stroke with a downward turn is written first from left to right and then downward.

9. The vertical stroke with a horizontal turn to the right is written first from the top downward and then horizontally to the right.

10. The horizontal stroke with a downward turn and hook is written first from left to right, then downward, and finally a turn is made toward the top-left by quickly lifting the pen to make the hook.

11. The vertical stroke with a right turn and a hook is written first from the top downward, then toward the right. Finally, an upward turn is added by quickly lifting the pen to make the hook.

12. The horizontal stroke with a turn to the bottom-left is written first from left to right and then toward the bottom-left.

Basic rules for stroke order

1. A horizontal stroke precedes a vertical stroke or a downward stroke either to the left or to the right.

shí 十: 1) 一 2) 十
tiān 天: 1) 一 2) 二 3) チ 4) 天

2. A downward stroke to the left precedes one to the right.

rén 人: 1) 丿 2) 人
mù 木: 1) 一 2) 十 3) 才 4) 木

3. The strokes are usually written from the top down.

liù 六: 1) 丶 2) 亠 3) 4) 六

yán 言: 1) 丶 2) 亠 3) 4)
5) 6) 7) 言

4. The strokes are usually written from left to right.

ér 儿: 1) 丿 2) 儿

shén 什: 1) 丿 2) 亻 3) 4) 什

5. When strokes are enclosed by another stroke or strokes on the top-right, top-left, or left-top-right sides (that is, with an open bottom), the enclosing strokes usually precede the enclosed strokes.

yīng 应: 1) 丶 2) 亠 3) 广 4) 5) 6)
7) 应

xí 习: 1) 𠃌 2) 3) 习

tóng 同: 1) 丨 2) 冂 3) 4) 5) 6) 同

6. When strokes are enclosed by another stroke or strokes on the bottom-left, or left-bottom-right sides (that is, with an open top), the enclosed strokes usually precede the enclosing strokes.

zhè 这: 1) 丶 2) 亠 3) 4) 文 5) 6) 这

huà 画: 1) 一 2) 3) 4) 5) 6)
7) 8) 画

7. When strokes are enclosed by other strokes on all four sides, the strokes on the left, top and right sides are written first, then the enclosed strokes, and finally the stroke at the bottom. This is commonly described as "putting everything inside before the door is closed".

mù 目: 1) 丨 2) 冂 3) 4) 5) 目

yīn 因: 1) 丨 2) 冂 3) 4) 5) 6) 因

8. A vertical stroke in the middle usually precedes strokes on either side.

xiǎo 小: 1) 亅 2) 3) 小

shuǐ 水: 1) 亅 2) 3) 4) 水

9. If a vertical stroke in the middle crosses other strokes, it is usually written last.

zhōng 中: 1) 丨 2) 3) 口 4) 中

fēng 丰: 1) 一 2) 二 3) 三 4) 丰

Aa

a, an *determiner* ▶ **157**
= yī 一
a dog = yìtiáo gǒu 一条狗
an exhibition = yíge zhǎnlǎnhuì 一个展览会
a crowd of people = yìqún rén 一群人

able *adjective*
• (*used as a modifier*) = nénggàn de 能干的
an able nurse = yíge nénggàn de hùshi 一个能干的护士
• (*having enough strength, skills or knowledge*) = néng 能
to be able to [**walk** | **type** | **translate**] = néng [zǒu | dǎzì | fānyì] 能 [走 | 打字 | 翻译]

aboard *adverb*

> ! *Note that the type of vehicle needs to be specified in Chinese.*

to go aboard = shàng [qìchē | huǒchē | fēijī] 上 [汽车 | 火车 | 飞机]

about

> ! *Often* **about** *occurs in combinations with verbs, for example:* **bring about, run about** *etc. To find the correct translations for this type of verb, look up the separate dictionary entries at* **bring, run**, *etc.*

1 *preposition*
= guānyú 关于
a book about China = yìběn guānyú Zhōngguó de shū 一本关于中国的书
2 *adverb*
• (*pre-modifier*) = dàyuē 大约
Oxford is about 40 km from here = Niújīn lí zhèr dàyuē sìshí gōnglǐ 牛津离这儿大约40公里
• (*post-modifier*) = zuǒyòu 左右
he goes to bed at about 11 o'clock = tā shíyī diǎn zuǒyòu shuìjiào 他十一点左右睡觉
3 to be about to = jiùyào...le 就要...了, kuàiyào...le 快要...了

> ! *Note that a sentence-final particle* le 了 *is needed here in Chinese.*

to be about to [**leave** | **cry** | **fall asleep**] = jiùyào [líkāi | kū | shuìzháo] le 就要 [离开 | 哭 | 睡着] 了

above
1 *preposition*
= zài...shàngbian 在... 上边
their office is above a shop = tāmende bàngōngshì zài yíge shàngdiàn shàngbian 他们的办公室在一个商店上边
2 *adverb*
= zài shàngbian 在上边
his room is just above = tāde fángjiān jiù zài shàngbian 他的房间就在上边
3 above all = shǒuxiān 首先

abroad *adverb*
• = guówài 国外
be abroad = zài guówài 在国外
return from abroad = cóng guówài huílai 从国外回来
• **go abroad** = chūguó 出国

absent *adjective*
• = méi lái 没来, méi qù 没去, bú zài 不在
she is absent from work = tā méi lái shàngbān 他没来上班
• **absent from classes** = quē kè 缺课

accent *noun*
= kǒuyīn 口音

accept *verb*
= jiēshòu 接受

accident *noun*
• (*causing injury or damage*)
an accident = yícì shìgù 一次事故
a car accident = yícì chēhuò 一次车祸
• (*by accident*) = ǒurán 偶然
I met him by accident = wǒ ǒurán yùjiànle tā 我偶然遇见了他

accommodation *noun*
= zhùchù 住处
look for accommodation = zhǎo zhùchù 找住处

accompany *verb*
= péitóng 陪同

account *noun*
• (*in a bank*)

an account = yíge zhànghù 一个帐户
there's money in my account = wǒde zhànghù lǐ yǒu qián 我的帐户里有钱
- (*consideration*)
take travelling expenses into account = kǎolǜ lǚxíng de huāfèi 考虑旅行的花费

accountant *noun* ▶ 344
an accountant = yíge kuàijì 一个会计

accuse *verb*
accuse someone of cheating = zhǐzé mǒurén qīpiàn 指责某人欺骗

across *preposition*
- (*to go across the road*) = guò mǎlù 过马路
to run across the road = pǎoguò mǎlù 跑过马路
a journey across the desert = chuānguò shāmò de lǚxíng 穿过沙漠的旅行
- (*on the other side of*) = zài...de nà yìbiān 在... 的那一边
he lives across the street = tā zhù zài mǎlù de nà yìbiān 他住在马路的那一边

act *verb*
- (*to do something*) = xíngdòng 行动
- (*to play a role*) = bànyǎn 扮演

activity *noun*
= huódòng 活动

actor *noun* ▶ 344
an actor = yíge nán yǎnyuán 一个男演员

actress *noun* ▶ 344
an actress = yíge nǚ yǎnyuán 一个女演员

actually *adverb*
= shíjìshang 实际上, shìshíshang 事实上
actually, she's a very good athlete = shíjìshang, tā shì yíge hěn hǎo de yùndòngyuán 实际上, 她是一个很好的运动员

adapt *verb*
= shǐ...shìyìng 使... 适应
I must adapt myself to the new environment = wǒ yídìng yào shǐ zìjǐ shìyìng xīn de huánjìng 我一定要使自己适应新的环境

add *verb*
= jiā 加

address *noun*
= dìzhǐ 地址

admire *verb*
= qīnpèi 钦佩, zànshǎng 赞赏

admit *verb*
- (*to own up or recognize as being true*) = chéngrèn 承认
he admitted that he was wrong = tā chéngrèn tā cuò le 他承认他错了
- to be admitted to (the) hospital = zhùjìn yīyuàn 住进医院

adolescent *noun*
= qīngshàonián 青少年

adopt *verb*
= cǎiyòng 采用, cǎinà 采纳

adult *noun*
= chéngniánrén 成年人, dàrén 大人

advantage *noun*
- (*a benefit*) = hǎochù 好处
- (*a favouring condition*) = yǒulì tiáojiàn 有利条件
- (*superiority over another*) = yōushì 优势
at the beginning of the game, the advantage was with the blue team = bǐsài kāishǐ de shíhou, lán duì zhàn yōushì 比赛开始的时候, 蓝队占优势
- to take advantage of... = lìyòng... 利用...

adventure *noun*
an adventure = yícì màoxiǎn 一次冒险

advertise *verb*
= wèi...dēng guǎnggào 为... 登广告
to advertise goods = wèi shāngpǐn dēng guǎnggào 为商品登广告

advertisement *noun*
= guǎnggào 广告

advice *noun*
= zhōnggào 忠告, quàngào 劝告

advise *verb*
= quàngào 劝告, jiànyì 建议

aerial *noun*
= tiānxiàn 天线

aerobics *noun* ▶ 390
= zēngyǎng jiànshēn fǎ 增氧健身法

affect *verb*
= yǐngxiǎng 影响

afford *verb*
- (*to bear the expense*) = mǎi de qǐ 买得起
  he [can | cannot] afford to buy this car = tā [mǎi de qǐ | mǎi bù qǐ] zhèliàng chē 他 [买得起 | 买不起] 这辆车
- (*to have the time*) = chōu de chū 抽得出
  I [can | cannot] afford the time to go to the cinema = wǒ [chōu de chū | chōu bù chū] shíjiān qù kàn diànyǐng 我 [抽得出 | 抽不出] 时间去看电影

> **!** *Note that to negate,* de 得 *in* mǎi de qǐ 买得起 *and* chōu de chū 抽得出 *has to be replaced with the negative particle* bù 不.

afraid *adjective*
- (*fearful*) = hàipà 害怕, pà 怕
  she is afraid of dogs = tā hàipà gǒu 她害怕狗
  she is afraid to lose this opportunity = tā pà diūle zhège jīhuì 她怕丢了这个机会
- (*regretfully thinking*) = kǒngpà 恐怕

> **!** *Note that in this usage, if the subject of the main clause is a first-person singular pronoun* (I = wǒ 我), *it has to be phonetically silent and the subject of the embedded clause can often be moved to the main clause.*

  I'm afraid that I won't be able to go = kǒngpà wǒ bù néng qù le 恐怕我不能去了, wǒ kǒngpà bù néng qù le 我恐怕不能去了
  I'm afraid that he has left = kǒngpà tā yǐjīng líkāi le 恐怕他已经离开了, tā kǒngpà yǐjīng líkāi le 他恐怕已经离开了

Africa *noun*
  = Fēizhōu 非洲

African ▶ 288
1 *adjective*
  = Fēizhōu de 非洲的
2 *noun*
  = Fēizhōurén 非洲人

after
1 *preposition*
  = (zài)...yǐhòu (在)... 以后
  after breakfast = zǎofàn yǐhòu 早饭以后
  the day after tomorrow = hòutiān 后天
2 *conjunction*
  = ...yǐhòu ... 以后
  after we had eaten, we went for a walk = chīle fàn yǐhòu, wǒmen chūqu sànbù 吃了饭以后, 我们出去散步
  they went in after the film had started = diànyǐng kāishǐ yǐhòu tāmen cái jìnqu 电影开始以后他们才进去
3 after all = bìjìng 毕竟

afternoon *noun* ▶ 204, ▶ 412
  = xiàwǔ 下午

afterwards, afterward (*US English*) *adverb*
- = yǐhòu 以后
- (*when talking about a past event*) = hòulái 后来

again *adverb*
- (*when the repetition has already happened*) = yòu 又
  he has come again = tā yòu lái le 他又来了
- (*when the repetition is to happen*) = zài 再
  please try it again = qǐng zài shì yícì 请再试一次

against *preposition*
- (*in the sense of being opposed to something*) = fǎnduì 反对
  I am against this plan = wǒ fǎnduì zhège jìhuà 我反对这个计划
- (*to resist the wind*) = dǐng 顶
  the ship is sailing against the wind = chuán zhèng dǐngzhe fēng xíngshǐ 船正顶着风行驶
- (*to resist a water current*) = nì 逆
  she swam against the current = tā nì shuǐ yóuyǒng 她逆水游泳
- (*to put pressure upon*) = kào 靠, yǐ 倚
  I was standing against the wall = wǒ kàozhe qiáng zhànzhe 我靠着墙站着

age *noun* ▶ 170
  = suì 岁, niánjì 年纪, niánlíng 年龄

aged *adjective*
- (*advanced in age*) = lǎo 老
- (*of the age of*) = ···suì de ···岁的
  children aged 10 = shí suì de háizi 十岁的孩子

ago *adverb*
  = yǐqián 以前
  two weeks ago = liǎng gè xīngqī yǐqián 两个星期以前
  long ago = hěn jiǔ yǐqián 很久以前

Age

How old?

- (when asking about a child's age) = jǐ suì (le) 几岁(了), duò dà (le) 多大(了)

  How old are you? = nǐ jǐ suì (le)? 你几岁(了)?

- (when asking about an elderly person's age) = duō dà niánjì (le) 多大年纪(了), duō dà suìshu (le) 多大岁数(了)

  how old is your grandmother? = nǐ nǎinai duō dà niánjì (le)? 你奶奶多大年纪(了)?

- (when asking about a person's age in a general situation) = duōshǎo suì (le) 多少岁(了)

  how old is he? = tā duōshǎo suì (le)? 他多少岁(了)?

- (when asking about the age of an inanimate entity) = yǒu duōshǎo nián de lìshǐ (le) 有多少年的历史(了)

  how old is the university? = zhèsuǒ dàxué yǒu duōshǎo nián de lìshǐ le? 这所大学有多少年的历史了?

In answering, the word **suì** 岁 (*years old*) can be omitted if the age is older than ten.

I am eight (years old) = wǒ bā suì (le) 我八岁(了)
she is seventy (years old) = tā qīshí (suì) (le) 她七十(岁)(了)
the university is a hundred years old = zhèsuǒ dàxué yǒu yìbǎi nián de lìshǐ (le) 这所大学有一百年的历史(了)

Note the use of **de** 的 when age is used as a modifier:

a woman aged thirty = yíge sānshí suì de nǚrén 一个三十岁的女人

Comparing ages

*I'm older **than** you* = wǒ **bǐ** nǐ dà 我比你大
*she's younger **than** he* = tā **bǐ** tā xiǎo 她比他小
*Anne's two years **younger*** = Ānní **xiǎo** liǎng suì 安妮小两岁
*Tom's five years **older than** Joe* = Tāngmǔ **bǐ** Qiáo **dà** wǔ suì 汤姆比乔大五岁

Approximate ages

*he's **about** fifty* = tā **dàyuē** wǔshí suì 他大约五十岁
*she's **just over** sixty* = tā **gāng guò** liùshí 她刚过六十
*games for **the under** twelves* = shí'èr suì **yǐxià** de bǐsài 十二岁以下的比赛
*only for **the over** eighteens* = zhǐ shìyú shíbā suì **yǐshàng** de rén 只适于十八岁以上的人

---

agree *verb*
- (*to have the same opinion*) = tóngyì 同意, zàntóng 赞同
  I don't agree with you = wǒ bù tóngyì nǐde yìjiàn 我不同意你的意见
- (*to consent to do*) = dāying 答应, yīngyǔn 应允
  he agrees to help us = tā dāying bāngzhù wǒmen 他答应帮助我们
- (*to decide jointly*) = shāngdìng 商定, yuēdìng 约定
  we have agreed on the date for the meeting = wǒmen shāngdìngle huìyì de rìqī 我们商定了会议的日期

agriculture *noun*
= nóngyè 农业

ahead *adverb*
- (*location*) = zài···qiánmian 在···前面
  he is ahead of others = tā zài biéren qiánmian 他在别人前面
- (*direction*) = xiàng qián 向前
  look ahead = xiàngqián kàn 向前看

Aids *noun* ▶ 277
= àizībìng 艾滋病

aim
1 *noun*
an aim (*an object aimed at*) = yī gè mùbiāo 一个目标
(*a purpose aimed at*) = yī gè mùdì 一个目的
2 *verb*
- (*to be directed at*)
  to be aimed at young people = zhēnduì niánqīngrén 针对年轻人
- (*when using a weapon*)
  to aim a rifle at someone = yòng qiāng miáozhǔn mǒurén 用枪瞄准某人

air *noun*
= kōngqì 空气
- **in the air** = zài kōngzhōng 在空中

air force *noun*
= kōngjūn 空军

air hostess *noun* ▶ 344 (*British English*)
an air hostess = yī wèi kōngzhōng xiǎojie 一位空中小姐

airmail *noun*
to send a letter by airmail = jì yī fēng hángkōngxìn 寄一封航空信

airport *noun*
an airport = yīgè fēijīchǎng 一个飞机场

alarm clock *noun*
an alarm clock = yīge nàozhōng 一个闹钟

alcohol *noun*
- (*chemical term*) = jiǔjīng 酒精
- (*drink containing alcohol*) = jiǔ 酒

alive *adjective*
= huózhe 活着

all
1 *determiner*
- (*whole*) = zhěnggè 整个
  I spent all week working = wǒ zhěnggè xīngqī dōu gōngzuò 我整个星期都工作
- (*every*) = suǒyǒu de 所有的, quánbù de 全部的
  all the men have left = suǒyǒu de nánrén dōu líkāi le 所有的男人都离开了

2 *pronoun*
- (*people*) = suǒyǒu de rén 所有的人
  all of us = wǒmen suǒyǒu de rén 我们所有的人
- (*things*) = yīqiè 一切, suǒyǒu de 所有的
  these are all I have = zhè shì wǒ yōngyǒu de yīqiè 这是我拥有的一切
  that's all = wán le 完了

3 *adverb*
to be all alone = dúzì yī rén 独自一人
he didn't go all along the street = tā méiyǒu yīzhí yánzhe mǎlù zǒu 他没有一直沿着马路走

allow *verb*
- = yǔnxǔ 允许, zhǔnxǔ 准许
  to allow someone to [work | play | leave...] = yúnxǔ mǒurén [gōngzuò | wán | líkāi···] 允许某人[工作 | 玩 | 离开···]
- **smoking is not allowed** = jìnzhǐ xīyān 禁止吸烟

all right *adjective*
- (*when giving your opinion*) = búcuò 不错, hái kěyǐ 还可以
  the film was all right = zhèbù diànyǐng bùcuò 这部电影不错
- (*when talking about health*)
  are you all right? = nǐ hái hǎo ma? 你还好吗?, nǐ hái xíng ma? 你还行吗?
- (*when asking someone's opinion*)
  is it all right if I come later? = wǒ wǎn diǎnr lái xíng ma? 我晚点儿来行吗?
  come at about nine, all right? = dàyuē jiǔ diǎn lái, xíng ma? 大约九点来, 行吗?
- (*when agreeing*) = xíng 行, hǎo 好

almond *noun*
= xìngrén 杏仁

almost *adverb*
= jīhū 几乎, chàbuduō 差不多
I almost forgot = wǒ jīhū wàng le 我几乎忘了

alone
1 *adjective*
= dāndú 单独, dúzì yìrén 独自一人

to be all alone = dúzì yìrén 独自一人
leave me alone! = bié guǎn wǒ! 别管我! bié dòng wǒ! 别动我!

2 *adverb*
[to work | to live | to travel...] alone = dúzì yìrén [gōngzuò | shēnghuó | lǚxíng...] 独自一人[工作 | 生活 | 旅行...]

along *preposition*
= yánzhe 沿着
there are trees along the river = yánzhe hébiān yǒu yìxiē shù 沿着河边有一些树

aloud *adverb*
= dàshēng de 大声地
to read aloud = lǎngdú 朗读

already *adverb*
= yǐjīng 已经
it's ten o'clock already = yǐjīng shí diǎn le 已经十点了

also *adverb*
- (*likewise*) = yě 也
  he also agrees with me = tā yě tóngyì wǒde yìjiàn 他也同意我的意见
- (*in addition*) = hái 还
  I also bought a bottle of wine = wǒ hái mǎile yìpíng jiǔ 我还买了一瓶酒

although *conjunction*
= suīrán 虽然, jǐnguǎn 尽管
although she's strict, she's fair = suīrán tā hěn yángé, dàn tā hěn gōngpíng 虽然她很严格, 但她很公平

always *adverb*
- (*every time*) = zǒngshì 总是, lǎoshì 老是
  I always go to China in (the) summer = wǒ zǒngshì xiàtiān qù Zhōngguó 我总是夏天去中国
- (*ever*) = yǒngyuǎn 永远
  I'll always remember him = wǒ jiāng yǒngyuǎn jìzhù tā 我将永远记住他

amazed *adjective*
= jīngyà 惊讶, jīngqí 惊奇

amazing *adjective*
= lìngrén jīngyà 令人惊讶, liǎobuqǐ 了不起

ambition *noun*
- (*aspiration for success or advancement*) = bàofù 抱负, xióngxīn 雄心
- (*inordinate desire for power, fame*) = yěxīn 野心, shēwàng 奢望

ambitious *adjective*
- (*aspiring*) = yǒu bàofù de 有抱负的, yǒu xióngxīn de 有雄心的
- (*inordinately longing for power, fame*) = yǒu yěxīn de 有野心的

ambulance *noun*
= jiùhùchē 救护车

America *noun*
= Měiguó 美国

American ▶ 288
1 *adjective*
= Měiguó de 美国的
2 *noun*
= Měiguórén 美国人

among, amongst *preposition*
- (*in the middle of*) = zài...zhōngjiān 在...中间
  she was sitting among the students = tā zuò zài xuésheng zhōngjiān 她坐在学生中间
- (*in a particular group*) = zài...zhōng 在...中
  unemployment among young people = zài niánqīng rén zhōng de shīyè qíngkuàng 在年轻人中的失业情况

amount *noun*
= shùliàng 数量

amusement arcade *noun*
= diànzǐ yóuxì fáng 电子游戏房

amusement park *noun*
= yùlè chǎng 娱乐场

an ▶ a

ancestor *noun*
= zǔzōng 祖宗, zǔxiān 祖先

and *conjunction*
- and = hé 和
  father and mother = bàba hé māma 爸爸和妈妈
- (and *is not translated when it is used to connect two verb phrases or two sentences*)
  she went to the shop and bought some fruit = tā qù shāngdiàn mǎile yìxiē shuǐguǒ 她去商店买了一些水果

- (*in numbers*, and *is not translated*)
  three hundred and sixty-five = sānbǎi liùshí wǔ 三百六十五

anger *noun*
= fènnù 愤怒, qìfèn 气愤

angry *adjective*
to be angry = shēngqì 生气
to be angry with someone = duì mǒurén shēngqì 对某人生气

animal *noun*
= dòngwù 动物
farm animals = sìyǎng de dòngwù 饲养的动物

ankle *noun* ▶ 189
= huáiguānjié 踝关节, jiǎobózi 脚脖子

announcement *noun*
an announcement = yíge tōnggào/tōngzhī 一个通告/通知

annoy *verb*
= shǐ...shēngqì 使...生气, shǐ... náohuǒ 使...恼火
to annoy someone = shǐ mǒurén shēngqì 使某人生气

annoyed *adjective*
to be annoyed with someone = duì mǒurén shēngqì 对某人生气

another
1 *determiner*
- **another** = zài...yī 再...一, lìng...yī 另...一
  another cup of coffee? = zài hē yìbēi kāfēi? 再喝一杯咖啡?
  I'll buy another ticket for her = wǒ gěi tā lìng mǎi yìzhāng piào 我给她另买一张票
- (*different*) = biéde 别的, lìngwài de 另外的
  there's another way of doing it = hái yǒu biéde fāngfǎ zuò zhèjiàn shì 还有别的方法做这件事
  he has become another person = tā biànchéngle lìngwài de yíge rén 他变成了另外的一个人

2 *pronoun*
I don't like [**this pen** | **this book** | **this coat...**]; **please show me another** = wǒ bù xǐhuān [zhèzhī bǐ | zhèběn shū | zhèjiàn shàngyī....], qǐng ná [lìng yìzhī | lìng yìběn | lìng yíjiàn...] gěi wǒ kànkan 我不喜欢[这支笔 | 这本书 | 这件上衣....], 请拿[另一支 | 另一本 | 另一件...] 给我看看

> ! *Note that it is necessary to use an appropriate measure word after* lìng yī... 另一..., *when* another *is translated as a pronoun.*

answer
1 *noun*
- = dáfù 答复, huídá 回答
  did you get an answer? = nǐ dédào dáfù le ma? 你得到答复了吗?
  there's no answer (at the door) = méi rén huídá 没人回答
- (*solution*) = dá'àn 答案
  answers to the exercises = liánxí dá'àn 练习答案

2 *verb*
- = huídá 回答
  to answer a question = huídá yíge wèntí 回答一个问题
- **to answer the phone** = jiē diànhuà 接电话

answering machine *noun*
an answering machine = yìtái lùyīn diànhuà 一台录音电话

ant *noun*
an ant = yìzhī mǎyǐ 一只蚂蚁

antique *noun*
an antique = yíjiàn gǔwù 一件古物, yíjiàn gǔdǒng 一件古董

antique shop *noun*
an antique shop = yìjiā gǔwù shāngdiàn 一家古物商店, yìjiā gǔdǒng diàn 一件古董店

anxious *adjective*
- (*uneasy with fear*) = dānxīn 担心, jiāolǜ 焦虑
  I'm anxious about her safety = wǒ wèi tāde ānquán dānxīn 我为她的安全担心
- (*eager*) = jíqiè 急切, kěwàng 渴望
  she is anxious to go with me = tā jíqiè xiǎng gēn wǒ yìqǐ qù 她急切想跟我一起去

any
1 *determiner*
- (*in questions*) = shénme 什么

> ! *Note that it is often unnecessary to translate* any *in questions.*

  do you have any questions? = nǐ yǒu (shénme) wèntí ma? 你有(什么)问题吗?
- (*with the negative*) = rènhé 任何

I didn't have any friends = wǒ méi yǒu rènhé péngyou 我没有任何朋友
• (*whatever*) = rènhé 任何
any pen will do = rènhé bǐ dōu xíng 任何笔都行
2 *pronoun*
do any of you know his telephone number? = nǐmen shéi zhīdao tāde diànhuà hàomǎ ma? 你们谁知道他的电话号码吗?
do you have any? = nǐ yǒu ma? 你有吗?
he doesn't have any = tā méi yǒu 他没有

> **!** *Note that it is often unnecessary to translate* **any** *when it is used as a pronoun in an object position.*

anyone *pronoun* (*also* **anybody**)
= rènhé rén 任何人
did you meet anyone? = nǐ yùjiàn rènhé rén le ma? 你遇见任何人了吗?
anyone could do it = rènhé rén dōu néng zuò zhèjiàn shì 任何人都能做这件事

anything *pronoun*
• (*in questions or with the negative*) = shénme shì 什么事, rènhé shì 任何事
can I do anything for you? = wǒ néng wèi nǐ zuò diánr shénme shì ma? 我能为你做点儿什么事吗?
there isn't anything to do here = zhèr méi yǒu rènhé shì kě zuò 这儿没有任何事可做
• (*everything*) = rènhé shìqing 任何事情, yíqiè 一切
he is willing to do anything for her = tā yuàn wèi tā zuò rènhé shìqing 他愿为她做任何事情

anyway *adverb*
= fǎnzhèng 反正
I didn't want to go there anyway = fǎnzhèng wǒ běnlái yě bù xiǎng qù nàr 反正我本来也不想去那儿

anywhere *adverb*
• (*in questions or with the negative*) = nǎr 哪儿, nǎli 哪里
can you see a telephone anywhere? = nǐ néng kànjian nǎr yǒu diànhuà ma? 你能看见哪儿有电话吗?
you can't go anywhere = nǐ nǎr yě bù néng qù 你哪儿也不能去
• (*any place*) = zài rènhé dìfang 在任何地方
we can meet anywhere you like = wǒmen kěyǐ zài rènhé dìfang jiànmiàn, suí nǐ biàn 我们可以在任何地方见面, 随你便

apart
1 *adjective*
they don't like being apart = tāmen bú yuànyì fēnkāi 他们不愿意分开
2 apart from = chúle...(yǐwài) 除了...(以外)
apart from Tom, I don't know anyone there = chúle Tāngmǔ (yǐwài), nàr wǒ shéi dōu bú rènshi 除了汤姆(以外), 那儿我谁都不认识

apartment *noun*
an apartment = yítào gōngyù fángjiān 一套公寓房间

apartment block *noun*
an apartment block = yìpái gōngyù lóu 一排公寓楼

apologize *verb*
= dàoqiàn 道歉
did you apologize to him? = nǐ xiàng tā dàoqiàn le ma? 你向他道歉了吗?

apology *noun*
= dàoqiàn 道歉, rèncuò 认错
to make an apology to him for coming late = wèi láiwǎnle xiàng tā dàoqiàn 为来晚了向他道歉

appear *verb*
• (*to seem*) = kànqilai 看起来, hǎoxiàng 好象
• (*to come into view*) = chūxiàn 出现, xiǎnlù 显露

appetite *noun*
= shíyù 食欲, wèikǒu 胃口
to have a good appetite = shíyù hǎo 食欲好

apple *noun*
an apple = yíge píngguǒ 一个苹果

apple juice *noun*
= píngguǒ zhī 苹果汁

appliance *noun*
= qìjù 器具, yòngjù 用具
an appliance = yíjiàn qìjù 一件器具

application *noun*
an application = yífèn shēnqǐng 一份申请

apply *verb*
= shēnqǐng 申请
to apply for a passport = shēnqǐng yìběn hùzhào 申请一本护照

appointment *noun*
= yuēhuì 约会
to make an appointment with someone = gēn mǒurén yuēhuì 跟某人约会

appreciate *verb*
I'd appreciate it if you could let me know = rúguǒ nǐ néng gàosu wǒ, wǒ huì fēicháng gǎnxiè 如果你能告诉我, 我会非常感谢

approach *verb*
= jiējìn 接近, kàojìn 靠近

approve *verb*
- = pīzhǔn 批准, tōngguò 通过
- **to approve of someone** = zànchéng mǒurén 赞成某人

apricot *noun*
an apricot = yíge xìng 一个杏

April *noun* ▶ 218
= sìyuè 四月

architect *noun* ▶ 344
an architect = yíge jiànzhùshī 一个建筑师

area *noun*
- (*a region*) = dìqū 地区
  an area = yíge dìqū 一个地区
- (*an academic field*) = lǐngyù 领域
  an area = yíge lǐngyù 一个领域

area code *noun* (*US English*)
= yóuzhèng biānmǎ 邮政编码

argue *verb*
= zhēnglùn 争论, biànlùn 辩论
to argue about politics = zhēnglùn zhèngzhì 争论政治

argument *noun*
an argument = yíge lùndiǎn 一个论点, yíge lǐyóu 一个理由
to have an argument with someone = gēn mǒurén zhēnglùn 跟某人争论

arm *noun* ▶ 189
the arm = gēbo 胳膊, bì 臂

armchair *noun*
an armchair = yíge fúshǒuyǐ 一个扶手椅

armed *adjective*
= wǔzhuāng de 武装的

arms *noun*
= wǔqì 武器

army *noun*
= jūnduì 军队
to join the army = cān jūn 参军

around

> **!** *Often* around *occurs in combinations with verbs, for example:* run around, turn around, *etc. To find the correct translations for this type of verb, look up the separate dictionary entries at* run, turn, *etc.*

1 *preposition*
= zài...zhōuwéi 在... 周围
there are trees all around the garden = zài huāyuán zhōuwéi dōu shì shù 在花园周围都是树
the people around me were speaking Chinese = zài wǒ zhōuwéi de rén shuō Hànyǔ 在我周围的人说汉语
to go around the world = zhōuyóu shìjiè 周游世界

2 *adverb*
- (*nearby*) = zhōuwéi 周围
  he looked around = tā xiàng zhōuwéi kàn le kàn 他向周围看了看
- (*approximately*) = dàyuē 大约
  we'll be there at around four o'clock = wǒmen dàyuē sì diǎn zhōng dào nàr 我们大约四点钟到那儿

arrange *verb*
- (*to make plans in advance*) = ānpái 安排
  to arrange a break in Italy = ānpái zài Yìdàlì xiūxi yíxià 安排在意大利休息一下
  to arrange to have lunch together = ānpái yìqǐ chī wǔfàn 安排一起吃午饭
- (*to put in order*) = zhěnglǐ 整理
  to arrange his books = zhěnglǐ tāde shū 整理他的书

arrest *verb*
= dàibǔ 逮捕

arrive *verb*
= dàodá 到达, dào 到
we arrived at the station at noon = wǒmen zhōngwǔ dàodá chēzhàn 我们中午到达车站

arrow *noun*
- (*missile*) = jiàn 箭
  an arrow = yìzhī jiàn 一支箭

- (*mark or object*) = jiàntóu 箭头
  an arrow = yíge jiàntóu 一个箭头

art *noun*
= yìshù 艺术

art gallery *noun*
an art gallery = yíge měishùguǎn 一个美术馆

artificial *adjective*
= réngōng 人工, rénzào 人造

artist *noun* ▶ 344
an artist = yíge yìshùjiā 一个艺术家

arts *noun*
arts and humanities = rénwén xuékē 人文学科

arts and crafts *noun*
= gōngyì měishù 工艺美术

as

1 *conjunction*

- **as** = ànzhào 按照
  do as he does = ànzhào tāde yàngzi zuò 按照他的样子做
- (*at the time when*) = ... de shíhou ...的时候
  the phone rang as I was getting out of the bath = wǒ zhèng cóng zǎopén chūlai de shíhou, diànhuà líng xiǎng le 我正从澡盆出来的时候,电话铃响了
  I used to live there as a child = wǒ xiǎo de shíhou zhù zài nàr 我小的时候住在那儿
- (*because, since*) = yīnwèi 因为, yóuyú 由于
  as you were out, I left a note = yīnwèi nǐ chūqu le, suǒyǐ wǒ jiù liúle zhāng tiáo 因为你出去了,所以我就留了张条
- (*when used with* **the same**) = gēn...yíyàng 跟...一样, hé...yíyàng 和...一样
  my coat is the same as yours = wǒde shàngyī gēn nǐde yíyàng 我的上衣跟你的一样

2 *preposition*
she's got a job as a teacher = tā zhǎodào le yíge jiàoshī de gōngzuò 她找到了一个教师的工作
he was dressed as a sailor = tā chuān de xiàng yíge shuǐshǒu 他穿得象一个水手

3 *adverb*
as [intelligent | rich | strong...] as he is = hé tā yíyàng [cōngming | yǒuqián | qiángzhuàng...] 和他一样 [聪明 | 有钱 | 强壮...]
go there as fast as you can = nǐ jìnkuài qù nàr 你尽快去那儿
I have as much work as you = wǒde gōngzuò hé nǐde yíyàng duō 我的工作和你的一样多
he plays the piano as well as his younger sister = tā tán gāngqín tán de hé tā mèimei yíyàng hǎo 他弹钢琴弹得和他妹妹一样好

4 as usual = xiàng wǎngcháng yíyàng 象往常一样, zhàolì 照例

ashamed *adjective*
to be ashamed = gǎndào cánkuì 感到惭愧, gǎndào hàisào 感到害臊

ashes *noun*
= huī(jìn) 灰(烬)
(*of a cigarette*) = yānhuī 烟灰
(*of a dead body*) = gǔhuī 骨灰

ashtray *noun*
an ashtray = yíge yānhuīgāng 一个烟灰缸

Asia *noun*
= Yàzhōu 亚洲

Asian ▶ 288

1 *adjective*
= Yàzhōu de 亚洲的

2 *noun*
= Yàzhōurén 亚洲人

ask *verb*

- **to ask** = wèn 问
  he asked me my name = tā wèn wǒ jiào shénme 他问我叫什么
  I'll ask them if they want to come = wǒ yào wèn tāmen xiǎng bù xiǎng lái 我要问他们想不想来
  to ask a question = wèn wèntí 问问题
- (*to request*) = ràng 让, jiào 叫, yāoqiú 要求
  to ask someone to [phone | come | do the shopping...] = ràng mǒurén [dǎ diànhuà | lái | mǎi dōngxi...] 让某人 [打电话 | 来 | 买东西...]
  to ask to speak to someone = yāoqiú gēn mǒurén jiǎnghuà 要求跟某人讲话
  to ask for money = yào qián 要钱
- (*to invite*) = yāoqǐng 邀请, qǐng 请
  to ask some friends to dinner = yāoqǐng yìxiē péngyou chī fàn 邀请一些朋友吃饭
- (*to look for information*) = xúnwèn 询问

did you ask about the tickets? = nǐ xúnwèn piào de shìqing le ma? 你询问票的事情了吗?

asleep *adjective*
to be asleep = zài shuìjiào 在睡觉
to fall asleep = shuìzháo 睡着

assemble *verb*
- (*to call together*) = jíhé 集合
all the students assembled in the school hall = xuésheng dōu zài xuéxiào lǐtáng lǐ jíhé 学生都在学校礼堂里集合
- (*to collect*) = shōují 收集
she has assembled some materials = tā yǐjīng shōují le yìxiē cáiliào 她已经收集了一些材料
- (*to put together the parts of*) = zhuāngpèi 装配
to assemble a machine = zhuāngpèi jīqì 装配机器

assignment *noun*
a school assignment = xuéxiào zuòyè 学校作业

assistant *noun*
an assistant = yíge zhùshǒu 一个助手
a shop assistant = yíge shòuhuòyuán 一个售货员
a teaching assistant = yíge zhùjiào 一个助教

at *preposition*

> **!** *There are many verbs which involve the use of* at, *like* look at, laugh at, point at, *etc. For translations, look up the entries at* look, laugh, point, *etc.*

- (*when talking about a position or place*) = zài 在
we'll meet at the concert = wǒmen zài yīnyuèhuì jiànmiàn 我们在音乐会见面
to be [at home | at school | at work...] = [zài jiā | zài xuéxiào | zài shàngbān...] [在家 | 在学校 | 在上班...]
- to be at one's desk = zài xuéxí 在学习, zài gōngzuò 在工作
- (*when talking about time and age*) = (zài)...(de shíhou) (在)...(的时候)
the film starts at nine o'clock = diànyǐng jiù diǎn kāiyǎn 电影九点开演
she was able to read at four years of age = tā (zài) sì suì (de shíhou) jiù néng kàn shū le 她(在)四岁(的时候)就能看书了
- (*when talking about speed and price*) = yǐ 以
the car goes at seventy miles an hour = qìchē yǐ měi xiǎoshí wǔshí yīnglǐ de sùdù xíngshǐ 汽车以每小时五十英里的速度行驶
at a low price = yǐ hěn dī de jiàqián 以很低的价钱

athlete *noun* ▶ 344
an athlete = yíge yùndòngyuán 一个运动员, yìmíng yùndòngyuán 一名运动员

athletics *noun* ▶ 390
(*in Britain*) = tiánjìng yùndòng 田径运动
(*in the US*) = tǐyù yùndòng 体育运动

Atlantic *noun*
the Atlantic = Dàxīyáng 大西洋

atmosphere *noun*
- (*the air*) = dàqì 大气, kōngqì 空气
- (*a mood, a feeling*) = qìfen 气氛

attach *verb*
to be attached to the wall = tiē zài qiáng shang 贴在墙上
attach a basket to the bike = bǎ yíge lánzi jì zài zìxíngchē shang 把一个篮子系在自行车上

attachment *noun*
an attachment = yíge fùjiàn 一个附件

attack *verb*
= gōngjī 攻击, jìngōng 进攻

attempt
1 *verb*
= shìtú 试图
2 *noun*
= chángshì 尝试, shìtú 试图

attend *verb*
- (*to be present*) = cānjiā 参加, chūxí 出席
to attend a meeting = cānjiā huìyì 参加会议
- (*to go regularly to*) = shàng 上
to attend evening classes = shàng yèxiào 上夜校

attention *noun*
= zhùyì 注意
to get someone's attention = yǐnqǐ mǒurén de zhùyì 引起某人的注意
to pay attention to the teacher = zhùyì tīng lǎoshī jiǎngkè 注意听老师讲课

attic *noun*
= gélóu 阁楼, fángdǐngshì 房顶室

attitude *noun*
= tàidu 态度
his attitude toward(s) me = tā duì wǒ de tàidu 他对我的态度

attract *verb*
- **to attract people** = xīyǐn rén 吸引人
- **to attract** [**attention** | **interest** | **appreciation**] = yǐnqǐ [zhùyì | xìngqu | zànshǎng] 引起 [注意 | 兴趣 | 赞赏]

attractive *adjective*
= yǒu xīyǐnlì de 有吸引力的, yòurén de 诱人的

auburn *adjective*
= jīn zōngsè de 金棕色的

audience *noun*
- (*assembly of hearers*) = tīngzhòng 听众
- (*assembly of spectators*) = guānzhòng 观众

August *noun* ▶ 218
= bāyuè 八月

aunt *noun*
- (*father's sister*) = gūmǔ 姑母, gūgu 姑姑
- (*mother's sister*) = yímǔ 姨母, yí 姨
- (*a respectful form of address to an elderly woman*) = dàmā 大妈, dàniáng 大娘
- (*a respectful form used by children to address an adult woman*) = āyí 阿姨

au pair *noun*
an au pair = yíge bāngshǒu 一个帮手, yíge bānggōng 一个帮工

Australia *noun*
= Àodàlìyà 澳大利亚

Australian ▶ 288
1 *adjective*
= Àodàlìyà de 澳大利亚的
2 *noun*
= Àodàlìyàrén 澳大利亚人

Austria *noun*
= Àodìlì 奥地利

Austrian ▶ 288
1 *adjective*
= Àodìlì de 奥地利的
2 *noun*
= Àodìlìrén 奥地利人

author *noun* ▶ 344
= zuòzhě 作者

automatic *adjective*
= zìdòng 自动

autumn *noun*
= qiūtiān 秋天, qiūjì 秋季

available *adjective*
- (*obtainable through purchase*) = néng mǎidào 能买到, mǎi de dào 买得到
  tickets for the concert are still available = yīnyuèhuì de piào hái néng mǎidào 音乐会的票还能买到
- (*accessible for use*) = kěyǐ yòng 可以用
  all the books are available to the students = suǒyǒu de shū xuésheng dōu kěyǐ yòng 所有的书学生都可以用

average *adjective*
- (*mean*) = píngjūn 平均
- (*ordinary*) = pǔtōng de 普通的, tōngcháng de 通常的
  the average man = pǔtōng de rén 普通的人

avoid *verb*
- (*to prevent*) = bìmiǎn 避免
  to avoid spending money = bìmiǎn huā qián 避免花钱
- (*to stay away from*) = duǒkāi 躲开, huíbì 回避

awake *adjective*
to be awake (*having slept*) = xǐngle 醒了
to stay awake = shuì bù zháo 睡不着
to keep someone awake = shǐ mǒurén shuì bù zháo 使某人睡不着

award *noun*
an award = yíge jiǎng(pǐn) 一个奖(品)
she got the award for best actress = tā huòdé zuìjiā nǚ yǎnyuán jiǎng 她获得最佳女演员奖

aware *adjective*
to be aware of the [**problem** | **danger** | **difficulty...**] = yìshídào zhège [wèntì | wēixiǎn | kùnnan...] 意识到这个 [问题 | 危险 | 困难...]

away *adverb*
- (*absent*)
  to be away = bú zài 不在
  she's away on business = tā chūchāi le 她出差了

- (*when talking about distances*)
  to be far away = zài hěn yuǎn 在很远
  London is 40 km away = Lúndūn lí zhèr sìshí gōnglǐ 伦敦离这儿四十公里

awful *adjective*
- (*no good*) = zāotòu le 糟透了, hěn zāogāo 很糟糕
  I thought the film was awful = wǒ juéde zhège diànyǐng zāotòu le 我觉得这个电影糟透了
- (*causing shock*) = kěpà 可怕
  an awful accident = yíge kěpà de shìgù 一个可怕的事故
- **I feel awful** = wǒ gǎndào fēicháng nánshòu 我感到非常难受

awkward *adjective*
- (*describing a situation, a problem*) = jìshǒu 棘手, nán chǔlǐ 难处理
- (*embarrassed*) = gāngà 尴尬
  I feel awkward about telling him = gàosu tā wǒ juéde hěn gāngà 告诉他我觉得很尴尬

axe *noun*
  an axe = yìbǎ fǔtóu 一把斧头, yìbǎ fǔzi 一把斧子

baby *noun*
  a baby = yíge yīng'ér 一个婴儿

babysit *verb*
  = zhàokàn háizi 照看孩子

back

> **!** *Often* back *occurs in combinations with verbs, for example:* come back, get back, give back, *etc. To find the correct translations for this type of verb, look up the separate dictionary entries at* come, get, give, *etc.*

1 *noun*
- (*part of the body*) ▶ 189
  the back = bèibù 背部, bèi 背
  I've hurt my back = wǒ bèibù shòule shāng 我背部受了伤
- (*the rear*) = hòumian 后面
  at the back of the supermarket = zài chāojí shìchǎng hòumian 在超级市场后面
  to sit in the back of the car = zuò zài chē hòumian 坐在车后面

2 *adverb*
- **to be back** = huílai 回来
  I'll be back in five minutes = wǒ guò wǔ fēnzhōng huílai 我过五分钟回来

back door *noun*
  the back door = hòumén 后门

background *noun*
- (*previous history of a person*) = lǚlì 履历
- (*upbringing of a person*) = chūshēn 出身
- (*of a picture or a story*)
  the background = bèijǐng 背景

backpack *noun*
  a backpack = yíge bèibāo 一个背包

back seat *noun*
  the back seat = hòumian de zuòwei 后面的坐位

back to front *adverb*
  = fǎn 反
  to put a sweater on back to front = bǎ máoyī chuānfǎn le 把毛衣穿反了

backwards, backward *adverb*
  = xiànghòu 向后

bacon *noun*
  bacon = xián zhūròu 咸猪肉

bad *adjective*
- **bad** = huài 坏, bù hǎo 不好
  a bad idea = yíge huài zhǔyì 一个坏主意
  a bad film = yíge bù hǎo de diànyǐng 一个不好的电影
  I have some bad news = wǒ yǒu yíge huài xiāoxi 我有一个坏消息
  to be bad at [**maths** | **tennis** | **chess...**] = bú shàncháng [shùxué | dǎ wǎngqiú | xià qí...] 不善长 [数学 | 打网球 | 下棋...]
  it's a bad time to go on holiday = zhège shíjiān dùjià bù hǎo 这个时间度假不好
  'was the film good?'—'not bad' = 'zhège diànyǐng hǎo ma?'—'bú cuò' '这个电影好吗?'—'不错'

smoking is bad for you = xīyān duì nǐ shēntǐ bù hǎo 吸烟对你身体不好
- (*serious*) = yánzhòng 严重
  a bad accident = yíge yánzhòng de shìgù 一个严重的事故
  to have a bad cold = dé zhòng gǎnmào 得重感冒
- (*when talking about food*)
  the milk has gone bad = niúnǎi huài le 牛奶坏了
- (*not kind, not honest*) = bú dàodé, 不道德, huài 坏

badger *noun*
a badger = yìzhī huān 一只獾

badly *adverb*
- (*not well*) = bù hǎo 不好
  she slept badly = tā shuì de bù hǎo 她睡得不好
- (*seriously*) = yánzhòng 严重
  he was badly injured = tā shāng de hěn yánzhòng 他伤得很严重
- (*naughty*) = tiáopí 调皮
  this child behaves badly = zhège háizi hěn tiáopí 这个孩子很调皮

badminton *noun* ▶ 390
= yǔmáoqiú 羽毛球

bad-tempered *adjective*
to be bad-tempered = píqì hěn huài 脾气很坏

bag *noun*
a bag = yíge bāo 一个包

baggage *noun*
a piece of baggage = yíjiàn xíngli 一件行李

bake *verb*
= kǎo 烤

baker *noun* ▶ 344
a baker = yíge miànbāoshī 一个面包师

bakery *noun* ▶ 344
a bakery = yìjiā miànbāodiàn 一家面包店

balance *noun*
- (*an instrument for weighing*) = chèng 称, tiānpíng 天平
- (*equilibrium*) = pínghéng 平衡
  to lose one's balance = shīqù pínghéng 失去平衡

balcony *noun*
a balcony = yíge yángtái 一个阳台

bald *adjective*
= tūdǐng 秃顶, tūtóu 秃头

ball *noun*
a ball = yíge qiú 一个球
to play ball = dǎ qiú 打球

ballet *noun*
ballet = bāléiwǔ 芭蕾舞

balloon *noun*
a balloon = yíge qìqiú 一个气球

ballpoint (*US English*) *noun*
a ballpoint pen = yìzhī yuánzhūbǐ 一支圆珠笔

ban *verb*
= jìnzhǐ 禁止

banana *noun*
a banana = yíge xiāngjiāo 一个香蕉

band *noun*
- (*a flat strip*)
  a band = yìgēn dàizi 一根带子
- (*a body of musicians*) = yíge yuèduì 一个乐队
- (*a group*) = qún 群
  a band of football fans = yìqún qiúmí 一群球迷

bandage *noun*
a bandage = yìgēn bēngdài 一根绷带

bang
1 *noun*
- (*a loud noise*)
  a bang = pēng de yìshēng 砰的一声
- (*US English*) (*fringe*)
  bangs = liúhǎir 刘海儿

2 *verb*
- (*to close with a bang*) = pēng de guānshang 砰地关上
- (*to strike with the head or body*) = měng zhuàng 猛撞
- (*to beat with the hand*) = měng qiāo 猛敲
  to bang one's fist on the table = yòng quántou měng qiāo zhuōzi 用拳头猛敲桌子

bank *noun*
- (*a financial institution*)
  a bank = yìjiā yínháng 一家银行
- (*blood bank*)
  a blood bank = yíge xuěkù 一个血库
- (*of a river*)
  a river bank = yíge hé'àn 一个河岸

bank account *noun*
a bank account = yíge yínháng zhànghù 一个银行帐户

B

bank holiday *noun* (*British English*)
a bank holiday = yíge gōngjiàrì 一个公假日

bar *noun*
- (*a place*)
a bar = yíge jiǔbā 一个酒吧
- (*made of metal*)
an iron bar = yìgēn tiěbàng 一根铁棒
- (*on a cage or window*)
a bar = yìgēn zhàlan 一根栅栏
- (*other uses*)
a bar of soap = yìtiáo féizào 一条肥皂
a bar of chocolate = yí dà kuài qiǎokèlì 一大块巧克力

barbecue *noun*
a barbecue = yícì shāokǎo yěcān 一次烧烤野餐

barely *adverb*
= miǎnqiáng 勉强
he was barely able to walk = tā miǎnqiáng nénggòu zǒulù 他勉强能够走路

bargain *noun*
a bargain = yìbǐ jiāoyì 一笔交易

bark
1 *noun*
- (*of a tree*)
= shùpí 树皮
- (*of a dog*)
the dog's bark = gǒu jiào de shēngyīn 狗叫的声音

2 *verb*
the dog is barking = gǒu zài jiào 狗在叫

barn *noun*
a barn = yíge gǔcāng 一个谷仓

barrel *noun*
a barrel of water = yìtǒng shuǐ 一桶水

base *verb*
- (*use as a basis for*)
= yǐ ... wéi jīchǔ 以 ... 为基础, yǐ ... wéi gēnjù 以 ... 为根据
to be based on a true story = yǐ yíge zhēnshí de gùshi wéi jīchǔ 以一个真实的故事为基础
- (*of a company or diplomatic mission*)
to be based in London = cháng zhù (zài) Lúndūn 常驻(在)伦敦

baseball *noun* ▶ 390
baseball = bàngqiú 棒球

basement *noun*
a basement = yíge dìxiàshì 一个地下室

basically *adverb*
= jīběnshang 基本上

basin *noun*
a basin = yíge pén 一个盆

basket *noun*
a basket = yíge lánzi 一个篮子

basketball *noun* ▶ 390
basketball = lánqiú 篮球

bat *noun*
- (*in cricket or baseball*)
a bat = yìgēn qiúbàng 一根球棒
- (*an animal*)
a bat = yíge biānfú 一个蝙蝠

bath *noun*
- to have a bath = xǐzǎo 洗澡
he's in the bath = tā zài xǐzǎo 他在洗澡
- (*a bathtub*)
a bath = yíge yùpén 一个浴盆

bathroom *noun*
- a bathroom = yíge yùshì 一个浴室
- (*US English*) (*the toilet*)
to go to the bathroom = shàng cèsuǒ 上厕所

battery *noun*
a battery (*for a torch*) = yìjié diànchí 一节电池
(*for a car*) = yíge diànchí 一个电池

battle *noun*
a battle = yìchǎng zhàndòu 一场战斗

bay *noun*
a bay = yíge hǎiwān 一个海湾

be *verb*
▶ *See the boxed note on* **be** ▶ 182 *for more information and examples.*
- to be = shì 是
he is a lawyer = tā shì yíge lǜshī 他是一个律师
- (*in the future tense or in the infinitive*)
= chéngwéi 成为
Tom will be a film star = Tāngmǔ jiāng chéngwéi yíge diànyǐng míngxīng 汤姆将成为一个电影明星
my son hopes to be a footballer = wǒ érzi xīwàng chéngwéi yíge zúqiú yùndòngyuán 我儿子希望成为一个足球运动员

be

As an ordinary verb

When **be** is used as a simple verb in a **subject + verb** sentence, it is generally translated as **shì** 是, which is not inflected for number, person, or tense. The tense is often indicated by the accompanying adverbial phrase in Chinese.

*she **is** a doctor*	= tā **shì** dàifu 她是大夫
*she **was** a doctor*	= tā yǐqián **shì** dàifu 她以前是大夫
*we **are** doctors*	= wǒmen **shì** dàifu 我们是大夫

- (No translation of **be**)

1 describing a physical or mental state

*I **am** tired*	= wǒ ___ lèi le 我 ___ 累了
*they **are** very happy*	= tāmen ___ hěn gāoxìng 他们 ___ 很高兴

2 indicating weather, age, location, cost

*it **is** cold today*	= jīntiān ___ hěn lěng 今天 ___ 很冷
*my daughter **is** seven years old*	= wǒ nǚ'ér ___ qī suì le 我女儿 ___ 七岁了
*her mother **was** not in the garden*	= tā māma bú ___ zài huāyuán li 她妈妈不___在花园里
*this book **is** twelve pounds*	= zhèběn shū ___ shí'èr yīngbàng 这本书 ___十二英镑

- (Required translation of **be**)

1 sentences expressing one's profession, identity, or nationality

*he **was** a teacher*	= tā yǐqián **shì** yíge lǎoshī 他以前是一个老师
*she **is** my younger sister*	= tā **shì** wǒ mèimei 她是我妹妹
*that **is** a hospital*	= nà **shì** yíge yīyuàn 那是一个医院
*my birthday **is** the 7th of May*	= wǒde shēngrì **shì** wǔyuè qīhào 我的生日是五月七号
*that year **was** 1948*	= nà nián **shì** yījiǔsìbā nián 那年是一九四八年
*they **are** Chinese*	= tāmen **shì** Zhōngguórén 他们是中国人

2 sentences expressing the colour or shape of something (in this use, **de** 的 is required at the end of the sentence)

*her coat **is** black*	= tāde dàyī **shì** hēi **de** 她的大衣是黑的
*the earth **is** round*	= dìqiú **shì** yuán **de** 地球是圆的

- (Optional translation of **be** in sentences expressing the time, day, date)

*it **is** 10 o'clock*	= xiànzài (**shì**) shí diǎn 现在(是)十点
*it **was** Wednesday yesterday*	= zuótiān (**shì**) xīngqīsān 昨天(是)星期三
*it **is** the 26th of June today*	= jīntiān (**shì**) liùyuè èrshíliù hào 今天(是)六月二十六号

As an auxiliary verb in progressive tenses

In English, **be** can be used in combination with another verb to form a progressive tense which allows us to express an idea of duration, of something happening over a period of time.

The present

= zhèngzài 正在, zài 在

I'm working	= wǒ zhèngzài gōngzuò 我正在工作
he's reading a newspaper	= tā zài kàn bào 他在看报

B

The future

= jiāngyào 将要, dǎsuàn 打算

we are going to Beijing next week = wǒmen xiàge xīngqī jiāngyào qù Běijīng 我们下个星期将要去北京

The past

(dāngshí /nàshí) zhèngzài (当时/那时) 正在

she was watching TV = tā dāngshí zhèngzài kàn diànshì 她当时正在看电视

In short questions

With questions like **aren't you?**, **wasn't she?**, **is he?**, a general Chinese translation is **shì bú shì?** 是不是?:

you are a doctor, ***aren't you****?* = nǐ shì yíge dàifu, **shì bú shì**? 你是一个大夫, 是不是?

he is not there, ***is he****?* = tā bú zài nàr, **shì bú shì**? 他不在那儿, 是不是?

In short answers

Shi 是 can be used as a short answer meaning **yes**.

'is she pretty?'—'yes, she is' = 'tā hěn piàoliang ma?'—'shì, tā hěn piàoliang' '她很漂亮吗?'—'是, 她很漂亮'

- (*when talking about travelling*)
  I've never been to Japan = wǒ cónglái méi qùguo Rìběn 我从来没去过日本
  have you ever been to Africa? = nǐ qùguo Fēizhōu ma? 你去过非洲吗?
- (*when talking about health*)
  how are you? = nǐ hǎo ma? 你好吗?
  I'm very well = wǒ hěn hǎo 我很好
  how is your mother? = nǐ māma hǎo ma? 你妈妈好吗?

beach *noun*
a beach =
(*on a sea*) = yíge hǎitān 一个海滩
(*on a river*) = yíge hétān 一个河滩
(*on a lake*) = yíge hútān 一个湖滩

beam *noun*
- (*in a building*)
  a beam = yìgēn liáng 一根梁
- (*a ray of light*)
  a beam of light = yíshù guāng 一束光, yídào guāng 一道光

bean *noun*
a bean = yíge dòuzi 一个豆子

bear
1 *noun*
a bear = yìzhī xióng 一只熊
2 *verb*
- (*to sustain*) = fùdān 负担, chéngdān 承担
- (*to endure*) = rěnshòu 忍受, róngrěn 容忍

beard *noun*
= húzi 胡子

beat *verb*
- (*to hit hard*) = dǎ 打
- (*in cooking*) = jiǎobàn 搅拌
- (*to win against*) = zhànshèng 战胜, dǎbài 打败
  Scotland beat England two to one = Sūgélán èr bǐ yī zhànshèng le Yīnggélán 苏格兰二比一战胜了英格兰

beautiful *adjective*
= měilì 美丽, piàoliang 漂亮
a beautiful garden = yíge měilì de huāyuán 一个美丽的花园
a beautiful girl = yíge piàoliang de gūniang 一个漂亮的姑娘

beauty *noun*
= měilì 美丽, měi 美

because
1 *conjunction*
= yīnwèi 因为

he didn't come because he was ill = yīnwèi tā bìngle, suǒyǐ tā méi lái 因为他病了, 所以他没来

2 because of = yīnwèi 因为

we didn't go out because of the rain = yīnwèi xiàyǔ, suǒyǐ wǒmen méi chūqu 因为下雨, 所以我们没出去

> **!** *Note that the clause or phrase introduced by* yīnwèi 因为 *usually appears before the main clause. Note also that when* yīnwèi 因为 *is used, the main clause is often preceded by* suǒyǐ 所以, *which means* therefore.

become *verb*

- (*followed by a noun*) = biànchéng 变成, chéngwéi 成为

  he has become an adult = tā biànchéng/chéngwéi dàrén le 他变成/成为大人了

- (*followed by an adjective*) = biàn 变, biànde 变得

  it has become cold = tiān biàn lěng le 天变冷了

bed *noun*

a bed = yìzhāng chuáng 一张床

to go to bed = shàng chuáng shuìjiào 上床睡觉

bed and breakfast *noun*

= zhùsù jiā zǎocān 住宿加早餐

bedroom *noun*

a bedroom = yíge wòshì 一个卧室, yíge qǐnshì 一个寝室

bee *noun*

a bee = yìzhī mìfēng 一只蜜蜂

beef *noun*

= niúròu 牛肉

roast beef = kǎo niúròu 烤牛肉

beer *noun*

- (*the product*)

  beer = píjiǔ 啤酒

- (*a glass of beer*)

  a beer = yìbēi píjiǔ 一杯啤酒

beet, beetroot *noun* (*British English*)

= tiáncài 甜菜

before

1 *preposition*

- (*referring to time*) = zài...yǐqián 在…以前, ...yǐqián …以前

  before 6 o'clock = (zài) liù diǎn yǐqián (在)六点以前

  the day before yesterday = qiántiān 前天

  the day before the exam = kǎoshì de qián yì tiān 考试的前一天

- (*in front of*) = zài...qiánmian 在…前面, zài...qiántou 在…前头

  he was before me in the queue = tā pái zài wǒ qiánmian 他排在我前面

2 *adverb*

= yǐqián 以前

have you been to Beijing before? = nǐ yǐqián qùguo Běijīng ma? 你以前去过北京吗?

3 *conjunction*

= zài...yǐqián 在…以前, zài...zhīqián 在… 之前

I'd like to phone him before he goes = (zài) tā zǒu yǐqián wǒ xiǎng gěi tā dǎ ge diànhuà (在)他走以前我想给他打个电话

beg *verb*

- (*for food, money, etc.*)

  beg for = yào 要, qǐtǎo 乞讨

- (*making requests*) = qǐqiú 乞求, kěnqiú 恳求

beggar *noun*

a beggar = yíge qǐgài 一个乞丐, yíge yào fàn de 一个要饭的

begin *verb*

= kāishǐ 开始

to begin [working | laughing | raining] = kāishǐ [gōngzuò | xiào | xiàyǔ] 开始[工作 | 笑 | 下雨]

beginner *noun*

a beginner = yíge chūxuézhě 一个初学者

beginning *noun*

- (*of an event, of an activity*) = kāishǐ 开始, kāiduān 开端

  a good beginning = yíge liánghǎo de kāiduān 一个良好的开端

- (*of a year, of a month*)

  the beginning of [the month | the year | May] = [yuè | nián | wǔyuè] chū [月 | 年 | 五月] 初

behave *verb*

- (*to act, to function*) = biǎoxiàn 表现

  he behaved badly = tā biǎoxiàn bù hǎo 他表现不好

- (*to conduct oneself well*) = shǒu guīju 守规矩

behave yourself! = guīju dian! 规矩点!

behaviour (*British English*), **behavior** (*US English*) *noun*
= xíngwéi 行为, biǎoxiàn 表现

behind
1 *preposition*
= zài...hòumian 在... 后面, zài...hòubian 在... 后边
my house is behind the school = wǒde jiā zài xuéxiào hòumian 我的家在学校后面
2 *adverb*
= zài hòumian 在后面, zài hòubian 在后边
she is sitting behind = tā zuò zài hòumian 她坐在后面

Belgian ▶ 288
1 *adjective*
= Bǐlìshí de 比利时的
2 *noun*
a Belgian
= yíge Bǐlìshírén 一个比利时人

Belgium *noun*
= Bǐlìshí 比利时

believe *verb*
= xiāngxìn 相信
believe in = xìnrèn 信任

bell *noun*
- (*in a church*) = zhōng 钟
- (*on a door or bicycle*) = líng 铃

belong *verb*
- (*to be the property of*) = shǔyú 属于
  that piece of land belongs to our college = nàkuài dì shǔyú wǒmen xuéyuàn 那块地属于我们学院
- (*be a member of*)
  belong to a party = shì yíge dǎng de dǎngyuán 是一个党的党员

belongings *noun*
- (*luggage*) = xíngli 行李
- (*things that one owns*) = dōngxi 东西
  his belongings = tāde dōngxi 他的东西

below
1 *preposition*
- (*in space*) = zài ... xiàmian 在 ... 下面
  the kitchen is below my bedroom = chúfáng zài wǒde wòshì xiàmian 厨房在我的卧室下面
- (*in rank, age, degree, etc.*) = (zài) ... yǐxià (在) ...以下
  below 60 years old = liùshí suì yǐxià 六十岁以下
  10 degrees below zero = língxià shí dù 零下十度

2 *adjective*
= xiàmian de 下面的
please do the exercises below = qǐng zuò xiàmian de liànxí 请做下面的练习

belt *noun*
- (*worn around the waist*) = yāodài 腰带, pídài 皮带
- (*in machinery*) = jīqì pídài 机器皮带

bench *noun*
= chángdèng 长凳

bend
1 *verb*
- (*to bend an object*) = wān 弯, nòngwān 弄弯
  he bent the iron bar with his bare hands = tā yòng shǒu bǎ tiěbàng nòngwān le 他用手把铁棒弄弯了
- (*to bend down or lower one's head*) = dīxia 低下
  to bend down one's head = dīxia tóu 低下头
- (*to bend down one's body*) = wānxia 弯下
  he bent down to pick up the coin = tā wānxia shēnzi bǎ qián jiǎnqǐlai 他弯下身子把钱捡起来

2 *noun*
= zhuǎnwān 转弯, guǎiwān 拐弯
there is a sharp bend in this road = zhètiáo lù shang yǒu yíge jí zhuǎnwān 这条路上有一个急转弯

beneath *preposition*
= zài...xiàmian 在... 下面, zài...dǐxia 在... 底下

beside *preposition*
= zài...pángbiān 在... 旁边
to sit beside me = zuò zài wǒ pángbiān 坐在我旁边
to live beside the sea = zhù zài hǎibiān 住在海边

best
1 *adjective*
= zuì hǎo 最好
my best friend = wǒ zuì hǎo de péngyou 我最好的朋友
this is the best hotel in the city = zhè shì zhège chéngshì zuì hǎo

de lǚguǎn 这是这个城市最好的旅馆

2 *adverb*

= zuì hǎo 最好

she sings the best = tā chàng de zuì hǎo 她唱得最好

• (*most*) = zuì 最

I like tennis best = wǒ zuì xǐhuan wǎngqiú 我最喜欢网球

3 *pronoun*

the best = zuì hǎo de... 最好的...

he's the best in his class = tā shì bān lǐ zuì hǎo de xuésheng 他是班里最好的学生

do one's best = jìnlì 尽力, jìn zuì dà nǔlì 尽最大努力

bet *verb*

• (*with money*) = tóng...dǎdǔ 同... 打赌

• (*predict*) = gǎn duàndìng 敢断定

I bet he'll win = wǒ gǎn duàndìng tā huì yíng 我敢断定他会赢

better

1 *adjective*

= gèng hǎo 更好

they will have a better future = tāmen huì yǒu yíge gèng hǎo de wèilái 他们会有一个更好的未来

is she better today? = tā jīntiān hǎo xiē le ma? 她今天好些了吗?

his Chinese is better than mine = tāde Hànyǔ bǐ wǒde hǎo 他的汉语比我的好

2 *adverb*

= gèng hǎo de 更好地

he swims better than I do = tā yóuyǒng yóu de bǐ wǒ hǎo 他游泳游得比我好

• = zuì hǎo 最好

we'd better go = wǒmen zuì hǎo háishì zǒu ba 我们最好还是走吧

it's better to go by bus = zuì hǎo zuò qìchē qù 最好坐汽车去

between *preposition*

= zài...zhījiān 在... 之间, zài...zhōngjiān 在... 中间

there is a stream between the two gardens = zài liǎngge huāyuán zhījiān yǒu yìtiáo xiǎo hé 在两个花园之间有一条小河

between 2 and 3 o'clock = liǎng diǎn dào sān diǎn zhījiān 两点到三点之间

beyond *preposition*

• (*on the further side of*) = zài...nà bian 在... 那边

beyond the mountain = zài shān nà bian 在山那边

• (*out of reach of*) = chāochū 超出

beyond my ability = chāochū wǒde nénglì 超出我的能力

bicycle *noun*

a bicycle = yíliàng zìxíngchē 一辆自行车

big *adjective*

• (*large*) = dà 大

a big garden = yíge dà huāyuán 一个大花园

• (*important*) = zhòngyào 重要

a big question = yíge zhòngyào wèntí 一个重要问题

• (*serious*) = yánzhòng 严重

a big mistake = yíge yánzhòng cuòwù 一个严重错误

• (*heavy, thick*) = hòu 厚, zhòng 重

a big book = yìběn hěn hòu de shū 一本很厚的书

bill *noun*

• (*for gas, electricity, telephone*) = dān 单

[**gas** | **electricity** | **telephone**] **bill** = [méiqì fèi | diàn fèi | diànhuà fèi] dān [煤气费 | 电费 | 电话费] 单

• (*in a restaurant or hotel*) = zhàngdān 帐单

could we have the bill, please? = qǐng gěi wǒmen jié yíxià zhàng hǎo ma? 请给我们结一下帐好吗?

• (*US English*) (*money*) = chāopiào 钞票

a 10-dollar bill = yìzhāng shí měiyuán de chāopiào 一张十美元的钞票

billiards *noun* ▶ **390**

billiards = táiqiú 台球

bin *noun* (*British English*)

a bin = yíge lājītǒng 一个垃圾桶

biology *noun*

biology = shēngwùxué 生物学

bird *noun*

a bird = yìzhī niǎo 一只鸟

bird flu *noun*

= qínliúgǎn 禽流感

biro® *noun* (*British English*)

a biro® = yìzhī yuánzhūbǐ 一支圆珠笔

birth *noun*
a birth = chūshēng 出生, dànshēng 诞生
a place of birth = chūshēng dì 出生地

birthday *noun*
= shēngri 生日
happy birthday! = shēngri kuàilè ! 生日快乐!

biscuit *noun* (*British English*)
a biscuit = yíkuài bǐnggān 一块饼干

bit
1 *noun*
a bit of [cheese | bread | paper] = yìdiǎnr [nǎilào | miànbāo | zhǐ] 一点儿[奶酪 | 面包 | 纸]
2 a bit (*British English*)
a bit [early | hot | odd] = yǒu diǎnr [zǎo | rè | qíguài] 有点儿[早 | 热 | 奇怪]

bite *verb*
= yǎo 咬

bitter *adjective*
= kǔ 苦

black *adjective*
= hēi 黑

blackberry *noun*
= hēiméi 黑莓
a blackberry = yíge hēiméi 一个黑莓

blackboard *noun*
a blackboard = yíkuài hēibǎn 一块黑板

blackcurrants *noun*
blackcurrants = hēi pútaogān 黑葡萄干

blade *noun*
- (*of a knife, a sword*) = dǎorèn 刀刃, dāokǒu 刀口
- a blade of grass = yíyè cǎopiàn 一叶草片

blame
1 *verb*
= zébèi 责备, zéguài 责怪
2 *noun*
to take the blame = fùzé 负责, shòuguò 受过

blank *adjective*
(*describing a page*) = kòngbái 空白
(*describing a cassette*) = kōng 空

blanket *noun*
a blanket = yìtiáo tǎnzi 一条毯子

blaze *noun*
= huǒyàn 火焰

bleed *verb*
= chū xuě/chū xiě 出血
my nose is bleeding = wǒde bízi zài chū xuě 我的鼻子在出血

blind
1 *adjective*
= shīmíng 失明, xiā 瞎
2 *verb*
- (*destroy someone's sight*) = shǐ ... shīmíng 使 ... 失明
  he was blinded in an accident = tā zài yícì shìgù zhōng shīmíng le 他在一次事故中失明了
- (*to dazzle*) = shǐ ... kànbújiàn 使 ... 看不见

3 *noun*
a blind = yíge bǎiyèchuāng 一个百叶窗

blink *verb*
= zhǎ yǎnjīng 眨眼睛

blister *noun*
a blister = yíge pāo 一个疱, yíge pào 一个泡

block
1 *noun*
- (*a building*)
  a block of apartments = yízhuàng gōngyùlóu 一幢公寓楼
- (*a group of houses*)
  a block of houses = yíge jiēqū 一个街区
- (*a large piece*)
  a block = yí dà kuài 一大块
  a block of ice = yí dà kuài bīng 一大块冰

2 *verb*
= zǔsāi 阻塞, dǔsāi 堵塞
to block a road = zǔsāi mǎlù 阻塞马路

blond, blonde *adjective*
= jīnsè 金色
he has blond hair = tāde tóufa shì jīnsè de 他的头发是金色的

blood *noun*
= xuè/xiě 血

blouse *noun*
a blouse = yíjiàn (nǚshì) chènshān 一件(女式)衬衫

blow
1 *verb*
- (*if it's the wind or a person*) = chuī 吹

the wind blew the door shut = fēng chuī de bǎ mén guānshang le 风吹得把门关上了
to blow a whistle = chuī shào 吹哨
• to blow one's nose = xǐng bízi 擤鼻子
2 *noun*
a blow = yíge dǎjī 一个打击
blow away
to be blown away = chuīzǒu le 吹走了
blow down
to be blown down = chuīdǎo le 吹倒了
blow out = chuīmiè 吹灭
to blow out a candle = chuīmiè làzhú 吹灭蜡烛
blow up
• (*to destroy*) = zhàhuǐ 炸毁, zhàdiào 炸掉
to blow up a car = zhàhuǐ yíliàng qìchē 炸毁一辆汽车
• (*to put air into*) = chōng qì 充气

blue *adjective*
= lán 蓝

blush *verb*
= liǎnhóng 脸红

board
1 *noun*
• (*a piece of wood*) = mùbǎn 木板
a board = yíkuài mùbǎn 一块木板
• (*in chess, draughts, checkers*) = qípán 棋盘
a board = yíkuài qípán 一块棋盘
• (*a blackboard*)
a board = yíkuài hēibǎn 一块黑板
2 *verb*
to board a ship = shàng chuán 上船
3 on board [a ship | a train | a plane...] = zài [chuán | huǒchē | fēijī...] shang 在 [船 | 火车 | 飞机...] 上

boarding school *noun*
a boarding school = yìsuǒ jìsù xuéxiào 一所寄宿学校

boast *verb*
= zìwǒ chuīxū 自我吹嘘, zìkuā 自夸, chuīniú 吹牛

boat *noun*
a boat = yìtiáo chuán 一条船

body *noun*
• (*the body*) = shēntǐ 身体
(*a dead body*) = shītǐ 尸体

boil *verb*
• (*an action done by a person*)
to boil water = shāo kāishuǐ 烧开水
to boil an egg = zhǔ jīdàn 煮鸡蛋
• (*referring to water or milk*) = kāi 开
the water is boiling = shuǐ kāi le 水开了

boiled egg *noun*
a boiled egg = yíge zhǔ jīdàn 一个煮鸡蛋

boiler *noun*
a boiler = yíge guōlú 一个锅炉

boiling *adjective*
(*when describing water or milk*) = fèiténg 沸腾
(*when describing the weather*) = hěn rè 很热

bomb
1 *noun*
a bomb = yìkē zhàdàn 一颗炸弹
2 *verb*
= hōngzhà 轰炸

bone *noun* ▶ 189
a bone
(*in the body, in meat*) = yíkuài gǔtou 一块骨头
(*in fish*) = yìgēn yúcì 一根鱼刺

bonnet *noun* (*British English*)
the bonnet (*in a car*) = qìchē yǐnqíng gàizi 汽车引擎盖子

book
1 *noun*
a book = yìběn shū 一本书
2 *verb*
= yùdìng 预订
to book a room = yùdìng yíge fángjiān 预订一个房间
the flight is fully booked = zhècì hángbān quánbù dìngmǎn le 这次航班全部订满了

booking *noun*
a booking = yùdìng 预订

bookshop, bookstore *noun* ▶ 344
a bookshop, a bookstore = yíge shūdiàn 一个书店

boot *noun*
• (*worn on the feet*)
a boot = yìzhī xuēzi 一只靴子
a pair of boots = yìshuāng xuēzi 一双靴子
• (*British English*) (*of a car*)
the boot = xínglixiāng 行李箱

B

The human body

Note that where a possessive pronoun is required in English, there is no such requirement in Chinese:

he raised **his** *hand* = tā jǔ ___ shǒu 他举___手
she closed **her** *eyes* = tā bìshang ___ yǎnjīng 她闭上___眼睛
he was washing **his** *hands* = tā zài xǐ ___ shǒu 他在洗___手

Describing people

Here are some ways of describing people in Chinese:

his hair is long = tāde tóufa hěn cháng 他的头发很长
he has long hair = tā liúzhe hěn cháng de tóufa 他留着很长的头发
a boy with long hair = liú cháng fà de nánháir 留长发的男孩儿
her eyes are blue = tāde yǎnjīng shì lánsè de 她的眼睛是蓝色的
she has blue eyes = tā shì lán yǎnjīng 她是蓝眼睛
the girl with blue eyes = lán yǎnjīng de nǚháir 蓝眼睛的女孩儿
he has a [long | round | apple-shaped] face = tā yǒu yìzhāng [cháng | yuán | píngguǒ] lián 他有一张[长 | 圆 | 苹果]脸
he has a red nose = tā shì hóng bízi 他是红鼻子

For other expressions relating to parts of the body ▶ 277

---

border *noun*
a border = yìtiáo biānjiè 一条边界
to cross the border = yuèguò biānjiè 越过边界

bore *verb*
= shǐ ... yànfán 使 ... 厌烦
her speech bored everyone = tāde jiǎnghuà shǐ dàjiā dōu gǎndào yànfán 他的讲话使大家都感到厌烦

bored *adjective*
to be bored, to get bored = gǎndào yànfán 感到厌烦

boring *adjective*
= lìng rén yànfán 令人厌烦

born *adjective*
to be born = chūshēng 出生
he was born in February = tā èryuè chūshēng 他二月出生
she was born in Italy = tā chūshēng zài Yìdàlì 她出生在意大利

borrow *verb*
= jiè 借
to borrow some money from someone = xiàng mǒurén jiè qián 向某人借钱

boss *noun*
the boss = lǎobǎn 老板

both
1 *determiner*
= liǎng ... dōu... 两 ... 都...
both girls have blonde hair = liǎngge gūniang dōu shì jīnsè de tóufa 两个姑娘都是金色的头发
both my daughter and my son came = wǒde nǚ'ér hé érzi dōu lái le 我的女儿和儿子都来了
2 *pronoun*
= liǎng ... dōu... 两 ... 都...
you are both wrong, both of you are wrong = nǐmen liǎngge rén dōu cuò le 你们两个人都错了

bother *verb*
- *(to take the trouble)*
don't bother calling back = bú bì huí diànhuà 不必回电话
- *(to worry, to upset)* = shǐ ... fánnǎo 使 ... 烦恼, shǐ ... cāoxīn 使 ... 操心
her health bothers her a lot = tāde shēntǐ shǐ tā hěn fánnǎo 她的身体使她很烦恼

- (*in polite apologies*)
  I'm sorry to bother you = duìbuqǐ, dǎrǎo nín 对不起, 打扰您

bottle *noun*
  a bottle = yíge píngzi 一个瓶子
  a bottle of [**wine** | **beer** | **water**] = yìpíng [jiǔ | píjiǔ | shuǐ ...] 一瓶 [酒 | 啤酒 | 水...]

bottle-opener *noun*
  a bottle-opener = yíge píngqǐzi 一个瓶起子

bottom
1 *noun*
- (*the lowest part*) = dǐ(bù) 底(部)
  the bottom of a bottle = píngzi dǐ(bù) 瓶子底(部)
  at the bottom [**of the lake** | **of the sea** | **of the river...**] = zài [hú | hǎi | hé...] dǐ 在 [湖 | 海 | 河...] 底
- (*of a mountain*) = jiǎo 脚
  the bottom of the hill = shānjiǎo 山脚
- (*of a page*) = xiàduān 下端
  at the bottom of the page = zài nà yíyè de xiàduān 在那一页的下端
- (*of a garden or street*) = jìntóu 尽头
  at the bottom of the garden = zài huāyuán de jìntóu 在花园的尽头
- (*at the lowest position*) = zuìhòu yìmíng 最后一名
  to be at the bottom of the class = quán bān zuìhòu yìmíng 全班最后一名
- (*part of the body*) ▶ 189
  the bottom = pìgu 屁股

2 *adjective*
  = zuì dǐxia de 最底下的
  the bottom [**shelf** | **drawer...**] = zuì dǐxia de [yìcéng shūjià | chōuti ...] 最底下的 [一层书架 | 抽屉...]

bound: to be bound to *verb*
  = kěndìng 肯定, bìdìng 必定
  it's bound to create problems = zhè kěndìng huì zàochéng yìxiē wèntí 这肯定会造成一些问题
  she's bound to complain = tā kěndìng huì bàoyuàn 她肯定会抱怨

bow¹ *noun*
- (*a knot*)
  a bow = yíge húdiéjié (lǐngdài) 一个蝴蝶结(领带)
- (*a weapon*)
  a bow = yìbǎ gōngzi 一把弓子
- (*used for playing a stringed instrument*)
  a bow = yìgēn qǐngōng 一根琴弓

bow² *verb*
  = jūgōng 鞠躬
  to bow one's head = dīxia tóu 低下头

bowl *noun*
  a bowl = yíge wǎn 一个碗

bowling *noun* ▶ 390
  bowling = bǎolíngqiú 保龄球

box *noun*
  = hézi 盒子, xiāngzi 箱子
  a box = yíge hézi 一个盒子

boxing *noun* ▶ 390
  = quánjī 拳击

boy *noun*
  a boy = yíge nánháir 一个男孩儿

boyfriend *noun*
  a boyfriend = yíge nánpéngyou 一个男朋友

bra *noun*
  a bra = yíge rǔzhào 一个乳罩

bracelet *noun*
  a bracelet = yíge shǒuzhuó 一个手镯

braid *noun* (*US English*)
  a braid = yìgēn biànzi 一根辫子

brain *noun* ▶ 189
  = nǎozi 脑子

brake *noun*
  a brake = yíge zhá 一个闸, yíge zhìdòngqì 一个制动器, yíge shāchē 一个刹车

branch *noun*
- **a branch** (*of a tree*) = yìgēn shùzhī 一根树枝
- (*of a river*) = yìtiáo zhīliú 一条支流
- (*of a bank*) = yíge fēnháng 一个分行
- (*of a department store*) = yíge fēndiàn 一个分店

brand-new *adjective*
  = zhǎnxīn 崭新

brandy *noun*
  brandy = báilándì jiǔ 白兰地酒

brave *adjective*
  = yǒnggǎn 勇敢

Brazil *noun*
  Brazil = Bāxī 巴西

bread *noun*
bread = miànbāo 面包

break
1 *verb*
• (*to be damaged*)
[**the window** | **the teapot** | **the bowl...**]
broke = [chuānghu | cháhú | wǎn...] pò le [窗户 | 茶壶 | 碗...] 破了
[**the leg of the chair** | **the needle** | **the rope...**] **broke** = [yǐzi tuǐ | zhēn | shéngzi...] duàn le [椅子腿 | 针 | 绳子...] 断了
• (*to crack, to smash or damage*)
to break [**the window** | **the teapot** | **the bowl...**] = bǎ [chuānghu | cháhú | wǎn...] dǎpò 把 [窗户 | 茶壶 | 碗...] 打破
to break [**the leg of the chair** | **the needle** | **the rope**] = bǎ [yǐzi tuǐ | zhēn | shéngzi...] nòngduàn 把 [椅子腿 | 针 | 绳子...] 弄断
• (*to injure*)
to break one's arm = bǎ gébo nòngduàn le 把胳膊弄断了
• (*not to keep*)
to break a promise = wéifǎn nuòyán 违反诺言
to break the rules = wéifǎn guīzé 违反规则
2 *noun*
• (*a short rest*) = xiūxi 休息
(*at school*) = kèjiān xiūxi 课间休息
to take a break = xiūxi yíxià 休息一下
• (*a holiday*) = xiūjià 休假
break down
• (*if it's a TV, a car*) = huàile 坏了
• (*to stop, as a negotiation or meeting*) = tíngzhǐ 停止, zhōngzhǐ 中止
• (*in health or spirit*) = kuǎxiàlai 垮下来
• (*to get upset*)
break down crying = nánguò de kū le 难过得哭了
break into (a house) = chuǎngrù 闯入
to be broken into by someone = bèi rén pò mén ér rù 被人破门而入
break out
(*if it's a fire*) = fāshēng 发生
a fire broke out = fāshēngle huǒzāi 发生了火灾
(*if it's violence*) = bàofā 爆发
break up
• (*to break up a crowd*) = qūsàn 驱散
• (*if it's a couple breaking up by themselves*) = fēnshǒu 分手
to break up with someone = gēn mǒurén duànjué láiwǎng 跟某人断绝来往
• (*if it's a third party breaking up a couple*) = chāisàn 拆散
• (*to end*) = jiéshù 结束
the meeting didn't break up until eight o'clock = huìyì bā diǎn cái jiéshù 会议八点才结束

breakfast *noun*
= zǎofàn 早饭
to have breakfast = chī zǎofàn 吃早饭

breast *noun* ▶ 189
a breast (*of a female*) = yíge rǔfáng 一个乳房
(*of a male or an animal*) = yíge xiōngpǔ 一个胸脯

breath *noun*
= hūxī 呼吸
to be out of breath = shàngqì bù jiē xiàqì 上气不接下气
to hold one's breath = bù chū shēng 不出声, bìngzhù qì 屏住气

breathe *verb*
= hūxī 呼吸
breathe in = xīrù 吸入
breathe out = hūchū 呼出

breeze *noun*
a breeze = wēifēng 微风

brick *noun*
a brick = yíkuài zhuān 一块砖

bride *noun*
a bride = yíge xīnniáng 一个新娘

bridegroom *noun*
a bridegroom = yíge xīnláng 一个新郎

bridge *noun*
a bridge = yízuò qiáo 一座桥

brief *adjective*
• (*in time*) = duǎnzàn 短暂
• (*in content*) = jiǎnduǎn 简短

bright *adjective*
• (*describing colours, light*) = xiānyàn 鲜艳
a bright red dress = yíjiàn xiānhóng de yīfu 一件鲜红的衣服
• (*having plenty of light, sun*) = míngliàng 明亮
this room is not very bright = zhège fángjiān bú tài míngliàng 这个房间不太明亮
• (*intelligent*) = cōngming 聪明

brilliant *adjective*
- (*very intelligent*) = zhuōyuè 卓越, cáihuá héngyì 才华横溢
- (*British English*) (*informal, for emphasis*) = tài hǎo le 太好了, miào jí le 妙极了

bring *verb*
- = dàilai 带来

  to bring someone a present = gěi mǒurén dàilai yíjiàn lǐwù 给某人带来一件礼物

  it will bring us good luck = tā jiāng gěi wǒmen dàilai hǎo yùnqi 它将给我们带来好运气

  bring about = dàilai 带来, zàochéng 造成

  to bring about a change = dàilai biànhuà 带来变化

  bring back = dàihuílai 带回来

  he brought me back some perfume = tā gěi wǒ dàihuílai yìxiē xiāngshuǐ 他给我带回来一些香水

  bring up = pēiyǎngchéng rén 培养成人

  to bring up a child = bǎ yíge háizi péiyǎngchéng rén 把一个孩子培养成人

Britain *noun*
= Yīngguó 英国

British ▶ 288
1 *adjective*
= Yīngguó de 英国的
2 *noun*
the British = Yīngguórén 英国人

broad *adjective*
- (*wide*) = kuān 宽
- (*covering a wide range*) = guǎngdà 广大

broadband *noun*
= kuāndài 宽带

broadcast *verb*
= guǎngbō 广播

brochure *noun*
a brochure = yìběn xiǎo cèzi 一本小册子

broke *adjective*
= fēnwén méi yǒu 分文没有, pòchǎn 破产

broken *adjective*
- (*if it's a window, a teapot, or a bowl*) = pò 破, suì 碎
- (*if it's a leg, a needle, or a rope*) = duàn 断
- (*if it's a car, a machine, or a watch*) = huài 坏

bronze *noun*
= qīngtóng 青铜

brother *noun*
a brother = yíge xiōngdì 一个兄弟
a younger brother = yíge dìdi 一个弟弟
an elder brother = yíge gēge 一个哥哥

brother-in-law *noun*
(*the husband of a younger sister*) = mèifu 妹夫
(*the husband of an elder sister*) = jiěfu 姐夫

brown *adjective*
= zōngsè de 棕色的, kāfēisè de 咖啡色的

bruise *noun* ▶ 277
a bruise = yíkuài qīngzhǒng 一块青肿, yíkuài shānghén 一块伤痕

brush
1 *noun*
- (*for clothes, shoes, hair, and for sweeping up*) = shuāzi 刷子

  a brush = yìbǎ shuāzi 一把刷子
  a toothbrush = yìbǎ yáshuā 一把牙刷
- (*for painting*) = huàbǐ 画笔

  a brush = yìzhī huàbǐ 一支画笔
- (*for writing*) = máobǐ 毛笔

  a writing brush = yìzhī máobǐ 一支毛笔

2 *verb*
= shuā 刷
to brush one's teeth = shuā yá 刷牙

Brussels *noun*
= Bùlǔsài'ěr 布鲁塞尔

bubble *noun*
a bubble = yíge shuǐpào 一个水泡

bucket *noun*
a bucket = yíge shuǐtǒng 一个水桶

Buddhism *noun*
= Fójiào 佛教

Buddhist
1 *adjective*
= Fójiào de 佛教的, Fó de 佛的
2 *noun*
a Buddhist = yíge Fójiàotú 佛教徒

build *verb*
- (*to construct as a house or a railway*) = jiàn 建, jiànzào 建造
- (*to establish as a society or a system*) = jiànlì 建立, jiànshè 建设

building *noun*
a building = yíge jiànzhùwù 一个建筑物

bull *noun*
a bull = yìtóu gōngniú 一头公牛

bullet *noun*
a bullet = yìkē zǐdàn 一颗子弹

bulletin *noun*
a bulletin = yí ge/fèn gōngbào 一个/份公报
a news bulletin = yìtiáo xīnwén bàodǎo 一条新闻报导
a bulletin board = yíge gōnggào lán 一个公告栏

bully *verb*
= qīfu 欺负, qīwǔ 欺侮

bump *verb*
= zhuàng 撞, pèngzhuàng 碰撞
he bumped his head against the wall = tāde tóu zhuàngzàile qiáng shang 他的头撞在了墙上
bump into
- (*to hit*) = zhuàng 撞, pèngzhuàng 碰撞
- (*to meet*) = yùjiàn 遇见, pèngjiàn 碰见

bunch *noun*
a bunch of flowers = yíshù huā 一束花
a bunch of grapes = yíchuàn pútao 一串葡萄
a bunch of keys = yíchuàn yàoshi 一串钥匙

burger *noun*
a burger = yíge jiā ròubǐng de miànbāo 一个夹肉饼的面包, yíge hànbǎobāo 一个汉堡包

burglar *noun*
a burglar = yíge qièzéi 一个窃贼

burglar alarm *noun*
a burglar alarm = yíge fángdào jǐngbàoqì 一个防盗警报器

burglary *noun*
a burglary = yìqǐ dàoqiè àn 一起盗窃案

burn
1 *verb*
- (*to destroy, to get rid of*) = shāohuǐ 烧毁, shāodiào 烧掉
  to burn rubbish = shāodiào lājī 烧掉垃圾
- (*to injure by fire*) = shāoshāng 烧伤
- (*to injure by boiling water or something hot*) = tàngshāng 烫伤
- (*to be on fire*) = ránshāo 燃烧
- (*when cooking*) = shāojiāo 烧焦
- (*in the sun*) = shàishāng 晒伤
  to burn easily = róngyì shàishāng 容易晒伤
  burn down = shāohuǐ 烧毁, shāodiào 烧掉

2 *noun*
- (*by a fire*) = shāoshāng 烧伤
- (*by boiling water or something very hot*) = tàngshāng 烫伤

burst *verb*
- (*if it's a balloon*) = bào 爆
- (*if it's a water pipe*) = liè 裂
- (*if it's a river dam*) = kuìjué 溃决
  to burst its banks = juékǒu 决口
  burst into
  to burst into [tears | laughter] = tūrán [kū | xiào] qǐlai 突然[哭|笑]起来
  burst out
  to burst out [laughing | crying] = tūrán [xiào | kū] qǐlai 突然[笑|哭]起来

bury *verb*
- (*to put in the grave as a dead body*) = máizàng 埋葬, mái 埋
- (*to hide in the ground*) = máicáng 埋藏, mái 埋

bus *noun*
a bus = yíliàng gōnggòng qìchē 一辆公共汽车

bus conductor *noun* ▶ 344
a bus conductor = yíge qìchē shòupiàoyuán 一个汽车售票员

bus driver *noun* ▶ 344
a bus driver = yíge gōnggòng qìchē sījī 一个公共汽车司机

bush *noun*
a bush = yíge guànmùcóng 一个灌木丛

business *noun*
- (*commercial activities*) = shāngyè 商业, shēngyi 生意
  to go to London on business = qù Lúndūn chūchāi 去伦敦出差
- (*a company*)
  a business = yìjiā shāngdiàn 一家商店, yíge gōngsī 一个公司
- (*when protecting one's privacy*)
  that's my business = nà shì wǒde shì 那是我的事
  it's none of your business = nǐ shǎo guǎn xiánshì 你少管闲事

businessman, businesswoman *noun* ▶ 344
a businessman, a businesswoman = yíge shāngrén 一个商人

bus station *noun*
a bus station, a bus stop = yíge (gōnggòng) qìchē zhàn 一个(公共)汽车站

busy *adjective*
= máng 忙, fánmáng 繁忙
to be busy working = mángzhe gōngzuò 忙着工作
a busy day = fánmáng de yì tiān 繁忙的一天
to lead a busy life = guòzhe mánglù de shēnghuó 过着忙碌的生活

but *conjunction*
= dànshì 但是, kěshì 可是
he can read Chinese but he doesn't speak it = tā néng kàndǒng Zhōngwén, dànshì tā bú huì shuō 他能看懂中文, 但是他不会说

butcher *noun* ▶ 344
a butcher
• (*one selling meat*) = yíge mài ròu de 一个卖肉的
• (*one whose business is to slaughter animals for food*) = yíge túzǎi gōngrén 一个屠宰工人
• (*one who delights in bloody deeds*) = yíge guìzishǒu 一个刽子手

butter *noun*
butter = huángyóu 黄油

butterfly *noun*
a butterfly = yìzhī húdié 一只蝴蝶

button *noun*
a button
• (*on clothes*) = yíge niǔkòu 一个钮扣
• (*on a machine*) = yíge diànniǔ 一个电钮

buy *verb*
= mǎi 买
to buy a present for someone = gěi mǒurén mǎi yíjiàn lǐwù 给某人买一件礼物
she bought herself a new coat = tā gěi zìjǐ mǎile yíjiàn xīn wàitào 她给自己买了一件新外套

buzz *verb*
= fāchū wēngwēng shēng 发出嗡嗡声

by *preposition*
• (*by means of*)
to travel by [bus | train | plane | boat] = zuò [qìchē | huǒchē | fēijī | chuán] lǚxíng 坐 [汽车 | 火车 | 飞机 | 船] 旅行
we went there by bicycle = wǒmen qí zìxíngchē qù nàr 我们骑自行车去那儿
to pay by cheque = yòng zhīpiào fù qián 用支票付钱
to book by phone = dǎ diànhuà yùdìng 打电话预订
to come in by the back door = cóng hòumén jìnlai 从后门进来
he succeeded by working hard = tā tōngguò nǔlì gōngzuò chénggōng le 他通过努力工作成功了
• (*beside*) = zài ... (páng)biān 在...(旁)边
by the sea = zài hǎi biān 在海边
by the side of the road = zài lù (páng)biān 在路(旁)边
• (*along a route passing*) = jīngguò 经过
to go by the post office = jīngguò yóujú 经过邮局
• (*indicating an author or painter*)
a book by Dickens = Dígēngsī xiě de shū 狄更斯写的书
a painting by his father = tā bàba huà de huà 他爸爸画的画
• (*in the passive voice*) = bèi 被, jiào 叫, ràng 让
he was bitten by a dog = tā jiào yìtiáo gǒu yǎo le 他叫一条狗咬了
the house was burnt down by a fire = nàzhuàng fángzi bèi yìchǎng huǒ shāohuǐ le 那幢房子被一场火烧毁了
• (*when talking about time*)
by next Thursday = xiàge xīngqīsì yǐqián 下个星期四以前
he should be here by now = xiànzài tā yīnggāi lái le 现在他应该来了
• (*when talking about figures, rates*)
to increase by 20% = zēngjiā bǎifēn zhī èrshí 增加百分之二十
to be paid by the hour = àn xiǎoshí fù qián 按小时付钱
8 metres by 4 metres = bā mǐ chéng sì mǐ 八米乘四米
• (*set phrases*)
by accident = ǒurán 偶然, pèngqiǎo 碰巧
by chance = ǒurán 偶然, pèngqiǎo 碰巧

[take... | see... | write...] by mistake = [ná | kàn | xiě] cuò... [拿 | 看 | 写] 错...
one by one = yíge jiē yíge 一个接一个
by and large = dàtǐshang 大体上
by oneself = dāndú 单独

cab *noun*
a cab = yíliàng chūzūchē 一辆出租车

cabbage *noun*
= juǎnxīncài 卷心菜
Chinese cabbage = dà báicài 大白菜

cable car *noun*
a cable car = yíliàng lǎnchē 一辆缆车

café *noun*
a café = yìjiā kāfēiguǎn 一家咖啡馆

cake *noun*
a cake = yíge dàngāo 一个蛋糕
a piece of cake = yíkuài dàngāo 一块蛋糕

calculator *noun*
a calculator = yíge jìsuànqì 一个计算器

calendar *noun*
a calendar = yíge rìlì 一个日历

calf *noun*
- (*the animal*)
  a calf = yìtóu xiǎoniú 一头小牛
- (*part of the leg*) ▶ 189
  the calf = xiǎotuǐ 小腿

call *verb*
- (*to name*) = jiào 叫
  he's called Mark = tā jiào Mǎkè 他叫马克
  it's called 'chá' in Chinese = Zhōngwén zhège jiào 'chá' 中文这个叫'茶'
  we call him 'Xiǎo Lǐ' = wǒmen jiào tā 'Xiǎo Lǐ' 我们叫他 '小李'
- (*to describe as*)
  to call someone a coward = rènwéi mǒurén shì ge dǎnxiǎoguǐ 认为某人是个胆小鬼
- (*to cry aloud*) = hǎn 喊
  the teacher is calling us at the window = lǎoshī zài chuānghu nàr hǎn wǒmen 老师在窗户那儿喊我们
- (*to phone*) = dǎ diànhuà 打电话
  he'll call me this evening = tā jīntiān wǎnshang gěi wǒ dǎ diànhuà 他今天晚上给我打电话
- (*to get to come*) = qǐng 请
  to call the doctor = qǐng dàifu 请大夫
- (*to wake*) = jiàoxǐng 叫醒
- (*to pay a visit*) = bàifǎng 拜访
  I called at his house yesterday = wǒ zuótiān qù tā jiā bàifǎng 我昨天去他家拜访

call back
- (*to command to return*) = jiào huílai 叫回来
- (*to phone back*) = huí diànhuà 回电话

call off = qǔxiāo 取消

call out
to call out the numbers for the lottery = dàshēng hǎn zhòngjiǎng hàomǎ 大声喊中奖号码

call centre *noun*
a call centre = yíge diànhuà zhōngxīn 一个电话中心

calm
1 *adjective*
- (*when talking about the weather, the sea*) = píngjìng 平静
- (*when talking about people*) = zhènjìng 镇静

2 *verb*
= píngjìng 平静, zhènjìng 镇静
calm down = píngjìng xiàlai 平静下来, zhènjìng xiàlai 镇静下来

camcorder *noun*
a camcorder = yíjià shèxiàngjī 一架摄像机

camel *noun*
a camel = yìtóu luòtuo 一头骆驼

camera *noun*
a camera (*for taking photos*) = yíjià zhàoxiàngjī 一架照相机
(*in a studio, for videos*) = yíjià shèyǐngjī 一架摄影机

camp
1 *noun*
= yěyíng 野营
a summer camp = yíge xiàlìngyíng 一个夏令营

2 *verb*
= yěyíng 野营
to go camping = qù yěyíng 去野营

campsite *noun*
a campsite = yíge yíngdì 一个营地

campus *noun*
a campus = yíge xiàoyuán 一个校园

can¹ *verb*
- (*to have the possibility*) = néng 能
can he come? = tā néng lái ma? 他能来吗?
where can I buy stamps? = wǒ zài nǎr néng mǎidào yóupiào 我在哪儿能买到邮票?
- (*to know how to*) = huì 会, néng 能
she can swim = tā huì yóuyǒng 她会游泳
he can't drive yet = tā hái bú huì kāi chē 他还不会开车
can/do you speak Chinese? = nǐ huì shuō Hànyǔ ma? 你会说汉语吗?

> **!** *Note that when talking about the ability to speak a language, whether or not* **can** *is used in English,* **huì 会** *is required in Chinese.*

- (*to be allowed to*) = kěyǐ 可以

> **!** *Note that to negate, you have to use* **bù néng 不能** *rather than* **bù kěyǐ 不可以**.

can I smoke? = wǒ kěyǐ xīyān ma? 我可以吸烟吗?
sorry, you can't smoke here = duìbuqǐ, nǐ bù néng zài zhèr xīyān 对不起, 你不能在这儿吸烟
we can't turn right here = wǒmen zài zhèr bù néng xiàng yòu guǎi 我们在这儿不能向右拐
- **can/may I help you?** = xūyào wǒ bāngmáng ma? 需要我帮忙吗? (*when asked by a shop assistant*) = nín yào mǎi shénme dōngxi ma? 您要买什么东西吗?

can² *noun*
a can = yìtīng guàntou 一听罐头

Canada *noun*
Canada = Jiānádà 加拿大

Canadian ▶ 288
1 *adjective*
= Jiānádà de 加拿大的
2 *noun*
= Jiānádàrén 加拿大人

canal *noun*
a canal = yìtiáo yùnhé 一条运河

cancel *verb*
= qǔxiāo 取消
he cancelled his room reservation = tā qǔxiāole yùdìng de fángjiān 他取消了预订的房间

cancer *noun* ▶ 277
cancer = ái 癌, áizhèng 癌症

candle *noun*
a candle = yìzhī làzhú 一支蜡烛

candy *noun* (*US English*)
- **candy** = tángguǒ 糖果
- (*a sweet*)
a candy = yíkuài táng 一块糖

canoe *noun*
a canoe = yìtiáo dúmùzhōu 一条独木舟

canoeing *noun* ▶ 390
canoeing = huá dúmùzhōu yùndòng 划独木舟运动

can-opener *noun*
a can-opener = yíge guàntou qǐzi 一个罐头起子

canteen *noun*
a canteen
- (*a dining hall*) = yíge shítáng 一个食堂
- (*a container of water*) = yíge shuǐhú 一个水壶

Cantonese ▶ 288
1 *adjective*
= Guǎngdōng de 广东的
2 *noun*
- (*the people*) = Guǎngdōngrén 广东人
- (*the dialect*) = Guǎngdōnghuà 广东话

cap *noun*
a cap = yìdǐng màozi 一顶帽子
a baseball cap = yìdǐng bàngqiú mào 一顶棒球帽

capable *adjective*
= yǒu nénglì 有能力
a very capable nurse = yíge hěn yǒu nénglì de hùshi 一个很有能力的护士
to be capable of looking after oneself = yǒu nénglì zhàogù zìjǐ 有能力照顾自己

capital
1 *noun*
= shǒudū 首都

Beijing is the capital of China = Běijīng shì Zhōngguó de shǒudū 北京是中国的首都

2 *adjective*
= dà xiě de 大写的
capital P = dà xiě de P 大写的P

captain *noun*
- (*of a ship*) = chuánzhǎng 船长
- (*of a team*) = duìzhǎng 队长

car *noun*
- (*a vehicle driven on a road*) = qìchē 汽车, jiàochē 轿车
  a car = yíliàng qìchē 一辆汽车
- (*a vehicle for railway travelling*) = chēxiāng 车厢
  a sleeping car = yìjié wòpù chēxiāng 一节卧铺车厢
  a dining car = yìjié cānchē 一节餐车

caravan *noun* (*British English*)
a caravan = yíliàng sùyíng chē 一辆宿营车

card *noun*
- (*for sending to someone*) = kǎpiàn 卡片
  a card = yìzhāng kǎpiàn 一张卡片
- (*for playing games*) = zhǐpái 纸牌
  a card = yìzhāng zhǐpái 一张纸牌
  to play cards = dǎ púkèpái 打扑克牌

care
1 *noun*
- (*watchfulness*) = xiǎoxīn 小心
  he takes great care crossing the street = tā guò mǎlù hěn xiǎoxīn 他过马路很小心
- (*charge*) = zhàoguǎn 照管
  to take care of someone = zhàoguǎn mǒurén 照管某人

2 *verb*
- (*to be concerned*) = guānxīn 关心
  to care about the environment = guānxīn huánjìng wèntí 关心环境问题
- (*to look after*) = zhàogù 照顾, guānhuái 关怀
  to care for the students = zhàogù xuésheng 照顾学生
- (*to mind*) = zàihu 在乎
  I don't care = wǒ bú zàihu 我不在乎

carer *noun*
a carer = yíwèi hùlǐyuán 一位护理员

career *noun*
- (*progress through life*) = shēngyá 生涯
- (*profession or occupation*) = zhíyè 职业

careful *adjective*
= xiǎoxīn 小心, zǐxì 仔细
he is very careful crossing the street = tā guò mǎlù hěn xiǎoxīn 他过马路很小心
to make a careful study of the problem = duì zhège wèntí jìnxíng zǐxì de yánjiū 对这个问题进行仔细的研究

careless *adjective*
= cūxīn 粗心, shūhu 疏忽

car ferry *noun*
a car ferry = yìsōu qìchē dùlún 一艘汽车渡轮

carnival *noun*
- (*British English*) (*a festival*)
  a carnival = yíge kuánghuānjié 一个狂欢节
- (*US English*) (*a fair*)
  a carnival = yíge yóuyì yúlè huì 一个游艺娱乐会

car park *noun* (*British English*)
a car park = yíge tíngchēchǎng 一个停车场

carpet *noun*
carpet = dìtǎn 地毯

car phone *noun*
a car phone = yíge chēyòng diànhuà 一个车用电话

carrot *noun*
a carrot = yíge húluóbo 一个胡萝卜

carry *verb*
- (*with one's hand*) = tí 提
  she was carrying a handbag = tā tízhe yíge shǒutíbāo 他提着一个手提包
- (*on one's shoulder*) = káng 扛
  he was carrying a box on his shoulder = tā kángzhe yíge xiāngzi 他扛着一个箱子
- (*in one's arms*) = bào 抱
  she was carrying her daughter in her arms = tā bàozhe tāde nǚ'ér 她抱着她的女儿
- (*on one's back*) = bēi 背

she was carrying her daughter on her back = tā bēizhe tāde nǚ'ér 她背着她的女儿
- to carry a bookbag on one's back = bēi shūbāo 背书包

carry on = jìxù 继续

cartoon *noun*

a cartoon (*a comic strip*) = yìzhāng mànhuà 一张漫画
(*a film*) = yíbù dònghuàpiān 一部动画片

case[1]: in case *conjunction*

- (*in the event that*) = jiǎshǐ 假使, jiǎrú 假如

in case you can't come, please phone me = jiǎshǐ nǐ bù néng lái, qǐng gěi wǒ dǎ diànhuà 假使你不能来, 请给我打电话
- (*lest*) = miǎnde 免得, yǐfáng 以防

I'll remind him again in case he forgets = wǒ yào zài tíxǐng tā yíxià, miǎnde tā wàng le 我要再提醒他一下, 免得他忘了

case[2] *noun*

a case
(*a box*) = yíge hézi 一个盒子
(*luggage*) = yíge xiāngzi 一个箱子

cash

1 *noun*

cash = xiànjīn 现金, xiànkuǎn 现款
to pay in cash = yòng xiànjīn fù kuǎn 用现金付款

2 *verb*

= duìhuànchéng xiànjīn 兑换成现金

cash dispenser *noun*

a cash dispenser = yíge zìdòng qǔkuǎnjī 一个自动取款机

cassette *noun*

a cassette = yíge hézi 一个盒子, yíge lùyīndài hé 一个录音带盒

cassette player *noun*

a cassette player = yìtái lùyīndài bōfàngjī 一台录音带播放机

castle *noun*

a castle = yízuò chéngbǎo 一座城堡

cat *noun*

a cat = yìzhī māo 一只猫

catch *verb*

- (*to capture*) = zhuō 捉

to catch a fish = zhuō yìtiáo yú 捉一条鱼
- (*to take hold of*) = zhuāzhù 抓住

catch my hand = zhuāzhù wǒde shǒu 抓住我的手
- (*to take hold of something in motion*) = jiēzhù 接住

he didn't catch the ball = tā méi jiēzhù nàge qiú 他没接住那个球
- (*to pinch, to stick*)

he caught his finger in the door = tāde shǒuzhǐ bèi mén jiāzhù le 他的手指被门夹住了
my shirt got caught by a nail = wǒde chènshān bèi yíge dīngzi guāzhù le 我的衬衫被一个钉子挂住了
- (*to be in time for*) = gǎn 赶

he was running to catch the train = tā pǎozhe qù gǎn huǒchē 他跑着去赶火车
- (*to take by surprise, to come upon*)

to catch someone stealing = fāxiàn mǒurén tōu dōngxi 发现某人偷东西
- (*to become ill with*) = dé 得

he caught flu = tā déle liúgǎn 他得了流感
- to catch fire = zháohuǒ 着火

catch up = gǎnshàng 赶上
to catch up with someone = gǎnshàng mǒurén 赶上某人

cathedral *noun*

a cathedral = yízuò dà jiàotáng 一座大教堂

cauliflower *noun*

= càihuā 菜花

cause *verb*

- to cause damage = zàochéng sǔnhuài 造成损坏
- to cause someone a lot of problems = gěi mǒurén dàilai hěn duō wèntí 给某人带来很多问题
- to cause one to be suspicious = yǐnqǐ mǒurén de huáiyí 引起某人的怀疑

cautious *adjective*

= xiǎoxīn 小心

cave *noun*

a cave = yíge shāndòng 一个山洞

CD, compact disk *noun*

a CD = yìzhāng guāngpán 一张光盘

CD player *noun*

a CD player = yìtái guāngpán bōfàngjī 一台光盘播放机

ceiling *noun*

the ceiling = tiānhuābǎn 天花板

celebrate *verb*
= qìngzhù 庆祝
to celebrate someone's birthday = qìngzhù mǒurén de shēngri 庆祝某人的生日

celery *noun*
= qíncài 芹菜

cell *noun*
- (*a unit of living matter*) = xìbāo 细胞
  a cell = yíge xìbāo 一个细胞
- (*a small room*) = xiǎo wū 小屋
  a cell = yìjiān xiǎo wū 一间小屋

cell phone, cellular phone *noun* (*US English*)
a cell phone = yíge shǒujī 一个手机

cellar *noun*
a cellar = yíge dìjiào 一个地窖

'cello *noun* ▶ 308
a 'cello = yìbǎ dàtíqín 一把大提琴

cement *noun*
= shuǐní 水泥

cemetery *noun*
a cemetery = yíge gōngmù 一个公墓

centimetre (*British English*), **centimeter** (*US English*) *noun* ▶ 300
a centimetre = yì gōngfēn 一公分, yì límǐ 一厘米

central heating *noun*
= jízhōng gòngrè 集中供热

centre (*British English*), **center** (*US English*) *noun*
= zhōngxīn 中心
a leisure centre = yíge yúlè zhōngxīn 一个娱乐中心
near the centre of London = kàojìn Lúndūn shì zhōngxīn 靠近伦敦市中心

century *noun* ▶ 412
a century = yíge shìjì 一个世纪

certain *adjective*
- (*sure*)
  = yídìng 一定
- (*some*)
  = mǒu 某
  a certain person = mǒu yíge rén 某一个人

certainly *adverb*
= yídìng 一定, kěndìng 肯定

chain *noun*
a chain = yìtiáo liànzi 一条链子

chair *noun*
a chair = yìbǎ yǐzi 一把椅子

chalk *noun*
= fěnbǐ 粉笔

champagne *noun*
= xiāngbīnjiǔ 香槟酒

champion *noun*
a champion = yíge guànjūn 一个冠军

chance *noun*
- (*a possibility*) = kěnéng 可能
  there is a chance that she'll have a job in Beijing = yǒu kěnéng tā huì zài Běijīng zhǎodào gōngzuò 有可能她会在北京找到工作
- (*an opportunity*) = jīhuì 机会
  to have a chance to meet him = yǒu jīhuì jiàndào tā 有机会见到他
- **by chance** = ǒurán 偶然

change
1 *noun*
- **a change** = yíge biànhuà 一个变化
  a change of temperature = wēndù de biànhuà 温度的变化
- (*cash*) = língqián 零钱
  have you got change for 50 pence? = nǐ yǒu wǔshí biànshì língqián ma? 你有五十便士零钱吗?

2 *verb*
- (*to become different*) = biànhuà 变化
  this city has changed a lot = zhège chéngshì biànhuà hěn dà 这个城市变化很大
- (*to make different*) = gǎibiàn 改变
  I've changed my mind = wǒ yǐjīng gǎibiànle zhǔyì 我已经改变了主意
- (*to replace, exchange, switch*) = huàn 换
  to change a wheel = huàn lúnzi 换轮子
  to change a shirt for a smaller size = huàn yíjiàn xiǎo yìdiǎn de chènshān 换一件小一点的衬衫
  to change places with someone = gēn mǒurén huàn dìfang 跟某人换地方
  to change channels = huàn píndào 换频道
  to get changed = huàn yīfu 换衣服
  to change trains = huàn chē 换车

to change dollars into pounds = bǎ měiyuán (duì)huànchéng yīngbàng 把美元(兑)换成英镑

changing room *noun*
a changing room = yìjiān gēngyīshì 一间更衣室

channel *noun*
a TV channel = yíge diànshì píndào 一个电视频道

Channel *noun*
the (English) Channel = Yīngjílì Hǎixiá 英吉利海峡

chapter *noun*
a chapter = yìzhāng 一章

charge
1 *verb*
that hotel charged him 10 pounds for the night = nàjiā lǚguǎn yíyè shōule tā shí bàng 那家旅馆一夜收了他十镑
they'll charge you for the electricity = tāmen huì xiàng nǐ shōu diànfèi 他们会向你收电费
2 *noun*
• (*a fee, a price*) = fèiyòng 费用, jiàqián 价钱
there is no charge = miǎnfèi 免费
3 in charge = fùzé 负责, zhǎngguǎn 掌管, zhǔguǎn 主管
to be in charge of the money = zhǎngguǎn qián 掌管钱

charming *adjective*
= mírén 迷人, kě'ài 可爱

chase *verb*
= zhuīgǎn 追赶
chase away = qūzhú 驱逐, qūgǎn 驱赶

chat
1 *verb*
= liáotiān 聊天, xiántán 闲谈
2 *noun*
a chat = liáotiān 聊天, xiántán 闲谈
chat up (*British English*) = hǒngpiàn 哄骗

cheap *adjective*
• (*not expensive*) = piányi 便宜
it's cheap = zhè hěn piányi 这很便宜
• (*of poor quality*) = dīliè 低劣

cheat *verb*
= piàn 骗, qīpiàn 欺骗

check
1 *verb*
= jiǎnchá 检查
you should check whether it's true = nǐ yīnggāi jiǎnchá yíxià zhè shìfǒu shì zhēn de 你应该检查一下这是否是真的
they didn't even check our passports = tāmen shènzhì méiyǒu jiǎnchá wǒmende hùzhào 他们甚至没有检查我们的护照
2 *noun*
• (*US English*) (*a bill*) = zhàngdān 帐单
a check = yìzhāng zhàngdān 一张帐单
• (*US English*) (*a cheque*) = zhīpiào 支票
a check = yìzhāng zhīpiào 一张支票
check in = dēngjì 登记
check out = jiézhàng líkāi 结帐离开

checkbook *noun* (*US English*)
a checkbook = yìběn zhīpiàobù 一本支票簿

checkers *noun* ▶ 390 (*US English*)
= tiàoqí 跳棋

check-in *noun*
• (*at an airport*) = bànlǐ dēngjī shǒuxù 办理登机手续
• (*at a hotel*) = bànlǐ zhùdiàn shǒuxù 办理住店手续

checkout *noun*
• (*at a hotel*) = bànlǐ lídiàn shǒuxù 办理离店手续

cheek *noun* ▶ 189
= miànjiá 面颊

cheeky *adjective*
= wúlǐ 无礼, hòuliǎnpí 厚脸皮

cheerful *adjective*
= kuàihuo 快活, gāoxìng 高兴

cheese *noun*
= nǎilào 奶酪, rǔlào 乳酪

chef *noun* ▶ 344
= chúshī 厨师

chemist *noun* ▶ 344
• (*in a shop*)
a chemist = yíge yàojìshī 一个药剂师
• (*in a laboratory*)
a chemist = yíge huàxuéjiā 一个化学家, yíge huàxué gōngzuòzhě 一个化学工作者

chemistry *noun*
= huàxué 化学

cheque *noun* (*British English*)
a cheque = yìzhāng zhīpiào 一张支票
to write a cheque for £50 = xiě yìzhāng wǔshí yīngbàng de zhīpiào 写一张五十英镑的支票

cheque book *noun* (*British English*)
a cheque book = yìběn zhīpiàobù 一本支票簿

cherry *noun*
a cherry = yíge yīngtáo 一个樱桃

chess *noun* ▶ 390
= xiàngqí 象棋

chest *noun* ▶ 189
- (*of the human body*) = xiōng 胸, xiōngqiāng 胸腔
- (*furniture*) = guìzi 柜子
  a chest = yíge guìzi 一个柜子

chestnut
1 *noun*
a chestnut = yíge lìzi 一个栗子
2 *adjective*
= zǎohóngsè 枣红色
she has chestnut hair = tā shì zǎohóngsè de tóufa 她是枣红色的头发

chew *verb*
= jiáo 嚼

chewing gum *noun*
= kǒuxiāngtáng 口香糖

chicken *noun*
- (*the bird*)
  a chicken = yìzhī jī 一只鸡
- (*the meat*) = jīròu 鸡肉

child *noun*
a child = yíge xiǎoháir 一个小孩儿

chilly *adjective*
= hánlěng 寒冷

chimney *noun*
a chimney = yíge yāncōng 一个烟囱

chin *noun* ▶ 189
= xiàba(kēr) 下巴(颏儿)

China *noun*
= Zhōngguó 中国

Chinese ▶ 288
1 *adjective*
= Zhōngguó de 中国的
2 *noun*
- (*the people*) = Zhōngguórén 中国人
- (*the language*) = Zhōngwén 中文, Zhōngguóhuà 中国话, Hànyǔ 汉语

Chinese New Year *noun*
= Chūnjié 春节, Zhōngguó Xīnnián 中国新年

Chinese New Year's Eve *noun*
= chúxī 除夕

chips *noun*
- (*British English*) (*fries, French fries*) = tǔdòutiáo 土豆条, shǔtiáo 薯条
- (*US English*) (*crisps*) = tǔdòupiàn 土豆片

chocolate *noun*
= qiǎokèlì 巧克力
a box of chocolates = yìhé qiǎokèlì 一盒巧克力

choice *noun*
= xuǎnzé 选择
he made a wrong choice = tā zuòle yíge cuòwù de xuǎnzé 他做了一个错误的选择

choir *noun*
- (*in a church*) = chàngshībān 唱诗班
- (*a chorus of singers*) = gēyǒngduì 歌咏队, héchàngduì 合唱队

choke *verb*
- he choked on a fish bone = tā bèi yìgēn yúcì qiǎzhùle hóulóng 他被一根鱼刺卡住了喉咙
- he choked her to death = tā bǎ tā qiāsǐ le 他把她掐死了

choose *verb*
= xuǎnzé 选择, tiāoxuǎn 挑选

chopsticks *noun*
= kuàizi 筷子
a pair of chopsticks = yìshuāng kuàizi 一双筷子

chore *noun*
= jiāwù 家务
to do the chores = zuò jiāwù 做家务

Christian
1 *noun*
= Jīdūjiàotú 基督教徒
2 *adjective*
= Jīdūjiào de 基督教的

Christian name *noun*
a Christian name = yíge jiàomíng 一个教名

C

Christmas *noun*
Christmas (Day) = Shèngdàn(jié) 圣诞(节)
Merry Christmas!, Happy Christmas! = Shèngdàn kuàilè! 圣诞快乐!

Christmas carol *noun*
a Christmas carol = yìshǒu Shèngdàn sònggē 一首圣诞颂歌

Christmas cracker *noun* (*British English*)
a Christmas cracker = yíge Shèngdàn cǎisè bàozhú 一个圣诞彩色爆竹

Christmas Eve *noun*
Christmas Eve = Shèngdàn qiányè 圣诞前夜

Christmas tree *noun*
a Christmas tree = yìkē Shèngdàn shù 一棵圣诞树

church *noun*
- (*building*)
  a church = yízuò jiàotáng 一座教堂
- (*a group of people*)
  a church = yíge jiàohuì 一个教会

cider *noun*
= guǒjiǔ 果酒

cigar *noun*
a cigar = yìzhī xuějiā(yān) 一支雪茄(烟)

cigarette *noun*
a cigarette = yìzhī xiāngyān 一支香烟

cigarette lighter *noun*
a cigarette lighter = yíge dǎhuǒjī 一个打火机

cinema *noun* (*British English*)
a cinema = yíge diànyǐngyuàn 一个电影院

circle *noun*
a circle = yíge yuánquān 一个圆圈
we were sitting in a circle = wǒmen zuòchéng yíge yuánquān 我们坐成一个圆圈

circus *noun*
a circus = yíge mǎxìtuán 一个马戏团

citizen *noun*
- (*of a country*)
  a citizen = yíge gōngmín 一个公民
- (*of a city or town*)
  a citizen = yíge shìmín 一个市民, yíge jūmín 一个居民

city *noun*
a city = yízuò chéngshì 一座城市

city centre (*British English*), **city center** (*US English*) *noun*
the city centre = shì zhōngxīn 市中心

civilized *adjective*
= wénmíng 文明

civil servant *noun* ▶ 344
a civil servant = yíge gōngwùyuán 一个公务员

clap *verb*
- (*to pat*) = pāi 拍
- (*to applaud*) = gǔzhǎng 鼓掌

clarinet *noun* ▶ 308
a clarinet = yíge dānhuángguǎn 一个单簧管

class *noun*
- (*a group of students*)
  a class = yíge bān 一个班
- (*a lesson*)
  a class = yìjié kè 一节课
  a history class = yìjié lìshǐ kè 一节历史课
- (*a social group*)
  a (social) class = yíge (shèhuì) jiējí 一个(社会)阶级

classical music *noun*
classical music = gǔdiǎn yīnyuè 古典音乐

classmate *noun*
a classmate = yíge tóngxué 一个同学

classroom *noun*
a classroom = yìjiān jiàoshì 一间教室

clean
1 *adjective*
= gānjìng 干净, qīngjié 清洁
my hands are clean = wǒde shǒu hěn gānjìng 我的手很干净
to keep the room clean = bǎochí fángjiān qīngjié 保持房间清洁
2 *verb*
= bǎ...nòng gānjìng 把...弄干净

> **!** *Note that the verb* nòng 弄 *can be replaced by another verb, such as* xǐ 洗 (= to wash) *or* cā 擦 (= to wipe), *depending on the way the object is cleaned.*

to have the clothes cleaned = bǎ yīfu xǐgānjìng 把衣服洗干净
I have cleaned the windows = wǒ bǎ chuānghu cāgānjìng le 我把窗户擦干净了

clear
1 *adjective*
- (*easy to understand, see, or hear*) = qīngchu 清楚
  is that clear? = qīngchu ma? 清楚吗?
- **his voice isn't clear** = tāde shēngyīn bù qīngchu 他的声音不清楚
- **your writing must be very clear** = nǐ bìxū xiě de hěn qīngchu 你必须写得很清楚
- (*obvious*) = xiǎnrán 显然, míngxiǎn 明显
  it is clear that he is unhappy = xiǎnrán tā bù gāoxìng 显然他不高兴
- (*with no rain or cloud*) = qínglǎng 晴朗
  a clear day = yíge qíng tiān 一个晴天

2 *verb*
- (*to empty, to remove from*)
  to clear the table = shōushi zhuōzi 收拾桌子
  to clear the house of everything in it = qīngchú fángzi lǐ suǒyǒu de dōngxi 清除房子里所有的东西
- (*about the sky or the weather*) = biànqíng 变晴

clever *adjective*
= cōngming 聪明
she is a clever girl = tā shì yíge cōngming de gūniang 她是一个聪明的姑娘
clever at = shàncháng 擅长
to be clever at mathematics = shàncháng shùxué 擅长数学

click *verb*
(*using a mouse*) = jī 击, diǎnjī 点击

cliff *noun*
a cliff = yíge xuányá 一个悬崖, yíge qiàobì 一个峭壁

climate *noun*
= qìhòu 气候

climb *verb*
- (*to ascend by clutching with hands and feet*) = pá 爬
  to climb (up) a tree = pá shù 爬树
  to climb a mountain = pá shān 爬山
  to climb over a wall = fānguò qiáng 翻过墙
- (*to rise higher*) = xiàng shàng pá 向上爬

climbing *noun* ▶ 390
= pāndēng 攀登

clinic *noun*
a clinic = yíge ménzhěnsuǒ 一个门诊所, yíge yīwùshì 一个医务室

cloakroom *noun*
a cloakroom = yíge xǐshǒujiān 一个洗手间, yíge yīmàojiān 一个衣帽间

clock *noun*
(*on a building, in a room, or as an ornament*) = zhōng 钟
(*in sporting events*) = miǎobiǎo 秒表

close[1]
1 *adjective*
- (*near*) = jìn 近
  the station is quite close = chēzhàn bǐjiào jìn 车站比较近
  is the house close to the school? = fángzi lí xuéxiào jìn ma? 房子离学校近吗?
- (*as a relative*) = jìn 近
  a close relative = yíge jìnqīn 一个近亲
- (*as a friend*) = qīnmì 亲密
  a close friend = yíge qīnmì de péngyou 一个亲密的朋友

2 *adverb*
to live close (by) = zhù zài fùjìn 住在附近
to follow close behind someone = jǐn gēn zài mǒurén hòumian 紧跟在某人后面

close[2] *verb*
- (*if it's a door or a window*) = guān 关
  to close the window = guān chuāng 关窗
  the door closed suddenly = mén tūrán guānshang le 门突然关上了
- (*if it's the eye or the mouth*) = bì 闭
  close your eyes = bìshang nǐde yǎnjīng 闭上你的眼睛
- (*if it's a shop or a bank*) = guānmén 关门
  the shop closes at noon = zhèjiā shāngdiàn zhōngwǔ guānmén 这家商店中午关门
  close down = guānbì 关闭, dǎobì 倒闭
  the factory has closed down = zhèjiā gōngchǎng guānbì le 这家工厂关闭了

closed *adjective*
= guānbì 关闭, guānmén 关门

cloth *noun*
- (*material*) = bù 布

The Clock

What time is it?

excuse me, what time is it? = qǐng wèn, jǐ diǎn le? 请问, 几点了?
it's exactly four o'clock = zhènghǎo sì diǎn 正好四点

There is no Chinese equivalent of "it is..." in expressions of time. Usually, **xiànzài** 现在 (= now) is used at the beginning of the Chinese sentence to indicate the time.

it is...	**xiànzài...** 现在...
4 o'clock	sì diǎn 四点
4 o'clock in the morning|4 am	zǎochén sì diǎn 早晨四点
4 o'clock in the afternoon|4 pm	xiàwǔ sì diǎn 下午四点
4:10|ten past four	sì diǎn shí fēn 四点十分
4:15	sì diǎn shíwǔ fēn 四点十五分
a quarter past four	sì diǎn yí kè 四点一刻
4:20	sì diǎn èrshí fēn 四点二十分
4:25	sì diǎn èrshíwǔ fēn 四点二十五分
4:30	sì diǎn sānshí fēn 四点三十分
half past four	sì diǎn bàn 四点半
4:35	sì diǎn sānshíwǔ fēn 四点三十五分
twenty-five to five	chà èrshíwǔ fēn wǔ diǎn 差二十五分五点
4:40	sì diǎn sìshí fēn 四点四十分
twenty to five	chà èrshí fēn wǔ diǎn 差二十分五点
4:45	sì diǎn sìshíwǔ fēn 四点四十五分
a quarter to five	chà yí kè wǔ diǎn 差一刻五点
4:50	sì diǎn wǔshí fēn 四点五十分
ten to five	chà shí fēn wǔ diǎn 差十分五点
4:55	sì diǎn wǔshíwǔ fēn 四点五十五分
five to five	chà wǔ fēn wǔ diǎn 差五分五点
5 o'clock	wǔ diǎn 五点
16:15	shíliù diǎn shíwǔ fēn 十六点十五分
8 o'clock in the evening|8 pm	wǎnshang bā diǎn 晚上八点
12:00	shí'èr diǎn 十二点
12 noon	zhōngwǔ shí'èr diǎn 中午十二点
12 midnight	bànyè shí'èr diǎn 半夜十二点, wǔyè shí'èr diǎn 午夜十二点

In timetables, etc., the twenty-four hour clock is used. For example, 4 pm is **shíliù diǎn** 十六点. In ordinary usage, one says **xiàwǔ sì diǎn** 下午四点.

When?

Chinese never drops the word **diǎn** 点; **at five** is **wǔ diǎn** 五点 and so on.

It is not necessary to translate the word **at** into Chinese, but other prepositions or adverbs are still necessary.

***at what time** will he come?* = tā ___ jǐ diǎn lái? 他 ___几点来?
*he'll come **at** four* = tā ___ sì diǎn lái 他 ___ 四点来
*he'll come **at about** five* = tā ___ **dàyuē** wǔ diǎn lái 他 ___ 大约五点来
*it must be ready **by** ten* = shí diǎn **yǐqián** yídìng yào zhǔnbèihǎo 十点以前一定要准备好
*closed **from** 1 **to** 2 pm* = **cóng** xiàwǔ yì diǎn **dào** liǎng diǎn guānmén 从下午一点到两点关门
*I'll go **after** 6* = wǒ liù diǎn **yǐhòu** qù 我六点以后去

- a cloth (*for dusting*) = yíkuài mābù 一块抹布
- a table cloth = yíkuài zhuōbù 一块桌布
- a cloth
  (*for dishes*) = yíkuài shuā wǎn bù 一块刷碗布
  (*for the floor*) = yíkuài cā dìbǎn bù 一块擦地板布

clothes *noun*
= yīfu 衣服
to put on one's clothes = chuānshang yīfu 穿上衣服
to take off one's clothes = tuōxia yīfu 脱下衣服
to have no clothes on = méi chuān yīfu 没穿衣服

cloud *noun*
a cloud = yìduǒ yún 一朵云

clown *noun*
a clown = yíge xiǎochǒu 一个小丑

club *noun*
- a club = yíge jùlèbù 一个俱乐部
  a tennis club = yíge wǎngqiú jùlèbù 一个网球俱乐部
- (*a nightclub*)
  a club = yíge yèzǒnghuì 一个夜总会

clue *noun*
a clue = yìtiáo xiànsuǒ 一条线索

clumsy *adjective*
= bènzhuō 笨拙

coach
1 *noun* (*British English*)
- (*a bus*)
  a coach = yī liàng chángtú qìchē 一辆长途汽车
- (*of a train*) (*British English*)
  a coach = yī jié chēxiāng 一节车厢
- (*a trainer in sports*)
  a coach = yī ge jiàoliàn 一个教练
- (*a private tutor*)
  a coach = yī ge sīrén jiàoshī 一个私人教师

2 *verb*
- (*in sports*) = xùnliàn 训练
- (*in academic studies*) = fǔdǎo 辅导

coach station *noun*
a coach station = yī ge chángtú qìchē zhàn 一个长途汽车站

coal *noun*
= méi 煤

coast *noun*
= hǎi'àn 海岸

coat *noun*
- a coat = yíjiàn wàitào 一件外套
- (*of an animal*) = pímáo 皮毛

coat hanger *noun*
a coat hanger = yī gè yījià 一个衣架

cobweb *noun*
a cobweb = yī ge zhīzhūwǎng 一个蜘蛛网

cock *noun*
a cock = yī zhī gōngjī 一只公鸡

cocoa *noun*
- (*the drink*) = kěkěchá 可可茶
- (*the product*) = kěkěfěn 可可粉

coconut *noun*
a coconut = yī gè yēzi 一个椰子

cod *noun*
= xuěyú 鳕鱼

coffee *noun*
- (*the product*) = kāfēi 咖啡
- (*a cup of coffee*)
  a coffee = yī bēi kāfēi 一杯咖啡

coffee machine *noun*
a coffee machine (*an appliance*) = yī gè kāfēiqì 一个咖啡器
(*a machine*) = yītái kāfēijī 一台咖啡机

coin *noun*
a coin = yī ge yìngbì 一个硬币
a ten-pence coin = yī gè shí biànshì de yìngbì 一个十便士的硬币

coincidence *noun*
a coincidence = yī gè qiǎohé 一个巧合

cold
1 *adjective*
= lěng 冷
I'm very cold = wǒ hěn lěng 我很冷
it's cold in the classroom = jiàoshì lǐ hěn lěng 教室里很冷
a cold meal = yī dùn liángfàn 一顿凉饭

2 *noun*
- (*the lack of heat*) = hánlěng 寒冷
- (*a common illness*) = gǎnmào 感冒

collapse *verb*
(*if it's a building, a wall*) = dǎotā 倒塌
(*in health*) = kuǎ 垮
(*when talking about a person falling down physically*) = dǎoxià 倒下

collar *noun*
- (*on a shirt or jacket*)
  a collar = yíge lǐngzi 一个领子

C

- (*for a pet*)
  a collar = yíge jǐngquān 一个颈圈

colleague *noun*
  a colleague = yíge tóngshì 一个同事

collect *verb*
- (*to gather*) = jí 集, shōují 收集
  to collect materials = shōují cáiliào 收集材料
  he collects stamps = tā jíyóu 他集邮
- (*to pick up or meet a person*) = jiē 接
  she is going to collect her son = tā yào qù jiē tā érzi 她要去接她儿子
- (*to collect money or rubbish*) = shōu 收
  to collect taxes = shōu shuì 收税
- **to collect my post** = qǔ wǒde xìnjiàn 取我的信件

collection *noun*
- (*a set*) = shōují 收集
  she has a great collection of posters = tā shōujíle hěn duō zhāotiēhuà 她收集了很多招贴画
- (*money collected*) = shōu de qián 收的钱

college *noun*
  a college = yíge xuéyuàn 一个学院
  to go to college = shàng dàxué 上大学
  to be at college = zài dàxué shàngxué 在大学上学

colour (*British English*), **color** (*US English*)
1 *noun*
  a colour = yìzhǒng yánsè 一种颜色
  what colour is the car? = chē shì shénme yánsè de? 车是什么颜色的?
2 *verb*
  = gěi...zhuósè 给...着色
  to colour the drawings (in...) = (yòng...) gěi huà zhuósè (用...) 给画着色

colourful (*British English*), **colorful** (*US English*) *adjective*
  = yànlì 艳丽, sècǎi fēngfù 色彩丰富
  a colourful shirt = yíjiàn yànlì de chènshān 一件艳丽的衬衫

colour television (*British English*), **color television** (*US English*) *noun*
  a colour television = yìtái cǎisè diànshìjī 一台彩色电视机

comb
1 *noun*
  a comb = yìbǎ shūzi 一把梳子
2 *verb*
  to comb one's hair = shū tóufa 梳头发

come *verb*
- **to come** = lái 来
  she's coming today = tā jīntiān lái 她今天来
  we'll come by bike = wǒmen qí zìxíngchē lái 我们骑自行车来
  I'm coming = wǒ zhè jiù lái 我这就来
  is the bus coming? = chē lái le ma? 车来了吗?
  be careful when you come down the stairs = xià lóutī de shíhou yào xiǎoxīn 下楼梯的时候要小心
  to come through the city centre = chuānguò shì zhōngxīn 穿过市中心
- (*to happen*) = fāshēng 发生
  whatever comes, I won't change my mind = bùguǎn fāshēng shénme shì, wǒ dōu bú huì gǎibiàn zhǔyì 不管发生什么事，我都不会改变主意
- (*to reach*) = dào 到
  turn left when you come to the traffic lights = nǐ dàole jiāotōng dēng de shíhou xiàng zuǒ guǎi 你到了交通灯的时候向左拐
- (*to attend*) = cānjiā 参加
  will you be able to come to the meeting? = nǐ néng cānjiā huìyì ma? 你能参加会议吗?
- (*to be a native or a product of*) = láizì 来自
  she comes from Japan = tā láizì Rìběn 他来自日本
  the strawberries all come from Spain = zhèxiē cǎoméi quánbù láizì Xībānyá 这些草莓全部来自西班牙
- (*in a contest*) = dé 得
  to come first = dé dìyī 得第一

come around ▶ **come round**

come back = huílai 回来
  when will you come back? = nǐ shénme shíhou huílai? 你什么时候回来?
  to come back home = huí jiā 回家

come in
- (*to enter*) = jìnlai 进来
- (*if it's a plane, a train*) = dàodá 到达

- the tide's coming in = zhèngzài zhǎngcháo 正在涨潮

come off = diào 掉

a button came off my shirt = wǒde chènshān diàole yíge kòuzi 我的衬衫掉了一个扣子

come on

- (*to start*) = kāishǐ 开始
  (*if it's heating*) = kāishǐ rè 开始热
  (*if it's a light*) = kāishǐ liàng 开始亮
- (*when encouraging someone*) = kuài 快, déla 得啦
  come on, hurry up! = kuài, gǎnjǐn! 快,赶紧!
  come on, you can do better than that! = déla, nǐ néng zuò de bǐ nà gèng hǎo! 得啦,你能做得比那更好!

come out

- (*to leave a place*) = chūlai 出来
  I saw him as I was coming out of the shop = wǒ cóng shāngdiàn chūlai de shíhou kànjiànle tā 我从商店出来的时候看见了他
- (*to become available*)
  (*if it's a film*) = shàngyǎn 上演
  (*if it's a book*) = chūbǎn 出版
- (*to wash out*) = xǐdiào 洗掉
- (*if it's a photo*)
  the photo didn't come out = zhèzhāng zhàopiàn méi zhàohǎo 这张照片没照好
- (*if it's smoke, fire*) = màochūlai 冒出来
  there are flames coming out of the windows = yǒu yìxiē huǒmiáo cóng chuānghu lǐ màochūlai 有一些火苗从窗户里冒出来

come round

- (*to visit*) = lái 来
- (*after a faint*) = sūxǐngguòlai 苏醒过来

come to (*to total*) = gòngjì 共计

the meal came to 75 pounds = fàn fèi gòngjì qīshíwǔ bàng 饭费共计七十五镑

how much does it come to? = gòngjì duōshǎo qián 共计多少钱

come up

- (*to be discussed*) = tíchūlai 提出来
  has this question come up? = zhège wèntí tíchūlai le ma? 这个问题提出来了吗?
- (*if it's the sun*) = chūlai 出来

comfortable *adjective*
= shūfu 舒服, shūshì 舒适

do you feel comfortable? = nǐ gǎnjué shūfu ma? 你感觉舒服吗?

comforter *noun* (*US English*)
a comforter

- (*if it's a person*) = yíge ānwèizhě 一个安慰者
- (*if it's a blanket*) = yìtiáo tǎnzi 一条毯子

comic strip *noun*
a comic strip = yítào liánhuán mànhuà 一套连环漫画

commercial
1 *adjective*
= shāngyè 商业, shāngwù 商务
2 *noun*
a commercial (*on TV or radio*) = yíge guǎnggào jiémù 一个广告节目

commit *verb*
to commit [a crime | a mistake | a murder] = fàn [zuì | cuò | móushā zuì] 犯[罪 | 错 | 谋杀罪]

common *adjective*

- (*public*) = gòngyǒu de 共有的, gòngtóng de 共同的
- (*ordinary*) = pǔtōng de 普通的, tōngcháng de 通常的

communicate *verb*

- (*to pass, to impart*) = chuándá 传达, chuánsòng 传送
- (*to have communication*) = liánxì 联系, liánluò 联络
  to communicate with someone by [letter | telephone | fax] = yǔ mǒurén tōngguò [xìnjiàn | diànhuà | chuánzhēn] liánxì 与某人通过[信件 | 电话 | 传真] 联系

community *noun*
a community = yíge shètuán 一个社团, yíge tuǎntǐ 一个团体

company *noun*

- (*a business*) = gōngsī 公司
  a company = yíge gōngsī 一个公司
- (*a group of actors*) = jùtuán 剧团
  a theatre company = yíge jùtuán 一个剧团
- (*other people*) = péibàn 陪伴
  to keep someone company = péibàn mǒurén 陪伴某人
  to part company with someone = gēn mǒurén fēnshǒu 跟某人分手

compare *verb*
= bǐjiào 比较

to compare China with Japan = ná Rìběn gēn Zhōngguó bǐjiào 拿日本跟中国比较
she compares herself to her older sister = tā ná zìjǐ gēn tā jiějie bǐjiào 她拿自己跟她姐姐比较

compass *noun*
a compass = yíge zhǐnánzhēn 一个指南针

competition *noun*
- = jìngzhēng 竞争
there's a lot of competition between the schools = zài gè xuéxiào zhījiān yǒu hěn duō jìngzhēng 在各学校之间有很多竞争
- (*a contest*) = bǐsài 比赛
a drawing competition = yícì huìhuà bǐsài 一次绘画比赛

competitive *adjective*
= jùyǒu jìngzhēng xìng de 具有竞争性的

complain *verb*
= bàoyuàn 抱怨
to complain about the food = bàoyuàn fàn bù hǎo 抱怨饭不好

complete
1 *adjective*
- (*entire*) = wánquán 完全
it was a complete disaster = zhè wánquán shì yìchǎng zāinàn 这完全是一场灾难
this is a complete waste of time = zhè wánquán shì làngfèi shíjiān 这完全是浪费时间
- (*finished*) = wánchéng 完成
the work must be complete by 10 o'clock = zhège gōngzuò shí diǎn yǐqián bìxū wánchéng 这个工作十点以前必须完成

2 *verb*
= wánchéng 完成
the project has not been completed yet = zhèxiàng gōngchéng hái méiyǒu wánchéng 这项工程还没有完成

completely *adverb*
= wánquán 完全

complicate *verb*
= shǐ...fùzá 使...复杂
this has further complicated the situation = zhè shǐ xíngshì gèng fùzá le 这使形势更复杂了

complicated *adjective*
= fùzá 复杂

compliment
1 *noun*
a compliment = zànyáng 赞扬, zànměi de huà 赞美的话
2 *verb*
= chēngzàn 称赞, zànměi 赞美
to compliment someone = chēngzàn mǒurén 称赞某人

compulsory *adjective*
- (*if it's education or military service*) = yìwù 义务
- (*if it's a school subject*) = bìxiū 必修
- (*if it's a way of handling something*) = qiángzhì 强制, qiángpò 强迫

computer *noun*
a computer = yìtái jìsuànjī 一台计算机, yìtái diànnǎo 一台电脑

computer game *noun*
a computer game = yíge jìsuànjī yóuxì 一个计算机游戏

computer programme *noun*
a computer programme = yíge jìsuànjī chéngxù 一个计算机程序

computer programmer *noun* ▶ 344
a computer programmer = yíge biān jìsuànjī chéngxù de rén 一个编计算机程序的人

computer scientist *noun* ▶ 344
a computer scientist = yíge jìsuànjī kēxuéjiā 一个计算机科学家

computer studies *noun*
= jìsuànjīxué 计算机学

concentrate *verb*
- (*to bring towards a centre*) = jízhōng 集中
- (*to direct one's thoughts towards one object*) = jízhōng jīnglì 集中精力

concert *noun*
a concert = yìchǎng yīnyuèhuì 一场音乐会

concert hall *noun*
a concert hall = yíge yīnyuètīng 一个音乐厅

concrete *noun*
= hùnníngtǔ 混凝土

condemn *verb*
- (*to censure or blame*) = qiǎnzé 谴责
- (*to sentence*) = pànchǔ 判处

to condemn someone to death = pànchǔ mǒurén sǐxíng 判处某人死刑

condition *noun*
- (*prerequisite*) = tiáojiàn 条件
  conditions of success = chénggōng de tiáojiàn 成功的条件
- (*a state*) = zhuàngkuàng 状况
  the car is in good condition = chē de zhuàngkuàng hěn hǎo 车的状况很好
  on condition that = rúguǒ 如果
  you can go on condition that her parents drive you home = rúguǒ tā fùmǔ kāi chē sòng nǐ huí jiā, nǐ jiù kěyǐ qù 如果她父母开车送你回家，你就可以去

! *Note that the conditional clause precedes the main clause in Chinese.*

condom *noun*
a condom = yíge bìyùntào 一个避孕套

conductor *noun* ▶ 344
- (*in an orchestra or a choir*)
  a conductor = yíge yuèduì zhǐhuī 一个乐队指挥
- (*in a bus*)
  a conductor = yíge shòupiàoyuán 一个售票员
- (*in a train*)
  a conductor = yíge lièchēyuán 一个列车员

conference *noun*
a conference = yícì huìyì 一次会议

confidence *noun*
- = xìnxīn 信心
- (*trust*) = xìnrèn 信任
  to have confidence in someone = xìnrèn mǒurén 信任某人

confident *adjective*
= yǒu xìnxīn 有信心

confidential *adjective*
- (*given in confidence*) = mìmì de 秘密的, jīmì de 机密的
- (*admitted into confidence*) = cānyù jīmì de 参与机密的
  a confidential secretary = yíge jīyào mìshū 一个机要秘书

confiscate *verb*
= mòshōu 没收

conflict *noun*
= chōngtū 冲突

Confucian
1 *adjective*
= Kǒngzǐ de 孔子的, Rújiā de 儒家的
1 *noun*
= Rújiā 儒家, Kǒngzǐ de méntú 孔子的门徒

confused *adjective*
= hútu 糊涂

congratulate *verb*
= zhùhè 祝贺

congratulations *noun (also exclamation)*
= zhùhè 祝贺
congratulations! = zhùhè nǐ ! 祝贺你!

connection *noun*
= guānxi 关系
it has no connection with the strike = zhè yǔ bàgōng méi yǒu guānxi 这与罢工没有关系

conscientious *adjective*
= rènzhēn 认真

conscious *adjective*
- (*aware*) = yìshìdào 意识到
- (*after an operation*) = shénzhì qīngxǐng 神志清醒

construct *verb*
= jiànzào 建造, jiànshè 建设

consult *verb*
- (*to discuss*) = shāngliang 商量
  to consult with him = gēn tā shāngliang 跟他商量
- (*to ask advice of*) = qǐngjiào 请教
  to consult the teacher = qǐngjiào lǎoshī 请教老师
- (*to look up for information*) = chá 查
  to consult a dictionary = chá zìdiǎn 查字典

contact
1 *noun*
to be in contact with someone = gēn mǒurén yǒu liánxi 跟某人有联系
to lose contact = shīqù liánxi 失去联系
2 *verb*
to contact someone = gēn mǒurén liánxi 跟某人联系

contact lens *noun*
= yǐnxíng yǎnjìng 隐形眼镜

C

contain *verb*
- (*if it's a substance*) = hányǒu 含有
  sea water contains salt = hǎishuǐ hányǒu yán 海水含有盐
- (*if it's a container*) = zhuāng 装
  this box contains apples = zhège xiāngzi zhuāngzhe píngguǒ 这个箱子装着苹果
- (*if it's a room or a hall*) = róngnà 容纳
  this room can contain 20 people = zhège fángjiān néng róngnà èrshíge rén 这个房间能容纳二十个人

content *adjective*
- (*satisfied*) = mǎnyì 满意
- (*not wanting more*) = mǎnzú 满足

contest *noun*
= bǐsài 比赛, jìngsài 竞赛

continent *noun*
- (*a large mass of land*)
  a continent = yíge dàlù 一个大陆
- (*British English*) (*Europe*)
  the Continent = Oūzhōu dàlù 欧洲大陆

continue *verb*
= jìxù 继续
to continue to talk, to continue talking = jìxù tánhuà 继续谈话

continuous *adjective*
= chíxù 持续, búduàn 不断
a continuous noise = chíxù de zàoyīn 持续的噪音

contraception *noun*
= bìyùn 避孕

contract *noun*
a contract = yíge hétong 一个合同
to have a two-year contract = huòdé yíge liǎng nián de hétong 获得一个两年的合同

contradict *verb*
- (*to oppose by words*) = fǎnbó 反驳
- (*to deny*) = fǒurèn 否认
- (*to be contrary to*) = yǔ...xiāng máodùn 与...相矛盾
  this document contradicts that one = zhège wénjiàn yǔ nàge wénjiàn xiāng máodùn 这个文件与那个文件相矛盾

contradiction *noun*
a contradiction = yíge máodùn 一个矛盾

contrast *noun*
= duìbǐ 对比, duìzhào 对照

contribute *verb*
- (*to give money*) = juān(xiàn) 捐(献)
- **to contribute one's share** = gòngxiàn zìjǐ de yífèn lìliang 贡献自己的一份力量

control
1 *noun*
= kòngzhì 控制
to take control of a situation = kòngzhì júshì 控制局势
to lose control of a car = duì chē shīqù kòngzhì 对车失去控制
2 *verb*
- = kòngzhì 控制
  to control a region = kòngzhì yíge dìqū 控制一个地区
- **to control traffic** = guǎnlǐ jiāotōng 管理交通

convenient *adjective*
= fāngbiàn 方便
it's more convenient to take the bus = zuò qìchē gèng fāngbiàn 坐汽车更方便
it's not convenient for me = zhè duì wǒ bù fāngbiàn 这对我不方便

conversation *noun*
= tánhuà 谈话
to have a conversation with someone = yǔ mǒurén tánhuà 与某人谈话

convince *verb*
- (*to persuade*) = shuōfú/shuìfú 说服
- (*to satisfy as to the truth of something*) = shǐ...xìnfú 使...信服, shǐ...quèxìn 使 ... 确信
  he convinced me of his innocence = tā shǐ wǒ quèxìn tā shì qīngbái de 他使我确信他是清白的

cook
1 *verb*
= zuò fàn 做饭
to cook a meal = zuò fàn 做饭
2 *noun* ▶ 344
a cook = yíge chúshī 一个厨师, yíge chuīshìyuán 一个炊事员

cooker *noun* (*British English*)
a cooker = yíge lúzào 一个炉灶

cookie *noun* (*US English*)
a cookie = yíkuài bǐnggān 一块饼干, yíge xiǎo tiánbǐng 一个小甜饼

cooking *noun*
= pēngtiáo 烹调, pēngrèn 烹饪
to do the cooking = zuò fàn 做饭

cool *adjective*
- (*fresh, not hot*) = liáng 凉, liángkuai 凉快
  a cool drink = yíge lěngyǐn 一个冷饮
  it's much cooler today = jīntiān liángkuai duō le 今天凉快多了
- (*calm*) = lěngjìng 冷静
- (*fashionable*) = kù 酷✖

cool down
- (*to get colder*) = biàn liáng 变凉
- (*to calm down*) = píngjìng xiàlai 平静下来

cooperate *verb*
= hézuò 合作
to cooperate with someone = yǔ mǒurén hézuò 与某人合作

cope *verb*
= yìngfu 应付, duìfu 对付
can he cope with this work? = tā néng yìngfu zhège gōngzuò ma? 他能应付这个工作吗?

copper *noun*
= tóng 铜

copy
1 *noun*
a copy = yíge fùzhìpǐn 一个复制品
(*if it's photocopy*) = yíge fùyìnjiàn 一个复印件, yíge yǐngyìnjiàn 一个影印件
2 *verb*
- (*to photocopy*) = fùyìn 复印, yǐngyìn 影印
- (*to reproduce a painting, a videotape, an antique*) = fùzhì 复制
- (*to plagiarize*) = chāoxí 抄袭
- (*to imitate*) = mófǎng 模仿

cork *noun*
- **a cork** = yíge ruǎnmù sāi 一个软木塞
- **cork** = ruǎnmù 软木

corkscrew *noun*
a corkscrew = yìbǎ kāisāizuàn 一把开塞钻

corner *noun*
- (*of a street*) = guǎijiǎo 拐角
- (*of a table, a room*) = jiǎo 角
  the corner of a table = zhuōzi jiǎo 桌子角
- (*in football, hockey*) = jiǎoqiú 角球
  a corner = yícì jiǎoqiú 一次角球

correct
1 *adjective*
= zhèngquè 正确
2 *verb*
to correct a mistake = gǎizhèng cuòwù 改正错误
to correct an essay = xiūgǎi wénzhāng 修改文章

correction *noun*
= gǎizhèng 改正, xiūgǎi 修改

corridor *noun*
a corridor = yíge zǒuláng 一个走廊

cost
1 *noun*
= fèiyòng 费用
2 *verb*
how much does it cost? = zhège duōshǎo qián? 这个多少钱?
it will cost a lot of money = zhè yào huā hěn duō qián 这要花很多钱

costume *noun*
a costume = yìzhǒng zhuāngshù 一种装束

cosy (*British English*), **cozy** (*US English*) *adjective*
a cosy room = yíge wēnnuǎn shūshì de fángjiān 一个温暖舒适的房间

cot *noun* (*British English*)
a cot = yìzhāng értóng chuáng 一张儿童床

cottage *noun*
a cottage = yìsuǒ xiǎo biéshù 一所小别墅, yìsuǒ cūnshè 一所村舍

cotton *noun*
- (*the material*) = miánhuā 棉花
- (*the thread*) = mián xiàn 棉线

cotton wool *noun* (*British English*)
= tuōzhīmián 脱脂棉, yàomián 药棉

couch *noun*
a couch = yíge cháng shāfā 一个长沙发

cough *verb*
= késou 咳嗽

could *verb*
- (*knew how to*) = néng 能

✖in informal situations

she could read at the age of three = tā sān suì jiù néng kàn shū 她三岁就能看书
he couldn't type = tā bú huì dǎzì 他不会打字

> **!** *Note that here in the negative sentence,* **bú huì 不会** *should be used instead of* **bù néng 不能**.

- (*when talking about speaking or writing in a foreign language*) = huì 会

he could speak Japanese but I couldn't = tā huì shuō Rìyǔ kěshì wǒ bú huì 他会说日语可是我不会

- (*in the negative sentence when talking about* **seeing, hearing, understanding, could** *is not translated*)

I couldn't see those words = wǒ kàn bú jiàn nàxiē zì 我看不见那些字
he couldn't hear me = tā tīng bú jiàn wǒde shēngyīn 他听不见我的声音
they couldn't understand English = tāmen bù dǒng Yīngyǔ 他们不懂英语

- (*when implying that something did not happen*)

she could have become a doctor = tā běnlái kěyǐ chéngwéi yíge yīshēng 他本来可以成为一个医生
you could have apologized! = nǐ dāngshí yīnggāi dàoqiàn! 你当时应该道歉!

- (*when indicating a possibility*) = kěnéng 可能

they could be wrong = tāmen kěnéng cuò le 他们可能错了
it could be very cold in Shanghai = Shànghǎi kěnéng hěn lěng 上海可能很冷

- (*when making a request or suggestion*)

could you tell me his address, please? = qǐng nín gàosu wǒ tāde dìzhǐ hǎo ma? 请您告诉我他的地址好吗?
we could go back by bus = wǒmen kěyǐ zuò chē huíqu 我们可以坐车回去

count *verb*
= shǔ 数
count on
to count on someone = yīkào mǒurén 依靠某人

counter *noun*

- (*a surface for putting things on*)
  a counter = yíge guìtái 一个柜台
- (*a device that counts*)
  a counter = yíge jìshùqì 一个计数器

country *noun*

- (*a state*)
  a country = yíge guójiā 一个国家
- (*the countryside*) = nóngcūn 农村, xiāngxia 乡下
  to live in the country = zhù zài nóngcūn 住在农村

countryside *noun*
the countryside = nóngcūn 农村, xiāngxia 乡下

couple *noun*

- (*husband and wife*) = fūfù 夫妇, fūqī 夫妻
  a couple = yíduì fūfù 一对夫妇
- (*when talking about the approximate number*) = liǎngsān 两三
  a couple of days = liǎngsān tiān 两三天
  a couple of books = liǎngsānběn shū 两三本书
- (*two, a pair*) = duì 对
  a couple of players = yíduì xuánshǒu 一对选手

courage *noun*
= yǒngqì 勇气

courageous *adjective*
= yǒnggǎn 勇敢

course
1 *noun*

- (*a series of lessons or lectures*) = kèchéng 课程
  a course = yìmén kèchéng 一门课程
  a language course = yìmén yǔyán kèchéng 一门语言课程
- (*part of a meal*)
  a course = yídào cài 一道菜
  what's the main course? = zhǔ cài shì shénme? 主菜是什么?

2 of course = dāngrán 当然

court *noun*

- (*of law*) = fǎyuàn 法院, fǎtíng 法庭
  a court = yíge fǎyuàn 一个法院
  to go to court = qǐsù 起诉
- (*for playing sports*) = chǎng 场
  a tennis court = yíge wǎngqiú chǎng 一个网球场

a basketball court = yíge lánqiú chǎng 一个篮球场

court case *noun*
a court case = yíge fǎtíng ànjiàn 一个法庭案件

cousin *noun*
- (*a male cousin, older than oneself*)
  a cousin = yíge biǎogē 一个表哥
- (*a male cousin younger than oneself*)
  a cousin = yíge biǎodì 一个表弟
- (*a female cousin older than oneself*)
  a cousin = yíge biǎojiě 一个表姐
- (*a female cousin younger than oneself*)
  a cousin = yíge biǎomèi 一个表妹

cover
1 *verb*
- = gài 盖, fùgài 覆盖
  he covered his daughter with his overcoat = tā bǎ dàyī gài zài tāde nǚ'ér shēn shang 他把大衣盖在女儿身上
- (*to cover a table, a bed*) = pū 铺
  he covered the bed with a white sheet = tā bǎ yìtiáo bái chuángdān pū zài chuáng shang 他把一条白床单铺在床上
  the table was covered with a blue cloth = zhuōzi shang pūzhe yíkuài lán zhuōbù 桌子上铺着一块蓝桌布

2 *noun*
- (*a lid*)
  a cover = yíge gàizi 一个盖子
- (*for a cushion, a quilt*)
  a cover = yíge tàozi 一个套子
- (*on a book, a magazine, an exercise book*)
  the front cover = fēngmiàn 封面
  the back cover = fēngdǐ 封底

cow *noun*
a cow = yìtóu mǔniú 一头母牛

coward *noun*
a coward = yíge dǎnxiǎoguǐ 一个胆小鬼

cowboy *noun*
a cowboy = yíge mùtóng 一个牧童, yíge niúzǎi 一个牛仔

cozy ▸ cosy

crab *noun*
a crab = yìzhī xiè 一只蟹

crack *verb*
- (*to fracture with the parts remaining in contact*) = nòngliè 弄裂
  the accident has cracked the walls of the house = zhècì shìgù bǎ fángzi de qiáng nòngliè le 这次事故把房子的墙弄裂了
- (*to be fractured with the parts remaining in contact*) = liè 裂
  the bottle cracked = píngzi liè le 瓶子裂了
- (*to break partially and suddenly*) = dǎpò 打破
  the ball cracked the window = qiú bǎ chuānghu dǎpò le 球把窗户打破了

cradle *noun*
a cradle = yíge yáolán 一个摇篮

cramp *noun*
a cramp = chōujīnr 抽筋儿, jīngluán 痉挛

crash
1 *noun*
= pèngzhuàng 碰撞
a car crash = yícì zhuàng chē shìgù 一次撞车事故

2 *verb*
to crash into a tree = zhuàng zài shù shang 撞在树上
the plane crashed = fēijī zhuìhuǐ le 飞机坠毁了

crayon *noun*
a crayon = yìzhī cǎi bǐ 一支彩笔

crazy *adjective*
= fāfēng 发疯, fākuáng 发狂

cream *noun*
= nǎiyóu 奶油

create *verb*
= chuàngzào 创造
to create employment = chuàngzào jiùyè jīhuì 创造就业机会

credit
1 *noun*
- (*honour, glory*) = shēngwàng 声望
  a scholar of the highest credit = yíge jí yǒu shēngwàng de xuézhě 一个极有声望的学者
- (*financial reliability and reputation*) = xìnyù 信誉
- (*belief, trust*) = xiāngxìn 相信, xìnrèn 信任

do you give credit to this report? = nǐ xiāngxìn zhètiáo bàodào ma? 你相信这条报道吗?
- (*merit*) = gōngláo 功劳, gōngjì 功绩
  she deserves all the credit for this = zhèjiàn shì suǒyǒu de gōngláo dōu yīnggāi guī tā 这件事所有的功劳都应该归她

2 *verb*
- (*to believe*) = xiāngxìn 相信
  I don't credit his words = wǒ bù xiāngxìn tāde huà 我不相信他的话
- (*to add to a bank account or financial statement*)
  to credit the money to someone's account = bǎ qián jìrù mǒurén de zhàng 把钱记入某人的账

credit card *noun*
a credit card = yìzhāng xìnyòng kǎ 一张信用卡

cricket *noun* ▶ 390
= bǎnqiú 板球

crime *noun*
= zuì 罪, zuìxíng 罪行

criminal
1 *noun*
a criminal = yíge zuìfàn 一个罪犯
2 *adjective*
= fànzuì de 犯罪的

crisis *noun*
a crisis = yícì wēijī 一次危机

crisps *noun* (*British English*)
= yóuzhá tǔdòupiàn 油炸土豆片

critical *adjective*
- (*relating to criticism*) = pīpíng de 批评的
- (*relating to a turning point or a crisis*) = guānjiànxìng de 关键性的, wēijí 危急

criticize *verb*
= pīpíng 批评

crocodile *noun*
a crocodile = yìtiáo èyú 一条鳄鱼

crooked *adjective*
- (*bent like a crook*) = wān 弯, wānqū 弯曲
  a crooked line = yìtiáo wānqū de xiàn 一条弯曲的线
- (*deviating from a right position*) = wāi 歪
  the picture is crooked = zhàopiàn wāi le 照片歪了

cross
1 *verb*
- (*to go across*)
  to cross the road = (chuān)guò mǎlù (穿)过马路
  to cross the Channel = dùguò Yīngjílì Hǎixiá 渡过英吉利海峡
  to cross the border = yuèguò biānjiè 越过边界
- (*other uses*)
  to cross one's legs = pántuǐ 盘腿
  our letters crossed = wǒmende xìn hùxiāng cuòguò le 我们的信互相错过了

2 *noun*
- (*a mark*)
  a cross = yíge shízì (biāojì) 一个十字(标记)
- (*of a church or as a religious symbol*)
  a cross = yíge shízìjià 一个十字架

3 *adjective*
to get cross with someone = duì mǒurén fā píqì 对某人发脾气
cross out = huádiào 划掉

crossroad *noun*
a crossroad = yíge shízì lùkǒu 一个十字路口

crossword puzzle *noun*
a crossword puzzle = yíge zònghéng zìmí 一个纵横字迷

crow *noun*
a crow = yìzhī wūyā 一只乌鸦

crowd *noun*
- (*a large number of people*)
  a crowd = yìqún rén 一群人
  crowds of people = xǔduō rén 许多人
- (*watching a game*)
  the crowd = guānzhòng 观众

crown *noun*
- (*on a king's head*) = wángguān 王冠
  a crown = yìdǐng wángguān 一顶王冠
- (*on a queen's head*) = huángguān 皇冠
  a crown = yìdǐng huángguān 一顶皇冠

cruel *adjective*
= cánkù 残酷

cruelty *noun*
= cánkù 残酷

cruise *noun*
= xúnyóu 巡游

crush *verb*
- (*to squeeze together*) = zhà 榨
- (*if it's an object*) = yāsuì 压碎
- (*if it's a person*) = yādǎo 压倒

crutch *noun*
a crutch = yìgēn guǎizhàng 一根拐杖

cry
1 *verb*
- (*to weep*) = kū 哭
- (*to utter loudly*) = hǎn 喊

2 *noun*
- (*a sound of weeping*) = kūshēng 哭声
- (*a shout*) = hǎnshēng 喊声

cub *noun*
a cub = yìzhī yòuzǎi 一只幼仔

cuckoo *noun*
a cuckoo = yìzhī bùgǔniǎo 一只布谷鸟

cucumber *noun*
a cucumber = yìgēn huángguā 一根黄瓜

cuddle *noun*
= yōngbào 拥抱
to give someone a cuddle = yōngbào mǒurén 拥抱某人

culprit *noun*
a culprit = yíge fànrén 一个犯人

cultural *adjective*
= wénhuà 文化

culture *noun*
= wénhuà 文化

cunning *adjective*
(*describing a person*) = jiǎohuá 狡猾
(*describing a plan*) = qiǎomiào 巧妙

cup *noun*
- **a cup** = yíge bēizi 一个杯子
  a cup of coffee = yìbēi kāfēi 一杯咖啡
- (*in sport*)
  a cup = yíge jiǎngbēi 一个奖杯

cupboard *noun*
a cupboard = yíge wǎnchú 一个碗橱

curb *noun*
the curb = lùbiān xiāngbiānshí 路边镶边石

cure
1 *verb*
= zhìhǎo 治好, zhìyù 治愈
2 *noun*
= zhìhǎo 治好

curious *adjective*
= hàoqí 好奇

curly *adjective*
= juǎnqū 卷曲
curly hair = juǎnqū de tóufa 卷曲的头发

currency *noun*
a currency = yìzhǒng huòbì 一种货币
foreign currency = wàibì 外币, wàihuì 外汇

curry *noun*
a curry = gālí 咖喱

curtain *noun*
a curtain = yíge chuānglián 一个窗帘
to draw the curtains = lā chuánglián 拉窗帘

cushion *noun*
a cushion = yíge diànzi 一个垫子

custard *noun*
= niǔnǎi dànhú 牛奶蛋糊

custom *noun*
a custom = yìzhǒng xíguàn 一种习惯

customer *noun*
a customer = yíge gùkè 一个顾客

customs *noun*
= hǎiguān 海关
to go through customs = tōngguò hǎiguān 通过海关

customs officer *noun* ▶ 344
a customs officer = yíge hǎiguān guānyuán 一个海关官员

cut
1 *verb*
- (*if it's an object*) = qiē 切, gē 割
  to cut an apple in half = bǎ píngguǒ qiēchéng liǎng bàn 把苹果切成两半
- (*if it's part of the body*) = gēpò 割破
  to cut [**one's fingers** | **one's knee** | **one's foot...**] = gēpò [shǒuzhǐ | xīgài | jiǎo...] 割破[手指|膝盖|脚...]
- (*to cut with scissors*) = jiǎn 剪
  to cut cloth = jiǎn bù 剪布
  she got her hair cut = tā jiǎn tóufa le 他剪头发了
  he got his hair cut = tā lǐfà le 他理发了

2 *noun*
- (*of the body*) = shāngkǒu 伤口
- (*in finance, expense*) = xuējiǎn 削减
- (*in a film, a book*) = shānjié 删节

cut down
- (*to bring down by cutting*) = kǎndǎo 砍倒
- (*to reduce, curtail*) = xuējiǎn 削减

cut out
to cut a photo out of a magazine = cóng zázhì shang jiǎnxià yìzhāng zhàopiàn 从杂志上剪下一张照片
cut up = qiēsuì 切碎

cute *adjective*
= kě'ài 可爱, dòu rén xǐ'ài 逗人喜爱

CV *noun*
a CV = yífèn jiǎnlì 一份简历

cycle *verb*
= qí zìxíngchē 骑自行车
to cycle to school = qí zìxíngchē shàngxué 骑自行车上学
to go cycling = qù qí zìxíngchē 去骑自行车

cycle lane, cycle path *noun*
a cycle lane = yìtiáo zìxíngchē dào 一条自行车道

cycling *noun* ▶ 390
cycling = zìxíngchē yùndòng 自行车运动

cyclist *noun*
a cyclist = yíge qí zìxíngchē de rén 一个骑自行车的人

cynical *adjective*
= wán shì bù gōng 玩世不恭, lěngcháo rèfěng 冷嘲热讽

Dd

---

dad, Dad *noun*
= bàba 爸爸

daffodil *noun*
a daffodil = yìkē shuǐxiānhuā 一棵水仙花

daisy *noun*
a daisy = yìkē chújú 一棵雏菊

damage
1 *verb*
- (*to damage*) = huǐhuài 毁坏

the building was damaged by the fire = fángzi bèi dàhuǒ huǐhuài le 房子被大火毁坏了
- (*to harm*) = sǔnhài 损害

it can damage your health = zhè huì sǔnhài nǐde jiànkāng 这会损害你的健康

2 *noun*
- = sǔnhuài 损坏
- (*loss*) = sǔnshī 损失
- (*harm*) = sǔnhài 损害

damp *adjective*
= cháoshī 潮湿

dance
1 *verb*
= tiàowǔ 跳舞
2 *noun*
a dance = yíge wǔdǎo 一个舞蹈

dancer *noun* ▶ 344
a dancer = yíge wǔdǎo yǎnyuán 一个舞蹈演员

dancing *noun*
= tiàowǔ 跳舞

danger *noun*
= wēixiǎn 危险
to be in danger = zài wēixiǎn zhōng 在危险中

dangerous *adjective*
= wēixiǎn 危险

Danish ▶ 288
1 *adjective*
= Dānmài de 丹麦的
2 *noun*
= Dānmàiyǔ 丹麦语

dare *verb*
- (*to have the courage*) = gǎn 敢
- (*when testing someone*)

I dare you to criticise her = wǒ gǎn shuō nǐ bù gǎn pīpíng tā 我敢说你不敢批评她
- (*when expressing anger*)

don't dare speak to me like that! = nǐ zěnme gǎn zhèyàng gēn wǒ jiǎnghuà! 你怎么敢这样跟我讲话!

dark
1 *adjective*
- (*lacking light*) = àn 暗, hēi'àn 黑暗

it's getting dark = tiān hēixiàlai le 天黑下来了
- (*black*) = hēi 黑

he's got dark hair = tā shì hēi tóufa 他是黑头发

- (*darkish*) = shēn 深
  a dark blue dress = yíjiàn shēn lánsè de yīfu 一件深蓝色的衣服

2 *noun*
- (*if it's a colour*) = hēisè 黑色, ànsè 暗色
- (*absence of light*) = hēi'àn 黑暗

darts *noun* ▶ 390
= fēibiāo 飞镖
a game of darts = fēibiāo yóuxì 飞镖游戏

date *noun* ▶ 218
- (*in a calendar*)
  a date = yíge rìqī 一个日期
  what date is today? = jīntiān jǐ hào? 今天几号?
- (*with a friend*) = yuēhuì 约会
  to go out on a date with someone = gēn mǒurén chūqu yuēhuì 跟某人出去约会

daughter *noun*
a daughter = yíge nǚ'ér 一个女儿

daughter-in-law *noun*
a daughter-in-law = yíge érxífu 一个儿媳妇

dawn *noun*
= límíng 黎明
at dawn = límíng shí 黎明时

day *noun* ▶ 412
a day = yì tiān 一天
what day is it today? = jīntiān xīngqījǐ? 今天星期几?
during the day = zài báitiān 在白天
we had a very nice day = wǒmen dùguòle měihǎo de yì tiān 我们度过了美好的一天
the next day, the day after = dì'èr tiān 第二天
the day before = qián yì tiān 前一天
the day after tomorrow = hòutiān 后天
the day before yesterday = qiántiān 前天
New Year's Day = Yuándàn 元旦, Xīnnián 新年
Christmas Day = Shèngdànjié 圣诞节

daylight *noun*
= rìguāng 日光
before daylight = tiān liàng qián 天亮前

dead *adjective*
- = sǐ 死
  he is dead = tā sǐ le 他死了
- (*more polite form*) = qùshì 去世, shìshì 逝世
  he is dead = tā qùshì le 他去世了

deaf *adjective*
= lóng 聋

deal
1 *noun*
- **a deal** (*in business*) = yìbǐ mǎimai 一笔买卖
  (*with a friend*) = yíge yuēdìng 一个约定
- **a great deal of** [**money** | **time** | **energy**] = dàliàng de [qián | shíjiān | jīnglì] 大量的 [钱 | 时间 | 精力]

2 *verb*
to deal the cards = fā pái 发牌
deal with = chǔlǐ 处理, duìfu 对付
to deal with a problem = chǔlǐ yíge wèntí 处理一个问题

dear
1 *adjective*
- (*in letters*) = qīn'ài de 亲爱的
  Dear Anne and Paul = Qīn'ài de Ānnī he Bǎoluó 亲爱的安妮和保罗
- (*expensive*) = guì 贵

2 *exclamation*
oh dear! = A! Tiān na! 啊! 天哪!

death *noun*
= sǐ 死, sǐwáng 死亡

death penalty *noun*
= sǐxíng 死刑

debate *noun*
a debate = yícì biànlùn 一次辩论

debt *noun*
a debt = yìbǐ zhài 一笔债
to be in debt = qiàn zhài 欠债

decade *noun*
a decade = shí nián 十年

decaffeinated *adjective*
= chúqu kāfēiyīn de 除去咖啡因的

deceive *verb*
= qīpiàn 欺骗

December *noun* ▶ 218
= shí'èryuè 十二月

decide *verb*
= juédìng 决定
he decided [**to accept** | **to go** | **to get married...**] = tā juédìng [jiéshòu | qù | jiéhūn...] 他决定 [接受 | 去 | 结婚...]

decision *noun*
a decision = yíxiàng juédìng 一项决定

D

Dates, days and months

The days of the week

Monday	= xīngqīyī 星期一
Tuesday	= xīngqī'èr 星期二
Wednesday	= xīngqīsān 星期三
Thursday	= xīngqīsì 星期四
Friday	= xīngqīwǔ 星期五
Saturday	= xīngqīliù 星期六
Sunday	= xīngqīrì 星期日, xīngqītiān 星期天

Xīngqīyī 星期一 in the terms below can be replaced by any day of the week. They all work the same way.

on Monday	= xīngqīyī 星期一
Monday afternoon	= xīngqīyī xiàwǔ 星期一下午
last/next Monday	= shàngge/xiàge xīngqīyī 上个 / 下个星期一
last Monday night	= shàngge xīngqīyī wǎnshang 上个星期一晚上
early on Monday	= xīngqīyī zǎoxiē shíhou 星期一早些时候
late on Monday	= xīngqīyī wǎnxiē shíhou 星期一晚些时候
a month from Monday	= cóng xīngqīyī kāishǐ de yíge yuè 从星期一开始的一个月
from Monday on	= cóng xīngqīyī kāishǐ 从星期一开始

The months of the year

January	= yīyuè 一月
February	= èryuè 二月
March	= sānyuè 三月
April	= sìyuè 四月
May	= wǔyuè 五月
June	= liùyuè 六月
July	= qīyuè 七月
August	= bāyuè 八月
September	= jiǔyuè 九月
October	= shíyuè 十月
November	= shíyīyuè 十一月
December	= shí'èryuè 十二月

May in the phrases below stands for any month; they all work in the same way.

in May	= wǔyuè 五月
next May	= míngnián wǔyuè 明年五月
last May	= qùnián wǔyuè 去年五月
in early/late May	= wǔyuè shàngxún/xiàxún 五月上旬 / 下旬

Dates

The order of dates in Chinese begins with the year, followed by the month, the date, and the day of the week.

Monday, May 1st, 1901	= yījiǔlíngyī nián wǔyuè yī rì, xīngqīyī 1901年 5 月1日, 星期一
What's the date?	= jīntiān jǐ hào? 今天几号?
it's the tenth of May	= jīntiān wǔyuè shí hào 今天五月十号
in 1968	= yījiǔliùbā nián 1968 年
in the year 2000	= èrlínglínglíng nián 2000 年
in October, 2002	= èrlínglíng'èr nián shíyuè 2002 年 10 月
in the seventeenth century	= zài shíqī shìjì 在十七世纪

Both **rì** 日 and **hào** 号 can be used to express the date. The former is usually used in written Chinese and the latter in spoken Chinese

May 1	= wǔyuè yī rì 五月一日
May 2	= wǔyuè èr rì 五月二日
from 4th to 16th May	= cóng wǔyuè sì rì dào shíliù rì 从五月四日到十六日
May 6, 2001	= èrlínglíngyī nián wǔyuè liù rì 2001 年 5 月 6 日
in the 1980s	= zài èrshí shìjì bāshí niándài 在 20 世纪 80 年代
the 16th century	= shíliù shìjì 十六世纪

Other Expressions

this week/month	= zhège xīngqī/yuè 这个星期 / 月
next week/month	= xiàge xīngqī/yuè 下个星期 / 月
last week/month	= shàngge xīngqī/yuè 上个星期 / 月
last Sunday	= shàngge xīngqīrì 上个星期日
next Sunday	= xiàge xīngqīrì 下个星期日
this year	= jīnnián 今年
next year	= míngnián 明年
last year	= qùnián 去年

---

to make a decision = zuò yíge juédìng 做一个决定

deck *noun*
= jiǎbǎn 甲板
on deck = zài jiǎbǎn shang 在甲板上

deckchair *noun*
a deckchair = yìbǎ zhédiéshì tǎngyǐ 一把折叠式躺椅

decorate *verb*
= zhuāngshì 装饰

decoration *noun*
= zhuāngshì 装饰

deep *adjective* ▶ 300
= shēn 深
how deep is the lake? = zhège hú yǒu duō shēn? 这个湖有多深?
the hole is three metres deep = zhège dòng yǒu sān mǐ shēn 这个洞有三米深

deer *noun*
a deer = yìtóu lù 一头鹿

defeat
1 *verb*
to defeat an enemy = zhànshèng dírén 战胜敌人
the team was defeated = zhège duì bèi dǎbài le 这个队被打败了
2 *noun*
a defeat = yícì shībài 一次失败

defence (*British English*), **defense** (*US English*) *noun*
- (*protection*) = bǎohù 保护
- (*guarding against attack*) = bǎowèi 保卫

defend *verb*
- (*to protect*) = bǎohù 保护
- (*to maintain against attack*) = bǎowèi 保卫

definite *adjective*
- (*describing an answer, a decision, a plan*) = míngquè 明确
- (*fixed*) = quèdìng 确定
  nothing is definite = shénme dōu méi quèdìng 什么都没确定
- (*obvious, visible*) = míngxiǎn 明显
  a definite improvement = míngxiǎn de gǎijìn 明显的改进

definitely *adverb*
= kěndìng 肯定
they're definitely lying = tāmen kěndìng zài shuōhuǎng 他们肯定在说谎
I'm definitely coming = wǒ kěndìng lái 我肯定来

defy *verb*
= mièshì 蔑视

degree *noun*
- (*from a university*)
  a degree = yíge xuéwèi 一个学位

- (*in measurements*) = dù 度
  5 degrees = wǔ dù 五度

delay
1 *verb*
= yánwù 延误, dānwù 耽误
2 *noun*
= yánwù 延误, dānwù 耽误

deliberate *adjective*
= gùyì 故意

deliberately *adverb*
= gùyì de 故意地

delicious *adjective*
= hǎochī 好吃

delighted *adjective*
= gāoxìng 高兴
to be delighted with a present = shōudào lǐwù hěn gāoxìng 收到礼物很高兴

deliver *verb*
- (*if it's something heavy*) = (yùn)sòng (运)送
  to deliver goods = (yùn)sòng huòwù (运)送货物
- (*if it's mail*) = tóudì 投递
  to deliver mail = tóudì xìnjiàn 投递信件

demand
1 *verb*
= yāoqiú 要求
2 *noun*
= yāoqiú 要求

demolish *verb*
= chāihuǐ 拆毁

demonstration *noun*
- (*a practical show or exhibition*) = shìfàn 示范
  a demonstration = yícì shìfàn 一次示范
- (*a public procession or movement*) = shìwēi 示威
  a demonstration = yícì shìwēi 一次示威

denim jacket *noun*
a denim jacket = yíjiàn láodòngbù jiákèshān 一件劳动布夹克衫

Denmark *noun*
= Dānmài 丹麦

dentist *noun* ▶ 344
a dentist = yíge yáyī 一个牙医

deny *verb*
= fǒurèn 否认

department *noun*
a department
(*in a firm*) = yíge bùmén 一个部门
(*in a university*) = yíge xì 一个系
(*in a large store*)
a [food | clothes | furniture] department = yíge [shípǐn | fúzhuāng | jiājù] bù 一个[食品 | 服装 | 家具] 部

department store *noun*
a department store = yíge bǎihuò shāngdiàn 一个百货商店

depend *verb*
- (*to rely*) = yīkào 依靠
  to depend on someone = yīkào mǒurén 依靠某人
- (*to be determined*)
  it depends on you = zhè yào qǔjué yú nǐ 这要取决于你
  it depends = zhè děi kàn qíngkuàng (ér dìng) 这得看情况(而定)

depressed *adjective*
= jǔsàng 沮丧, xiāochén 消沉

depressing *adjective*
= lìng rén jǔsàng 令人沮丧, lìng rén xiāochén 令人消沉

deprive *verb*
= bōduó 剥夺

depth *noun* ▶ 300
= shēnchù 深处, shēndù 深度

describe *verb*
- (*in writing*) = miáoxiě 描写
- (*in speaking*) = miáoshù 描述

description *noun*
- (*in writing*) = miáoxiě 描写
- (*in speaking*) = miáoshù 描述

desert *noun*
a desert = yíge shāmò 一个沙漠

deserve *verb*
= yīnggāi shòudào 应该受到
he deserves to be punished = tā yīnggāi shòudào chéngfá 他应该受到惩罚

design
1 *verb*
- (*to contrive*) = shèjì 设计
  to design clothes = shèjì fúzhuāng 设计服装
  that bridge was designed by him = nàzuò qiáo shì tā shèjì de 那座桥是他设计的

- (*to plan*) = cèhuà 策划, jìhuà 计划
  she designed the art exhibition = zhècì yìshù zhǎnlǎnhuì shì tā cèhuà de 这次艺术展览会是她策划的

2 *noun*

- (*drawing or sketching*) = shèjì 设计
  fashion design = fúzhuāng shèjì 服装设计
- (*a pattern*) = tú'àn 图案
  a design = yíge tú'àn 一个图案

desk *noun*
a desk = yìzhāng shūzhuō 一张书桌

desperate *adjective*

- (*in a state of despair*) = juéwàng 绝望
- (*despairingly reckless*) = búgù yíqiè 不顾一切

dessert *noun*
= tiánshí 甜食

destroy *verb*
= cuīhuǐ 摧毁, huǐhuài 毁坏

detail *noun*
a detail = yíge xìjié 一个细节
to go into detail = xiángxì xùshù 详细叙述

detective *noun* ▶ 344
a detective = yíge zhēntàn 一个侦探
a private detective = yíge sījiā zhēntàn 一个私家侦探

detective story *noun*
a detective story = yíge zhēntàn gùshi 一个侦探故事

determined *adjective*
= jiānjué 坚决, yǒu juéxīn de 有决心的
to be determined to go = juéxīn yào qù 决心要去

develop *verb*

- (*to evolve*) = fāzhǎn 发展
  to develop a friendly relationship = fāzhǎn yǒuhǎo guānxi 发展友好关系
- (*to bring out what is latent or potential in*) = kāifā 开发
  to develop a new market = kāifā xīn shìchǎng 开发新市场

development *noun*
the rapid development of computer science = jìsuànjī kēxué de xùnsù fāzhǎn 计算机科学的迅速发展
the development of natural resources = zìrán zīyuán de kāifā 自然资源的开发

diagram *noun*
a diagram = yìzhāng túbiǎo 一张图表

dial *verb*
to dial a number = bō yíge hàomǎ 拨一个号码

dialling code *noun* (*British English*)
a dialling code = yíge bōhào 一个拨号

dialling tone (*British English*), **dial tone** (*US English*) *noun*
a dialling tone = yíge bōhào yīn 一个拨号音

diamond *noun*
a diamond = yíkuài zuànshí 一块钻石

diary *noun*
a diary = yìběn rìjì 一本日记

dice *noun*
a pair of dice = yíduì tóuzi 一对骰子

dictionary *noun*
a dictionary = yìběn cídiǎn 一本词典, yìběn zìdiǎn 一本字典

die *verb*

- (*to die*) = sǐ 死
  he died in the war = tā zài zhànzhēng zhōng sǐ le 他在战争中死了
  she is dying of cancer = tā yīn déle áizhèng kuàiyào sǐ le 她因得了癌症快要死了
- (*to indicate extreme desire*)
  I'm dying to go on holiday = wǒ kěwàng qù dùjià 我渴望去度假

diet *noun*
= yǐnshí 饮食
to go on a diet = jié shí 节食

difference *noun*
= chābié 差别
I can't tell the difference = wǒ kàn bù chū yǒu shénme chābié 我看不出有什么差别
it won't make any difference = zhè bú huì yǒu shénme guānxi 这不会有什么关系
what difference does it make? = zhè yǒu shénme guānxi? 这有什么关系?

different *adjective*
= bùtóng 不同

difficult *adjective*
= nán 难
Chinese is not difficult to learn = Zhōngwén bù nán xué 中文不难学

it is difficult to get along with someone = gēn mǒurén hěn nán xiāngchǔ 跟某人很难相处

difficulty *noun*
a difficulty = yíge kùnnan 一个困难
to have difficulty concentrating = hěn nán jízhōng jīnglì 很难集中精力

dig *verb*
= wā 挖
dig up
- (*when gardening*) = wāchūlai 挖出来
- (*to find what was buried*) = wājué chūlai 挖掘出来

digital *adjective*
= shùmǎ 数码, shùzì 数字

dim *adjective*
- (*describing a light*) = àndàn 暗淡
- (*describing a room*) = hūn'àn 昏暗

diner (*US English*) *noun*
a diner = yíge kuàicāndiàn 一个快餐店

dining room *noun*
a dining room = yíge fàntīng 一个饭厅

dinner *noun*
- a dinner (*the chief meal of the day*) = yídùn zhèngcān 一顿正餐
- (*a feast*) = yícì yànhuì 一次宴会

dip *verb*
= zhàn 蘸

direct
1 *adjective* = zhíjiē 直接
2 *verb*
- (*when talking about direction*)
could you direct me to the station? = nǐ néng gàosu wǒ qù chēzhàn zěnme zǒu ma? 你能告诉我去车站怎么走吗?
- (*in cinema or theatre*) = dǎoyǎn 导演
to direct [a film | a play] = dǎoyǎn [yíbù diànyǐng | yìchū xì] 导演 [一部电影 | 一出戏]

direction *noun*
a direction = yíge fāngxiàng 一个方向
is this the right direction? = zhège fāngxiàng duì ma? 这个方向对吗?

directions *noun*
- = zhǐshì 指示
to give someone directions = xiàng mǒurén fāchū zhǐshì 向某人发出指示
to ask someone for directions = xiàng mǒurén qǐng(qiú zhǐ)shì 向某人请(求指)示
- (*directions for use*) = shǐyòng shuōmíng 使用说明

director *noun* ▶ 344
- (*of a film or play*) = dǎoyǎn 导演
a director = yíge dǎoyǎn 一个导演
- a director
(*of a research institute or department*) = yíge suǒzhǎng 一个所长, yíge zhǔrèn 一个主任
(*of a factory*) = yíge chǎngzhǎng 一个厂长
(*of a company*) = yíge zǒngcái 一个总裁

dirt *noun*
= zāng dōngxi 脏东西

dirty
1 *adjective*
= zāng 脏
2 *verb*
= nòngzāng 弄脏

disabled *adjective*
= shāngcán 伤残, cánjí 残疾

disadvantage *noun*
a disadvantage = yíge búlì tiáojiàn 一个不利条件

disagree *verb*
= bù tóngyì 不同意
I disagree with you = wǒ bù tóngyì nǐde yìjiàn 我不同意你的意见

disappear *verb*
= bújiàn 不见, xiāoshī 消失

disappoint *verb*
to disappoint someone = shǐ mǒurén shīwàng 使某人失望

disappointed *adjective*
= shīwàng 失望

disappointing *adjective*
= lìng rén shīwàng 令人失望

disappointment *noun*
= shīwàng 失望

disapprove *verb*
to disapprove of someone = bú zànchéng mǒurén 不赞成某人

disaster *noun*
a disaster = yìchǎng zāinàn 一场灾难

discipline *noun*
= jìlǜ 纪律

disco *noun*
- (*a party*) = dísīkē wǔhuì 迪斯科舞会
  a disco = yíge dísīkē wǔhuì 一个迪斯科舞会
- (*the dance*) = dísīkē(wǔ) 迪斯科(舞)

disconnect *verb*
- (*to cut off*) = qiēduàn 切断
- (*to separate*) = chāikāi 拆开

discourage *verb*
- (*dishearten*) = xièqì 泄气
  to discourage someone = shǐ mǒurén xièqì 使某人泄气
  he was discouraged by the difficulties he met = tā yīnwèi yùdào kùnnan ér xièqì 他因为遇到而泄气
- (*oppose by showing disfavour*) = zǔzhǐ 阻止, quànzǔ 劝阻
  to discourage someone = zǔzhǐ mǒurén 阻止某人

discover *verb*
= fāxiàn 发现

discovery *noun*
a discovery = yíge fāxiàn 一个发现

discreet *adjective*
= jǐnshèn 谨慎

discrimination *noun*
- (*distinction*) = qūbié 区别
- (*different treatment of a group of people*) = qíshì 歧视

discuss *verb*
= tǎolùn 讨论
to discuss politics = tǎolùn zhèngzhì 讨论政治

discussion *noun*
a discussion = yícì tǎolùn 一次讨论

disease *noun* ▶ 277
a disease = yìzhǒng (jí)bìng 一种(疾)病

disguise
1 *noun*
= wěizhuāng 伪装
2 *verb*
to disguise oneself as a woman = bǎ zìjǐ zhuāngbànchéng nǚ de 把自己装扮成女的

disgusting *adjective*
= lìng rén ěxin 令人恶心

dish *noun*
- (*food*)
  a dish = yìpán cài 一盘菜
- (*object on which to place food for eating*) = yíge pánzi 一个盘子
  to wash the dishes = xǐ pánzi 洗盘子

dishonest *adjective*
= bù chéngshí 不诚实

dishwasher *noun*
a dishwasher = yìtái xǐwǎnjī 一台洗碗机

dislike *verb*
= bù xǐhuan 不喜欢
I dislike him = wǒ bù xǐhuan tā 我不喜欢他

dismiss *verb*
- (*to remove from office*) = chè...de zhí 撤...的职
  to dismiss someone from his post = chè mǒurén de zhí 撤某人的职
  he was dismissed = tā bèi chèzhí le 他被撤职了
- (*to remove from employment*) = jiěgù 解雇
  to dismiss a worker = jiěgù yíge gōngrén 解雇一个工人
- (*to send away*)
  the teacher didn't dismiss the class until 6 o'clock = lǎoshī liù diǎn cái xiàkè 老师六点才下课

disobedient *adjective*
- = bù fúcóng de 不服从的
- (*when talking about children*) = bù tīnghuà de 不听话的
  a disobedient child = yíge bù tīnghuà de háizi 一个不听话的孩子

disobey *verb*
= wéikàng 违抗, bù fúcóng 不服从
to disobey someone = wéikàng mǒurén 违抗某人

display *noun*
= zhǎnlǎn 展览, chénliè 陈列
a window display = yíge chúchuāng zhǎnlǎn 一个橱窗展览

dispute *noun*
- (*an argument or a debate*) = zhēnglùn 争论, biànlùn 辩论
  a dispute = yícì zhēnglùn 一次争论
- (*a quarrel*) = jiūfēn 纠纷, zhēngduān 争端
  a dispute = yícì jiūfēn 一次纠纷

disqualify *verb*
to disqualify someone = qǔxiāo mǒurén de zīgé 取消某人的资格

disrupt *verb*
• (*to break up*) = fēnliè 分裂
to disrupt a country = fēnliè yíge guójiā 分裂一个国家
• (*to interrupt*) = dǎluàn 打乱, rǎoluàn 扰乱
to disrupt the traffic = rǎoluàn jiāotōng 扰乱交通

dissatisfied *adjective*
= bù mǎnyì 不满意

distance *noun*
= jùlí 距离
in the distance = zài yuǎnchù 在远处
to keep one's distance = bǎochí shūyuǎn 保持疏远

distinct *adjective*
• (*distinguished*) = dútè 独特
• (*clear*) = qīngchu 清楚

distinguish *verb*
= qūbié 区别
to distinguish between truth and lies = qūbié zhēnlǐ yú huǎngyán 区别真理与谎言

distract *verb*
= fēnsàn...de zhùyìlì 分散...的注意力
to distract someone from working = fēnsàn mǒurén de zhùyìlì shǐ tā bù néng gōngzuò 分散某人的注意力使他不能工作

distressed *adjective*
= kǔnǎo 苦恼, tòngkǔ 痛苦

distribute *verb*
• (*to divide and deal out among several*) = fēn 分
• (*to spread out*) = sànfā 散发

disturb *verb*
= dǎrǎo 打扰

disturbing *adjective*
= lìng rén bù ān 令人不安

dive *verb* ▶ 390
= tiàoshuǐ 跳水
to go diving = qù tiàoshuǐ 去跳水

divide *verb*
• (*in arithmetic*) = chú 除
• (*to share*) = fēn 分

diving board *noun*
a diving board = yíge tiào(shuǐ) tái 一个跳(水)台

divorce
1 *noun*
= líhūn 离婚
2 *verb*
she divorced him = tā gēn tā líhūn le 她跟他离婚了

DIY, Do-It-Yourself *noun*
(*British English*)
= zìjǐ zhìzuò 自己制作

dizzy *adjective*
= tóuyūn 头晕
to feel dizzy = gǎndào tóuyūn 感到头晕

do *verb*
• (*to do*) = zuò 做, gàn 干
to do the cooking = zuò fàn 做饭
to do one's homework = zuò zuòyè 做作业
what is he doing? = tā zài gàn shénme? 他在干什么?
do as I told you = ànzhào wǒ gàosu nǐ de nàyàng zuò 按照我告诉你的那样做
• (*in questions, negatives*)

> **!** *Note that in Chinese questions and negatives, there is no auxiliary like the word* do *in English.*

when did you come? = nǐ shénme shíhou lái de? 你什么时候来的?
do you like cats? = nǐ xǐhuan māo ma? 你喜欢猫吗?
I didn't go = wǒ méi qù 我没去
she doesn't live in Beijing = tā bú zhù zài Běijīng 他不住在北京
• (*in imperatives*)
don't shout! = bié hǎn! 别喊!
don't shut the door = bié guān mén 别关门
do come on time = yídìng yào zhǔnshí lái 一定要准时来
• (*in emphatic uses*) = quèshí 确实, díquè 的确
I do like your dress = wǒ quèshí xǐhuan nǐde yīfu 我确实喜欢你的衣服
I do think you should go = wǒ quèshí rènwéi nǐ yīnggāi qù 我确实认为你应该去
• (*in short answers*)

> **!** *Note that when* do *is used in English to refer to a previous verb, in Chinese the previous verb is normally repeated in short answers.*

'Do you like strawberries?' — 'Yes, I do' = 'Nǐ xǐhuan cǎoméi ma?' — '(Duì, wǒ) xǐhuan' '你喜欢草莓吗?'—'(对, 我)喜欢'
'I never said I liked him' — 'Yes, you did' = 'Wǒ cónglái méi shuōguo wǒ xǐhuan tā' — 'Bù, nǐ shuōguo' '我从来没说过我喜欢他'.—'不, 你说过'.
'I love chocolate' — 'So do I' = 'Wǒ xǐhuan qiǎokèlì' — 'Wǒ yě xǐhuan' '我喜欢巧克力'.— '我也喜欢'.
'May I sit here?' — 'Of course, please do' = 'Wǒ kěyǐ zuò zài zhèr ma?' — 'Dāngrán kěyǐ, qǐng zuò' '我可以坐在这儿吗?' — '当然可以, 请坐'.
'Who wrote it?' — 'I did' = 'Shéi xiě de?' — 'Wǒ xiě de' '谁写的?' — '我写的'.

• (*in tag questions*)

> ! *Note that tag questions in English are usually translated as* shì bú shì 是不是 *or* duì bú duì 对不对 *in Chinese.*

he lives in London, doesn't he? = tā zhù zài Lúndūn, shì bú shì? 他住在伦敦,是不是?
you didn't phone, did you? = nǐ méi dǎ diànhuà, duì bú duì? 你没打电话,对不对?

• (*to be enough*)
ten pounds will do = shí bàng jiù gòu le 10镑就够了
that box will do = nàge hézi jiù xíng 那个盒子就行

• (*to perform*)
(*when talking about a task, a project*) = gàn 干
he did well = tā gàn de hěn hǎo 他干得很好
he did badly = tā gàn de bù hǎo 他干得不好
(*when talking about an exam*) = kǎo 考
you did well = nǐ kǎo de hěn hǎo 你考得很好
(*when talking about a performance, a show*) = yǎn 演
she did well = tā yǎn de hěn hǎo 她演得很好

do up
to do up one's buttons = bǎ kòuzi kǒuhǎo 把扣子扣好
to do up a house = zhěngxiū fángzi 整修房子

do with
it's got something to do with computers = zhè yǔ jìsuànjī yǒuguān 这与计算机有关

do without
= méi yǒu...yě xíng 没有... 也行
I can do without a television = wǒ méi yǒu diànshìjī yě xíng 我没有电视机也行

dock *noun*
a dock = yíge mǎtou 一个码头, yíge chuánwū 一个船坞

doctor *noun* ▶ 344
a doctor (*of medicine*) = yíge yīshēng 一个医生, yíge dàifu 一个大夫
• (*Ph.D.*) = yíge bóshì 一个博士

document *noun*
a document = yífèn wénjiàn 一份文件

documentary *noun*
a documentary = yíbù jìlùpiān 一部纪录片

dog *noun*
a dog = yìtiáo gǒu 一条狗

doll *noun*
a doll = yíge (yáng)wáwa 一个(洋)娃娃

dollar *noun*
a [US | Canadian | Hong Kong] dollar = yíkuài [měiyuán | jiāyuán | gǎngbì] 一块[美元 | 加元 | 港币]

dolphin *noun*
a dolphin = yìtiáo hǎitún 一条海豚

dominoes *noun* ▶ 390
= duōmǐnuò gǔpái 多米诺骨牌

donkey *noun*
a donkey = yìtóu lǘ 一头驴

door *noun*
a door = yíge mén 一个门

doorbell *noun*
a doorbell = yíge ménlíng 一个门铃

dormitory *noun*
a dormitory = yíge sùshè 一个宿舍

dose *noun*
a dose of medicine = yíjì yào 一剂药
a dose of Chinese medicine = yífù zhōngyào 一服中药

double
1 *adjective*
• (*for two people*) = shuāngrén 双人

D

a double bed = yìzhāng shuāngrén chuáng 一张双人床
a double room = yíge shuāngrén fángjiān 一个双人房间
• (*twice as much*) = shuāngbèi de 双倍的, liǎngbèi de 两倍的
to pay double the money = fù shuāngbèi de qián 付双倍的钱
• (*when spelling or giving a number*) = liǎngge 两个
a double 'n' = liǎngge 'n' 两个 'n'
three double five (*British English*) = sān wǔ wǔ 三五五
2 *verb*
= zēngjiā yíbèi 增加一倍
the number of students has been doubled = xuésheng rénshù zēngjiāle yíbèi 学生人数增加了一倍

double bass *noun* ▶ 308
a double bass = yìbǎ dīyīn tíqín 一把低音提琴

double-decker *noun*
a double-decker = yíliàng shuāngcéng qìchē 一辆双层汽车

doubt
1 *noun*
= huáiyí 怀疑, yíwèn 疑问
I have some doubt that it's true = wǒ huáiyí zhè shì zhēn de 我怀疑这是真的
there is no doubt that he is innocent = háowú yíwèn tā shì wúgū de 毫无疑问他是无辜的
2 *verb*
= huáiyí 怀疑
I doubt if she'll come = wǒ huáiyí tā huì lái 我怀疑她会来

dough *noun*
= shēngmiàntuán 生面团

doughnut, donut (*US English*) *noun*
a doughnut = yíge zhá miànbǐngquānr 一个炸面饼圈儿

down

> **!** *Often* down *occurs in combination with verbs. For example:* calm down, let down, slow down, *etc. To find the correct translations for this type of verb, look up the separate dictionary entries at* calm, let, slow, *etc.*

1 *preposition*
to go down the street = yánzhe mǎlù wǎng xià zǒu 沿着马路往下走
he walked down the corridor = tā yánzhe zǒuláng zǒuqu 他沿着走廊走去
he ran down the hill = tā pǎo xià shān qu 他跑下山去
the kitchen is down those stairs = chúfáng zài lóutī xiàmian 厨房在楼梯下面
2 *adverb*
she's down in the cellar = tā zài xiàmian dìjiào li 她在下面地窖里
to go down = xiàjiàng 下降
to fall down = dǎoxia 倒下
down there = zài xiàmian nàr 在下面那儿

downstairs *adverb*
= lóuxià 楼下
to go downstairs = xià lóu 下楼
to bring the boxes downstairs = bǎ hézi nádào lóuxià lai 把盒子拿到楼下来

dozen *noun* ▶ 349
a dozen = yìdá 一打
a dozen eggs = yìdá jīdàn 一打鸡蛋
dozens of people = jǐshíge rén 几十个人

draft *noun*
a draft
• (*a preliminary sketch, version, plan*) = yífèn cǎogǎo 一份草稿
• (*an order for the payment of money*) = yìzhāng huìpiào 一张汇票

drag *verb*
= tuō 拖

drain *verb*
• (*to discharge*) = páidiào 排掉
to drain away the water = bǎ shuǐ páidiào 把水排掉
• (*to drink dry*) = hēwán 喝完
he drained his glass of wine = tā bǎ tā nàbēi jiǔ hēwán le 他把他那杯酒喝完了

drama *noun*
• (*a play*) = xì 戏
a drama = yìchū xì 一出戏
• (*theatre*) = xìjù 戏剧

dramatic
• (*belonging to the drama*) = xìjù de 戏剧的
• (*with the force and vividness of the drama*) = xìjùxìng de 戏剧性的

drapes *noun* (*US English*)
= bùlián 布帘, chuānglián 窗帘

draught *noun* (*British English*)
a draught = chuāntáng fēng 穿堂风

draughts *noun* ▶ 390 (*British English*)
= tiàoqí 跳棋

draw
1 *verb*
- (*with a pen or pencil*) = huà 画
  to draw a rabbit = huà yìzhī tùzi 画一只兔子
  to draw a line = huà yìtiáo xiàn 画一条线
- (*to pull*) = lā 拉
  to draw the curtains = lā chuānglián 拉窗帘
- (*to take out*)
  to draw a knife = chōuchū yìbǎ dāo 抽出一把刀
  to draw a nail from the door = cóng mén shang báchū yíge dīngzi 从门上拔出一个钉子
- (*in a lottery*) = chōu 抽
  to draw a ticket = chōu yìzhāng cǎipiào 抽一张彩票
- (*to attract*) = xīyǐn 吸引
  the circus drew a large crowd = mǎxìtuán xīyǐnle hěn duō rén 马戏团吸引了很多人
- (*in sports*) (*British English*) = sàichéng píngjú 赛成平局
- **Christmas is drawing near** = Shèngdànjié kuài dào le 圣诞节快到了

2 *noun*
- (*in sports*) = píngjú 平局
- (*in a lottery*) = chōujiǎng 抽奖

draw aside
to draw someone aside = bǎ mǒurén lādào pángbiān 把某人拉到旁边

draw back
to draw back the curtain = bǎ chuānglián lāhuílai 把窗帘拉回来

draw up
to draw up a list = lièchū yíge míngdān 列出一个名单

drawer *noun*
a drawer = yíge chōuti 一个抽屉

drawing *noun*
= huàr 画儿

dread *verb*
= jùpà 惧怕

dreadful *adjective*
- (*producing great fear*) = kěpà 可怕, hàipà 害怕
- (*very bad, unpleasant*) = jíhuài de 极坏的, zāotòu de 糟透的

dream ▶ 238
1 *noun*
  a dream = yíge mèng 一个梦
  to have a dream = zuò yíge mèng 做一个梦

2 *verb*
  to dream of going to Japan = zuò mèng qù Rìběn 做梦去日本

dress
1 *noun*
  a dress = yíjiàn nǚzhuāng 一件女装

2 *verb*
- (*to put one's own clothes on*) = chuān yīfu 穿衣服
- **to dress someone** = gěi mǒurén chuān yīfu 给某人穿衣服

dress up
- (*in good clothes*) = dǎbàn 打扮
- (*in a disguise*) = zhuāngbàn 装扮

dressing gown *noun*
a dressing gown = yíjiàn chényī 一件晨衣

drill
1 *noun*
- (*a training exercise*) = cāoliàn 操练
  a drill = yícì cāoliàn 一次操练
- (*an instrument for boring hard substances*) = zuàntóu 钻头
  a drill = yíge zuàntóu 一个钻头

2 *verb*
  to drill a hole = zuān yíge kǒng 钻一个孔
  to drill through the wall = zuāntòu qiáng 钻透墙

drink
1 *verb*
  = hē 喝

2 *noun*
  = yǐnliào 饮料
  give me a drink of water = gěi wǒ yìxiē shuǐ hē 给我一些水喝

drive
1 *verb*
- (*in a car*) = kāi chē 开车
  to learn to drive = xué kāi chē 学开车
  he drives to work = tā kāi chē qù shàngbān 他开车去上班
  to drive someone home = kāi chē sòng mǒurén huí jiā 开车送某人回家
- (*to make*) = shǐ 使
  to drive someone mad = shǐ mǒurén qì de fāfēng 使某人气得发疯

2 *noun*
to go for a drive = qù kāi chē wányiwán 去开车玩一玩, qù dōufēng 去兜风
drive away
- (*in a car*) = kāi chē líkāi 开车离开
- (*to chase away*) = gǎnzǒu 赶走

drive back = kāi chē huílai 开车回来

driver *noun*
a driver = yíge sījī 一个司机, yíge jiàshǐyuán 一个驾驶员

driver's license (*US English*), **driving licence** (*British English*) *noun*
a driver's license = yíge jiàshǐ zhízhào 一个驾驶执照

drizzle *verb*
= xià xiǎo yǔ 下小雨, xià máomaoyǔ 下毛毛雨

drop
1 *verb*
- (*to come down*) = xiàjiàng 下降
  the temperature has dropped = wēndù xiàjiàng le 温度下降了
- (*to let fall*) = rēngxia 扔下
  she dropped her suitcase = tā rēngxia xiāngzi 她扔下箱子
- (*to fall*) = diàoxia 掉下, luòxia 落下
  the paper has dropped = zhǐ diàoxiàlai le 纸掉下来了
- (*to fall in drops*) = dīxia 滴下

2 *noun*
- (*a fall*) = xiàjiàng 下降
  a drop in temperature = wēndù xiàjiàng 温度下降
- (*of liquid*)
  a drop = yìdī 一滴

drop in = shùnbiàn fǎngwèn 顺便访问
he dropped in to see me = tā shùnbiàn lái kànkan wǒ 他顺便来看看我
drop off = bǎ...fàngxia 把...放下
could you drop me off at the railway station? = zài huǒchē zhàn bǎ wǒ fàngxia, hǎo ma? 在火车站把我放下, 好吗?
drop out = tuìchū 退出
to drop out of school = tuìxué 退学
to drop out of a race = tuìchū bǐsài 退出比赛

drought *noun*
a drought = yìchǎng gānhàn 一场干旱

drown *verb*
= yānsǐ 淹死

drug
1 *noun*
- = dúpǐn 毒品
  to be on drugs = xīdú 吸毒
- (*for medical use*) = yào 药, yàopǐn 药品

2 *verb*
to drug someone = shǐ mǒurén xīdú 使某人吸毒

> **!** *Note that Chinese uses the verb* xī 吸*, specifying the method by which the drugs are ingested, i.e. by smoking. However,* xīdú 吸毒 *generally means to take drugs, whether by smoking, injecting, or taking them as a pill.*

drug addict *noun*
a drug addict = yíge xīdú chéngyǐn de rén 一个吸毒成瘾的人

drum *noun* ▶ **308**
a drum = yíge gǔ 一个鼓
to play drums = dǎ gǔ 打鼓, qiāo gǔ 敲鼓

drunk *adjective*
= (hē)zuì (喝)醉

dry
1 *adjective*
= gān 干, gānzào 干燥
the clothes are not dry yet = yīfu hái bù gān 衣服还不干
a dry climate = gānzào de qìhòu 干燥的气候

2 *verb*
- (*to dry in the sun*) = shàigān 晒干
- (*to dry by a heater or fire*) = kǎogān 烤干
- (*to dry with a towel or cloth*) = cāgān 擦干

duck
a duck = yìzhī yāzi 一只鸭子
a Peking roast duck = yìzhī Běijīng kǎoyā 一只北京烤鸭

due
1 due to = yīnwèi 因为, yóuyú 由于
the game was cancelled due to bad weather = yóuyú tiānqì bù hǎo, bǐsài qǔxiāo le 由于天气不好, 比赛取消了

> **!** *Note that the phrase introduced by* yóuyú 由于 *or* yīnwèi 因为 *comes at the beginning of the sentence in Chinese.*

2 *adjective*
- (*expected*)
  the train is due (in) at two o'clock = huǒchē yùdìng liǎng diǎn dào 火车预定两点到
- (*that ought to be paid or done*)
  the amount of money due to someone = yīnggāi fùgěi mǒurén de qián 应该付给某的人钱
  the rent is due tomorrow = míngtiān yīnggāi jiāo fángzū le 明天应该交房租了
- (*proper*)
  in due time = zài shìdàng de shíhou 在适当的时候
  to pay due attention = jǐyǔ yīngyǒu de zhùyì 给予应有的注意

dull *adjective*
- (*describing a person*) = chídùn 迟钝, dāibèn 呆笨
- (*describing a colour*) = àndàn 暗淡
- (*describing the weather or a landscape*) = yīnchén 阴沉
- (*not interesting, boring*) = dāndiào fáwèi 单调乏味

dumb *adjective*
- (*unable to speak*) = yǎ 哑
- (*stupid*) = bèn 笨

dump
1 *verb*
- (*to unload*) = qīngdào 倾倒
- (*to get rid of*) = pāoqì 抛弃

2 *noun*
a dump
- (*a rubbish heap*) = yíge lājīduī 一个垃圾堆
- (*an untidy place*) (*US English*)
  her room is a dump = tāde fángjiān luànqībāzāo 她的房间乱七八糟

during *preposition*
= zài...qījiān 在...期间, zài...de shíhou 在...的时候
during the examination = zài kǎoshì qījiān 在考试期间

dust
1 *noun*
= huīchén 灰尘
2 *verb*
= qùdiào...shang de huīchén 去掉...上的灰尘
to dust off one's clothes = qùdiào yīfu shang de huīchén 去掉衣服上的灰尘

dustbin *noun* (*British English*)
a dustbin = yíge lājītǒng 一个垃圾桶

dustman *noun* (*British English*)
a dustman = yíge qīngjiégōng 一个清洁工

dustpan *noun*
a dustpan = yíge bòji 一个簸箕, yíge běnjī 一个畚箕

Dutch *noun* ▶ 288
1 *adjective*
= Hélán de 荷兰的
2 *noun*
- (*the language*) = Hélányǔ 荷兰语
- (*the people*) = Hélánrén 荷兰人

duty *noun*
- (*a task, part of one's job*) = zhízé 职责
  a duty = yíxiàng zhízé 一项职责
- (*to be on duty*) = zhíbān 值班
- (*what one must do*) = yìwù 义务, zérèn 责任
  it is our duty to protect the environment = bǎohù huánjìng shì wǒmende yìwù 保护环境是我们的义务
- (*a tax*) = shuì 税
  customs duties = guānshuì 关税
  duty-free = miǎnshuì 免税

DVD *noun*
a DVD = yìzhāng yǐngdié 一张影碟

DVD player *noun*
a DVD player = yìtái yǐngdié bōfàngjī 一台影碟播放机

dye *noun*
= rǎn 染
to dye one's hair = rǎn tóufa 染头发

each
1 *determiner*
= měi 每
each time I see him = měicì wǒ kànjiàn tā 每次我看见他
2 *pronoun*

> **!** *Note that when the pronoun* **each** *is translated into Chinese, it functions as a modifier rather than a pronoun.*

= měi 每

E

each of the boys = měi (yí)ge nánháir 每(一)个男孩儿
I wrote to each of them = wǒ gěi tāmen měi (yí)ge rén dōu xiěle xìn 我给他们每(一)个人都写了信
each of the books = měi (yì)běn shū 每(一)本书

each other
= hùxiāng 互相, xiānghù 相互
they know each other already = tāmen hùxiāng yǐjīng rènshi le 他们互相已经认识了
we write to each other every year = wǒmen měi nián dōu hùxiāng tōng xìn 我们每年都互相通信

eager *adjective*
= kěwàng 渴望

ear *noun* ▶ 189
an ear = yìzhī ěrduo 一只耳朵

early *adverb*
- = zǎo 早
  to get up early = zǎo qǐchuáng 早起床
  early in the afternoon = xiàwǔ zǎoxiē shíhou 下午早些时候
- **early [last month | next month | last year | next year | this year]** = [shàngge yuè | xiàge yuè | qùnián | míngnián | jīnnián] chū [上个月 | 下个月 | 去年 | 明年 | 今年] 初

earn *verb*
= zhèng 挣, zhuàn 赚
to earn lots of money = zhèng hěn duō qián 挣很多钱

earring *noun*
an earring = yíge ěrhuán 一个耳环

earth *noun*
- (*the planet*) = dìqiú 地球
- (*soil*) = tǔ 土
- (*land as opposed to sea*) = lùdì 陆地, dìmiàn 地面

easily *adverb*
= róngyì de 容易地

east
1 *noun*
- (*the eastern part of the heavens*) = dōngfāng 东方
  the sun rises in the east = tàiyáng cóng dōngfāng shēngqǐ 太阳从东方升起
  the Far East = Yuǎndōng 远东
- (*the eastern part of a region*) = dōngbù 东部
  in the east of Asia = zài Yàzhōu dōngbù 在亚洲东部

2 *adverb*
to go east = wǎng dōng qù 往东去
to live east of Beijing = zhù zài Běijīng dōngmian 住在北京东面

3 *adjective*
= dōng 东
to work in east London = zài dōng Lúndūn gōngzuò 在东伦敦工作

Easter *noun*
= Fùhuó jié 复活节
Happy Easter! = Fùhuó jié kuàilè! 复活节快乐!

Easter egg *noun*
an Easter egg = yíge Fùhuó jié cǎidàn 一个复活节彩蛋

easy *adjective*
= róngyì 容易
it's easy to fix = hěn róngyì xiūlǐ 很容易修理
it's not easy to find work there = zài nàr zhǎo gōngzuò bù róngyì 在那儿找工作不容易

eat *verb*
= chī 吃
eat out = shàng fàndiàn chīfàn 上饭店吃饭

EC *noun*
= European Community
the EC = Oūzhōu Gòngtóngtǐ 欧洲共同体

echo *noun*
an echo = yíge huíshēng 一个回声, yíge huíyīn 一个回音

economic *adjective*
= jīngjì 经济

economics *noun*
= jīngjìxué 经济学

economy *noun*
= jīngjì 经济

edge *noun*
- (*of a road, table, forest, an object*) = biān 边
  the edge of the lake = húbiān 湖边
  at the edge of the town = zài chéngbiān 在城边
- (*of a blade or knife*) = dāokǒu 刀口, dāorèn 刀刃

educate *verb*
= jiàoyù 教育
he was educated in America = tā shì zài Měiguó shòu de jiàoyù 他是在美国受的教育

education *noun*
= jiàoyù 教育

effect *noun*
= jiéguǒ 结果, xiàoguǒ 效果
an effect = yíge jiéguǒ 一个结果

effective *adjective*
= yǒuxiào 有效

efficient *adjective*
= gāo xiàolǜ de 高效率的

effort *noun*
= nǔlì 努力
to make an effort = zuòchū nǔlì 作出努力

egg *noun*
an egg (a hen's egg) = yíge jīdàn 一个鸡蛋

eggcup *noun*
an eggcup = yíge dànbēi 一个蛋杯

eight *number* ▶ 170, ▶ 204
= bā 八
eight apples = bāge píngguǒ 八个苹果

eighteen *number* ▶ 170, ▶ 204 = shíbā 十八

eighteenth *number*
- (*in a series*) = dìshíbā 第十八
- (*in dates*) ▶ 218

the eighteenth of August = bāyuè shíbā hào 八月十八号

eighth *number*
- (*in a series*) = dìbā 第八
- (*in dates*) ▶ 218

the eighth of August = bāyuè bā hào 八月八号

eighty *number* ▶ 170
= bāshí 八十

either
1 *conjunction*
= either...or...
- (*in the affirmative*) = huòzhě...huòzhě... 或者...或者..., yàome...yàome... 要么...要么...

they're coming on either Tuesday or Wednesday = tāmen yàome xīngqī'èr lái, yàome xīngqīsān lái 他们要么星期二来, 要么星期三来
- (*in the negative*) = (yě)...yě... (也)...也...

> **!** *Note that in the negative, the translation of* **either** *is sometimes optional and* **or** *is translated as* yě 也.

He didn't contact either Helen or Paul = tā (yě) méi gēn Hǎilún liánxì yě méi gēn Bǎoluó liánxì 他(也)没跟海伦联系也没跟保罗联系

2 *pronoun*
- (*in the affirmative*) = rènhé yi... 任何一...

you can borrow either of the books = zhè liǎngběn shū nǐ jiè rènhé yìběn dōu xíng 这两本书你借任何一本都行
- (*in the negative*) = dōu bù 都不

I don't know either of them = tāmen liǎngge rén wǒ dōu bú rènshi 他们两个人我都不认识

3 *determiner*
- (*in the affirmative*) = rènhé yi... 任何一...

you can take either road = nǐ kěyǐ zǒu rènhé yìtiáo lù 你可以走任何一条路
- (*in the negative*) = dōu bù 都不

I don't want to live in either country = zhè liǎngge guójiā wǒ dōu bù xiǎng zhù 这两个国家我都不想住

4 *adverb*
= yě 也
she can't come either = tā yě bù néng lái 她也不能来

elbow *noun* ▶ 189
= gēbozhǒu 胳膊肘

elder *adjective*
= niánlíng jiào dà de 年龄较大的
his [elder brother | elder sister] = tā [gēge | jiějie] 他 [哥哥 | 姐姐]

elderly *adjective*
= shàngle niánji de 上了年纪的, lǎo 老

eldest *adjective*
= zuì niánzhǎng de 最年长的
the eldest [daughter | son | granddaughter | grandson] = dà [nǚ'ér | érzi | sūnnǚ | sūnzi] 大 [女儿 | 儿子 | 孙女 | 孙子]

elect *verb*
= xuǎnjǔ 选举

E

election *noun*
an election = yícì xuǎnjǔ 一次选举
to win an election = xuǎnjǔ zhōng huòshèng 选举中获胜

electric *adjective*
= diàn 电

electrician *noun* ▶ 344
an electrician = yíge diàngōng 一个电工

electricity *noun*
= diàn 电

electronic *adjective*
= diànzǐ 电子

elegant *adjective*
= yǎzhì 雅致, yōuyǎ 优雅

elephant *noun*
an elephant = yìtóu dàxiàng 一头大象

elevator *noun*
an elevator = yíge diàntī 一个电梯

eleven *number* ▶ 170, ▶ 204
= shíyī 十一
eleven apples = shíyīge píngguǒ 十一个苹果

eleventh *number*
- (*in a series*) = dìshíyī 第十一
- (*in dates*) ▶ 218
  the eleventh of May = wǔyuè shíyī hào 五月十一号

else *adjective*
= biéde 别的, qítā de 其他的
someone else = bié(de) rén 别(的)人
there is nothing else = méi yǒu biéde dōngxi 没有别的东西
what else did you say? = nǐ hái shuō shénme le? 你还说什么了?
something else = biéde dōngxi 别的东西
everything else = qítā de suǒyǒu dōngxi 其他的所有东西
or else = fǒuzé 否则, yàobù 要不
be quiet or else I'll get angry = ānjìng yìdiǎnr, fǒuzé wǒ huì shēngqì de 安静一点儿, 否则我会生气的

elsewhere *adverb*
= biéde dìfang 别的地方

e-mail *noun*
an e-mail = yíge diànzǐ yóujiàn 一个电子邮件

embarrassed *adjective*
= nánwéiqíng 难为情, bùhǎoyìsi 不好意思

embarrassing *adjective*
= lìng rén nánwéiqíng 令人难为情

embassy *noun*
an embassy = yíge dàshǐguǎn 一个大使馆

emergency *noun*
an emergency = yíge jǐnjí qíngkuàng 一个紧急情况

emergency exit *noun*
an emergency exit = yíge jǐnjí chūkǒu 一个紧急出口

emigrate *verb*
= yíjū 移居

emotion *noun*
= jīdòng 激动

emotional *adjective*
- (*describing a scene or moment*) = dòngrén de 动人的
- (*describing a person*) = jīdòng de 激动的

emperor *noun*
an emperor = yíge huángdì 一个皇帝

employ *verb*
- (*to give work to*) = gùyòng 雇用, gù 雇
- (*to use as a means*) = yòng 用, shǐyòng 使用

employed *adjective*
to be employed by someone = shòu gù yú mǒurén 受雇于某人

employee *noun*
an employee = yíge gùyuán 一个雇员

employer *noun*
an employer = yíge gùzhǔ 一个雇主

employment *noun*
- (*the act of employing*) = gùyòng 雇用
- (*occupation*) = gōngzuò 工作, zhíyè 职业

empty
1 *adjective*
= kōng 空
2 *verb*
to empty the dustbin = bǎ lājītǒng dàokōng 把垃圾桶倒空
they emptied three bottles of wine = tāmen hēguāngle sānpíng jiǔ 他们喝光了三瓶酒

encourage *verb*
= gǔlì 鼓励

end
1 *noun*

- (*of a novel, film, play, speech*) = jiéwěi 结尾
  the end of the book = shū de jiéwěi 书的结尾
- (*of a month, year*) = dǐ 底
  the end of next year = míngnián dǐ 明年底
- **in the end** = zuìhòu 最后, zhōngyú 终于
- (*the furthest part*) = jìntóu 尽头
  at the end of the street = zài mǎlù jìntóu 在马路尽头

2 *verb*
- (*to come to an end*) = jiéshù 结束
- (*to put an end to, to finish*) = jiéshù 结束
  to end the war = jiéshù zhànzhēng 结束战争
  to end a concert = jiéshù yīnyuèhuì 结束音乐会

end up *verb*
  he ended up in London = tā zuìhòu dāizàile Lúndūn 他最后呆在了伦敦
  to end up going abroad = zuìhòu qùle guówài 最后去了国外

ending *noun*
  = jiéjú 结局, jiéwěi 结尾

enemy *noun*
  an enemy = yíge dírén 一个敌人

energetic *adjective*
  = jīnglì wàngshèng de 精力旺盛的

energy *noun*
- (*vigour*) = jīnglì 精力
- (*the power of doing work*) = néngliàng 能量

engaged *adjective*
- (*to be married*) = dìnghūn 订婚
  to be engaged (to someone) = (yǔ mǒurén) dìnghūn (与某人)订婚
- (*occupied*)
  she is engaged in writing a new novel = tā zhèng mángzhe xiě yíbù xīn xiǎoshuō 她正忙着写一部新小说
- (*British English*) (*describing a phone, a toilet*)
  the line is engaged = diànhuà zhànxiàn 电话占线
  the toilet is engaged = cèsuǒ yǒu rén 厕所有人

engine *noun*
  an engine = yìtái fādòngjī 一台发动机

engineer *noun* ▶ 344
  an engineer = yíge gōngchéngshī 一个工程师

England *noun*
  = Yīnggélán 英格兰

English ▶ 288

1 *adjective*
  = Yīnggélán de 英格兰的

2 *noun*
- (*the people*) = Yīnggélánrén 英格兰人
- (*the language*) = Yīngyǔ 英语

enjoy *verb*
- (*to like*) = xǐhuan 喜欢, xǐ'ài 喜爱
  he enjoys fishing = tā xǐhuan diàoyú 他喜欢钓鱼
  did you enjoy your holiday? = nǐ jiàqī guò de hǎo ma? 你假期过得好吗?
- (*to use with delight*) = xiǎngshòu 享受
  to enjoy social benefits = xiǎngshòu shèhuì fúlì 享受社会福利
- (*to have a good time*) ▶ 238
  enjoy yourself! = zhù nǐ wánr de kuàihuo! 祝你玩儿得快活!

enjoyable *adjective*
  = yúkuài 愉快, kuàilè 快乐

enormous *adjective*
  = jùdà 巨大, pángdà 庞大

enough

1 *adjective*
  = zúgòu 足够
  I don't have enough [money | time | friends...] = wǒ méi yǒu zúgòu de [qián | shíjiān | péngyou...] 我没有足够的 [钱 | 时间 | 朋友...]
  there is enough wine for everyone = yǒu zúgòu de jiǔ gòng dàjiā hē 有足够的酒供大家喝

2 *adverb*
  = gòu 够, zúgòu 足够
  is it big enough? = zhè gòu dà ma? 这够大吗?
  you are not old enough = nǐde niánlíng hái bú gòu dà 你的年龄还不够大

3 *pronoun*
  we have enough to eat = wǒmen yǒu zúgòu de dōngxi chī 我们有足够的东西吃
  I've had enough = wǒ yǐjīng shòu gòu le 我已经受够了
  that's enough = zúgòu le 足够了

enquire *verb*
  = xúnwèn 询问

I'll enquire about the price = wǒ xúnwèn yíxià jiàqián 我询问一下价钱

enter *verb*
- (*to go into*) = jìnrù 进入
- (*to take part in*) = cānjiā 参加
  to enter a competition = cānjiā bǐsài 参加比赛

entertain *verb*
- (*to treat hospitably*) = kuǎndài 款待, zhāodài 招待
- (*to amuse*) = shǐ...gāoxìng 使…高兴
  his performance entertained everyone = tāde biǎoyǎn shǐ dàjiā dōu hěn gāoxìng 他的表演使大家都很高兴

entertaining *adjective*
= yǒuqù 有趣

entertainment *noun*
- (*the act of entertaining guests*) = kuǎndài 款待, zhāodài 招待
- (*amusement*) = yùlè 娱乐, lèqù 乐趣

enthusiasm *noun*
= rèqíng 热情

enthusiastic *adjective*
= rèqíng 热情

entrance *noun*
an entrance = yíge rùkǒu 一个入口
the entrance to the castle = chéngbǎo de rùkǒu 城堡的入口

envelope *noun*
an envelope = yíge xìnfēng 一个信封

environment *noun*
= huánjìng 环境

envy
1 *noun*
- (*a feeling of chagrin at the fortune of another*) = jìdu 忌妒, dùji 妒忌
- (*a person or an object being envied*) = jìdu de duìxiàng 忌妒的对象, jìdu de mùbiāo 忌妒的目标

2 *verb*
= jìdu 忌妒, dùji 妒忌

episode *noun*
an episode (*an event or an incident in a story, a novel, a film*) = yíge qíngjié 一个情节
(*an event*) = yíge shìjiàn 一个事件

equal
1 *adjective*
- (*identical in quality, value, proportion, etc*) = xiāngděng 相等, jūnděng 均等
- (*in social status*) = píngděng 平等
  to fight for equal rights = wèi píngděng quánlì ér dòuzhēng 为平等权利而斗争

2 *verb*
= děngyú 等于
six plus four equal ten = liù jiā sì děngyú shí 六加四等于十

equality *noun*
= píngděng 平等, tóngděng 同等

equator *noun*
= chìdào 赤道

equipment *noun*
- (*in a factory, laboratory, or office*) = shèbèi 设备
- (*in military forces*) = zhuāngbèi 装备

eraser *noun*
- (*for a blackboard*)
  an eraser = yíge hēibǎn cā 一个黑板擦
- (*a pencil rubber*) (*US English*)
  an eraser = yíkuài xiàngpí 一块橡皮

escalator *noun*
an escalator = yíge diàndòng fútī 一个电动扶梯

escape *verb*
- (*to get away*) = táopǎo 逃跑
  he escaped from prison = tā cóng jiānyù li táopǎo le 他从监狱里逃跑了
- (*to avoid*) = táobì 逃避, táotuō 逃脱
  to escape punishment = táobì chéngfá 逃避惩罚

especially *adverb*
= tèbié 特别, yóuqí 尤其

essay *noun*
an essay = yìpiān wénzhāng 一篇文章

essential *adjective*
- (*relating to the essence*) = shízhì de 实质的, běnzhì de 本质的
- (*indispensable*) = bìyào 必要, bìbùkěshǎo 必不可少

ethnic *adjective*
= zhǒngzú de 种族的

EU, European Union *noun*
= Ōuzhōu Liánméng 欧洲联盟

euro *noun*
= ōuyuán 欧元

Europe *noun*
= Ōuzhōu 欧洲

European *adjective* ▶ 288
= Ōuzhōu de 欧洲的

evacuate *verb*
• (*to withdraw*) = chèlí 撤离
• (*to clear out inhabitants from*) = shūsàn 疏散

even[1]
1 *adverb*
• (*when expressing surprise*) = shènzhì 甚至, lián...yě... 连... 也...
he didn't even believe his mother = tā shènzhì bù xiāngxìn tāde māma 他甚至不相信他的妈妈
she even works on weekends = tā lián zhōumò yě gōngzuò 她连周末也工作
• (*in comparison*) = gèng 更, hái 还
it's even colder today = jīntiān gèng lěng 今天更冷
• (*when used with the conjunction* **if** *or* **though**)
even if/though = jíshǐ 即使, jíbiàn 即便
even if it rains tomorrow, you still have to go = jíshǐ míngtiān xià yǔ, nǐ yě děi qù 即使明天下雨, 你也得去

even[2] *adjective*
• (*flat, smooth*) = píng de 平的, píngtǎn de 平坦的
• (*when talking about numbers*)
an even number = yíge shuāng shù 一个双数, yíge ǒu shù 一个偶数

evening *noun* ▶ 204, ▶ 412
an evening = yíge wǎnshang 一个晚上
at eight o'clock in the evening = (zài) wǎnshang bā diǎn (在)晚上八点

event *noun*
• (*an incident*) = shìjiàn 事件
an event = yíge shìjiàn 一个事件
• (*in a sports programme*) = xiàngmu 项目
an event = yíge xiàngmu 一个项目

eventually *adverb*
= zhōngyú 终于, zuìhòu 最后

ever *adverb*
• (*at any time*)
nothing ever happens here = zhèr cónglái bù fāshēng shénme shì 这儿从来不发生什么事
have you ever been to Thailand? = nǐ qùguo Tàiguó ma? 你去过泰国吗?
I hardly ever go there = wǒ jīhū cónglái bú qù nàr 我几乎从来不去那儿
for ever = yǒngyuǎn 永远
we'll remember him for ever = wǒmen jiāng yǒngyuǎn jìzhù tā 我们将永远记住他

every *determiner* ▶ 412
= měi 每
every time I meet her = měi cì wǒ jiàndào tā 每次我见到她
every [day | week | month | year] = měi [tiān | zhōu | yuè | nián] 每[天|周|月|年]
every other [day | week | month | year] = měi gé [yì tiān | yì zhōu | yíge yuè | yì nián] 每隔[一天|一周|一个月|一年]
two out of every three people are men = měi sānge rén zhōng yǒu liǎngge shì nánrén 每三个人中有两个是男人

everyone, everybody *pronoun*
= měi ge rén 每个人, dàjiā 大家
everyone else = suǒyǒu qítā de rén 所有其他的人

everything *pronoun*
• (*every single matter*) = měi jiàn shì 每件事, suǒyǒu de shì 所有的事
• (*every single thing*) = měi jiàn dōngxi 每件东西, suǒyǒu de dōngxi 所有的东西

everywhere *adverb*
• = dàochù 到处
there are flowers everywhere = dàochù dōu shì xiānhuā 到处都是鲜花
• (*when used to introduce a clause*)
everywhere I went, I would buy some souvenirs = wǒ měi dào yíge dìfang dōu yào mǎi yìxiē jìniànpǐn 我每到一个地方都要买一些纪念品

evidence *noun*
• (*support for a belief*) = zhèngjù 证据
a piece of evidence = yíge zhèngjù 一个证据
to give evidence = tígòng zhèngjù 提供证据
• (*indications or signs*) = jìxiàng 迹象

evil *noun*
= xié'è 邪恶, zuì'è 罪恶

exact *adjective*
= quèqiè 确切, jīngquè 精确

exactly *adverb*
= quèqiè de 确切地, jīngquè de 精确地

exaggerate *verb*
= kuādà 夸大, kuāzhāng 夸张

exam *noun*
an exam = yícì kǎoshì 一次考试
to pass an exam = kǎoshì jígé 考试及格
to take an exam = cānjiā kǎoshì 参加考试

examine *verb*
- (*to check*) = jiǎnchá 检查
- (*to test in schools or universities*) = kǎo 考, kǎochá 考查

example *noun*
an example = yíge lìzi 一个例子
for example = lìrú 例如, bǐrú 比如

excellent *adjective*
- = yōuxiù 优秀, jiéchū 杰出
- (*in an exclamation*)
excellent! = hǎo jíle! 好极了!

except *preposition*
= chúle...(yǐwài)...dōu 除了...(以外)...都

exchange *verb*
- to exchange [books | students | gifts] = jiāohuàn [shū | xuésheng | lǐwù] 交换[书 | 学生 | 礼物]
- to exchange [foreign currency | US dollars | British pounds] = duìhuàn [wàibì | měiyuán | yīngbàng] 兑换[外币 | 美元 | 英镑]
- to exchange seats = diàohuàn zuòwei 调换座位

exchange rate *noun*
= duìhuàn huìlǜ 兑换汇率

excited *adjective*
= jīdòng 激动, xìngfèn 兴奋

exciting *adjective*
= lìng rén jīdòng 令人激动, lìng rén xìngfèn 令人兴奋

exclude *verb*
- (*hinder from participation*)
I excluded him from the meeting = wǒ méiyǒu ràng tā cānjiā zhège huì 我没有让他参加这个会
- (*to rule out*)
= páichú 排除
I cannot exclude this possibility = wǒ bù néng páichú zhèzhǒng kěnéngxìng 我不能排除这种可能性

excuse
1 *noun*
an excuse = yíge jièkǒu 一个借口
to make excuses = zhìzào jièkǒu 制造借口
2 *verb*
= yuánliàng 原谅
excuse me! = duìbuqǐ! 对不起!, láojià! 劳驾!

exercise *noun*
- (*physical exercise*) = duànliàn 锻炼
to take exercise, to do exercise = jìnxíng duànliàn 进行锻炼
- (*a piece of work*)
an exercise = yíge liànxí 一个练习

exercise book *noun*
an exercise book = yìběn liànxí běn 一本练习本

exhausted *adjective*
- (*tired out*) = jīnpílìjìn 筋疲力尽
- (*consumed*) = yòngwán 用完, hàojìn 耗尽

exhibition *noun*
an exhibition = yíge zhǎnlǎnhuì 一个展览会

exit *noun*
an exit = yíge chūkǒu 一个出口

expect *verb*
- (*to be prepared for*) = qīdài 期待
to expect bad news = qīdài huài xiāoxi 期待坏消息
they expect to win = tāmen qīdàizhe yíng 他们期待着赢
- (*to wait for*) = děngdài 等待, děng 等
- (*to want*) = pànwàng 盼望, qīwàng 期望
they expect us to do the work = tāmen qīwàng wǒmen zuò zhège gōngzuò 他们期望我们做这个工作

expenses *noun*
= huāfèi 花费, zhīchū 支出

expensive *adjective*
= guì 贵, ángguì 昂贵

experience *noun*
- (*passing through an event or events*) = jīnglì 经历

an experience = yícì jīnglì 一次经历
- (*practical acquaintance with any matter*) = jīngyàn 经验

experienced *adjective*
= yǒu jīngyàn de 有经验的

experiment
1 *noun*
an experiment = yícì shíyàn 一次实验, yícì shìyàn 一次试验
2 *verb*
= shíyàn 实验, shìyàn 试验

expert *noun*
an expert = yíge zhuānjiā 一个专家

explain *verb*
= jiěshì 解释, shuōmíng 说明
to explain a rule to someone = xiàng mǒurén jiěshì yíge guīzé 向某人解释一个规则

explanation *noun*
an explanation = yíge jiěshì 一个解释, yíge shuōmíng 一个说明

explode *verb*
- (*if it's a bomb*) = bàozhà 爆炸
- (*in personal emotion or feeling*)
to explode with laughter = hōngtáng dàxiào 哄堂大笑

exploit *verb*
- (*to turn to use*) = kāifā 开发, kāicǎi 开采
- (*to make gain at the expense of*) = bōxuē 剥削

explosion *noun*
an explosion = yícì bàozhà 一次爆炸

export *verb*
= chūkǒu 出口, shūchū 输出

express
1 *verb*
= biǎoshì 表示, biǎodá 表达
2 *adjective*
= tèkuài 特快
an express train = yítàng kuài chē 一趟快车
an express letter = yìfēng kuài xìn 一封快信

expression *noun*
a happy expression = yífù gāoxìng de biǎoqíng 一副高兴的表情
the expression of different opinions = bùtóng yìjiàn de biǎodá 不同意见的表达

extinct *adjective*
(*describing an animal or a plant*) = juézhǒng de 绝种的, mièjué de 灭绝的
(*describing a volcano*) = xīmiè de 熄灭的, sǐ 死

extra
1 *adjective*
- (*beyond or more than the usual*) = éwài 额外
to pay an extra ten pounds = éwài duō fù shí bàng qián 额外多付十镑钱
- (*additional*) = wàijiā 外加
an extra bed = yìzhāng jiā chuáng 一张加床
1 *adverb*
to pay extra for wine = jiǔ qián lìng fù 酒钱另付

extraordinary *adjective*
= tèbié 特别, fēicháng 非常

extreme *adjective*
- (*most remote*) = jìntóu de 尽头的
- (*highest in degree*) = jíduān 极端
- (*extraordinary in opinions or behaviour*) = jījìn 激进, piānjī 偏激

extremely *adverb*
= jíduān 极端, fēicháng 非常

eye *noun* ▶ 189
an eye = yìzhī yǎnjing 一只眼睛

eyebrow *noun* ▶ 189
= méimao 眉毛

eyelash *noun* ▶ 189
= jiémáo 睫毛

eyelid *noun* ▶ 189
= yǎnjiǎn 眼睑, yǎnpí 眼皮

eye shadow *noun*
= yǎnyǐng 眼影

eyesight *noun*
= shìlì 视力

E

Useful everyday expressions in Spoken Chinese

When things are going well

well done! = gàn de hǎo! 干得好!
congratulations! = zhùhè nǐ! 祝贺你!
excellent!, brilliant! = tài hǎo le! 太好了!✖

When things are not so good

hard luck!, bad luck! = zhēn bù zǒuyùn! 真不走运!
too bad! = zhēn zāogāo! 真糟糕!
cheer up!, chin up! = dǎqǐ jīngshén lai! 打起精神来!
oh, dear! = ā, tiān na! 啊, 天哪!✖
damn! = zāogāo! 糟糕!✖
blast! = gāisǐ! 该死!●
good luck! (you'll need it) = zhù nǐ shí lái yùn zhuǎn! 祝你时来运转!
shit! = zhēn chòu! 真臭!●
get well soon! = zhù nǐ zǎo rì kāngfù! 祝你早日康复!

Coming

Welcome! = huānyíng , huānyíng! 欢迎, 欢迎!
nice to meet you, pleased to meet you = hěn gāoxìng jiàndào nǐ 很高兴见到你
= jiàndào nǐ hěn gāoxìng 见到你很高兴
hello! = nǐ hǎo! 你好!
hi! = nǐ hǎo! 你好!

Going

goodbye! = zàijiàn! 再见!
bye! = zàijiàn! 再见!
cheers! (British English)
(goodbye) = zàijiàn! 再见!
(thank you) = xièxie! 谢谢!
see you soon! = xīwàng hěn kuài jiàndào nǐ! 希望很快见到你!
see you [later|tomorrow|next week]! = [回头/明天/下周]见!
see you around! = huítóu jiàn! 回头见!✖
(have a) safe journey! = yílù píng'ān! 一路平安!
all the best! = zhù nǐ yíqiè shùnlì! 祝你一切顺利!
= zhù nǐ yìfān fēng shùn! 祝你一帆风顺!

Wishing someone well

have a nice day! = zhù nǐ dùguo měihǎo de yì tiān! 祝你度过美好的一天!
have a good weekend! = zhōumò kuàilè! 周末快乐!
have a great holiday|vacation! = jiàqī kuàilè! 假期快乐!

✖in informal situations

● may be considered offensive

have a good time! enjoy yourself! = zhù nǐ wánr de kuàihuo! 祝你玩儿得快活!

have a good trip! = zhù nǐ lǚtú yúkuài! 祝你旅途愉快!

Special greetings

Happy birthday! = zhù nǐ shēngri kuàilè! 祝你生日快乐!
Merry Christmas! = Shèngdàn kuàilè! 圣诞快乐!
Happy New Year! = xīnnián kuàilè! 新年快乐!
Happy Chinese New Year! = gōngxǐ fācái! 恭喜发财!

F

In reply to "Thank you"

You're very welcome = bú kèqi! 不客气!
don't mention it = bú yòng xiè! 不用谢!
not at all = bú xiè! 不谢!*

Eating and drinking

help yourself! = qǐng suíbiàn chī! 请随便吃!
enjoy your meal! = xīwàng nǐmen chī de kāixīn! 希望你们吃得开心!
cheers! (as a toast) = gānbēi! 干杯!

Sleeping

good night! = wǎn'ān! 晚安!
sleep well! = zhù nǐ shuì ge hǎo jiào! 祝你睡个好觉!

face
1 *noun*
the face = liǎn 脸, miànkǒng 面孔
to make a face = zuò guǐliǎnr 做鬼脸儿
2 *verb*
• (*to be opposite*) = miànduì 面对
she was facing me = tā miànduìzhe wǒ 面对着我
• (*to have to deal with*) = zhèngshì 正视, duìfu 对付
we have to face these difficulties = wǒmen bìxū zhèngshì zhèxiē kùnnan 我们必须正视这些困难
• (*to look toward(s)*) = cháo 朝, miànxiàng 面向
my room faces the sea = wǒde fángjiān cháo hǎi 我的房间朝海
face up to = yǒnggǎn de duìfu 勇敢地对付

fact
1 *noun*
a fact = yíge shìshí 一个事实
2 in fact = qíshí 其实, shíjìshang 实际上

factory *noun*
a factory = yíge gōngchǎng 一个工厂

fade *verb*
(*if it's a flower or tree leaf*) = kūwěi 枯萎, diāoxiè 凋谢
(*if it's a colour*) = tuìsè 褪色

fail *verb*
• (*in an examination*) = bù jígé 不及格
to fail an exam = kǎoshì bù jígé 考试不及格
• (*miss an achievement*) = shībài 失败
his plan failed = tāde jìhuà shībài le 他的计划失败了
• (*to prove deficient*)

*in informal situations

the plane failed to arrive on time = fēijī méiyǒu zhǔnshí dàodá 飞机没有准时到达
she never fails to remember my birthday = tā cónglái méi wàngjì wǒde shēngri 她从来没忘记我的生日
- (*in health, sight or hearing*) = shuāituì 衰退, shuāiruò 衰弱

failure *noun*
a failure (*an event, an attempt*) = yícì shībài 一次失败
(*a person in an exam*) = bù jígé 不及格

faint *verb*
= hūndǎo 昏倒, yūndǎo 晕倒

fair
1 *adjective*
- (*just*) = gōngpíng 公平, gōngzhèng 公正

it's not fair = zhè bù gōngpíng 这不公平
- (*in colour*)

fair hair = jīnhuángsè de tóufa 金黄色的头发
fair skin = báinèn de pífū 白嫩的皮肤
2 *noun*
- (*British English*) (*a funfair*)

a fair = yíge yóulèhuì 一个游乐会
- (*a display of goods*)

a (trade) fair = yíge shāngpǐn jiāoyìhuì 一个商品交易会

fairly *adverb*
- (*justly*) = gōngpíng de 公平地, gōngzhèng de 公正地
- (*quite*) = xiāngdāng 相当

faith *noun*
- (*trust or confidence*) = xìnrèn 信任, xiāngxìn 相信

to have faith in someone = xìnrèn mǒurén 信任某人
- (*in religion*) = xìnyǎng 信仰

faithful *adjective*
= zhōngchéng 忠诚, zhōngshí 忠实

fall
1 *verb*
- (*if it's a person*) = shuāidǎo 摔倒, diēdǎo 跌倒

she fell to the ground = tā shuāidǎo zài dì shang 她摔倒在地上
- (*to drop*) = luò 落, diào 掉

an apple fell onto his head = yíge píngguǒ diào zài tāde tóu shang 一个苹果掉在他的头上
- (*in price, temperature*) = xiàjiàng 下降, jiàngdī 降低
- (*other uses*)

to fall asleep = shuìzháo 睡着
to fall ill = bìng le 病了
to fall in love with someone = àishang mǒurén 爱上某人
2 *noun*
- (*in price, temperature*) = xiàjiàng 下降, jiàngdī 降低
- (*US English*) (*autumn*) = qiūtiān 秋天

fall down
- (*if it's a person*) = dǎoxia 倒下, shuāidǎo 摔倒
- (*if it's a building*) = dǎotā 倒塌, tāntā 坍塌

fall off
to fall off a chair = cóng yǐzi shang diēxiàlai 从椅子上跌下来
fall out
- (*from somewhere*) = diàochūlai 掉出来

the letter fell out of his pocket = xìn cóng tā kǒudài li diàochūlai 信从他口袋里掉出来
- (*to quarrel*) = chǎojià 吵架, nàofān 闹翻

fall over = diējiāo 跌跤, diēdǎo 跌倒
fall through = shībài 失败

false *adjective*
- (*untrue, not real*) = jiǎ 假
- (*wrong, erroneous*) = cuòwù de 错误的, miùwù de 谬误的

familiar *adjective*
= shúxī 熟悉

family *noun*
a family = yíge jiātíng 一个家庭

famous *adjective*
= zhùmíng 著名, yǒumíng 有名

fan *noun*
- (*of a pop star, an actor, a sport*) = mí 迷

a football fan = yíge zúqiú mí 一个足球迷
- (*for cooling*)

a fan (*electric*) = yìtái (diàn)fēngshàn 一台(电)风扇
(*hand-held*) = yìbǎ shànzi 一把扇子

fancy dress party *noun* (*British English*)
a fancy dress party = yíge huàzhuāng wǔhuì 一个化妆舞会

fantastic *adjective*
- (*fanciful*) = huànxiǎng de 幻想的

- (*weird, odd*) = qíyì 奇异, gǔguài 古怪
- **fantastic!** = tài hǎo le! 太好了!

far
1 *adverb*
- **▶ 300**
  far (away) = yuǎn 远
  how far is it to London? = dào Lúndūn yǒu duō yuǎn? 到伦敦有多远?
  how far is Oxford from London? = Niújīn lí Lúndūn yǒu duō yuǎn? 牛津离伦敦有多远?
  we went as far as the coast = wǒmen yìzhí zǒudàole hǎibiān 我们一直走到了海边
- (*in time*)
  as far back as 1950 = yuǎn zài yījiǔwǔlíng nián 远在1950年
- (*very much*)
  you're eating far too much bread = miànbāo nǐ chī de tài duō le 面包你吃得太多了
  far [better | colder | earlier...] = [hǎo | lěng | zǎo...] de duō [好 | 冷 | 早...] 得多

2 *adjective*
- (*farther*) = nàyibiān 那一边
  at the far side of the room = zài fángjiān de nàyibiān 在房间的那一边
- **the Far East** = Yuǎndōng 远东

3 so far = dào mùqián wéizhǐ 到目前为止

fare *noun*
the fare (*on a bus, train, or underground*) = chēfèi 车费
(*on a boat*) = chuánfèi 船费

farm *noun*
a farm (*for cultivation*) = yíge nóngchǎng 一个农场
(*for pasture*) = yíge xùmùchǎng 一个畜牧场

farmer *noun* **▶ 344**
a farmer = yíge nóngchǎngzhǔ 一个农场主

fascinating *adjective*
= mírén 迷人

fashion *noun*
- (*form or pattern*) = yàngzi 样子
- (*prevailing mode or shape of dress*) = liúxíng shìyàng 流行式样
  to be in fashion = zhèng shíxīng 正时兴
  to go out of fashion = guòshí 过时, bù shíxīng 不时兴

fashionable *adjective*
= shímáo 时髦, liúxíng 流行

fast
1 *adjective*
- (*rapid*) = kuài 快, xùnsù 迅速
- (*as a clock or watch*) = kuài 快
  my watch is ten minutes fast = wǒde shǒubiǎo kuài shí fēnzhōng 我的手表快十分钟

2 *adverb*
= kuài 快, xùnsù 迅速

fasten *verb*
= jìláo 系牢, jìhǎo 系好
to fasten a seatbelt = jìhǎo ānquándài 系好安全带

fast-forward *verb*
to fast-forward a cassette = kuàisù xiàngqián zhuàn cídài 快速向前转磁带

fat *adjective*
- (*describing a person*) = pàng 胖
- (*describing animals or meat*) = féi 肥

fatal *adjective*
- (*causing death*) = zhìmìng de 致命的
- (*decided by fate*) = mìngzhōng zhùdìng de 命中注定的
- (*determining fate*) = juédìng mìngyùn de 决定命运的
  a fatal decision for me = juédìng wǒ mìngyùn de juédìng 决定我命运的决定

father *noun*
a father = yíge bàba 一个爸爸, yíge fùqin 一个父亲

Father Christmas *noun* (*British English*)
Father Christmas = Shèngdàn Lǎorén 圣诞老人

father-in-law *noun*
- (*husband's father*) = gōnggong 公公
- (*wife's father*) = yuèfù 岳父

faucet *noun* (*US English*)
a faucet = yíge shuǐlóngtóu 一个水龙头

fault *noun*
a fault (*a mistake made by someone*) = yíge guòcuò 一个过错
(*in a mechanical, electrical or electronic system*) = yíge gùzhàng 一个故障

F

favour (*British English*), **favor** (*US English*)
1 *noun*
to do someone a favour = bāng mǒurén yíge máng 帮某人一个忙
to ask someone a favour = qǐng mǒurén bāng ge máng 请某人帮个忙
2 in favour of
to be in favour of the new law = zànchéng xīn de fǎlǜ 赞成新的法律

favourite (*British English*), **favorite** (*US English*) *adjective*
= tèbié xǐhuan de 特别喜欢的
it's my favourite film = zhè shì wǒ tèbié xǐhuan de diànyǐng 这是我特别喜欢的电影

fax *noun*
a fax = yífèn chuánzhēn 一份传真

fear *noun*
= hàipà 害怕, kǒngjù 恐惧

feather *noun*
a feather = yìgēn yǔmáo 一根羽毛

February *noun* ▶ 218
= èryuè 二月

fed up *adjective*
be fed up = fēicháng yànjuàn 非常厌倦

fee *noun*
(*for attending an event, a show*) = fèi 费
(*for joining a club, a union*) = huìfèi 会费

feeble *adjective*
= xūruò 虚弱, wúlì 无力

feed *verb*
- (*if it's a person*) = wèi 喂
- (*if it's an animal*) = sìyǎng 饲养, wèi(yǎng) 喂(养)

feel *verb*
- (*referring to an emotion, an impression, or a physical feeling*) = juéde 觉得, gǎndào 感到
  to feel happy = gǎndào gāoxìng 感到高兴
  he's feeling uncomfortable = tā juéde bù shūfu 他觉得不舒服
  to feel afraid = juéde hàipà 觉得害怕
  I feel as if I'm being followed = wǒ gǎndào hǎoxiàng yǒu rén gēnzhe wǒ 我感到好像有人跟着我
  to feel [hot | cold | sleepy] = juéde [rè | lěng | kùn] 觉得 [热 | 冷 | 困]
  to feel ill = gǎnjué shēntǐ bù shūfu 感觉身体不舒服
  I don't feel a thing = wǒ shénme dōu gǎnjué bú dào 我什么都感觉不到
- (*describing how something seems*)
  the box felt very heavy = nàge hézi náqǐlai hěn zhòng 那个盒子拿起来很重
  the room feels very cold = zhège fángjiān ràng rén juéde hěn lěng 这个房间让人觉得很冷
- (*to touch*) = mō 摸
  the doctor felt her head = dàifu mōle yíxià tāde tóu 大夫摸了一下她的头
- **to feel like [going out | eating | dancing...]** = xiǎngyào [chūqu | chī dōngxi | tiàowǔ...] 想要 [出去 | 吃东西 | 跳舞...]
  I don't feel like it
  (*if it's about going out*) = wǒ bù xiǎng (chū)qù 我不想(出)去
  (*if it's about eating something*) = wǒ bù xiǎng chī 我不想吃
  (*if it's about doing something*) = wǒ bù xiǎng zuò 我不想做

feeling *noun*
- (*emotional*) = gǎnqíng 感情
  a feeling = yìzhǒng gǎnqíng 一种感情
  to hurt someone's feelings = shānghài mǒurén de gǎnqíng 伤害某人的感情
- (*physical*) = gǎnjué 感觉
  a feeling = yìzhǒng gǎnjué 一种感觉
- **I have a feeling he's right** = wǒ juéde tā shì duì de 我觉得他是对的

felt-tip pen *noun*
a felt-tip pen = yìzhī zhāntóubǐ 一支毡头笔

female *adjective*
- (*in biology*) = cíxìng de 雌性的
- (*relating to women*) = nǚ 女, nǚxìng de 女性的
- (*relating to animals*) = mǔ 母

feminine *adjective*
- (*female*) = nǚxìng de 女性的

- (*effeminate*) = nǚzǐqì de 女子气的, jiāoróu de 娇柔的

fence *noun*
a fence = yíge líba 一个篱笆, yíge wéilán 一个围栏

fencing *noun* ▶ 390
= jījiàn 击剑

festival *noun*
a festival day = yíge jié(rì) 一个节(日)

fetch *verb*
= ná 拿, qǔ 取
go and fetch some water = qù ná diǎn shuǐ lai 去拿点水来
fetch a doctor = qǐng ge dàifu lai 请个大夫来

fever *noun*
to have a fever = fāshāo 发烧, fārè 发热

few ▶ 349
1 a few = yìxiē 一些, jǐge 几个
a few [**people** | **houses** | **books...**] = yìxiē [rén | fángzi | shū...] 一些[人 | 房子 | 书...]
a few of them speak Cantonese = tāmen dāngzhōng de jǐge rén huì shuō Guǎngdōnghuà 他们当中的几个人会说广东话
2 *determiner*
- (*not many*) = jīhū méi yǒu 几乎没有, hěn shǎo 很少
few [**people** | **letters** | **cars...**] = jīhū méi yǒu [rén | xìn | chē...] 几乎没有 [人 | 信 | 车...]
- (*several*) = jǐge 几个
the first few weeks = kāishǐ de jǐge xīngqī 开始的几个星期

3 *pronoun*
few of us succeeded = wǒmen dāngzhōng jīhū méi yǒu rén chénggōng 我们当中几乎没有人成功

field *noun*
- (*open country in general*) = tiányě 田野, tiándì 田地
a field = yíkuài tiándì 一块田地
- (*a piece of ground enclosed for sports, construction, entertainment, etc.*)
a field = yíge chǎngdì 一个场地
- (*an area of knowledge or speciality*) = lǐngyù 领域
a field = yíge lǐngyù 一个领域

fifteen *number* ▶ 170, ▶ 204
= shíwǔ 十五

fifteenth *number*
- (*in a series*) = dìshíwǔ 第十五
- (*in dates*) ▶ 218
the fifteenth of May = wǔyuè shíwǔ hào 五月十五号

fifth *number*
- (*in a series*) = dìwǔ 第五
- (*in dates*) ▶ 218
the fifth of June = liùyuè wǔ hào 六月五号

fifty *number* ▶ 170, ▶ 204
= wǔshí 五十

fight
1 *verb*
- **to fight (against) prejudice** = yǔ piānjiàn zuò dòuzhēng 与偏见作斗争
to fight for justice = wèi zhèngyì ér fèndòu 为正义而奋斗
- (*in war*) = yǔ...zhàndòu 与... 战斗, yǔ...zuòzhàn 与... 作战
to fight (against) the enemy = yǔ dírén zhàndòu 与敌人战斗
- (*physically*) = yǔ...dǎzhàng 与... 打仗
- (*to quarrel*) = yǔ...zhēngchǎo 与... 争吵

2 *noun*
- (*a campaign*) = dòuzhēng 斗争
a fight = yìchǎng dòuzhēng 一场斗争
- (*physical*)
a fight = yìchǎng zhàndòu 一场战斗, yìchǎng bódòu 一场搏斗
fight back = huánjī 还击

figure *noun*
- (*a number*) = shùzì 数字
a figure = yíge shùzì 一个数字
- **to have a good figure** = yǒu yíge hǎo de tǐxíng 有一个好的体型

file *noun*
- **a file** (*for documents*) = yíge ànjuàn 一个案卷, yíge juànzōng 一个卷宗
(*in a computer*) = yíge wénjiàn 一个文件

fill *verb*
- (*to fill a container*) = zhuāngmǎn 装满
- (*if it's people filling a room or a hall*) = jǐmǎn 挤满
fill in (*if it's a form*) = tiánxiě 填写
(*if it's a hole or a sunken place*) = tián 填

film
1 *noun*
- (*in a cinema or on TV*)
  a film = yíbù diànyǐng 一部电影
- (*for a camera*)
  a film = yíge jiāojuǎn 一个胶卷

2 *verb*
= pāishè 拍摄

filthy *adjective*
= āngzāng 肮脏

final
1 *adjective*
= zuìhòu 最后, zuìzhōng 最终
2 *noun*
a final (*in sports*) = yícì juésài 一次决赛
(*an examination*) = zuìhòu dàkǎo 最后大考

finally *adverb*
= zuìhòu 最后, zuìzhōng 最终

find *verb*
- (*to reach the thing or person one has looked for*) = zhǎodào 找到
- (*to discover*) = fāxiàn 发现
- (*to come to perceive*) = fājué 发觉, gǎnjué 感觉

find out
to find out the truth = chámíng zhēnxiàng 查明真相
if he ever finds out he'll be furious = rúguǒ tā fāxiànle, tā huì dà fā léitíng 如果他发现了, 他会大发雷霆

fine
1 *adjective*
- (*describing a person's character*) = yōuliáng 优良, yōuxiù 优秀
- (*describing the weather*) = qínglǎng 晴朗, búcuò 不错
- (*describing the appearance of a person, a building, or a scene*) = hǎokàn 好看, piàoliang 漂亮
- (*in good health*)
  I feel fine = wǒ gǎnjué hěn hǎo 我感觉很好
- (*expressing agreement*)
  (that's) fine = xíng 行

2 *noun*
a fine = yífèn fákuǎn 一份罚款

finger *noun* ▶ 189
= shǒuzhǐ 手指

finish
1 *verb*
- (*to complete*) = wánchéng 完成
  to finish one's [homework | task | experiment] = wánchéng [zuòyè | rènwu | shíyàn] 完成[作业 | 任务 | 实验]
- (*used after a verb to indicate a result of an action*) = wán 完
  to finish [cooking | eating] supper = [zuò | chī] wán wǎnfàn [做 | 吃] 完晚饭
- (*to come to an end*) = jiéshù 结束
  the film finishes at 8:00 = diànyǐng bā diǎn jiéshù 电影八点结束

2 *noun*
the finish (*the last part in a film, a race, or a certain process*) = zuìhòu yíduàn 最后一段

fire
1 *noun*
= huǒ 火
a fire (*for heat*) = lúhuǒ 炉火
(*causing damage*) = yìchǎng huǒzāi 一场火灾
to catch fire = zháohuǒ 着火, qǐhuǒ 起火
to be on fire = zháohuǒ 着火, qǐhuǒ 起火
2 *verb*
- (*to shoot*) = kāiqiāng 开枪
- (*to dismiss*) = jiěgù 解雇, kāichú 开除

fire alarm *noun*
a fire alarm = yíge huǒjǐng bàojǐngqì 一个火警报警器

fire brigade (*British English*), **fire department** (*US English*) *noun*
= xiāofángduì 消防队

fire engine *noun*
a fire engine = yíliàng xiāofángchē 一辆消防车

fireman *noun* ▶ 344
a fireman = yíge xiāofáng duìyuán 一个消防队员

fire station *noun*
a fire station = yíge xiāofángzhàn 一个消防站

fireworks display *noun*
a fireworks display = yìchǎng yānhuǒ wǎnhuì 一场烟火晚会

firm
1 *noun*
a firm = yíge gōngsī 一个公司

2 *adjective*
- (*when describing a structure, foundation, or frame*) = jiēshi 结实, láogù 牢固
- (*when describing one's attitude, position*) = jiāndìng 坚定, jiānjué 坚决

first
1 *adjective*
the first [time | lesson | day] = dìyī [cì | kè | tiān] 第一[次 | 课 | 天]
the first [three weeks | two months | few days] = tóu [sān zhōu | liǎngge yuè | jǐ tiān] 头[三周 | 两个月 | 几天]
2 *adverb*
- (*to begin with*) = shǒuxiān 首先
  first of all = shǒuxiān 首先
- (*for the first time*) = dìyīcì 第一次
- **to arrive first** = dìyīge dàodá 第一个到达

3 *noun*
- (*in a series or group*)
  the first = dìyīge 第一个
  he was the first to congratulate us = tā shì dìyīge zhùhè wǒmen de rén 他是第一个祝贺我们的人
- (*in dates*) ▶ 218
  the first of June = liùyuè yī hào 六月一号

4 at first = qǐchū 起初, kāishǐ de shíhou 开始的时候

first aid *noun*
= jíjiù 急救

first class *adverb*
to travel first class (*in a boat or a plane*) = zuò tóuděng cāng lǚxíng 坐头等舱旅行
(*in a train*) = zuò tóuděng chēxiāng lǚxíng 坐头等车厢旅行

first floor *noun*
(*in Britain*) = èrlóu 二楼
(*in the US*) = yīlóu 一楼

first name *noun*
= jiàomíng 教名, míng 名

fish
1 *noun*
a fish = yìtiáo yú 一条鱼
2 *verb*
to go fishing (*with a rod*) = qù diàoyú 去钓鱼
(*with a net*) = qù bǔ yú 去捕鱼

fisherman *noun* ▶ 344
a fisherman = yíge yúmín 一个渔民

fishing *noun* ▶ 390
(*with a rod*) = diàoyú 钓鱼
(*with a net*) = bǔ yú 捕鱼

fishing rod *noun*
a fishing rod = yìgēn diàoyú gānr 一根钓鱼杆儿

fist *noun* ▶ 189
= quántou 拳头

fit
1 *verb*
the shoes don't fit me = zhèshuāng xié wǒ chuān bù héshì 这双鞋我穿不合适
the photo won't fit into the envelope = zhèzhāng zhàopiàn zhuāng bú jìn zhègè xìnfēng li qu 这张照片装不进这个信封里去
will the table fit here? = zhèzhāng zhuōzi fàng zài zhèr héshì ma? 这张桌子放在这儿合适吗?
2 *adjective*
- (*suitable*) = héshì 合适, shìhé 适合
  the house isn't fit to live in = zhè(zhuàng) fángzi bú shìhé jūzhù 这(幢)房子不适合居住
  to be fit to drive = shìhé kāi chē 适合开车
  he is not fit to be a leader = tā bù héshì zuò lǐngdǎo 他不合适做领导
- (*healthy*)
  to be fit = jiànkāng 健康

fit in

> **!** *Note that the translation varies with the context, which determines the verb that is used.*

- (*in a car*)
  can you all fit in? = nǐmen dōu néng zuòjìnqu ma? 你们都能坐进去吗?
- (*in a group or team*)
  can he fit in? = tā néng gēn qítā rén hé de lái ma? 他能跟其他人合得来吗?

fitness *noun*
(physical) fitness = (shēntǐ) jiànkāng (身体)健康

five *number* ▶ 170, ▶ 204
= wǔ 五
five apples = wǔge píngguǒ 五个苹果

fix *verb*
- (*to decide on*) = quèdìng 确定, juédìng 决定

F

- (*to fasten or attach*) = gùdìng 固定, ānzhuāng 安装
- (*to repair*) = xiūlǐ 修理
- (*to prepare*) = zhǔnbèi 准备

flag *noun*
a flag = yímiàn qí 一面旗

flame *noun*
= huǒyàn 火焰

flash
1 *noun*
a flash (*for a camera*) = yíge shǎnguāngdēng 一个闪光灯
2 *verb*
to flash (on and off) = shǎnliàng 闪亮, shǎnguāng 闪光

flashlight *noun*
a flashlight = yíge shǎnguāngdēng 一个闪光灯

flat
1 *noun* (*British English*)
a flat = yíge tàofáng 一个套房, yítào dānyuán fángjiān 一套单元房间
2 *adjective*
- (*smooth and level*) = píng 平, píngtǎn 平坦
- **to have a flat tyre** = chētāi biě le 车胎瘪了

flavour (*British English*), **flavor** (*US English*) *noun*
a flavour = yìzhǒng wèidào 一种味道

flea *noun*
a flea = yíge tiàozǎo 一个跳蚤

flight *noun*
- **a flight** (*a regular air journey, numbered and at a fixed time*) = yíge hángbān 一个航班, yíge bānjī 一个班机
- (*the act of flying*) = fēi 飞, fēixíng 飞行

flight attendant *noun* ▶ 344
a flight attendant = yìmíng jīshang fúwùyuán 一名机上服务员

float *verb*
- (*in the air*) = piāo 飘
to float up into the air = piāodào kōng zhōng qu 飘到空中去
- (*in the water*) = piāo 漂
to float in the river = zài hé li piāo 在河里漂

flock *noun*
a flock of [sheep | geese | birds...] = yìqún [yáng | é | niǎo...] 一群[羊 | 鹅 | 鸟...]

flood *noun*
a flood = yícì hóngshuǐ 一次洪水, yícì shuǐzāi 一次水灾

floor *noun*
- (*a surface*)
a floor = dìbǎn 地板
to sit on the floor = zuò zài dìbǎn shang 坐在地板上
- (*a storey*) = céng 层, lóu 楼
the ground floor (*British English*) = yīcéng 一层, yīlóu 一楼

florist *noun* ▶ 344
a florist = yíge mài huā de rén 一个卖花的人, yíge huāshāng 一个花商

flour *noun*
= miàn 面, miànfěn 面粉

flow *verb*
= liú 流, liúdòng 流动

flower
1 *noun*
a flower (*if it's a single flower*) = yìzhī huā 一枝花
(*if it's a plant*) = yìkē huā 一棵花
2 *verb*
= kāihuā 开花

flu *noun* ▶ 277
= liúxíngxìng gǎnmào 流行性感冒, liúgǎn 流感

fluently *adverb*
= liúlì de 流利地

flush *verb*
to flush the toilet = chōng cèsuǒ 冲厕所

flute *noun* ▶ 308
a flute = yìgēn chángdí 一根长笛

fly
1 *noun*
a fly = yìzhī cāngying 一只苍蝇
2 *verb*
- (*if it's a bird, plane*) = fēi 飞
to fly from London to Beijing = cóng Lúndūn fēidào Běijīng 从伦敦飞到北京
- **to fly a plane** = jiàshǐ yíjià fēijī 驾驶一架飞机
- (*if it's a flag*) = piāoyáng 飘扬
fly away = fēizǒu 飞走

fog *noun*
= wù 雾

fold *verb*
- (*if it's a chair, bed, or table*) = zhédié 折叠
- (*if it's clothes, a handkerchief, a bed sheet*) = dié 叠
- **to fold one's arms** = bǎ shuāngbì zài xiōngqián jiāochāqǐlai 把双臂在胸前交叉起来

folder *noun*
a folder = yíge wénjiànjiā 一个文件夹

follow *verb*
- (*to go or come after*) = gēnsuí 跟随
- (*to pursue*) = zhuīgǎn 追赶, zhuīzōng 追踪
- (*to understand*) = dǒng/lǐjiě...de yìsi 懂/理解... 的意思
- (*to obey*) = tīngcóng 听从, zūnxún 遵循
- (*to imitate*) = fǎngxiào 仿效
- (*to keep an eye fixed on*) = zhùshì 注视
- (*to keep one's hearing fixed on*) = qīngtīng 倾听
- (*to keep one's attention fixed on*) = zhùyì 注意

following *adjective*
the following (*below*) = xiàmian 下面
the following paragraph = xiàmian yíduàn 下面一段
the following names = xiàliè míngzi 下列名字
(*when talking about the day, the week, the month, the year*) = dì'èr 第二
the following day = dì'èr tiān 第二天

fond *adjective*
I'm very fond of you = wǒ hěn xǐhuan nǐ 我很喜欢你

food *noun*
= shíwù 食物, shípǐn 食品

fool
1 *verb*
= qīpiàn 欺骗, yúnòng 愚弄
2 *noun*
a fool = yíge shǎzi 一个傻子, yíge shǎguā 一个傻瓜

foot *noun*
- (*part of the leg*) ▶ 189
= jiǎo 脚
on foot = bùxíng 步行
- (*in measurements*) ▶ 300
a foot = yì yīngchǐ 一英尺

football *noun* ▶ 390
- (*soccer*) = zúqiú 足球
(*American football*) = gǎnlǎnqiú 橄榄球
- (*a ball*)
a football = yíge zúqiú 一个足球

footballer (*British English*), **football player** (*US English*) *noun* ▶ 344
a footballer = yíge zúqiú yùndòngyuán 一个足球运动员

footprint *noun*
a footprint = yíge jiǎoyìn 一个脚印

footstep *noun*
a footstep = yíge jiǎobù 一个脚步

for *preposition*
- (*indicating the purpose of*) = wèile 为了, wèi 为
to fight for national interests = wèile guójiā lìyì ér dòuzhēng 为了国家利益而斗争
- (*indicating the beneficiary*) = wèi 为, gěi 给
to work for a company = wèi yíge gōngsī gōngzuò 为一个公司工作
he cooked dinner for us = tā gěi wǒmen zuò fàn 他给我们做饭
- (*indicating time and distance*)

> **!** *Note that when indicating time and distance,* **for** *is not translated into Chinese.*

we've been living here for two years = wǒmen zài zhèr zhùle liǎng nián le 我们在这儿住了两年了
he's going to Shanghai for a year = tā yào qù Shànghǎi yì nián 他要去上海一年
we drove for 80 kilometres = wǒmen kāile bāshí gōnglǐ 我们开了80公里
- (*indicating the price of a purchase*) = huā 花
he bought the bag for £50 = tā huā wǔshí yīngbàng mǎile zhège bāo 他花50英镑买了这个包
- (*indicating the selling price*) = yǐ 以
he sold his bike for £40 = tā yǐ sìshí yīngbàng màile tāde zìxíngchē 他以40英镑卖了他的自行车
- (*in favour of*) = zànchéng 赞成, yōnghù 拥护
are you for or against his suggestion? = nǐ zànchéng háishì

fǎnduì tāde jiànyì? 你赞成还是反对他的建议?

- (*indicating to whom or what something or somebody is intended or destined*)

> ! *Note that in this use* for *is usually not translated into Chinese.*

a letter for you = nǐde xìn 你的信
the Minister for Education = Jiàoyù Bùzhǎng 教育部长
the money is for buying a new car = zhè qián shì mǎi xīn chē yòng de 这钱是买新车用的

- (*on behalf of, in place of*) = tì 替, dài 代

let me do it for you = ràng wǒ tì nǐ zuò ba 让我替你做吧
say hello to her for me = dài wǒ xiàng tā wèn hǎo 代我向她问好

- (*indicating the direction or the destination*)

the plane for Beijing = fēi wǎng Běijīng de fēijī 飞往北京的飞机
[the train | the bus | the boat] for London = kāi wǎng Lúndūn de [huǒchē | qìchē | chuán] 开往伦敦的[火车 | 汽车 | 船]

- (*other uses*)

a cheque for £20 = yìzhāng èrshí yīngbàng de zhīpiào 一张20英镑的支票
what is the Chinese for 'badger'? = Hànyǔ 'badger' zěnme shuō? 汉语'badger'怎么说?
we went [for a swim | for a run | for a walk...] = wǒmen qù [yóuyǒng | pǎobù | sànbù...] 我们去[游泳 | 跑步 | 散步...]

forbid *verb*
= jìnzhǐ 禁止, bùxǔ 不许
to forbid someone to go out = bùxǔ mǒurén chūqu 不许某人出去
smoking is forbidden = jìnzhǐ xīyān 禁止吸烟

force
1 *verb*
= qiángpò 强迫, bī 逼
to force someone to leave = qiángpò mǒurén líkāi 强迫某人离开
2 *noun*

- (*strength*) = lì 力, lìliang 力量
- (*influence*) = shìlì 势力
- **by force** = tōngguò wǔlì 通过武力
- **[police | air] force** = [jǐngchá | kōngjūn] [警察 | 空军]

forecast *noun*
= yùbào 预报
the forecast is for rain = yùbào shuō yǒu yǔ 预报说有雨

forehead *noun* ▶ 189
= qián'é 前额

foreign *adjective*
= wàiguó de 外国的

foreigner *noun*
a foreigner = yíge wàiguórén 一个外国人

forest *noun*
a forest = yíge sēnlín 一个森林

forever, for ever *adverb*
= yǒngyuǎn 永远

forget *verb*
= wàng 忘, wàngjì 忘记
to forget about someone = wàngle mǒurén 忘了某人
to forget [to do the shopping | to eat | to call...] = wàngle [mǎi dōngxi | chī fàn | dǎ diànhuà...] 忘了[买东西 | 吃饭 | 打电话...]

forgive *verb*
= yuánliàng 原谅

fork *noun*
a fork = yìbǎ chāzi 一把叉子

form
1 *noun*

- **a form** (*a shape*) = yìzhǒng xíngzhuàng/yàngzi 一种形状/样子
- (*a style*) = yìzhǒng xíngshì/fāngshì 一种形式/方式
- (*a document*) = yìzhāng biǎogé 一张表格
- (*referring to mood or fitness*)

to be in good form = zhuàngtài liánghǎo 状态良好

- (*British English*) (*a year in a school*)

a form = yíge niánjí 一个年级
to be in the sixth form = zài (zhōngxué) liù niánjí 在(中学)六年级
2 *verb*

- (*to create, to make*) = xíngchéng 形成, gòuchéng 构成

to form a circle = xíngchéng yíge yuánquān 形成一个圆圈

- (*to establish, set up*) = zǔchéng 组成, jiànlì 建立

F

Forms of address (Miss, Mr., Mrs.)

The order of the given name, surname and title in Chinese

Unlike the order in English names, Chinese surnames precede given names. For example, in the Chinese name below, **Wáng** 王 is the surname and **Tiěshān** 铁山 is the given name:

Wáng Tiěshān 王铁山

In Chinese, the title follows the surname or the full name:

Mr. Wang	= Wáng xiānsheng 王先生
Mr. Tieshan Wang	= Wáng Tiěshān xiānsheng 王铁山先生

Titles frequently used in addressing people

Miss Jones	= Qióngsī xiǎojiě 琼斯小姐
Mr. Smith	= Shǐmìsī xiānsheng 史密斯先生
Mrs. Davis	= Dàiwéisī tàitai 戴维斯太太
Ms. Lambert	= Lánbótè nǚshì 兰伯特女士
Professor Hull	= Hè'ěr jiàoshòu 赫尔教授
Dr. Brown (medical)	= Bùlǎng dàifu 布朗大夫
Dr. Brown (academic)	= Bùlǎng bóshì 布朗博士

Titles frequently used in addressing people in China

Comrade Wang	= Wáng tóngzhì 王同志
Teacher Wang	= Wáng lǎoshī 王老师
Master (master worker) Wang	= Wáng shīfu 王师傅
Master (schoolmaster) Wang	= Wáng xiàozhǎng 王校长
Manager Wang	= Wáng jīnglǐ 王经理

The following two forms are also frequently used by Chinese friends and colleagues in addressing each other:

Little Wang (to a person younger than the speaker)	= Xiǎo Wáng 小王
Old Wang (to a person older than the speaker)	= Lǎo Wáng 老王

---

formal *adjective*
- (*describing language*) = guīfàn 规范
- **to wear formal clothes** (*for the evening*) = chuān wǎnlǐfú 穿晚礼服
- (*official*) = zhèngshì 正式

former *adjective*
- (*before in time, past*) = yǐqián de 以前的, cóngqián de 从前的
- (*the first of the two mentioned*) = qiánzhě 前者

fortnight *noun* ▶ 412 (*British English*)
a fortnight = liǎngge xīngqī 两个星期

fortunately *adverb*
= xìngyùn de shì 幸运的是, xìngkuī 幸亏

fortune *noun*
- **a fortune** = yìbǐ cáichǎn 一笔财产
  to make a fortune = fā yìbǐ cái 发一笔财
- **to tell someone's fortune** = gěi mǒurén suàn mìng 给某人算命

forty *number* ▶ 170, ▶ 204
forty = sìshí 四十

forward
1 *adverb*
= xiàngqián 向前
to step forward = xiàngqián zǒu 向前走
2 *verb*
to forward a letter to someone = bǎ yìfēng xìn zhuǎn gěi mǒurén 把一封信转给某人

found *verb*
- (*to found an organisation, a system, an institution*) = jiànlì 建立, chuànglì 创立
- (*to found a building, a city*) = jiànshè 建设, jiànzhù 建筑

fountain *noun*
a fountain = yíge pēnquán 一个喷泉

four *number* ▶ 170, ▶ 204
= sì 四

fourteen *number* ▶ 170, ▶ 204
= shísì 十四

fourteenth *number*
- (*in a series*) = dìshísì 第十四
- (*in dates*) ▶ 218
  the fourteenth of July = qīyuè shísì hào 七月十四号

fourth *number*
- (*in a series*) = dìsì 第四
- (*in dates*) ▶ 218
  the fourth of July = qīyuè sì hào 七月四号

fox *noun*
a fox = yìzhī húli 一只狐狸

fragile *adjective*
- (*easily broken*) = yìsuì 易碎
- (*delicate, frail*) = cuìruò 脆弱

frame *noun*
a frame (*a structure*) = yíge gòujià 一个构架, yíge jiégòu 一个结构
(*a case made to enclose, border, or support something*) = yíge kuàngzi 一个框子, yíge kuàngjià 一个框架
(*the body*) = yíge shēnqū 一个身躯

France *noun*
= Fǎguó 法国

frank *adjective*
= tǎnshuài 坦率, zhíshuài 直率

freckle *noun*
a freckle = yíge quèbān 一个雀斑

free
1 *adjective*
- (*costing nothing*) = miǎnfèi 免费
  he gets free medical treatment = tā jiēshòu miǎnfèi zhìliáo 他接受免费治疗
- (*independent, not bound by rules*) = zìyóu 自由
  free trade = zìyóu màoyì 自由贸易
  he is free to do what he likes = tā kěyǐ zuò rènhé tā xiǎng zuò de shì 他可以做任何他想做的事
- (*not occupied, available*) = yǒu kòngr 有空儿, kòngxián 空闲
  are you free on Monday? = nǐ xīngqīyī yǒu kòngr ma? 你星期一有空儿吗?

2 *verb*
to free the prisoners = shìfàng qiūfàn 释放囚犯

freedom *noun*
= zìyóu 自由

freeway *noun* (*US English*)
a freeway = yìtiáo (gāosù)gōnglù 一条(高速)公路

freeze *verb*
- (*if it is water, river*) = jiébīng 结冰
  the river froze = hé jiébīng le 河结冰了
- (*to freeze something*) = dòng 冻
  to freeze the chicken in the freezer = bǎ jī fàng zài bīngxiāng li dòngqǐlai 把鸡放在冰箱里冻起来
  the ground was frozen hard = dì dòng de hěn yìng 地冻得很硬
- (*to stop as if by cold*) = dòngjié 冻结
  to freeze the prices = dòngjié wùjià 冻结物价
- **to freeze to death** = dòngsǐ 冻死

freezer *noun*
a freezer = yíge lěngdòngguì 一个冷冻柜, yíge lěngcángguì 一个冷藏柜

freezing *adjective*
= hěn lěng 很冷, jí lěng 极冷
it's freezing = tiānqì hěn lěng 天气很冷

French ▶ 288
1 *adjective*
= Fǎguó de 法国的
2 *noun*
- (*the people*) = Fǎguórén 法国人
- (*the language*) = Fǎyǔ 法语, Fǎwén 法文

French fries *noun* (*US English*)
= yóuzhá tǔdòutiáo 油炸土豆条

fresh *adjective*
- (*when describing food, vegetables, fruits, fish*) = xīnxiān 新鲜
- (*new*) = xīn 新
  fresh paint = xīn (shuā) de yóuqī 新(刷)的油漆

Friday *noun* ▶ 218
Friday = xīngqīwǔ 星期五

fridge *noun*
a fridge = yíge bīngxiāng 一个冰箱

fried *adjective*
= yóujiān de 油煎的, yóuzhá de 油炸的

fried egg *noun*
a fried egg = yíge jiān jīdàn 一个煎鸡蛋

friend *noun*
a friend = yíge péngyou 一个朋友
to make friends with someone = hé mǒurén jiāo péngyou 和某人交朋友

friendly *adjective*
= yǒuhǎo 友好

fright *noun*
to get a fright = chī yìjīng 吃一惊, xià yítiào 吓一跳
to give someone a fright = xià mǒurén yítiào 吓某人一跳, shǐ mǒurén chī yìjīng 使某人吃一惊

frightened *adjective*
to be frightened = hàipà 害怕

fringe *noun*
- (*of the hair*) (*British English*) = liǔhǎir 刘海儿
- (*border*) = biānyuán 边缘, biānyán 边沿

frog *noun*
a frog = yìzhī qīngwā 一只青蛙

from *preposition*

> **!** *There are many verbs which involve the use of* from, *like* borrow from, escape from, *etc. For translations, look up the entries at* borrow, escape, *etc.*

- (*indicating a location, a place, a time, etc., which is the starting point of an activity, journey, period of time, etc.*) = cóng 从
  the boy from London = cóng Lúndūn lái de nánháir 从伦敦来的男孩儿
  where did she come from? = tā cóng nǎr lái? 她从哪儿来?
  to come back from the office = cóng bàngōngshì huílai 从办公室回来
  the shop is open from eight to six = zhège shāngdiàn cóng bā diǎn dào liù diǎn kāimén 这个商店从八点到六点开门
  from Monday to Saturday = cóng xīngqīyī dào xīngqīliù 从星期一到星期六
  from April on = cóng sìyuè qǐ 从四月起
- (*indicating a location, a place, an object from which distance is stated*) = lí 离
  we live ten minutes from the city centre = wǒmen zhù de dìfang lí shì zhōngxīn yǒu shí fēnzhōng de lù 我们住的地方离市中心有十分钟的路
  my house is not very far from the seaside = wǒ jiā lí hǎibiān bú tài yuǎn 我家离海边不太远
- (*indicating a basis on which a point of view, an assumption, an idea is formed*) = gēnjù 根据
  from this information, I think we should let him go = gēnjù zhège xìnxī, wǒ rènwéi wǒmen yīnggāi ràng tā qù 根据这个信息, 我认为我们应该让他去
  from his point of view = gēnjù tāde guāndiǎn 根据他的观点

front
1 *noun*
- (*of a building*) = qiánmian 前面, zhèngmiàn 正面
  my room is at the front of the house = wǒde fángjiān zài fángzi de zhèngmiàn 我的房间在房子的正面
- (*of a car, a train or queue*) = qiánmian 前面
  at the front of the bus = zài qìchē qiánmian 在汽车前面

2 in front of = zài...qiánmian 在... 前面

front door *noun*
= qián mén 前门

front page *noun*
- (*of a newspaper*) = tóubǎn 头版
- (*of a book*) = biāotí yè 标题页

front seat *noun*
= qiánpái zuòwèi 前排座位

frost *noun*
= shuāngdòng 霜冻, shuāng 霜

frozen *adjective*
- (*turned solid by fall of temperature*) = bīngdòngle de 冰冻了的
- (*stopped as if by cold*) = dòngjiē de 冻结的

fruit *noun*
a piece of fruit = yíkuài shuǐguǒ 一块水果
he likes fruit = tā xǐhuan shuǐguǒ 他喜欢水果

frustrated *adjective*
= huīxīn 灰心, huīxīn sàngqì 灰心丧气

fry *verb*
= (yóu)jiān (油)煎, (yóu)zhá (油)炸

frying pan *noun*
a frying pan = yíge jiānguō 一个煎锅

full *adjective*
- (*of people*) = jǐmǎn 挤满
  the streets were full of people = jiē shang jǐmǎnle rén 街上挤满了人
- (*describing a flight, a hotel, or maximum possible marks in an examination*) = mǎn 满
  to get full marks = dé mǎn fēn 得满分
- (*unable to eat any more*) = bǎo 饱
  I'm full = wǒ bǎo le 我饱了, wǒ chībǎo le 我吃饱了
- (*complete*) = quán 全
  to pay the full fare = fù quán fèi 付全费
  his full name = tāde quán míng 他的全名
  at full speed = quán sù 全速

full-time
1 *adjective*
= zhuānzhí 专职, quánrì 全日
a full-time job = yíge zhuānzhí gōngzuò 一个专职工作
2 *adverb*
to work full-time = quánrì gōngzuò 全日工作

fumes *noun*
- (*smoke*) = yān 烟
- (*of wine, chemicals*) = qì 气, qìwèi 气味

fun *noun*
- (*amusement*) = hǎowánr 好玩儿, yǒuqù 有趣
  it's fun = zhè zhēn hǎowánr 这真好玩儿
  skiing is fun = huáxuě hěn yǒuqù 滑雪很有趣
  she is fun = tā hěn yǒuqù 她很有趣
- **to have fun** = wán de tòngkuai 玩得痛快

function
1 *noun*
- (*the role played by a part in a system*) = yíge gōngnéng 一个功能, yíge zuòyòng 一个作用
- (*duty peculiar to any office*) = yíxiàng zhínéng 一项职能, yíxiàng zhízé 一项职责

2 *verb*
- (*to work*) = gōngzuò 工作
- (*to perform a function*) = qǐ zuòyòng 起作用

funeral *noun*
a funeral = yíge zànglǐ 一个葬礼

funfair *noun* (*British English*)
a funfair = yíge yóulèhuì 一个游乐会

funny *adjective*
- (*amusing*) = hǎowánr 好玩儿, yǒuqù 有趣
- (*odd*) = gǔguài 古怪, qíguài 奇怪

fur *noun*
- (*on an animal's coat*) = pímáo 皮毛
- (*on a garment*) = máopí 毛皮, pízi 皮子

furious *adjective*
- (*describing a person*) = dànù 大怒, kuángnù 狂怒
- (*violent*) = měngliè 猛烈, jùliè 剧烈

furniture *noun*
= jiājù 家具
a piece of furniture = yíjiàn jiājù 一件家具

further *adverb*
- (*when talking about distance*) = gèng yuǎn 更远
  he lives further away from the school = tā zhù de lí xuéxiào gèng yuǎn 他住的离学校更远
- (*in addition, to a greater degree*) = jìn yíbù de 进一步地
  to improve quality further = jìn yíbù de tígāo zhìliàng 进一步地提高质量

fuss *noun*
to make a fuss about something = yīnwèi mǒushì dàjīng-xiǎoguài 因为某事大惊小怪

future
1 *noun*
- (*prospects*) = qiántú 前途
- (*time to come*) = jiānglái 将来, jīnhòu 今后

in (the) future = jiānglái 将来, jīnhòu 今后

2 *adjective*
= jiānglái de 将来的, wèilái de 未来的

my future wife = wǒ wèilái de tàitai 我未来的太太

Gg

gallery *noun*
- (*a building for displaying works of art*)
  a gallery = yíge měishùguǎn 一个美术馆, yíge huàláng 一个画廊
- (*a long passage*)
  a gallery = yìtiáo chángláng 一条长廊

game *noun*
- (*a contest for recreation*) = yóuxì 游戏
  a game = yíge yóuxì 一个游戏
- (*in sport*) = bǐsài 比赛
  a game = yìchǎng bǐsài 一场比赛
  a game of [football | tennis] = yìchǎng [zúqiú | wǎngqiú] bǐsài 一场[足球 | 网球] 比赛

games *noun*
= yùndònghuì 运动会

the Olympic Games = Àolínpíkè Yùndònghuì 奥林匹克运动会

gang *noun*
a gang (*a group of friends, young people*) = yìhuǒ 一伙
(*of criminals*) = yìbāng 一帮

gap *noun*
- **a gap** (*in a fence or hedge*) = yíge quēkǒu 一个缺口, yíge huōkǒu 一个豁口
  (*between buildings, cars*) = yíduàn jiàngé 一段间隔, yíduàn jùlí 一段距离
  (*a period of time*) = yíduàn jiàngé 一段间隔

garage *noun*
a garage (*for keeping a car*) = yíge chēkù 一个车库
(*for fixing a car*) = yíge qìchē xiūlǐchǎng 一个汽车修理厂

garbage *noun* (*US English*)
= lājī 垃圾

garden

1 *noun*
a garden = yíge huāyuán 一个花园

2 *verb*
= cōngshì yuányì 从事园艺

gardener *noun* ▶ 344
a gardener = yíge yuánlín gōngrén 一个园林工人

gardening *noun*
= yuányì 园艺

garlic *noun*
= suàn 蒜, dàsuàn 大蒜

gas *noun*
- (*for cooking, heating*) = méiqì 煤气
- (*US English*) (*gasoline*) = qìyóu 汽油

gas station *noun* (*US English*)
a gas station = yíge jiāyóuzhàn 一个加油站

gate *noun*
a gate = yíge mén 一个门, yíge dàmén 一个大门

gather *verb*
- (*to come together*) = jíhé 集合, jùjí 聚集
- (*to collect*) = sōují 搜集, shōují 收集
  to gather information = sōují zīliào 搜集资料
- (*to pick up*) = cǎijí 采集
  to gather fruit = cǎijí shuǐguǒ 采集水果

gay *adjective*
= tóngxìngliàn 同性恋

gear *noun*
- (*in a car or bus, on a bike*)
  a gear = yíge dǎng 一个挡
- (*equipment*) = yòngjù 用具
  fishing gear = diàoyú yòngjù 钓鱼用具
- (*clothes*)
  my football gear = wǒde zúqiú fú 我的足球服
  your swimming gear = nǐde yóuyǒng yī 你的游泳衣

general

1 *noun*
a general = yíge jiāngjūn 一个将军

2 *adjective*
- (*common, not special*) = yìbān 一般, pǔtōng 普通

G

Get

A multi-purpose verb

Chinese has no single, multi-purpose equivalent to the word *get* in English. As a result, it is often necessary to select different Chinese words to translate **get**, or no word at all, depending on the meaning of the sentence.

Main senses

When changing from one state (of mind) to another

It is often unnecessary to translate **get** in the various combinations of **to get + adjective**. In this case, Chinese employs a sentence-final particle **le** 了 to indicate the change of state.

to get old/angry/hot/jealous = lǎo le / shēngqì le / rè le / jìdu le 老了/生气了/热了/忌妒了

When asking or telling

The translations **ràng** 让 and **jiào** 叫 are helpful here:

__get__ him to call me = **jiào** tā gěi wǒ dǎ diànhuà 叫他给我打电话
I'll __get__ her to help me = wǒ yào **ràng** tā bāngzhù wǒ 我要让她帮助我

When persuading

The translation of **quàn** 劝 is helpful here:

__get__ him to see a doctor = **quàn** tā qù kàn yīshēng 劝他去看医生

When getting things done by someone else

The construction **qǐng rén** 请人 **+ verb** is useful here:

to __get__ the car __cleaned__ = **qǐng rén qīngxǐ** chē 请人清洗车
to __get__ a TV __repaired__ = **qǐng rén xiūlǐ** diànshìjī 请人修理电视机

But:

to __get__ one's hair __cut__ = **lǐfà** 理发

When "to get" means to obtain

to __get__ (or __buy__) someone a present = gěi mǒurén **mǎi** ge lǐwù 给某人买个礼物
I __got__ (or __found__) a job in Taiwan = wǒ zài Táiwān **zhǎodàole** yíge gōngzuò 我在台湾找到了一个工作

When "to get" means to receive

If it is a material object, the best translation is **shōudào** 收到:

we __got__ a letter from Mark = wǒmen **shōudào** Mǎkè de yìfēng xìn 我们收到马克的一封信

If it is not a material object, the best translation is **dédào** 得到

to __get__ good marks = **dédào** hǎo fēnshù 得到好分数
to __get__ a promotion = **dédào** tíshēng 得到提升

When cooking

A translation which will work well is **zhǔnbèi** 准备:

to __get__ dinner = **zhǔnbèi** fàn 准备饭

With illnesses

In this context, **dé** 得 or **huàn** 患 is useful:

to __get__ measles = **dé** mázhěn 得麻疹
to __get__ a cold = **huàn** gǎnmào 患感冒

When using transport

The most useful translations are **chéng** 乘 and **zuò** 坐:

*we can **get** the bus*	= wǒmen kěyǐ **chéng** qìchē 我们可以乘汽车
*to **get** a taxi to the station*	= **zuò** chūzūchē qù chēzhàn 坐出租车去车站

▶ To find translations for other expressions using **get** — **to get sick**, **to get a surprise**, **to get better**, etc. — look up the entries at **sick**, **surprise**, **better**, etc.

▶ You will also find translations for **phrasal verbs** using **get** (**get down**, **get away**, **get on**, **get up**) listed separately in the dictionary.

G

general knowledge = yìbān zhīshi 一般知识, chángshí 常识
- (*whole or all*) = quántǐ 全体
  a general meeting = yícì quántǐ dàhuì 一次全体大会
- (*vague*) = dàtǐ 大体, lóngtǒng 笼统
  a general idea = yíge dàtǐ de xiǎngfǎ 一个大体的想法
- (*widespread*) = pǔbiàn 普遍
  a matter of general concern = yíge pǔbiàn guānxīn de wèntí 一个普遍关心的问题

3 in general = dàtǐshang 大体上, yìbān shuōlái 一般说来

generation *noun*
a generation = yídài rén 一代人

generous *adjective*
= kāngkǎi 慷慨, dàfang 大方

Geneva *noun*
Geneva = Rìnèiwǎ 日内瓦

genius *noun*
a genius = yíge tiāncái 一个天才

gentle *adjective*
- (*when describing manners or actions*) = wényǎ 文雅, wēnróu 温柔
- (*when describing a person's disposition*) = wēnróu 温柔
- (*amiable*) = yǒushàn 友善

gentleman *noun*
- (*a polite term used for men in general*)
  a gentleman = yíwèi xiānsheng 一位先生
- (*a man of refined manners*)
  a gentleman = yíwèi shēnshì 一位绅士

geography *noun*
= dìlí 地理

germ *noun*
= xìjūn 细菌

German ▶ 288
1 *adjective*
= Déguó de 德国的
2 *noun*
- (*the people*) = Déguórén 德国人
- (*the language*) = Déyǔ 德语, Déwén 德文

Germany *noun*
= Déguó 德国

get *verb*
▶ *See the boxed note on* get **▶ 254** *for more information and examples.*

get away
- (*to escape*) = táotuō 逃脱
- **he won't get away with it** = tā zuò de zhèjiàn shì kěndìng huì bèi fājué 他做的这件事肯定会被发觉

get back
- (*to come back*) = huílai 回来
- (*to go back*) = huíqu 回去
- (*to have back after being stolen*) = zhǎohuílai 找回来
  I got my bike back = wǒ bǎ zìxíngchē zhǎohuílai le 我把自行车找回来了
  (*to have back after being borrowed*) = huánhuílai 还回来
  he's got his book back = tāde shū huánhuílai le 他的书还回来了

get down
- (*to go down*) = xiàqu 下去
- (*to come down*) = xiàlai 下来
  can you get down from the tree? = nǐ néng cóng shù shang xiàlai ma? 你能从树上下来吗?
- (*to take down*) = náxiàlai 拿下来
  I got the box down from the shelf = wǒ bǎ hézi cóng jiàzi shang náxiàlai 我把盒子从架子上拿下来
- (*to be depressed over something*) = shǐ...jǔsàng 使... 沮丧
  it gets him down = zhè shǐ tā hěn jǔsàng 这使他很沮丧

get in
- (*to enter*) = jìnrù 进入
- (*to arrive*) = dàodá 到达

get off
- (*to leave a bus or train*) = xià chē 下车

  I'm getting off at the next stop = wǒ xià yi zhàn xià chē 我下一站下车

  he fell as he was getting off the train = tā xià huǒchē de shíhou shuāidǎo le 他下火车的时候摔倒了
- (*to remove*) = bǎ...nòngxiàlai 把...弄下来

  to get a stain off = bǎ wūdiǎn nòngxiàlai 把污点弄下来

get on
- (*to climb on board a bus or train*) = shàng chē 上车

  to get on the bus = shàng qìchē 上汽车
- **to get on well** = xiāngchǔ de hěn hǎo 相处得很好

  I get on well with her = wǒ gēn tā xiāngchǔ de hěn hǎo 我跟她相处得很好
- (*in polite enquiries*)

  how did you get on? = nǐ guò de zěnmeyàng? 你过得怎么样?

  how is she getting on at school? = tā zài xuéxiào zěnmeyàng? 她在学校怎么样?

get out
- **she got out of the building** = tā cóng dàlóu li chūlai 她从大楼里出来
- **to get the furniture out of the house** = bǎ jiājù cóng fángzi li náchūlai 把家具从房子里拿出来

get over

to get over a shock = cóng zhènjīng zhōng huīfuguòlai 从震惊中恢复过来

get through to

to get through to someone = chuándào mǒurén 传到某人

get together = jùjí 聚集, jùhuì 聚会

get up

when do you get up? = nǐ shénme shíhou qǐchuáng? 你什么时候起床?

ghost *noun*

a ghost = yíge guǐ 一个鬼

gift *noun*
- (*a present*) = yíge lǐwù 一个礼物
- (*an ability*)

  a gift = tiānfù 天赋

  to have a gift for languages = yǒu yǔyán tiānfù 有语言天赋

ginger

1 *noun*

(*a vegetable used for spices*) = jiāng 姜

2 *adjective*

= jiānghuángsè de 姜黄色的

ginger hair (*British English*) = jiānghuángsè de tóufa 姜黄色的头发

girl *noun*

a girl = yíge nǚhái(zi) 一个女孩(子), yíge gūniang 一个姑娘

girlfriend *noun*

a girlfriend = yíge nǚpéngyou 一个女朋友

give *verb*

> **!** *For translations of expressions like* to give someone a lift, to give someone an injection, to give someone a fright, *etc, look up the entries* lift, injection, fright.

- **to give** = gěi 给

  to give someone a book = gěi mǒurén yìběn shū 给某人一本书

  I gave him the photos = wǒ bǎ nàxiē zhàopiàn gěile tā 我把那些照片给了他
- (*to offer as a gift*) = sònggěi 送给

  to give someone a present = sònggěi mǒurén yíge lǐwù 送给某人一个礼物
- **to give someone a message** = (chuán)gěi mǒurén yíge kǒuxìn (传)给某人一个口信

give away
- (*to make a present of ...*) = sònggěi biéren ... 送给别人...
- **to give away a secret** = xièlòu mìmì 泄漏秘密

give back = huángěi 还给

give in = ràngbù 让步, qūfú 屈服

give off

to give off fumes = màochū yān lai 冒出烟来

give out

to give out the exercise books = fēnfā liànxíběn 分发练习本

give up
- (*to stop*)

  to give up smoking = jiè yān 戒烟

to give up the idea of working abroad = fàngqì qù guówài gōngzuò de xiǎngfǎ 放弃去国外工作的想法
- to give oneself up to the police = xiàng jǐngchá zìshǒu 向警察自首

glad *adjective*
= gāoxìng 高兴

glass *noun*
a glass = yíge bōlibēi 一个玻璃杯
a glass of water = yìbēi shuǐ 一杯水

glasses *noun*
= yǎnjìng 眼镜

glove *noun*
a pair of gloves = yífù shǒutào 一副手套

glow *verb*
= fāguāng 发光

glue
1 *noun*
= jiāo 胶
2 *verb*
= zhān 粘

go *verb*
▶ *See the boxed note on* go ▶ 258 *for more information and examples.*
go across = chuānguò 穿过
go after
- (*physically*) = zhuī 追
- (*when talking about pursuing an abstract goal*) = zhuīqiú 追求

go ahead
- (*if it's an event*) = zhàocháng jìnxíng 照常进行
  the concert's going ahead = yīnyuèhuì jiāng zhàocháng jìnxíng 音乐会将照常进行
- (*if it's a person*)
  go ahead (*when about to do something*) = gàn ba 干吧
  (*when about to say something*) = shuō ba 说吧
  (*when about to walk somewhere*) = zǒu ba 走吧

go around = **go round**
go around with = **go round with**
go away = zǒu 走, líkāi 离开
go away! = nǐ zǒukāi! 你走开! gǔn! 滚!✖
go back = huí 回, huíqu 回去
Gary went back to London = Jiālǐ huí Lúndūn le 加里回伦敦了
to go back to school = huíqu shàngxué 回去上学
to go back to work = huíqu gōngzuò 回去工作
go by = guòqu 过去
go by... = lùguò... 路过...
go down
- (*if it's quality, a price, a salary*) = xiàjiàng 下降
- (*if it's a person*)
  she went down to have a look = tā xiàqu kànkàn 她下去看看
  they went down the hill = tāmen xià shān le 他们下山了
- (*if it's the sun or moon*) = luòxia 落下
- (*if it's a computer*) = huài le 坏了

go in = jìnqu 进去
he didn't go in = tā méi jìnqu 他没进去
go off
- (*to explode*) = bàozhà 爆炸
- (*to ring*) = xiǎng 响
- (*to leave*) = líqù 离去, zǒudiào 走掉
- (*when talking about food becoming bad*) = biànhuài 变坏
  the milk will go off = niúnǎi huì biànhuài 牛奶会变坏
- (*to be switched off*) = guāndiào 关掉, tíngdiào 停掉

go on
- (*to continue*) = jìxù 继续
  to go on talking = jìxù jiǎnghuà 继续讲话
- (*to happen*)
  what's going on? = fāshēngle shénme shì? 发生了什么事?
- (*to keep talking*)
  he goes on (and on) about his work = tā yígejìnr de tán tāde gōngzuò 他一个劲儿地谈他的工作
- (*to be switched on*) = dǎkāi 打开

go out
- (*to leave the house*) = chūqu 出去
  are you going out this evening? = jīntiān wǎnshang nǐ chūqu ma? 今天晚上你出去吗?
- (*as with a boyfriend, a girlfriend*) = chūqu tán péngyou 出去谈朋友
  to go out with someone = gēn mǒurén chūqu tán péngyou 跟某人出去谈朋友

✖an offensive word

Go

▶ You will find translations for phrasal verbs like **go away**, **go back**, **go round**, etc. listed separately in the dictionary.

▶ For translations of expressions like **I'm going to leave** / **go to London** / **learn to drive**, see the entry **going**.

Getting from A to B

Generally **go** is translated by **qù 去**:

we went to his house	= wǒmen qù tā jiā 我们去他家
to go to Germany|to Japan	= qù Déguó/Rìběn 去德国/日本
to go swimming|fishing	= qù yóuyǒng/diàoyú 去游泳/钓鱼
to go for a coffee|for a walk	= qù hē kāfēi/sànbù 去喝咖啡/散步
to go to the dentist's|the doctor's	= qù kàn yá/bìng 去看牙/病

But:

to go to town	= jìn chéng 进城
to go to school	= shàngxué 上学
to go home	= huí jiā 回家
to go outside	= chūqu 出去
to go upstairs	= shàng lóu 上楼

Go meaning *to become*

This can be translated as **biàn 变**, but the translation is usually unnecessary in Chinese. The sentence-final particle **le 了** indicates a change of state:

her face went pale|red	= tāde liǎn (biàn) bái/hóng le 她的脸(变)白/红了
he has gone blind	= tāde yǎnjīng xiā le 他的眼睛瞎了
the light went red	= dēng (biàn) hóng le 灯(变)红了
he won't go crazy	= tā bú huì fāfēng 他不会发疯

In polite inquiries

how's it going?	= zěnmeyàng? 怎么样?
everything's going very well	= yíqiè dōu hěn hǎo 一切都很好
how did the exam go?	= kǎoshì zěnmeyàng? 考试怎么样?

Talking about time, money, food...

the time goes so quickly	= shíjiān guò de zhēn kuài 时间过得真快
the money's gone	= qián huāwán le 钱花完了
the bread's gone	= miànbāo chīwán le 面包吃完了
the petrol's gone	= qìyóu yòngwán le 汽油用完了

Describing how (and if) something works

is the machine going?	= jīqì gōngzuò ma? 机器工作吗?
it's still not going	= réngrán bù gōngzuò 仍然不工作
to get the heating going	= shǐ nuǎnqì bù tíng de gōngzuò 使暖气不停地工作

- (*to be switched off as a fire, to stop burning*) = xīmiè 熄灭

go over

- (*to check*) = jiǎnchá 检查

  to go over some grammar = jiǎnchá yìxiē yǔfǎ 检查一些语法

- (*to revise*) = fùxí 复习

go round

- (*British English*) (*to call on*) = shùnbiàn qù 顺便去

  to go round to see someone = shùnbiàn qù kànwàng mǒurén 顺便去看望某人

- (*to walk around, to visit*) = guàng 逛

  to go round the museums = guàng bówùguǎn 逛博物馆

  to go round the shops = guàng shāngdiàn 逛商店

- (*to be enough*)

  is there enough bread to go round? = miànbāo gòu fēn de ma? 面包够分的吗?

go round with

- (*British English*) (*to spend time with*)

  to go round with someone = gēn mǒurén jiāowǎng 跟某人交往

go through

- (*to have, to live through*)

  to go through a difficult time = jīnglì yíduàn kùnnan shíqī 经历一段困难时期

- (*to search*) = sōuchá 搜查
- (*to check*) = jiǎnchá 检查

go together = xiāngpèi 相配

the skirt and blouse go well together = qúnzi hé chènshān hěn xiāngpèi 裙子和衬衫很相配

go up

- (*if it's a person*) = shàng 上

  he went up the stairs = tā shàng lǒu le 他上楼了

  to go up to the top of the hill = shàng shāndǐng 上山顶

- (*if it's a price, a salary*) = zhǎng 涨

go with = yǔ...xiāngpèi 与... 相配

the trousers don't really go with the jacket = kùzi yǔ jiákè bù xiāngpèi 裤子与夹克不相配

goal *noun*

- (*an end or aim*) = yíge mùdì 一个目的, yíge mùbiāo 一个目标
- (*a score in some ball games*) = yìfēn 一分
- (*in a football field*) = qiúmén 球门

goalkeeper *noun*

a goalkeeper = yíge shǒuményuán 一个守门员

goat *noun*

a goat = yìzhī shānyáng 一只山羊

god *noun*

a god = yíge shén 一个神

God = Shàngdì 上帝

goddaughter *noun*

a goddaughter = yíge jiàonǚ 一个教女

godfather *noun*

a godfather = yíge jiàofù 一个教父

godmother *noun*

a godmother = yíge jiàomǔ 一个教母

godson *noun*

a godson = yíge jiàozǐ 一个教子

going: to be going to

= zhǔnbèi 准备, dǎsuàn 打算

I'm going to [**leave** | **go to Ireland** | **learn to drive...**] = wǒ zhǔnbèi [líkāi | qù Ài'ěrlán | xué kāi chē...] 我准备 [离开 | 去爱尔兰 | 学开车...]

gold

1 *noun*

gold = jīn 金, huángjīn 黄金

2 *adjective*

= jīn de 金的

a gold ring = yíge jīn jièzhi 一个金戒指

goldfish *noun*

a goldfish = yìtiáo jīnyú 一条金鱼

golf *noun* ▶ 390

= gāo'ěrfūqiú 高尔夫球

golf course *noun*

a golf course = yíge gāo'ěrfūqiú chǎng 一个高尔夫球场

good

1 *adjective*

- **good** = hǎo 好

  a good book = yìběn hǎo shū 一本好书

- **to be good at** [**chemistry** | **drawing** | **chess...**] = shàncháng [huàxué | huà huà | xià qí...] 擅长 [化学 | 画画 | 下棋...]
- (*beneficial*) = yǒuyì 有益, yǒu hǎochù 有好处

  exercise is good for you = duànliàn duì nǐ yǒuyì 锻炼对你有益

G

- (*pleasant*)
  I had a good time = wǒ guò de hěn yúkuài 我过得很愉快
- (*healthy*)
  to look good = kànshangqu shēntǐ hěn hǎo 看上去身体很好
  I don't feel too good = wǒ gǎnjué shēntǐ bù tài hǎo 我感觉身体不太好
- (*talking about food*) = hǎochī 好吃
- (*obedient*) = tīnghuà 听话
- (*when expressing gratitude*)
  it's very good of you to let me know = xièxiè nǐ gàosu wǒ 谢谢你告诉我

2 *noun*
it's no good [**shouting** | **crying** | **going there...**] = [hǎn | kū | qù nàr...] méi yǒu yòng [喊 | 哭 | 去哪儿...] 没有用
he is no good at Latin = tāde Lādīngyǔ hěn zāogāo 他的拉丁语很糟糕
the change will do you good = zhège biànhuà huì duì nǐ yǒu hǎochù 这个变化会你有好处

3 *exclamation*
Good heavens! = tiān a! 天啊!
Good for you! = gàn de hǎo! 干得好!

4 for good = yǒngjiǔ 永久, yǒngyuǎn 永远

good afternoon *noun* (also *exclamation*)
(*when meeting*) = xiàwǔ hǎo 下午好
(*when leaving*) = zàijiàn 再见

goodbye *noun* (also *exclamation*)
= zàijiàn 再见

good evening *noun* (also *exclamation*)
= wǎnshang hǎo 晚上好

good-looking *adjective*
= hǎokàn 好看

good morning *noun* (also *exclamation*)
(*when meeting*) = zǎoshang hǎo 早上好
(*when leaving*) = zàijiàn 再见

goodnight *noun* (also *exclamation*)
= wǎn'ān 晚安

goods *noun*
= huòwù 货物

goose *noun*
a goose = yìzhī é 一只鹅

gooseberry *noun*
a gooseberry = yíge cùlì 一个醋栗

gorilla *noun*
a gorilla = yíge dà xīngxing 一个大猩猩

gossip *verb*
- (*to chat*) = xiánliáo 闲聊
- (*to talk in a harmful way*) = sànbù liúyán fēiyǔ 散布流言蜚语

got: to have got *verb*
▶ *See the boxed note on* **get ▶ 254** *for more information and examples.*
- (*to have*) = yǒu 有
  I've got work to do = wǒ yǒu gōngzuò yào zuò 我有工作要做
- **have you got a cold?** = nǐ gǎnmào le ma? 你感冒了吗?
- (*to be obliged to*)
  to have got to = bìxū 必须, děi 得
  I've got to [**go** | **work** | **buy a new computer...**] = wǒ bìxū [zǒu | gōngzuò | mǎi yìtái xīn jìsuànjī...] 我必须[走 | 工作 | 买一台新计算机...]

government *noun*
a government = yíge zhèngfǔ 一个政府

GP, General Practitioner (medicine) *noun* **▶ 344**
a GP = yíge jiātíng yīshēng 一个家庭医生

grab *verb*
to grab someone by the arm = zhuāzhù mǒurén de gēbo 抓住某人的胳膊
he tried to grab my handbag = tā shìtú qiǎng wǒde shǒutíbāo 他试图抢我的手提包

grade *noun*
- (*a mark on an examination or in a class or course of study*)
  a grade = yíge fēnshù 一个分数
- (*US English*) (*a class in school*)
  a grade = yíge niánjí 一个年级
  he's in the eighth grade = tā zài bā niánjí 他在八年级

grade school *noun* (*US English*)
a grade school = yìsuǒ xiǎoxué 一所小学

gradually *adverb*
= zhújiàn 逐渐, jiànjiàn 渐渐

gram(me) *noun* **▶ 300**
a gram = yí kè 一克

grammar *noun*
= yǔfǎ 语法

grandchild *noun*
a grandchild
(*a son's son*) = yíge sūnzi 一个孙子
(*a son's daughter*) = yíge sūnnǚ 一个孙女
(*a daughter's son*) = yíge wàisūn 一个外孙
(*a daughter's daughter*) = yíge wàisūnnǚ 一个外孙女

granddaughter *noun*
a granddaughter
(*a son's daughter*) = yíge sūnnǚ 一个孙女
(*a daughter's daughter*) = yíge wàisūnnǚ 一个外孙女

grandfather *noun*
(*father's father*) = yéye 爷爷, zǔfù 祖父
(*mother's father*) = wàigōng 外公, lǎoyé 姥爷, wàizǔfù 外祖父

> ! *Note that* zǔfù 祖父, wàizǔfù 外祖父 *cannot be used in direct address.*

grandmother *noun*
(*father's mother*) = nǎinai 奶奶, zǔmǔ 祖母
(*mother's mother*) = wàipó 外婆, lǎolao 姥姥, wàizǔmǔ 外祖母

> ! *Note that* zǔmǔ 祖母, wàizǔmǔ 外祖母 *cannot be used in direct address.*

grandparents *noun*
(*father's parents*) = yéye (he) nǎinai 爷爷(和)奶奶
(*mother's parents*) = lǎolao (he) lǎoyé 姥姥(和)姥爷, wàigōng (he) wàipó 外公(和)外婆

grandson *noun*
a grandson
(*a son's son*) = yíge sūnzi 一个孙子
(*a daughter's son*) = yíge wàisūn 一个外孙

grapefruit *noun*
= pútaoyòu 葡萄柚
a grapefruit = yíge pútaoyòu 一个葡萄柚

grapes *noun*
= pútao 葡萄
a bunch of grapes = yíchuàn pútao 一串葡萄

grass *noun*
= cǎo 草
to cut the grass = gē cǎo 割草

grasshopper *noun*
a grasshopper = yìzhī zhàměng 一只蚱蜢

grateful *adjective*
= gǎnjī 感激, gǎnxiè 感谢
I would be grateful if you could let me know = rúguǒ nǐ néng gàosu wǒ, wǒ huì hěn gǎnjī 如果你能告诉我, 我会很感激

grave *noun*
a grave = yíge fénmù 一个坟墓

gray (*US English*) ▶ **grey**

grease *noun*
= yóuzhī 油脂

greasy *adjective*
= (yǒu) yóuzhī de (有)油脂的

great *adjective*
- (*stressing size, amount*) = dà 大
  a great improvement = yíge hěn dà de tígāo 一个很大的提高
  to have great difficulty reading = yuèdú yǒu hěn dà de kùnnan 阅读有很大的困难
- (*when describing a country or an outstanding person*) = wěidà 伟大
  your great country = nǐmen wěidà de guójiā 你们伟大的国家
- (*showing enthusiasm*)
  that's great! = hǎo jíle! 好极了!
  I had a great time = wǒ wán de fēicháng yúkuài 我玩得非常愉快

Great Britain *noun*
= Dàbùlièdiān 大不列颠

great grandfather *noun*
(*if it's on the father's side*) = zēngzǔfù 曾祖父
(*if it's on the mother's side*) = wàizēngzǔfù 外曾祖父

great grandmother *noun*
(*if it's on the father's side*) = zēngzǔmǔ 曾祖母
(*if it's on the mother's side*) = wàizēngzǔmǔ 外曾祖母

Greece *noun*
= Xīlà 希腊

greedy *adjective*
(*having a voracious appetite*) = tānchī 贪吃, tānzuǐ 贪嘴

G

(*inordinately desirous of increasing one's own share*) = tānlǎn 贪婪, tānxīn 贪心

Greek ▶ 288
1 *adjective*
= Xīlà de 希腊的
2 *noun*
- (*the people*) = Xīlàrén 希腊人
- (*the language*) = Xīlàyǔ 希腊语, Xīlàwén 希腊文

green *adjective*
= lǜ 绿, lǜsè de 绿色的

greenhouse *noun*
a greenhouse = yíge wēnshì 一个温室

grey (*British English*), **gray** (*US English*) *adjective*
- = huī 灰, huīsè de 灰色的
- **grey hair** = bái tóufa 白头发

grill *verb*
= zài kǎojià shang kǎo 在烤架上烤

grin *verb*
= liěkāi zuǐ xiào 咧开嘴笑

grocer *noun* ▶ 344
a grocer = yíge záhuòshāng 一个杂货商

grocery *noun* ▶ 344
a grocery = yíge záhuòdiàn 一个杂货店

ground *noun*
- = dì 地
the ground is hard in winter = dōngtiān dì hěn yìng 冬天地很硬
- (*land used for sports*)
a sports ground = yíge yùndòngchǎng 一个运动场

ground floor *noun* (*British English*)
the ground floor = yīlóu 一楼, yīcéng 一层

group *noun*
- (*a number of persons or things put together in a certain way*)
= zǔ 组
we are divided into 3 groups = wǒmen bèi fēnchéng sān zǔ 我们被分成三组
- (*a crowd*) = qún 群
a group of children = yìqún háizi 一群孩子
- (*a band*)
a rock group = yíge yáogǔnyuèduì 一个摇滚乐队

grow *verb*
- (*to get big, strong, long, tall*) = zhǎng 长, chéngzhǎng 成长
the tree grows fast = shù zhǎng de hěn kuài 树长得很快
- (*as a gardener, a farmer*) = zhòng 种
to grow vegetables = zhòng cài 种菜
- (*to let grow*)
to grow a beard = liú húzi 留胡子
- (*to become*) = biàn de 变得

> **!** *Note that it's often unnecessary to translate* **grow** *here.*

she's grown more cynical = tā (biàn de) gèngjiā wán shì bù gōng 她(变得)更加玩世不恭
he has grown old = tā lǎo le 他老了
- (*to increase*) = zēngzhǎng 增长
the population will grow = rénkǒu jiānghuì zēngzhǎng 人口将会增长
- (*to develop*) = fāzhǎn 发展
that place is growing into a city = nàge dìfang zhèngzài fāzhǎn chéngwéi yíge chéngshì 那个地方正在发展成为一个城市
grow up = zhǎngdà 长大
when I grow up, I want to be a doctor = wǒ zhǎngdà le yào dāng yīshēng 我长大了要当医生

grumble *verb*
= bàoyuàn 抱怨, fā láosāo 发牢骚

guard *noun*
a guard (*in a prison*) = yíge kānshǒu(yuán) 一个看守(员)
(*in a bank or important institution*) = yíge bǎowèi rényuán 一个保卫人员
(*in the army*) = yíge wèibīng 一个卫兵
- **to be on guard** = zhàngǎng 站岗

guard dog *noun*
a guard dog = yìtiáo jǐngquǎn 一条警犬

guess *verb*
= cāi 猜

guest *noun*
a guest = yíwèi kèren 一位客人

guesthouse *noun*
a guesthouse = yíge zhāodàisuǒ 一个招待所

guide
1 *noun*
a guide =
(*for tourists*) = yíge dǎoyóu 一个导游
(*for travellers, mountaineers*) = yíge xiàngdǎo 一个向导

2 *verb*
= yǐndǎo 引导

guide book *noun*
a guide book = yìběn lǚxíng zhǐnán 一本旅行指南

guided tour *noun*
a guided tour = yícì yǒu dǎoyóu de lǚxíng 一次有导游的旅行

guilty *adjective*
- (*having broken the law*) = yǒu zuì de 有罪的
- to feel guilty = gǎndào nèijiù 感到内疚

guitar *noun* ▶ 308
a guitar = yìbǎ jítā 一把吉它

gum *noun*
- (*part of the mouth*) = chǐyín 齿龈, yáchuáng 牙床
- (*for chewing*) = kǒuxiāngtáng 口香糖

gun *noun*
a gun = yìzhī qiāng 一支枪

gym, gymnasium *noun*
a gym/gymnasium = yíge tǐyùguǎn 一个体育馆

gymnastics *noun* ▶ 390
= tǐcāo 体操

Hh

habit *noun*
a habit = yíge xíguàn 一个习惯

hail *noun*
= bīngbáo 冰雹

hair *noun*
- (*on the head*) = tóufa 头发
- (*on the body*) = máo 毛

hairbrush *noun*
a hairbrush = yìbǎ tóufashuā 一把头发刷

hairdresser *noun* ▶ 344
a hairdresser = yíge lǐfàshī 一个理发师

hairdryer *noun*
a hairdryer = yíge chuīfàjī 一个吹发机

hairstyle *noun*
a hairstyle = yìzhǒng fàxíng 一种发.

half ▶ 349
1 *noun*
- a half = yí bàn 一半
  to cut a melon in half = bǎ guā qiēchéng liǎng bàn 把瓜切成两半
- (*in a game*)
  the first half = shàng bàn chǎng 上半场

2 *adjective*
= bàn 半
a half-litre of milk, half a litre of milk = bàn shēng niúnǎi 半升牛奶

3 *pronoun*
- (*when talking about quantities, numbers*) = yí bàn 一半
  to spend half of one's pocket money = huā yí bàn de línghuāqián 花一半的零花钱
  half the pupils speak Japanese = yí bàn de xuésheng shuō Rìyǔ 一半的学生说日语
- (*when talking about time, age*) ▶ 170, ▶ 204 = bàn 半
  an hour and a half = yíge bàn xiǎoshí 一个半小时
  he's three and a half = tā sān suì bàn 他三岁半
  it's half (past) three = sān diǎn bàn 三点半

4 *adverb*
Sam's half Chinese and half English = Sàmǔ shì yí bàn Zhōngguó xuètǒng yí bàn Yīngguó xuètǒng 萨姆是一半中国血统一半英国血统

half hour *noun* ▶ 412
a half hour = bànge xiǎoshí 半个小时

half term *noun* (*British English*)
= qīzhōng jià 期中假

hall *noun*
- (*in a house, an apartment*)
  a hall = yíge tīng 一个厅
- (*for public events*)
  a hall = yíge dàtīng 一个大厅, yíge lǐtáng 一个礼堂

ham *noun*
= huǒtuǐ 火腿

hamburger *noun*
a hamburger = yíge Hànbǎobāo 一个汉堡包

hammer *noun*
a hammer = yìbǎ chuízi 一把锤子

H

hamster *noun*
a hamster = yìzhī cāngshǔ 一只仓鼠

hand
1 *noun*
- (*the part of the body*) ▶ 189 = shǒu 手
he had a pencil in his hand = tā shǒu lǐ názhe yìzhī qiānbǐ 他手里拿着一支铅笔
to hold someone's hand = lāzhe mǒurén de shǒu 拉着某人的手
- (*help*)
a hand = bāngzhù 帮助
- (*on a clock or watch*)
a hand = yìgēn zhǐzhēn 一根指针
- (*when judging a situation or subject*)
on the one hand..., on the other... = yì fāngmiàn..., lìng yì fāngmiàn... 一方面..., 另一方面...

2 *verb*
(*to pass with the hand*) = dì 递, gěi 给

handbag *noun*
a handbag = yíge shǒutíbāo 一个手提包

handball *noun* ▶ 390
= shǒuqiú 手球

handicapped *adjective*
= cánjí 残疾

handkerchief *noun*
a handkerchief = yìtiáo shǒujuàn(r) 一条手绢(儿)

handle *noun*
a handle = yíge bǎshǒu 一个把手

handsome *adjective*
= piàoliang 漂亮, yīngjùn 英俊
a handsome young man = yíge yīngjùn de niánqīngrén 一个英俊的年轻人

handwriting *noun*
= shūxiě 书写, bǐjì 笔迹

handy *adjective*
- (*convenient*) = fāngbiàn 方便
- (*near*) = jìnbian 近便

hang *verb*
- (*on a hook, a coat hanger, a line*) = guà 挂
to hang clothes (up) in a wardrobe = bǎ yīfu guà zài yīguì li 把衣服挂在衣柜里
- (*for drying*) = liàng 晾
to hang clothes on a line = bǎ yīfu liàng zài shéngzi shang 把衣服晾在绳子上
- (*to suspend*) = diào 吊
to hang the light above the table = bǎ dēng diào zài zhuōzi shàng fāng 把灯吊在桌子上方
- (*to kill*) = diàosǐ 吊死, jiǎosǐ 绞死

hang around
- (*walking around doing nothing*) = xiánguàng 闲逛
- (*stay around out of affection or respect*) = jù zài...pángbiān 聚在...旁边
the children hung around the old man = háizimen jù zài lǎorén pángbiān 孩子们聚在老人旁边

hang on to = jǐnjǐn wòzhù 紧紧握住
she was hanging on to the rope = tā jǐnjǐn wòzhù shéngzi 她紧紧握住绳子

hang up
- (*on a hook, a coat hanger, a line*) = guà 挂
to hang up one's coat = guà yīfu 挂衣服
- your coat's hanging up in the hall = nǐde wàiyī guà zài tīng li 你的外衣挂在厅里
- (*for drying*) = liàng 晾
drying clothes = liàng yīfu 晾衣服
- (*when phoning*) = guàduàn 挂断

happen *verb*
- (*to occur*) = fāshēng 发生
what happened? = fāshēng shénme shì le? 发生什么事了?
the accident happened last week = zhège shìgù shì shàng xīngqī fāshēng de 这个事故是上星期发生的
- (*to affect someone*)
what happened to you? = nǐ zěnme le? 你怎么了?
something odd happened to me = wǒ yùdàole yíjiàn qíguài de shì 我遇到了一件奇怪的事
- (*to chance*) = pèngqiǎo 碰巧
I happened to be out when he came = tā lái de shíhou, wǒ pèngqiǎo chūqu le 他来的时候, 我碰巧出去了

happy *adjective*
- (*delighted*) = gāoxìng 高兴
  to make someone happy = shǐ mǒurén gāoxìng 使某人高兴
  they were happy to receive your letter = tāmen hěn gāoxìng shōudào nǐde xìn 他们很高兴收到你的信
- (*content*) = mǎnyì 满意
  he's happy with the language course = tā duì yǔyán kè hěn mǎnyì 他对语言课很满意
- (*in greetings*) = kuàilè 快乐
  Happy Birthday! = Shēngri kuàilè! 生日快乐!
  Happy New Year! = Xīnnián kuàilè! 新年快乐!

hard
1 *adjective*
- (*firm, stiff*) = yìng 硬
  the ground is hard = dì hěn yìng 地很硬
- (*difficult*) = nán 难
  a hard question = yíge hěn nán de wèntí 一个很难的问题
  it's hard to explain this problem = hěn nán jiěshì zhège wèntí 很难解释这个问题
- (*harsh, tough*)
  we were having a hard time during the war = zhànzhēng qījiān wǒmen guòzhe jiānnán de rìzi 战争期间我们过着艰难的日子
- (*severe*)
  it's a hard blow to her = zhè duì tā shì ge chénzhòng de dǎjī 这对她是个沉重的打击

2 *adverb*
- (*diligently*) = nǔlì 努力
  to work hard = nǔlì gōngzuò 努力工作
- (*severely*)
  it's raining hard = yǔ xià de hěn dà 雨下得很大

hardly *adverb*
- (*not quite*) = bú tài 不太
  I hardly know them = wǒ bú tài rènshi tāmen 我不太认识他们
- (*scarcely*) = jīhū...bù 几乎... 不, jiǎnzhí...bù 简直... 不
  she could hardly recognize me = tā jīhū rèn bù chū wǒ lai le 她几乎认不出我来了

hardware *noun*
  hardware (*for computers*) = (jìsuànjī) yìngjiàn (计算机)硬件

hard-working *adjective*
  = qínfèn 勤奋, nǔlì 努力

hare *noun*
  a hare = yìzhī yětù 一只野兔

harm *verb*
  to harm someone = shānghài mǒurén 伤害某人
  to harm the environment = sǔnhài huánjìng 损害环境

harmful *adjective*
  = yǒuhài 有害

harmless *adjective*
  = wúhài 无害

harp *noun* ▶ 308
  a harp = yíjià shùqín 一架竖琴

harvest *noun*
  = shōuhuò 收获, shōuchéng 收成

hat *noun*
  a hat = yìdǐng màozi 一顶帽子

hate *verb*
- (*to feel a strong dislike for*) = bù xǐhuan 不喜欢
  she hates pork = tā bù xǐhuan zhūròu 她不喜欢猪肉
- (*to feel hatred for*) = hèn 恨
  to hate somebody = hèn mǒurén 恨某人

hatred *noun*
  = (zēng)hèn (憎)恨

have
1 *verb*
  ▶ *See the boxed note on* **have** ▶ 266 *for more information and examples.*
- (*to possess or be in a special relation to*) = yǒu 有
  she doesn't have much money = tā méi yǒu hěn duō qián 她没有很多钱
  they have three children = tāmen yǒu sānge háizi 他们有三个孩子
- (*to eat*) = chī 吃
  to have a sandwich = chī yíkuài sānmíngzhì 吃一块三明治
  to have dinner = chī fàn 吃饭
- (*to drink*) = hē 喝
  to have a glass of wine = hē yìbēi jiǔ 喝一杯酒

H

have

As an ordinary verb:

- When **have** or **have got** is used as a verb meaning **possess**, it is generally translated by **yǒu** 有:

  I have (got) a car = wǒ yǒu yíliàng qìchē 我有一辆汽车
  do they have problems? = tāmen yǒu wèntí ma? 他们有问题吗?

- In negative sentences, **do not have** or **have no** is translated as **méi yǒu** 没有 rather than **bù yǒu** 不有

  she does not have any Chinese friends = tā méi yǒu Zhōngguó péngyou 她没有中国朋友
  this school has no foreign students = zhège xuéxiào méi yǒu wàiguó xuésheng 这个学校没有外国学生

- **Have** is also used with certain noun objects where the whole expression is equivalent to a verb: **to have dinner** = to dine; **to have a chat** = to chat; **to have a swim** = to swim. In such cases, the verb **have** is usually not translated into Chinese:

  to have a chat = liáotiān 聊天
  to have a swim = yóuyǒng 游泳
  to have a look = kànkan 看看

As an auxiliary verb

- When used as an auxiliary with a verb indicating a change of state or location, the Chinese translation is the Chinese equivalent verb followed by the aspect marker **le** 了:

  *he **has** left* = tā zǒu **le** 他走了
  *she **has** fallen asleep* = tā shuìzháo **le** 她睡着了
  *they **had** changed their clothes* = tāmen huàn yīfu **le** 他们换衣服了

- In a negative sentence, where **méi** 没 (= not) is used, the aspect marker **le** 了 should not be used:

  he hasn't left = tā méi zǒu 他没走
  she hasn't fallen asleep = tā méi shuìzháo 她没睡着
  I hadn't changed my clothes = wǒ méi huàn yīfu 我没换衣服

- When used as an auxiliary with a verb indicating an experience one has had, the Chinese translation is usually the Chinese equivalent verb followed by the experiencial aspect marker **guo** 过:

  ***have** you seen any Chinese films?* = nǐ kàn**guo** Zhōngguó diànyǐng ma? 你看过中国电影吗?
  *No, I **haven't*** = méiyǒu, wǒ méi kàn**guo** 没有, 我没看过
  ***have** you been to Japan?* = nǐ qù**guo** Rìběn ma? 你去过日本吗?
  *Yes, I **have*** = shìde, wǒ qù**guo** (Rìběn) 是的, 我去过(日本)

have (got) to

- have (got) to, meaning **must**, is generally translated as **bìxū** 必须 or **bùdébù** 不得不:

  I have to leave now = wǒ xiànzài **bìxū** líkāi 我现在必须离开
  = wǒ xiànzài **bùdébù** líkāi 我现在不得不离开

you've got to come = nǐ **bìxū** lái 你必须来
= nǐ **bùdébù** lái 你不得不来

- In negative sentences, **not to have to** is usually translated as **búbì 不必**:

*you **don't have** to go* = nǐ búbì qù 你不必去
*we **don't have** to accept* = wǒmen búbì jiēshòu 我们不必接受

For **have** used with illnesses ▶ 277

- (*to get*)
I had a letter from Bob yesterday = wǒ zuótiān shōudàole Bàobó de yìfēng xìn 我昨天收到了鲍勃的一封信
I'll let you have the money soon = wǒ huì hěn kuài ràng nǐ nádào qián 我会很快让你拿到钱
- (*to hold or organize*) = jǔxíng 举行
to have a party = jǔxíng yíge jùhuì 举行一个聚会
to have a competition = jǔxíng yícì bǐsài 举行一次比赛
- (*to spend*)
▶ 238
we had a nice day at the beach = wǒmen zài hǎibiān dùguòle yúkuài de yì tiān 我们在海边度过了愉快的一天
I'll have a good time in Beijing = wǒ huì zài Běijīng guò de hěn yúkuài 我会在北京过得很愉快
- (*to suffer*)
he had [a headache | a toothache | a stomach ache...] = tā [tóuténg | yátòng | dùzi téng...] 他[头疼 | 牙疼 | 肚子疼...]

> **!** *Note that in this case,* **have** *is not translated into Chinese.*

- (*to catch a disease*) = dé 得
to have [flu | cancer | heart disease...] = dé [liúgǎn | áizhèng | xīnzàng bìng...] 得[流感 | 癌症 | 心脏病...]
- (*to get something done*)
to have the house painted = shuā fángzi 刷房子
she had her hair cut = tā jiǎn tóufa le 她剪头发了

2 *auxiliary verb*

> **!** *For a detailed note on the use of* **have** *as an auxiliary verb, see the boxed note on* **have**.

you've seen her, haven't you? = nǐ jiànguo tā, shì ba? 你见过她, 是吧?
they've already left, haven't they? = tāmen yǐjīng zǒu le, shì ba? 他们已经走了, 是吧?

3 to have to = bùdébù 不得不, bìxū 必须
I have to [study hard | go home | go to see a doctor] = wǒ bùdébù [nǔlì xuéxí | huí jiā | qù kàn yīshēng] 我不得不[努力学习 | 回家 | 去看医生]
you have to come = nǐ bìxū lái 你必须来

hay *noun*
= gāncǎo 干草

hazel *adjective*
= dàn hèsè de 淡褐色的

hazelnut *noun*
a hazelnut
= yíge zhēnzi 一个榛子

he *pronoun*
= tā 他

head
1 *noun*
- (*the part of the body*) ▶ 189
= tóu 头
- (*the mind*)
= nǎozi 脑子
he's got lots of ideas in his head = tā nǎozi li zhǔyì hěn duō 他脑子里主意很多
- **a head of cabbage** = yìkē juǎnxīn cài 一棵卷心菜
a head of lettuce = yìkē shēngcài 一棵生菜
- (*the person in charge*)
the head of a delegation = dàibiǎotuán tuánzhǎng 代表团团长
the head of the Chinese Department = Zhōngwén xì xìzhǔrèn 中文系系主任
a head of State = yíwèi guójiā yuánshǒu 一位国家元首

H

2 *verb*

- (*to be in charge of*)
  to head a team = shuàilǐng yíge duì 率领一个队
- (*in soccer*)
  to head the ball = (yòng tóu) dǐng qiú (用头)顶球
  head for... = xiàng...qu 向... 去
  the car headed for the city centre = qìchē xiàng shì zhōngxīn shǐqu 汽车向市中心驶去

headache *noun* ▶ 277
he has a headache = tā tóuténg 他头疼

> **!** *Note that in* **have a headache**, **have** *is not translated into Chinese.*

my headache's gone = wǒde tóuténg hǎo le 我的头疼好了

headlamp, headlight
a headlamp = yíge qiándēng 一个前灯

headline *noun*
a headline = yíge biāotí 一个标题
to hit the headlines = chéngwéi tóutiáo xīnwén 成为头条新闻
the news headlines = xīnwén tíyào 新闻提要

headquarters *noun*
(*of a company, an organization*) = zǒngbù 总部
(*of an army*) = sīlìngbù 司令部

headteacher *noun* ▶ 344
a headteacher = yíge xiàozhǎng 一个校长

health *noun*
= jiànkāng 健康

healthy *adjective*

- (*in good health*) = jiànkāng 健康
- (*good for the health*) = yǒuyìyú jiànkāng de 有益于健康的

hear *verb*

- **to hear** = tīngjian 听见
  he can't hear anything = tā tīng bú jiàn rènhé shēngyīn 他听不见任何声音
  I heard someone coming in = wǒ tīngjian yǒu rén jìnlai 我听见有人进来
  you can hear him practising the piano = nǐ néng tīngjian tā liànxí gāngqín de shēngyīn 你能听见他练习钢琴的声音
- (*to learn, to discover*)
  to hear the news = tīngdào zhège xiāoxi 听到这个消息
  I've heard about that school = wǒ tīngshuōguo nàge xuéxiào 我听说过那个学校
- (*to listen to*) = tīng 听
  he'd like to hear our opinions = tā xiǎng tīng wǒmende yìjiàn 他想听我们的意见
  hear from... = shōudào...de xìn 收到... 的信
  have you heard from her? = nǐ shōudàoguo tāde xìn ma? 你收到过她的信吗?
  hear of = tīngshuōguo 听说过
  I've never heard of the place = wǒ cónglái méi tīngshuōguo nàge dìfang 我从来没听说过那个地方

heart *noun*

- (*part of the body*) ▶ 189
  = xīnzàng 心脏
- (*the centre*) = zhōngxīn 中心
  right in the heart of London = jiù zài Lúndūn zhōngxīn 就在伦敦中心
- **to learn...by heart** = jìzhù... 记住..., bèixialai... 背下来...

heart attack *noun* ▶ 277
a heart attack = yícì xīnzàngbìng fāzuò 一次心脏病发作

heat
1 *verb*
= bǎ...jiārè 把... 加热
to heat the water = bǎ shuǐ jiārè 把水加热
2 *noun*

- (*a high temperature, or hotness*) = gāowēn 高温, rè 热
  I can't stand the heat in Hong Kong = wǒ shòu bù liǎo Xiānggǎng de rè 我受不了香港的热
- (*a degree of hotness*) = rèdù 热度
  the heat in the oven = kǎoxiāng de rèdù 烤箱的热度
- (*in a sporting contest*)
  a heat = yícì jìngsài 一次竞赛

heat up

- (*to cook*) = shāorè 烧热
- (*to warm up again*) = chóngxīn jiārè 重新加热

heater *noun*
a heater = yìtái fārèqì 一台发热器

heating *noun*
- (*a system*) = gòng nuǎn xìtǒng 供暖系统
- (*providing the heat*) = gòng rè 供热

heatwave *noun*
a heatwave = yìgǔ rèlàng 一股热浪

heaven *noun*
= tiāntáng 天堂

heavy *adjective*
- (*in weight*) ▶ 300
= zhòng 重
- (*in quantity, intensity*)
the traffic is very heavy = jiāotōng hěn yōngjǐ 交通很拥挤
a heavy smoker = yíge chōuyān hěn duō de rén 一个抽烟很多的人
to have a heavy cold = dé zhòng gǎnmào 得重感冒
- (*describing food*) = nán xiāohuà de 难消化的
- **it's very heavy today** = jīntiān tiānqì hěn yīnchén 今天天气很阴沉
the air is heavy = kōngqì hěn chénmèn 空气很沉闷

hedge *noun*
a hedge = yìpái shùlí 一排树篱

hedgehog *noun*
a hedgehog = yìzhī cìwei 一只刺猬

heel *noun*
- (*part of the foot*) ▶ 189
= jiǎohòugēn 脚后跟
- (*part of the shoe*) = hòugēn 后跟

height *noun* ▶ 300
- (*of a person*) = shēngāo 身高
- (*of a building, a tree*) = gāodù 高度, gāo 高
to be afraid of heights = hàipà dēng gāo 害怕登高

helicopter *noun*
a helicopter = yíjià zhíshēngfēijī 一架直升飞机

hell *noun*
= dìyù 地狱

hello *noun* (also *exclamation*) ▶ 238
hello!
(*when greeting someone*) = nǐ hǎo! 你好!
(*on the phone*) = wèi! 喂!

helmet *noun*
a helmet = yíge tóukuī 一个头盔

help
1 *verb*
- **to help** = bāngzhù 帮助
to help someone [study | do the housework | escape...] = bāngzhù mǒurén [xuéxí | zuò jiāwù | táopǎo...] 帮助某人[学习|做家务|逃跑...]
to help each other = hùxiāng bāngzhù 互相帮助
- (*to remedy*) =
the medicine helps to cure the illness = zhèzhǒng yào zhìliáo zhèzhǒng bìng 这种药治疗这种病
- (*at a meal*)
help yourselves! = qǐng suíbiàn chī! 请随便吃!
- **I couldn't help laughing** = wǒ jīnbúzhù xiàole qǐlai 我禁不住笑了起来

2 *exclamation*
help!
(*when the speaker is in danger*) = jiùmìng a! 救命啊!
(*when someone else is in danger*) = jiù rén a! 救人啊!

3 *noun*
- (*assistance*) = bāngzhù 帮助
to ask someone for help = qǐng mǒurén bāngzhù 请某人帮助
- (*one who assists*) = bāngshǒu 帮手, zhùshǒu 助手
she is quite a help to me = tā shì wǒde yíge hǎo bāngshǒu 她是我的一个好帮手

help out
help someone out = bāngzhù mǒurén bǎituō kùnjìng 帮助某人摆脱困境

helpful *adjective*
- (*giving help*) = yǒu bāngzhù de 有帮助的
- (*useful*) = yǒu yòng de 有用的

helping *noun*
a helping of food = yífèn fàn 一份饭

helpless *adjective*
- (*having no one to help*) = méi yǒu rén bāngzhù de 没有人帮助的
she was left helpless = tā bèi rēng zài nàr méi yǒu rén bāngzhù 他被扔在那儿没有人帮助
- (*because of weakness, ill health*) = gūruò de 孤弱的

hen *noun*
a hen = yìzhī mǔjī 一只母鸡

H

her
1 *pronoun*
= tā 她
I know her = wǒ rènshi tā 我认识她
2 *determiner*
= tāde 她的
I don't like her dog = wǒ bù xǐhuan tāde gǒu 我不喜欢她的狗

herd *noun*
a herd of cattle = yìqún niú 一群牛

here *adverb*
• (*when talking about location*) = zhèr 这儿, zhèlǐ 这里
is your house far from here? = nǐde jiā lí zhèr yuǎn ma? 你的家离这儿远吗?
he doesn't live here = tā bú zài zhèlǐ zhù 他不在这里住
• (*when drawing attention*)
here's the post office = zhè jiùshì yóujú 这就是邮局
here they are = tāmen lái le 他们来了
here comes the train = huǒchē lái le 火车来了
here's my telephone number = zhè shì wǒde diànhuà hàomǎ 这是我的电话号码

hers *pronoun*
= tāde 她的
the green pen is hers = nàzhī lǜ bǐ shì tāde 那支绿笔是她的
my room is smaller than hers = wǒde fángjiān bǐ tāde xiǎo 我的房间比她的小

herself *pronoun*
• (*when used as a reflexive pronoun*) = (tā) zìjǐ (她)自己
she's cut herself with a knife = tā yòng dāo gēshāngle zìjǐ 她用刀割伤了自己
will she forgive herself? = tā huì yuánliàng zìjǐ ma? 她会原谅自己吗?
• (*when used for emphasis*)
she said it herself = tā qīnzì shuō de zhèjiàn shì 她亲自说的这件事
she did it all by herself = zhè dōu shì tā yíge rén zuò de 这都是她一个人做的

hesitate *verb*
= yóuyù 犹豫

hi *exclamation*
hi! = nǐ hǎo! 你好!

hiccups *noun*
to have hiccups = dǎgér 打嗝儿

hidden *adjective*
= yǐncáng de 隐藏的

hide *verb*
= (yǐn)cáng (隐)藏
she hid the money in her shoes = tā bǎ qián cáng zài xié li 她把钱藏在鞋里

hi-fi *noun*
a hi-fi = yítào zǔhé yīnxiǎng 一套组合音响

high
1 *adjective* ▶ 300
= gāo 高
[the mountain | the price | the speed...] is high = [shān | jiàgé | sùdù...] hěn gāo [山 | 价格 | 速度...] 很高
to get high grades = dé gāo fēn 得高分
2 *adverb*
don't go any higher = bié wǎng shàng qù le 别往上去了

high rise block *noun*
a high rise block = yízuò duōcéng gāolóu 一座多层高楼

high school *noun*
a high school
(*in the US*) = yìsuǒ zhōngxué 一所中学
(*in Britain*) = yìsuǒ gāozhōng 一所高中

hijack *verb*
= jiéchí 劫持

hike *verb*
to go hiking = qù túbù lǚxíng 去徒步旅行

hiking *noun* ▶ 390
= túbù lǚxíng 徒步旅行

hill *noun*
a hill = yízuò xiǎo shān 一座小山
(*a rise in the road*) = yíge xiépō 一个斜坡

him *pronoun*
= tā 他
I know him = wǒ rènshi tā 我认识他

himself *pronoun*
• (*when used as a reflexive pronoun*) = (tā) zìjǐ (他)自己
he's cut himself with a knife = tā yòng dāo gēshāng le (tā) zìjǐ 他用刀割伤了(他)自己

will he forgive himself? = tā huì yuánliàng (tā) zìjǐ ma? 他会原谅(他)自己吗?
- (*when used for emphasis*)
he said it himself = tā qīnzì shuō de zhèjiàn shì 他亲自说的这件事
he did it all by himself = zhè dōu shì tā yíge rén zuò de 这都是他一个人做的

hip *noun* ▶ 189
= túnbù 臀部

hire *verb*
- (*to employ*) = gù 雇
- (*British English*) (*to rent*) = zū 租
to hire a car = zū yíliàng chē 租一辆车
- (*to lend for a fee*) = chūzū 出租
they hire (out) bikes = tāmen chūzū zìxíngchē 他们出租自行车

his
1 *determiner*
= tāde 他的
I don't like his dog = wǒ bù xǐhuan tāde gǒu 我不喜欢他的狗
2 *pronoun*
= tāde 他的
the blue pen is his = lán de bǐ shì tāde 蓝的笔是他的

history *noun*
= lìshǐ 历史

hit
1 *verb*
- (*to strike on purpose*) = dǎ 打
to hit someone on the head = dǎ mǒurén de tóu 打某人的头
- (*to strike accidentally*) = pèng 碰
she hit her head on a chair = tāde tóu pèng zài yìbǎ yǐzi shang 她的头碰在一把椅子上
- (*to crash into*) = zhuàng 撞
to hit a wall = zhuàngdào qiáng shang 撞到墙上
2 *noun*
a hit (*a song*) = yìshǒu liúxíng gēqǔ 一首流行歌曲
(*a film or a play*) = yíbù fēngxíng yìshí de zuòpǐn 一部风行一时的作品
(*in baseball*) = dé fēn 得分
hit back = huíjī 回击
to hit someone back = huíjī mǒurén 回击某人

hitchhike *verb*
- (*to have a free lift in a vehicle*) = miǎnfèi dā tārén de chē 免费搭他人的车
- (*to request a free lift in a vehicle*) = yāoqiú miǎnfèi dā chē 要求免费搭车

hitchhiker *noun*
a hitchhiker = yíge yāoqiú miǎnfèi dā chē de rén 一个要求免费搭车的人

hoarse *adjective*
= sīyǎ 嘶哑

hobby *noun*
a hobby = yíge shìhào 一个嗜好

hockey *noun* ▶ 390
= qūgùnqiú 曲棍球

hold
1 *verb*
- **to hold** = názhe 拿着
he held some keys in his hand = tā shǒu lǐ názhe yìxiē yàoshi 他手里拿着一些钥匙
- **to hold someone's hand** = wòzhe mǒurén de shǒu 握着某人的手
- (*when used to mean to have meetings, competitions, parties*) = jǔxíng 举行
to hold a competition = jǔxíng bǐsài 举行比赛
the party will be held in the school = jùhuì jiāng zài xuéxiào jǔxíng 聚会将在学校举行
- (*to detain*) = kòuliú 扣留
hold someone hostage = kòuliú mǒurén zuò rénzhì 扣留某人作人质
- (*to keep back*) = (bǎo)liú (保)留
to hold a seat for someone = wèi mǒurén (bǎo)liú yíge zuòwèi 为某人(保)留一个座位
- (*other uses*)
to hold the world record = bǎochí shìjiè jìlù 保持世界纪录
to hold someone responsible = yào mǒurén fùzé 要某人负责
please hold the line! = qǐng bié guàduàn (diànhuà)! 请别挂断(电话)!
2 *noun*
- **to get hold of the ball** = zhuāzhù qiú 抓住球

H

- **to get hold of someone** = zhǎodào mǒurén 找到某人

hold on

- (*to wait*) = děngyiděng 等一等
- **hold on tight!** = jǐnjǐn zhuāzhù! 紧紧抓住!

  hold on to the rope = zhuāzhù shéngzi 抓住绳子

hold up

- (*to raise*) = jǔqǐ 举起

  to hold up one's hand = jǔqǐ shǒu lai 举起手来
- (*to delay*)

  to hold someone up = tuōzhù mǒurén 拖住某人

  to hold up the traffic = zǔsè jiāotōng 阻塞交通
- (*to rob*) = qiǎngjié 抢劫

hole *noun*

a hole (*if it's a pit in the ground*) = yíge kēng 一个坑

(*if it's a round-shaped gap*) = yíge kǒng 一个孔, yíge dòng 一个洞

(*in a wall, clothes*) = yíge kūlong 一个窟窿

holiday *noun*

- (*British English*) (*a vacation*)

  a holiday = yíge jiàqī 一个假期

  to go on holiday = qù dù jià 去度假
- (*a national or religious festival*) = jiàrì 假日

  a (public) holiday = yíge (gōngxiū) jiàrì 一个(公休)假日
- (*British English*) (*time taken off work*) = jià 假

  to take two weeks' holiday = xiū liǎngge xīngqī de jià 休两个星期的假

Holland *noun*

= Hélán 荷兰

home

1 *noun*

- **a home** (*a place to live*) = yíge jiā 一个家

  (*a house*) = yíge zhùzhái 一个住宅

  to leave home = líkāi jiā 离开家

  to work from home = zài jiā shàngbān 在家上班
- **a home for elderly people** = yìsuǒ yǎnglǎoyuàn 一所养老院
- **a home for handicapped children** = yíge cánjí értóng zhī jiā 一个残疾儿童之家

2 *adverb*

to go home (*to one's house*) = huí jiā 回家

(*to one's home country*) = huí guó 回国

on my way home = zài wǒ huí jiā de lù shang 在我回家的路上

to be home (*from school, work*) = dào jiā 到家

I can take you home = wǒ kěyǐ sòng nǐ huí jiā 我可以送你回家

3 at home

- (*in one's house*) = zài jiā 在家

  she's working at home = tā zài jiā gōngzuò 她在家工作

  he lives at home = tā zài jiā zhù 他在家住
- **to feel at home** = wú jūshù 无拘束

  make yourselves at home = bú yào jūshù 不要拘束
- (*when talking about a sports team*) = zài běndì 在本地

homeless *adjective*

= wú jiā kě guī 无家可归

homesick *adjective*

= xiǎng jiā 想家

homework *noun*

= zuòyè 作业

homosexual *noun*

a homosexual = yíge tóngxìngliànzhě 一个同性恋者

honest *adjective*

- = chéngshí 诚实
- (*frank, sincere*) = tǎnshuài 坦率

  to be honest, I'd rather stay here = tǎnshuài de shuō, wǒ níngyuàn dāi zài zhèr 坦率地说, 我宁愿呆在这儿

honestly *adverb*

= chéngshí de 诚实地

honey *noun*

= fēngmì 蜂蜜

honeymoon *noun*

= mìyuè 蜜月

Hong Kong *noun*

= Xiānggǎng 香港

hood *noun*

- (*to cover the head*)

  a hood = yìdǐng dōumào 一顶兜帽
- (*US English*) (*of a car*)

  the hood = chēpéng 车篷

hoof *noun*
a hoof = yìzhī tízi 一只蹄子

hook *noun*
• (*for hanging clothes, pictures*)
a hook = yíge gōu(zi) 一个钩(子)
• (*for fishing*)
a hook = yíge diàoyúgōu 一个钓鱼钩

hooligan *noun*
a hooligan = yíge liúmáng 一个流氓

hoover *verb* (*British English*)
to hoover the house = gěi fángzi xīchén 给房子吸尘

hop *verb*
= tiào 跳

hope
1 *verb*
= xīwàng 希望
I hope you don't mind = wǒ xīwàng nǐ bú jièyì 我希望你不介意
I hope so = wǒ xīwàng rúcǐ 我希望如此
2 *noun*
= xīwàng 希望
she is my only hope = tā shì wǒde wéiyī xīwàng 她是我的唯一希望

hopeless *adjective*
• (*without hope of success*) = méi yǒu xīwàng 没有希望
• (*without any ability*) = méi yǒu zàojiù 没有造就
to be hopeless at cooking = zài zuò fàn fāngmiàn méi yǒu zàojiù 在做饭方面没有造就

horn *noun*
• (*on a car, a bus*) = lǎbā 喇叭
to blow a horn = àn lǎbā 按喇叭
• (*of an animal*)
a horn = yìzhī jiǎo 一只角
• (*an instrument*) ▶ 308
a horn = yíge hào 一个号

horoscope *noun*
= xīngzhàn 星占

horrible *adjective*
• (*exciting horror*) = kěpà 可怕, kǒngbù 恐怖
• (*very bad*) = zāogāo 糟糕, huài 坏

horror film *noun*
a horror film = yíbù kǒngbù diànyǐng 一部恐怖电影

horse *noun*
a horse = yìpí mǎ 一匹马

horseracing *noun* ▶ 390
= sài mǎ 赛马

horseriding *noun* ▶ 390
= qí mǎ 骑马

hospital *noun*
a hospital = yìjiā yīyuàn 一家医院
he's still in (the) hospital = tā hái zài yīyuàn li 他还在医院里
to be taken to (the) hospital = bèi sòngjìn yīyuàn 被送进医院

host *noun*
a host = yíge zhǔrén 一个主人

hostage *noun*
a hostage = yìmíng rénzhì 一名人质

hostel *noun*
a hostel = yíge zhāodàisuǒ 一个招待所

hostess *noun*
a hostess (*a female host*) = yíge nǚ zhǔrén 一个女主人
(*in a plane*) = yíge kōngzhōng xiǎojie 一个空中小姐

hot *adjective*
• (*very warm*) = rè 热
I'm very hot = wǒ hěn rè 我很热
a hot meal = yídùn rè cān 一顿热餐
• (*strong, with a lot of spices*) = là 辣
a very hot dish = yídào hěn là de cài 一道很辣的菜

hot air balloon *noun*
a hot air balloon = yíge rè qìqiú 一个热气球

hot dog *noun*
a hot dog = yíge hóngcháng miànbāo 一个红肠面包

hotel *noun*
a hotel = yìjiā lǚguǎn 一家旅馆

hour *noun* ▶ 204, ▶ 412
an hour = yíge xiǎoshí 一个小时, yíge zhōngtóu 一个钟头
I earn two pounds an hour = wǒ yíge xiǎoshí zhèng liǎng bàng qián 我一个小时挣两镑钱

house *noun*
• (*a building*) = fángzi 房子
a house = yízuò fángzi 一座房子
• (*a dwelling place*) = jiā 家
to go to someone's house = qù mǒurén de jiā 去某人的家

H

the bike is at my house = zìxíngchē zài wǒ jiā li 自行车在我家里

housewife *noun* ▶ 344
a housewife = yíge jiātíng fùnǚ 一个家庭妇女

housework *noun*
= jiāwùhuór 家务活儿
to do the housework = zuò jiāwùhuór 做家务活儿

housing estate (*British English*), **housing development** (*US English*) *noun*
a housing estate = yíge zhùzhái qū 一个住宅区

hovercraft *noun*
a hovercraft = yìsōu qìdiànchuán 一艘气垫船

how *adverb*
- (*in what way*) = zěnme 怎么, zěnyàng 怎样
  how did you find us? = nǐ zěnme zhǎodào de wǒmen? 你怎么找到的我们?
  I know how [to swim | to ride a horse | to cook a curry...] = wǒ zhīdào zěnyàng [yóuyǒng | qí mǎ | zuò gālí cài...] 我知道怎样[游泳 | 骑马 | 做咖喱菜...]
- (*in polite questions*)
  how are you? = nǐ hǎo ma? 你好吗?
  how is your mother? = nǐ māma hǎo ma? 你妈妈好吗?
  how was your holiday? = nǐ jiàqī wánr de hǎo ma? 你假期玩儿得好吗?
- (*in questions requiring specific information*)
  how long will it take? = zhè yào huā duō cháng shíjiān? 这要花多长时间?
  how tall are you? = nǐ yǒu duō gāo? 你有多高?
  how old is he? = tā duōshǎo suì? 他多少岁? ▶ 170
- (*when making a suggestion*)
  how would you like to eat out? = chūqu chī fàn zěnmeyàng? 出去吃饭怎么样?

however *adverb*
- (*nevertheless*) = kěshì 可是, búguò 不过
- however hard I try, I can't understand grammar = bùguǎn zěnme nǔlì, wǒ yě nòng bù dǒng yǔfǎ 不管怎么努力, 我也弄不懂语法

how many ▶ 349
1 *pronoun*
= duōshǎo 多少
how many do you want? = nǐ yào duōshǎo? 你要多少?
how many of you are there? = nǐmen yǒu duōshǎo rén? 你们有多少人?
2 *determiner*
= duōshǎo 多少
how many children are going on the trip? = yǒu duōshǎo háizi qù lǚxíng? 有多少孩子去旅行?

how much ▶ 349
1 *pronoun*
= duōshǎo 多少
how much does it come to? = yígòng duōshǎo? 一共多少?
2 *determiner*
= duōshǎo 多少
how much money do you have left? = nǐ hái shèng duōshǎo qián? 你还剩多少钱?

huge *adjective*
= jùdà 巨大

human being *noun*
= rén 人

humour (*British English*), **humor** (*US English*) *noun*
= yōumò 幽默
to have a sense of humour = yǒu yōumò gǎn 有幽默感

hundred *number* ▶ 170
one hundred, a hundred = yìbǎi 一百
three hundred = sānbǎi 三百
five hundred and fifty dollars = wǔbǎi wǔshí měiyuán 五百五十美元
about a hundred people = dàyuē yìbǎi rén 大约一百人

hungry *adjective*
= è 饿
I'm very hungry = wǒ hěn è 我很饿

hunt *verb* ▶ 390
= dǎliè 打猎
to go hunting = qù dǎliè 去打猎

hurdles *noun* ▶ 390
= kuàlán 跨栏

hurrah, hurray *noun* (also *exclamation*)
hurrah! = hǎo wa! 好哇!

hurry
1 *verb*
- = gǎnjǐn 赶紧
  hurry home! = gǎnjǐn huí jiā! 赶紧回家!
- **to hurry someone** = cuī mǒurén 催某人

2 *noun*
be in a hurry = hěn cōngmáng 很匆忙
there's no hurry = bú yòng zháojí 不用着急
hurry up = gǎnjǐn 赶紧

hurt *verb*
- (*to injure*)
  I hurt myself = wǒ shòule shāng 我受了伤
  she hurt her leg = tāde tuǐ shòule shāng 她的腿受了伤
- (*to be painful*) = téng 疼
  my throat hurts = wǒde sǎngzi téng 我的嗓子疼
  that hurts = nà hěn téng 那很疼
- (*to upset*) = shānghài 伤害
  to hurt someone's feelings = shānghài mǒurén de gǎnqíng 伤害某人的感情

husband *noun*
= zhàngfu 丈夫

Ii

I *pronoun*
= wǒ 我
Mr. Li and I are going to Hong Kong tomorrow = wǒ hé Lǐ xiānsheng míngtiān qù Xiānggǎng 我和李先生明天去香港

ice *noun*
= bīng 冰

ice cream *noun*
an ice cream = yíge bīngqílín 一个冰淇淋

ice hockey *noun* ▶ 390
= bīngqiú 冰球

ice rink *noun*
an ice rink = yíge huábīngchǎng 一个滑冰场

ice-skate *noun*
a pair of ice-skates = yìshuāng bīngxié 一双冰鞋

ice-skating *noun* ▶ 390
= huábīng 滑冰

icing *noun*
= tángshuāng 糖霜

ID, identity card *noun*
an identity card = yíge shēnfènzhèng 一个身份证

idea *noun*
- **an idea** (*a thought*) = yìzhǒng sīxiǎng 一种思想
  (*a view*) = yìzhǒng kànfa 一种看法
  (*a plan*) = yíge zhǔyì 一个主意
  what a good idea! = duōme hǎo de zhǔyì a! 多么好的主意啊!
- **I've got no idea how much it costs** = wǒ bù zhīdào zhè yào duōshǎo qián 我不知道这要多少钱

idiot *noun*
an idiot = yíge báichī 一个白痴, yíge shǎzi 一个傻子

if *conjunction*
- (*on condition that*) = rúguǒ 如果
  you'll get good marks if you study hard = rúguǒ nǐ nǔlì xuéxí, nǐ huì qǔdé hǎo chéngji 如果你努力学习, 你会取得好成绩
- (*in case that*) = yàoshì 要是
  we won't go if it rains = yàoshì xiàyǔ, wǒmen jiù bú qù 要是下雨, 我们就不去
- (*supposing that*) = jiǎrú 假如, yàoshì 要是
  I would travel if I were rich = jiǎrú wǒ hěn yǒuqián, wǒ huì qù lǚxíng 假如我很有钱, 我会去旅行
  I'd refuse if I were you = yàoshì wǒ shì nǐ, wǒ jiù jùjué 要是我是你, 我就拒绝

> **!** *Note that the conditional clause introduced by* **if** *precedes the main clause in Chinese.*

- (*whether*) = shìfǒu 是否
  I don't know if they'll come = wǒ bù zhīdào tāmen shìfǒu huì lái 我不知道他们是否会来

> **!** *Note that* **shìfǒu 是否** *appears after the subject of the subordinate clause in Chinese.*

ignore *verb*
to ignore someone = bù lǐ mǒurén 不理某人
to ignore a problem = hūshì yíge wèntí 忽视一个问题

ill *adjective*
= bìng 病, yǒu bìng 有病
she is ill = tā bìng le 她病了

illegal *adjective*
= fēifǎ 非法

illness *noun*
an illness = yìzhǒng (jí)bìng 一种(疾)病

imagination *noun*
- (*the act of imagining*) = xiǎngxiàng 想象
  this is only my imagination = zhè zhǐ shì wǒde xiǎngxiàng 这只是我的想象
- (*the ability to imagine*) = xiǎngxiànglì 想象力
  he has no imagination = tā méi yǒu xiǎngxiànglì 他没有想象力

imagine *verb*
- (*to form an image in one's mind*) = xiǎngxiàng 想象
- (*to think vainly or falsely*) = shèxiǎng 设想

imitate *verb*
= mófǎng 模仿, fǎngxiào 仿效

immediately *adverb*
= lìjí 立即, mǎshàng 马上

impatient *adjective*
= bú nàifán 不耐烦
to get impatient = biànde bú nàifán 变得不耐烦

import *verb*
= jìnkǒu 进口

important *adjective*
= zhòngyào 重要
it is important to keep fit = bǎochí jiànkāng hěn zhòngyào 保持健康很重要

impossible *adjective*
= bù kěnéng 不可能
it's impossible to change this plan = gǎibiàn zhège jìhuà shì bù kěnéng de 改变这个计划是不可能的

impress *verb*
I'm impressed by his speech = tāde jiǎnghuà gěi wǒ liúxià hěn shēn de yìnxiàng 他的讲话给我留下很深的印象

impression *noun*
= yìnxiàng 印象
she made a good impression on me = tā gěi wǒ liúxià hěn hǎo de yìnxiàng 她给我留下很好的印象

improve *verb*
- (*to make better*) = tígāo 提高, gǎishàn 改善
  to improve living conditions = gǎishàn shēnghuó tiáojiàn 改善生活条件
  to improve one's spoken Chinese = tígāo zìjǐde Hànyǔ kǒuyǔ shuǐpíng 提高自己的汉语口语水平
- (*to get better*) = hǎozhuǎn 好转
  the economic situation is improving = jīngjì xíngshì zhèngzài hǎozhuǎn 经济形势正在好转

improvement *noun*
= gǎijìn 改进, gǎishàn 改善

in

> **!** *Often* **in** *occurs in combination with verbs, for example:* **drop in, fit in, move in**, *etc. To find the correct translations for this type of verb, look up the separate dictionary entries at* **drop, fit, move**, *etc.*

1 *preposition*
- (*inside*) = zài...li 在...里
  in the house = zài fángzi li 在房子里
  there is a letter in the envelope = (zài) xìnfēng li yǒu yìfēng xìn (在)信封里有一封信
- (*when talking about being in print*) = zài...shang 在...上
  the woman in the photograph = (zài) zhàopiàn shang de nǚrén (在)照片上的女人
  I saw your picture in the newspaper = wǒ zài bàozhǐ shang kàndào le nǐde zhàopiàn 我在报纸上看到了你的照片
- **in the world** = zài shìjiè shang 在世界上

> **!** *Note that when* **zài** 在 *appears at the beginning of a sentence or when a phrase introduced by* **zài** 在 *is used to modify a noun phrase, the use of* **zài** 在 *is optional.*

Illnesses, aches, and pains

Where does it hurt?

where does it hurt?	= nǎr téng? 哪儿疼?
his leg hurts	= tāde tuǐ téng 他的腿疼
he has a pain in his leg	= tāde tuǐ téng 他的腿疼

Note that **his leg hurts** and **he has a pain in his leg** share the same Chinese translation.

Aches

he has [a headache|a sore throat|a stomach ache...]	= tā [tóuténg/sǎngzi téng/dùzi téng...] 他[头疼/嗓子疼/肚子疼...]

Note that **have** is not translated into Chinese.

Accidents

*she broke **her** leg*	= tā shuāiduànle ___ tuǐ 她摔断了__腿
*I twisted **my** ankle*	= wǒ niǔshāngle ___ jiǎobózi 我扭伤了__脚脖子

Note that, unlike English, Chinese doesn't require a possessive before the part of the body.

Being ill

to have|to catch [flu|measles|cold...]	= dé [liúgǎn/mázhěn/gǎnmào...] 得[流感/麻疹/感冒...]
to have cancer	= dé áizhèng 得癌症

Treatment

to be treated for rabies	= yīn kuángquǎnbìng ér jīeshòu zhìliáo 因狂犬病而接受治疗
to take tablets for indigestion	= yīn xiāohuà bùliáng ér chī yào 因消化不良而吃药
to be operated on for cancer	= yīn áizhèng ér zuò shǒushù 因癌症而做手术

- (*at*) = zài 在
  I am learning Japanese in school = wǒ zài xuéxiào xuéxí Rìyǔ 我在学校学习日语
  in the countryside = zài nóngcūn 在农村
- (*when talking about countries or cities*) = zài 在
  to live in [America | Japan | Shanghai...] = zhù zài [Měiguó | Rìběn | Shànghǎi...] 住在[美国|日本|上海...]
- (*dressed in*) = chuānzhe 穿着
  in a skirt = chuānzhe qúnzi 穿着裙子
  to be dressed in black = chuānzhe hēisè de yīfu 穿着黑色的衣服
- (*showing the way in which something is done*) = yòng 用
  to write a letter in Chinese = yòng Zhōngwén xiě xìn 用中文写信
  we paid in cash = wǒmen yòng xiànjīn fù qián 我们用现金付钱
  in ink = yòng mòshuǐ(r) 用墨水(儿)
- (*during*) = zài 在
  in October = zài shíyuè 在十月
  in the night = zài yèli 在夜里
  in the morning = zài zǎochén 在早晨
- (*within*) = guò 过, zài...zhīnèi 在... 之内
  I'll be ready in ten minutes = wǒ zài shí fēnzhōng zhīnèi huì zhǔnbèihǎo 我在十分钟之内会准备好

she'll be back in half an hour = tā guò bàn xiǎoshí huílai 她过半小时回来
- (*other uses*)

to stay in the rain = dāi zài yǔ zhōng 呆在雨中
she is in her twenties = tā èrshíjǐ suì 她二十几岁
one in ten = shíge dāngzhōng yǒu yíge 十个当中有一个
to cut an apple in two = bǎ yíge píngguǒ qiēchéng liǎng bàn 把一个苹果切成两半

2 *adverb*
- (*at home*) = zài jiā 在家
- (*available*) = zài 在

tell her I'm not in = gàosu tā wǒ bú zài 告诉她我不在
- (*arrived*)

the train is in = huǒchē dào le 火车到了

inch *noun* ▶ 300
an inch = yì yīngcùn 一英寸

> **!** *Note that an* inch *= 2.54 cm.*

include *verb*
= bāokuò 包括
service is included in the bill = zhàngdān li bāokuò fúwùfèi 帐单里包括服务费

including *preposition*
= bāokuò 包括
they were all invited, including the children = tāmen dōu shòudào yāoqǐng , bāokuò háizi 他们都受到邀请, 包括孩子

income *noun*
an income = yífèn shōurù 一份收入

income tax *noun*
= suǒdéshuì 所得税

inconvenient *adjective*
= bù fāngbiàn 不方便

increase
1 *verb*
= zēngjiā 增加
to increase by 10% = zēngjiā bǎifēn zhī shí 增加百分之十
2 *noun*
= zēngjiā 增加

incredible *adjective*
= nányǐzhìxìn 难以置信

independent *adjective*
= dúlì de 独立的

India *noun*
= Yìndù 印度

Indian ▶ 288
1 *adjective*
= Yìndù de 印度的
2 *noun*
- (*the people from India*) = Yìndùrén 印度人
- (*the indigenous people of America*) = Yìndì'ānrén 印地安人

indicate *verb*
- (*to show*) = biǎoshì 表示
- (*to point out*) = zhǐchū 指出

indifferent *adjective*
- (*unconcerned*) = bú zàihu 不在乎, bù guānxīn 不关心
- (*of a middle quality*) = zhíliàng bù gāo 质量不高

indigestion *noun* ▶ 277
to have indigestion = xiāohuà bùliáng 消化不良

individual
1 *adjective*
- (*pertaining to one only or to each one separately*) = gèrén de 个人的
- (*separate*) = gèbié de 个别的

2 *noun*
an individual = yígè rén 一个人

indoor *adjective*
= shìnèi 室内
an indoor swimming pool = yíge shìnèi yóuyǒngchí 一个室内游泳池

indoors *adverb*
- = zài wū li 在屋里
- go indoors = jìn wū li 进屋里

industrial *adjective*
= gōngyè de 工业的

industry *noun*
= gōngyè 工业

inevitable *adjective*
= bùkě bìmiǎn de 不可避免的

infant school *noun*
(*British English*)
an infant school = yíge xuéqiánbān 一个学前班

infection *noun*
- (*the act of tainting*) = gǎnrǎn 感染
- (*the act of imparting some disease*) = chuánrǎn 传染
- (*an infectious disease*) = chuánrǎnbìng 传染病

influence
1 *noun*
an influence = yìzhǒng yǐngxiǎng 一种影响
to have influence over = duì... yǒu yǐngxiǎng 对... 有影响
2 *verb*
= yǐngxiǎng 影响
to influence someone = yǐngxiǎng mǒurén 影响某人
to be influenced by someone = shòudào mǒurén de yǐngxiǎng 受到某人的影响

inform *verb*
- (*to tell*) = gàosu 告诉
  to inform them of the news = gàosu tāmen zhège xiāoxi 告诉他们这个消息
- (*to impart knowledge*) = tōngzhī 通知
  to inform the police of the accident = bǎ zhège shìgù tōngzhī gěi jǐngchá 把这个事故通知给警察
  to keep someone informed = suíshí xiàng mǒurén bàogào 随时向某人报告

informal *adjective*
- (*describing a person, a person's manner*) = suíbiàn 随便
- (*describing a word, a language*) = rìcháng shǐyòng de 日常使用的
- (*describing a discussion or an interview*) = fēi zhèngshì de 非正式的

information *noun*
- **a piece of information** = yìtiáo xiāoxi 一条消息
- **thank you for your information** = xièxie nǐ gàosu wǒ zhètiáo xìnxī 谢谢你告诉我这条信息

information desk *noun*
= wènxùn chù 问讯处

information technology *noun*
= xìnxī jìshù 信息技术

ingredient *noun*
an ingredient = yìzhǒng pèiliào 一种配料

inhabitant *noun*
an inhabitant = yíge jūmín 一个居民

injection *noun*
- **an injection** = yìzhī zhùshèjì 一支注射剂
- **to give someone an injection** = gěi mǒurén dǎ yìzhēn 给某人打一针

injured *adjective*
= shòushāng 受伤

injury *noun*
= sǔnshāng 损伤, shāng 伤

ink *noun*
= mòshuǐ(r) 墨水(儿)

innocent *adjective*
- (*not legally guilty*) = wúzuì 无罪
- (*harmless*) = wúhài 无害
- (*naïve*) = tiānzhēn 天真
- (*ignorant of evil*) = yòuzhì 幼稚

inquiry *noun*
- (*a question*) = xúnwèn 询问, dǎtīng 打听
- (*an investigation*) = diàochá 调查
- (*a search for knowledge*) = tànjiū 探究

insect *noun*
an insect = yíge kūnchóng 一个昆虫

inside
1 *preposition*
= zài...lǐmian 在...里面
inside the house = zài fángzi lǐmian 在房子里面
2 *adverb*
= lǐmian 里面
he's inside = tā zài lǐmian 他在里面
I looked inside = wǒ xiàng lǐmian kàn 我向里面看
let's bring the chairs inside = wǒmen bǎ yǐzi nádào lǐmian qu ba 我们把椅子拿到里面去吧
3 *noun*
= lǐmian 里面
the inside of the house = fángzi lǐmian 房子里面
4 *adjective*
= lǐmian de 里面的
5 inside out
to put one's shirt on inside out = bǎ chènshān chuān fǎn le 把衬衫穿反了

inspect *verb*
- (*to examine*) = jiǎnchá 检查
- (*to look at officially*) = shìchá 视察
- (*to look at ceremonially*) = jiǎnyuè 检阅
  the president inspected the guard of honour = zǒngtǒng jiǎnyuèle yízhàngduí 总统检阅了仪仗队

inspector *noun*
an inspector (*an examining officer*) = yíge jiǎncháyuán 一个检察员

(*one who inspects officially*) = yíge shìcházhě 一个视察者
(*one who inspects ceremonially*) = yíge jiǎnyuèzhě 一个检阅者

instantly *adverb*
= lìjí 立即

instead
1 instead of
• (*rather than*) = ér búshì 而不是
he hired a van instead of a car = tā zūle yíliàng huòchē ér búshì yíliàng jiàochē 他租了一辆货车而不是一辆轿车
instead of working he watched TV = tā kàn diànshì ér búshì gōngzuò 他看电视而不是工作
• (*in place of*) = dàitì 代替
use oil instead of butter = yòng yóu dàitì huángyóu 用油代替黄油
his wife came instead of him = tā tàitai dàitì tā lái le 他太太代替他来了
2 *adverb*
I don't feel like going to the cinema—let's stay at home instead = wǒ bù xiǎng qù kàn diànyǐng—zánmen dāi zài jiāli ba 我不想去看电影—咱们呆在家里吧

instruction *noun*
an instruction = yíxiàng zhǐshì 一项指示, yíxiàng mìnglìng 一项命令
to give someone instructions to check the baggage = zhǐshì mǒurén jiǎnchá xínglǐ 指示某人检查行李
instructions for use = shǐyòng shuōmíng 使用说明

instrument *noun* ▶ 308
an instrument
• (*an indicating device*) = yíge yíqì 一个仪器
• (*a tool*) = yíjiàn gōngjù 一件工具
• (*for hospital operations*) = yíjiàn qìxiè 一件器械
• (*for playing music*) = yíjiàn yuèqì 一件乐器

insult *verb*
= wǔrǔ 侮辱

insurance *noun*
= bǎoxiǎn 保险

insure *verb*
= bǎoxiǎn 保险
is your car insured? = nǐde qìchē bǎoxiǎn le ma? 你的汽车保险了吗?

intelligent *adjective*
= cōngming 聪明

intend *verb*
he intends to [leave | learn Cantonese | travel abroad...] = tā dǎsuàn [zǒu | xué Guǎngdōnghuà | qù guówài lǚxíng...] 他打算 [走 | 学广东话 | 去国外旅行...]

intense *adjective*
• (*when describing a pain*) = jùliè 剧烈
• (*when describing feelings*) = qiángliè 强烈
• (*when describing an earnestly or deeply emotional person or manner*) = rèqiè 热切

intensive care *noun*
to be in intensive care = jiēshòu tèbié jiānhù 接受特别监护

interest
1 *noun*
• (*enthusiasm*) = xìngqù 兴趣
to have an interest in music = duì yīnyuè gǎn xìngqù 对音乐感兴趣
• (*premium paid for money borrowed from or saved in a bank*) = lìxī 利息
(*benefit*) = lìyì 利益
2 *verb*
to interest somebody = shǐ mǒurén gǎn xìngqù 使某人感兴趣

interested *adjective*
= gǎn xìngqù 感兴趣
to be interested in [politics | sports | painting...] = duì [zhèngzhì | tǐyù | huì huà...] gǎn xìngqù 对 [政治 | 体育 | 绘画...] 感兴趣
are you interested? = nǐ gǎn xìngqù ma? 你感兴趣吗?

interesting *adjective*
= yǒuqù 有趣, yǒu yìsi 有意思

interfere *verb*
• (*to get involved in*) = gānshè 干涉
to interfere in someone's business = gānshè mǒurén de shì 干涉某人的事
• (*to have a bad effect on*) = fáng'ài 妨碍
it's going to interfere with his work = zhè yào fáng'ài tāde gōngzuò 这要妨碍他的工作

intermission *noun*
= jiànxiē 间歇, xiūxi 休息

international *adjective*
= guójì 国际

internet *noun*
the internet = hùliánwǎng 互联网, yīntèwǎng 因特网

interpreter *noun* ▶ 344
an interpreter = yíge fānyì 一个翻译, yíge kǒuyì 一个口译

interrupt *verb*
- (*to break in upon someone's action, speech, etc.*) = dǎduàn 打断
- (*to disturb by breaking in upon*) = dǎrǎo 打扰
- (*to stop continuity in*) = zhōngduàn 中断

interval *noun*
- (*in time*) = jiàngé 间隔
  at regular intervals = měi gé yídìng shíjiān 每隔一定时间
- (*at a location*) = jiàngé 间隔
  at regular intervals = měi gé yídìng jùlí 每隔一定距离
- (*British English*) (*during a play, a show*) = mùjiān xiūxi 幕间休息

interview
1 *noun*
an interview (*for a job*) = yícì miànshì 一次面试
(*with a journalist*) = yícì cǎifǎng 一次采访
2 *verb*
to interview someone (*if it's an employer*) = miànshì mǒurén 面试某人
(*if it's a journalist*) = cǎifǎng mǒurén 采访某人
(*if it's the police*) = shěnwèn mǒurén 审问某人

intimidate *verb*
= dònghè 恫吓, kǒnghè 恐吓

into *preposition*
- (*when talking about a location*)
  to walk into the garden = zǒu jìn huāyuán 走进花园
  to get into a car = jìndào qìchē li 进到汽车里
  to get into bed = shàngchuáng 上床
- (*indicating a change*) = chéng 成
  to translate a letter into French = bǎ yìfēng xìn fānyìchéng Fǎwén 把一封信翻译成法文
  to turn someone into a frog = bǎ mǒurén biànchéng yìzhī qīngwā 把某人变成一只青蛙

introduce *verb*
- (*to bring in*)
  to introduce a new technique = yǐnjìn yíxiàng xīn jìshù 引进一项新技术
- (*when people meet, or on radio or television*) = jièshào 介绍
  he introduced me to Peter = tā bǎ wǒ jièshào gěi Bǐdé 他把我介绍给彼得
  to introduce a programme = jièshào yíge jiémù 介绍一个节目

invade *verb*
= qīnfàn 侵犯, qīnrù 侵入

invent *verb*
= fāmíng 发明

invention *noun*
an invention = yíxiàng fāmíng 一项发明

investigate *verb*
= diàochá 调查

investigation *noun*
an investigation = yíxiàng diàochá 一项调查

invisible *adjective*
= kàn bú jiàn de 看不见的

invitation *noun*
- (*the act of inviting*) = yāoqǐng 邀请
- (*a written form*) = qǐngtiě 请帖, qǐngjiǎn 请柬
  an invitation = yífèn qǐngtiě 一份请帖, yífèn qǐngjiǎn 一份请柬

invite *verb*
= yāoqǐng 邀请
to invite someone to dinner = yāoqǐng mǒurén chīfàn 邀请某人吃饭

involve *verb*
to be involved in an accident = juǎnrù yícì shìgù 卷入一次事故
this activity involves both teachers and students = zhèxiàng huódòng bāokuò lǎoshī hé xuésheng 这项活动包括老师和学生

Ireland *noun*
= Ài'ěrlán 爱尔兰

Irish ▶ 288
1 *adjective*
= Ài'ěrlán de 爱尔兰的
2 *noun*
- (*the people*) = Ài'ěrlánrén 爱尔兰人
- (*the language*) = Ài'ěrlányǔ 爱尔兰语

iron
1 *noun*
- **iron** = tiě 铁
- **an iron** = yíge yùndǒu 一个熨斗

It

In most cases, when used as a subject or an object, **it** is not translated into Chinese.

- When **it** is used as a subject pronoun

*'where is the book/chair?' — '**it**'s in the kitchen'*	= 'shū/yǐzi zài nǎr?' — '__ zài chúfáng li' '书/椅子在哪儿?' — '__在厨房里'

- When **it** is used as an object pronoun

*Look at this shirt. Do you like **it**?*	= kàn zhèjiàn chènshān, nǐ xǐhuan __ ma? 看这件衬衫, 你喜欢 __ 吗?
*That's my book. Don't give **it** to him!*	= nà shì wǒde shū, bié gěi tā __ ! 那是我的书, 别给他 __ !

When used after a preposition indicating a location or after bǎ 把, **it** is often translated as **tā** 它 in Chinese.

- After a preposition indicating a location

*please don't put the suitcase on **it***	= qǐng bié bǎ xiāngzi fàng zài **tā** shàngbian 请别把箱子放在它上边

- After **bǎ** 把

*I have sold **it***	= wǒ bǎ **tā** mài le 我把它卖了
*don't throw **it** away*	= bié bǎ **tā** rēng le 别把它扔了

It can be translated as a noun phrase or a demonstrative

*we talked about **it***	= wǒmen tánle **zhèjiàn shì** 我们谈了这件事
***it's** a small city*	= **zhè** shì yíge xiǎo chéngshì 这是一个小城市

- When used in expressions like **it's raining**, **it will snow**, etc., **it** can be translated as **tiān** 天 or not translated at all. See the entry for the verb in question.

For translations of **it's Friday**, **it's five o'clock**, etc. ▶ 218, ▶ 204

---

2 *verb*
= yùn 熨

island *noun*
an island = yíge dǎo(yǔ) 一个岛(屿)

it *pronoun*
▶ *See the boxed note on* it ▶ **282** *for more information and examples.*
where is it? = zài nǎr? 在哪儿?
who is it? = shéi (a)? 谁(啊)?
it's me = (shì) wǒ (a) (是)我(啊)
it's a large school = zhè shì yíge hěn dà de xuéxiào 这是一个很大的学校
it is [difficult | easy | interesting...] to learn Chinese = xuéxí Zhōngwén [hěn nán | hěn róngyi | hěn yǒu yìsi...] 学习中文 [很难 | 很容易 | 很有意思...]
it doesn't matter = méi guānxi 没关系
it's [cold | warm | mild...] = (tiān qì) [hěn lěng | hěn rè | hěn nuǎnhuo...] (天气) [很冷 | 很热 | 很暖和...]
I've heard about it = wǒ tīngshuōle zhèjiàn shì 我听说了这件事

Italian ▶ 288
1 *adjective*
= Yìdàlì de 意大利的
2 *noun*
- *(the people)*
= Yìdàlìrén 意大利人
- *(the language)*
= Yìdàlìyǔ 意大利语, Yìdàlìwén 意大利文

Italy *noun*
= Yìdàlì 意大利

itchy *adjective*
my leg is itchy = wǒde tuǐ fāyǎng 我的腿发痒

its *determiner*
= tāde 它的
its [nose | tail | eyes] = tāde [bízi | wěiba | yǎnjīng] 它的 [鼻子 | 尾巴 | 眼睛]

itself *pronoun*
- (*when used as a reflexive pronoun*) = (tā)zìjǐ (它)自己
  the dog is going to wash itself = zhèzhī gǒu yào gěi (tā)zìjǐ xǐzǎo 这只狗要给(它)自己洗澡
- (*when used for emphasis*)
  the car itself was not damaged = chē běnshēn méiyǒu sǔnhuài 车本身没有损坏
  the heating comes on by itself = nuǎnqì zìdòng kāi le 暖气自动开了

Jj

jacket *noun*
a jacket = yíjiàn duǎn shàngyī 一件短上衣
(*gathered at the waist*) = yíjiàn jiákè 一件夹克

jail *noun*
a jail = yìsuǒ jiānyù 一所监狱

jam *noun*
jam = guǒjiàng 果酱

January *noun* ▶ 218
January = yīyuè 一月

Japan *noun*
= Rìběn 日本

Japanese ▶ 288
1 *adjective*
= Rìběn de 日本的
2 *noun*
- (*the people*)
  = Rìběnrén 日本人
- (*the language*)
  = Rìyǔ 日语, Rìwén 日文

jaw *noun* ▶ 189
= è 颚

jazz *noun*
= juéshìyuè 爵士乐

jealous *adjective*
= jìdu 忌妒, dùjì 妒忌
he is jealous of her = tā jìdu tā 他妒忌她

jeans *noun*
= niúzǎikù 牛仔裤

jeer *verb*
to jeer someone = cháoxiào mǒurén 嘲笑某人

jelly *noun*
- (*US English*) (*jam*)
  = guǒjiàng 果酱
- (*British English*) (*a gelatinized dessert*)
  = guǒzidòng 果子冻

Jesus *noun*
= Yēsū 耶稣

jet *noun*
a jet (*an aircraft*) = yíjià pēnqìshì fēijī 一架喷气式飞机

jewellery (*British English*), **jewelry** (*US English*) *noun*
= zhūbǎo 珠宝
a piece of jewellery = yíjiàn zhūbǎo 一件珠宝

Jewish *adjective*
= Yóutàirén de 犹太人的

jigsaw puzzle *noun*
a jigsaw puzzle = yíge pīnbǎn wánjù 一个拼板玩具

job *noun*
- (*work*) = gōngzuò 工作
  a job = yíge gōngzuò 一个工作
  to look for a job = zhǎo gōngzuò 找工作
- (*a task*) = rènwù 任务
  a job = yíxiàng rènwù 一项任务

jogging *noun* ▶ 390
= mànpǎo 慢跑

join *verb*
- (*become a member of*) = cānjiā 参加, jiārù 加入
  to join a club = cānjiā yíge jùlèbù 参加一个俱乐部
  to join a company = jiārù yíge gōngsī 加入一个公司
- (*meet up with*)
  I'll join you for lunch tomorrow = míngtiān wǒ hé nǐmen yìqǐ chī wǔfàn 明天我和你们一起吃午饭
- **to join the army** = cānjūn 参军
  join in
  to join in a game = cānjiā bǐsài 参加比赛

joke
1 *noun*
a joke = yíge wánxiào 一个玩笑, yíge xiàohua 一个笑话
2 *verb*
= kāi wánxiào 开玩笑

journalist *noun* ▶ 344
a journalist = yíge jìzhě 一个记者

journey *noun*
a journey = yícì lǚxíng 一次旅行
to go on a journey = qù lǚxíng 去旅行

joy *noun*
= huānlè 欢乐, lèqù 乐趣

judge
1 *noun* ▶ 344
a judge (*in a court*) = yíge fǎguān 一个法官
(*in competitions*) = yíge cáipàn 一个裁判
2 *verb*
- (*in a court*) = shěnpàn 审判
- (*in competitions*) = píngpàn 评判
- (*to determine the truth*) = duàndìng 断定

judo *noun* ▶ 390
= róudào 柔道

jug *noun*
a jug = yíge guànzi 一个罐子

juice *noun*
= zhī 汁
fruit juice = guǒzhī 果汁

July *noun* ▶ 218
= qīyuè 七月

jump *verb*
- = tiào 跳
  the children were jumping on the bed = háizimen zài chuáng shang tiào 孩子们在床上跳
  to jump across the stream = tiàoguò xiǎo hé 跳过小河
  to jump a rope = tiào shéng 跳绳
  to jump out of the window = tiàodào chuāng wài qu 跳到窗外去
- **to jump the queue** (*British English*) = chāduì 插队

jumper *noun* (*British English*)
a jumper = yíjiàn tàotóushān 一件套头衫

June *noun* ▶ 218
= liùyuè 六月

junior high school *noun* (*US English*)
a junior high school = yìsuǒ chūjí zhōngxué 一所初级中学

junior school *noun* (*British English*)
a junior school = yìsuǒ xiǎoxué 一所小学

jury *noun*
- (*in a court*) = péishěntuán 陪审团
- (*in a competition*) = píngjiǎngtuán 评奖团

just[1] *adverb*
- (*very recently*) = gāng 刚
  I have just [arrived | seen her | received the letter...] = wǒ gāng [dào | kànjiàn tā | shōudào xìn...] 我刚 [到 | 看见她 | 收到信...]
  I had just turned on the TV = wǒ gāng dǎkāi diànshìjī 我刚打开电视机
- (*at this or that very moment*) = zhènghǎo 正好
  I was just about to phone you = wǒ zhènghǎo yào gěi nǐ dǎ diànhuà 我正好要给你打电话
  I arrived just as he was leaving = tā zhènghǎo yào zǒu de shíhou, wǒ dào le 他正好要走的时候, 我到了
- (*only*) = jǐnjǐn 仅仅, zhǐbúguò 只不过
  just two days ago = jǐnjǐn liǎng tiān yǐqián 仅仅两天以前
  he's just a child = tā zhǐbúguò shì ge háizi 他只不过是个孩子
- (*barely*)
  I got there just in time = wǒ chàyìdiǎnr méi ànshí dào nàr 我差一点儿没按时到那儿
  she's just 18 = tā gānggāng shíbā suì 她刚刚十八岁
- (*when comparing*)
  she is just as intelligent as he is = tā hé tā yíyàng cōngming 她和他一样聪明
- (*immediately*) = jiù 就
  just before the weekend = jiù zài zhōumò yǐqián 就在周末以前

just[2] *adjective*
- (*righteous*) = zhèngyì 正义
- (*impartial, fair*) = gōngzhèng 公正, gōngpíng 公平

justice *noun*
- (*rightness*) = zhèngyì 正义
- (*impartiality*) = gōngzhèng 公正, gōngpíng 公平

Kk

kangaroo *noun*
a kangaroo = yìzhī dàishǔ 一只袋鼠

karate *noun* ▶ 390
= Rìběn kōngshǒudào 日本空手道

keen *adjective*
a keen teacher = yíwèi rèxīn de lǎoshī 一位热心的老师
to be keen on swimming = xǐhuan yóuyǒng 喜欢游泳

keep *verb*
- (*to maintain*) = bǎochí 保持
  to keep a speed of 30 miles an hour = bǎochí měi xiǎoshí sānshí yīnglǐ de sùdu 保持每小时三十英里的速度
- (*to reserve*) = bǎoliú 保留
  could you keep this seat for me? = qǐng nǐ gěi wǒ bǎoliú zhège zuòwèi, hǎo ma? 请你给我保留这个座位,好吗?
- (*to restrain from departure*) = liú 留
  to keep someone in (the) hospital = bǎ mǒurén liú zài yīyuàn 把某人留在医院
- (*to preserve*) = (bǎo)cún (保)存
  we keep the wine in the cellar = wǒmen bǎ jiǔ cún zài dìjiào li 我们把酒存在地窖里
- (*to cause to remain in a state or position*)
  this sweater will keep you warm = zhèjiàn máoyī huì shǐ nǐ nuǎnhuo 这件毛衣会使你暖和
  to keep someone waiting = ràng mǒurén děnghòu 让某人等候
- (*to delay*) = dānge 耽搁
  I won't keep you long = wǒ bú huì dānge nǐ hěn jiǔ 我不会耽搁你很久
  what kept you? = shénme shì dāngele nǐ? 什么事耽搁了你?
- (*to put away*) = fàng 放
  where do you keep the cups? = nǐ bǎ chábēi fàng zài nǎr? 你把茶杯放在哪儿?
- (*not to break, not to reveal*)
  to keep a promise = lǚxíng nuòyán 履行诺言
  to keep a secret = bǎoshǒu mìmì 保守秘密, bǎo mì 保密
- (*to continue*)
  keep (on) = bù tíng de 不停地
  to keep (on) [walking | talking | running...] = bù tíng de [zǒu | jiǎng | pǎo...] 不停地 [走 | 讲 | 跑...]
  keep away = bié kàojìn 别靠近
  keep away from the fire! = bié kàojìn huǒ! 别靠近火!
  keep back = liúxia 留下
  he kept the children back after school = fàngxué yǐhòu tā bǎ háizimen liúxia 放学以后他把孩子们留下
  keep out
  to keep out of the sun = búyào jiēchù yángguāng 不要接触阳光
  to keep the rain out = bú ràng yǔshuǐ liújìnlai 不让雨水流进来
  keep up = gǎnshàng 赶上
  to keep up with the other pupils = gǎnshàng biéde xuésheng 赶上别的学生

kerb (*British English*) *noun*
= lùbiān xiāngbiānshí 路边镶边石

kettle *noun*
a kettle = yíge shuǐhú 一个水壶

key *noun*
a key (*of a lock*) = yìbǎ yàoshi 一把钥匙
(*of a keyboard*) = yíge jiàn 一个键

keyhole *noun*
a keyhole = yíge yàoshikǒng 一个钥匙孔

kick *verb*
= tī 踢
to kick someone = tī mǒurén 踢某人
he didn't kick the ball = tā méi tī qiú 他没踢球
kick off (*in a football match*) = kāiqiú 开球
kick out
to kick someone out = bǎ mǒurén gǎnchūqu 把某人赶出去

kid *noun*
- (*a child*)
  a kid = yíge xiǎoháir 一个小孩儿
- (*a young goat*)
  a kid = yìtóu xiǎo shānyáng 一头小山羊

kidnap *verb*
= bǎngjià 绑架

kill *verb*
- = shāsǐ 杀死
  kill [someone | a pig | a chicken...] = shāsǐ [mǒurén | yìtóu zhū | yìzhī jī...] 杀死 [某人 | 一头猪 | 一只鸡...]
- (*to kill in a certain way*) = ...sǐ ...死
  the poison killed lots of animals = dúyào dúsǐle xǔduō dòngwù 毒药毒死了许多动物
  the frost tonight will kill those plants = jīn yè de yánshuāng huì dòngsǐ nàxiē zhíwù 今夜的严霜会冻死那些植物
- (*to kill oneself*) = zìshā 自杀

kilo, kilogram(me) *noun* ▶ 300
a kilo = yì gōngjīn 一公斤

kilometre (*British English*), **kilometer** (*US English*) *noun* ▶ 300
a kilometre = yì gōnglǐ 一公里

kind
1 *noun*
= zhǒng 种
it's a kind of [fish | novel | hotel...] = zhè shì yìzhǒng [yú | xiǎoshuō | lǚguǎn...] 这是一种[鱼 | 小说 | 旅馆...]
this kind of film = zhèzhǒng diànyǐng 这种电影
2 *adjective*
= shànliáng 善良, hé'ǎi 和蔼

king *noun*
a king = yíge guówáng 一个国王

kingdom *noun*
a kingdom = yíge wángguó 一个王国

kiss
1 *verb*
= wěn 吻
to kiss someone = wěn mǒurén 吻某人
2 *noun*
= wěn 吻, jiēwěn 接吻

kitchen *noun*
a kitchen = yíge chúfáng 一个厨房

kite *noun*
a kite = yìzhī fēngzheng 一只风筝

kitten *noun*
a kitten = yìzhī xiǎomāo 一只小猫

knee *noun*
= xīgài 膝盖

kneel down *verb*
= guìxia 跪下

knife *noun*
a knife = yìbǎ dāo 一把刀

knit *verb*
to knit a sweater out of wool = zhī máoyī 织毛衣

knock
1 *verb*
= qiāo 敲
to knock on the door = qiāo mén 敲门
2 *noun*
to get a knock on the head = tóu bèi qiāole yíxià 头被敲了一下

knock down
- (*in an accident*) = zhuàngdǎo 撞倒
- (*to demolish*) = chāichú 拆除

knock out
- (*to make unconscious*) = dǎhūn 打昏
- (*in a contest*) = táotài 淘汰

knock over = zhuàngdǎo 撞倒

knot *noun*
a knot (*of a cord, a piece of ribbon or lace*) = yíge jié 一个结
(*of wood*) = yíge jiébā 一个节疤

know *verb*
- (*to be acquainted with*) = rènshi 认识
  do you know her? = nǐ rènshi tā ma? 你认识她吗?
- (*when talking about languages*) = dǒng 懂, huì 会
  he knows five languages = tā dǒng wǔzhǒng yǔyán 他懂五种语言
- (*to have the knowledge of*) = zhīdao 知道
  I know why he phoned = wǒ zhīdao tā wèishénme dǎ diànhuà 我知道他为什么打电话
  does he know about the party? = tā zhīdao zhège jùhuì ma? 他知道这个聚会吗?
- **he knows how to [swim | ride a bike | play chess...]** = tā huì [yóuyǒng | qí zìxíngchē | xià qí...] 他会[游泳 | 骑自行车 | 下棋...]
- **please let me know** = qǐng gàosu wǒ 请告诉我

knowledge *noun*
- (*learning*) = zhīshi 知识
- (*that which is known*) = zhīdào 知道, liǎojiě 了解

laboratory *noun*
a laboratory = yíge shíyànshì 一个实验室

lace *noun*
- (*the material*) = huābiānr 花边儿
- (*for tying shoes*) = xiédài 鞋带
  to tie one's laces = jì xiédài 系鞋带

lack
1 *noun*
a lack of [food | money | air...] = quēshǎo [shípǐn | qián | kōngqì...] 缺少[食品 | 钱 | 空气...]
2 *verb*
= quēshǎo 缺少, quēfá 缺乏
he lacks confidence = tā quēshǎo xìnxīn 他缺少信心

ladder *noun*
a ladder = yíge tīzi 一个梯子

lady *noun*
a lady = yíwèi nǚshì 一位女士

lake *noun*
a lake = yíge hú 一个湖

lamb *noun*
a lamb = yìzhī xiǎo yáng 一只小羊

lamp *noun*
a lamp = yìzhǎn dēng 一盏灯

lampshade *noun*
a lampshade = yíge dēngzhào 一个灯罩

land
1 *noun*
- (*as opposed to the sea*) = lùdì 陆地
- (*for farming*) = tiándì 田地
- (*property*) = tǔdì 土地
  a piece of land = yíkuài tǔdì 一块土地
  to own land = yōngyǒu tǔdì 拥有土地

2 *verb*
- (*to fall*) = luò 落
- (*if it's a plane*) = jiàngluò 降落, zhuólù 着陆
- (*to set on shore*) = shàng àn 上岸

landscape *noun*
- (*scenery*) = fēngjǐng 风景, jǐngsè 景色
- (*a painting*) = fēngjǐnghuà 风景画

language *noun*
- a language = yìzhǒng yǔyán 一种语言
  foreign languages = wàiyǔ 外语
- bad language = cūhuà 粗话, zānghuà 脏话

laptop *noun*
a laptop = yìtái shǒutí diànnǎo 一台手提电脑

large *adjective*
- = dà 大
  a large garden = yíge dà huāyuán 一个大花园
  a large sum of money = yí dà bǐ qián 一大笔钱
- a large population = rénkǒu hěn duō 人口很多

last
1 *adjective*
- (*final*) = zuìhòu 最后
  the last month of the year = yì nián de zuìhòu yíge yuè 一年的最后一个月
  the last person to leave = zuìhòu líkāi de nàge rén 最后离开的那个人
  that's the last time I saw her = nà shì wǒ zuìhòu yícì kànjiàn tā 那是我最后一次看见她
- (*the most recent*)
  last [time | week | month] = shàng [yícì | ge xīngqī | ge yuè] 上[一次 | 个星期 | 个月]
  last year = qùnián 去年

2 *adverb*
- (*most recently*) = shàng yícì 上一次
  when I was last here = wǒ shàng yícì lái zhèr de shíhou 我上一次来这儿的时候
- (*at the end*) = zuìhòu 最后
  I'll do the Chinese homework last (of all) = wǒ zuìhòu zuò Zhōngwén zuòyè 我最后做中文作业
  he came last in the race = tā bǐsài dé zuìhòu yìmíng 他比赛得最后一名

3 *pronoun*
they were the last to arrive = tāmen shì zuìhòu dào de 他们是最后到的
[the night | the day | the year] before last = qián [tiān wǎnshang | tiān | nián] 前[天晚上 | 天 | 年]
[the week | the month] before last = dà shàngge [xīngqī | yuè] 大上个[星期 | 月]

Languages and nationalities

Languages

The names of languages in Chinese always end with **wén** 文 or **yǔ** 语. The former usually emphasizes the written language while the latter usually emphasizes the spoken language.

Chinese	= Zhōngwén 中文, Hànyǔ 汉语
Japanese	= Rìwén 日文, Rìyǔ 日语
English	= Yīngwén 英文, Yīngyǔ 英语
French	= Fǎwén 法文, Fǎyǔ 法语

A certain language *versus* a certain country

a teacher from China	= yíge Zhōngguó lǎoshī 一个中国老师
a teacher of Chinese	= yíge Zhōngwén lǎoshī 一个中文老师
a film from Japan	= yíbù Rìběn diànyǐng 一部日本电影
a film in Japanese	= yíbù Rìwén diànyǐng 一部日文电影
a student from France	= yíge Fǎguó xuésheng 一个法国学生
a student of French	= yíge xué Fǎyǔ de xuésheng 一个学法语的学生

Nationalities

The expression of one's nationality in Chinese is always the name of the country followed by **rén** 人.

Chinese person	= Zhōngguórén 中国人
Japanese person	= Rìběnrén 日本人
British person	= Yīngguórén 英国人
Englishman/woman	= Yīnggélánrén 英格兰人
Scotsman/woman	= Sūgélánrén 苏格兰人
German	= Déguórén 德国人
American	= Měiguórén 美国人

---

4 *verb*
= chíxù 持续
the film lasts two hours = diànyǐng chíxùle liǎngge xiǎoshí 电影持续了两个小时

late
1 *adverb*
• (*far into the day or night*)
late in the afternoon = xiàwǔ wǎn xiē shíhou 下午晚些时候
late in the night = shēnyè 深夜
• (*not on time*) = wǎn 晚, chí 迟
to arrive half an hour late = wǎn dào bànge xiǎoshí 晚到半个小时
2 *adjective*
= wǎn 晚, chídào 迟到
to be late for work = shàngbān chídào 上班迟到
the train was two hours late = huǒchē wǎnle liǎngge xiǎoshí 火车晚了两个小时
to make someone late = shǐ mǒurén chídào 使某人迟到

later *adverb*
I'll tell you later = wǒ yǐhòu zài gàosu nǐ 我以后再告诉你
see you later = huítóu jiàn 回头见, zàijiàn 再见

latest *adjective*
• (*the most up-to-date*) = zuì xīn 最新
the latest news = zuì xīn xiāoxi 最新消息
• **at the latest** = zuì chí 最迟

Latin *noun*
= Lādīngyǔ 拉丁语, Lādīngwén 拉丁文

laugh
1 *verb*
- = xiào 笑
  they laughed loudly = tāmen dàshēng de xiào 他们大声地笑
- **to laugh at somebody** = xiàohua mǒurén 笑话某人

2 *noun*
= xiào 笑

laundry *noun*
- (*when referring to the place*) = xǐyīfáng 洗衣房
- **clean laundry** = xǐhǎo de yīfu 洗好的衣服
- **to do the laundry** = xǐ yīfu 洗衣服

law *noun*
- (*a set of rules in a country*) = fǎlǜ 法律
  to obey the law = zūnshǒu fǎlǜ 遵守法律
  it's against the law = zhè shì wéifàn fǎlǜ de 这是违犯法律的
- (*physical or scientific law*) = dìnglǜ 定律
  a law = yìtiáo dìnglǜ 一条定律
- (*as a subject*) = fǎxué 法学

lawn *noun*
a lawn = yíkuài cǎodì 一块草地

lawnmower *noun*
a lawnmower = yíge gēcǎojī 一个割草机

lawyer *noun*
a lawyer = yíge lǜshī 一个律师

lay *verb*
- (*to put*) = fàng 放
  to lay some newspapers on the floor = bǎ yìxiē bàozhǐ fàng zài dì shang 把一些报纸放在地上
- (*when talking about setting the table for dinner*) = bǎi 摆
  to lay the table = bǎihǎo cānjù 摆好餐具
- (*of a chicken*) = xià 下
  to lay an egg = xià yíge jīdàn 下一个鸡蛋
  lay down = fàngxia 放下
  he laid the tray down gently = tā bǎ pánzi qīngqīng fàngxia 他把盘子轻轻放下
  lay off = jiěgù 解雇

lazy *adjective*
= lǎn 懒, lǎnduò 懒惰

lead¹ *verb*
- (*to act as a head*) = lǐngdǎo 领导
  to lead a political party = lǐngdǎo yíge zhèngdǎng 领导一个政党
- (*to guide*)
  he led us through the forest = tā dàilǐng wǒmen chuānguò sēnlín 他带领我们穿过森林
- (*in a match or a race*) = lǐngxiān 领先
- (*to live*) = guò 过
  to lead a busy life = guò fánmáng de shēnghuó 过繁忙的生活
- (*to have as a result*) = dǎozhì 导致
  to lead to an accident = dǎozhì yìchǎng shìgù 导致一场事故

lead² *noun*
= qiān 铅

leader *noun*
a leader (*of a political party*) = yíge lǐngxiù 一个领袖
(*of a state*) = yíge lǐngdǎorén 一个领导人

leaf *noun*
a leaf = yípiàn yèzi 一片叶子

leak *verb*
= lòu 漏
the pipe leaks = guǎnzi lòule 管子漏了

lean
1 *verb*
- (*to rest sideways against*) = kào 靠
  to lean against the wall = kào zài qiáng shang 靠在墙上
  to lean a bicycle against the wall = bǎ zìxíngchē kào zài qiáng shang 把自行车靠在墙上
- **to lean out of the window** = bǎ shēnzi tànchū chuāng wài 把身子探出窗外

2 *adjective*
(*not fat*) = shòu 瘦
lean on = yīkào 依靠

learn *verb*
= xué 学, xuéxí 学习
to learn how to drive = xué kāichē 学开车

least
1 *adjective*
= zuì shǎo 最少
they have the least money = tāmende qián zuì shǎo 他们的钱最少

2 *pronoun*

it was the least I could do! = wǒ qǐmǎ kěyǐ zuò zhèjiàn shì! 我起码可以做这件事!

3 *adverb*

> ! *Note that when* **the least** *is used to modify an adjective, the opposite of that adjective is used in Chinese, along with the word* **zuì 最** (= *the most*).

the least expensive shop = zuì piányi de shāngdiàn 最便宜的商店

the least difficult question = zuì róngyi de wèntí 最容易的问题

4 at least

= zhìshǎo 至少

he's at least thirty = tā zhìshǎo sānshí suì 他至少三十岁

leather *verb*

= pí 皮, pígé 皮革

leave *verb*

- (*to depart or go away from*) = líkāi 离开

she left the room = tā líkāile fángjiān 她离开了房间

- (*to allow to remain*)

leave your coat here = bǎ wàiyī fàng zài zhèr 把外衣放在这儿

she left the window open = tā ràng chuānghu kāizhe 她让窗户开着

- (*to put, to give*) = liúxia 留下

he didn't leave a message = tā méi liúxia shénme huà 他没留下什么话

she left him some money = tā gěi tā liúxia yìxiē qián 她给他留下一些钱

- (*to put off*)

leave the work until tomorrow = děngdào míngtiān zài zuò zhège gōngzuò 等到明天再做这个工作

- (*to forget*) = wàng 忘

I left my bag on the train = wǒ bǎ wǒde bāo wàng zài huǒchē shang le 我把我的包忘在火车上了

- (*to remain*) = shèngxia 剩下

there's nothing left = shénme yě méi shèngxia 什么也没剩下

we've got only ten minutes left = wǒmen zhǐ shèngxia shí fēnzhōng le 我们只剩下十分钟了

- (*to let*) = ràng 让

I left them to clean the room = wǒ ràng tāmen dǎsǎo fángjiān 我让他们打扫房间

leave behind

= liúxia 留下

he left his belongings behind = tā bǎ xíngli liúxia le 他把行李留下了

leave me alone

= bié guǎn wǒ 别管我

leave out

- (*not to show or talk about*) (*by accident*) = lòudiào 漏掉

(*deliberately*) = shěngqù 省去, lüèqù 略去

- (*to exclude*) = páichú 排除

to leave out this possibility = páichú zhège kěnéngxìng 排除这个可能性

leave over

= shèngxia 剩下

there is some food left over = shèngxia yìxiē fàn 剩下一些饭

lecture *noun*

a lecture (*as part of the curriculum*) = yìtáng kè 一堂课

(*specially arranged*) = yíge jiǎngzuò 一个讲座

left

1 *noun*

- (*when referring to the direction*) = zuǒ 左

to turn to the left = xiàng zuǒ zhuǎnwān 向左转弯

- (*when referring to the side*) = zuǒbian 左边

she sat on my left = tā zuò zài wǒde zuǒbian 她坐在我的左边

2 *adjective*

= zuǒ 左

his left hand = tāde zuǒ shǒu 他的左手

3 *adverb*

= xiàng zuǒ 向左

to turn left = xiàng zuǒ guǎi 向左拐

leg *noun* ▶ **189** *noun*

= tuǐ 腿

legal *adjective*

- (*pertaining to law*) = fǎlǜ de 法律的
- (*lawful*) = héfǎ 合法

leisure *noun*

= kòngxián 空闲

leisure centre *noun*

a leisure centre = yíge yùlè zhōngxīn 一个娱乐中心

lemon *noun*

a lemon = yíge níngméng 一个柠檬

lemonade *noun*
= níngméngshuǐ 柠檬水

lend *verb*
= jiègěi 借给
to lend someone money = jiègěi mǒurén qián 借给某人钱

length *noun* ▶ 300
- (*in measurements*) = chángdù 长度
- (*of a book, a film, a list, an event*) = cháng 长

leopard *noun*
a leopard = yìzhī bào 一只豹

less ▶ 349
1 *determiner*
= shǎo 少
drink less coffee = shǎo hē kāfēi 少喝咖啡
I have less work than he does = wǒde gōngzuò bǐ tāde shǎo 我的工作比他的少
2 *pronoun*
= shǎo 少
to pay less = shǎo fù qián 少付钱
he has less than you = tāde bǐ nǐde shǎo 他的比你的少
3 *adverb*
we travel less in winter = wǒmen dōngtiān lǚxíng bǐjiào shǎo 我们冬天旅行比较少
4 *preposition*
(*minus*) = jiǎnqù 减去
5 less and less
less and less often = yuèlái yuè bù jīngcháng 越来越不经常
6 less than
= bú dào 不到
less than half an hour = bú dào bànge xiǎoshí 不到半个小时

lesson *noun*
a lesson = yìjié kè 一节课
an English lesson = yìjié Yīngyǔ kè 一节英语课

let *verb*
- (*when making suggestions*)
  let's go home = zánmen huí jiā ba 咱们回家吧
  let's go! = zánmen zǒu ba! 咱们走吧!
- (*to rent out*) (*British English*) = chūzū 出租
- (*to allow*) = ràng 让
  he let me help him = tā ràng wǒ bāngzhù tā 他让我帮助他
  I let him use my computer = wǒ ràng tā yòng wǒde jìsuànjī 我让他用我的计算机
  she wouldn't let me go = tā bú ràng wǒ zǒu 她不让我走

let down
let someone down = shǐ mǒurén shīwàng 使某人失望
let go
- (*to stop holding*) = fàngkāi 放开
  he let go of me = tā fàngkāile wǒ 他放开了我
- (*to release*) = shìfàng 释放
  he let the prisoners go = tā shìfàngle nàxiē fànrén 他释放了那些犯人

let in
- (*to a room or house*)
  he didn't let me in = tā méi ràng wǒ jìn 他没让我进
- **to let in the rain** = lòu yǔ 漏雨

let out
- (*to allow to go out*) = fàng (...) chūqu 放(...)出去
  let me out! = fàng wǒ chūqu! 放我出去!
- **to let out a scream** = fāchū yìshēng jiānjiào 发出一声尖叫

let through
to let someone through = ràng mǒurén guòqu 让某人过去

letter *noun*
a letter = yìfēng xìn 一封信

letter box *noun*
a letter box = yíge xìnxiāng 一个信箱

lettuce *noun*
a head of lettuce = yìkē shēngcài 一棵生菜

level
1 *noun*
- (*a horizontal position*) = shuǐpíng 水平
- (*a horizontal plane*) = shuǐpíng miàn 水平面
- (*a horizontal line*) = shuǐpíng xiàn 水平线

2 *adjective*
= píng 平

library *noun*
a library = yíge túshūguǎn 一个图书馆

licence (*British English*), **license** (*US English*) *noun*
a licence = yíge zhízhào 一个执照

license plate (*US English*) *noun*
a license plate = yíge qìchē páizhào 一个汽车牌照

lick *verb*
= tiǎn 舔

lid *noun*
a lid = yíge gàizi 一个盖子

lie
1 *verb*
• (*on the ground, on a bed*) = tǎng 躺
he lay down on the sofa = tā tǎngdào shāfā shang 他躺到沙发上
he was lying on the sofa = tā tǎng zài shāfā shang 他躺在沙发上
• (*to be situated*) = wèiyú 位于
• (*not to tell the truth*) = shuōhuǎng 说谎, sāhuǎng 撒谎
2 *noun*
= huǎnghuà 谎话
to tell a lie = shuō huǎnghuà 说谎话
lie around
he always leaves his keys lying around = tā zǒngshì bǎ tāde yàoshi dàochù luàn diū 他总是把他的钥匙到处乱丢
lie down = tǎngxia 躺下

life *noun*
• (*a living being*) = shēngmìng 生命
• (*the stretch of time between birth and death*) = shòumìng 寿命
• (*manner of living*) = shēnghuó 生活

lifestyle *noun*
a lifestyle = yìzhǒng shēnghuó fāngshì 一种生活方式

lift
1 *verb*
to lift one's arm = táiqǐ gēbo 抬起胳膊
to lift a suitcase = tíqǐ yíge xiāngzi 提起一个箱子
2 *noun*
• (*British English*) (*an elevator*)
a lift = yíge diàntī 一个电梯
• (*in a car*)
can you give me a lift to the station? = wǒ néng dā nǐde chē qù chēzhàn ma? 我能搭你的车去车站吗?

light
1 *noun*
• (*from the sun, moon*) = guāng 光
• (*in a room, on a machine*) = dēng 灯
to switch on the light = dǎkāi dēng 打开灯
traffic lights = jiāotōng dēng 交通灯, hónglǜdēng 红绿灯
• **have you got a light?** = nǐ yǒu huǒ ma? 你有火吗?
2 *adjective*
• (*not dark in colour*) = qiǎn 浅
a light blue dress = yíjiàn qiǎn lánsè de yīfu 一件浅蓝色的衣服
• (*bright*) = míngliàng 明亮
a light room = yìjiān míngliàng de fángjiān 一间明亮的房间
• (*not heavy*) = qīng 轻
3 *verb*
• (*to set fire to*) = diǎn 点, diǎnrán 点燃
he lit a cigarette = tā diǎn yān 他点烟
to light a fire = diǎnhuǒ 点火
• (*to give light to*) = zhàoliàng 照亮
the lamp lit the room = dēng zhàoliàng le fángjiān 灯照亮了房间

light bulb *noun*
a light bulb = yíge dēngpào 一个灯泡

lighthouse *noun*
a lighthouse = yízuò dēngtǎ 一座灯塔

lightning *noun*
a lightning = yíge shǎndiàn 一个闪电

like¹ *preposition*
• (*with a resemblance to*) = xiàng 像
he looks like a foreigner = tā kànshangqu xiàng ge wàiguórén 他看上去像个外国人
• (*in the same manner as*) = xiàng...yíyàng 像... 一样
all his sons work like him = tāde érzimen dōu xiàng tā yíyàng gōngzuò 他的儿子们都像他一样工作

like² *verb*
• (*when expressing an interest*) = xǐhuan 喜欢
I like [swimming | reading | dancing...] = wǒ xǐhuan [yóuyǒng | kàn shū | tiàowǔ...] 我喜欢 [游泳 | 看书 | 跳舞...]
• **how do you like America?** = nǐ juéde Měiguó zěnmeyàng? 你觉得美国怎么样?
• (*when expressing a wish*) = xiǎng 想, xīwàng 希望
I'd like coffee = wǒ xiǎng hē kāfēi 我想喝咖啡
I'd like to live here = wǒ xīwàng zhù zài zhèr 我希望住在这儿

limit *noun*
- (*boundary*) = jièxiàn 界限
- (*that which may not be passed*) = xiàndù 限度
- (*restriction*) = xiànzhì 限制

line *noun*
- = xiàn 线
  a line (*a thread, string, cord*) = yìgēn xiàn 一根线
- (*a long, narrow mark*) = yìtiáo xiàn 一条线
  a straight line = yìtiáo zhí xiàn 一条直线
- (*US English*) (*a queue*)
  to stand in line = páiduì 排队
- (*a row*) = pái 排
- **the line is engaged** = diànhuà zhàn xiàn 电话占线

link *verb*
- (*physically*) = liánjiē 连接
  to link London to Paris = bǎ Lúndūn gēn Bālí liánjiēqǐlai 把伦敦跟巴黎连接起来
- (*to relate to*) = liánxì 联系
  the two murders are linked = zhè liǎngcì móushā shì yǒu liánxì de 这两次谋杀是有联系的

lion *noun*
  a lion = yìtóu shīzi 一头狮子

lip *noun*
  = chún 唇, zuǐchún 嘴唇

lipstick *noun*
  = kǒuhóng 口红

list *noun*
- **a list** (*a catalogue*) = yíge mùlù 一个目录
  (*an enumeration*) = yìzhāng biǎo 一张表, yìlánbiǎo 一览表
- **a list of names** = yífèn míngdān 一份名单

listen *verb*
  = tīng 听
  to listen to music = tīng yīnyuè 听音乐

litre (*British English*), **liter** (*US English*) *noun*
  a litre = yì shēng 一升

little
1 *adjective*
- (*in quantity*)
  little [food | wine | money...] = méi yǒu duōshǎo [fàn | jiǔ | qián...] 没有多少[饭 | 酒 | 钱...]
  there is very little time = méi yǒu duōshǎo shíjiān le 没有多少时间了
- (*in size, age*) = xiǎo 小
  a little girl = yíge xiǎo nǚhái 一个小女孩
  the little finger = xiǎo shǒuzhǐ 小手指

2 *pronoun*
  a little = yìdiǎnr 一点儿
  I only ate a little = wǒ zhǐ chīle yìdiǎnr 我只吃了一点儿

3 *adverb*
  he is little known = hěn shǎo yǒu rén zhīdào tā 很少有人知道他

4 a little (bit) = yìxiē 一些, yìdiǎnr 一点儿
  to add a little (bit of) sugar = jiā yìxiē táng 加一些糖
  I can speak a little (bit of) Chinese = wǒ huì shuō yìdiǎnr Hànyǔ 我会说一点儿汉语

5 little by little = yìdiǎn yìdiǎn de 一点一点地, zhújiàn de 逐渐地

live[1] *verb*
- (*to have one's home*) = zhù 住
  he lives in Beijing = tā zhù zài Běijīng 他住在北京
- (*to be alive*) = huó 活
  to live to be a hundred = huódào yìbǎi suì 活到一百岁
- (*to spend or pass*) = guò 过
  to live a happy life = guò xìngfú de shēnghuó 过幸福的生活

live[2] *adjective*
- (*alive*) = huó 活
- (*of a broadcast*) = shíkuàng 实况, xiànchǎng 现场

lively *adjective*
- (*active*) = huóyuè 活跃
- (*vital*) = chōngmǎn huólì 充满活力
- (*vivacious*) = huópō 活泼
- (*vivid*) = shēngdòng 生动

living room *noun*
  a living room = yìjiān qǐjūshì 一间起居室

load *noun*
- (*burden*) = fùdān 负担
- (*weight that can be carried*) = zhuāngzàiliàng 装载量
- **loads of money** = dàliàng de qián 大量的钱

loaf *noun*
  a loaf (of bread) = yìtiáo (miànbāo) 一条(面包)

L

loan *noun*
(*money lent*) = dàikuǎn 贷款
a loan = yìbǐ dàikuǎn 一笔贷款
on loan
the book is on loan = zhèběn shū jièchūqu le 这本书借出去了

lobster *noun*
a lobster = yìzhī lóngxiā 一只龙虾

local *adjective*
= dāngdì 当地, běndì 本地
a local newspaper = yífèn dāngdì bàozhǐ 一份当地报纸
the local people = běndì rén 本地人

lock
1 *verb*
= suǒ 锁
she locked the door = tā suǒshangle mén 她锁上了门
2 *noun*
a lock = yìbǎ suǒ 一把锁
lock in
to lock someone in = bǎ mǒurén suǒ zài lǐmian 把某人锁在里面
to lock oneself in = bǎ zìjǐ guān zài lǐmian 把自己关在里面

locker *noun*
a locker = yíge yǒu suǒ de xiǎo chú 一个有锁的小橱

logical *adjective*
= fúhé luójí de 符合逻辑的

London *noun*
= Lúndūn 伦敦

lonely *adjective*
= gūdú 孤独

long
1 *adjective* ▶ 300
= cháng 长
a long letter = yìfēng cháng xìn 一封长信
long hair = cháng tóufa 长头发
the film is two hours long = zhèbù diànyǐng yǒu liǎngge xiǎoshí cháng 这部电影有两个小时长
I haven't seen him for a long time = wǒ hěn cháng shíjiān méi kànjiàn tā le 我很长时间没看见他了
2 *adverb*
= jiǔ 久
long ago = hěn jiǔ yǐqián 很久以前
you can stay as long as you like = nǐ yuànyì dāi duō jiǔ jiù dāi duō jiǔ 你愿意呆多久就呆多久
3 as long as = zhǐyào 只要
as long as the weather is nice = zhǐyào tiānqì hǎo 只要天气好

look
1 *verb*
• = kàn 看
to look at a photograph = kàn zhàopiàn 看照片
to look out of the window = kàn chuāng wài 看窗外
• (*to appear*) = kànshangqu 看上去
to look tired = kànshangqu hěn lèi 看上去很累
to look well = kànshangqu hěn hǎo 看上去很好
he looks young = tā kànshangqu hěn niánqīng 他看上去很年青
she looks like her mother = tā kànshangqu xiàng tā māma 她看上去像她妈妈
what does he look like? = tā (kànshangqu) shénmeyang? 他(看上去)什么样?
2 *noun*
have a look = kàn (yi) kàn 看(一)看
let me have a look = ràng wǒ kàn (yi) kàn 让我看(一)看
look after = zhàogù 照顾, zhàoliào 照料
to look after a child = zhàogù yíge háizi 照顾一个孩子
look down on = kànbuqǐ 看不起
look down on someone = kànbuqǐ mǒurén 看不起某人
look for = zhǎo 找
he is looking for a job = tā zài zhǎo gōngzuò 他在找工作
look forward to = qīdài 期待, pànwàng 盼望
I am looking forward to meeting her = wǒ qīdàizhe gēn tā jiànmiàn 我期待着跟她见面
look into = diàochá 调查
he has looked into this problem = tā diàochále zhège wèntí 他调查了这个问题
look out! = dāngxīn! 当心!, xiǎoxīn! 小心!
look through
to look through a book = cháyuè yìběn shū 查阅一本书
look up
to look up a word in a dictionary = zài cídiǎn li chá yíge cí 在词典里查一个词

loose *adjective*
- (*describing clothes*) = kuānsōng 宽松
- (*describing a screw, a tooth*) = sōng 松

lorry *noun* (*British English*)
a lorry = yíliàng kǎchē 一辆卡车

lose *verb*
- (*when talking about a thing*) = diū(shī) 丢(失)
  to lose [**a pen** | **a key** | **a bag...**] = diūshī [yìzhī bǐ | yìbǎ yàoshi | yíge bāo...] 丢失 [一支笔 | 一把钥匙 | 一个包...]
- (*when talking about friendship or a psychological state*) = shīqù 失去
  to lose [**friends** | **interest** | **confidence**] = shīqù [péngyou | xìngqù | xìnxīn] 失去 [朋友 | 兴趣 | 信心]
- (*be defeated* [*in*]) = shū 输
  we lost the game = wǒmen shūle zhèchǎng bǐsài 我们输了这场比赛
- **to lose face** = diū liǎn 丢脸, diū miànzi 丢面子
- **to lose one's temper** = fā píqì 发脾气

lost *adjective*
to get lost = mílù 迷路

lot *pronoun* ▶ 349
a lot = hěn duō 很多
he eats a lot = tā chī de hěn duō 他吃得很多
a lot of [**money** | **time** | **books...**] = hěn duō [qián | shíjiān | shū...] 很多 [钱 | 时间 | 书...]
there is not a lot left = shèngxia de bù duō le 剩下的不多了

lottery *noun*
= cǎijiǎng 彩奖
a lottery ticket = yìzhāng cǎipiào 一张彩票

loud *adjective*
= dàshēng de 大声的
to talk in a loud voice = dàshēng de jiǎnghuà 大声地讲话

loudspeaker *noun*
a loudspeaker = yíge lǎba 一个喇叭

lounge *noun*
a lounge = yìjiān xiūxishì 一间休息室

love
1 *verb*
- (*when talking about people*) = ài 爱
  do you love her? = nǐ ài tā ma? 你爱她吗?
- (*when talking about things, activities*) = àihào 爱好, xǐhuan 喜欢

2 *noun*
to be in love = zài tán liàn'ài 在谈恋爱
to make love = zuò ài 做爱

lovely *adjective*
- (*beautiful*) = měilì 美丽
  a beautiful view = měilì de jǐngsè 美丽的景色
  you've got lovely eyes = nǐ yǒu yìshuāng měilì de yǎnjīng 你有一双美丽的眼睛
- (*very nice*) = (lìng rén) yúkuài de (令人)愉快的
  a lovely weekend = yíge (lìng rén) yúkuài de zhōumò 一个(令人)愉快的周末

low *adjective*
- (*when talking about temperature, voice, position*) = dī 低
  to speak in a low voice = dī shēng shuōhuà 低声说话
- (*when talking about heights*) = ǎi 矮
  a low wall = yìdǔ ǎi qiáng 一堵矮墙

lower *verb*
to lower a flag = bǎ qí qiàngxiàlai 把旗降下来
to lower the price = jiàng/jiǎn jià 降/减价

loyal *adjective*
= zhōngchéng 忠诚, zhōngshí 忠实

luck *noun* ▶ 238
- = yùnqi 运气
  good luck! = zhù nǐ hǎo yùnqi! 祝你好运气!
  to bring someone (good) luck = gěi mǒurén dàilái hǎo yùnqi 给某人带来好运气
- **to have bad luck** = bù zǒuyùn 不走运

lucky *adjective*
= xìngyùn 幸运, yùnqi hǎo 运气好
he is lucky = tā hěn xìngyùn 他很幸运

lunch *noun*
= wǔfàn 午饭

Luxembourg *noun*
= Lúsēnbǎo 卢森堡

luxury
1 *noun*
= shēchǐ 奢侈
2 *adjective*
a luxury hotel = yìjiā háohuá lǚguǎn 一家豪华旅馆

Mm

machine *noun*
a machine = yìtái jīqì 一台机器

mad *adjective*
- (*insane*) = fēng 疯
  the dog went mad = zhètiáo gǒu fēng le 这条狗疯了
- (*infatuated*)
  to be mad about [something | somebody] = kuángrè de míliàn [mǒushì | mǒurén] 狂热地迷恋 [某事 | 某人]
- (*very angry*) = fēicháng shēngqì 非常生气

magazine *noun*
a magazine = yìběn zázhì 一本杂志

magic
1 *adjective*
= yǒu mólì de 有魔力的
2 *noun*
(*referring to the magical arts*) = móshù 魔术, xìfǎ 戏法

maiden name *noun*
= niángjiā de xìng 娘家的姓

mail
1 *noun*
- (*the postal system*) = yóudì 邮递, yóuzhèng xìtǒng 邮政系统
- (*letters*) = xìnjiàn 信件

2 *verb* (*US English*)
to mail a letter to someone = gěi mǒurén jì yìfēng xìn 给某人寄一封信

mailbox *noun* (*US English*)
a mailbox = yíge xìnxiāng 一个信箱

mailman *noun* ▶ 344
a mailman = yíge yóudìyuán 一个邮递员

main *adjective*
= zhǔyào 主要

main course *noun*
a main course = yídào zhǔ cài 一道主菜

major
1 *adjective*
= zhǔyào 主要
major industries = zhǔyào gōngyè 主要工业
2 *noun*
a major (*a military rank*) = yíge shàoxiào 一个少校
(*in university or college*) = yìmén zhuānyè 一门专业
my major is mathematics = wǒde zhuānyè shì shùxué 我的专业是数学

majority *noun*
= duōshù 多数, dàduōshù 大多数

make *verb*

> **!** *Note that the word* make *can be translated by* zuò 做, zào 造, *or* shǐ 使, *etc., depending on the meaning to be expressed. Very often the translation of the word* make *is decided by other words with which it is collocated, such as* make a phone call *or* make friends. *To find translations for other expressions like* to make a mess, to make a mistake, to make sure, *etc., look up the entries at* mess, mistake, sure, *etc.*

- = zuò 做
  to make [breakfast | furniture | a dress...] = zuò [zǎofàn | jiājù | yíjiàn yīfu...] 做 [早饭 | 家具 | 一件衣服...]
- (*to produce*) = zào 造
  to be made of [gold | metal | wood...] = shì [jīnzi | jīnshǔ | mùtou...] zào de 是 [金子 | 金属 | 木头...] 造的
- (*to cause a particular reaction*) = shǐ 使
  to make someone [happy | angry | jealous...] = shǐ mǒurén [gāoxìng | shēngqì | jìdù...] 使某人 [高兴 | 生气 | 嫉妒...]
- to make someone wait = ràng mǒurén děnghòu 让某人等候
- to make a bed = pū chuáng 铺床
- to make a film = shèzhì yíbù diànyǐng 摄制一部电影
- to make coffee = chōng kāfēi 冲咖啡
- to make room = téngchū dìfang 腾出地方
- to make a phone call = dǎ yíge diànhuà 打一个电话
- to make friends = jiāo péngyou 交朋友
- (*to earn*)
  to make a lot of money = zhuàn hěn duō qián 赚很多钱

to make a living = wéichí shēnghuó 维持生活
to make a profit = huò(dé) lì(rùn) 获(得)利(润)
make do = còuhe 凑合
make out
to make out a list of names = liè yìzhāng míngdān 列一张名单
to make a cheque out to someone = gěi mǒurén kāi yìzhāng zhīpiào 给某人开一张支票
make up
- (*to be friends again*) = héhǎo 和好, héjiě 和解
- to make up an excuse = biānzào yíge jièkǒu 编造一个借口
- to make up a parcel = bāochéng yíge bāoguǒ 包成一个包裹
- to make up for lost time = bǔshàng sǔnshī de shíjiān 补上损失的时间

make-up *noun*
= huàzhuāng 化妆
she wears make-up = tā huàzhe zhuāng 她化着妆

male *adjective*
- (*in biology*) = xióng 雄
- (*relating to men*) = nán 男

man *noun*
- a man = yíge nánrén 一个男人
- (*humankind*) = rénlèi 人类

manage *verb*
- (*to run*) = guǎnlǐ 管理
to manage [a school | a hospital | a factory] = guǎnlǐ [yíge xuéxiào | yíge yīyuàn | yíge gōngchǎng] 管理 [一个学校 | 一个医院 | 一个工厂]
- to manage to finish one's homework = shèfǎ zuòwán zuòyè 设法做完作业

manager *noun*
a manager = yíge jīnglǐ 一个经理

mandarin *noun*
- (*standard Chinese*) = Hànyǔ pǔtōnghuà 汉语普通话
- (*the fruit*) = gānjú 柑橘
a mandarin = yíge gānjú 一个柑橘

manner *noun*
a manner (*the way in which something is done*) = yìzhǒng fāngshì 一种方式
(*method*) = yìzhǒng fāngfǎ 一种方法
(*personal style of acting*) = yìzhǒng fēngdù 一种风度

manners *noun*
- (*good behaviour*) = lǐmào 礼貌
she has no manners = tā méi yǒu lǐmào 她没有礼貌
- (*social conduct*) = guījù 规矩

manufacture *verb*
= zhìzào 制造

many ▶ 349
1 *determiner*
- (*a lot of*) = xǔduō 许多, hěn duō 很多
were there many shops? = yǒu xǔduō shāngdiàn ma? 有许多商店吗?
there weren't many people there = nàr méi yǒu hěn duō rén 那儿没有很多人
- (*when used with* how, *and the anticipated number is above nine*)
how many? = duōshǎo? 多少?
how many dictionaries do you have? = nǐ yǒu duōshǎoběn cídiǎn? 你有多少本词典?
- (*when used with* how, *and the anticipated number is below ten*)
how many? = jǐ 几
how many elder brothers do you have? = nǐ yǒu jǐge gēge? 你有几个哥哥?
too many = tài duō 太多
so many = zhème duō 这么多, nàme duō 那么多
as many as = hé...yíyàng duō 和...一样多

2 *pronoun*
are there many left? = shèngxia hěn duō ma? 剩下很多吗?
I've got too many = wǒde tài duō le 我的太多了
take as many as you like = nǐ yuànyì ná duōshǎo jiù ná duōshǎo 你愿意拿多少就拿多少
many of them speak English = tāmen xǔduō rén huì shuō Yīngyǔ 他们许多人会说英语

map *noun*
a map = yìzhāng dìtú 一张地图

marble *noun*
- (*a kind of stone*) = dàlǐshí 大理石
- (*a toy*) = dànzi 弹子
a marble = yíge dànzi 一个弹子

march *verb*
= xíngjìn 行进

March *noun* ▶ 218
= sānyuè 三月

margarine *noun*
= rénzào huángyóu 人造黄油

mark
1 *noun*
- **a mark** (*a symbol*) = yíge biāojì 一个标记, yíge jìhào 一个记号
- (*British English*) (*a grade*) = chéngjì 成绩, fēnshù 分数
  to get good marks = dé hǎo chéngjì 得好成绩

2 *verb*
- **to mark homework** = pàn zuòyè 判作业
- (*to indicate*) = biāomíng 标明

marker *noun*
- **a marker** (*an examiner*) = yíge kǎoguān 一个考官
- (*a pen*) = yìzhī zhāntóubǐ 一支毡头笔
- (*a bookmark*) = yíge shūqiān 一个书签

market *noun*
= shìchǎng 市场
a market = yíge shìchǎng 一个市场
a flea market = yíge tiàozǎo shìchǎng 一个跳蚤市场
the job market = láowù shìchǎng 劳务市场

marmalade *noun*
= júzi jiàng 橘子酱, guǒjiàng 果酱

marriage *noun*
= hūnyīn 婚姻, jiéhūn 结婚

married *adjective*
- = jiéle hūn de 结了婚的, yǐ hūn de 已婚的
- **to be married to someone** = gēn mǒurén jiéhūn 跟某人结婚

marry *verb*
to marry someone = gēn mǒurén jiéhūn 跟某人结婚

marsh *noun*
a marsh = yíkuài zhǎozédì 一块沼泽地

mashed potatoes *noun*
= tǔdòu ní 土豆泥

mask *noun*
a mask = yíge miànjù 一个面具

mat *noun*
a mat = yíge diànzi 一个垫子

match
1 *noun*
- (*a game*)
  a match = yìchǎng bǐsài 一场比赛
  a football match (*British English*) = yìchǎng zúqiú bǐsài 一场足球比赛
- (*a matchstick*)
  a match = yìgēn huǒchái 一根火柴

2 *verb*
the shoes match the belt = xié hé pídài hěn xiāngpèi 鞋和皮带很相配

mate *noun*
a mate (*a friend, good buddy, pal*) (*British English*) = yíge péngyou 一个朋友, yíge huǒbàn 一个伙伴
(*a partner, husband, or wife*) = yíge duìxiàng 一个对象, yíge bànlǚ 一个伴侣
(*for animals*) = dòngwù de pèiduì 动物的配对

material *noun*
a material (*for making things*) = yìzhǒng cáiliào 一种材料
(*in written form*) = yífèn cáiliào 一份材料

math (*US English*), **maths** (*British English*) *noun*
= shùxué 数学

mathematics *noun*
= shùxué 数学

matter
1 *noun*
what's the matter (with her)? = (tā) zěnme le? (她)怎么了?

2 *verb*
does it really matter? = zhè zhēn de hěn yàojǐn ma? 这真的很要紧吗?
it doesn't matter = méi guānxi 没关系, bú yàojǐn 不要紧

maximum
1 *adjective*
- (*the highest*) = zuì gāo 最高
  the maximum price = zuì gāo jiàgé 最高价格
  a maximum temperature = zuìgāo wēndù 最高温度
- (*greatest in quantity*) = zuì dà 最大, zuì duō 最多
  the maximum amount of work = zuì dà de gōngzuò liàng 最大的工作量

2 *noun*
the maximum (*of quantity*) = zuì dà liàng 最大量
(*of space*) = zuì dà kōngjiān 最大空间

(*of speed*) = zuì gāo sùdu 最高速度

> **!** *Note that the expression* **the maximum** *is translated into Chinese as a modifier, which differs according to the noun it modifies.*

may *verb*
- (*when talking about a possibility*) = kěnéng 可能, yěxǔ 也许
  this may be true = zhè kěnéng shì zhēn de 这可能是真的
  he may have got lost = tā yěxǔ mílù le 他也许迷路了
- (*when asking for or giving permission*) = kěyǐ 可以
  may I come in? = wǒ kěyǐ jìnlai ma? 我可以进来吗?
  you may sit down = nǐ kěyǐ zuòxia 你可以坐下

May *noun* ▶ 218
= wǔyuè 五月

maybe *adverb*
= dàgài 大概, yěxǔ 也许

mayor *noun* ▶ 344
a mayor = yíge shìzhǎng 一个市长

me *pronoun*
= wǒ 我
they know me = tāmen rènshi wǒ 他们认识我

meal *noun*
a meal = yídùn fàn 一顿饭

mean
1 *verb*
- **to mean** = shì...yìsi 是...意思
  what does it mean? = zhè shì shénme yìsi? 这是什么意思?
  what does this word mean? = zhège cí shì shénme yìsi? 这个词是什么意思?
  what do you mean? = nǐ shì shénme yìsi? 你是什么意思?
- (*to have as a result*) = yìwèizhe 意味着
  it means giving up my job = zhè yìwèizhe fàngqì wǒde gōngzuò 这意味着放弃我的工作
- (*to intend*)
  I meant to buy a new car = wǒ yuánlái dǎsuàn mǎi yíliàng xīn qìchē 我原来打算买一辆新汽车
  she didn't mean to upset you = tā bú shì gùyì ràng nǐ bù gāoxìng 她不是故意让你不高兴
- (*to be of much|little importance*)
  her work means a lot to her = tāde gōngzuò duì tā hěn zhòngyào 她的工作对她很重要
  money doesn't mean much to him = qián duì tā bìng bú zhòngyào 钱对他并不重要

2 *adjective*
- (*British English*) (*not generous*) = lìnsè 吝啬, xiǎoqi 小气
- (*unfriendly*)
  to be mean to someone = duì mǒurén bù yǒuhǎo 对某人不友好

meaning *noun*
a meaning = yìzhǒng yìsi 一种意思, yìzhǒng hányì 一种含义

means *noun*
- (*an instrument*) = gōngjù 工具
  a means of transport = yìzhǒng yùnshū gōngjù 一种运输工具
- (*a way to an end*) = fāngfǎ 方法
  a means of earning money = yìzhǒng zhuàn qián de fāngfǎ 一种赚钱的方法

meanwhile *adverb*
= tóngshí 同时

measles *noun* ▶ 277
= mázhěn 麻疹

measure *verb*
= liáng 量, cèliáng 测量

meat *noun*
= ròu 肉

mechanic *noun* ▶ 344
a mechanic = yíge jìgōng 一个技工

medal *noun*
a medal = yíge jiǎngzhāng 一个奖章, yíge jiǎngpái 一个奖牌
a gold medal = yíkuài jīn pái 一块金牌, yíkuài jīnzhì jiǎngzhāng 一块金质奖章

media *noun*
the media = xīnwén méijiè 新闻媒介

medical *adjective*
- = yīxué de 医学的
  a medical college = yíge yīxuéyuàn 一个医学院
- **to have medical treatment** = jiēshòu zhìliáo 接受治疗

medicine *noun*
- (*the study*) = yīxué 医学
- (*a drug*) = yào 药
  a type of Chinese medicine = yìzhǒng zhōngyào 一种中药

Length and Weight Measurements

Length measurements

1 inch	= 2.54 cm	*1 yard*	= 91.44 cm
1 foot	= 30.48 cm	*1 mile*	= 1.61 km

Length

how long is the rope? = zhègēn shéngzi yǒu duō cháng? 这根绳子有多长?
it's ten metres long = yǒu shí mǐ cháng 有十米长
the rope is three metres too short = zhègēn shéngzi duǎnle sān mǐ 这根绳子短了三米

Height

People: *how tall is he?* = tā (yǒu) duō gāo? 他(有)多高?
he's six feet tall = tā (yǒu) liù yīngchǐ gāo 他(有)六英尺高
he's taller|smaller than I am = tā bǐ wǒ gāo/ǎi 他比我高/矮
Things: *how high is the tower?* = nàzuò tǎ yǒu duō gāo? 那座塔有多高?
it's 100 metres high = yǒu yìbǎi mǐ gāo 有一百米高
A is higher than B = A bǐ B gāo A 比B高
A is lower than B = A bǐ B ǎi/dī A 比B矮/低

Distance

how far is it from your home to your school = nǐde jiā lí nǐde xuéxiào (yǒu) duō yuǎn? 你的家离你的学校(有)多远?
it's about 5 miles = dàyuē (yǒu) wǔ yīnglǐ 大约(有)五英里

Width/breadth

how wide is the river? = zhètiáo hé yǒu duō kuān? 这条河有多宽?
it's seven metres wide = yǒu qī mǐ kuān 有七米宽

Depth

how deep is the lake? = zhège hú yǒu duō shēn? 这个湖有多深?
it's four metres deep = yǒu sì mǐ shēn 有四米深

Note that a construction with **de** 的 always comes before the noun it describes:

a street two kilometres long = yìtiáo liǎng gōnglǐ cháng **de** mǎlù 一条两公里长的马路
a 100-metre-high tower = yízuò yìbǎi mǐ gāo **de** tǎ 一座一百米高的塔
a river 50 metres wide = yìtiáo wǔshí mǐ kuān **de** hé 一条五十米宽的河

Weight measurements

1 ounce	= 28.35 g (grammes)	*1 stone*	= 6.35 kg (kilos)
*1 pound**	= 453.60 g	*1 ton*	= 1014.60 kg

* **a pound** (£1) is translated as **yì yīngbàng** 一英镑, and **a pound** (1 lb) is translated as **yí bàng** 一磅.

People: *how much does he weigh?* = tā yǒu duō zhòng? 他有多重?
he weighs 82 kilos = tā (yǒu) bāshí'èr gōngjīn zhòng 他有八十二公斤重
Things: *what does the parcel weigh?* = zhège bāoguǒ yǒu duō zhòng? 这个包裹有多重?

how heavy is it?	= zhè yǒu duō zhòng? 这有多重?
it weighs 10 kilos	= yǒu shí gōngjīn zhòng 有十公斤重
A weighs more than B	= A bǐ B zhòng A 比 B 重
sold by the kilo	= àn gōngjīn chūshòu 按公斤出售

Mediterranean *noun*
= Dìzhōnghǎi 地中海

medium *adjective*
= zhōngděng 中等

meet *verb*
- (*by accident*) = yùjiàn 遇见, pèngshang 碰上
  she met him on the street = tā zài jiē shang yùjiànle tā 她在街上遇见了他
- (*by appointment*) = jiànmiàn 见面
  can we meet next week? = wǒmen xià xīngqī jiànmiàn, hǎo ma? 我们下星期见面, 好吗?
- (*to become acquainted with*) = rènshi 认识 jiéshí 结识
  she met him at a wedding = tā zài yícì hūnlǐ shang rènshile tā 她在一次婚礼上认识了他
- (*to come face to face with*) = jiàn 见
  have you met Tom? = nǐ jiànguo Tāngmǔ ma? 你见过汤姆吗?
- (*to fetch*) = jiē 接
  I can come to the station to meet you = wǒ kěyǐ lái chēzhàn jiē nǐ 我可以来车站接你
- (*to satisfy*) = mǎnzú 满足
  can this meet your requirements? = zhè néng mǎnzú nǐde yāoqiú ma? 这能满足你的要求吗?
- (*to have a meeting*) = kāihuì 开会
  the whole school will meet in the hall this afternoon = jīntiān xiàwǔ quán xiào zài lǐtáng kāihuì 今天下午全校在礼堂开会

meeting *noun*
a meeting = yícì huì(yì) 一次会(议)

melon *noun*
a melon = yíge guā 一个瓜

melt *verb*
- = rónghuà 融化
  the snow is starting to melt = xuě kāishǐ rónghuà le 雪开始融化了
- (*cause to melt*) = rónghuà 溶化
  the salt will melt the ice = yán huì shǐ bīng rónghuà 盐会使冰溶化

member *noun*
a member (*of a party*) = yíge dǎngyuán 一个党员
(*of a team*) = yíge duìyuán 一个队员
(*of an association*) = yíge huìyuán 一个会员
(*of the Congress, Parliament*) = yíge yìyuán 一个议员
a member of staff (*in a school*) = yíge jiàoyuán 一个教员
(*in a bank, a firm*) = yíge zhíyuán 一个职员

memory *noun*
- = jìyìlì 记忆力
  he's got a good memory = tāde jìyìlì hěn hǎo 他的记忆力很好
- (*of a person, a place, or time*) = huíyì 回忆
  a memory of one's childhood = duì tóngnián de huíyì 对童年的回忆

mend *verb*
- (*to fix*) = xiūlǐ 修理
- (*by sewing*) = féngbǔ 缝补

mental *adjective*
- (*pertaining to the mind*) = jīngshén de 精神的
- (*done in the mind*) = nǎolì de 脑力的
  mental labour = nǎolì láodòng 脑力劳动
- (*relating to a disease of the mind*) = jīngshénbìng de 精神病的
  a mental patient = yíge jīngshénbìngrén 一个精神病人
  a mental hospital = yíge jīngshénbìngyuàn 一个精神病院

menu *noun*
a menu = yífèn càidān 一份菜单, yífèn càipǔ 一份菜谱

mess *noun*
a mess = yìtuánzāo 一团糟, luànqībāzāo 乱七八糟
your room is (in) a mess = nǐde fángjiān luànqībāzāo 你的房间乱七八糟
to make a mess in the kitchen = bǎ chúfáng nòng de yìtuánzāo 把厨房弄得一团糟

M

message *noun*
a message (*if it's verbal*) = yíge kǒuxìn 一个口信
(*if it's written on a piece of paper*) = yìzhāng tiáo 一张条
(*a piece of information*) = yìtiáo xiāoxi 一条消息

metal *noun*
a type of metal = yìzhǒng jīnshǔ 一种金属

method *noun*
a method = yìzhǒng fāngfǎ 一种方法

metre (*British English*), **meter** (*US English*) *noun*
a metre = yì mǐ 一米

Mexico *noun*
= Mòxīgē 墨西哥

microphone *noun*
a microphone = yíge màikèfēng 一个麦克风

microwave *noun*
a microwave = yíge wēibōlú 一个微波炉

midday *noun* ▶ 204, ▶ 412
= zhèngwǔ 正午, zhōngwǔ 中午
at midday = zài zhèngwǔ 在正午

middle *noun*
- = zhōngjiān 中间
  in the middle of the road = zài mǎlù zhōngjiān 在马路中间
- **to be in the middle of cooking a meal** = zhèngzài zuò fàn 正在做饭

middle-aged *adjective*
= zhōngnián 中年

midnight *noun* ▶ 204, ▶ 412
= wǔyè 午夜
at midnight = zài wǔyè 在午夜

might *verb*
- (*when talking about a possibility*) = yěxǔ 也许, kěnéng 可能
  she might be right = tā yěxǔ shì duì de 她也许是对的
  he said he might not come = tā shuō tā kěnéng bù lái 他说他可能不来
- (*when implying something didn't happen*)
  you might have been late = nǐ běnlái huì chídào de 你本来会迟到的
  she might have told us = tā běnlái kěyǐ gàosu wǒmen 她本来可以告诉我们
- (*when making suggestions*)
  you might like to phone him = nǐ yěxǔ kěyǐ gěi tā dǎ ge diànhuà 你也许可以给他打个电话
  it might be better to wait = zuìhǎo děng yi děng 最好等一等

mild *adjective*
- (*in temper and disposition*) = wēnhé 温和
- (*of weather*) = wēnnuǎn 温暖, nuǎnhuo 暖和
  the weather's mild, it's mild = tiānqì hěn nuǎnhuo 天气很暖和

mile *noun* ▶ 300
a mile = yì yīnglǐ 一英里

> **!** *Note that one* **mile** *is 1609 metres.*

military *adjective*
= jūnshì de 军事的

milk
1 *noun*
- (*of a cow*) = niúnǎi 牛奶
- (*of a mother*) = mǔnǎi 母奶

2 *verb*
= jǐ'nǎi 挤奶

milkman *noun* ▶ 344
a milkman = yíge sòng niúnǎi de ren 一个送牛奶的人

million *number*
one million, a million = yìbǎiwàn 一百万
three million American dollars = sānbǎiwàn měiyuán 三百万美元
a million inhabitants = yìbǎiwàn jūmín 一百万居民

mind
1 *noun*
- = tóunǎo 头脑
  to have a logical mind = yǒu luóji tóunǎo 有逻辑头脑
- **to make up one's mind to change jobs** = xià juéxīn huàn gōngzuò 下决心换工作
- **to change one's mind** = gǎibiàn zhǔyì 改变主意

2 *verb*
- (*when expressing an opinion*)
  'where shall we go?'—'I don't mind' = 'wǒmen qù nǎr?'—'wǒ wúsuǒwèi' '我们去哪儿?'—'我无所谓'
  she doesn't mind the heat = tā bú zàihu rè 她不在乎热
- (*in polite questions or requests*)
  do you mind if I smoke? = wǒ chōu yān nǐ jièyì ma? 我抽烟你介意吗?

would you mind turning on the light? = qǐng nǐ dǎkāi dēng, hǎo ma? 请你打开灯, 好吗?
- (*to be careful*) = xiǎoxīn 小心, dāngxīn 当心
  mind the steps = xiǎoxīn lóutī 小心楼梯
  mind you don't break the plates = dāngxīn bié dǎpò pánzi 当心别打破盘子
- (*to take care of*) = zhàoliào 照料, zhàokàn 照看
  to mind a few children = zhàoliào jǐge háizi 照料几个孩子
- **never mind, she'll get the next train** = méiguānxi, tā huì zuò xià yítàng huǒchē 没关系, 她会坐下一趟火车

mine[1] *pronoun*
= wǒde 我的
the green pen is mine = nàzhī lǜ de bǐ shì wǒde 那支绿的笔是我的

mine[2] *noun*
(*for extracting minerals from the ground*) = yíge kuàng 一个矿

miner *noun* ▶ 344
a miner = yíge kuànggōng 一个矿工

mineral water *noun*
a bottle of mineral water = yìpíng kuàngquánshuǐ 一瓶矿泉水

minimum
1 *adjective*
- (*lowest*) = zuì dī 最低
  the minimum price = zuì dī jiàgé 最低价格
- (*smallest in quantity*) = zuì xiǎo 最小, zuì shǎo 最少
  the minimum amount of work = zuì xiǎo gōngzuò liàng 最小工作量

2 *noun*
the minimum (*of quantity*) = zuì xiǎo liàng 最小量, zuì shǎo liàng 最少量
(*of space*) = zuì xiǎo kōngjiān 最小空间
(*of speed*) = zuì dī sùdu 最低速度

> **!** *Note that the expression* **the minimum** *is translated into Chinese as a modifier, which differs according to the noun it modifies.*

minister *noun* ▶ 344
- (*in government*) = bùzhǎng 部长
  a minister = yíge bùzhǎng 一个部长
  the minister for education = jiàoyù bùzhǎng 教育部长
- (*in religion*) = mùshī 牧师
  a minister = yíge mùshī 一个牧师

minor *adjective*
- (*small*) = xiǎo 小
  a minor operation = yíge xiǎo shǒushù 一个小手术
- (*not serious*) = qīng 轻
  a minor injury = yícì qīng shāng 一次轻伤

minority *noun*
- (*the smaller number*) = shǎoshù 少数
- (*in a population*) = shǎoshù mínzú 少数民族
  a minority = yíge shǎoshù mínzú 一个少数民族

minus *preposition*
- (*in temperature*) = língxià 零下
  it's minus four outside = wàimian língxià sì dù 外面零下四度
- (*in calculation*) = jiǎn 减
  10 minus 5 is 5 = shí jiǎn wǔ děngyú wǔ 十减五等于五

minute *noun* ▶ 204, ▶ 412
- (*a minute*) = yì fēnzhōng 一分钟
- **wait a minute, please** = qǐng děng yíhuìr 请等一会儿

mirror *noun*
a mirror = yímiàn jìngzi 一面镜子

miserable *adjective*
- (*extremely unhappy*) = tòngkǔ 痛苦
  to feel miserable = gǎndào tòngkǔ 感到痛苦
- (*extremely poor*) = pínkùn 贫困
  to have a miserable life = guò pínkùn de shēnghuó 过贫困的生活

miss *verb*
- (*to fail to hit*) = méi dǎzhòng 没打中
- (*to fail to see*)
  you can't miss it = nǐ bú huì kàn bú dào de 你不会看不到的
- (*to fail to take*) = cuòguò 错过
  to miss an opportunity = cuòguò yíge jīhuì 错过一个机会
- (*to feel sad not to see*) = xiǎng(niàn) 想(念)
  I miss you = wǒ xiǎng nǐ 我想你
- (*other uses*)
  don't miss this film = bié cuòguò zhège diànyǐng 别错过这个电影

M

she missed her plane = tā wùle fēijī 她误了飞机
to miss school = quēkè 缺课

Miss *noun*
▶ 249
= xiǎojie 小姐

missing *adjective*
- (*not to be found*) = shīzōng 失踪
  missing soldiers = shīzōng de shìbīng 失踪的士兵
- (*lacking*) = quē(shǎo) 缺(少)
  a dictionary with two pages missing = yìběn quēle liǎngyè de cídiǎn 一本缺了两页的词典

mist *noun*
= wù 雾, wùqì 雾气

mistake *noun*
a mistake = yíge cuòwù 一个错误
to make a mistake = fàn cuòwù 犯错误

mix *verb*
- (*to put together*) = hùn 混, huò 和
  to mix blue paint with yellow paint = bǎ lán yóuqī hé huáng yóuqī hùn zài yìqǐ 把蓝油漆和黄油漆混在一起
  he mixed flour and water = tā bǎ miàn hé shuǐ huò zài yìqǐ 他把面和水和在一起
- (*to associate*) = láiwǎng 来往
  to mix with the other students = hé bié de xuésheng láiwǎng 和别的学生来往
  mix up = gǎohùn 搞混
  to get the two languages mixed up = bǎ liǎngzhǒng yǔyán gǎohùn le 把两种语言搞混了
  I'm always mixing him up with his brother = wǒ zǒngshì bǎ tā hé tā gēge gǎohùn 我总是把他和他哥哥搞混

mixture *noun*
a mixture = yìzhǒng hùnhéwù 一种混合物

model *noun*
- (*of a train, a car, a building*) = móxíng 模型
  a model = yíge móxíng 一个模型
- a (fashion) model = yíge (shízhuāng) mótèr 一个(时装)模特儿 ▶ 344

modern *adjective*
= xiàndài 现代

mole *noun*
a mole (*if it's a small and round mark*) = yíge hēizhì 一个黑痣
(*if it's a large mark*) = yíkuài hēizhì 一块黑痣

moment *noun*
- a moment = yíhuìr 一会儿
  please wait a moment = qǐng děng yíhuìr 请等一会儿
- there's no-one there at the moment = xiànzài nàr méi yǒu rén 现在那儿没有人

Monday *noun* ▶ 218
= xīngqīyī 星期一, lǐbàiyī 礼拜一

money *noun*
= qián 钱

monkey *noun*
a monkey = yìzhī hóuzi 一只猴子

month *noun* ▶ 218, ▶ 412
a month = yíge yuè 一个月
he'll be back in two months' time = tā liǎngge yuè yǐhòu huílai 他两个月以后回来

monument *noun*
a monument (*if it's a pillar, a stone*) = yízuò jìniànbēi 一座纪念碑
(*if it's an object*) = yíge jìniànwù 一个纪念物

mood *noun*
(*state of emotions*) = xīnqíng 心情, qíngxù 情绪
to be in a good mood = qíngxù hěn hǎo 情绪很好
I'm in a very bad mood = wǒde qíngxù hěn bù hǎo 我的情绪很不好

moon *noun*
- (*the earth's satellite*) = yuèqiú 月球
- (*that which gives moonlight*) = yuèliàng 月亮
- a moon cake = yíkuài yuèbǐng 一块月饼
- the Moon Festival = Zhōngqiūjié 中秋节

moonlight *noun*
= yuèguāng 月光

moral *adjective*
- (*conforming to the right or the virtuous*) = yǒu dàodé de 有道德的
- (*relating to ethics*) = dàodéshang de 道德上的

more ▶ 349
1 *determiner*
- = gèng duō de 更多的
  to have more [**friends** | **money** | **time**] = yǒu gèng duō de [péngyou | qián | shíjiān] 有更多的 [朋友 | 钱 | 时间]
- **more...than someone** = ...bǐ mǒurén duō... 比某人多
  I have more work than he does = wǒde gōngzuò bǐ tā duō 我的工作比他多
  he bought more books than I did = tā mǎi de shū bǐ wǒ duō 他买的书比我多
- **there's no more** [**bread** | **milk** | **money**] = méi yǒu [miànbāo | niúnǎi | qián] le 没有 [面包 | 牛奶 | 钱] 了
- **there's more** [**bread** | **milk** | **money**] = hái yǒu [miànbāo | niúnǎi | qián] 还有 [面包 | 牛奶 | 钱]
- **would you like more** [**coffee** | **wine** | **vegetables**]? = nǐ hái yào [kāfēi | jiǔ | cài] ma? 你还要 [咖啡 | 酒 | 菜] 吗?
- **he bought two more tickets** = tā yòu mǎile liǎngzhāng piào 他又买了两张票

2 *pronoun*
please give me a little more = qǐng zài gěi wǒ yìxiē 请再给我一些
to cost more = gèng guì 更贵
I did more than you = wǒ zuò de bǐ nǐ duō 我做的比你多
she spends more of her time studying Chinese now = xiànzài tā huā gèng duō de shíjiān xuéxí Hànyǔ 现在她花更多的时间学习汉语

3 *adverb*
- (*when comparing*) = gèng 更
  it's more complicated than that = zhè bǐ nàge gèng fùzá 这比那个更复杂
- (*when talking about time*)
  not...any more = búzài... 不再...
  he doesn't smoke any more = tā búzài chōu yān le 他不再抽烟了

4 more and more = yuèlái yuè 越来越
more and more people can afford to buy cars = yuèlái yuè duō de rén mǎi de qǐ qìchē le 越来越多的人买得起汽车了
more and more expensive = yuèlái yuè guì 越来越贵

5 more or less = huò duō huò shǎo 或多或少

6 more than = duō 多
there were more than 20 people there = nàr yǒu èrshí duō ge rén 那儿有二十多个人

morning *noun* ▶ 204, ▶ 412
- **a morning** (*between dawn and 8 or 9 am*) = yíge zǎochén 一个早晨
  (*between dawn and 12:00 noon*) = yíge shàngwǔ 一个上午
- **at three o'clock in the morning** = língchén sān diǎn zhōng 凌晨三点钟

mosquito *noun*
a mosquito = yíge wénzi 一个蚊子

most
1 *determiner*
- (*the majority of*) = dàduōshù 大多数, dàbùfen 大部分
  most schools start next week = dàduōshù xuéxiào xiàge xīngqī kāixué 大多数学校下个星期开学
- (*in quantity*) = zuì duō 最多
  who has the most money? = shéide qián zuì duō 谁的钱最多
- (*in degree*) = zuì 最
  who has the most need of help? = shéi zuì xūyào bāngzhù? 谁最需要帮助?

2 *pronoun*
- = dàduōshù 大多数, dàbùfen 大部分
  most of them are Chinese = tāmen dāngzhōng dàduōshù shì Zhōngguórén 他们当中大多数是中国人
- **he did the most he could** = tā jìnle zuì dà de nǔlì 他尽了最大的努力

3 *adverb*
= zuì 最
the most expensive shop in London = Lúndūn zuì guì de shāngdiàn 伦敦最贵的商店
the most beautiful city in China = Zhōngguó zuì měilì de chéngshì 中国最美丽的城市

4 at (the) most = zhìduō 至多, zuì duō 最多

mostly *adverb*
= dàbùfen 大部分, duōbàn 多半

mother *noun*
a mother = yíge māma 一个妈妈
(*more formal*) = yíwèi mǔqīn 一位母亲

M

mother-in-law *noun*
- (*wife's mother*) = yuèmǔ 岳母
- (*husband's mother*) = pópo 婆婆

motor *noun*
a motor (*a machine*) = yìtái fādòngjī 一台发动机
(*a motor-car*) = yíliàng jīdòngchē 一辆机动车

motorbike *noun*
a motorbike = yíliàng mótuōchē 一辆摩托车

motorcyclist *noun*
a motorcyclist = yíge qí mótuōchē de rén 一个骑摩托车的人

motorist *noun*
a motorist = yíge kāi qìchē de rén 一个开汽车的人

motor racing *noun* ▶ 390
= qìchē bǐsài 汽车比赛

motorway *noun*
a motorway = yìtiáo gāosù gōnglù 一条高速公路

mountain *noun*
a mountain = yízuò shān 一座山

mountain bike *noun*
a mountain bike = yíliàng shāndì zìxíngchē 一辆山地自行车

mountain climbing *noun* ▶ 390
= dēngshān 登山

mouse *noun*
a mouse
- (*the animal*) = yìzhī lǎoshǔ 一只老鼠, yìzhī hàozi 一只耗子
- (*for a computer*) = yíge shǔbiāo 一个鼠标

moustache, mustache *noun*
a moustache = yízuǒ bāzìhú 一撮八字胡

mouth *noun*
- (*of a person or an animal*) = zuǐ 嘴, kǒu 口
  open your mouth = bǎ kǒu zhāngkāi 把口张开
- (*of a river or a volcano*) = kǒu 口
  the mouth of [a river | a volcano] = [hé | huǒshān] kǒu [河 | 火山] 口

move *verb*
- (*to make a movement*)
  don't move! = bié dòng! 别动!
  the train's starting to move = huǒchē kāishǐ kāidòng 火车开始开动
- (*to make a movement with*)
  to move the car = yídòng qìchē 移动汽车
  to move the chair (out of the way) = bǎ yǐzi bānkai 把椅子搬开
  don't move the camera = bié dòng zhàoxiàngjī 别动照相机
- to move (house) = bānjiā 搬家
  move away (*to live elsewhere*) = bānzǒu 搬走
  (*to make a movement away*) = líkāi 离开
  to move away from the window = líkāi chuānghu 离开窗户
  move back (*in house-moving*) = bānhuí 搬回
  (*to step back*) = hòutuì 后退
  move forward = qiánjìn 前进
  move in = bānjìn 搬进
  he moved in yesterday = tā zuótiān bānjìnqu le 他昨天搬进去了
  move out = bānchū 搬出

moved *adjective*
to be moved to tears = gǎndòng de liú lèi 感动得流泪

movement *noun*
- (*a current of action*) = yùndòng 运动
  a students' movement = yícì xuésheng yùndòng 一次学生运动
- (*an act of moving*) = yídòng 移动, huódòng 活动

movie (*US English*) *noun*
a movie = yíbù diànyǐng 一部电影

movies (*US English*) *noun*
the movies = diànyǐng 电影

movie theatre (*US English*) *noun*
a movie theatre = yíge diànyǐngyuàn 一个电影院

moving *adjective*
- (*affecting the feelings*) = dòngrén 动人, lìng rén gǎndòng 令人感动
- (*changing position*) = huódòng 活动

mow *verb*
- = gē 割
- to mow the lawn = xiūjiǎn cǎopíng 修剪草坪

MP, Member of Parliament *noun* ▶ 344
an MP = yíge yìyuán 一个议员

Mr *noun*
▶ 249
= xiānsheng 先生

Mrs *noun*
▶ 249
= fūrén 夫人, tàitai 太太

much ▶ 349
1 *adverb*
• (*in comparison*) = ...duō ...多
he is much taller than you = tā bǐ nǐ gāo duō le 他比你高多了
her work is much more tiring = tāde gōngzuò lèi duō le 她的工作累多了
• (*often*) = chángcháng 常常, jīngcháng 经常
they don't go out much = tāmen bù chángcháng chūqu 他们不常常出去
• (*when used with* **very** *or* **so**) = hěn 很, fēicháng 非常
he misses her very much = tā hěn xiǎngniàn tā 他很想念她
2 *pronoun*
(*in questions*) = hěn duō 很多
is there much to be done? = yǒu hěn duō shì yào zuò ma? 有很多事要做吗?
(*in negative statements*) = duō 多
he doesn't eat much = tā chī de bù duō 他吃得不多
3 *determiner*
• (*a lot of*) (*in questions*) = hěn duō 很多
do you have much work? = nǐ yǒu hěn duō gōngzuò ma? 你有很多工作吗?
(*in negative statements*) = duō 多
we haven't got much time = wǒmende shíjiān bù duō le 我们的时间不多了
• (*when used with* **how**, **very**, **too**, **so**, *or* **as**)
how much money have you got? = nǐ yǒu duōshǎo qián? 你有多少钱?
she doesn't eat very much meat = tā chī ròu chī de bù duō 她吃肉吃得不多
I spent too much money = wǒ huā qián huā de tài duō le 我花钱花得太多了
don't drink so much wine = bié hē zhème duō jiǔ 别喝这么多酒
she has as much work as I do = tāde gōngzuò hé wǒde yíyàng duō 她的工作和我的一样多

mud *noun*
= ní 泥

mug *noun*
a mug = yíge bēizi 一个杯子

multiply *verb*
• (*in arithmetic*) = chéng 乘
multiply three by five = sān chéng wǔ 三乘五
• (*to increase*) = zēngjiā 增加
the population has multiplied there = nàr rénkǒu zēngjiāle hěn duō 那儿人口增加了很多

mum, Mum (*British English*) *noun*
= māma 妈妈

murder
1 *noun*
a murder = yìqǐ móushā àn 一起谋杀案
2 *verb*
= móushā 谋杀

murderer *noun*
a murderer = yíge shārénfàn 一个杀人犯

muscle *noun*
a muscle = yíkuài jīròu 一块肌肉

museum *noun*
a museum = yíge bówùguǎn 一个博物馆

mushroom *noun*
a mushroom = yíge mógu 一个蘑菇

music *noun*
= yīnyuè 音乐

musical instrument *noun*
a musical instrument = yíjiàn yuèqì 一件乐器

musician *noun* ▶ 344
a musician (*a person who works with music*) = yíge yīnyuè gōngzuòzhě 一个音乐工作者
(*a person who is famed for working with music*) = yíge yīnyuèjiā 一个音乐家

Muslim *adjective*
= Mùsīlín 穆斯林

mussel *noun*
a mussel = yíge gébèi 一个蛤贝

must *verb*
• (*when indicating obligation*) = bìxū 必须, yídìng děi 一定得
you must come on time = nǐ yídìng děi zhǔnshí lái 你一定得准时来

M

Musical instruments

Playing an instrument

If it is an instrument played with the fingers, **play** is translated as **tán** 弹.

*to **play** the piano*	= **tán** gāngqín 弹钢琴
*to **play** the guitar*	= **tán** jítā 弹吉它

If it is a stringed instrument played with a bow, **play** is translated as **lā** 拉.

*to **play** the violin*	= **lā** xiǎotíqín 拉小提琴
*to **play** the 'cello*	= **lā** dàtíqín 拉大提琴

If it is an instrument played by blowing it with the mouth, **play** is translated as **chuī** 吹.

*to **play** the flute*	= **chuī** dízi 吹笛子
*to **play** the saxophone*	= **chuī** sàkèsīguǎn 吹萨克斯管

Players

English **-ist** can be translated into Chinese as **shǒu** 手 or **jiā** 家. The former refers to a person who plays the instrument, and the latter to a person who is famed for playing the instrument.

*a pian**ist*** = yíge gāngqín**shǒu** 一个钢琴手, yíge gāngqín**jiā** 一个钢琴家
*a violin**ist*** = yíge xiǎotíqín**shǒu** 一个小提琴手, yíge xiǎotíqín**jiā** 一个小提琴家

Used with another noun

to take piano lessons	= shàng gāngqín kè 上钢琴课
a guitar solo	= jítā dúzòu 吉它独奏
a violin teacher	= yíge xiǎo tíqín lǎoshī 一个小提琴老师

---

she must take the exam in June = tā bìxū cānjiā liùyuè de kǎoshì 她必须参加六月的考试

- (*when indicating necessity*) = yídìng yào 一定要
  you must go to the doctor = nǐ yídìng yào qù kàn yīshēng 你一定要去看医生
  we mustn't tell anyone = wǒmen yídìng bú yào gàosu rènhé rén 我们一定不要告诉任何人
- (*when assuming something is true*) = yídìng 一定, hěn kěnéng 很可能
  he must be kidding = tā yídìng shì zài kāi wánxiào 他一定是在开玩笑
  they must have left = tāmen hěn kěnéng yǐjīng zǒu le 他们很可能已经走了
- (*when indicating prohibition, with 'not'*) = bùzhǔn 不准, jìnzhǐ 禁止
  cars mustn't be parked in front of the gate = mén qián bùzhǔn tíng chē 门前不准停车

mustard *noun*
= jièmo 芥末

mutton *noun*
= yángròu 羊肉

my *determiner*
- = wǒde 我的
  this is my car = zhè shì wǒde chē 这是我的车
- **I broke my leg** = wǒ bǎ tuǐ shuāiduàn le 我把腿摔断了

> **!** *Note that when talking about parts of the body*, wǒde 我的 *is not used. See the usage note on* The human body *►* **189** *for further examples.*

myself *pronoun*
- (*when used as a reflexive pronoun*) = zìjǐ 自己
  I didn't hurt myself = wǒ méiyǒu shāngzhe zìjǐ 我没有伤着自己
  I bought myself a new watch = wǒ gěi zìjǐ mǎile yíkuài xīn shǒubiǎo 我给自己买了一块新手表

- (*when used for emphasis*)
  I told them myself = shì wǒ qīnzì gàosu tāmen de 是我亲自告诉他们的
  I did it all by myself = zhè dōu shì wǒ yíge rén zuò de 这都是我一个人做的

mystery *noun*
a mystery = yíge mí 一个迷

Nn

nail *noun* ▶ 189
- (*for use in attaching, repairing*) = dīngzi 钉子
  a nail = yìkē dīngzi 一颗钉子
- (*on the fingers or toes*) = zhījia 指甲
  a nail = yíge zhījia 一个指甲

nail polish *noun*
= zhījiāyóu 指甲油

naked *adjective*
- (*when describing the body*) = luǒtǐ de 裸体的, guāngzhe 光着
- **naked trees** = guāngtūtū de shù 光秃秃的树
- **a naked light** = yìzhǎn méi yǒu zhào de dēng 一盏没有罩的灯

name *noun*
a name = yíge míngzi 一个名字
what's your name? = nǐ jiào shénme míngzi? 你叫什么名字?
my name is Louis = wǒ(de míngzi) jiào Lùyìsī 我(的名字)叫路易斯

narrow *adjective*
= zhǎi 窄, xiázhǎi 狭窄

nasty *adjective*
- (*when referring to a smell*) = nánwén 难闻, chòu 臭
- (*threatening, dangerous*) = xiōngxiǎn 凶险
- (*ill natured*) = bēibǐ 卑鄙
- **nasty weather** = huài tiānqì 坏天气

national *adjective*
- (*of a country*) = guójiā de 国家的
  the national team = guójiā duì 国家队
- (*nation-wide*) = quánguóxìng de 全国性的
  a national newspaper = quánguóxìng de bàozhǐ 全国性的报纸
- **national income** = guómín shōurù 国民收入
- **national economy** = guómín jīngjì 国民经济
- **national anthem** = guógē 国歌
- (*referring to a group of people marked by common descent, language, culture, or historical tradition*) = mínzú de 民族的
  national costume = mínzú fúzhuāng 民族服装

native *adjective*
a native language = yìzhǒng mǔyǔ 一种母语
a native Chinese speaker = mǔyǔ shì Hànyǔ de rén 母语是汉语的人

natural *adjective*
- (*not made by humans*)
  natural gas = tiānránqì 天然气
  natural resources = zìrán zīyuán 自然资源
- (*happening in the usual course of things*) = zìrán 自然
  a natural voice = shēngyīn zìrán 声音自然
- (*normal*) = zhèngcháng 正常
  a natural death = zhèngcháng sǐwáng 正常死亡

naturally *adverb*
- (*in a natural manner*) = zìrán 自然
  she acted very naturally = tā biǎoyǎn de hěn zìrán 她表演得很自然
- (*of course*) = dāngrán 当然
  he'll naturally be sad when he hears the news = tā tīngdào xiāoxi hòu dāngrán huì nánguò 他听到消息后当然会难过

nature *noun*
- (*the external world untouched by human beings*) = zìránjiè 自然界, dàzìrán 大自然
- (*inborn mind*) = běnxìng 本性
- (*disposition of a person*) = gèxìng 个性
- (*kind, sort*) = zhǒng 种, lèi 类
  mistakes of this nature = zhèzhǒng cuòwu 这种错误
- (*character of a certain matter*) = xìngzhi 性质
  this incident is quite serious in nature = zhèjiàn shì de xìngzhi xiāngdāng yánzhòng 这件事的性质相当严重

the two questions are different in nature = zhè liǎngge wèntí de xìngzhi bù tóng 这两个问题的性质不同

naughty *adjective*
= táoqì 淘气, tiáopí 调皮

navy *noun*
= hǎijūn 海军

navy blue *adjective*
= zàngqīngsè 藏青色, hǎijūn lán 海军蓝

near
1 *preposition*
• (*in proximity*)
he lives near us = tā zhù zài wǒmen fùjìn 他住在我们附近
• (*with respect to a goal*)
the new house is near completion = zhèzuò xīn fángzi jiùyào wángōng le 这座新房子就要完工了
2 *adverb*
• (*close by*) = jìn 近
they live quite near = tāmen zhù de hěn jìn 他们住得很近
• (*in time*)
Christmas is drawing near = Shèngdànjié kuài dào le 圣诞节快到了
3 *adjective*
• (*close*) = jìn 近
the school is quite near = xuéxiào hěn jìn 学校很近
a near relative = yíge jìnqīn 一个近亲
• **in the near future** = bùjiǔ 不久, bùjiǔ de jiānglái 不久的将来

nearby *adverb*
= zài fùjìn 在附近

nearly *adverb*
• = chàbuduō 差不多, jīhū 几乎
I nearly [forgot | gave up | fell asleep] = wǒ jīhū [wàng le | fàngqì le | shuìzháo le] 我几乎[忘了|放弃了|睡着了]
• **we're nearly there** = wǒmen kuài dào nàr le 我们快到那儿了

neat *adjective*
(*when describing a room, someone's clothing*) = zhěngjié 整洁
(*when describing someone's handwriting*) = gōngzhěng 工整
(*when describing objects that have been arranged*) = zhěngqí 整齐

necessary *adjective*
• (*when referring to something that must be or happen*) = bìxū 必须, yǒu bìyào 有必要
it's necessary to tell him immediately = bìxū lìjí gàosu tā 必须立即告诉他
• (*when used with* **not**) = búbì 不必
it is not necessary for you to come = nǐ búbì lái 你不必来
• (*indispensable*) = bìxū 必需
I'll only take the necessary tools = wǒ zhǐ dài nàxiē bìxū de gōngjù 我只带那些必需的工具
• (*unavoidable*) = bìrán 必然
a necessary outcome = yíge bìrán jiéguǒ 一个必然结果
• **if necessary** = rúguǒ yǒu bìyào (de huà) 如果有必要(的话)
I'll phone you if necessary = rúguǒ yǒu bìyào, wǒ huì gěi nǐ dǎ diànhuà, 如果有必要, 我会给你打电话

neck *noun* ▶ 189
= bózi 脖子

necklace *noun*
a necklace = yìtiáo xiàngliàn 一条项链

need *verb*
• (*used with* **not** *to mean* **not have to**) = búbì 不必, bù xūyào 不需要
you don't need to ask him = nǐ búbì wèn tā 你不必问他
the house doesn't need to be sold = zhèzuò fángzi bù xūyào mài 这座房子不需要卖
• (*to have to or want*) = xūyào 需要
they'll need to come early = tāmen xūyào zǎo lái 他们需要早来
they need [money | help | friends...] = tāmen xūyào [qián | bāngzhù | péngyou...] 他们需要[钱|帮助|朋友...]
we need to see the doctor = wǒmen xūyào kàn yīshēng 我们需要看医生

needle *noun*
a needle = yìgēn zhēn 一根针

negative
1 *adjective*
• (*expressing denial, refusal, or prohibition*) = fǒudìng de 否定的
a negative answer = yíge fǒudìng de huídá 一个否定的回答
• (*unconstructive*) = xiāojí 消极
• (*in mathematics and when referring to an electrical charge*) = fù 负

2 *noun*

- (*a word that expresses denial*) = fǒudìngcí 否定词
  a negative = yíge fǒudìngcí 一个否定词
- (*in photography*) = dǐpiàn 底片
  a negative = yìzhāng dǐpiàn 一张底片

neighbour (*British English*), **neighbor** (*US English*) *noun*
a neighbour = yíge línjū 一个邻居

neither

1 *conjunction*

- (*in* **neither... nor** *sentences*) = jì bù... yě bù 既不...也不, jì méi...yě méi 既没...也没
  she speaks neither Chinese nor Japanese = tā jì bú huì shuō Hànyǔ yě bú huì shuō Rìyǔ 她既不会说汉语也不会说日语
  I have neither the time nor the energy to argue with him = wǒ jì méi yǒu shíjiān yě méi yǒu jīnglì gēn tā zhēnglùn 我既没有时间也没有精力跟他争论
  I bought neither fruits nor vegetables = wǒ jì méi mǎi shuǐguǒ yě méi mǎi qīngcài 我既没买水果也没买青菜
- (*nor*) = yě bù 也不, yě méi 也没
  'I don't agree'—'neither do I' = 'wǒ bù tóngyì'—'wǒ yě bù tóngyì' '我不同意'—'我也不同意'
  'I didn't come'—'neither did she' = 'wǒ méi lái'—'tā yě méi lái' '我没来'—'她也没来'

> ! *Note that in sentences using the verb* **yǒu 有**, *or sentences indicating past events*, **(neither...) nor...** *is translated as* **(jì méi...) yě méi... (既没...) 也没....**

2 *determiner*
= liǎng... dōu bù/méi 两... 都/没
neither book is mine = liǎngběn shū dōu bú shì wǒde 两本书都不是我的
neither girl came = liǎngge nǚháir dōu méi lái 两个女孩儿都没来

3 *pronoun*
= liǎng... dōu bù 两... 都不, liǎng... dōu méi 两... 都没
neither of them is coming = tāmen liǎngge dōu bù lái 他们两个都不来
neither of us has met her = wǒmen liǎngge dōu méi jiànguo tā 我们两个都没见过她

> ! *Note that in sentences with the verb* **yǒu 有** *or sentences indicating past events, the determiner* **neither** *and the pronoun* **neither** *are translated as* **liǎng... dōu méi 两... 都没**.

nephew *noun*

- (*brother's son*) = zhízi 侄子
  a nephew = yíge zhízi 一个侄子
- (*sister's son*) = wàisheng 外甥
  a nephew = yíge wàisheng 一个外甥

nerves *noun*

- = shénjīng 神经
- **to get on someone's nerves** = shǐ mǒurén xīnfán 使某人心烦

nervous *adjective*

- (*frightened*) = hàipà 害怕
- (*anxious*) = jǐnzhāng 紧张
  to feel nervous = gǎndào jǐnzhāng 感到紧张

nest *noun*
a nest
(*for birds*) = yíge cháo 一个巢, yíge wō 一个窝
(*for mice, wasps*) = yíge wō 一个窝

N

net *noun*

- (*for fishing*) = yúwǎng 鱼网
  a net = yìzhāng yúwǎng 一张鱼网
- (*in sports*) = wǎng 网

Netherlands *noun*
= Hélán 荷兰

network *noun*
= wǎng 网
a [radio | TV | railway...] network = yíge [guǎngbō | diànshì | tiělù...] wǎng 一个[广播 | 电视 | 铁路...] 网

neutral *adjective*

- (*not siding with either party*) = zhōnglì 中立
  a neutral nation = yíge zhōnglì guó 一个中立国
- (*belonging to neither of two opposites in chemistry or electronics*) = zhōngxìng 中性

never *adverb*

- (*for future events or actions*) = jué bù 决不, yǒngyuǎn bù 永远不
  I'll never go back again = wǒ jué bú huì zài huíqu 我决不会再回去
  she'll never forget that day = tā yǒngyuǎn bú huì wàngjì nà yì tiān 她永远不会忘记那一天

- (*for habitual events or actions*) = cónglái bù 从来不
  they never come to see us = tāmen cónglái bù lái kàn wǒmen 他们从来不来看我们
- (*for past events or actions*) = cónglái méi (yǒu) 从来没(有)
  she's never been to China = tā cónglái méi(yǒu) qùguo Zhōngguó 她从来没(有)去过中国
  never in my life have I read such a good novel = wǒ cónglái méi(yǒu) kànguo zhème hǎo de xiǎoshuō 我从来没(有)看过这么好的小说

nevertheless *adverb*
= rán'ér 然而, búguò 不过

new *adjective*
= xīn 新
a new bike = yíliàng xīn zìxíngchē 一辆新自行车

newborn baby *noun*
a newborn baby = yíge xīnshēng yīng'ér 一个新生婴儿

news *noun*
- **a piece of news** = yìtiáo xiāoxi 一条消息
  have you heard the news? = nǐ tīngdào zhètiáo xiāoxi le ma? 你听到这条消息了吗?
- (*on radio, TV*) = xīnwén 新闻

newsagent's *noun* ▶ 344
(*British English*)
a newsagent's = yìjiā bàokān xiāoshòudiàn 一家报刊销售店

newspaper *noun*
a newspaper (*a sheet*) = yìzhāng bàozhǐ 一张报纸
(*if it consists of more than one sheet*) = yífèn bàozhǐ 一份报纸

New Year *noun*
= Xīnnián 新年
Happy New Year! = Xīnnián Kuàilè! 新年快乐!

New Year's Day, New Year's (*US English*) *noun*
= Yuándàn 元旦

New Year's Eve *noun*
= Xīnnián chúxī 新年除夕

New Zealand *noun*
= Xīnxīlán 新西兰

next
1 *adjective*
- (*when talking about what is still to come or what followed*) = xià 下
  I'll take the next train to London = wǒ zuò xià (yi)bān huǒchē qù Lúndūn 我坐下(一)班火车去伦敦
  we chatted while waiting for the next bus = wǒmen yìbiān liáotiān yìbiān děng xià (yi)tàng qìchē 我们一边聊天一边等下(一)趟汽车
  'who's next?' —'I'm next' = 'shéi shì xià yige?' —'wǒ shì xià yige' '谁是下一个?' —'我是下一个'
- (*when talking about future time*)
  next [week | month | term] = xiàge [xīngqī | yuè | xuéqī] 下个 [星期 | 月 | 学期]
  next year = míngnián 明年
  next time = xià yicì 下一次
- (*when talking about the past*) = dì'èr 第二
  the next [day | week | month | year], we went to Shanghai = dì'èr [tiān | ge xīngqī | ge yuè | nián], wǒmen qùle Shànghǎi 第二[天 | 个星期 | 个月 | 年], 我们去了上海

2 *adverb*
- (*in the past*) = ránhòu 然后, jiēzhe 接着
  what happened next? = ránhòu fāshēngle shénme shì? 然后发生了什么事?
- (*now*) = xiàmian 下面, jiēxialai 接下来
  what'll we do next? = wǒmen xiàmian zuò shénme? 我们下面做什么?
- (*in the future*) = xià (yi)cì 下(一)次
  when will you go to China next? = nǐ xià (yi)cì shénme shíhou qù Zhōngguó? 你下(一)次什么时候去中国?

3 next to
- (*adjacent to*) = jǐn'āi 紧挨, jǐnkào 紧靠
- (*in rank*) = jǐn cìyú 仅次于

next door *adverb*
= gébì 隔壁

nice *adjective*
- (*when talking about the weather*) = hǎo 好
  it's a nice day today = jīntiān tiānqì hěn hǎo 今天天气很好
- (*kind, friendly*) = hǎo 好
  a nice girl = yíge hǎo gūniang 一个好姑娘

to be nice to someone = duì mǒurén hěn hǎo 对某人很好
- (*pleasant, delightful*) = lìng rén yúkuài 令人愉快

we had a nice holiday = wǒmen dùguòle yíge lìng rén yúkuài de jiàqī 我们度过了一个令人愉快的假期

nickname *noun*

a nickname (*given in contempt*) = yíge wàihào 一个外号, yíge chuòhào 一个绰号

(*given to express affection*) = yíge àichēng 一个爱称

niece *noun*

a niece (*brother's daughter*) = yíge zhínǚ 一个侄女

(*sister's daughter*) = yíge wàishengnǚ 一个外甥女

night *noun* ▶ 412
- (*as opposed to day*) = yè 夜

a night = yí yè 一夜

I didn't sleep last night = wǒ zuótiān yí yè méi shuì 我昨天一夜没睡

he stayed out all night = tā yì zhěng yè dōu zài wàimian 他一整夜都在外面
- (*evening*) = wǎnshang 晚上

a night = yíge wǎnshang 一个晚上

last night = zuótiān wǎnshang 昨天晚上
- at night = zài yè li 在夜里
- late at night = zài shēnyè 在深夜

nightclub *noun*

a nightclub = yíge yèzǒnghuì 一个夜总会

nightdress (*British English*), **nightgown** (*US English*) *noun*

a nightdress = yíjiàn shuìyī 一件睡衣

nightmare *noun*

a nightmare = yíge èmèng 一个恶梦

to have a nightmare = zuò yíge èmèng 做一个恶梦

nil *noun*

= líng 零

nine *number* ▶ 170, ▶ 204

= jiǔ 九

nineteen *number* ▶ 170, ▶ 204

= shíjiǔ 十九

nineteenth *number*
- (*in a series*) = dìshíjiǔ 第十九
- (*in dates*) ▶ 218

the nineteenth of July = qīyuè shíjiǔ rì 七月十九日

ninety *number* ▶ 170

= jiǔshí 九十

ninth *number*
- (*in a series*) = dìjiǔ 第九
- (*in dates*) ▶ 218

the ninth of December = Shí'èryuè jiǔ rì 十二月九日

no

1 *adverb*
- (*in negative answers*) = bù 不

'do you like it?'—'no, I don't' = 'nǐ xǐhuan ma?'—'bù, wǒ bù xǐhuan' '你喜欢吗?'—'不, 我不喜欢'
- (*in a negative response to a negative statement or question*) = shìde 是的, duì 对

'is he not coming?'—'no, he is not' = 'tā bù lái ma?'—'shìde, tā bù lái' '他不来吗?'—'是的,他不来'

'you didn't go, did you?'—'no, I didn't' = 'nǐ méi qù, duì ma?'—'duì, wǒ méi qù' '你没去, 对吗?'—'对, 我没去'
- no longer = bú zài 不再

he no longer smokes = tā bú zài chōu yān le 他不再抽烟了

2 *determiner*
- (*not any*) = méi yǒu 没有

we have no money = wǒmen méi yǒu qián 我们没有钱

there are no trains = méi yǒu huǒchē 没有火车

it's no problem = méi yǒu wèntí 没有问题
- (*when refusing permission*) = bùxǔ 不许, jìnzhǐ 禁止

no smoking = jìnzhǐ xīyān 禁止吸烟

no talking! = bùxǔ jiǎnghuà! 不许讲话!

nobody ▶ no-one

noise *noun*
- (*sound of any kind*) = xiǎngshēng 响声
- (*excessively loud or disturbing sound*) = zàoyīn 噪音

noisy *adjective*

= cáozá 嘈杂, zàoshēng dà 噪声大

N

none *pronoun*

- **none of** = yíge yě bù 一个也不, dōu bù 都不

  none of [**us** | **you** | **them...**] **can speak German** = [wǒmen | nǐmen | tāmen...] yíge yě bú huì shuō Déyǔ [我们 | 你们 | 他们...] 一个也不会说德语

  none of the [**books** | **gifts** | **clothes...**] **is mine** = zhèxiē [shū | lǐwù | yīfu...] dōu bú shì wǒde 这些 [书 | 礼物 | 衣服...] 都不是我的
- (*when used in sentences with the verb* yǒu 有, *or in sentences indicating past events or actions*) = yíge yě méi yǒu 一个也没有, dōu méi yǒu 都没有

  none of the girls went to the class = nǚháizi yíge yě méiyǒu qù shàngkè 女孩子一个也没有去上课

  none of us has his telephone number = wǒmen dōu méi yǒu tāde diànhuà hàomǎ 我们都没有他的电话号码
- (*when referring to something uncountable*) = yìdiǎnr yě méi yǒu 一点儿也没有

  I wanted some bread but there was none left in the house = wǒ xiǎng chī miànbāo, kěshì jiā li yìdiǎnr yě méi yǒu le 我想吃面包, 可是家里一点儿也没有了

> **!** *Note that the measure word* gè 个 *in* yíge yě bù 一个也不 *and* yíge yě méi yǒu 一个也没有 *is replaced by a different measure word, such as* jiàn 件 *and* běn 本, *when certain nouns, such as* yīfu 衣服 *and* shū 书, *are used.*

noodles *noun*
= miàntiáo 面条

nonsense *noun*
= húshuō 胡说, fèihuà 废话

noon *noun* ▶ 204, ▶ 412
= zhōngwǔ 中午

no-one *pronoun* (*also* **nobody**)

> **!** *Note that in sentences with the verb* yǒu 有, *or in sentences describing past events or actions, the negative* méi 没 *is used instead of* bù 不.

- (*when used as a subject*) = shéi yě bù 谁也不, méi yǒu rén 没有人

  no-one has a Japanese dictionary = shéi yě méi yǒu Rìwén cídiǎn 谁也没有日文词典

  no-one tells me anything = shéi yě bú gàosu wǒ rènhé shìqing 谁也不告诉我任何事情

  no-one saw him = méi yǒu rén kànjian tā 没有人看见他
- (*when used as an object*) = shéi yě bù 谁也不

  I know no-one = wǒ shéi yě bú rènshi 我谁也不认识

  I saw no-one = wǒ shéi yě méi kànjian 我谁也没看见

nor *conjunction*

> **!** *For translations of* nor *when used in combination with* neither, *look at the entry for* neither *in this dictionary.*

- = yě bù 也不

  'I don't like him'—'nor do I' = 'wǒ bù xǐhuan tā'—'wǒ yě bù xǐhuan tā' '我不喜欢他'—'我也不喜欢他'
- (*when used with the verb* yǒu 有 *or to describe past events or actions*) = yě méi (yǒu) 也没(有)

  I don't have any money and nor does he = wǒ méi yǒu qián, tā yě méi yǒu qián 我没有钱, 他也没有钱

  he didn't come and nor did his wife = tā méi(yǒu) lái, tā tàitai yě méi(yǒu) lái 他没(有)来, 他太太也没(有)来

normal *adjective*
= zhèngcháng 正常

normally *adverb*
= yìbān 一般, tōngcháng 通常

north

1 *noun*

- (*when talking about the direction*) = běi 北
- (*when talking about the region*) = běifāng 北方, běibù 北部

  in the north of China = zài Zhōngguó de běifāng 在中国的北方

2 *adverb*

- (*when talking about the direction*) = xiàng běi 向北, wǎng běi 往北

  to drive north = xiàng běi kāi 向北开
- (*when talking about the region*) = zài...běibianr 在...北边儿

  to live north of Beijing = zhù zài Běijīng běibianr 住在北京北边儿

3 *adjective*
= běi 北
to work in north London = zài běi Lúndūn gōngzuò 在北伦敦工作

North America *noun*
North America = Běi Měizhōu 北美洲

northeast *noun*
= dōngběi 东北

Northern Ireland *noun*
Northern Ireland = Běi Ài'ěrlán 北爱尔兰

northwest *noun*
the northwest = xīběi 西北

Norway *noun*
= Nuówēi 挪威

Norwegian ▶ 288
1 *adjective*
= Nuówēide 挪威的
2 *noun*
the Norwegians = Nuówēirén 挪威人

nose *noun* ▶ 189
= bízi 鼻子

not
▶ *See the boxed note on* **not** ▶ 316 *for more information and examples.*
1 *adverb*
• = bù 不
this film is not bad = zhèbù diànyǐng búcuò 这部电影不错
we are going to go out whether it rains or not = bùguǎn xià bú xià yǔ, wǒmen dōu yào chūqu 不管下不下雨, 我们都要出去
• = méi 没
hasn't he phoned you? = tā hái méi gěi nǐ dǎ diànhuà ma? 他还没给你打电话吗?
2 not at all
• (*in no way*) = yìdiǎnr yě bù 一点也不
he's not at all worried = tā yìdiǎnr yě bù dānxīn 他一点儿也不担心
• **'thanks a lot'—'not at all'** = 'fēicháng gǎnxiè'—'bú kèqi' '非常感谢'—'不客气'

note
1 *noun*
• (*to remind oneself*) = bǐjì 笔记, jìlù 记录
• (*a message*) = biàntiáo 便条
a note = yìzhāng biàntiáo 一张便条
I left you a note = wǒ gěi nǐ liúle yìzhāng biàntiáo 我给你留了一张便条
• (*an explanation attached to a text*) = zhùshì 注释
a note = yìtiáo zhùshì 一条注释
• (*British English*) (*money*) = chāopiào 钞票, zhǐbì 纸币
a note = yìzhāng chāopiào 一张钞票
a 50-pound note = yìzhāng wǔshí yīngbàng de zhǐbì 一张五十英镑的纸币
2 *verb*
• (*to make a note of*) = jìlù 记录, jìxia 记下
• (*to notice*) = zhùyì 注意

notebook *noun*
a notebook = yìběn bǐjìběn 一本笔记本

nothing *pronoun*

> **!** *Note that* **shénme 什么** *often appears at the beginning of the sentence or after the subject.*

• = shénme (...) yě méiyǒu 什么(...)也没有
nothing has changed = shénme yě méiyǒu biàn 什么也没有变
there's nothing left = shénme yě méi yǒu le 什么也没有了
she said nothing = tā shénme yě méiyǒu shuō 她什么也没有说
• (*when used with verbs indicating the current state*) = shénme... yě bù 什么... 也不
I know nothing = wǒ shénme yě bù zhīdào 我什么也不知道
she is interested in nothing modern = xiàndài de dōngxi tā shénme yě bù gǎn xìngqu 现代的东西她什么也不感兴趣
he likes nothing = tā shénme yě bù xǐhuan 他什么也不喜欢
• **to have nothing to do with** = hé...wú guān 和... 无关
I had nothing to do with it = wǒ hé zhèjiàn shì wú guān 我和这件事无关
it's nothing to do with us = zhèjiàn shì hé wǒmen wú guān 这件事和我们无关

notice
1 *verb*
• (*to observe*) = zhùyì 注意
• (*to write or publish a notice of*) = tōngzhī 通知

Not

Used to translate the verb *to be* or verbs in the present or future tense

When **not** is used with the verb **to be** or verbs in the present or future tense, it is translated as **bù** 不.

> *I* ***was not*** *in China then* = nàshí wǒ **bú** zài Zhōngguó 那时我不在中国
> *She* ***is not*** *a doctor* = tā **bú** shì yīshēng 她不是医生
> *he* ***doesn't*** *smoke* = tā **bù** chōuyān 他不抽烟
> *it* ***isn't*** *going to rain* = tiān **bú** huì xià yǔ 天不会下雨
> *I* ***won't*** *forget you* = wǒ **bú** huì wàngjì nǐ 我不会忘记你

Used to translate the verb *to have* or verbs in the perfect and continuous forms

When **not** is used with the verb **to have** or verbs in the perfective and continous forms, it is translated as **méi** 没. When used with verbs in the past tense, **not** is often translated as **méi** 没.

> *she* ***doesn't*** *have much money* = tā **méi** yǒu hěn duō qián 她没有很多钱
> *he* ***didn't*** *go to Shanghai* = tā **méi** qù Shànghǎi 他没去上海
> *I* ***haven't*** *found my key yet* = wǒ hái **méi** zhǎodào wǒde yàoshi 我还没找到我的钥匙
> *he* ***isn't*** *studying Chinese* = tā **méi** zài xuéxí Zhōngwén 他没在学习中文

In orders, instructions, prohibitions, or suggestions

When **not** is used in giving orders, instructions, prohibitions, or suggestions, it is translated as **bié** 别.

> ***don't*** *turn left* = **bié** wǎng zuǒ guǎi 别往左拐
> ***don't*** *laugh* = **bié** xiào 别笑
> *he told me* ***not*** *to come* = tā ràng wǒ **bié** lái 他让我别来

With *all*, *both*, *every* for a partial negation

When **not** is used with **all**, **both**, and **every** for partial negation, it is translated as **bù (...) dōu** 不(...)都.

> ***not all*** *the students are pleased* = **bú** shì suǒyǒu de xuésheng **dōu** gāoxìng 不是所有的学生都高兴
> *her brothers are* ***not*** *both in the US* = tāde liǎngge gēge **bù dōu** zài Měiguó 她的两个哥哥不都在美国
> ***not every*** *teacher uses this textbook* = **bú** shì měige lǎoshī **dōu** shǐyòng zhèběn kèběn 不是每个老师都使用这本课本

For complete negation

For a complete negation, Chinese uses **dōu bù** 都不.

> *none of the students is pleased* = xuéshengmen **dōu bù** gāoxìng 学生们都不高兴
> *neither of her brothers is in the US* = tāde liǎngge gēge **dōu bú** zài Měiguó 她的两个哥哥都不在美国
> *none of the teachers uses this textbook* = lǎoshīmen **dōu bú** yòng zhèběn kèběn 老师们都不用这本课本

In short questions

When **not** is used in short questions, the whole question can usually be translated as **shì bú shì** 是不是 or **duì ma** 对吗.

you were there too, ***weren't you****?* = nǐ yě zài nàr, **shì bú shì**? 你也在那儿, 是不是?
he's got a lot of money, ***hasn't he****?* = tā yǒu hěn duō qián, **duì ma**? 他有很多钱, 对吗?
you'll come too, ***won't you****?* = nǐ yě huì lái, **shì bú shì**? 你也会来, 是不是?
he likes fish, ***doesn't he****?* = tā xǐhuan chī yú, **duì ma**? 他喜欢吃鱼, 对吗?

For more examples, see the entry **not**.

---

2 *noun*
- (*an announcement circulated internally*) = tōngzhī 通知
  a notice = yífèn tōngzhī 一份通知
- (*an announcement to the public*) = tōnggào 通告, bùgào 布告
  a notice = yìzhāng tōnggào 一张通告
- (*a warning*) = (yùxiān) ... tōngzhī (预先)... 通知
  my landlord gave me a month's notice to move out = wǒde fángdōng yùxiān yíge yuè tōngzhī wǒ bānchūqu 我的房东预先一个月通知我搬出去
  the meeting was cancelled at short notice = huìyì línshí tōngzhī qǔxiāo le 会议临时通知取消了
- **don't take any notice of this matter** = bié lǐhuì zhèjiàn shì 别理会这件事

novel *noun*
a novel = yìběn xiáoshuō 一本小说

November *noun* ▶ 218
= shíyīyuè 十一月

now
1 *adverb*
- (*at the present time*) = xiànzài 现在
  he is in his office now = tā xiànzài zài bàngōngshì li 他现在在办公室里
  from now on = cóng xiànzài qǐ 从现在起
- (*immediately*) = mǎshàng 马上, lìkè 立刻
  we have to do it now = wǒmen bìxū mǎshàng zuò zhèjiàn shì 我们必须马上做这件事
  do it right now = xiànzài mǎshàng zuò 现在马上做

2 now and again, now and then
= shícháng 时常, chángcháng 常常

nowhere
1 *adverb*
- (*not to any place*) = nǎr dōu bù 哪儿都不, rènhé dìfang dōu bù 任何地方都不
  I go nowhere without my dog = méi yǒu wǒde gǒu wǒ nǎr dōu bú qù 没有我的狗我哪儿都不去
- (*in sentences describing past actions*) = nǎr dōu méi 哪儿都没, rènhé dìfang dōu méi 任何地方都没
  she went nowhere = tā rènhé dìfang dōu méi qù 她任何地方都没去

2 *noun*
= méi yǒu dìfang 没有地方
there is nowhere to sit = méi yǒu dìfang zuò 没有地方坐

nuclear *adjective*
- (*central*) = héxīn de 核心的, zhōngxīn de 中心的
- (*pertaining to the nucleus of an atom*)
  a nuclear bomb = yìkē yuánzǐdàn 一颗原子弹
  a nuclear power-station = yízuò hédiànzhàn 一座核电站
  a nuclear war = yìchǎng hézhànzhēng 一场核战争
  nuclear weapons = héwǔqì 核武器

nuisance *noun*
these flies are a nuisance = zhèxiē cāngying zhēn tǎoyàn 这些苍蝇真讨厌

N

it's a nuisance having to pay in cash = zhēn máfan, hái děi fù xiànjīn 真麻烦, 还得付现金

numb *adjective*
• = mámù 麻木
my hands are numb = wǒde shǒu mámù le 我的手麻木了
• (*anaesthetized*) = shīqù gǎnjué 失去感觉

number
1 *noun*
• **a number** (*a figure*) = yíge shù(zì) 一个数(字)
(*of a house, a bus, a telephone, a passport*) = yíge hàomǎ 一个号码
• (*when talking about quantities*) ▶ 349
a number of = yìxiē 一些
a number of people = yìxiē rén 一些人
a small number of tourists = wéishù bù duō de lǚyóuzhě 为数不多的旅游者
a large number of new products = dàliàng de xīn chǎnpǐn 大量的新产品
2 *verb*
• (*to give a number to*) = gěi...biānhào 给...编号
to number the documents = gěi wénjiàn biānhào 给文件编号
• (*to amount to*) = zǒngjì 总计

number plate *noun* (*British English*)
a number plate = yíge hàomǎpái 一个号码牌

nun *noun* ▶ 344
a nun (*Christian*) = yíge xiūnǚ 一个修女
(*Buddhist*) = yíge nígū 一个尼姑

nurse *noun* ▶ 344
a nurse = yíge hùshi 一个护士

nursery *noun*
a nursery = yíge tuō'érsuǒ 一个托儿所

nursery school *noun*
a nursery school = yíge yòu'éryuán 一个幼儿园

nut *noun*
a nut (*a walnut*) = yíge hútao 一个胡桃
(*a chestnut*) = yíge lìzi 一个栗子

nylon *noun*
= nílóng 尼龙

Oo

oak *noun*
• (*a tree*) = xiàngshù 橡树
an oak = yìkē xiàngshù 一棵橡树
• (*for making furniture, etc.*) = zuòmù 柞木, xiàngmù 橡木

oar *noun*
an oar = yìgēn jiǎng 一根桨

obedient *adjective*
= shùncóng 顺从, gōngshùn 恭顺

obey *verb*
• = fúcóng 服从, tīngcóng 听从
to obey someone = fúcóng mǒurén 服从某人
• **to obey the law** = zūnshǒu fǎlǜ 遵守法律

object
1 *noun*
an object (*a thing*) = yíge dōngxi 一个东西
(*something on which attention, interest, or emotion is fixed*) = yíge duìxiàng 一个对象
(*an end or goal*) = yíge mùdì 一个目的
(*part of a sentence*) = yíge bīnyǔ 一个宾语
2 *verb*
= fǎnduì 反对, bú zànchéng 不赞成
I object to this plan = wǒ fǎnduì zhège jìhuà 我反对这个计划

oblige *verb*
• **to be obliged to leave** = bèipò líkāi 被迫离开
• **to oblige someone to apologize** = qiángpò mǒurén dàoqiàn 强迫某人道歉

obtain *verb*
= dédào 得到, huòdé 获得

observe *verb*
• (*to watch attentively*) = guānchá 观察, kàn 看
• (*to notice*) = zhùyì 注意
• (*to act according to*) = zūnshǒu 遵守

obvious *adjective*
= míngxiǎn 明显, xiǎn'éryìjiàn 显而易见

obviously *adverb*
= xiǎnrán 显然

occasion *noun*
• (*an event*)
an occasion = yíge chǎnghé 一个场合
on special occasions = zài tèshū chǎnghé xia 在特殊场合下
• (*an opportunity*) = yíge jīhuì 一个机会

occasionally *adverb*
= ǒu'ěr 偶尔, ǒurán 偶然

occupy *verb*
• (*when talking about taking over a piece of land or a place*) = zhànlǐng 占领, zhànjù 占据
• (*when talking about taking up space or time*) = zhànyòng 占用, zhàn 占
• **she is occupied in writing a novel** = tā zhèng máng yú xiě xiǎoshuō 她正忙于写小说

occur *verb*
• (*to happen*) = fāshēng 发生
a traffic accident has occurred = fāshēngle yìqǐ jiāotōng shìgù 发生了一起交通事故
• (*to come to mind*)
a good idea occurred to me = wǒ xiǎngchūle yíge hǎo zhǔyì 我想出了一个好主意
it suddenly occurred to him that he had to phone his wife = tā tūrán xiǎngdào tā děi gěi tā tàitai dǎ diànhuà 他突然想到他得给他太太打电话

ocean *noun*
= hǎiyáng 海洋

o'clock *adverb* ▶ 204
= diǎn (zhōng) 点(钟)
it's five o'clock now = xiànzài wǔ diǎn (zhōng) 现在五点(钟)

October *noun* ▶ 218
= shíyuè 十月

octopus *noun*
an octopus = yìtiáo zhāngyú 一条章鱼

oculist *noun* ▶ 344
an oculist (*an eye doctor*) = yíge yǎnkē yīshēng一个眼科医生

odd *adjective*
• (*strange*) = qíguài 奇怪, gǔguài 古怪
• (*unpaired*) = dānzhī de 单只的, bù chéngduì de 不成对的
• (*when talking about numbers*)
an odd number (*in mathematics*) = yíge jīshù 一个奇数
(*of a house, cinema seat or room*) = yíge dānhào 一个单号

odour (*British English*), **odor** (*US English*) *noun*
= wèir 味儿
an odour = yìzhǒng wèir 一种味儿

of *preposition*
• = de 的
the sound of an engine = fādòngjī de shēngyīn 发动机的声音
in the centre of Beijing = zài Běijīng de shì zhōngxīn 在北京的市中心
the names of the pupils = xuésheng de míngzi 学生的名字
• (*when talking about quantities*) ▶ 349

> **!** **Of** *is usually not translated in this use.*

a kilo of potatoes = yì gōngjīn tǔdòu 一公斤土豆
a bottle of mineral water = yì píng kuàngquánshuǐ 一瓶矿泉水
• (*when talking about a smaller number out of a larger whole*)
six of them = tāmen dāngzhōng de liùge rén 他们当中的六个人
only three of the students came = xuésheng zhǐ láile sānge 学生只来了三个
• (*when the number or group mentioned is the entire whole*)

> **!** **Of** *is usually not translated in this use.*

there were six of them = tāmen yígòng liùge rén 他们一共六个人
all of us agree = wǒmen dōu tóngyì 我们都同意
• (*when talking about cause*)
he died of cancer = tā sǐ yú áizhèng 他死于癌症
• (*when talking about the material or substance used*)
the bottle is made of plastic = zhège píngzi shì sùliào zuò de 这个瓶子是塑料做的

off

> **!** *Frequently* **off** *occurs in combinations with verbs, for example:* **get off, go off, take off,** *etc. To find the correct translations for this type of verb, look up the separate dictionary entries at* **get, go, take,** *etc.*

1 *adverb*
- (*leaving*) = zǒu 走
  I'm off = wǒ yào zǒu le 我要走了
- (*going*) = qù 去
  they are off to Japan tomorrow = tāmen míngtiān yào qù Rìběn 他们明天要去日本
  where are you off to? = nǐ qù nǎr? 你去哪儿?
- (*away*)
  the coast is a long way off = hǎibiān lí zhèr hěn yuǎn 海边离这儿很远
  Christmas is only a month off = lí Shèngdànjié zhǐyǒu yíge yuè le 离圣诞节只有一个月了
- (*free*)
  to take a day off = xiūjià yìtiān 休假一天
  today's her day off = jīntiān tā xiūxi 今天她休息
- (*not working, switched off*)
  the lights are all off = diàndēng quán miè le 电灯全灭了

2 *adjective*
  the milk is off = niúnǎi huài le 牛奶坏了

offence (*British English*), **offense** (*US English*) *noun*
- (*a crime*) = fànzuì 犯罪, fànfǎ xíngwéi 犯法行为
  an offence = yìzhǒng fànzuì 一种犯罪
- **to take offence** = shēngqì 生气

offend *verb*
- (*to displease, to make angry*) = dézuì 得罪, chùnù 触怒
- **offend against** = wéifǎn 违犯
  did he offend against the law? = tā wéifǎn fǎlǜ le ma? 他违犯法律了吗?

offer *verb*
- (*if what is offered is money, a job, an opportunity, a glass of wine, etc.*) = tígòng 提供, gěi 给
  to offer someone a job = gěi mǒurén tígòng yíge gōngzuò jīhuì 给某人提供一个工作机会
  to offer someone a cup of coffee = gěi mǒurén yìbēi kāfēi 给某人一杯咖啡
- (*if what is offered is an opinion, an idea, a suggestion, a resignation, etc.*) = tíchū 提出
  to offer a suggestion = tíchū yìtiáo jiànyì 提出一条建议
- (*to propose a price*) = chūjià 出价
  he offered 1000 pounds for the car = tā chūjià yìqiān bàng mǎi zhèliàng qìchē 他出价一千镑买这辆汽车
- (*to express willingness*) = biǎoshì yuànyì 表示愿意
  to offer to help the children = biǎoshì yuànyì bāngzhù háizi 表示愿意帮助孩子

office *noun*
  an office (*a room*) = yíge bàngōngshì 一个办公室
  (*a department*) = yíge bànshìchù 一个办事处

office block *noun* (*British English*)
  an office block = yízuò bànggōnglóu 一座办公楼

officer *noun*
  an officer (*in the government*) = yíge guānyuán 一个官员
  (*in the army or navy*) = yíge jūnguān 一个军官
  (*in the police force*) = yíge jǐngguān 一个警官

office worker *noun* ▶ 344
  an office worker = yíge kēshì rényuán 一个科室人员

official *adjective*
- (*issued or authorized by a public authority*)
  = guānfāng 官方
  an official explanation = guānfāng de jiěshì 官方的解释
- (*pertaining to an office*)
  official duties = gōngwù 公务

often *adverb*
  = jīngcháng 经常, chángcháng 常常

oil *noun*
- (*in general*) = yóu 油
- (*from a mineral deposit*) = shíyóu 石油

okay, OK

1 *adjective*
- (*when asking or giving opinions*) = kěyǐ 可以
  is it okay if I come later? = wǒ wǎndiǎnr lái kěyǐ ma? 我晚点儿来可以吗?
  it's okay to invite them = kěyǐ yāoqǐng tāmen 可以邀请他们

- (*when talking about health*)
  to feel okay = gǎnjué búcuò 感觉不错
  are you okay? = nǐ méi shìr ba? 你没事儿吧?

2 *adverb*
okay = hǎo 好, xíng 行
'please tell me'—'ok, I'll tell you' = 'qǐng gàosu wǒ'—'hǎo, wǒ gàosu nǐ' '请告诉我'—'好, 我告诉你'

old *adjective*
- (*not new*) = jiù 旧
  old clothes = jiù yīfu 旧衣服
- (*not young*) = lǎo 老
  old people = lǎo rén 老人
- (*with a long history*) = gǔlǎo 古老, lìshǐ yōujiǔ 历史悠久
  an old church = yízuò gǔlǎo de jiàotáng 一座古老的教堂
- (*when talking about a person's age*) ▶ 170
  how old are you? (*to a child*) = nǐ jǐsuì le 你几岁了?
  (*to an older person*) = nǐ duōdà niánjì le 你多大年纪了?
  (*to others*) = nǐ duōshǎo suì le 你多少岁了?
  a three-year old girl = yíge sān suì de nǚháir 一个三岁的女孩儿
  I'm as old as he is = wǒ hé tā yíyàng dà 我和他一样大
  she's eight years older than her brother = tā bǐ tā dìdì dà bā suì 她比她弟弟大八岁
  he is the oldest = tāde niánlíng zuì dà 他的年龄最大
- (*previous*)
  that's my old address = nà shì wǒ yǐqián de dìzhǐ 那是我以前的地址
  in the old days = zài guòqù 在过去

old-fashioned *adjective*
(*when describing attitudes, ideas, clothes*) = guòshí de 过时的
(*when describing people*) = shǒujiù de 守旧的

olive
1 *noun*
an olive = yíge gǎnlǎn 一个橄榄
2 *adjective*
= gǎnlǎnsè de 橄榄色的

olive oil *noun*
= gǎnlǎn yóu 橄榄油

Olympics *noun*
= Àolínpǐkè 奥林匹克

omelette *noun*
an omelette = yíge jiāndànbǐng 一个煎蛋饼

on

> **!** *Frequently* **on** *occurs in combinations with verbs, for example:* **count on, get on, keep on,** *etc. To find the correct translations for this type of verb, look up the separate dictionary entries for* **count, get, keep,** *etc.*

1 *preposition*
- (*when the prepositional phrase specifies a location*) = (zài)...shang (在)... 上

> **!** *Note that when* **zài...shang 在... 上** *occurs at the beginning of the sentence* **zài 在** *is often omitted.*

  the book is on the table = shū zài zhuōzi shang 书在桌子上
  the hat is on top of the wardrobe = màozi zài yīguì dǐng shang 帽子在衣柜顶上
  on the shelf there are lots of dictionaries = (zài) shūjià shang yǒu hěnduō cídiǎn (在)书架上有很多词典
  you've got a spot on your nose = (zài) nǐ bízi shang yǒu ge hēidiǎnr (在)你鼻子上有个黑点儿
- (*when the prepositional phrase is a modifier indicating a location*) = ...shang ...上
  I like the picture on the wall = wǒ xǐhuan qiáng shang de nàzhāng huà 我喜欢墙上的那张画
  the pen on the desk is not mine = shūzhuō shang de gāngbǐ bú shì wǒde 书桌上的钢笔不是我的
- (*when followed by the name of a street*) = zài 在
  to live on Park Avenue = zhù zài Gōngyuán Dàjiē 住在公园大街
- (*when talking about transport*)
  to travel on the bus = zuò gōnggòng qìchē lǚxíng 坐公共汽车旅行
  I'm on my bike today = wǒ jīntiān qí zìxíngchē 我今天骑自行车
- (*about*) = guānyú 关于
  it's a book on Africa = zhè shì yìběn guānyú Fēizhōu de shū 这是一本关于非洲的书

O

a TV programme on primary school pupils = yíge guānyú xiǎoxuéshēng de diànshì jiémù 一个关于小学生的电视节目
- (*when talking about time*)

> ! *Note that* **on** *is usually not translated in this use.*

she was born on the sixth of December = tā shí'èryuè liù hào chūshēng 她十二月六号出生
I'll go there on Saturday = wǒ xīngqīliù qù nàr 我星期六去那儿
- (*when talking about the media*)
on television = zài diànshì shang 在电视上
I saw you on the news = wǒ zài xīnwén jiémù li kànjiànle nǐ 我在新闻节目里看见了你
- (*when talking about an ongoing activity*) = zài 在
the workers are on strike = gōngrénmen zài bàgōng 工人们在罢工
they are on holiday at the moment = tāmen mùqián zài dùjià 他们目前在度假

2 *adverb*
- (*when talking about what one wears*)
to have a sweater on = chuānshang yíjiàn máoyī 穿上一件毛衣
she has make-up on = tā huàle zhuāng 她化了妆
- (*working, switched on*) = kāizhe 开着
why are all the lights on? = wèishénme suǒyǒu de dēng dōu kāizhe? 为什么所有的灯都开着?
the radio was on all evening = zhěnggè wǎnshang shōuyīnjī yìzhí kāizhe 整个晚上收音机一直开着
- (*showing*) = yǎn 演
what's on? (*on TV*) = diànshì shang yǎn shénme? 电视上演什么?
(*in the cinema*) = diànyǐngyuàn yǎn shénme? 电影院演什么?
- (*when talking about a starting point*) = qǐ 起, kāishǐ 开始
from Tuesday on = cóng xīngqī'èr qǐ 从星期二起
- (*continuously*)
go on = jìxù xiàqu 继续下去
I kept on asking questions = wǒ búduàn de wèn wèntí 我不断地问问题

once

1 *adverb*
- (*one time*) = yícì 一次
once a day = yì tiān yícì 一天一次
- (*formerly*) = cóngqián 从前, céngjīng 曾经
I once studied Japanese = wǒ cóngqián xuéguo Rìyǔ 我从前学过日语

2 *conjunction*
= yídàn...jiù 一旦... 就
life will be easier once I've found a job = wǒ yídàn zhǎodào gōngzuò, shēnghuó jiù róngyi le 我一旦找到工作, 生活就容易了

3 at once = lìkè 立刻, mǎshàng 马上

one

1 *number* ▶ 170, ▶ 204
= yī 一
one child = yíge háizi 一个孩子
one of my colleagues = wǒde yíge tóngshì 我的一个同事
one hundred = yìbǎi 一百

2 *determiner*
- (*the only*) = wéiyī 唯一
she's the one person who can help you = tā shì wéiyī nénggòu bāngzhù nǐ de rén 她是唯一能够帮助你的人
it's the one thing that annoys me = zhè shì wéiyī shǐ wǒ fánnǎo de shì 这是唯一使我烦恼的事
- (*the same*) = tóngyī 同一
the two birds are flying in one direction = liǎngzhī niǎo zài cháo tóngyī fāngxiàng fēi 两只鸟在朝同一方向飞
- (*a certain*) = mǒuyī 某一
one [day | evening | morning] = mǒuyì [tiān | tiān wǎnshang | tiān shàngwǔ] 某一 [天 | 天晚上 | 天上午]

3 *pronoun*
- (*when referring to something generally*)

> ! *Note that when* **one** *refers to something generally, it is often not translated.*

I need an umbrella—have you got one? = wǒ xūyào yìbǎ yǔsǎn, nǐ yǒu ma? 我需要一把雨伞, 你有吗?
- (*when referring to a specific person or thing*)

> ! *Note that when* the one *refers to a specific person or thing, the definite article* the *is often translated as* zhè(yi) 这(一) *or* nà(yi) 那(一) *followed by an appropriate measure word.* One *is often either not translated or is translated as the noun it refers to.*

I like this new house but she prefers that old one = wǒ xǐhuan zhèzuò xīn fángzi, kěshì tā xǐhuan nàzuò jiù de 我喜欢这座新房子, 可是她喜欢那座旧的
he's the one who helped me = tā jiù shì bāngzhù wǒ de nàge rén 他就是帮助我的那个人
which one? (*referring to a* [**book** | **bus** | **table**]) = nǎ [yìběn | yíliàng | yìzhāng] 哪[一本 | 一辆 | 一张]?
this one (*referring to a* [**book** | **bus** | **table**]) = zhè [yìběn | yíliàng | yìzhāng] 这[一本 | 一辆 | 一张]
• (*when used to mean* **you** *or* **people**)
in the room, one can see the sea = zài fángjiān li, nǐ kěyi kàndào dàhǎi 在房间里, 你可以看到大海
4 one by one = yíge yíge de 一个一个地

one another *pronoun*
= hùxiāng 互相, bícǐ 彼此
to help one another = hùxiāng bāngzhù 互相帮助

oneself *pronoun*
= zìjǐ 自己
to hurt oneself = shānghài zìjǐ 伤害自己

onion *noun*
an onion = yíge yángcōng 一个洋葱
a spring onion = yìkē cōng 一棵葱

online *adjective*
= zàixiàn 在线

only
1 *adverb*
• (*merely*) = búguò 不过, jǐnjǐn 仅仅
it's only a game = zhè búguò shì yìchǎng bǐsài 这不过是一场比赛
• (*not more than*) = zhǐ 只, cái 才
they've only met once = tāmen zhǐ jiànguo yícì (miàn) 他们只见过一次(面)
2 *adjective*
= wéiyī 唯一
she was the only one who didn't speak French = tā shì wéiyī bú huì jiǎng Fǎyǔ de rén 她是唯一不会讲法语的人
an only daughter = yíge dúshēngnǚ 一个独生女
3 only just
I've only just [**arrived** | **heard the news** | **moved house...**] = wǒ gānggāng [dào | tīngdào zhège xiāoxi | bānjiā...] 我刚刚[到 | 听到这个消息 | 搬家...]

onto *preposition*
= dào...shang 到...上
to jump onto the table = tiàodào zhuōzi shang 跳到桌子上

open
1 *verb*
• **to open** = dǎkāi 打开
to open a letter = dǎkāi yìfēng xìn 打开一封信
the door opens very easily = mén hěn róngyì dǎkāi 门很容易打开
• (*when talking about the eyes*) = zhēngkāi 睁开
to open one's eyes = zhēngkāi yǎnjīng 睁开眼睛
• (*when talking about starting business for the day*) = kāi mén 开门
what time do you open? = nǐmen jǐ diǎn kāi mén 你们几点开门
(*when talking about beginning a film, a play*) = kāiyǎn 开演
(*when talking about starting a new business*) = kāi 开
she opened a Chinese restaurant here = tā zài zhèr kāile yìjiā Zhōngguó cānguǎn 她在这儿开了一家中国餐馆
2 *adjective*
• (*not closed*) = kāizhe 开着
leave the door open = ràng mén kāizhe 让门开着
an open window = kāizhe de chuāng 开着的窗
• (*when talking about the eyes*) = zhēngzhe 睁着
with open eyes = zhēngzhe yǎnjīng 睁着眼睛
• (*public*) = gōngkāi 公开
an open letter = yìfēng gōngkāi xìn 一封公开信
• (*frank*) = tǎnshuài 坦率
3 *noun*
in the open

(*outside the room*) = zài shìwài 在室外
(*outside in the country or in a field*) = zài yěwài 在野外

opener *noun*
an opener = yìbǎ qǐzi 一把起子

open-minded *adjective*
- (*free from prejudice*) = méi yǒu piānjiàn 没有偏见
- (*ready to receive and consider new ideas*) = sīxiǎng kāifàng 思想开放

opera *noun*
an opera = yíbù gējù 一部歌剧

operate *verb*
- (*to make something work*) = cāozuò 操作, kāidòng 开动
- (*to carry out an operation*) = zuò shǒushù 做手术

to operate on someone = gěi mǒurén zuò shǒushù 给某人做手术

operation *noun*
- (*when talking about a person running a machine*) = cāozuò 操作
- (*when talking about the machine working*) = yùnzhuǎn 运转
- (*when talking about a surgical procedure*) = shǒushù 手术

an operation = yíge shǒushù 一个手术
to have an operation = zuò shǒushù 做手术, kāidāo 开刀

operator *noun* ▶ 344
an operator (*a person running a machine*) = yíge cāozuò rényuán 一个操作人员
(*a person employed to connect calls*) = yíge diànhuà jiēxiànyuán 一个电话接线员

opinion *noun*
an opinion = yìzhǒng kànfa 一种看法
(*when stating one's view*)
in my opinion = yī wǒ kàn 依我看, wǒ rènwéi 我认为
in my opinion, they're lying = wǒ rènwéi tāmen zài sāhuǎng 我认为他们在撒谎

opponent *noun*
an opponent (*in a physical game or contest*) = yíge duìshǒu 一个对手
(*in an argument or debate*) = yíge fǎnduìzhě 一个反对者

opportunity *noun*
an opportunity = yíge jīhuì 一个机会
take the opportunity = jiè zhège jīhuì 借这个机会, chèn zhège jīhuì 趁这个机会
to take the opportunity to visit Beijing = jiè cǐ jīhuì fǎngwèn Běijīng 借此机会访问北京

oppose *verb*
= fǎnduì 反对
to oppose a plan = fǎnduì yíge jìhuà 反对一个计划
to be opposed to nuclear weapons = fǎnduì héwǔqì 反对核武器

opposite
1 *preposition*
= zài...duìmiàn 在... 对面
she was sitting opposite me = tā zuò zài wǒ duìmiàn 她坐在我对面
2 *adjective*
- (*directly contrary*) = xiāngfǎn 相反

the opposite direction = xiāngfǎn de fāngxiàng 相反的方向
my answer is just opposite = wǒde dá'àn zhènghǎo xiāngfǎn 我的答案正好相反
- (*facing, on the other side*) = duìmiàn 对面

he was on the opposite side of the street = tā zài mǎlù de duìmiàn 他在马路的对面
- the opposite sex = yì xìng 异性

4 *noun*
- (*that which is contrary*) = xiāngfǎn 相反

his view is completely the opposite = tāde guāndiǎn wánquán xiāngfǎn 他的观点完全相反
- (*a word with an opposite meaning*) = fǎnyìcí 反义词

what is the opposite of 'big'? = 'dà' de fǎnyìcí shì shénme? '大'的反义词是什么?

optician *noun* ▶ 344
an optician (*one who sells glasses*) = yíge yǎnjìng shāng 一个眼镜商
(*one who makes glasses*) = yíge yǎnjìng zhìzhàozhě 一个眼镜制造者

optimist *noun*
an optimist = yíge lèguānzhǔyìzhě 一个乐观主义者

optimistic *adjective*
= lèguān 乐观, lèguānzhǔyì de 乐观主义的

or *conjunction*
- = huò(zhě) 或(者)
  once or twice a week = yíge xīngqī yícì huò(zhě) liǎngcì 一个星期一次或(者)两次
- (*when offering alternatives*) = háishì 还是
  would you like tea or coffee? = nǐ xiǎng hē chá háishì kāfēi? 你想喝茶还是咖啡?
- **either...or...** = huòzhě...huòzhě... 或者...或者..., yàome...yàome... 要么...要么...
  I'll come either on Saturday or on Sunday = wǒ huòzhě xīngqīliù huòzhě xīngqītiān lái 我或者星期六或者星期天来
- (*otherwise*) = fǒuzé 否则, bùrán 不然
  you have to come or she'll be angry = nǐ yídìng děi lái, bùrán tā huì shēngqì 你一定得来, 不然她会生气

oral *adjective*
- (*spoken, not written*) = kǒutóu de 口头的
- (*relating to the mouth*) = kǒubù de 口部的
- (*taken by mouth*) = kǒufú de 口服的

orange
1 *noun*
  an orange = yíge júzi 一个橘子, yíge chéngzi 一个橙子
2 *adjective*
  = júsè 橘色, chéngsè 橙色

orange juice *noun*
  = júzhī 橘汁, chéngzhī 橙汁

orchard *noun*
  an orchard = yíge guǒyuán 一个果园

orchestra *noun*
  an orchestra = yíge guǎnxián yuèduì 一个管弦乐队

order
1 *verb*
- (*to command*) = mìnglìng 命令
  to order someone to leave = mìnglìng mǒurén líkāi 命令某人离开
- (*to request the supply of*) = dìnggòu 定购
  to order goods from a shop = xiàng yíge shāngdiàn dìnggòu huòwù 向一个商店定购货物
- (*to ask for food in a restaurant*) = diǎn cài 点菜

2 *noun*
- (*a command*) = mìnglìng 命令
  an order = yíxiàng mìnglìng 一项命令
  to give orders = xià mìnglìng 下命令
- (*a sequence*) = shùnxù 顺序
  in the right order = àn zhèngquè shùnxù 按正确顺序

3 in order to
- (*when used at the beginning of a sentence*) = wèile 为了
  in order to get a good seat, he arrived very early = wèile dédào yíge hǎo zuòwei, tā hěn zǎo jiù dào le 为了得到一个好座位, 他很早就到了
- (*when used in mid-sentence*) = yǐbiàn 以便
  he arrived very early in order to get a good seat = tā hěn zǎo jiù dào le, yǐbiàn dédào yíge hǎo zuòwei 他很早就到了, 以便得到一个好座位

ordinary *adjective*
  = pǔtōng 普通, yìbān 一般
  an ordinary family = yíge pǔtōng de jiātíng 一个普通的家庭

organ *noun*
- (*the musical instrument*) ▶ 308 = fēngqín 风琴
  an organ = yíjià fēngqín 一架风琴
- (*a part of the body*) = qìguān 器官
  an organ = yíge qìguān 一个器官

organization *noun*
  an organization = yíge zǔzhī 一个组织

organize *verb*
- (*to form into a whole*) = zǔzhī 组织
- (*to arrange*) = ānpái 安排

original *adjective*
- (*first*) = zuìchū de 最初的, zuì zǎo de 最早的
- (*not copied or derived*) = yuán(lái) 原(来)
  an original manuscript = yífèn yuángǎo 一份原稿
- (*new, fresh*) = xīnyǐng 新颖, yǒu dúdào jiànjiě de 有独到见解的

ornament *noun*
  an ornament = yíge zhuāngshìpǐn 一个装饰品

orphan *noun*
  an orphan = yíge gū'ér 一个孤儿

other

1 *adjective*

= lìng(wài) 另(外), qítā 其他, bié 别

> **!** *Note that* qítā 其他 *and* bié 别 *are used with plural nouns, and that* lìng(wài) 另(外) *can be used with both plural and singular nouns.*

not that dress, the other one = búshì nàjiàn yīfu, shì lìng(wài) yíjiàn 不是那件衣服, 是另(外)一件

they sold the other three cars = tāmen bǎ lìng(wài) sānliàng chē mài le 他们把另(外)三辆车卖了

to help the other pupils = bāngzhù qítā de xuésheng 帮助其他的学生

every other day = měi gé yìtiān 每隔一天

2 *pronoun*

he makes others angry = tā shǐ biéren shēngqì 他使别人生气

this book is mine, the others are his = zhèběn shū shì wǒde, lìngwài de shū dōu shì tāde 这本书是我的, 另外的书都是他的

they came in one after the other = tāmen yíge jiē yíge de jìnlai 他们一个接一个地进来

otherwise *conjunction*

= fǒuzé 否则, bùrán 不然

it's not dangerous, otherwise I wouldn't go = zhè bù wēixiǎn, fǒuzé wǒ bú huì qù 这不危险, 否则我不会去

otter *noun*

an otter = yíge (shuǐ)tǎ 一个水獭

ought *verb*

- (*when saying what should be done or what may happen*) = yīngdāng 应当, yīnggāi 应该

you ought not to say things like that = nǐ bù yīngdāng nàme jiǎnghuà 你不应当那么讲话

they ought to arrive tomorrow = tāmen yīnggāi míngtiān dào 他们应该明天到

- (*when saying that something didn't happen*) = běn yīng(gāi) 本应(该), běn gāi 本该

he ought to have gone with them = tā běn yīng(gāi) gēn tāmen yìqǐ qù 他本应该跟他们一起去

our *determiner*

= wǒmende 我们的

what do you think of our house? = nǐ juéde wǒmende fángzi zěnmeyàng? 你觉得我们的房子怎么样?

ours *pronoun*

= wǒmende 我们的

the grey car is ours = nàliàng huī chē shì wǒmende 那辆灰车是我们的

ourselves *pronoun*

- (*when used as a reflexive pronoun*) = (wǒmen) zìjǐ (我们)自己

we didn't hurt ourselves = wǒmen méiyǒu shāngzhe zìjǐ 我们没有伤着自己

- (*when used for emphasis*)

we will go to buy the train tickets ourselves = wǒmen zìjǐ qù mǎi huǒchē piào 我们自己去买火车票

he wants us to solve the problem by ourselves = tā yào wǒmen zìjǐ jiějué zhège wèntí 他要我们自己解决这个问题

out

> **!** *Often* out *occurs in combinations with verbs, for example:* blow out, come out, find out, give out, *etc. To find the correct translations for this type of verb, look up the separate dictionary entries at* blow, come, find, give, *etc.*

1 *adverb*

- (*outside*) = zài wàibian 在外边

to stay out in the rain = dāi zài wàibian yǔ li 呆在外边雨里

she is out in the garden = tā zài wàibian huāyuán li 她在外边花园里

- (*away from the inside*) = chū 出

to go out = chūqu 出去

to come out = chūlai 出来

- (*absent*) = bú zài 不在, chūqu 出去

he is out = tā bú zài 他不在

someone phoned you while you were out = nǐ chūqu de shíhou, yǒu rén gěi nǐ dǎ diànhuà 你出去的时候, 有人给你打电话

- (*not lit, switched off*) = (xī)miè (熄)灭

all the lights were out = suǒyǒu de dēng dōu (xī)miè le 所有的灯都(熄)灭了

2 out of

to walk out of the building = cóng dàlóu li zǒuchūlai 从大楼里走出来

please get out of this room = qǐng líkāi zhège fángjiān 请离开这个房间

outdoor *adjective*
= shìwài 室外
an outdoor swimming pool = yíge shìwài yóuyǒngchí 一个室外游泳池

outdoors *adverb*
- (*outside the house or building*) = zài shìwài 在室外
- (*out in the field*) = zài yěwài 在野外

outer space *noun*
= wàicéng kōngjiān 外层空间

outside
1 *preposition*
= zài...wàibian 在... 外边
to wait outside the school = zài xuéxiào wàibian děng 在学校外边等
2 *adverb*
let's go outside = zánmen chūqu ba 咱们出去吧
let's bring the chairs outside = zánmen bǎ yǐzi bānchūlai ba 咱们把椅子搬出来吧
3 *noun*
the outside = wàibian 外边, wàimian 外面
the outside of the building = dàlóu de wàibian 大楼的外边
4 *adjective*
= wàibù de 外部的

oven *noun*
an oven = yíge kǎoxiāng 一个烤箱

over

> **!** *Often* **over** *occurs in combinations with verbs, for example:* **get over**, **move over**, *etc. To find the correct translations for this type of verb, look up the separate dictionary entries at* **get**, **move**, *etc.*

1 *preposition*
- (*on*) = zài...shang 在... 上
to spread a cloth over the table = bǎ yíkuài táibù pū zài zhuōzi shang 把一块台布铺在桌子上
- (*from one side to the other*) = guò 过
to climb over a wall = páguò yìdǔ qiáng 爬过一堵墙
come over here = guòlai 过来
- (*above*) = zài...shàngfāng 在... 上方
the picture is over the piano = huà zài gāngqín de shàngfāng 画在钢琴的上方
- (*above in age, value, quantity, number*) = ...yǐshàng ...以上
young people over 18 = shíbā suì yǐshàng de niánqīngrén 十八岁以上的年青人
over 20 kilograms = èrshí gōngjīn yǐshàng 二十公斤以上
- (*during*)
we saw them over the weekend = wǒmen zhōumò kànjiàn tāmen le 我们周末看见他们了
- (*everywhere*)
I've looked all over the house for my keys = zài zhèzuò fángzi li, wǒ dàochù dōu zhǎoguo wǒde yàoshi 在这座房子里, 我到处都找过我的钥匙
all over the world = shìjiè gèdì 世界各地
2 *adverb*
- (*finished*) = jiéshù 结束, wán 完
the term is over = xuéqī jiéshù le 学期结束了
is the film over? = diànyǐng wán le ma? 电影完了吗?
- (*to one's home*)
to ask someone over = qǐng mǒurén dào jiā li lái 请某人到家里来
- **to start all over again** = chóngxīn kāishǐ 重新开始

overdose *noun*
= guòliàng yòng yào 过量用药

overtake *verb*
- (*when talking about driving*) = chāo chē 超车
- (*to catch up with*) = gǎnshàng 赶上

overweight *adjective*
= chāozhòng 超重

owe *verb*
(*to be indebted to*) = qiàn 欠
to owe money to someone = qiàn mǒurén qián 欠某人钱

owl *noun*
an owl = yìzhī māotóuyīng 一只猫头鹰

own
1 *adjective*
= zìjǐ de 自己的
your own room = nǐ zìjǐ de fángjiān 你自己的房间

2 *pronoun*
= zìjǐ de 自己的
I didn't use his pencil—I've got my own = wǒ méi yòng tāde qiānbǐ—wǒ yǒu wǒ zìjǐ de 我没用他的铅笔—我有我自己的
they have a house of their own = tāmen yǒu tāmen zìjǐ de fángzi 他们有他们自己的房子
3 *verb*
• (*to possess*) = yǒu 有, yōngyǒu 拥有
he owns a shop in town = tā zài chéngli yǒu yìjiā shāngdiàn 他在城里有一家商店
4 on one's own = dúzì de 独自地, dúlì de 独立地
own up = tǎnbái 坦白, chéngrèn 承认
he owned up that he was wrong = tā chéngrèn tā cuò le 他承认他错了

owner *noun*
an owner = yíge zhǔrén 一个主人

ox *noun*
an ox = yìtóu gōngniú 一头公牛

oxygen *noun*
= yǎngqì 氧气

oyster *noun*
an oyster = yíge mǔlì 一个牡蛎

Pacific *noun*
the Pacific Ocean = Tàipíngyáng 太平洋

pack
1 *verb*
• (*to fill a space or container*) = zhuāng 装
he's packing his clothes into the suitcase = tā zhèngzài bǎ tāde yīfu zhuāngjìn xiāngzi li 他正在把他的衣服装进箱子里
I've got to pack my suitcase = wǒ děi zhuāng xiāngzi 我得装箱子
• (*to wrap up and bundle together*) = bāozhuāng 包装
to pack the china = bāozhuāng cíqì 包装瓷器
• (*to get one's things together and ready to move*)
to pack up one's belongings = shōushi zìjǐ de xíngli 收拾自己的行李
2 *noun*
a pack = yìbāo 一包, yìhé 一盒
a pack of cigarettes = yìbāo xiāngyān 一包香烟
a pack of cards = yìhé pūkèpái 一盒扑克牌

package *noun*
a package
• (*a bundle*) = yìkǔn 一捆
• (*a parcel*) = yíjiàn bāoguǒ 一件包裹
• (*a packet*) = yìbāo 一包

packed *adjective*
• (*with people*) = jǐmǎn 挤满
the classroom was packed with students = jiàoshì li jǐmǎnle xuésheng 教室里挤满了学生
• (*with things*) = zhuāngmǎn 装满
the box is packed with old newspapers = hézi li zhuāngmǎnle jiù bàozhǐ 盒子里装满了旧报纸

packet *noun*
a packet = yìbāo 一包

page *noun*
a page = yíyè 一页
on page six = zài dìliùyè 在第六页

pain *noun*
= téng 疼
I've got a pain in my back = wǒ hòubèi téng 我后背疼
to be in pain = tòngkǔ 痛苦

painful *adjective*
• (*full of pain*) = téngtòng 疼痛
• (*distressing*) = tòngkǔ 痛苦

paint
1 *noun*
(*for furniture, doors, windows, etc.*) = yóuqī 油漆
2 *verb*
• (*to produce a picture*) = huà 画
• (*to apply paint to furniture, doors, windows, etc.*) = yóu 油

paintbrush *noun*
a paintbrush
• (*for producing a picture*) = yìzhī huàbǐ 一支画笔

• (*for painting surfaces*) = yìbǎ shuāzi 一把刷子

painter *noun* ▶ 344

a painter

• (*an artist*) = yíge huàjiā 一个画家

• (*one whose job is painting surfaces*) = yíge yóuqījiàng 一个油漆匠

painting *noun*

• (*a picture*) = huà 画

a painting = yìfú huà 一幅画

• (*the activity of painting pictures*) = huìhuà 绘画

pair *noun*

a pair of shoes = yìshuāng xié 一双鞋

a pair of spectacles = yífù yǎnjìng 一副眼镜

a pair of vases = yíduì huāpíng 一对花瓶

pajamas ▶ **pyjamas**

Pakistan *noun*

= Bājīsītǎn 巴基斯坦

palace *noun*

= gōngdiàn 宫殿, gōng 宫

a palace = yíge gōngdiàn 一个宫殿

pale *adjective*

• (*when describing the face*) = cāngbái 苍白

• (*when describing the moon*) = àndàn 暗淡

pancake *noun*

a pancake = yíge báojiānbǐng 一个薄煎饼

panic *verb*

= kǒnghuāng 恐慌, jīnghuāng 惊慌

pants *noun*

• (*underwear*) (*British English*) = yìtiáo nèikù 一条内裤

• (*trousers*) (*US English*) = yìtiáo kùzi 一条裤子

pantyhose *noun* (*US English*)

= jǐnshēnkù 紧身裤

paper *noun*

• (*for writing or drawing on*) = zhǐ 纸

a piece of paper = yìzhāng zhǐ 一张纸

• (*a newspaper*) = bàozhǐ 报纸

a paper (*a sheet*) = yìzhāng bàozhǐ 一张报纸

• (*consisting of more than one sheet*) = yífèn bàozhǐ 一份报纸

parachuting *noun* ▶ 390

= tiàosǎn 跳伞

parade *noun*

a parade = yícì yóuxíng 一次游行

paralysed (*British English*), **paralyzed** (*US English*) *adjective*

= tānhuàn 瘫痪

parcel *noun*

a parcel = yíge bāoguǒ 一个包裹

parents *noun*

= fùmǔ 父母

Paris *noun*

Paris = Bālí 巴黎

park

1 *noun*

a park = yíge gōngyuán 一个公园

2 *verb*

to park a car = tíngchē 停车

to park near the office = zài bàngōngshì fùjìn tíngchē 在办公室附近停车

parking lot *noun* (*US English*)

a parking lot = yíge tíngchēchǎng 一个停车场

parking meter *noun*

a parking meter = yíge tíngchē jìshíqì 一个停车计时器

parliament *noun*

= guóhuì 国会, yìhuì 议会

parrot *noun*

a parrot = yìzhī yīngwǔ 一只鹦鹉

part

• **a part** = yíbùfen 一部分

part of the [book | programme | job] = [shū | jiémù | gōngzuò] de yíbùfen [书 | 节目 | 工作] 的一部分

• (*region, area*) = dìqū 地区

in this part of China = zài Zhōngguó de zhè yī dìqū 在中国的这一地区

• (*for a machine, a car, etc.*) = língjiàn 零件, bùjiàn 部件

a part = yíge língjiàn 一个零件

• (*a role*) = juésè 角色

to play the part of Tom = bànyǎn Tāngmǔ de juésè 扮演汤姆的角色

participate *verb*

= cānjiā 参加

to participate in the discussion = cānjiā tǎolùn 参加讨论

P

particular
1 *adjective*
= tèbié 特别, tèshū 特殊
2 in particular = tèbié 特别, yóuqí 尤其

partner *noun*
a partner (*in a love relationship*) = yíge bànlǚ 一个伴侣
(*in dancing*) = yíge wǔbàn 一个舞伴
(*in sports and games*) = yíge dádàng 一个搭档
(*in business*) = yíge hézuòzhě 一个合作者

part-time *adverb*
= fēi quánrì 非全日
to work part-time = fēi quánrì gōngzuò 非全日工作

party *noun*
- (*a social event*) = jùhuì 聚会
  a party = yícì jùhuì 一次聚会
- (*held in the evening*) = wǎnhuì 晚会
  a birthday party = yícì shēngri wǎnhuì 一次生日晚会
- **a political party** = yíge zhèngdǎng 一个政党

pass *verb*
- (*to go through*) = guò 过, tōngguò 通过
  to let someone pass = ràng mǒurén guòqu 让某人过去
- (*to go by*) = lùguò 路过, jīngguò 经过
  to pass the school = lùguò xuéxiào 路过学校
- (*to overtake*) = chāoguò 超过, chāoyuè 超越
  to pass a car = chāoguò yíliàng chē 超过一辆车
- (*to hand*) = dì 递
  pass me the salt, please = qǐng bǎ yán dìgěi wǒ 请把盐递给我
- (*to transfer to another person*) = chuán 传
  to pass the ball to him = bǎ qiú chuángěi tā 把球传给他
  please pass the word to my mother = qǐng bǎ zhège huà chuángěi wǒ māma 请把这个话传给我妈妈
- (*to spend*) = yòng 用
  I pass my time [**reading** | **painting** | **listening to the radio** ...] = wǒ bǎ wǒde shíjiān yòng lái [dú shū | huà huà | tīng shōuyīnjī...] 我把我的时间用来[读书 | 画画 | 听收音机 ...]
- (*to succeed in an exam*) = tōngguò 通过
  to pass an exam = tōngguò yícì kǎoshì 通过一次考试
- (*to succeed in an exam, just barely, and without honours*) = jígé 及格
  he narrowly passed the test = tā kǎoshì miǎnqiáng jígé 他考试勉强及格
- (*to approve*) = tōngguò 通过, pīzhǔn 批准
  the parliament has passed a new law = yìhuì tōngguòle yíxiàng xīnde fǎlǜ 议会通过了一项新的法律

passage *noun*
- (*a way or a route for going through*) = tōngdào 通道
  a passage = yìtiáo tōngdào 一条通道
- (*a piece of writing*) = duàn 段
  a passage in a book = shū zhōng de yíduàn 书中的一段

passenger *noun*
a passenger = yíge chéngkè 一个乘客

passport *noun*
a passport = yìběn hùzhào 一本护照

past
1 *noun*
the past = guòqù 过去
in the past = zài guòqù 在过去
2 *adjective*
= guòqù 过去
the past few days = guòqù jǐtiān 过去几天
3 *preposition*
- (*when talking about time*) = guò 过
  ▶ **204**

> **!** *Note that when* past *means* after the hour of, *it is often not translated.*

it's five past four = xiànzài sì diǎn (guò) wǔ fēn 现在四点(过)五分
it's past midnight = yǐjīng guòle wǔyè le 已经过了午夜了
- (*by*)
  to go past someone = cóng mǒurén pángbiān guòqu 从某人旁边过去
  she ran past me = tā cóng wǒ pángbiān pǎoguòqu 她从我旁边跑过去
- (*beyond*) = zài ... nàbian 在... 那边
  it's just past the traffic lights = jiù zài hónglǜdēng nàbian 就在红绿灯那边

4 *adverb*
to go past = guòqu 过去
to walk past = zǒuguòqu 走过去
to run past = pǎoguòqu 跑过去

pasta *noun*
pasta = Yìdàlì fěn 意大利粉

pastry *noun*
• (*for baking*) = miànhú 面糊
• (*a cake*) = gāodiǎn 糕点
a pastry = yíkuài gāodiǎn 一块糕点

patch *noun*
• (*on a garment or a tyre*) = bǔdìng 补丁
a patch = yíkuài bǔdìng 一块补丁
• (*a plaster for a cut or sore*) = gāoyào 膏药
a patch = yíkuài gāoyào 一块膏药

path *noun*
• (*a narrow way for pedestrians*) = xiǎodào 小道, lù 路
a path = yìtiáo xiǎodào 一条小道
• (*a route for a thing to move along*) = guǐdào 轨道
a path = yìtiáo guǐdào 一条轨道

patience *noun*
= nàixīn 耐心
to lose patience with someone = duì mǒurén shīqù nàixīn 对某人失去耐心

patient
1 *noun*
a patient = yíge bìngrén 一个病人
2 *adjective*
= nàixīn 耐心

patrol *verb*
= xúnluó 巡逻

patrol car *noun*
a patrol car = yíliàng xúnluó chē 一辆巡逻车

pattern *noun*
a pattern (*a thing to be copied as in dressmaking, carpentry, etc.*) = yíge yàngbǎn 一个样板
(*a decorative design*) = yíge shìyàng 一个式样
(*a particular disposition of forms and colours*) = yíge tú'àn 一个图案

pavement *noun*
• (*British English*) **the pavement** = rénxíngdào 人行道
• (*US English*) **the pavement** (*a paved road*) = pūguo de lùmiàn 铺过的路面, pūguo de dàolù 铺过的道路
(*a paved surface*) = pūguo de dìmiàn 铺过的地面

paw *noun*
a paw = yìzhī zhuǎzi 一只爪子

pay
1 *verb*
• **to pay** = fù 付
to pay the bills = fù zhàng 付帐
how much did you pay him? = nǐ fùgěi tā duōshǎo qián? 你付给他多少钱?
• **to pay for**
he paid for my meal = tā fùle wǒde fàn qián 他付了我的饭钱
my father paid for her education = wǒ bàba gòng tā shàngxué 我爸爸供她上学
• (*when talking about wages*)
the work doesn't pay very well = zhège gōngzuò gōngzī bù gāo 这个工作工资不高
I'm paid eight pounds an hour = wǒ měige xiǎoshí zhèng bā bàng qián 我每个小时挣八镑钱
• (*to give*)
to pay attention to the teacher = zhùyì lǎoshī 注意老师
to pay someone a visit = bàifǎng mǒurén 拜访某人
to pay someone a compliment = zànyáng mǒurén 赞扬某人

> **!** *Note that when* to pay *means* to give, *it is usually not translated. In most cases, the object, such as* attention, visit, *or* compliment, *is translated by the verb in Chinese.*

2 *noun*
= gōngzī 工资, xīnshuǐ 薪水
the pay is very good = gōngzī hěn hǎo 工资很好
pay back
• (*when in debt*) = chánghuán 偿还
• (*when in gratitude*) = bàodá 报答

PE, physical education *noun*
= tǐyù kè 体育课

pea *noun*
a pea = yílì wāndòu 一粒豌豆
green peas = qīngdòu 青豆

peace *noun*
• (*freedom from war*) = hépíng 和平
• (*a state of quiet*) = píngjìng 平静
• (*freedom from disturbance*) = ān'níng 安宁

P

peach *noun*
a peach = yíge táozi 一个桃子

peacock *noun*
a peacock = yìzhī kǒngquè 一只孔雀

peanut *noun*
a peanut = yílì huāshēng 一粒花生

pear *noun*
a pear = yíge lí 一个梨

pearl *noun*
a pearl = yìkē zhēnzhū 一颗珍珠

pebble *noun*
a pebble = yíge shízǐ 一个石子, yíge é'luǎnshí 一个鹅卵石

pedestrian *noun*
a pedestrian = yíge xíngrén 一个行人

pedestrian crossing *noun*
a pedestrian crossing = yìtiáo rénxíng héngdào 一条人行横道

peel *verb*
- (*to use one's hands to strip off an outer covering*) = bāo...pí 剥... 皮
  to peel an orange = bāo júzi pí 剥橘子皮
- (*to use a knife to strip off an outer covering*) = xiāo...pí 削... 皮
  to peel an apple = xiāo píngguǒ pí 削苹果皮

pen *noun*
a pen = yìzhī gāngbǐ 一只钢笔

penalty *noun*
- (*punishment*) = chùfá 处罚, chěngfá 惩罚
  a penalty = yíge chùfá 一个处罚
- (*in football*) = diǎnqiú 点球
  a penalty = yícì diǎnqiú 一次点球

pencil *noun*
a pencil = yìzhī qiānbǐ 一只铅笔

pencil case *noun*
a pencil case = yíge qiānbǐhé 一个铅笔盒

pencil sharpener *noun*
a pencil sharpener = yíge qiānbǐ dāo 一个铅笔刀

penfriend (*British English*), **penpal** (*US English*) *noun*
a penfriend = yíge bǐyǒu 一个笔友

penguin *noun*
a penguin = yìzhī qǐ'é 一只企鹅

penknife *noun*
a penknife = yìbǎ xiāobǐdāo 一把削笔刀

pensioner *noun*
a pensioner (*a retired person entitled to a pension*) = yíge tuìxiū de rén 一个退休的人
(*a person receiving an allowance for being disabled, widowed, orphaned, etc.*) = yíge lǐngqǔ fǔxùjīn de rén 一个领取抚恤金的人

people *noun*
- (*in general*) = rén 人
  we met some very nice people = wǒmen yùjiànle yìxiē hěn hǎo de rén 我们遇见了一些很好的人
  most people don't know what's happened = dàduōshù rén bù zhīdào fāshēngle shénme shì 大多数人不知道发生了什么事
- (*those from a city, from a nation, or of the world*) = rénmín 人民
  the people of the world = shìjiè rénmín 世界人民
- (*a nation, race, tribe, or ethnic group*) = mínzú 民族
  a people = yíge mínzú 一个民族

pepper *noun*
- (*the spice*) = hújiāo 胡椒
- (*the general term for the vegetable, usually green*) = qīngjiāo 青椒
  (*when the colour is specified*)
  a [green | red | yellow] pepper = yíge [qīng | hóng | huáng] jiāo 一个 [青 | 红 | 黄] 椒

per *preposition*
= měi 每
per [person | hour | week...] = měi ge [rén | xiǎoshí | xīngqī...] 每个 [人 | 小时 | 星期 ...]

per cent *noun*
= bǎifēn zhī 百分之, %
30% = bǎifēn zhī sānshí 百分之三十

perfect *adjective*
- (*extremely good*) = jí hǎo de 极好的
  to speak perfect Chinese = jiǎng yìkǒu jí hǎo de Hànyǔ 讲一口极好的汉语
- (*flawless*) = wánměi de 完美的, wúxiá de 无瑕的

nothing is perfect = méi yǒu dōngxi shì wánměi (wúxiá) de 没有东西是完美(无瑕)的

perform *verb*
- (*to do*)
  to perform an operation = zuò yíge shǒushù 做一个手术
  to perform a task = wánchéng yíxiàng rènwù 完成一项任务
- (*to play an instrument in a performance*) = yǎnzòu 演奏
  to perform a piece of music = yǎnzòu yìzhī qǔzi 演奏一支曲子
- (*to act*) = biǎoyǎn 表演
  to perform for the children = wèi háizimen biǎoyǎn 为孩子们表演

perfume *noun*
- (*if it's a liquid*) = xiāngshuǐ 香水
  to spray perfume = pēn xiāngshuǐ 喷香水
- (*if it's a fragrance*) = xiāng wèir 香味儿

perhaps *adverb*
= kěnéng 可能, yěxǔ 也许

period *noun*
a period of time = yíduàn shíjiān 一段时间
- (*a stage or phase in history*) = shíqī 时期
  the period of the Cold War = lěng zhàn shíqī 冷战时期
- (*in the course of an event*) = qījiān 期间
  in the period of the experiment = zài shíyàn qījiān 在实验期间
- (*a full stop*) = jùhào 句号
  a period = yíge jùhào 一个句号
- (*for women*) = yuèjīngqī 月经期
  a period = yícì yuèjīngqī 一次月经期
- (*a school lesson*) = kè 课
  a period = yìjié kè 一节课

permanent *adjective*
= yǒngjiǔ 永久

permission *noun*
= xǔkě 许可, yǔnxǔ 允许
to get permission to leave the hospital = dédào chū yuàn de xǔkě 得到出院的许可

person *noun*
a person = yíge rén 一个人

personal *adjective*
- (*one's own*) = gèrén de 个人的
- (*of private concerns*) = sīrén de 私人的

personality *noun*
(*distinctive character*) = xìnggé 性格, gèxìng 个性
a person with a strong personality = yíge xìnggé hěn qiáng de rén 一个性格很强的人

perspire *verb*
= chūhàn 出汗

persuade *verb*
= quàn 劝, shuōfú 说服
to persuade someone to buy a car = quàn mǒurén mǎi yíliàng chē 劝某人买一辆车

pessimist *noun*
a pessimist = yíge bēiguānzhě 一个悲观者, yíge bēiguānzhǔyìzhě 一个悲观主义者

pessimistic *adjective*
= bēiguān 悲观, bēiguānzhǔyì de 悲观主义的

pet *noun*
a pet = yíge chǒngwù 一个宠物

petrol *noun* (*British English*)
= qìyóu 汽油
to run out of petrol = qìyóu yòngwán le 汽油用完了

petrol station *noun* (*British English*)
a petrol station = yíge jiāyóuzhàn 一个加油站

pet shop *noun* ▶ 344
a pet shop = yíge chǒngwù shāngdiàn 一个宠物商店

phone
1 *noun*
a phone = yìtái diànhuà 一台电话
the phone's ringing = diànhuà xiǎng le 电话响了
to answer the phone = jiē diànhuà 接电话
he's on the phone = tā zài dǎ diànhuà 他在打电话
2 *verb*
= dǎ diànhuà 打电话
to phone someone = gěi mǒurén dǎ diànhuà 给某人打电话

phone book *noun*
a phone book = yìběn diànhuàbù 一本电话簿

phone booth *noun*
a phone booth = yíge diànhuàtíng 一个电话亭

phone call *noun*
a phone call = yíge diànhuà 一个电话
to receive a phone call = jiēdào yíge diànhuà 接到一个电话

phone card *noun*
a phone card = yìzhāng diànhuà cíkǎ 一张电话磁卡

phone number *noun*
a phone number = yíge diànhuà hàomǎ 一个电话号码

photo *noun*
a photo = yìzhāng zhàopiàn 一张照片, yìzhāng xiàngpiàn 一张相片

photocopier *noun*
a photocopier = yìtái fùyìnjī 一台复印机

photocopy
1 *noun*
a photocopy = yífèn fùyìnjiàn 一份复印件
1 *verb*
= fùyìn

photograph *noun*
a photograph = yìzhāng zhàopiàn 一张照片, yìzhāng xiàngpiàn 一张相片
to take a photograph of someone = gěi mǒurén zhào yìzhāng xiàng 给某人照一张相

photographer *noun* ▶ 344
a photographer = yíge shèyǐngshī 一个摄影师

physical *adjective*
- (*material*) = wùzhì de 物质的
  the physical world = wùzhì shìjiè 物质世界
- (*pertaining to natural science*) = wùlǐ de 物理的
  physical changes = wùlǐ biànhuà 物理变化
- (*bodily*) = shēntǐ de 身体的
  physical examinations = shēntǐ jiǎnchá 身体检查

physics *noun*
= wùlǐxué 物理学, wùlǐ 物理

piano *noun* ▶ 308
a piano = yíjià gāngqín 一架钢琴

pick *verb*
- (*to choose*) = tiāoxuǎn 挑选, xuǎnzé 选择
  to pick a number = tiāoxuǎn yíge hàomǎ 挑选一个号码
- (*to collect*) = zhāi 摘, cǎi 采
  to pick blackberries = zhāi hēiméi 摘黑莓
- (*to take*) = ná 拿
  to pick a book off the shelf = cóng shūjià shang náxia yìběn shū 从书架上拿下一本书

pick on
- (*to find fault with*) = tiāotì 挑剔
- (*to single out for something unpleasant*) = tiāochūlai pīpíng 挑出来批评
  he's always picking on me = tā zǒngshì bǎ wǒ tiāochūlai pīpíng 他总是把我挑出来批评

pick out
- (*to select*) = tiāoxuǎnchu 挑选出
- (*to make out, to distinguish*) = biànbiéchu 辨别出

pick up
- (*to lift*) = shíqǐ 拾起, jiǎnqǐ 捡起
  to pick the clothes up off the floor = bǎ yīfu cóng dì shang jiǎnqǐlai 把衣服从地上捡起来
  to pick a baby up = bǎ yíge háizi bàoqǐlai 把一个孩子抱起来
  to pick up the phone = náqǐ diànhuà lai 拿起电话来
- (*to collect*) = jiē 接
  to pick up passengers = jiē chéngkè 接乘客
  he's coming to pick me up = tā lái jiē wǒ 他来接我
- (*to buy*) = mǎi 买
  I stopped to pick up some milk = wǒ tíngxiàlai mǎi diǎnr niúnǎi 我停下来买点儿牛奶
- (*to learn*) = xuéhuì 学会
  to pick up a little German = xuéhuì yìdiǎnr Déyǔ 学会一点儿德语

picnic *noun*
a picnic = yícì yěcān 一次野餐
to go on a picnic = qù yěcān 去野餐

picture *noun*
- **a picture** (*a painting or a drawing*) = yìfú huà 一幅画
  (*a photograph*) = yìzhāng zhàopiàn 一张照片, yìzhāng xiàngpiàn 一张相片
  (*an image on a television screen*) = yíge túxiàng 一个图象
- **the pictures (cinema)** = diànyǐng 电影

piece *noun*
a piece of paper = yìzhāng zhǐ 一张纸
a piece of cheese = yíkuài nǎilào 一块奶酪
a piece of string = yìgēn xiànshéng 一根线绳
a piece of furniture = yíjiàn jiājù 一件家具
a piece of [**news** | **information** ...] = yìtiáo [xiāoxi | xìnxī ...] 一条[消息 | 信息...]
• (*a part of a machine*) = bùjiàn 部件
a piece = yíge bùjiàn 一个部件
• (*a coin*) = yìngbì 硬币
a 50-pence piece = yíge wǔshí biànshì de yìngbì 一个五十便士的硬币
• (*broken fragments of something thin*) = suìpiàn 碎片
pieces of broken glass = yìxiē suì bōli piàn 一些碎玻璃片
• (*portion of a solid object*) = kuài 块
to cut an apple into four pieces = bǎ píngguǒ qiēchéng sìkuài 把苹果切成四块

pierce *verb*
• (*to make a hole through*) = chuānkǒng 穿孔, chuāndòng 穿洞
• (*to thrust*) = cìchuān 刺穿, cìpò 刺破

pig *noun*
a pig = yìtóu zhū 一头猪

pigeon *noun*
a pigeon = yìzhī gézi 一只鸽子

pile
• **a pile** (*in a somewhat regular shape*) = yìluó 一摞
a pile of books = yìluó shū 一摞书
(*a heap*) = yìduī 一堆
a pile of logs = yìduī mùtou 一堆木头
• (*a large amount, lots*) = xǔduō 许多, dàliàng 大量
piles of [**toys** | **records** | **money**] = xǔduō [wánjù | chàngpiàn | qián] 许多[玩具 | 唱片 | 钱]

pill *noun*
• (*a tablet*)
a pill = yípiàn yào 一片药
• (*a method of contraception*)
the pill = bìyùnyào 避孕药

pillow *noun*
a pillow = yíge zhěntou 一个枕头

pilot *noun* ▶ 344
a pilot = yìmíng fēixíngyuán 一名飞行员, yìmíng fēijī jiàshǐyuán 一名飞机驾驶员

pin
1 *noun*
a pin = yìgēn biézhēn 一根别针, yìgēn dàtóuzhēn 一根大头针
2 *verb*
= yòng zhēn bié 用针别, yòng zhēn dīng 用针钉
to pin the flower to the dress = bǎ huā yòng zhēn bié zài yīfu shang 把花用针别在衣服上

PIN *noun*
a PIN = yíge mìmǎ 一个密码

pinch *verb*
• **to pinch** = níng 拧, niē 捏
he pinched my arm, he pinched me on the arm = tā níng wǒde gébo 他拧我的胳膊
• (*to hurt ... by being too tight*) = jǐ...tòng 挤...痛
my shoes are pinching = wǒde xié jǐ de wǒ jiǎo tòng 我的鞋挤得我脚痛

pineapple *noun*
a pineapple = yíge bōluó 一个菠萝

pine tree *noun*
a pine tree = yìkē sōngshù 一棵松树

pink *adjective*
= fěnhóngsè de 粉红色的

pint *noun*
• (*the quantity*)
a pint = yì pǐntuō 一品脱

> **!** *Note that a* **pint** *= 0.57 l in Britain and 0.47 l in the US.*

a pint of milk = yì pǐntuō niúnǎi 一品脱牛奶
• (*British English*) (*a drink*)
to go for a pint = qù hē yìbēi (jiǔ) 去喝一杯(酒)

pipe *noun*
• (*for gas, water*) = guǎnzi 管子
a pipe = yìgēn guǎnzi 一根管子
• (*for smoking*) = yāndǒu 烟斗
a pipe = yíge yāndǒu 一个烟斗

pirate
1 *noun*
a pirate (*on the high seas*) = yíge hǎidào 一个海盗
2 *verb*
(*print or publish illegally*)
= dàoyìn 盗印

a pirated edition = yíge dàobǎn 一个盗版

pitch
1 *noun (British English)*
a pitch = yíge chǎngdì 一个场地
a football pitch = yíge zúqiú chǎng 一个足球场
2 *verb*
(*in baseball*) = tóuzhì qiú 投掷球

pity
1 *noun*
- = liánmǐn 怜悯, tóngqíng 同情
- (*when expressing regret*) = yíhàn 遗憾, kěxī 可惜
what a pity! = zhēng yíhàn! 真遗憾!
it's a pity you can't come = kěxī nǐ bù néng lái 可惜你不能来

2 *verb*
= tóngqíng 同情, kělián 可怜

pizza *noun*
a pizza = yíge (Yìdàlì) bǐsàbǐng 一个(意大利)比萨饼

place
1 *noun*
- **a place** = yíge dìfang 一个地方
Oxford is a nice place = Niújīn shì yíge hěn hǎo de dìfang 牛津是一个很好的地方
this place is dirty = zhège dìfang hěn zāng 这个地方很脏
- (*a home*) = jiā 家
at Alison's place = zài Àilìsēn de jiā 在艾利森的家
I'd like a place of my own = wǒ xiǎng yǒu yíge zìjǐ de jiā 我想有一个自己的家
- (*on a bus, at a table*) = wèizi 位子, zuòwèi 座位
a place = yíge zuòwèi 一个座位
is this place free? = zhège wèizi yǒu rén ma? 这个位子有人吗?
to take someone's place = zhànle mǒurén de zuòwèi 占了某人的座位
- (*in a car park, in a queue*) = dìfang 地方, wèizhi 位置
a place = yíge wèizhi 一个位置
to find a place to park = zhǎo yíge wèizhi tíng chē 找一个位置停车
- (*as an employee in a firm, university, hospital*) = zhíwèi 职位, gōngzuò 工作
a place = yíge zhíwèi 一个职位
to get a place at the university = zài dàxué zhǎodào yíge zhíwèi 在大学找到一个职位
- (*on a course, a team*) = wèizi 位子
a place = yíge wèizi 一个位子
to get a place in a Chinese course = dédào yíge shàng Zhōngwén kè de wèizi 得到一个上中文课的位子
- (*in a contest*)
a place = yíge míngcì 一个名次
to win first place = dé dìyīmíng 得第一名

2 *verb*
- (*to put*) = fàng 放
- (*to arrange*) = ānzhì 安置, ānfàng 安放

plain
1 *adjective*
- (*simple*) = jiǎndān 简单, pǔsù 朴素
a plain dress = yíjiàn pǔsù de yīfu 一件朴素的衣服
- (*not good-looking*) = bù hǎo kàn 不好看
- (*ordinary*) = pǔtōng 普通, píngcháng 平常

2 *noun*
a plain = yíge píngyuán 一个平原

plait *noun (British English)*
a plait = yìgēn biànzi 一根辫子

plan
1 *noun*
- (*what one intends to do*) = jìhuà 计划, dǎsuàn 打算
a plan = yíge jìhuà 一个计划
we need a plan = wǒmen xūyào yíge jìhuà 我们需要一个计划
- (*what one has arranged to do*) = ānpái 安排
a plan = yíge ānpái 一个安排
I don't have any plans for tonight = wǒ jīntiān wǎnshang méi yǒu shénme ānpái 我今天晚上没有什么安排

2 *verb*
- (*to prepare, to organize*) = ānpái 安排
to plan [**a trip** | **a timetable** | **a meeting**] = ānpái [yícì lǚxíng | yíge shíjiānbiǎo | yícì huìyì] 安排[一次旅行 | 一个时间表 | 一次会议]
- (*to intend*) = jìhuà 计划, dǎsuàn 打算
I'm planning to visit Scotland = wǒ jìhuà fǎngwèn Sūgélán 我计划访问苏格兰

plane *noun*
- (*aeroplane*) = fēijī 飞机
  a plane = yíjià fēijī 一架飞机
- (*flat or level surface*) = píngmiàn 平面
  a plane = yíge píngmiàn 一个平面

planet *noun*
a planet = yíge xíngxīng 一个行星

plant
1 *noun*
- (*member of the vegetable kingdom*) = zhíwù 植物
  a plant = yìkē zhíwù 一棵植物
- (*factory*) = gōngchǎng 工厂
  a plant = yíge gōngchǎng 一个工厂

2 *verb*
- (*to put into the ground for growth*) = zhòng 种, zāi 栽
- (*to insert*) = chā 插, ānchā 安插

plaster *noun* (*British English*)
a plaster = yìtiē gāoyào 一贴膏药

plastic
1 *noun*
= sùliào 塑料
2 *adjective*
- (*made of plastic*) = sùliào de 塑料的
- (*flexible and malleable*) = kěsù de 可塑的, yǒu sùxìng de 有塑性的

plate *noun*
a plate = yíge pánzi 一个盘子

platform *noun*
a platform (*at a train station*) = yíge zhàntái 一个站台
on platform 4 = zài sìhào zhàntái 在四号站台
(*a raised floor for speakers*) = yíge jiǎngtái 一个讲台
(*a raised floor for singers, dancers, musicians*) = yíge wǔtái 一个舞台

play
1 *verb*
- (*to have fun*) = wánr 玩儿
  to play with friends = gēn péngyoumen yìqǐ wánr 跟朋友们一起玩儿
  to play a trick on someone = zhuōnòng mǒurén 捉弄某人
- (*when talking about sports*) ▶ 390
  to play [**football** | **cricket** | **basketball** | **tennis** | **cards** | **chess...**] = [tī zúqiú | dǎ bǎnqiú | dǎ lánqiú | dǎ wǎngqiú | dǎ pūkè | xià qí...] [踢足球 | 打板球 | 打篮球 | 打网球 | 打扑克 | 下棋...]
  England is playing (against) America = Yīnggélán duì zài gēn Měiguó duì bǐsài 英格兰队在跟美国队比赛
- (*when talking about music*) ▶ 308
  [**to play the piano** | **to play the flute** | **to play the violin** | **to play drums**] = [tán gāngqín | chuī dízi | lā xiǎotíqín | qiāo gǔ...] [弹钢琴 | 吹笛子 | 拉小提琴 | 敲鼓...]
- (*to put on music, etc.*) = (bō)fàng (播)放
  to play [**a video** | **a CD** | **a record**] = fàng [lùxiàng | guāngpán | chàngpiàn] 放 [录相 | 光盘 | 唱片]
- (*to act in a role, a part, etc.*) = bànyǎn 扮演
  to play the role of someone = bànyǎn mǒurén 扮演某人
- (*to be in a show in the theatre, cinema, etc.*) = shàngyǎn 上演
  the film will soon be playing at this cinema = zhèbù diànyǐng jiāng hěn kuài zài zhèjiā diànyǐngyuàn shàngyǎn 这部电影将很快在这家电影院上演

2 *noun*
a play (*a drama, a dramatic performance*) = yìchū xì 一出戏, yìchū jù 一出剧
(*a script of a play*) = yíge jùběn 一个剧本

play back
to play back a tape = dào cídài 倒磁带

player *noun* ▶ 390
a player (*in sports*) = yíge yùndòngyuán 一个运动员
(*in a musical performance*) = yíge yǎnzòuzhě 一个演奏者, yíge yǎnyuán 一个演员

playground *noun*
a playground (*for children to play in*) = yíge yóuxì chǎngdì 一个游戏场地
(*a field at a school*) = yíge cāochǎng 一个操场

please *adverb*
= qǐng 请
please come in = qǐng jìn 请进
'more cake?'—'yes please' = 'nǐ hái yào dàngāo ma?'—'hǎo, qǐng zài gěi wǒ yìdiǎnr' '你还要蛋糕吗?'—'好, 请再给我一点儿'

pleased *adjective*
- (*happy, delighted*) = gāoxìng 高兴, yúkuài 愉快

P

pleased to meet you = hěn gāoxìng jiàndào nǐ 很高兴见到你
- (*content, satisfied*) = mǎnyì 满意
  I was very pleased with myself = wǒ duì zìjǐ hěn mǎnyì 我对自己很满意

plenty *pronoun*
to have plenty of [**time** | **money** | **friends...**] = yǒu hěn duō [shíjiān | qián | péngyou...] 有很多 [时间 | 钱 | 朋友...]

plot *noun*
- (*a secret plan*) = mìmì jìhuà 秘密计划, yīnmóu 阴谋
  a plot = yíge yīnmóu 一个阴谋
- (*the story in a film, a novel, a play*) = qíngjié 情节
  a plot = yíge qíngjié 一个情节

plug *noun*
a plug (*on an appliance*) = yíge chātóu 一个插头
(*in a sink or bath*) = yíge sāizi 一个塞子
plug in = bǎ chātóu chāshang 把插头插上

plum *noun*
a plum = yíge lǐzi 一个李子

plumber *noun* ▶ 344
a plumber = yíge guǎnzigōng 一个管子工

plus *preposition*
= jiā 加
three plus three are six = sān jiā sān děngyú liù 三加三等于六

pocket *noun*
a pocket = yíge kǒudài 一个口袋, yíge yīdōu 一个衣兜

pocketbook *noun* (*US English*)
a pocketbook (*for keeping money*) = yíge qiánbāo 一个钱包
(*for taking notes*) = yíge xiǎo bǐjìběn 一个小笔记本

pocket money *noun*
pocket money = línghuāqián 零花钱, língyòngqián 零用钱

poem *noun*
a poem = yìshǒu shī 一首诗

point
1 *noun*
- (*a statement in a discussion*) = lùndiǎn 论点
  a point = yíge lùndiǎn 一个论点
  to make a point = zhèngmíng yíge lùndiǎn 证明一个论点
- (*the most important idea*) = yàodiǎn 要点
  that's not the point = nà bú shì yàodiǎn 那不是要点
- (*use, purpose*) = yòng 用
  there's no point in shouting = hǎn méi yǒu yòng 喊没有用
- (*when talking about time*)
  to be on the point of [**moving** | **leaving** | **selling the house**] = zhèngyào [dòngshēn | líkāi | mài fángzi] de shíhou 正要 [动身 | 离开 | 卖房子] 的时候
- (*the sharp end*) = jiān 尖
  the point of a pencil = qiānbǐ jiān 铅笔尖
- (*in a contest, a game*) = fēn 分
  a point = yì fēn 一分

2 *verb*
- (*to indicate*) = zhǐ 指
  to point (one's finger) at someone = (yòng shǒu) zhǐzhe mǒurén (用手) 指着某人
  to point at a house = zhǐ xiàng yízuò fángzi 指向一座房子
  to point the way to the station = zhǐdiǎn qù chēzhàn de lù 指点去车站的路
- (*to aim*)
  to point a gun at someone = bǎ qiāng duìzhǔn mǒurén 把枪对准某人
  point out = zhǐchū 指出
  to point out his mistakes = zhǐchū tāde cuòwù 指出他的错误

poison
1 *noun*
- (*drug*) = dúyào 毒药
- (*substance*) = dúwù 毒物

2 *verb*
- (*to kill with poison*) = dúsǐ 毒死
- (*to injure with poison*) = shǐ...zhòngdú 使... 中毒
  to poison someone = shǐ mǒurén zhòngdú 使某人中毒
  she got food-poisoning = tā shíwù zhòngdú 她食物中毒
- (*to corrupt*) = dúhài 毒害
  to poison young people's minds = dúhài niánqīng rén de sīxiǎng 毒害年轻人的思想

pole *noun*
a pole = yìgēn gān 一根杆

police *noun*
the police = jǐngchá 警察

policeman *noun* ▶ 344
a policeman = yíge jǐngchá 一个警察

police station *noun*
a police station = yíge jǐngchájú 一个警察局

policewoman *noun* ▶ 344
a policewoman = yíge nǚ jǐngchá 一个女警察

polish *verb*
to polish [shoes | the car | the furniture...] = cā [xié | qìchē | jiājù...] 擦 [鞋 | 汽车 | 家具...]

polite *adjective*
= yǒu lǐmào 有礼貌, kèqi 客气

political *adjective*
= zhèngzhì de 政治的, zhèngzhì shang de 政治上的

politician *noun* ▶ 344
a politician (*in a neutral sense*) = yíge zhèngzhìjiā 一个政治家
(*in a negative sense*) = yíge zhèngkè 一个政客

politics *noun*
politics = zhèngzhì 政治

pollute *verb*
= wūrǎn 污染

pollution *noun*
= wūrǎn 污染

pond *noun*
a pond = yíge chítáng 一个池塘

pony *noun*
a pony = yìpí xiǎomǎ 一匹小马

ponytail *noun*
a ponytail = yìzhǒng mǎwěi fàxíng 一种马尾发型

pool *noun*
- (*a swimming pool*)
  a pool = yíge yóuyǒngchí 一个游泳池
- (*on the ground, the floor*)
  a pool of water = yìtān shuǐ 一滩水
- (*the game*) ▶ 390 = dànzixì 弹子戏

poor *adjective*
- (*not wealthy*) = qióng 穷, pínqióng 贫穷
- (*not satisfactory*) = chà 差, bù hǎo 不好
  a poor memory = bù hǎo de jìyìlì 不好的记忆力
- (*expressing sympathy*) = kělián 可怜
  the poor boy is very ill = zhè kělián de háizi bìng de hěn lìhài 这可怜的孩子病得很厉害

popular *adjective*
- (*prevailing among the people*) = liúxíng 流行
  a popular hobby = yìzhǒng hěn liúxíng de shìhào 一种很流行的嗜好
  a popular song = yìshǒu liúxíng gēqǔ 一首流行歌曲
- (*enjoying the favour of*) = shòu...huānyíng 受... 欢迎, shòu...xǐhuan 受... 喜欢
  a popular writer = yíge shòu (rén) huānyíng de zuòjiā 一个受(人)欢迎的作家
  to be popular with the girls = shòu nǚháizi xǐhuan 受女孩子喜欢

population *noun*
= rénkǒu 人口

> **!** *Note that* rénkǒu 人口 *is uncountable and does not have a measure word.*

a population of one million = yìbǎiwàn rénkǒu 一百万人口

pork *noun*
= zhūròu 猪肉

port *noun*
a port = yíge gǎngkǒu 一个港口

portrait *noun*
a portrait = yìzhāng huàxiàng 一张画像, yìzhāng xiāoxiàng 一张肖像

Portugal *noun*
= Pútáoyá 葡萄牙

Portuguese ▶ 288
1 *adjective*
= Pútáoyá de 葡萄牙的
2 *noun*
- (*the people*) = Pútáoyárén 葡萄牙人
- (*the language*) = Pútáoyáyǔ 葡萄牙语, Pútáoyáwén 葡萄牙文

position *noun*
a position (*place occupied*) = yíge wèizhi 一个位置, yíge fāngwèi 一个方位
(*status or place in society*) = yíge dìwèi 一个地位, yìzhǒng shēnfèn 一种身份
(*post or appointment*) = yíge zhíwèi 一个职位, yíge zhíwù 一个职务

P

(*attitude or ground taken in an argument*) = yìzhǒng tàidù 一种态度
(*situation*) = yìzhǒng xíngshì 一种形势, yìzhǒng zhuàngkuàng 一种状况
(*posture*) = yìzhǒng zīshì 一种姿势

positive *adjective*
- (*definitely and explicitly laid down*) = míngquè 明确, quèshí 确实
- (*beyond possibility of doubt*) = kěndìng 肯定
- (*fully convinced*) = quèxìn 确信
- (*having a good and constructive attitude*) = jījí 积极, jiànshèxìng de 建设性的

possibility *noun*
a possibility = yìzhǒng kěnéng(xìng) 一种可能(性)

possible *adjective*
= kěnéng 可能
it's possible that it'll rain tomorrow = míngtiān kěnéng xiàyǔ 明天可能下雨
as quickly as possible = jìn kuài 尽快
please come as quickly as possible = qǐng jìn kuài lái 请尽快来

post (*British English*)
1 *noun*
the post (*the system*) = yóuzhèng 邮政
(*the letters*) = yóujiàn 邮件
has the post come yet? = yóujiàn lái le ma? 邮件来了吗?
2 *verb*
= jì 寄, yóujì 邮寄
to post a letter = jì yìfēng xìn 寄一封信

postbox *noun* (*British English*)
a postbox = yíge xìnxiāng 一个信箱

postcard *noun*
a postcard = yìzhāng míngxìnpiàn 一张明信片

postcode *noun* (*British English*)
a postcode = yíge yóuzhèng biānmǎ 一个邮政编码

poster *noun*
a poster (*giving information*) = yìzhāng zhāotiē 一张招贴, yìzhāng guǎnggào 一张广告
(*used as a picture*) = yìzhāng zhāotiē huà 一张招贴画

postman *noun* ▶ **344** (*British English*)
a postman = yíge yóudìyuán 一个邮递员

post office *noun*
a post office = yíge yóujú 一个邮局

postpone *verb*
= tuīchí 推迟, yánqī 延期
let's postpone the party until next week = zánmen bǎ jùhuì tuīchídào xiàge xīngqī ba 咱们把聚会推迟到下个星期吧
the concert has been postponed = yīnyuèhuì yánqī le 音乐会延期了

pot *noun*
- (*a container for making coffee or tea*) = hú 壶
  a pot = yíge hú 一个壶
- (*a container for preserving something*) = guàn(zi) 罐(子)
  a pot = yíge guànzi 一个罐子
- (*a saucepan*) = guō 锅
  a pot = yíge guō 一个锅

potato *noun*
a potato = yíge tǔdòu 一个土豆

pottery *noun*
= táoqì 陶器

pound *noun*
- (*the currency*) = yīngbàng 英镑
  a pound = yì (yīng)bàng 一(英)镑
- (*in weight*) = bàng 磅
  a pound = yí bàng 一磅
  two pounds of apples = liǎng bàng píngguǒ 两磅苹果

pour *verb*
- (*from a container*) = dào 倒
  to pour milk into a bowl = bǎ niúnǎi dàojìn wǎn li 把牛奶倒进碗里
  to pour wine for someone = gěi mǒurén dào jiǔ 给某人倒酒
- (*to flow*) = liú 流, tǎng 淌
  the water was pouring into the kitchen = shuǐ liújìnle chúfáng 水流进了厨房
- (*to escape*) = mào 冒
  there is smoke pouring out of the window = yǒu yìxiē yān cóng chuānghu li màochūlai 有一些烟从窗户里冒出来
- (*to rain*) = xià dà yǔ 下大雨
  it's pouring (with rain) = zhèngzài xià dà yǔ 正在下大雨

- (*to enter in large numbers*) = yǒngjìn 涌进
  to pour into the city = yǒngjìn chéngshì 涌进城市
- (*to leave in large numbers*) = yǒngchu 涌出
  to pour out of the stadium = yǒngchu tǐyùchǎng 涌出体育场

powder *noun*
= fěn 粉

power *noun*
- (*control*) = quánlì 权力
  to be in power = zhí zhèng 执政, zhǎng quán 掌权
- (*influence*) = shìlì 势力
  to have great power = yǒu hěn dà de shìlì 有很大的势力
- (*electricity*) = diàn 电

practical *adjective*
- (*given to action rather than theory*) = shíjiàn de 实践的
- (*relating to real existence or action*) = shíjì de 实际的
- (*workable*) = kěxíng de 可行的
- (*useful*) = shíyòng de 实用的

practically *adverb*
= shíjìshang 实际上, shìshíshang 事实上

practise (*British English*), **practice** (*US English*) *verb*
- (*to work at improving a skill*) = liànxí 练习
  to practise [the piano | one's Chinese | a song | playing basketball...] = liànxí [gāngqín | Zhōngwén | yìshǒu gē | dǎ lánqiú...] 练习[钢琴 | 中文 | 一首歌 | 打篮球...]
- (*to carry out*) = shíxíng 实行, shíshī 实施
  to practise economy = shíxíng jiéyuē 实行节约

praise *verb*
= biǎoyáng 表扬, zànyáng 赞扬
to praise someone = biǎoyáng mǒurén 表扬某人

prawn *noun* (*British English*)
a prawn = yìzhī duìxiā 一只对虾

pray *verb*
- (*in a religious sense*) = qídǎo 祈祷, dǎogào 祷告
- (*to hope*) = (yīnqiè) pànwàng (殷切) 盼望, qíqiú 祈求
  they are praying for rain = tāmen pànwàngzhe xiàyǔ 他们盼望着下雨

prayer *noun*
= dǎowén 祷文, dǎogào 祷告

precaution *noun*
a precaution = yíxiàng yùfáng cuòshī 一项预防措施

precious *adjective*
= bǎoguì 宝贵, zhēnguì 珍贵

precise *adjective*
= jīngquè 精确, zhǔnquè 准确

predict *verb*
= yùyán 预言, yùgào 预告

prediction *noun*
= yùyán 预言, yùgào 预告

prefer *verb*
= xǐhuan 喜欢, yuànyì 愿意
to prefer Chinese food to English food = xǐhuan Zhōngguó fàn, bù xǐhuan Yīngguó fàn 喜欢中国饭, 不喜欢英国饭

> **!** *Note that in stating a preference for one thing over another, the thing that is less preferred is expressed in a negative phrase in Chinese, as in* bù xǐhuan Yīngguó fàn 不喜欢英国饭 *above.*

I'd prefer to phone = wǒ yuànyì dǎ diànhuà 我愿意打电话

pregnant *adjective*
= huáiyùn 怀孕
she's become pregnant = tā huáiyùn le 她怀孕了

prejudice *noun*
a prejudice (*against someone or something*) = yìzhǒng piānjiàn 一种偏见
(*in favour of someone or something*) = yìzhǒng piān'ài 一种偏爱
he has [a prejudice against | a prejudice in favour of] Japanese wine = tā duì Rìběn jiǔ yǒu [yìzhǒng piānjiàn | yìzhǒng piān'ài] 他对日本酒有[一种偏见 | 一种偏爱]

prepare *verb*
- (*to get something or someone ready*) = shǐ...zuòhǎo zhǔnbèi 使... 做好准备
  to prepare pupils for an exam = shǐ xuésheng wèi kǎoshì zuòhǎo zhǔnbèi 使学生为考试做好准备

P

- (*to get ready*) = zhǔnbèi 准备
  to prepare for [**an exam** | **a trip** | **a party...**] = zhǔnbèi [yícì kǎoshì | yícì lǚxíng | yícì jùhuì...] 准备 [一次考试 | 一次旅行 | 一次聚会...]

prepared *adjective*

- (*willing*) = yuànyì 愿意
  to be prepared to wait = yuànyì děng 愿意等
- (*ready*) = zuòhǎo zhǔnbèi 做好准备
  to be prepared for an exam = wèi kǎoshì zuòhǎo zhǔnbèi 为考试做好准备

prescription *noun*

a prescription = yíge chùfāng 一个处方, yíge yàofāng 一个药方

present

1 *noun*

- (*a gift*) = lǐwù 礼物, lǐpǐn 礼品
  a present = yíge lǐwù 一个礼物
  to give someone a present = sònggěi mǒurén yíge lǐwù 送给某人一个礼物
- (*now*)
  the present = xiànzài 现在, mùqián 目前
  I'm staying here at present = mùqián wǒ dāi zài zhèr 目前我呆在这儿

2 *adjective*

- (*in a place*)
  to be present (*at a formal event*) = chūxí 出席, dàochǎng 到场
  to be present at the meeting = chūxí huìyì 出席会议
  (*in an informal situation*) = zài 在
  he was not present then = dāngshí tā bú zài 当时他不在
- (*now under consideration*) = mùqián de 目前的, xiànzài de 现在的
  the present situation = mùqián de xíngshì 目前的形势

3 *verb*

- (*to give as a gift*) = zèngsòng 赠送
  to present a book to him = zèngsòng gěi tā yìběn shū 赠送给他一本书
- (*to give as an award*) = fāgěi 发给, jǐyǔ 给予
  to present a gold medal to someone = fāgěi mǒurén yíkuài jīnzhì jiǎngpái 发给某人一块金质奖牌
- (*to give to someone who is one's senior*) = xiàngěi 献给
  a girl presented the hero with a bunch of flowers = yíge gūniang xiàngěi nàge yīngxióng yíshù huā 一个姑娘献给那个英雄一束花
- (*to introduce formally or to introduce on radio or TV*) = jièshào 介绍
  may I present Mr.Wang to you? = qǐng yúnxǔ wǒ bǎ Wáng xiānsheng jièshào gěi nín 请允许我把王先生介绍给您
  to present a programme = jièshào yíge jiémù 介绍一个节目
- (*to hand something to someone formally*) = dìjiāo 递交
  to present a report to the committee = xiàng wěiyuánhuì dìjiāo yífèn bàogào 向委员会递交一份报告
- (*to put forward*) = tíchū 提出
  to present a proposal to the government = xiàng zhèngfǔ tíchū yíge jiànyì 向政府提出一个建议
- (*to put on a drama, a play*) = shàngyǎn 上演
  when will the play be presented? = zhège huàjù shénme shíhou shàngyǎn? 这个话剧什么时候上演?

president *noun* ▶ **344**

a president (*of a country*) = yíge zǒngtǒng 一个总统
(*of an association or a board*) = yíge huìzhǎng 一个会长
(*of a university*) = yíge xiàozhǎng 一个校长
(*of a college*) = yíge yuànzhǎng 一个院长

press

1 *verb*

- (*with the hand*) = àn 按
  to press the button = àn diànniǔ 按电钮
- (*to compress*) = yā 压
- (*to urge strongly*) = dūncù 敦促
  to press him to change his mind = dūncù tā gǎibiàn zhǔyì 敦促他改变主意

2 *noun*

the press = xīnwénjiè 新闻界

pressure *noun*

= yālì 压力
to put pressure on someone = xiàng mǒurén shījiā yālì 向某人施加压力

pretend *verb*

= jiǎzhuāng 假装
he's pretending to be annoyed = tā jiǎzhuāng shēngqì le 他假装生气了

pretty
1 *adjective*
= piàoliang 漂亮, měilì 美丽
• (*when talking about music or voice*) = yōuměi 优美, hǎotīng 好听
2 *adverb*
= xiāngdāng 相当, tǐng 挺
that's pretty good = nà xiāngdāng hǎo 那相当好

prevent *verb*
• (*to keep from happening*) = fángzhǐ 防止, bìmiǎn 避免
to prevent a war = fángzhǐ zhànzhēng 防止战争
• (*to stop or hinder*) = zǔzhǐ 阻止, zhìzhǐ 制止
to prevent someone from [**working** | **smoking** | **going out...**] = zǔzhǐ mǒurén [gōngzuò | xīyān | chūqu...] 阻止某人 [工作 | 吸烟 | 出去...]
• (*make unable*) = shǐ...bù néng 使...不能
the noise prevented him from sleeping = zàoyīn shǐ tā bù néng shuìjiào 噪音使他不能睡觉

previous *adjective*
the previous [**night** | **year** | **headmaster**] = qián [yíge wǎnshang | yìnián | yíge xiàozhǎng] 前 [一个晚上 | 一年 | 一个校长]
previous problems = yǐqián de wèntí 以前的问题

price *noun*
• (*the amount for which a thing is bought or sold*) = jiàqián 价钱, jiàgé 价格
• (*the cost one suffers in order to gain something*) = dàijià 代价

pride *noun*
• = jiāo'ào 骄傲, zìháo 自豪
• (*self-respect*) = zìzūnxīn 自尊心

priest *noun* ▶ 344
a priest
(*protestant*) = yíge mùshī 一个牧师
(*Roman Catholic*) = yíge shénfù 一个神父

primary school *noun*
a primary school = yìsuǒ xiǎoxué 一所小学

primary school teacher *noun* ▶ 344
a primary school teacher = yíge xiǎoxué jiàoshī 一个小学教师

prime minister *noun* ▶ 344
a prime minister = yíwèi shǒuxiàng 一位首相

prince *noun*
a prince = yíge wángzǐ 一个王子

princess *noun*
a princess = yíge gōngzhǔ 一个公主

principal *noun*
a principal = yíge xiàozhǎng 一个校长

print
1 *verb*
= yìn 印, yìnshuā 印刷
to print a book = yìn yìběn shū 印一本书
2 *noun*
• (*of a photo*)
a print = yìzhāng zhàopiàn 一张照片
• (*of a finger*)
a print = yíge shǒuyìn 一个手印
• (*of a foot*)
a print = yíge jiǎoyìn 一个脚印

printer *noun*
a printer = yìtái dǎyìnjī 一台打印机

priority *noun*
a priority (*something given special attention*) = yíge zhòngdiǎn 一个重点
(*the privilege of preferential treatment*) = yíge yōuxiānquán 一个优先权

prison *noun*
a prison = yìsuǒ jiānyù 一所监狱
to put someone in prison = bǎ mǒurén guānjìn jiānyù 把某人关进监狱

prisoner *noun*
a prisoner (*one confined in prison*) = yíge fànrén 一个犯人, yíge qiúfàn 一个囚犯
(*a captive*) = yíge fúlǔ 一个俘虏
to be taken prisoner = bèi fúlǔ le 被俘虏了

private
1 *adjective*
• (*personal*) = sīrén de 私人的, gèrén de 个人的
my private life = wǒde sīrén shēnghuó 我的私人生活
• (*independent*) = sīlì 私立
a private school = yìsuǒ sīlì xuéxiào 一所私立学校

Shops, trades and professions

Work and jobs

what does she do? = tā zuò shénme gōngzuò? 她做什么工作?
what's his occupation? = tāde zhíyè shì shénme? 他的职业是什么?

In describing a person's job, the English article "a" does not normally have to be translated. Note the following examples:

he works as a translator = tā dāng fānyì 他当翻译
Paul is a dentist = Bǎoluó shì yáyī 保罗是牙医
I want to be a policeman = wǒ yào dāng jǐngchá 我要当警察

When the English article "a" is expressed, it is rendered as "yi 一", followed by an appropriate measure word. In this case, "yi 一" is optional.

she's a teacher = tā shì (yí)ge lǎoshī 她是 (一) 个老师
he is a good doctor = tā shì (yí)ge hěn hǎo de yīshēng 他是 (一)个很好的医生

Shops

In English you can say **at the baker's**, but in Chinese you have to add the word **diàn** 店 for "shop":

at the baker's = zài miànbāodiàn 在面包店
I'm going to the chemist's = wǒ qù yàodiàn 我去药店

- (*not owned by the state*) = sīyǒu 私有
  private property = sīyǒu cáichǎn 私有财产
- (*not run by the state*) = sīyíng 私营
  private industry = sīyíng gōngyè 私营工业

2 in private = sīxià 私下, mìmì 秘密

prize *noun*
a prize = yíge jiǎng(pǐn) 一个奖(品)

probably *adverb*
= hěn kěnéng 可能, dàgài 大概

problem *noun*
a problem = yíge wèntí 一个问题

process *noun*
a process = yíge guòchéng 一个过程
to be in the process of writing a letter = zhèngzài xiě yìfēng xìn 正在写一封信

produce
1 *verb*
- (*to make*) = shēngchǎn 生产, zhìzào 制造
- (*to bring about*) = chǎnshēng 产生, yǐnqǐ 引起
  to produce good results = chǎnshēng hǎo de jiéguǒ 产生好的结果
- (*to create*)
  to produce a film = shèzhì yíbù diànyǐng 摄制一部电影
  to produce a play = páiyǎn yìchū xì 排演一出戏

2 *noun*
produce = chǎnpǐn 产品

product *noun*
a product (*a thing produced*) = yíge chǎnpǐn 一个产品
(*a result*) = yíge jiéguǒ 一个结果

production *noun*
(*of food, cars, clothes, etc.*) = shēngchǎn 生产
(*of a film*) = shèzhì 摄制, pāishè 拍摄
(*of a play*) = yǎnchū 演出

profession *noun*
a profession = yìzhǒng zhíyè 一种职业

professional *adjective*
- (*pertaining to a profession*) = zhuānyè de 专业的
  professional knowledge = zhuānyè zhīshì 专业知识
- (*not amateur*) = zhíyè de 职业的

a professional athlete = yíge zhíyè yùndòngyuán 一个职业运动员

professor *noun* ▶ **344**
a professor = yíwèi jiàoshòu 一位教授

profit *noun*
a profit (*benefit*) = yíge yìchù 一个益处
(*advantage*) = yíge hǎochù 一个好处
(*capital gain*) = yífèn lìrùn 一份利润

program
1 *noun*
• (*for a computer*) = chéngxù 程序
a program = yíge chéngxù 一个程序
• (*US English*) ▶ **programme**
2 *verb*
• (*a computer*) = biān chéngxù 编程序
• (*a concert, a show, a radio or TV broadcast*) = ānpái jiémù 安排节目

programme (*British English*), **program** (*US English*) *noun*
• (*on radio, TV*) = jiémù 节目
a programme = yíge jiémù 一个节目
a programme about China = yíge guānyú Zhōngguó de jiémù 一个关于中国的节目
• (*for a play, a concert*) = jiémùdān 节目单
a programme = yìzhāng jiémùdān 一张节目单
• (*for a conference, a course*) = ānpái 安排
the programme of the conference = huìyì de ānpái 会议的安排

progress *noun*
• (*forward movement*) = qiánjìn 前进
• (*advance to something better or higher in development*) = jìnbù 进步
to make progress = jìnbù 进步

project *noun*
a project (*for study or research*) = yíge kètí 一个课题
(*in construction*) = yíxiàng gōngchéng 一项工程
(*a scheme*) = yíxiàng guīhuà 一项规划, yíge jìhuà 一个计划

promise
1 *verb*
= dāyìng 答应, yǔnnuò 允诺
to promise to [come | repay a loan | say nothing] = dāyìng [lái | huán dàikuǎn | shénme yě bù shuō] 答应 [来 | 还贷款 | 什么也不说]
2 *noun*
a promise = yíge nuòyán 一个诺言, yíge yǔnnuò 一个允诺
[to keep | to break] one's promise = [zūnshǒu | bù zūnshǒu] nuòyán [遵守 | 不遵守] 诺言

pronounce *verb*
• (*to articulate*) = fā...de yīn 发... 的音, niàn 念
how do you pronounce this character? = nǐ zěnme fā zhège zì de yīn? 你怎么发这个字的音?

proof *noun*
= zhèngmíng 证明, zhèngjù 证据

properly *adverb*
• (*in an appropriate manner*) = shìdàng de 适当地, qiàdàng de 恰当地
• (*strictly*) = yángé de 严格地

property *noun*
• (*something that is owned*) = cáichǎn 财产
• (*house that is owned*) = fángchǎn 房产
• (*land that is owned*) = dìchǎn 地产

protect *verb*
• (*to guard*) = bǎohù 保护
to protect oneself = bǎohù zìjǐ 保护自己
• (*to defend*) = bǎowèi 保卫

protest *verb*
• (*to make a declaration against*) = kàngyì 抗议, fǎnduì 反对
• (*assert formally*) = duànyán 断言, biǎoshì 表示
he protested his innocence = tā duànyán zìjǐ wúzuì 他断言自己无罪

protester *noun*
a protester = yíge kàngyìzhě 一个抗议者

proud *adjective*
= jiāo'ào 骄傲, zìháo 自豪
she's proud of herself = tā wèi zìjǐ gǎndào jiāo'ào 她为自己感到骄傲

prove *verb*
= zhèngmíng 证明, zhèngshí 证实

provide *verb*
= tígòng 提供
to provide meals = tígòng fàn 提供饭

to provide a transport service = tígòng jiāotōng fúwù 提供交通服务

provided *conjunction*
= jiǎrú 假如
I'll lend you my car provided you pay me = jiǎrú nǐ fù gěi wǒ qián, wǒ jiù bǎ chē jiè gěi nǐ 假如你付给我钱，我就把车借给你

> **!** *Note that the clause introduced by* jiǎrú 假如 *comes before the main clause and* jiù 就 *is often used after the subject in the main clause.*

psychiatrist *noun* ▶ 344
a psychiatrist = yíge jīngshénbìng yīshēng 一个精神病医生

psychologist *noun* ▶ 344
a psychologist
(*one who does research*) = yíge xīnlǐxuéjiā 一个心理学家
(*one who sees patients*) = yíge xīnlǐ yīshēng 一个心理医生

pub *noun* (*British English*)
a pub = yíge jiǔguǎn(r) 一个酒馆(儿)

public
1 *noun*
the public = gōngzhòng 公众, mínzhòng 民众
2 *adjective*
- (*open to all*) = gōnggòng 公共
  a public library = yíge gōnggòng túshūguǎn 一个公共图书馆
- (*used by all*) = gōngyòng 公用
  a public telephone = yíge gōngyòng diànhuà 一个公用电话
- (*known to all*) = gōngkāi 公开
  to make their relationship public = bǎ tāmende guānxi gōngkāi 把他们的关系公开

3 in public = gōngkāi 公开, dāngzhòng 当众

public holiday *noun*
a public holiday = yíge gōngdìng jiàrì 一个公定假日

public transport *noun*
= gōnggòng jiāotōng 公共交通

pudding *noun*
a pudding = yíge bùdīng 一个布丁
(*general term for a dessert*) (*British English*) = yíge tiánshí 一个甜食

puddle *noun*
a puddle = yíge xiǎo shuǐkēng 一个小水坑

pull *verb*
- (*to move something toward oneself*) = lā 拉
  to pull on a rope = lā yìgēn shéngzi 拉一根绳子
- (*if there is a means to facilitate the action, such as wheels or rollers, or if it's a person walking*) = lā 拉
  to pull the piano into the sitting room = bǎ gāngqín lā dào kètīng li 把钢琴拉到客厅里
  to pull someone away from the door = bǎ mǒurén cóng ménkǒu lāzǒu 把某人从门口拉走
- (*if there is no means to facilitate the pulling action*) = tuō 拖
  to pull the dead body out of the river = bǎ shītǐ cóng hé li tuōchūlai 把尸体从河里拖出来
  the demonstrators were pulled away by the policeman = shìwēizhě bèi jǐngchá tuōzǒu le 示威者被警察拖走了
- (*to extract something that is fixed*) = bá 拔
  to pull [a tooth | a nail | the weeds] = bá [yìkē yá | yíge dīngzi | cǎo] 拔[一颗牙 | 一个钉子 | 草]
- **to pull a face** (*British English*) = zuò guǐliǎnr 做鬼脸儿

pull down
- (*to knock down*) = chāidiào 拆掉
- (*to lower*) = jiàngdī 降低

pull out
to pull a tooth out = báchū yìkē yá 拔出一棵牙

pull up
- (*to stop*) = tíngxia 停下
- (*to remove*)
  to pull up the weeds = bá cǎo 拔草
- **to pull up one's socks** = bǎ wàzi lāqǐlai 把袜子拉起来

pullover *noun*
a pullover = yíjiàn tàoshān 一件套衫

pump *noun*
- (*for moving or raising fluids*) = bèng 泵
  a pump = yíge bèng 一个泵
- (*for transferring air*)
  a bicycle pump = yíge dǎqìtǒng 一个打气筒

pump up = dǎ qì 打气

pumpkin *noun*
a pumpkin = yíge nánguā 一个南瓜

punch *verb*
= yòng quán dǎ 用拳打
she punched him in the face = tā yòng quán dǎ tāde liǎn 她用拳打他的脸

puncture *noun*
a puncture = yíge cìkǒng 一个刺孔

punish *verb*
= chǔfá 处罚, chěngfá 惩罚

pupil *noun*
a pupil = yíge xuésheng 一个学生

puppet *noun*
a puppet = yíge mù'ǒu 一个木偶

puppy *noun*
a puppy = yìzhī xiǎogǒu 一只小狗

pure *adjective*
- (*unmixed and untainted*) = chún 纯
pure gold = chún jīn 纯金
- (*clean*) = chúnjìng 纯净, jiéjìng 洁净
pure air = chúnjìng de kōngqì 纯净的空气
- (*free from bad taste, bad ideas, evil thinking*) = chúnjié 纯洁
pure love = chúnjié de àiqíng 纯洁的爱情
- (*sheer*) = wánquán 完全 chúncuì 纯粹
it's pure nonsense = zhè wánquán shì húshuōbādào 这完全是胡说八道
- (*when talking about the use of a language*) = chúnzhèng 纯正
a pure Beijing accent = chúnzhèng de Běijīng kǒuyīn 纯正的北京口音

purple *adjective*
= zǐsè de 紫色的

purpose
1 *noun*
a purpose (*intention*) = yíge yìtú 一个意图
(*aim*) = yíge mùdì 一个目的
(*a useful function*) = yíge yòngchù 一个用处
2 on purpose = gùyì 故意
you did it on purpose! = nǐ shì gùyì zhèyàng zuò de! 你是故意这样做的!

purse *noun*
- (*for money*) = qiánbāo 钱包
a purse = yíge qiánbāo 一个钱包
- (*US English*) (*a handbag*) = shǒutíbāo 手提包
a purse = yíge shǒutíbāo 一个手提包

push *verb*
- (*press or move forward by pressure*) = tuī 推
to push a car = tuī chē 推车
to push someone down the stairs = bǎ mǒurén tuīxià lóutī 把某人推下楼梯
- (*to urge*) = cuī(cù) 催(促)
don't push her too hard = bié cuī tā tài jǐn 别催她太紧
- (*sell*) = fànmài 贩卖
to push drugs = fànmài dúpǐn 贩卖毒品

pushchair *noun* (*British English*)
a pushchair = yíge yīnghái tuīchē 一个婴孩推车

pusher *noun*
a pusher (*a drug seller*) = yíge fàn dú de rén 一个贩毒的人

put *verb*
- (*to place or to add*) = fàng 放
to put the book on the table = bǎ shū fàng zài zhuōzi shang 把书放在桌子上
don't put sugar in my coffee = bié wǎng wǒde kāfēi li fàng táng 别往我的咖啡里放糖
- (*to raise*) = tíchū 提出
to put a question to him = xiàng tā tíchū yíge wèntí 向他提出一个问题
- (*to cause to be in a position or state*)
to put someone in prison = bǎ mǒurén guānjìn jiānyù 把某人关进监狱
to put someone in a bad mood = shǐ mǒurén xīnqíng bù hǎo 使某人心情不好

put away
- (*to pack up*) = shōuqǐlai 收起来
put your tools away = bǎ nǐde gōngjù shōuqǐlai 把你的工具收起来
- (*to put into a proper or desirable place*) = fànghǎo 放好
to put the money away = bǎ qián fànghǎo 把钱放好

put back
- (*to return to its place*) = fànghuí 放回
to put the book back on the shelf = bǎ shū fànghuí shūjià 把书放回书架
- (*to change the time*)
to put the clock back = bǎ zhōngbiǎo wǎng huí bō 把钟表往回拨

P

put down

- (*to lay down*) = fàngxia 放下
  put the knife down! = bǎ dāo fàngxia! 把刀放下!
- (*when phoning*) = guàduàn 挂断
  to put the phone down = guàduàn diànhuà 挂断电话
- (*British English*) (*to give a lethal injection to*) = gěi...zhùshè yàopǐn shǐ tā ānlè sǐqù 给... 注射药品使它安乐死去
  our dog had to be put down = zhǐhǎo gěi wǒmende gǒu zhùshè yàopǐn shǐ tā ānlè sǐqù 只好给我们的狗注射药品使它安乐死去
- (*to write down*) = xiěxia 写下
  please put your name down on this paper = qǐng zài zhèzhāng zhǐ shang xiěxia nǐde míngzi 请在这张纸上写下你的名字

put forward

- (*to propose*) = tíchū 提出
  to put forward a suggestion = tíchū yíge jiànyì 提出一个建议
- (*to change the time*)
  to put the clocks forward = bǎ biǎo wǎng qián bō 把表往前拨

put off

- (*to delay*) = tuīchí 推迟
  to put off the meeting till next week = bǎ huìyì tuīchí dào xiàge xīngqī 把会议推迟到下个星期
- (*to switch off*) = guānshang 关上

put on

- (*if it's clothes, shoes, socks*) = chuānshang 穿上
  to put jeans on = chuānshang niúzǎikù 穿上牛仔裤
- (*if it's a hat, gloves, glasses, a scarf*) = dàishang 戴上
  to put on one's watch = dàishang shǒubiǎo 戴上手表
- (*to switch on*) = dǎkāi 打开
  to put the heating on = bǎ nuǎnqì dǎkāi 把暖气打开
- **to put a CD on** = fàngshang yìzhāng guāngpán 放上一张光盘
- **to put on weight** = zēngjiā tǐzhòng 增加体重
- (*to organize, to produce*) = shàngyǎn 上演
  to put on a play = shàngyǎn yìchū xì 上演一出戏

put out

- **to put out a cigarette** = mièdiào yānjuǎnr 灭掉烟卷儿
- (*to switch off*) = guāndiào 关掉
  to put out the lights = bǎ dēng guāndiào 把灯关掉

put up

- (*to raise*) = jǔqǐ 举起, táiqǐ 抬起
  to put up one's hand = jǔqǐ shǒu 举起手
- **to put a sign up** = guàqǐ yíge zhāopái 挂起一个招牌
- (*to erect*) = dāqǐ 搭起
  to put up a tent = dāqǐ yíge zhàngpeng 搭起一个帐篷
- (*British English*) (*to raise*) = tígāo 提高
  to put the rent up = tígāo fángzū 提高房租
- (*to give someone a place to stay*)
  to put someone up = gěi mǒurén tígòng zhùchù 给某人提供住处

put up with = rěnshòu 忍受, róngrěn 容忍

puzzle *noun*

a puzzle (*a riddle*) = yíge míyǔ 一个谜语
(*a question*) = yíge nántí 一个难题
(*a bewildering situation*) = yíge mí 一个谜
(*a jigsaw puzzle*) = yíge pīnbǎn wánjù 一个拼板玩具

pyjamas *noun*

- = shuìyī 睡衣
- (*if it's trousers only*) = shuìkù 睡裤

Qq

qualified *adjective*

- (*having the right qualifications*) = yǒu zīgé de 有资格的
- (*competent and fit*) = shèngrèn 胜任

quality *noun*

- (*grade of goodness*) = zhìliàng 质量
- (*attribute*) = pǐnzhì 品质
- (*characteristic*) = tèxìng 特性

quantity *noun* ▶ 349
= liàng 量, shùliàng 数量

Quantities

How much?

how much is there? = yǒu duōshǎo? 有多少?
there is a lot = yǒu hěn duō 有很多
there is not much = méi yǒu hěn duō 没有很多
there are two kilos = yǒu liǎng gōngjīn 有两公斤
how much sugar do you have? = nǐ yǒu duōshǎo táng? 你有多少糖?
I've got a lot = wǒ yǒu hěn duō 我有很多
I haven't got (very)much = wǒ méi yǒu hěn duō 我没有很多
I've got two kilos = wǒ yǒu liǎng gōngjīn 我有两公斤

How many?

how many (apples) are there? = yǒu duōshǎo(ge píngguǒ)? 有多少(个苹果)?
there are a lot = yǒu hěn duō 有很多
there aren't many = méi yǒu hěn duō 没有很多
there are twenty = yǒu èrshíge 有二十个
how many (apples) do you have? = nǐ yǒu duōshǎo(ge píngguǒ)? 你有多少(个苹果)?
I have twenty = wǒ yǒu èrshíge 我有二十个
I have a lot = wǒ yǒu hěn duō 我有很多
I haven't got many = wǒ méi yǒu hěn duō 我没有很多

Comparison

Tim has more than Tom = Dìmǔde bǐ Tāngmǔde duō 蒂姆的比汤姆的多
Tim has more money than Tom = Dìmǔde qián bǐ Tāngmǔde duō 蒂姆的钱比汤姆的多
much more than = bǐ...duō de duō 比...多得多
a little more than = bǐ...duō yìdiǎnr 比...多一点儿
Tim has more apples than Tom = Dìmǔde píngguǒ bǐ Tāngmǔde duō 蒂姆的苹果比汤姆的多
he has many more apples than I = tāde píngguǒ bǐ wǒde duō hěn duō 他的苹果比我的多很多
he has a few more apples than I = tāde píngguǒ bǐ wǒde duō jǐge 他的苹果比我的多几个
Tom has less than Tim = Tāngmǔde bǐ Dìmǔde shǎo 汤姆的比蒂姆的少
Tom has less money than Tim = Tāngmǔde qián bǐ Dìmǔde shǎo 汤姆的钱比蒂姆的少
much less than... = bǐ...shǎo de duō 比...少得多
a little less than... = bǐ...shǎo yìdiǎnr 比...少一点儿
he has fewer (apples) than I = tāde (píngguǒ) bǐ wǒde shǎo 他的(苹果)比我的少
he has many fewer than I = tāde bǐ wǒde shǎo hěn duō 他的比我的少很多

Relative Quantities

how many are there to the kilo? = yì gōngjīn yǒu jǐgè? 一公斤有几个?

there are ten to the kilo	= yì gōngjīn yǒu shíge 一公斤有十个
how many can you buy for one pound?	= yì yīngbàng mǎi jǐge? 一英镑买几个?
you can buy five for one pound	= yì yīngbàng mǎi wǔge 一英镑买五个
how much does the oil cost a litre?	= yóu yì shēng duōshǎo qián? 油一升多少钱?
it costs £2 a litre	= yóu yì shēng liǎng bàng qián 油一升两镑钱
how much do apples cost per kilo?	= píngguǒ yì gōngjīn duōshǎo qián? 苹果一公斤多少钱?
how many glasses do you get to the bottle?	= yì píng néng dào duōshǎo bēi? 一瓶能倒多少杯?
you get six glasses to the bottle	= yì píng néng dào liù bēi 一瓶能倒六杯

a [small | large] quantity of oil = [shǎo | dà] liàng de yóu [少 | 大] 量的油
large quantity of bananas = dà liàng de xiāngjiāo 大量的香蕉

quarrel
1 *noun*
a quarrel = yícì zhēngchǎo 一次争吵, yícì chǎojià 一次吵架
2 *verb*
= zhēngchǎo 争吵, chǎojià 吵架
to quarrel with someone = gēn mǒurén zhēngchǎo 跟某人争吵

quarter
1 *noun*
a quarter of an hour = yí kè zhōng 一刻钟
to divide the tomatoes in quarters = bǎ xīhóngshì fēnchéng sì fèn 把西红柿分成四份
2 *pronoun*
• (*when talking about quantities, numbers*) ▶ **349**
a quarter = sìfēn zhī yī 四分之一
a quarter of the population can't read = sìfēn zhī yī de rénkǒu bù shí zì 四分之一的人口不识字
• (*when talking about time*) ▶ **204**
a quarter = yí kè (zhōng) 一刻(钟), shíwǔ fēn (zhōng) 十五分(钟)
an hour and a quarter = yì xiǎoshí (líng) yí kè zhōng 一小时(零)一刻钟
it's a quarter past five = wǔ diǎn shíwǔ (fēn) 五点十五(分)

> **!** *Note that when talking about a point of time*, zhong 钟 *is not used.*

quay *noun*
a quay = yíge mǎtou 一个码头

queen *noun*
a queen = yíge nǚwáng 一个女王

question
1 *noun*
a question = yíge wèntí 一个问题
to ask someone a question = wèn mǒurén yíge wèntí 问某人一个问题
to answer a question = huídá yíge wèntí 回答一个问题
2 *verb*
• (*to put questions to*) = xúnwèn 询问, xùnwèn 讯问
• (*when handling a suspect or a criminal*) = shěnwèn 审问

queue (*British English*)
1 *noun*
a queue = yìtiáo duì 一条队
to join the queue = cānjiā pái duì 参加排队
to jump the queue = chāduì 插队, bú àn cìxù pái duì 不按次序排队, jiāsāir 加塞儿
2 *verb*
= pái duì 排队

quick *adjective*
= kuài 快, xùnsù 迅速
a quick answer = yíge hěn kuài de dáfù 一个很快的答复
it's quicker to go by train = zuò huǒchē qù gèng kuài 坐火车去更快
it's the quickest way [to get to London | to save money | to make friends] =

zhè shì [qù Lúndūn | shěng qián | jiāo péngyou] de zuì kuài fāngfǎ 这是[去伦敦 | 省钱 | 交朋友] 的最快方法

quickly *adverb*
= kuài 快, hěn kuài de 很快地

quiet
1 *adjective*
• (*silent*) = jìng 静, ānjìng 安静
to keep quiet = bǎochí ānjìng 保持安静
be quiet! = ānjìng! 安静!
• (*not talkative*) = wénjìng 文静
• (*calm*) = píngjìng 平静, níngjìng 宁静
a quiet little village = yíge níngjìng de xiǎo cūnzhuāng 一个宁静的小村庄
2 *noun*
= ānjìng 安静, píngjìng 平静
quiet please! = qǐng ānjìng! 请安静!

quietly *adverb*
to speak quietly = qīngshēng de jiǎnghuà 轻声地讲话
[**to sit there** | **to read newspapers** | **to drink tea**] **quietly** = jìngjìng de [zuò zài nàr | kàn bào | hē chá] 静静地 [坐在那儿 | 看报 | 喝茶]

quit *verb*
• (*to resign*) = cí zhí 辞职
• (*US English*) (*to give up*)
to quit [**smoking** | **drinking** | **taking drugs**] = jiè [yān | jiǔ | dú] 戒 [烟 | 酒 | 毒]
to quit school = tuìxué 退学

quite *adverb*
• (*rather*) = xiāngdāng 相当, tǐng 挺
I quite like Chinese food = wǒ tǐng xǐhuan Zhōngguó fàn 我挺喜欢中国饭
she earns quite a lot of money = tā zhèng de qián xiāngdāng duō 她挣的钱相当多
• (*completely*) = wánquán 完全, shífēn 十分
I'm not quite ready yet = wǒ hái méi wánquán zhǔnbèihǎo 我还没完全准备好
you're quite right = nǐ wánquán duì 你完全对
I'm not quite sure what he does = wǒ bù shífēn qīngchu tā zuò shénme 我不十分清楚他做什么

quiz *noun*
a quiz = yícì wèndá bǐsài 一次问答比赛

Rr

rabbit *noun*
a rabbit = yìzhī tùzi 一只兔子

rabies *noun* ▶ 277
= kuángquǎnbìng 狂犬病

race
1 *noun*
• (*a contest*) = bǐsài 比赛
a race = yícì bǐsài 一次比赛
to have a race = jìnxíng yícì bǐsài 进行一次比赛
• (*for horse-racing*)
the races = sàimǎ 赛马
• (*a group of people*) = rénzhǒng 人种, zhǒngzú 种族
a race = yíge rénzhǒng 一个人种
2 *verb*
• (*to compete with*) = gēn...bǐsài 跟...比赛
to race (against) someone = gēn mǒurén bǐsài 跟某人比赛
I'll race you to the car = wǒ gēn nǐ bǐsài, kàn shéi xiān pǎodào nàliàng qìchē 我跟你比赛, 看谁先跑到那辆汽车
• (*to take part in a contest*) = cānjiā bǐsài 参加比赛

racehorse *noun*
a racehorse = yìpí bǐsài yòng de mǎ 一匹比赛用的马

racetrack *noun*
a racetrack = yìtiáo pǎodào 一条跑道
(*for cars*) = yìtiáo (sài)chēdào 一条(赛)车道

racism *noun*
= zhǒngzú zhǔyì 种族主义, zhǒngzú qíshì 种族歧视

racket, racquet *noun*
a racket = yíge pāizi 一个拍子, yíge qiúpāi 一个球拍

radiator *noun*
a radiator
(*for heating*) = yíge nuǎnqì 一个暖气

radio *noun*
a radio = yìtái shōuyīnjī 一台收音机
on the radio = zài guǎngbō li 在广播里

radio station *noun*
a radio station = yíge (guǎngbō) diàntái 一个(广播)电台

rage *noun*
= kuángnù 狂怒, dànù 大怒
to fly into a rage = bórán dànù 勃然大怒

raid *verb*
= xíjī 袭击
to raid a bank = xíjī yìjiā yínháng 袭击一家银行
the police raided the building = jǐngchá xíjīle nàzuò dàlóu 警察袭击了那座大楼

rail *noun*
- (*for holding on to*) = fúshǒu 扶手, lángān 栏杆
a rail = yíge fúshǒu 一个扶手
- (*for trains*)
rails = tiěguǐ 铁轨, tiělù 铁路

railway (*British English*), **railroad** (*US English*) *noun*
- (*a track*) = tiělù 铁路, tiědào 铁道
a railway = yìtiáo tiělù 一条铁路
- (*the rail system*)
the railway = tiělù xìtǒng 铁路系统

railway line *noun* (*British English*)
a railway line = yìtiáo tiělùxiàn 一条铁路线

railway station *noun* (*British English*)
a railway station = yíge huǒchēzhàn 一个火车站

rain
1 *noun*
= yǔ 雨
to stand in the rain = zhàn zài yǔ zhōng 站在雨中
2 *verb*
= xiàyǔ 下雨
it's raining = zhèngzài xiàyǔ 正在下雨

rainbow *noun*
a rainbow = yídào cǎihóng 一道彩虹

raincoat *noun*
a raincoat = yíjiàn yǔyī 一件雨衣

raise *verb*
- (*to lift*) = jǔqǐ 举起, táiqǐ 抬起
- (*to increase*) = tígāo 提高
to raise prices = tígāo jiàqián 提高价钱
to raise one's voice = tígāo shēngyīn 提高声音
- (*to bring up, as an issue or question*) = tíchū 提出
to raise a question = tíchū yíge wèntí 提出一个问题
- (*to bring up, as a child*) = fúyǎng 抚养
to raise children = fúyǎng háizi 抚养孩子

range *noun*
- (*variation between limits*) = fúdù 幅度
a range = yíge fúdù 一个幅度
the range of increase in temperature = qìwēn shēnggāo de fúdù 气温升高的幅度
- (*scope*) = fànwéi 范围
a range = yíge fànwéi 一个范围
your range of choices = nǐ kěyǐ xuǎnzé de fànwéi 你可以选择的范围
- (*of mountains*) = shānmài 山脉
a mountain range = yíge shānmài 一个山脉
- (*US English*) (*for cooking*)
a range = yíge lúzào 一个炉灶

rare *adjective*
- (*not common*) = hǎnjiàn 罕见, xīyǒu 稀有
- (*very slightly cooked*) = bàn shú de 半熟的

rarely *adverb*
= hěn shǎo 很少, nándé 难得

rasher *noun* (*British English*)
a rasher (of bacon) = yípiàn xiánròu 一片咸肉

raspberry *noun*
a raspberry = yíge mùméi 一个木莓

rat *noun*
a rat = yìzhī lǎoshǔ 一只老鼠, yìzhī hàozi 一只耗子

rather *adverb*
- (*when saying what one would prefer*)
I'd rather [leave | stay here | read the paper...] = wǒ níngyuàn [zǒu | dāizài zhèr | kàn bàozhǐ...] 我宁愿[走 | 呆在这儿 | 看报纸...]
I'd rather you go with me = wǒ dào xīwàng nǐ hé wǒ yìqǐ qù 我倒希望你和我一起去
I'd rather go than stay here = wǒ xiǎng zǒu, bù xiǎng dāi zài zhèr 我想走，不想呆在这儿
- (*quite*) = xiāngdāng 相当, tǐng 挺
I think he's rather nice = wǒ rènwéi tā xiāngdāng hǎo 我认为他相当好

raw *adjective*
- (*uncooked*) = shēng 生
  raw fish = shēng yú 生鱼
- (*not manufactured*)
  raw materials = yuán cáiliào 原材料

razor *noun*
  a razor = yìbǎ guāliǎndāo 一把刮脸刀, yìbǎ guāhúdāo 一把刮胡刀

razor blade *noun*
  a razor blade = yíge dāopiàn 一个刀片

reach *verb*
- (*to arrive at*) = dàodá 到达
  they reached the school at midnight = tāmen bànyè dàodá xuéxiào 他们半夜到达学校
- (*to be delivered to*)
  the letter never reached me = wǒ cónglái jiù méi shōudào nàfēng xìn 我从来就没收到那封信
- (*by stretching*) = gòu 够
  I can't reach the shelf = wǒ gòu bù zháo shūjià 我够不着书架
- (*to come to*)
  to reach an agreement = dáchéng yíge xiéyì 达成一个协议
- (*to contact*) = gēn...liánxì 跟... 联系
  you can reach me at this number = nǐ kěyǐ dǎ zhège diànhuà hàomǎ gēn wǒ liánxì 你可以打这个电话号码跟我联系
  reach out = shēnchū 伸出
  to reach out one's hand = shēnchū shǒu 伸出手

react *verb*
  = fǎnyìng 反应
  the audience reacted warmly to his speech = tīngzhòng duì tāde jiǎnghuà fǎnyìng rèliè 听众对他的讲话反应热烈

read *verb*
- (*to look at and comprehend*) = kàn 看, dú 读
  to read the newspaper = kàn bào 看报
- (*to read aloud*) = niàn 念, dú 读
  she is reading a story to her children = tā zài gěi tāde háizi niàn yíge gùshi 她在给她的孩子念一个故事
- (*to study*) = xuéxí 学习
  she's reading medicine at a university = tā zài yìsuǒ dàxué xuéxí yīxué 她在一所大学学习医学
- (*understand by reading*) = kàndǒng 看懂
  can you read Chinese? = nǐ kàn de dǒng Zhōngwén ma? 你看得懂中文吗?
  read out
  to read out the names = niàn míngzi 念名字
  read through = tōngdú 通读, cóng tóu dú dào wěi 从头读到尾

reading *noun*
- (*the action of reading*) = yuèdú 阅读, dúshū 读书
- (*material for reading*) = yuèdú cáiliào 阅读材料

ready *adjective*
- (*prepared*) = zhǔnbèihǎo 准备好
  are you ready? = nǐ zhǔnbèihǎo le ma? 你准备好了吗?
  to get the meal ready = bǎ fàn zhǔnbèihǎo 把饭准备好
- (*happy*) = lèyì 乐意, yuànyì 愿意
  I'm ready to help you = wǒ hěn lèyì bāngzhù nǐ 我很乐意帮助你

real *adjective*
- (*genuine*) = zhēn 真, zhēnzhèng 真正
  real diamonds = zhēn zuànshí 真钻石
- (*actual*) = xiànshí 现实, zhēnshí 真实
  real life = xiànshí shēnghuó 现实生活
- **it's a real shame** = zhè zhēn kěxī 这真可惜

reality *noun*
  = xiànshí 现实, shíjì cúnzài 实际存在

realize *verb*
- (*make real*) = shíxiàn 实现
  he has realized his goal = tā shíxiànle tāde mùbiāo 他实现了他的目标
- (*to comprehend completely*) = rènshidào 认识到
  he didn't realize that he was wrong = tā méiyǒu rènshidào tā cuò le 他没有认识到他错了

really *adverb*
- (*truly, actually*) = quèshí 确实
  it's really easy to make = zhè quèshí hěn róngyì zuò 这确实很容易做
- **really?** = zhēn de ma? 真的吗?

rear
1 *noun*
- (*back part*) = hòubù 后部, hòumian 后面

2 *verb*
- (*to care for and educate*) = fǔyǎng 抚养, yǎngyù 养育
  to rear the children = fǔyǎng háizi 抚养孩子
- (*to breed*) = sìyǎng 饲养
  to rear pigs = sìyǎng zhū 饲养猪

reason *noun*
- (*ground or cause*) = yuányīn 原因, lǐyóu 理由
  a reason = yíge yuányīn 一个原因
  the reason for being late = chídào de yuányīn 迟到的原因
- (*sensible or logical thought or view*) = dàolǐ 道理
  there is reason in what he said = tā shuō de yǒu dàolǐ 他说的有道理

reassure *verb*
the policeman reassured me about my daughter's safety = jǐngchá ràng wǒ bú yào wèi wǒ nǚ'ér de ānquán dānyōu 警察让我不要为我女儿的安全担忧
this letter reassured me = zhèfēng xìn shǐ wǒ fàngxīn le 这封信使我放心了

receipt *noun*
a receipt = yìzhāng shōujù 一张收据

receive *verb*
- (*to obtain from someone by delivery*) = shōudào 收到, jiēdào 接到
  we received a letter from the teacher = wǒmen shōudào lǎoshī de yìfēng xìn 我们收到老师的一封信
- (*to get*) = dédào
  to receive help from someone = dédào mǒurén de bāngzhù 得到某人的帮助
- (*meet and welcome*) = jiēdài 接待
  the delegation was well received = dàibiǎotuán shòudàole hěn hǎo de jiēdài 代表团受到了很好的接待

recent *adjective*
= zuìjìn de 最近的, jìnlái de 近来的

recently *adverb*
= zuìjìn 最近, jìnlái 近来

reception *noun*
- (*in a hotel, a hospital, a company*)
  the reception (area) = jiēdàichù 接待处
  ask at reception = zài jiēdàichù xúnwèn 在接待处询问
- (*a formal event*)
  a reception = yíge zhāodàihuì 一个招待会
- (*the act of receiving or being received*) = jiēdài 接待

receptionist *noun* ▶ **344**
a receptionist = yíge jiēdàiyuán 一个接待员

recipe *noun*
a recipe (*instructions for cooking a dish*) = yìzhǒng pēngtiáo fāngfǎ 一种烹调方法
(*medical prescription*) = yíge yàofāng 一个药方

recognize *verb*
- (*to identify as known*) = rènchū 认出
- (*to acknowledge*) = chéngrèn 承认

recommend *verb*
- (*to command or introduce as suitable*) = tuījiàn 推荐
- (*to advise*) = quàngào 劝告, jiànyì 建议

record
1 *noun*
- (*details about a fact or proceeding*) = jìlù 记录
- (*information about a person's past*) = lǚlì 履历, jīnglì 经历
- (*the best recorded achievement*)
  a record = yíxiàng jìlù 一项记录
  to break the world record = dǎpò shìjiè jìlù 打破世界记录
- (*for playing music*)
  a record = yìzhāng chàngpiàn 一张唱片

2 *verb*
- (*to put in writing*) = jìlù 记录
- (*to make a recording of music, speech, etc.*) = lùyīn 录音

recorder *noun* ▶ **308**
a recorder (*a musical instrument*) = yìzhī dízi 一支笛子
(*a machine for recording sounds*) = yìtái lùyīnjī 一台录音机

record player *noun*
a record player = yìtái diànchàngjī 一台电唱机, yìtái liúshēngjī 一台留声机

recover *verb*
- (*to regain one's health*) = huīfù 恢复
  the patient has completely recovered from his illness = bìngrén yǐjīng

wánquán huīfù le 病人已经完全恢复了
- (*get back or find again*) = zhǎohuí 找回
  I have recovered the money I lost = wǒ bǎ wǒ diū de qián zhǎohuílai le 我把我丢的钱找回来了

recycle *verb*
- (*to reprocess and reuse*) = huíshōu chǔlǐ 回收处理, xúnhuán shǐyòng 循环使用
  to recycle newspapers = huíshōu chǔlǐ bàozhǐ 回收处理报纸
  to recycle these bottles = xúnhuán shǐyòng zhèxiē píngzi 循环使用这些瓶子

red *adjective*
= hóng 红, hóngsè de 红色的
to go red, to turn red = biàn hóng 变红

red-haired *adjective*
= hóng tóufa de 红头发的

reduce *verb*
- (*to lower*) = jiǎn 减, jiǎnshǎo 减少
  to reduce prices = jiǎn jià 减价
- (*to diminish in weight, pain, pressure*) = jiǎnqīng 减轻
  to reduce one's weight = jiǎnqīng tǐzhòng 减轻体重
- (*to slow down*) = jiǎndī 减低, jiǎnmàn 减慢
  to reduce speed = jiǎndī sùdù 减低速度

reduction *noun*
= jiǎnshǎo 减少, suōjiǎn 缩减

redundant *adjective*
- (*British English*) (*of worker, no longer needed and therefore dismissed*) = bèi cáijiǎn de 被裁减的
  to be made redundant = bèi cáijiǎn 被裁减
- (*superfluous*) = guòshèng 过剩, duōyú 多余

referee *noun* ▶ 344
a referee (*in matches and games*) = yìmíng cáipàn 一名裁判
(*one who testifies to someone's character, knowledge, etc.*) = yìmíng jiàndìngrén 一名鉴定人, yìmíng shěncharén 一名审查人
(*an arbitrator*) = yìmíng zhòngcáirén 一名仲裁人

reflection *noun*
a reflection (*a conscious thought*) = yìzhǒng xiǎngfǎ 一种想法, yìzhǒng jiànjiě 一种见解
(*an image reflected in water, etc.*) = yíge dàoyǐng 一个倒影
(*an expression*) = yìzhǒng fǎnyìng 一种反映, yìzhǒng biǎoxiàn 一种表现
a reflection of the living standards in this country = zhège guójiā shēnghuó shuǐpíng de yìzhǒng fǎnyìng 这个国家生活水平的一种反映

refreshing *adjective*
- (*pleasantly cooling*) = qīngshuǎng 清爽, liángshuǎng 凉爽
- (*invigorating*) = shǐ rén zhènzuò de 使人振作的

refrigerator *noun*
a refrigerator = yìtái (diàn)bīngxiāng 一台(电)冰箱

refugee *noun*
a refugee = yíge bìnànzhě 一个避难者, yíge nànmín 一个难民

refuse[1] *verb*
= jùjué 拒绝, bùkěn 不肯
to refuse [**to listen** | **to accept a gift** | **to pay the money...**] = jùjué [tīng | jiēshòu lǐwù | fù qián...] 拒绝 [听 | 接受礼物 | 付钱...]

refuse[2] *noun*
= lājī 垃圾, fèiwù 废物

regards *noun*
= wènhòu 问候, zhìyì 致意
give her my regards = dài wǒ xiàng tā wènhòu 代我向她问候

region *noun*
a region (*area, district*) = yíge dìqū 一个地区
(*part of the body*) = yíge bùwèi 一个部位

regional *adjective*
= dìqū de 地区的, júbù de 局部的

register *noun*
a register (*a written record regularly kept*) = yìběn dēngjìbù 一本登记簿
to take the register = dēngjì 登记

regret *verb*
- (*to wish something had not happened*) = hòuhuǐ 后悔, àohuǐ 懊悔

I regret changing my mind = wǒ hòuhuǐ gǎibiànle zhǔyì 我后悔改变了主意
- (*feel sorry*) = yíhàn 遗憾

he regrets that he can't come = tā hěn yíhàn tā bù néng lái 他很遗憾他不能来

regular *adjective*
- (*habitual or according to rule*) = yǒu guīlǜ de 有规律的, guīzé de 规则的
- (*periodical*) = dìngqī 定期
- (*normal*) = zhèngcháng 正常

regularly *adverb*
- (*habitually, by rule*) = yǒu guīlǜ de 有规律地, guīzé de 规则地
- (*periodically*) = dìngqī de 定期地

rehearsal *noun*

a rehearsal (*a trial or practise performance*) = yícì páiliàn 一次排练, yícì páiyǎn 一次排演

rehearse *verb*

(*to perform privately for trial or practice*) = páiliàn 排练, páiyǎn 排演

reject *verb*
- (*to refuse to accept*) = jùjué (jiēshòu) 拒绝(接受)

to reject someone's advice = jùjué (jiēshòu) mǒurén de quàngào 拒绝(接受)某人的劝告
- (*to refuse to pass, as a bill, proposal, etc.*) = fǒujué 否决

to reject a candidate = fǒujué yìmíng hòuxuǎnrén 否决一名候选人

relationship *noun*

= guānxì 关系

she has a good relationship with her parents = tā gēn tāde fùmǔ guānxì hěn hǎo 她跟她的父母关系很好

> **!** *Note that the indefinite article* **a** *in this sentence is not translated.*

relative *noun*

a relative = yíge qīnqi 一个亲戚

relax *verb*
- (*to make less rigid or strict*) = fàngkuān 放宽, fàngsōng 放松

to relax a rule = fàngkuān yíxiàng guīdìng 放宽一项规定
- (*to make less tense*) = fàngsōng 放松

to relax [**one's grip** | **one's muscles** | **one's efforts**] = [sōng shǒu | fàngsōng jīròu | sōng jìn(r)] [松手 | 放松肌肉 | 松劲(儿)]
- (*to become loose or slack*) = fàngsōng 放松

you can relax now = nǐ xiànzài kěyǐ fàngsōng le 你现在可以放松了
- (*to become less tense*) = sōngxiè 松懈, fàngsōng 放松

their efforts have started to relax = tāmende nǔlì kāishǐ sōngxiè le 他们的努力开始松懈了
- (*to have a rest*) = xiūxi 休息

let's stop and relax for a while = zánmen tíngxiàlai xiūxi yíhuìr ba 咱们停下来休息一会儿吧

relaxed *adjective*
- (*loosened, slackened*) = fàngsōng de 放松的
- (*becoming less tense, severe*) = huǎnhé de 缓和的

relay race *verb*

a relay race = yíxiàng jiēlì bǐsài 一项接力比赛

release *verb*
- (*to set free*) = shìfàng 释放

he was released = tā bèi shìfàng le 他被释放了
- (*to relieve*) = jiěchú 解除

to release him from his pain = jiěchú tāde téngtòng 解除他的疼痛
- (*to make available or known widely*)

(*if it's a film, a CD, a video*) = fāxíng 发行

to release a Chinese film = fāxíng yíbù Zhōngguó diànyǐng 发行一部中国电影

(*if it's an announcement, a piece of news*) = fābiǎo 发表, fābù 发布

the government is going to release a piece of important news = zhèngfǔ zhǔnbèi fābù yìtiáo zhòngyào xiāoxi 政府准备发布一条重要消息

reliable *adjective*
- (*dependable*) = kěkào 可靠

is this news reliable? = zhè xiāoxi kěkào ma? 这消息可靠吗?
- (*trustworthy*) = kěyǐ xìnlài de 可以信赖的

a reliable lawyer = yíwèi kěyǐ xìnlài de lǜshī 一位可以信赖的律师

relieved *adjective*
= kuānwèi 宽慰
my mother was relieved to receive my letter = wǒ māma shōudào wǒde xìn gǎndào hěn kuānwèi 我妈妈收到我的信感到很宽慰

religion *noun*
= zōngjiào 宗教

religious education, RE (*British English*) *noun*
= zōngjiào kè 宗教课

rely *verb*
- (*to lean on as a support*) = yīkào 依靠
- (*to count on*) = yīlài 依赖, zhǐwàng 指望
can we rely on you? = wǒmén kěyǐ yīlài nǐ ma? 我们可以依赖你吗?

remain *verb*
- (*to stay or be left behind*) = liúxia 留下
only I remained = zhǐyǒu wǒ yíge rén liúxia le 只有我一个人留下了
- (*to be left over*) = shèngxia 剩下
you can take all those things that remain = nǐ kěyǐ bǎ shèngxia de dōngxi dōu názǒu 你可以把剩下的东西都拿走
- (*to continue in the same place*) = hái zài 还在, réngrán cúnzài 仍然存在
that old building remains = nàzuò gǔlǎo jiànzhù hái zài 那座古老建筑还在
- (*to dwell or abide*) = dāi 呆/待, dòuliú 逗留
I'll remain in Shanghai for a week = wǒ yào zài Shànghǎi dāi yíge xīngqī 我要在上海呆一个星期
- (*to continue to be*) = réngrán 仍然
she remained unhappy = tā réngrán bù gāoxìng 她仍然不高兴

remark *noun*
a remark (*a comment*) = yíge pínglùn 一个评论
(*a statement*) = yíduàn chénshù 一段陈述
(*something said on a subject*) = yíduàn huà 一段话

remarkable *adjective*
= fēifán 非凡, zhuóyuè 卓越

remember *verb*
- (*to have in mind*) = jìde 记得
do you remember her? = nǐ jìde tā ma? 你记得她吗?
- (*to recall*) = xiǎngqǐ 想起
now I remember = xiànzài wǒ xiǎngqǐlai le 现在我想起来了
- (*to retain in one's memory*) = jìzhù 记住
to remember to turn off the lights = jìzhù bǎ dēng guānshang 记住把灯关上

remind *verb*
- (*to put in mind of*) = tíxǐng 提醒
to remind someone to buy milk = tíxǐng mǒurén mǎi niúnǎi 提醒某人买牛奶
- (*to cause to remember*) = shǐ...xiǎngqǐ 使... 想起
she reminds me of my younger sister = tā shǐ wǒ xiǎngqǐ wǒde mèimei 她使我想起我的妹妹

remote control *noun*
a remote control = yíge yáokòngqì 一个遥控器

remove *verb*
- (*to take or put away by hand*) = nákāi 拿开, bānzǒu 搬走
to remove these books = bǎ zhèxiē shū nákāi 把这些书拿开
- (*to clean off*) = qùdiào 去掉, nòngdiào 弄掉
to remove stains from a carpet = bǎ wūjī cóng dìtǎn shang nòngdiào 把污迹从地毯上弄掉
- **to remove someone from his post** = chèdiào mǒurén de zhíwù 撤掉某人的职务
- **to remove this wall** = bǎ zhèdǔ qiáng chāichú 把这堵墙拆除

rent
1 *verb*
= zū 租, zūyòng 租用
to rent a house = zū yídòng fángzi 租一栋房子
2 *noun*
a rental payment = yífèn zūjīn 一份租金
rent out = chūzū 出租

repair *verb*
- (*if it's something mechanical, electrical, electronic, or a piece of furniture*) = xiūlǐ 修理
to repair [a bicycle | a TV set | a bed...] = xiūlǐ [yíliàng zìxíngchē | yìtái diànshìjī | yìzhāng chuáng...] 修理 [一辆自行车 | 一台电视机 | 一张床...]

R

- (*to patch*) = bǔ 补, xiūbǔ 修补
- **to repair the damage** = míbǔ sǔnshī 弥补损失

repeat *verb*
- (*to say again*) = chóngfù 重复, chóngshuō 重说
- (*to do again*) = chóngzuò 重做
- **don't repeat this mistake** = bié zài fàn zhège cuòwù le 别再犯这个错误了

replace *verb*
- (*put back*) = fànghuí yuánchù 放回原处

  please replace the magazine after reading = zázhì kànwán hòu qǐng fànghuí yuánchù 杂志看完后请放回原处
- (*substitute for*) = dàitì 代替, tìhuàn 替换

  can computers replace human beings? = jìsuànjī néng dàitì rén ma? 计算机能代替人吗?
- **they replaced the fence with a wall** = tāmen bǎ líba chāi le, jiànle yìdǔ qiáng 他们把篱笆拆了, 建了一堵墙

reply

1 *verb*
- = huídá 回答

  to reply to [**someone** | **a question**] = huídá [mǒurén | yíge wèntí] 回答[某人 | 一个问题]
- **to reply to** [**a letter** | **a fax**] = huí [xìn | chuánzhēn] 回[信 | 传真]

2 *noun*

  a reply = yíge huídá 一个回答, yíge dáfù 一个答复

report

1 *verb*
- (*to tell about*) = bàogào 报告

  to report an accident = bàogào yícì shìgù 报告一次事故
- (*in the news*) = bàodǎo 报导

  to report on a demonstration = bàodǎo yícì shìwēi yóuxíng 报导一次示威游行
- (*to lay a charge against*) = gàofā 告发, jiēfā 揭发

  to report someone to the police = xiàng jǐngchá gàofā mǒurén 向警察告发某人

2 *noun*
- (*in the news*)

  a report = yìtiáo bàodào 一条报道
- (*an official document*)

  a report = yífèn bàogào 一份报告
- (*British English*) (*from school*)

  a (school) report = yífèn xuéxiào chéngjì bàogào 一份学校成绩报告

report card *noun* (*US English*)

  a report card = yífèn xuésheng chéngjì bàogào 一份学生成绩报告

reporter *noun* ▶ 344

  a reporter (*a journalist*) = yíge jìzhě 一个记者

  (*a person who reports*) = yíge bàogàorén 一个报告人

represent *verb*
- (*to act on behalf of*) = dàibiǎo 代表

  would you like her to represent you? = nǐ yuànyì tā dàibiǎo nǐ ma? 你愿意她代表你吗?
- (*stand for, symbolize*) = biǎoshì 表示, xiàngzhēng 象征

  this gift represents our friendship = zhège lǐwù biǎoshì wǒmende yǒuyì 这个礼物表示我们的友谊

republic *noun*

  a republic = yíge gònghéguó 一个共和国

request *noun*

  a request = yíge qǐngqiú 一个请求

rescue *verb*

  (*from danger*) = yuánjiù 援救, yíngjiù 营救

resemble *verb*

  = xiàng 象

  the two brothers resemble each other = xiōngdì liǎ zhǎngde hěn xiàng 兄弟俩长得很象

resent *verb*

  = duì...bùmǎn 对... 不满, duì...bù gāoxìng 对... 不高兴

  to resent someone = duì mǒurén bùmǎn 对某人不满

  he resents me for winning = tā duì wǒ yíng le bù gāoxìng 他对我赢了不高兴

reservation *noun*

  a reservation (*a booking at a restaurant, theatre, etc.*) = yùdìng 预订

  to make a reservation for two people = yùdìng liǎngge rén de zuòwèi 预订两个人的座位

(*an uncertainty about something*) = yíge bǎoliú yìjiàn 一个保留意见 yìzhǒng bǎoliú tàidù 一种保留态度

I have serious reservations about this contract = wǒ duì zhège hétóng chí yánsù de bǎoliú yìjiàn 我对这个合同持严肃的保留意见

(*limiting condition*) = yíxiàng bǎoliú 一项保留

we accept your proposal with some reservations = wǒmen yǒu bǎoliú de jiēshòu nǐde tíyì 我们有保留地接受你的提议

reserve *verb*

• (*to book*) = dìng 订, yùdìng 预订

I've reserved rooms for my whole family in that hotel = wǒ yǐjīng zài nàjiā lǚguǎn wèi wǒ quán jiā yùdìngle fángjiān 我已经在那家旅馆为我全家预订了房间

• (*to hold back or set aside*) = bǎoliú 保留, liúchū 留出

we've reserved ten seats for the delegation = wǒmen wèi dàibiǎotuán liúchūle shíge zuòwèi 我们为代表团留出了十个座位

• (*to save up for a future occasion*) = chǔbèi 储备, chǔcún 储存

resign *verb*

• (*to give up*) = cíqù 辞去

I've resigned my position as head of department = wǒ yǐjīng cíqùle xì zhǔrèn de gōngzuò 我已经辞去了系主任的工作

• (*to give up office, employment*) = cízhí 辞职

are you going to resign? = nǐ yào cízhí ma? 你要辞职吗?

resist *verb*

• (*to strive against*) = dǐkàng 抵抗, fǎnkàng 反抗

to resist violence = fǎnkàng bàolì 反抗暴力

• (*to withstand*) = kàng 抗, nài 耐

does this kind of material resist heat? = zhèzhǒng cáiliào nài rè ma? 这种材料耐热吗?

• (*to hinder the action of*) = rěnzhù 忍住

> **!** *Note that the negative form of* rěnzhù 忍住 *is* rěn bú zhù 忍不住.

she could not resist laughing = tā rěn bú zhù xiào le 她忍不住笑了

respect

1 *verb*

= zūnzhòng 尊重, zūnjìng 尊敬

2 *noun*

• (*deferential esteem*) = zūnzhòng 尊重, zūnjìng 尊敬

out of respect = chūyú zūnzhòng 出于尊重

• (*point, aspect*) = fāngmiàn 方面

in this respect = zài zhège fāngmiàn 在这个方面

responsibility *noun*

• (*a duty on a job, a task*) = zhízé 职责

• (*obligation*) = zérèn 责任

responsible *adjective*

• (*personally accountable for*) = fùzé 负责

to be responsible for the damage = duì zàochéng de sǔnhuài fùzé 对造成的损坏负责

• (*in charge*) = fùzé 负责

to be responsible for organizing a trip = fùzé zǔzhī lǚxíng 负责组织旅行

rest

1 *noun*

• (*a break, time to recover*) = xiūxi 休息

to need rest = xūyào xiūxi 需要休息

to have a rest = xiūxi yíhuìr 休息一会儿

• (*what is left*)

the rest = shèngxia de 剩下的, qíyú de 其余的

we spent the rest of the day in the garden = zhè yì tiān shèngxia de shíjiān wǒmen shì zài huāyuán li dùguo de 这一天剩下的时间我们是在花园里度过的

2 *verb*

= xiūxi 休息

restaurant *noun*

a restaurant = yìjiā fànguǎnr 一家饭馆儿, yìjiā fàndiàn 一家饭店

result *noun*

• (*effect, consequence*) = jiéguǒ 结果

a good result = yíge hǎo de jiéguǒ 一个好的结果

• (*outcome of an exam, a race, a competition*) = chéngjì 成绩, fēnshù 分数

the results of the competition = bǐsài chéngjì 比赛成绩

the examination results = kǎoshì fēnshù 考试分数

R

- **as a result of an accident** = yīnwèi yícì shìgù 因为一次事故, yóuyú yícì shìgù 由于一次事故

résumé *noun* (*US English*)
a résumé = yífèn jiǎnlì 一份简历

retire *verb*
- (*to give up office or work because of old age*) = tuìxiū 退休
  my father retired at the age of 60 = wǒ bàba liùshí suì tuìxiū 我爸爸六十岁退休
- (*to go away*) = líkāi 离开
  after dinner, all the ladies retired = chīwán fàn hòu, nǚshìmen dōu líkāi le 吃完饭后，女士们都离开了
- (*to go to bed*) = shuìjiào 睡觉, jiùqǐn 就寝

return *verb*
- (*to go back*) = huí 回, huíqu 回去
- (*to come back*) = huí 回, huílai 回来
- (*from abroad, to one's home country*) = huí guó 回国
- (*to give back*) = huán 还
  can you return my book? = nǐ bǎ wǒde shū huángěi wǒ hǎo ma? 你把我的书还给我好吗?
- (*to send back*) = tuìhuán 退还
  to return goods = tuìhuán huòwù 退还货物
- (*to start again*)
  to return to work = huīfù gōngzuò 恢复工作
  to return to school = fù kè 复课

return ticket *noun* (*British English*)
a return ticket = yìzhāng wǎngfǎn piào 一张往返票, yìzhāng láihuí piào 一张来回票

reveal *verb*
to reveal a secret = xièlù yíge mìmì 泄露一个秘密

revenge *noun*
= bàochóu 报仇, bàofù 报复
to have one's revenge on someone for something = wèi mǒushì xiàng mǒurén bàochóu 为某事向某人报仇

revolution *noun*
a revolution = yìchǎng gémìng 一场革命

reward
1 *noun*
a reward = yìbǐ chóujīn 一笔酬金, yìbǐ bàochóu 一笔报酬
2 *verb*
- (*to give a reward in return for a deed or service rendered*) = chóuxiè 酬谢
- (*to give as a reward*) = jiǎngshǎng 奖赏, jiǎnglì 奖励

rewind *verb*
(*for video/audio tapes*) = dào(zhuàn)(cí)dài 倒(转)(磁)带

rhythm *noun*
= jiézòu 节奏, jiépāi 节拍

rib *noun* ▶ 189
a rib (*in the human body*) = yìgēn lèigǔ 一根肋骨
(*as in* **spare rib**) = yìgēn páigǔ 一根排骨

rice *noun*
- (*raw*) = dàmǐ 大米
- (*cooked*) = mǐfàn 米饭

rich *adjective*
= fù 富, fùyù 富裕, yǒuqián 有钱
to get rich = fùqǐlai 富起来, zhìfù 致富

rid: to get rid of *verb*
= qùdiào 去掉, chúqù 除去

ride
1 *verb* ▶ 390
- (*on a horse or a bicycle*) = qí 骑
  to ride a horse = qí mǎ 骑马
  to go riding = qù qí mǎ 去骑马
  he is riding a bike = tā zài qí zìxíngchē 他在骑自行车
- (*in a plane, on a train, or on a bus*) = chéng 乘, zuò 坐
  to ride [on a train | in a plane | on a bus] = zuò [huǒchē | fēijī | qìchē] 坐[火车 | 飞机 | 汽车]

2 *noun*
to go for a ride (*in a car*) = qù kāi yíhuìr chē 去开一会儿车, qù dōufēng 去兜风
(*on a bike*) = qù qí yíhuìr zìxíngchē 去骑一会儿自行车
(*on a horse*) = qù qí yíhuìr mǎ 去骑一会儿马

ridiculous *adjective*
= huāngmiù 荒谬, huāngtáng 荒唐

rifle *noun*
a rifle = yìzhī bùqiāng 一枝步枪

right
1 *adjective*
- (*not left*) = yòu 右, yòubian de 右边的
  his right hand = tāde yòu shǒu 他的右手
- (*proper*) = héshì 合适, qiàdàng 恰当
  is she the right person for this job? = tā zuò zhège gōngzuò héshì ma? 她做这个工作合适吗?
- (*correct*) = duì 对, zhèngquè 正确
  the right answer = zhèngquè de dá'àn 正确的答案
  is this the right direction? = zhège fāngxiàng duì ma? 这个方向对吗?
  what's the right time? = xiànzài zhǔnquè de shíjiān shì jǐ diǎn? 现在准确的时间是几点?
  you're right = nǐ shì duì de 你是对的
  that's right = duì 对

2 *noun*
- (*the direction*)
  the right = yòu 右, yòubian 右边
  the first road on the right = yòubian dìyītiáo mǎlù 右边第一条马路
- (*what one is entitled to*)
  a right = yíge quánlì 一个权力
  to have a right to education = yǒu quánlì shòu jiàoyù 有权力受教育
  human rights = rénquán 人权

3 *adverb*
- (*correctly*) = duì 对
  did I do it right? = wǒ zuò de duì ma? 我做得对吗?
- (*to the right side*) = xiàng yòu 向右
  to turn right = xiàng yòu zhuǎn 向右转
- (*for emphasis*)
  right now = mǎshàng 马上, lìkè 立刻
  she stood right in the centre of the garden = tā zhàn zài huāyuán zhèng zhōngyāng 她站在花园正中央

ring
1 *verb*
- (*British English*) (*to phone*) = dǎ diànhuà 打电话
  to ring for a taxi = dǎ diànhuà jiào chūzūchē 打电话叫出租车
- (*to make a sound*) = xiǎng 响
  the telephone rang = diànhuà líng xiǎng le 电话铃响了
- (*to activate a door or bicycle bell*) = àn líng 按铃
  to ring the doorbell = àn ménlíng 按门铃
- (*to sound a church bell*) = qiāo zhōng 敲钟

2 *noun*
- (*a piece of jewellery*)
  a ring = yìzhī jièzhi 一只戒指
  a wedding ring = yìzhī jiēhūn jièzhi 一只结婚戒指
- (*a circle*)
  a ring = yíge yuánquān 一个圆圈, yíge huán 一个环
- (*in a circus*)
  the ring = yuánxíng chǎngdì 圆形场地
  ring up (*British English*) = dǎ diànhuà 打电话

rinse *verb*
= chōngxǐ 冲洗, qīngxǐ 清洗

ripe *adjective*
= shú 熟, chéngshú 成熟

rise *verb*
- (*if it's the sun or moon*) = shēngqǐ 升起
- (*if it's smoke, a balloon, a plane*) = shàngshēng 上升
- (*if it's a price, a water level*) = shàngzhǎng 上涨
- (*if it's temperature*) = shēnggāo 升高

risk
1 *noun*
= wēixiǎn 危险
2 *verb*
= mào...wēixiǎn 冒... 危险
to risk losing one's job = mào shīqù gōngzuò de wēixiǎn 冒失去工作的危险

river *noun*
a river = yìtiáo hé 一条河

riverbank *noun*
a riverbank = yìtiáo hé'àn 一条河岸

road *noun*
a road = yìtiáo (dào)lù 一条(道)路
the road to London = qù Lúndūn de lù 去伦敦的路

road sign *noun*
a road sign = yíge lùbiāo 一个路标

roadworks *noun*
= xiū lù gōngchéng 修路工程

roar *verb*
(*if it's a lion*) = hǒu 吼, hǒujiào 吼叫
(*if it's a person*) = hūhǎn 呼喊, dàhǎndàjiào 大喊大叫

R

(*if it's an engine*) = hōngmíng 轰鸣
(*if it's the wind*) = hūxiào 呼啸

roast
1 *verb*
= kǎo 烤
2 *adjective*
= kǎo 烤
to eat Peking duck = chī Běijīng kǎo yā 吃北京烤鸭
3 *noun*
a roast = yíkuài kǎoròu 一块烤肉

rob *verb*
= qiǎng 抢, qiǎngjié 抢劫
to rob someone of his money = qiǎng mǒurén de qián 抢某人的钱
to rob a bank = qiǎngjié yínháng 抢劫银行

robbery *noun*
a robbery = yícì qiǎngjié (àn) 一次抢劫(案)

robin *noun*
a robin = yìzhī zhīgēngniǎo 一只知更鸟

robot *noun*
a robot = yíge jīqìrén 一个机器人

rock *noun*
• (*a large stone*)
a rock = yíkuài shítou 一块石头, yíkuài yánshí 一块岩石
• (*as a material for construction*) = yánshí 岩石, shítou 石头
• (*a type of music*) = yáogǔn yīnyuè 摇滚音乐

rock climbing *noun* ▶ 390
= pānshí yùndòng 攀石运动

rocket *noun*
a rocket = yìkē huǒjiàn 一颗火箭

role *noun*
• (*an actor's part*) = jiǎosè 角色
a role = yíge jiǎosè 一个角色
• (*a function*) = zuòyòng 作用
he played an important role in organizing this conference = tā zài zǔzhī zhècì huìyì zhōng qǐle zhòngyào de zuòyòng 他在组织这次会议中起了重要的作用

roll
1 *verb*
• (*to move by turning over and over*) = gǔn(dòng) 滚(动)
the ball rolled under a car = qiú gǔndàole yíliàng qìchē xiàmian 球滚到了一辆汽车下面
to roll the pastry into a ball = bǎ miàn gǔnchéng yíge qiú 把面滚成一个球
2 *noun*
• (*of paper, cloth, plastic*) = juǎn 卷
a roll of film = yìjuǎn jiāojuǎn 一卷胶卷
• (*bread*)
a roll = yíge miànbāojuǎn 一个面包卷
• (*US English*) (*at school*)
to call the roll = diǎn míng 点名
roll about, roll around (*if it's an object*) = dàochù gǔn 到处滚
roll over = fān 翻
roll up = juǎn 卷
to roll up a newspaper = juǎnqǐ bàozhǐ 卷起报纸

roller coaster *noun*
a roller coaster = yíliè yóulè tiānchē 一列游乐天车

roller-skate *noun*
= hànbīng xié
a pair of roller-skates = yìshuāng hànbīng xié 一双旱冰鞋

roller-skating *noun* ▶ 390
= huá hànbīng 滑旱冰

romantic *adjective*
• (*characterized by romance*) = luómàndìkè 罗曼蒂克, làngmàn 浪漫
• (*passionate and imaginative*) = fùyú huànxiǎng 富于幻想, xiǎngrùfēifēi 想入非非

roof *noun*
a roof = yíge wūdǐng 一个屋顶, yíge fángdǐng 一个房顶

room *noun*
• **a room** = yíge fángjiān 一个房间
• (*space*) = kōngjiān 空间, dìfang 地方
to make room = kòngchū dìfang 空出地方
is there room? = hái yǒu kōngjiān ma? 还有空间吗?
• (*scope*) = yúdì 余地
there is still room for improvement = hái yǒu gǎijìn de yúdì 还有改进的余地

root *noun*
- (*of a plant*) = yíge gēn 一个根
- (*source, origin, cause*) = yíge gēnyuán 一个根源

rope *noun*
a rope = yìgēn shéngzi 一根绳子

rose *noun*
a rose (*a plant*) = yìkē méiguì 一棵玫瑰
(*a flower*) = yìzhī méiguìhuā 一支玫瑰花

rosy *adjective*
- (*rose-red*) = méiguìsè de 玫瑰色的
- **rosy cheeks** = hóngrùn de liǎnjiá 红润的脸颊

rotten *adjective*
= fǔlàn de 腐烂的, fǔxiǔ de 腐朽的

rough *adjective*
- (*not smooth*) = bù píng 不平, bù guānghuá 不光滑
- (*when talking about the skin, paper*) = cūcào 粗糙
rough skin = cūcào de pífū 粗糙的皮肤
- (*when talking about roads*) = qíqū bù píng 崎岖不平
the road is rough = zhètiáo lù qíqū bù píng 这条路崎岖不平
- (*not gentle*) = cūbào 粗暴, cūlǔ 粗鲁
- (*tough*)
to live in a rough area = zhù zài yíge zhì'ān chà de dìqū 住在一个治安差的地区
- (*not exact, precise*) = cūlüè 粗略
a rough figure = yíge cūlüè de shùzì 一个粗略的数字
- (*difficult*) = jiānnán 艰难
he had a rough time there = tā zài nàr guòle yíduàn hěn jiānnán de rìzi 他在那儿过了一段很艰难的日子
- (*caused by bad weather*)
a rough sea = bōtāo xiōngyǒng de hǎimiàn 波涛汹涌的海面

round

> **!** *Often* **round** *occurs in combinations with verbs. For more information, see the note at* **around**.

1 *preposition*
- (*on every side of*) = wéizhe 围着
to sit round a table = wéizhe zhuōzi zuò 围着桌子坐
- (*to complete a circuit*) = rào 绕, wéirào 围绕
to sail round the world = wéirào dìqiú hángxíng 围绕地球航行
- (*all over*) = zài.. gè chù 在... 各处, zài...dàochù 在... 到处
we walked round Oxford = wǒmen zài Niújīn gè chù zǒulezǒu 我们在牛津各处走了走

2 *adverb*
- (*on a circular or circuitous course*) = zhuàn quān 转圈
to run round the track on the sports ground = zài cāochǎng shang zhuàn quān pǎo 在操场上转圈跑
- **to go round to John's** = ràodào qù Yuēhàn jiā 绕道去约翰家
- **to invite someone round** = yāoqǐng mǒurén dào jiā li lái 邀请某人到家里来

3 *noun*
a round (*in a quiz show or showjumping*) = yìchǎng 一场
(*in boxing*) = yíge huíhé 一个回合
(*in an election, a negotiation, a tournament*) = yìlún 一轮

4 *adjective*
- (*circular*) = yuán 圆, yuánxíng de 圆形的
- (*spherical*) = qiúxíng de 球形的
- (*plump*) = fēngmǎn 丰满

roundabout *noun*
- (*British English*) (*in a playground or at a fair*)
a roundabout = yíge mùmǎ xuánzhuǎn pán 一个木马旋转盘
- (*for traffic*)
a roundabout = yíge huánxíng lùkǒu 一个环形路口

route *noun*
- (*on land*) = lùxiàn 路线
a route = yìtiáo lùxiàn 一条路线
a [**bus** | **train**] **route** = yìtiáo [qìchē | huǒchē] lùxiàn 一条 [汽车 | 火车] 路线
- (*for planes and ships*) = hángxiàn 航线
a route = yìtiáo hángxiàn 一条航线

routine *noun*
= chánggui 常规, guànlì 惯例

row[1]

1 *noun*
- (*a line of persons or things*) = pái 排
a row of [**people** | **seats** | **cars...**] = yìpái [rén | zuòwèi | qìchē...] 一排 [人 | 座位 | 汽车...]

R

the pupils were sitting in rows = xuéshengmen yìpái yìpái de zuòzhe 学生们一排一排地坐着
- **in a row** = liánxù 连续, yìlián 一连
  to arrive late five days in a row = liánxù wǔ tiān chí dào 连续五天迟到

2 *verb*
- (*to propel with an oar*) = huá 划
  to row a boat = huá chuán 划船
- (*to transport by rowing*) = huá chuán sòng 划船送
  I can row you across the river = wǒ kěyǐ huá chuán sòng nǐ guò hé 我可以划船送你过河
- (*as a sport*) ▶ 390 = huá chuán bǐsài 划船比赛
  Oxford University rowed against Cambridge University on the river Thames = Niújīn Dàxué gēn Jiànqiáo Dàxué zài Tàiwùshìhé shang jìnxíngle huá chuán bǐsài 牛津大学跟剑桥大学在泰晤士河上进行了划船比赛

row² *noun* (*British English*)
a row = yícì chǎojià 一次吵架, yícì chǎozuǐ 一次吵嘴
to have a row with someone = gēn mǒurén chǎojià 跟某人吵架

rowing *noun* ▶ 390
= huá chuán 划船

rowing boat (*British English*), **rowboat** (*US English*) *noun*
a rowing boat = yìtiáo huátǐng 一条划艇

royal *adjective*
the Royal Family = wángshì 王室, huángjiā 皇家
the Royal Navy = Huángjiā Hǎijūn 皇家海军
[**Your** | **His** | **Her**] **Royal Highness** = Diànxià 殿下
a royal palace (*for a queen*) = yízuò huánggōng 一座皇宫
(*for a king*) = yízuò wánggōng 一座王宫

rub *verb*
(*to apply pressure to with a circular or backward and forward movement*) = róu 揉
to rub one's eyes = róu yǎnjīng 揉眼睛
rub out (*British English*) = cādiào 擦掉
to rub out that character = cādiào nàge zì 擦掉那个字

rubber *noun*
- (*the material*) = xiàngjiāo 橡胶
- (*British English*) (*an eraser*)
  a rubber = yíkuài xiàngpí 一块橡皮

rubbish *noun*
- (*refuse*) = lājī 垃圾
- (*anything worthless*) = fèiwù 废物
- (*nonsense*) = fèihuà 废话

rubbish bin *noun* (*British English*)
a rubbish bin = yíge lājītǒng 一个垃圾桶

rucksack *noun*
a rucksack = yíge bèibāo 一个背包

rude *adjective*
- (*not polite*) = cūlǔ 粗鲁, wúlǐ 无礼
  to be rude to someone = duì mǒurén hěn wúlǐ 对某人很无礼
- (*vulgar*) = dījí 低级, xiàliú 下流
  a rude story = yíge xiàliú gùshi 一个下流故事

rug *noun*
a rug (*a floor mat*) = yíkuài xiǎo dìtǎn 一块小地毯
(*a thick covering or wrap*) = yìtiáo máotǎn 一条毛毯

rugby *noun* ▶ 390
= gǎnlǎnqiú 橄榄球

ruin
1 *verb*
- (*to spoil*) = gǎozāo 搞糟
  he's ruined this meal = tā bǎ zhèdùn fàn gǎozāo le 他把这顿饭搞糟了
- (*to damage*) = huǐhuài 毁坏
  you'll ruin your shoes = nǐ huì huǐhuài nǐde xié 你会毁坏你的鞋
- (*to destroy completely*) = huǐmiè 毁灭
  his hope was ruined = tāde xīwàng (bèi) huǐmiè le 他的希望(被)毁灭了

2 *noun*
- (*destruction*) = huǐmiè 毁灭
- (*damage*) = huǐhuài 毁坏
- (*a fallen or broken state*) = fèixū 废墟
  the whole school is now in ruins = zhěnggè xuéxiào xiànzài chéngle yípiàn fèixū 整个学校现在成了一片废墟

rule
1 *noun*
a rule (*of a game, a language*) = yìtiáo guīzé 一条规则
(*in a school, an organization*) = yìtiáo guīdìng 一条规定
it's against the rules = zhè wéifǎn guīdìng 这违反规定
2 *verb*
• (*to govern*) = tǒngzhì 统治
to rule a country = tǒngzhì yíge guójiā 统治一个国家
• (*to control*) = kòngzhì 控制 ✕
he ruled his family with an iron hand = tā jǐnjǐn de kòngzhìzhe quán jiā 他紧紧地控制着全家
• (*to determine or decree*) = cáijué 裁决, cáidìng 裁定
the court ruled that he was guilty = fǎyuàn cáijué tā yǒu zuì 法院裁决他有罪

ruler *noun*
a ruler (*for measuring or ruling lines*) = yíge chǐzi 一个尺子
(*a person who governs*) = yíge tǒngzhìzhě 一个统治者

rumour (*British English*), **rumor** (*US English*) *noun*
a rumour (*a statement of doubtful accuracy*) = yíge yáoyán 一个谣言
(*hearsay*) = yíge chuánwén 一个传闻

run
1 *verb*
• **to run** = pǎo 跑
to run across the street = pǎoguò mǎlù 跑过马路
• (*compete in a race*) = sàipǎo 赛跑
to run a race = cānjiā sàipǎo 参加赛跑
• (*from danger*) = táopǎo 逃跑
• (*to manage*) = guǎnlǐ 管理
to run a school = guǎnlǐ yíge xuéxiào 管理一个学校
• (*to work, to operate*) = yùnzhuǎn 运转, yùnxíng 运行
the machine is running well = jīqì yùnzhuǎn liánghǎo 机器运转良好
• (*if it's a vehicle*) = xíngshǐ 行驶
the car is running at 80 kilometres per hour = qìchē zài yǐ měi xiǎoshí bāshí gōnglǐ de sùdù xíngshǐ 汽车在以每小时八十公里的速度行驶
• (*to organize*) = bàn 办
to run a competition = bàn yíge bǐsài 办一个比赛
• (*to flow*) = liú 流
• (*to fill with water*)
to run a bath = wǎng zǎopén li fàng shuǐ 往澡盆里放水
• (*to come off, as stains or make-up*) = diào 掉
the rain has made her make-up run = yǔshuǐ bǎ tā liǎn shang de huàzhuāng chōngdiào le 雨水把她脸上的化妆冲掉了
• (*in an election*) = jìngxuǎn 竞选
to run for president = jìngxuǎn zǒngtǒng 竞选总统
• (*other uses*)
it is running late = shíjiān bù duō le 时间不多了
he is running a temperature = tā zài fāshāo 他在发烧
2 *noun*
to go for a run = qù pǎobù 去跑步
run about, run around = dàochù pǎo 到处跑, sìchù pǎo 四处跑
run away (*to escape*) = táopǎo 逃跑, qiántáo 潜逃
(*to gallop away uncontrollably*) = shīqù kòngzhì 失去控制
run off (*to escape*) = táopǎo 逃跑

runner *noun*
a runner (*one who runs*) = yíge pǎobù de rén 一个跑步的人
(*one who runs in a race*) = yìmíng sàipǎo yùndòngyuán 一名赛跑运动员

rush
1 *verb*
• (*to hurry*) = jímáng 急忙, cōngcōng 匆匆, cōngmáng 匆忙

> **!** *Note that in this sense, the force of the word* **rush** *is often carried by such adverbs as those in the translations above. Where necessary, another verb functions as the predicate.*

to rush to finish one's homework = jímáng zuòwán zuòyè 急忙做完作业
he rushed into a shop = tā cōngcōng de jìnle yìjiā shāngdiàn 他匆匆地进了一家商店
to rush out of the house = cōngmáng chōngchū fángzi 匆忙冲出房子
to be rushed to the hospital = jímáng bèi sòngjìn yīyuàn 急忙被送进医院

R

• (*to put pressure on*) = cuī 催, cuīcù 催促
please don't rush me = qǐng búyào cuī wǒ 请不要催我

2 *noun*
to be in a rush = cōngmáng 匆忙, mánglù 忙碌
to do one's homework in a rush = cōngmáng de zuò zuòyè 匆忙地做作业

rush hour *noun*
the rush hour = jiāotōng gāofēng shíjiān 交通高峰时间

Russia *noun*
= Éguó 俄国, Éluósī 俄罗斯

Russian ▶ 288
1 *adjective*
= Éguó de 俄国的, Éluósī de 俄罗斯的
2 *noun*
• (*the people*)
the Russians = Éguórén 俄国人, Éluósīrén 俄罗斯人
• (*the language*)= Éyǔ 俄语, Éwén 俄文

rusty *adjective*
= (shēng)xiù de (生)锈的

Ss

---

sad *adjective*
• (*sorrowful*) = nánguò 难过, bēishāng 悲伤
he feels sad = tā gǎndào nánguò 他感到难过
• (*grave, saddening*) = lìng rén nánguò de 令人难过的, lìng rén bēishāng de 令人悲伤的
sad news = lìng rén nánguò de xiāoxi 令人难过的消息
• (*regrettable*) = yíhàn 遗憾, kěxī 可惜
it's sad that you didn't get a scholarship = hěn yíhàn, nǐ méiyǒu dédào jiǎngxuéjīn 很遗憾, 你没有得到奖学金

saddle *noun*
a saddle = yíge ānzi 一个鞍子, yíge mǎ'ān 一个马鞍

safe
1 *adjective* ▶ 238
• (*free from danger, without risk*) = ānquán 安全
a safe place = yíge ānquán de dìfang 一个安全的地方
is it safe to go there? = qù nàr ānquán ma? 去那儿安全吗?
to feel safe = gǎndào ānquán 感到安全
• (*sure, reliable*) = yǒu bǎwò 有把握, yídìng 一定
it is safe to say that she will get the scholarship = tā yídìng huì dédào jiǎngxuéjīn 她一定会得到奖学金
2 *noun*
a safe = yíge bǎoxiǎnxiāng 一个保险箱

safety *noun*
= ānquán 安全

sail
1 *noun*
a sail = yíge fān 一个帆
to set sail = kāiháng 开航, chūháng 出航
2 *verb*
= (chéng chuán) hángxíng (乘船)航行
to sail around the world = wéirào shìjiè hángxíng 围绕世界航行
to go sailing = qù chéng chuán hángxíng 去乘船航行

sailing *noun* ▶ 390
• (*in sports*) = hánghǎi yùndòng 航海运动
• (*travelling by boat*) = chéng chuán lǚxíng 乘船旅行

sailing boat (*British English*), **sailboat** (*US English*) *noun*
a sailing boat = yìsōu fānchuán 一艘帆船

sailor *noun* ▶ 344
a sailor = yìmíng shuǐshǒu 一名水手, yìmíng hǎiyuán 一名海员

saint *noun*
a saint = yíge shèngrén 一个圣人, yíge shèngtú 一个圣徒

salad *noun*
= sèlā 色拉, xīcān liángbàncài 西餐凉拌菜

salary *noun*
a salary = yífèn gōngzī 一份工资, yífèn xīnshuǐ 一份薪水

sale *noun*
• **to be on sale at a reduced price** = jiǎnjià chūshòu 减价出售

for sale = chūshòu 出售, dàishòu 待售

- **the total sales of this year** = quán nián xiāoshòu é 全年销售额

sales assistant *noun* ▶ 344

(*British English*)

a sales assistant = yíge tuīxiāoyuán 一个推销员, yíge xiāoshòuyuán 一个销售员

salmon *noun*

a salmon = yìtiáo sānwényú 一条三文鱼, yìtiáo guīyú 一条鲑鱼

salt *noun*

= yán 盐

same

1 *adjective*

- (*identical*) = tóngyī 同一

they go to the same school = tāmen zài tóngyīge xuéxiào shàngxué 他们在同一个学校上学

- (*similar in style or type*) = tóngyàng 同样, yíyàng 一样

she has the same coat as I do = tāde shàngyī gēn wǒde yíyàng 她的上衣跟我的一样

I made the same mistake as he did = wǒ hé tā fànle tóngyàng de cuòwù 我和他犯了同样的错误

the houses all look the same = zhèxiē fángzi kànshangqu dōu yíyàng 这些房子看上去都一样

2 *pronoun*

> **!** *Note that in this sense, the meaning conveyed by* **same** *in English has to be stated overtly in Chinese.*

I bought my girlfriend a bottle of perfume, and he did the same = wǒ gěi wǒ nǚpéngyou mǎile yì píng xiāngshuǐ, tā yě gěi tā nǚpéngyou mǎile yì píng 我给我女朋友买了一瓶香水, 他也给他女朋友买了一瓶

to do the same as the others = xiàng biéren nàyàng zuò 象别人那样做

'Happy New Year!'—'the same to you!' = 'Xīnnián kuàilè!'—'yě zhù nǐ Xīnnián kuàilè!' '新年快乐!'—'也祝你新年快乐!'

sand *noun* = shāzi 沙子, shā 沙

sandal *noun*

a sandal = yìzhī liángxié 一只凉鞋

a pair of sandals = yìshuāng liángxié 一双凉鞋

sandwich *noun*

a sandwich = yíkuài sānmíngzhì 一块三明治

a ham sandwich = yíkuài huǒtuǐ sānmíngzhì 一块火腿三明治

Santa (Claus) *noun*

Santa (Claus) = Shèngdàn lǎorén 圣诞老人

sardine *noun*

a sardine = yìtiáo shādīngyú 一条沙丁鱼

satellite TV *noun*

= wèixīng diànshì 卫星电视

satisfactory *adjective*

= lìng rén mǎnyì de 令人满意的

satisfied *adjective*

= mǎnyì 满意

Saturday *noun* ▶ 218

= xīngqīliù 星期六, lǐbàiliù 礼拜六

sauce *noun*

a sauce = yìzhǒng jiàngzhī 一种酱汁, yìzhǒng tiáowèizhī 一种调味汁

saucepan *noun*

a saucepan = yíge (chángbǐng) píngdǐguō 一个(长柄)平底锅

saucer *noun*

a saucer = yíge chábēidié 一个茶杯碟

sausage *noun*

a sausage = yìgēn xiāngcháng 一根香肠

save *verb*

- (*to rescue*) = jiù 救

they saved his life = tāmen jiùle tāde mìng 他们救了他的命

- (*to avoid spending*) = chǔxù 储蓄, zǎn 攒

to save (up) = chǔxù 储蓄

to save money = zǎnqián 攒钱

- (*to avoid wasting*) = jiéshěng 节省, jiéyuē 节约

to save [time | energy | money...] = jiéshěng [shíjiān | jīnglì | qián...] 节省[时间 | 精力 | 钱...]

- (*to keep*) = liú 留

to save a piece of cake for someone = gěi mǒurén liú yíkuài dàngāo 给某人留一块蛋糕

- (*to preserve in the computer*) = cún 存, chǔcún 储存

S

to save a file = cún yíge wénjiàn 存一个文件
- (*to spare*)
  to save someone a lot of work = jiéshěng mǒurén hěn duō gōngzuò 节省某人很多工作
  it will save us from having to write to him again = zhè kěyǐ shǐ wǒmen miǎnde zài gěi tā xiě xìn 这可以使我们免得再给他写信

savings *noun*
= chǔxù 储蓄, cúnkuǎn 存款

saw *noun*
a saw = yìbǎ jù 一把锯

saxophone *noun* ▶ 308
a saxophone = yìgēn sàkèsīguǎn 一根萨克斯管

say *verb*
- (*to utter in words*) = shuō 说
  to say goodbye = shuō zàijiàn 说再见
  she says (that) she can't go out tonight = tā shuō jīnwǎn tā bù néng chūqu 她说今晚她不能出去
  he said to wait here = tā shuō zài zhèr děng 他说在这儿等
- (*to express*) = shuōmíng 说明, biǎomíng 表明
  what do these figures say? = zhèxiē shùzì shuōmíng shénme? 这些数字说明什么?
- (*to report in the newspaper, on the radio, TV*) = bàodǎo shuō 报导说, bàogào shuō 报告说
  the radio said the Queen was going to visit China = shōuyīnjī bàodǎo shuō Nǚwáng yào fǎngwèn Zhōngguó 收音机报导说女王要访问中国
- (*to suppose*) = jiǎdìng 假定, jiǎshè 假设
  let's say there will be twenty people at the party = zánmen jiǎdìng yǒu èrshíge rén cānjiā zhège jùhuì 咱们假定有二十个人参加这个聚会

scandal *noun*
a scandal = yíjiàn chǒuwén 一件丑闻, yíjiàn chǒushì 一件丑事

scare *verb*
= xià 吓, jīngxià 惊吓
you scared me! = nǐ xiàle wǒ yítiào 你吓了我一跳
scare away = bǎ...xiàpǎo 把... 吓跑
to scare someone away = bǎ mǒurén xiàpǎo 把某人吓跑

scared *adjective*
I am scared = wǒ hàipà 我害怕

scarf *noun*
a scarf = yìtiáo wéijīn 一条围巾

scenery *noun*
= fēngjǐng 风景, jǐngsè 景色

school *noun*
a school = yìsuǒ xuéxiào 一所学校
to be a student at school = zài shàngxué 在上学
a school bus = yíliàng xiàochē 一辆校车

schoolbag *noun*
a schoolbag = yíge shūbāo 一个书包

schoolboy *noun*
a schoolboy = yíge nán xuésheng 一个男学生

schoolgirl *noun*
a schoolgirl = yíge nǚ xuésheng 一个女学生

schoolwork *noun*
= gōngkè 功课, zuòyè 作业

science *noun*
= kēxué 科学
to study science = xuéxí kēxué 学习科学

scientist *noun* ▶ 344
a scientist = yìmíng kēxuéjiā 一名科学家

scissors *noun*
= jiǎnzi 剪子, jiǎndāo 剪刀
a pair of scissors = yìbǎ jiǎnzi 一把剪子

score
1 *verb*
to score a goal = jìn yíge qiú 进一个球
to score a point = dé yì fēn 得一分
2 *noun*
- (*points gained in a game or competition*) = bǐfēn 比分
  the final score of the football match = zúqiú bǐsài de zuìhòu bǐfēn 足球比赛的最后比分
- (*result of a test or examination*)
  a score = yíge chéngji 一个成绩

Scotland *noun*
= Sūgélán 苏格兰

Scottish *adjective* ▶ 288
= Sūgélán(rén) de 苏格兰(人)的

scratch *verb*
- (*when itchy*) = náo 挠, sāo 搔
  to scratch one's arm = náo gēbo 挠胳膊
- (*if it's a person or an animal*) = zhuā 抓
- (*if it's by a bush, a thorn*) = guā 刮, huá 划
- (*to mark with a knife or something hard*) = kè 刻

scream *verb*
= jiānjiào 尖叫, dàjiào 大叫

screen *noun*
a screen (*of a TV set or a computer*) = yíge píngmù 一个屏幕
(*of a cinema*) = yíge yínmù 一个银幕

screw *noun*
a screw = yìkē luósī(dīng) 一颗螺丝(钉)

sea *noun*
= hǎi 海, hǎiyáng 海洋
beside the sea, by the sea = zài hǎi biān 在海边

seagull *noun*
a seagull = yìzhī hǎi'ōu 一只海鸥

seal
1 *noun*
a seal
- (*the animal*) = yìzhī hǎibào 一只海豹
- (*a tool used to impress*) = yìméi túzhāng 一枚图章

2 *verb*
- (*to close up*) = fēng 封
  to seal the envelope = bǎ xìnfēng fēngqǐlai 把信封封起来
- **to seal up** = mìfēng 密封
- (*to stamp*) = gài zhāng 盖章
  to seal a document = zài wénjiàn shang gài zhāng 在文件上盖章

search *verb*
- **to search** = xúnzhǎo 寻找
  to search for someone = xúnzhǎo mǒurén 寻找某人
- (*to examine a place, a person*) = sōuchá 搜查
  they searched my luggage at the airport = tāmen zài fēijīchǎng sōuchále wǒde xíngli 他们在飞机场搜查了我的行李

seashell *noun*
a seashell = yíge bèiké 一个贝壳

seasick *adjective*
to be seasick, to get seasick = yūnchuán 晕船

seaside *noun*
= hǎibiān
at the seaside = zài hǎibiān 在海边

season *noun*
- (*one of the four divisions of the year*) = jì 季, jìjié 季节
  a season = yí jì 一季, yíge jìjié 一个季节
- **strawberries are in season** = xiànzài shì cǎoméi wàngjì 现在是草莓旺季

seat *noun*
a seat (*something to sit on*) = yíge zuòwèi 一个座位, yíge wèizi 一个位子
(*a right to sit in a council or committee*) = yíge xíwèi 一个席位

seatbelt *noun*
a seatbelt = yíge ānquándài 一个安全带

second
1 *adjective*
- = dì'èr 第二
  it's the second time I've called her = zhè shì wǒ dì'èrcì gěi tā dǎ diànhuà 这是我第二次给她打电话
- (*of lower quality*) = èrděng de 二等的
  a second class cabin = èrděng cāng 二等舱

2 *noun*
- (*in a series*)
  the second = dì'èr 第二
- (*in time*)
  a second = yì miǎo 一秒, yì miǎo zhōng 一秒钟
  (*a very short time*) = yíhuìr 一会儿, piànkè 片刻
- (*in dates*) ▶ 218 = èr rì 二日, èr hào 二号
  the second of May = wǔyuè èr rì 五月二日

3 *adverb*
= dì'èr 第二
to come second in the race = zài sàipǎo zhōng dé dì'èr 在赛跑中得第二

secondary school *noun*
a secondary school = yìsuǒ zhōngxué 一所中学

second-hand *adjective*
= (biéren) yòngguo de (别人)用过的, èrshǒu 二手
a second-hand table = yìzhāng yòngguo de zhuōzi 一张用过的桌子
a second-hand car = yíliàng èrshǒu chē 一辆二手车
a second-hand coat = yíjiàn biéren chuānguo de wàiyī 一件别人穿过的外衣

secret
1 *adjective*
= mìmì 秘密
2 *noun*
a secret = yíge mìmì 一个秘密
to tell someone a secret = gàosu mǒurén yíge mìmì 告诉某人一个秘密
3 in secret = mìmì de 秘密地

secretary *noun* ▶ 344
a secretary
(*in an office, dealing with papers, keeping records, etc.*) = yíge mìshū 一个秘书
(*of a political party or party organization*) = yíge shūjì 一个书记
(*a government minister*) = yíge dàchén 一个大臣

see *verb* ▶ 238
• **to see** = kànjian 看见, kàndào 看到
what can you see? = nǐ néng kànjian shénme? 你能看见什么?
I didn't see them = wǒ méi jiàndào tāmen 我没见到他们
she can't see the words on the blackboard = tā kàn bú jiàn hēibǎn shang de zì 她看不见黑板上的字

> **!** *Note that to negate* **kànjian 看见**, *the negative* **bù 不** *comes between* **kàn 看** *and* **jiàn 见**.

• (*to meet*) = jiànmiàn 见面
do you see each other often? = nǐmen chángcháng hùxiāng jiànmiàn ma? 你们常常互相见面吗?
see you tomorrow! = míngtiān jiàn! 明天见!
• (*to look at*) = kàn 看
please let me see your ticket = qǐng ràng wǒ kàn yíxià nǐde piào 请让我看一下你的票
• (*to visit*) = kàn 看
I'm going to see a doctor = wǒ qù kàn yīshēng 我去看医生
he came to see me yesterday = tā zuótiān lái kàn wǒ le 他昨天来看我了
• (*to watch*) = kàn 看
to see [a film | a play | an exhibition] = kàn [diànyǐng | xì | zhǎnlǎnhuì] 看[电影 | 戏 | 展览会]
• (*to understand, apprehend*) = dǒng 懂, lǐjiě 理解, míngbai 明白
do you see what I mean? = nǐ dǒng wǒde yìsi ma? 你懂我的意思吗?
• (*to accompany*) = péi 陪
I'll see you home = wǒ péi nǐ huí jiā 我陪你回家

seem *verb*
• (*to appear*) = hǎoxiàng 好像, sìhū 似乎
she seems [happy | annoyed | tired...] = tā hǎoxiàng [hěn gāoxìng | hěn nǎohuǒ | hěn lèi...] 她好像[很高兴 | 很恼火 | 很累...]
• (*when talking about one's impressions*) = kànlai 看来, kànyàngzi 看样子
it seems (that) there are many problems = kànlai yǒu hěn duō wèntí 看来有很多问题

seldom *adverb*
= hěn shǎo 很少, bù cháng 不常

self-confident *adjective*
= yǒu zìxìnxīn 有自信心

selfish *adjective*
= zìsī 自私

sell *verb*
= mài 卖, chūshòu 出售
to sell books to the students = mài shū gěi xuésheng 卖书给学生
he sold me his car = tā bǎ tāde chē màigěile wǒ 他把他的车卖给了我
water is sold in bottles = shuǐ àn píng chūshòu 水按瓶出售

send *verb*
• (*to direct someone to go on a mission*) = pài 派, pàiqiǎn 派遣
to send someone to post a letter = pài mǒurén qū jì xìn 派某人去寄信
• (*to cause to be conveyed by post*) = jì 寄
to send a package to someone = jìgěi mǒurén yíge bāoguǒ 寄给某人一个包裹

he sent her a letter = tā jìgěi tā yìfēng xìn 他寄给她一封信

- (*to cause to be conveyed by electronic means*) = fā 发

to send an e-mail message to someone = gěi mǒurén fā yíge diànzǐ yóujiàn 给某人发一个电子邮件

- **to send a pupil home from school** = bǎ yíge xuésheng cóng xuéxiào dǎfā huí jiā 把一个学生从学校打发回家

send away (*to dismiss*) = jiěgù 解雇 (*to expel*) = qūzhú 驱逐

send back = tuìhuán 退还, sònghuán 送还

send for = qù jiào 去叫

to send for the doctor = qù jiào yīshēng 去叫医生

send off

to send a player off = bǎ yìmíng duìyuán fáxia chǎng 把一名队员罚下场

send on

to send on baggage = tíqián yùnsòng xíngli 提前运送行李

to send on post = zhuǎnsòng xìnjiàn 转送信件

senior high school (*US English*), **senior school** (*British English*) *noun*

a senior (high) school = yìsuǒ gāozhōng 一所高中

sense *noun*

- (*the body's capacity for perception*)

the sense of [**sight** | **hearing** | **taste** | **smell** | **touch**] = [shì | tīng | wèi | xiù | chù] jué [视 | 听 | 味 | 嗅 | 触] 觉

- (*meaning, significance*) = yìyì 意义, yìsi 意思

it doesn't make sense = zhè méi yǒu yìyì 这没有意义

- (*reasonableness*) = dàoli 道理

it makes sense to check first = xiān jiǎnchá yíxià shì yǒu dàoli de 先检查一下是有道理的

to have the sense not to go = bú qù shì yǒu dàoli de 不去是有道理的

- **common sense** = chángshí 常识, chánglǐ 常理
- (*mental attitude*)

a sense of [**honour** | **justice** | **humour** | **beauty**] = yìzhǒng [róngyù | zhèngyì | yōumò | měi] gǎn 一种 [荣誉 | 正义 | 幽默 | 美] 感

- (*consciousness*) = zhījué 知觉

he is still in hospital but has recovered his senses = tā hái zài yīyuàn li, dàn yǐjīng huīfù zhījué 他还在医院里, 但已经恢复知觉

- (*feeling for what is appropriate*) = lǐzhì 理智, lǐxìng 理性

he has obviously lost his senses = tā xiǎnrán shīqùle lǐzhì 他显然失去了理智

sensible *adjective*

(*when describing a person*) = dǒngshì 懂事, míngzhì 明智

(*when describing a decision, a plan*) = qièhé shíjì 切合实际, hélǐ 合理

(*when describing clothes*) = shíyòng 实用

sensitive *adjective*

(*easily affected*) = mǐngǎn 敏感

he is very sensitive to criticism = tā duì pīpíng fēicháng mǐngǎn 他对批评非常敏感

a sensitive market = yíge mǐngǎn de shìchǎng 一个敏感的市场

sentence

1 *noun*

- (*in language*) = jùzi 句子

a sentence = yíge jùzi 一个句子, yíjù huà 一句话

- (*for a crime*) = pànjué 判决, pànxíng 判刑

a (prison) sentence = yíxiàng pànjué 一项判决

2 *verb*

= pàn 判, pànjué 判决

to sentence someone to one year in prison = pàn mǒurén yì nián túxíng 判某人一年徒刑

separate

1 *adjective*

- (*individual*) = dāndú 单独

the children have separate rooms = háizimen yǒu dāndú de fángjiān 孩子们有单独的房间

- (*distinct*) = bù tóng 不同

there are two separate problems = yǒu liǎngge bù tóng de wèntí 有两个不同的问题

2 *verb*

- (*if it's a couple*) = fēnjū 分居

her parents separated two years ago = tā fùmǔ liǎng nián qián fēnjū le 她父母两年前分居了

- to separate the meat from the fish = bǎ ròu gēn yú fēnkāi 把肉跟鱼分开

separated *adjective*
= fēnkāi de 分开的, gékāi de 隔开的

separately *adverb*
- (*apart*) = fēnkāi de 分开地
- (*individually*) = fēnbié de 分别地

September *noun* ▶ 218
= jiǔyuè 九月

serial *noun*
a serial (*if it's a novel*) = yíbù liánzǎi xiǎoshuō 一部连载小说
(*if it's a periodical publication*) = yífèn qīkān 一份期刊
(*if it's a TV play*) = yíbù diànshì liánxùjù 一部电视连续剧

series *noun*
- (*sequence*) = xìliè 系列
  a series of problems = yíxìliè wèntí 一系列问题
- (*set*)
  a series of stamps = yítào yóupiào 一套邮票
  a new series of Chinese language textbooks = yítào xīn de Zhōngwén jiàokēshū 一套新的中文教科书

serious *adjective*
- (*causing worry*) = yánzhòng 严重
  a serious accident = yícì yánzhòng shìgù 一次严重事故
- (*when describing a personality*) = rènzhēn 认真
- **to be serious about** [**football** | **going to college**] = duì [zúqiú | shàng dàxué] hěn zhòngshì 对[足球 | 上大学]很重视

serve *verb*
- (*in a shop*)
  are you being served? = yǒu rén zài jiēdài nín ma? 有人在接待您吗?
- (*at table*)
  to serve the soup = shàng tāng 上汤
  he served the guest a cup of Chinese tea = tā gěi kèrén duānshang yìbēi Zhōngguó chá 他给客人端上一杯中国茶
- (*to work for*) = wèi...fúwù 为... 服务
  can computers serve agriculture? = jìsuànjī kěyǐ wèi nóngyè fúwù ma? 计算机可以为农业服务吗?
- (*in tennis, badminton, etc.*) = fāqiú 发球

service *noun*
- (*the act of serving*) = fúwù 服务
- (*the act of helping or assisting*) = bāngzhù 帮助
- (*in a church*) = yíshì 仪式
- (*other uses*)
  military service = bīngyì 兵役
  public services = gōnggòng shìyè 公共事业
  there are eight bus services to Beijing everyday = měi tiān yǒu bābān gōnggòng qìchē qù Běijīng 每天有八班公共汽车去北京

service station *noun*
a service station = yíge jiāyóuzhàn 一个加油站

set
1 *noun*
- (*a collection*) = tào 套
  a set of [**keys** | **stamps** | **plates**] = yítào [yàoshi | yóupiào | pánzi] 一套[钥匙 | 邮票 | 盘子]
- (*in tennis*) = pán 盘
  a set = yìpán 一盘

2 *verb*
- (*to decide on*) = (guī)dìng (规)定
  to set [**a date** | **a price** | **a goal...**] = (guī)dìng [yíge rìqī | yíge jiàgé | yíge mùbiāo...] (规)定[一个日期 | 一个价格 | 一个目标...]
- (*to adjust for a specific time or condition*) = tiáo 调
  to set [**an alarm clock** | **a video** | **a camera lens**] = tiáo [nàozhōng | lùxiàngjī | zhàoxiàngjī jìngtóu] 调[闹钟 | 录像机 | 照相机镜头]
- (*for assignments or exams*)
  to set homework = bùzhì zuòyè 布置作业
  to set an exam = chū kǎojuàn 出考卷
- (*to create*) = chuàngzào 创造
  to set a new world record = chuàngzào yíxiàng xīn de shìjiè jìlù 创造一项新的世界记录
- (*to establish*) = shùlì 树立
  to set a good example for someone = wèi mǒurén shùlì yíge hǎo bǎngyàng 为某人树立一个好榜样

- (*when talking about a story, a film, or the physical stage for a play*) = yǐ...wéi bèijǐng 以... 为背景
  the film is set in Shanghai = zhèbù diànyǐng yǐ Shànghǎi wéi bèijǐng 这部电影以上海为背景
- (*when talking about the sun*) = luò 落
- (*other uses*)
  to set the table = bǎi cānzhuō 摆餐桌
  to set fire to a house = fàng huǒ shāo yízuò fángzi 放火烧一座房子
  to set someone free = shìfàng mǒurén 释放某人

set off
- (*to leave*) = chūfā 出发, dòngshēn 动身
- (*to cause to go off*)
  to set off fireworks = ránfàng yānhuǒ 燃放烟火
  to set off a bomb = shǐ yìkē zhàdàn bàozhà 使一颗炸弹爆炸
  to set off a burglar alarm = nòngxiǎng fángdào bàojǐngqì 弄响防盗报警器

set up
- (*establish*) = jiànlì 建立, shèlì 设立
  to set up an organization = jiànlì yíge zǔzhī 建立一个组织
- (*to start and manage*) = kāibàn 开办
  to set up a company = kāibàn yìjiā gōngsī 开办一家公司
- (*to place in position*) = shùqǐ 竖起, dāqǐ 搭起
  to set up a tent = tāqǐ yíge zhàngpeng 搭起一个帐篷

settle *verb*
- (*to end*) = jiějué 解决, tiáotíng 调停
  to settle [an argument | a dispute | a problem] = jiějué [yìchǎng zhēnglùn | yíge jiūfēn | yíge wèntí] 解决 [一场争论 | 一个纠纷 | 一个问题]
- (*to decide on*) = dìng 定, juédìng 决定
  nothing is settled yet = yíqiè dōu hái méi dìng 一切都还没定
- (*to make one's home*) = dìngjū 定居

settle down
- (*to live comfortably in one's new home*) = ānjū 安居
- (*to calm down*) = píngjìngxialai 平静下来, ānxia xīn lai 安下心来
  she settled down to her homework = tā ānxia xīn lai zuò zuòyè 她安下心来做作业

settle in = āndùn 安顿

seven *number* ▶ 170, ▶ 204
= qī 七

seventeen *number* ▶ 170, ▶ 204
= shíqī 十七

seventeenth *number*
- (*in a series*) = dìshíqī 第十七
- (*in dates*) ▶ 218
  the seventeenth of May = wǔyuè shíqī rì 五月十七日, wǔyuè shíqī hào 五月十七号

seventh *number*
- (*in a series*) = dìqī 第七
- (*in dates*) ▶ 218
  the seventh of July = qīyuè qī rì 七月七日, qīyuè qī hào 七月七号

seventy *number* ▶ 170
= qīshí 七十

several *determiner*
= jǐge 几个
several tables = jǐzhāng zhuōzi 几张桌子
several books = jǐběn shū 几本书

> ! *Note that in* jǐge 几个, ge 个 *is a measure word that may be replaced by a different measure word, depending on the noun that follows.*

severe *adjective*
- (*harsh*) = yánlì 严厉
- (*giving cause for concern*) = yánzhòng 严重
- (*strict*) = yángé 严格

sew *verb*
= féng 缝, féngzhì 缝制

sewing *noun*
= féngrèn 缝纫

sewing machine *noun*
a sewing machine = yìtái féngrènjī 一台缝纫机

sex *noun*
- (*state of being male or female*) = xìngbié 性别
- (*sexual intercourse*) = xìngjiāo 性交
  to have sex with someone = hé mǒurén fāshēng xìng guānxi 和某人发生性关系, hé mǒurén xìngjiāo 和某人性交

shade *noun*
- (*out of the sun*) = yīn 荫, yīnliángchù 荫凉处

to sit in the shade of a tree = zuò zài shùyīn xia 坐在树荫下
• (*a colour*) = nóngdàn 浓淡
a shade = yìzhǒng nóngdànsè 一种浓淡色
• (*for a lamp*) = dēngzhào 灯罩
a shade = yíge dēngzhào 一个灯罩

shadow *noun*
a shadow = yíge yǐngzi 一个影子

shake *verb*
• (*to move with quick vibrations*) = yáo(huàng) 摇(晃), yáo(dòng) 摇(动)
to shake a bottle = yáohuàng yíge píngzi 摇晃一个瓶子
• (*to grasp the hand of another in greeting*) = wò 握
to shake hands with someone = hé mǒurén wò shǒu 和某人握手
• (*when saying no*) = yáo 摇
to shake one's head = yáo tóu 摇头
• (*with cold, fear, shock*) = fādǒu 发抖
he was shaking with fear = tā xià de fādǒu 他吓得发抖
• (*during an explosion, an earthquake*) = zhèndòng 震动
the earthquake shook the building = dìzhèn bǎ zhěnggè dàlóu dōu zhèndòng le 地震把整个大楼都震动了

shall *verb*
• (*when talking about the future*) = huì 会, jiāng(yào) 将(要)
I shall see you next Tuesday = xiàge xīngqī'èr wǒ huì jiàndào nǐ 下个星期二我会见到你
we shall arrive there on time = wǒmen jiāng ànshí dàodá nàr 我们将按时到达那儿
• (*when making suggestions*) = ...hǎo ma ...好吗, yào bu yào... 要不要...
shall I set the table? = yào bú yào wǒ bǎi cānzhuō? 要不要我摆餐桌?
shall we go to the cinema? = wǒmen qù kàn diànyǐng hǎo ma? 我们去看电影好吗?

shame *noun*
• (*emotion caused by a humiliating feeling*) = xiūkuì 羞愧, xiūchǐ 羞耻
she felt shame at having failed the exam = tā yīn kǎoshì bù jígé ér gǎndào xiūkuì 她因考试不及格而感到羞愧
• (*disgrace or dishonour*) = chírǔ 耻辱, xiūrǔ 羞辱
to bring shame on someone = gěi mǒurén dàilai chírǔ 给某人带来耻辱
shame on you! = nǐ zhēn diūrén! 你真丢人!
• (*when expressing regret*) = yíhàn 遗憾, kěxī 可惜
that's a shame = zhēn yíhàn 真遗憾

shampoo *noun*
= xǐfàjì 洗发剂, xiāngbō 香波

shape *noun*
• (*a form*) = xíng 形, xíngzhuàng 形状
a shape = yíge xíngzhuàng 一个形状
a square shape = yíge fāngxíng 一个方形
in the shape of an apple = chéng píngguǒ (de) xíngzhuàng 呈苹果(的)形状
• (*when talking about health*) = qíngkuàng 情况, zhuàngtài 状态
she is in good shape after the operation = tā shǒushù hòu shēntǐ qíngkuàng hěn hǎo 她手术后身体情况很好
to get in shape = chǔyú liánghǎo zhuàngtài 处于良好状态

share
1 *verb*
• (*to join with others in using*) = héyòng 合用
to share a house = héyòng/hézhù yídòng fángzi 合用/合住一栋房子
• (*when talking about dividing costs, rent, work*) = fēndān 分担
to share [**the cost** | **the petrol** | **the work**] **(with someone)** = (hé mǒurén) fēndān [fèiyòng | qìyóufèi | zhèxiàng gōngzuò] (和某人)分担[费用 | 汽油费 | 这项工作]
• (*to take a share of*) = fēnxiǎng 分享
he shared [**the profit** | **the money** | **her joy**] **(with his sister)** = tā (hé tā mèimei) fēnxiǎng [lìrùn | qián | tāde huānlè] 他(和他妹妹)分享[利润 | 钱 | 她的欢乐]
2 *noun*
• (*portion*) = fènr 份儿
a share = yífènr 一份儿
to pay one's fair share = fù yīng fù de nà yífènr 付应付的那一份儿
• (*unit of ownership in a public company*) = gǔpiào 股票

a share = yìgǔ 一股
share out (*British English*) (*amongst others*) = fēn 分

shark *noun*
a shark = yìtiáo shāyú 一条鲨鱼

sharp *adjective*
- (*when speaking of knives, blades, etc.*) = kuài 快
- (*pointed*) = jiān 尖
- (*sudden, extreme*) = jí 急
  a sharp bend = yíge jí zhuǎnwān 一个急转弯
- (*intelligent*) = jīngmíng 精明
- (*aggressive*) = jiānkè 尖刻, kēkè 苛刻
- (*when talking about a pain*) = jùliè 剧烈

shave *verb*
= guā liǎn 刮脸, tì xū 剃须

she *pronoun*
= tā 她

sheep *noun*
a sheep = yìzhī yáng 一只羊

sheet *noun*
- (*for a bed*) = chuángdān 床单
  a sheet = yìzhāng chuángdān 一张床单
- (*a piece*)
  a sheet (*of paper*) = yìzhāng zhǐ 一张纸
  (*of glass*) = yíkuài bōli 一块玻璃

shelf *noun*
a shelf = yíge jiàzi 一个架子
a book shelf = yíge shūjià 一个书架

shell *noun*
a shell = yíge ké 一个壳

shelter
1 *noun*
- (*from rain, danger*)
  a shelter = yíge duǒbìchù 一个躲避处
- (*for homeless people*)
  a shelter = yíge qīshēn zhī dì 一个栖身之地
- **a bus shelter** = yíge gōnggòng qìchē hòuchētíng 一个公共汽车候车亭

2 *verb*
- (*to take shelter*) = duǒbì 躲避
- (*to give protection to*) = bìhù 庇护, bǎohù 保护

shin *noun* ▶ 189
the shin = xiǎotuǐ 小腿

shine *verb*
- (*if it's the sun*) = zhàoyào 照耀
  the sun is shining = yángguāng zhàoyào 阳光照耀
- (*to give off light*) = fā guāng 发光
  the light in the lighthouse is shining = dēngtǎ li de dēng zài shǎnshǎn fā guāng 灯塔里的灯在闪闪发光
- (*to reflect light*) = fāliàng 发亮, fā guāng 发光
  the ring on her hand shone in the sun = tā shǒu shang de jièzhi zài yángguāng xia shǎnshǎn fāliàng 她手上的戒指在阳光下闪闪发亮
- (*to point a light at*)
  to shine a torch at someone = yòng shǒudiàntǒng zhào mǒurén 用手电筒照某人

ship *noun*
a ship = yìsōu chuán 一艘船
a passenger ship = yìsōu kèlún 一艘客轮

shirt *noun*
a shirt = yíjiàn chènshān 一件衬衫, yíjiàn chènyī 一件衬衣

shiver *verb*
= fādǒu 发抖, duōsuo 哆嗦

shock
1 *noun*
- (*an upsetting experience*) = zhènjīng 震惊, dǎjī 打击
  a shock = yíge zhènjīng 一个震惊, yíge dǎjī 一个打击
  to get a shock = shòudào zhènjīng 受到震惊
  to give someone a shock = gěi mǒurén yíge dǎjī 给某人一个打击
- (*the medical state*) = xiūkè 休克, zhòngfēng 中风
  to be in shock = chǔyú xiūkè zhuàngtài 处于休克状态
- (*from electricity*)
  a shock = yícì diànjī 一次电击
  to get a shock = chù diàn 触电

2 *verb*
- (*to upset*) = shǐ...zhènjīng 使… 震惊
  to shock someone = shǐ mǒurén zhènjīng 使某人震惊
  we were shocked by the news = duì zhège xiāoxi wǒmen dōu gǎndào

zhènjīng 对这个消息我们都感到震惊
- (*to cause a scandal*) = **shǐ...fènkǎi** 使… 愤慨
  to shock someone = shǐ mǒurén gǎndào fènkǎi 使某人感到愤慨

shoe *noun*
- (*for a person*) = xié 鞋
  a shoe = yìzhī xié 一只鞋
  a pair of shoes = yìshuāng xié 一双鞋
- (*for a horse*) = títiě 蹄铁
  a shoe = yíge títiě 一个蹄铁

shoot *verb*
- (*to aim and fire a weapon*) = shèjī 射击, kāi qiāng 开枪
  to shoot at someone = xiàng mǒurén shèjī 向某人射击
- (*to hit with a missile from a weapon*) = jīzhòng 击中, shèzhòng 射中
  they shot him in the leg = tāmen jīzhòngle tāde tuǐ 他们击中了他的腿
  to shoot someone dead = kāi qiāng dǎsǐ mǒurén 开枪打死某人
- (*to move very fast*)
  his car shot past me = tāde chē cóng wǒ pángbiān fēisù kāiguoqu 他的车从我旁边飞速开过去
- (*when talking about film production*) = pāishè 拍摄
  to shoot a film = pāishè yíbù diànyǐng 拍摄一部电影

shop
1 *noun*
  a shop = yìjiā shāngdiàn 一家商店
2 *verb*
  to go shopping = qù mǎi dōngxi 去买东西

shop assistant *noun* ▶ 344
(*British English*)
  a shop assistant = yìmíng shòuhuòyuán 一名售货员

shopkeeper *noun* ▶ 344
  a shopkeeper = yíge diànzhǔ 一个店主

shopping *noun*
  = mǎi dōngxi 买东西
  to do the shopping = mǎi dōngxi 买东西

shopping cart *noun* (*US English*)
  a shopping cart = yíliàng gòuwù shǒutuīchē 一辆购物手推车

shopping centre (*British English*), **shopping center** (*US English*)
noun
  a shopping centre, a shopping mall = yíge gòuwù zhōngxīn 一个购物中心

shopping trolley *noun* (*British English*)
  a shopping trolley = yíliàng gòuwù shǒutuīchē 一辆购物手推车

shop window *noun*
  a shop window = yíge chúchuāng 一个橱窗

shore *noun*
- (*the edge of the sea*) = hǎi'àn 海岸
- (*dry land*) = hǎibīn 海滨

short
1 *adjective*
- (*not long*) = duǎn 短
  the days are getting shorter = tiān yuèlái yuè duǎn le 天越来越短了
  a short skirt = yìtiáo duǎn qún 一条短裙
  he has short hair = tā shì duǎn tóufa 他是短头发
- (*not tall*) = ǎi 矮
  he's shorter than I = tā bǐ wǒ ǎi 他比我矮
- (*brief*) = jiǎnduǎn 简短
  a short speech = yíge jiǎnduǎn de jiǎnghuà 一个简短的讲话
- (*lacking, wanting*) = quē(shǎo) 缺(少)
  to be short of [**money** | **food** | **ideas...**] = quēshǎo [qián | shípǐn | zhǔyì...] 缺少[钱 | 食品 | 主意...]

2 in short = zǒngzhī 总之

short cut *noun*
  a short cut = yíge jiéjìng 一个捷径

shortly *adverb*
- (*soon*) = lìkè 立刻, mǎshàng 马上
- (*not long*) = bùjiǔ 不久
  shortly before we left = wǒmen líkāi qián bùjiǔ 我们离开前不久

shorts *noun*
  = duǎnkù 短裤
  a pair of shorts = yìtiáo duǎnkù 一条短裤

shot *noun*
- (*from a gun*)
  a shot = (kāi) yì qiāng (开)一枪, yícì shèjī 一次射击

to fire a shot at someone = xiàng mǒurén kāi yì qiāng 向某人开一枪

- (*in sports*) ▶ 390

a shot (*in football*) = yícì shèmén 一次射门

should *verb*

- (*when talking about what is right, what one ought to do*) = yīnggāi 应该, yīngdāng 应当

she should learn to drive = tā yīnggāi xué kāi chē 她应该学开车

you shouldn't be late = nǐ bù yīngdāng chídào 你不应当迟到

- (*when saying something may happen*) = yīnggāi huì 应该会, kěnéng huì 可能会

we should be there by midday = zhōngwǔ yǐqián wǒmen yīnggāi huì dàodá nàr 中午以前我们应该会到达那儿

it shouldn't be too difficult = zhè kěnéng bú huì tài nán 这可能不会太难

- (*when implying that something, though likely, didn't happen*) = běnlái (yīnggāi) 本来(应该)

the letter should have arrived yesterday = zhèfēng xìn běnlái yīnggāi zuótiān dào 这封信本来应该昨天到

- (*when implying that something happened though it ought not to have*) = běnlái bù (yīng)gāi 本来不(应)该

you shouldn't have said that = nǐ běnlái bù yīnggāi nàme shuō 你本来不应该那么说

- (*when used in a conditional clause to express a hypothetical condition*) = wànyī 万一

if it should rain tomorrow, we shall have to change our plans = míngtiān wànyī xiàyǔ, wǒmen jiù děi gǎibiàn jìhuà 明天万一下雨, 我们就得改变计划

- (*when asking for permission*) = kě(yǐ) bù kěyǐ 可(以)不可以

should I call him? = wǒ kě bù kěyǐ gěi tā dǎ diànhuà? 我可不可以给他打电话?

- (*when asking for advice*) = yīng(gāi) bù yīnggāi 应(该)不应该, hǎo ma 好吗

should I call the doctor? = wǒ yīng bù yīnggāi jiào yīshēng? 我应不应该叫医生?

- (*when expressing a past expectation of a future event*) = jiāng 将, huì 会

they didn't expect that I should come and attend the meeting = tāmen méi xiǎngdào wǒ huì lái cānjiā huì 他们没想到我会来参加会

- (*when expressing surprise at something unexpected*) = huì 会, jìng(huì) 竟(会)

it is surprising that he should be so foolish = tā jìnghuì zhème shǎ, zhēn ràng rén chījīng 他竟会这么傻, 真让人吃惊

- (*when used after such verbs as* **propose**, **suggest**, *or such adjectives as* **necessary**, **important**)

> **!** *Note that in these cases,* **should** *is often not translated.*

I suggest that he should discuss this matter with you = wǒ jiànyì tā hé nǐ tǎolùn zhège wèntí 我建议他和你讨论这个问题

shoulder *noun* ▶ 189

= jiān 肩, jiānbǎng 肩膀

to wear a sweater over one's shoulders = bǎ yíjiàn máoyī pī zài jiān shang 把一件毛衣披在肩上

he has strong shoulders = tāde jiānbǎng hěn jiēshi 他的肩膀很结实

shout

1 *verb*

= hǎn 喊, jiào 叫

to shout at someone = duì mǒurén hǎn 对某人喊

2 *noun*

= hūhǎn 呼喊, hǎnjiào 喊叫

a shout = yìshēng hūhǎn 一声呼喊

shout out = hǎnchūlai 喊出来, dàshēng shuōchūlai 大声说出来

shovel *noun*

a shovel = yìbǎ tiěxiān 一把铁锨, yìbǎ tiěchǎn 一把铁铲

show

1 *verb*

- (*to let someone see*) = gěi...kàn 给... 看

to show someone a photo = gěi mǒurén kàn yìzhāng zhàopiàn 给某人看一张照片

- (*to guide*) = dài 带, (dài)lǐng (带)领
  I'll show you to your room = wǒ dài nǐ qù nǐde fángjiān 我带你去你的房间
- (*to point to*)
  to show someone where to go = gàosu mǒurén wǎng nǎr zǒu 告诉某人往哪儿走
  there's a sign showing the way to the swimming pool = yǒu yíge lùbiāo gàosu nǐ qù yóuyǒngchí de lù zénme zǒu 有一个路标告诉你去游泳池的路怎么走
- (*to be on TV, at the cinema*) = fàngyìng 放映
  the film is showing at that cinema = zhèbù diànyǐng zhèngzài nàjiā diànyǐngyuàn fàngyìng 这部电影正在那家电影院放映
  to be shown on TV = zài diànshì shang fàngyìng/bōfàng 在电视上放映/播放
- (*to indicate*) = biǎomíng 表明, shuōmíng 说明
  this shows that he doesn't agree with our plan = zhè biǎomíng tā bù tóngyì wǒmende jìhuà 这表明他不同意我们的计划
- (*to demonstrate*) = gěi...shìfàn 给…示范, zuògěi...kàn 做给…看
  let me show you how to use this computer = wǒ lái gěi nǐ shìfàn zěnme yòng zhètái jìsuànjī 我来给你示范怎么用这台计算机

2 *noun*

- **a show** (*on a stage*) = yìchǎng yǎnchū 一场演出
  (*on TV*) = yíge diànshì jiémù 一个电视节目
  (*on radio*) = yíge guǎngbō jiémù 一个广播节目
  (*at a cinema*) = yìchǎng diànyǐng 一场电影
- (*an exhibition*)
  a show = yíge zhǎnlǎn 一个展览

show off = màinòng 卖弄, xuànyào 炫耀

show round

to show someone round the town = dài mǒurén cānguān chéngqū 带某人参观城区

show up

- (*to be present*) = dàochǎng 到场
- (*to appear*) = xiǎnlù 显露, xiǎnchū 显出
- (*to expose*) = jiēlù 揭露, jiēchuān 揭穿

shower *noun*

- (*for washing*) = línyù 淋浴
  a shower = yíge línyù 一个淋浴
  to have a shower = xǐ línyù 洗淋浴
- (*rain*) = zhènyǔ 阵雨
  a shower = yìchǎng zhènyǔ 一场阵雨

showjumping *noun* ▶ 390
= qí mǎ yuè zhàng yùndòng 骑马越障运动

shrimp *noun*
a shrimp = yíge (xiǎo)xiā 一个小虾

shrink *verb*

- (*when talking about clothing*) = shōusuō 收缩
  the shirt shrank after washing = zhèjiàn chènshān xǐ hòu shōusuō le 这件衬衫洗后收缩了
- (*when talking about an economy, etc.*) = suōxiǎo 缩小, jiǎnshǎo 减少

shut

1 *adjective*

- (*when referring to a book*) = héshang de 合上的
  the book was shut = shū shì héshang de 书是合上的
- (*when describing the eyes, the mouth*) = bìshang 闭上
  my eyes were shut = wǒ bìzhe yǎnjīng 我闭着眼睛
- (*when describing a door, a shop*) = guānmén 关门
  all the shops are shut = suóyǒu de shāngdiàn dōu guānmén le 所有的商店都关门了

2 *verb*

- (*if it's a window, a door*) = guān 关
  to shut [**the window** | **the door**] = guān [chuānghu | mén] 关 [窗户 | 门]
  the door does not shut properly = zhè mén guān bú shàng 这门关不上
- (*if it's a book, a dictionary, a magazine to be closed*) = héshang 合上
  to shut [**the book** | **the dictionary**] = héshang [shū | cídiǎn] 合上 [书 | 词典]
- (*if it's the eyes, the mouth to be closed*) = bìshang 闭上
  to shut [**one's eyes** | **one's mouth**] = bìshang [yǎnjīng | zuǐ] 闭上 [眼睛 | 嘴]

shut down (*to close*) = guānbì 关闭
the factory shut down in May last year = zhèjiā gōngchǎng qùnián wǔyuè guānbì le 这家工厂去年五月关闭了
shut out
to shut someone out = bǎ mǒurén guān zài wàimian 把某人关在外面
shut up
- (*to be quiet*) = zhùzuǐ 住嘴, zhùkǒu 住口
- (*to lock inside*)
to shut someone up = bǎ mǒurén guānqilai 把某人关起来
to shut something up = bǎ mǒuwù shōucángqilai 把某物收藏起来

shy *adjective*
- (*bashful*) = hàixiū 害羞, miǎntiǎn 腼腆
- (*easily frightened*) = dǎnqiè 胆怯

sick *adjective*
- (*ill*) = bìng 病, shēngbìng 生病
he got sick = tā bìng le 他病了
she felt sick = tā juézhe bù shūfu 她觉着不舒服
to be sick (*British English*) (*to vomit*) = ěxīn 恶心, yào ǒutù 要呕吐
- (*fed up*) = fán le 烦了, yànjuàn le 厌倦了
he's sick of his neighbours = tā duì tāde línjū yànjuàn le 他对他的邻居厌倦了

sickness *noun*
a sickness = yìzhǒng jíbìng 一种疾病

side *noun*
- (*a line forming part of a boundary or the part near the boundary*) = biān 边
a side = yì biān 一边
there are shops on either side of the road = mǎlù liǎng biān dōu yǒu shāngdiàn 马路两边都有商店
by the side of the river = zài hé biān 在河边
the north side of Beijing = Běijīng de běi biān 北京的北边
- (*of a person's body*) = cè 侧
to be lying on one's side = cèzhe shēnzi tǎngzhe 侧着身子躺着
on my right side = wǒ shēntǐ de yòu cè 我身体的右侧
- (*a surface of something flat*) = miàn 面
a side = yí miàn 一面
please read the other side of the page = qǐng kàn zhè yíyè de lìng yí miàn 请看这一页的另一面
- (*aspect*) = fāngmiàn 方面
a side = yíge fāngmiàn 一个方面
to consider all sides of the problem = kǎolǜ zhège wèntí de gègè fāngmiàn 考虑这个问题的各个方面
- (*in a conflict, a contest*) = pài 派, fāng 方
a side = yí pài 一派, yì fāng 一方
- (*a team*) = duì 队, fāng 方
a side = yí duì 一队
side with = zhàn zài...de yì biān 站在...的一边, zhīchí 支持

sidewalk *noun* (*US English*)
a sidewalk = yìtiáo rénxíngdào 一条人行道

sigh *verb*
= tànxī 叹息, tànqì 叹气

sight *noun*
- (*faculty of seeing*) = shìlì 视力, shìjué 视觉
to have good sight = shìlì hǎo 视力好
to be [**long** | **short**] **-sighted** = huàn [yuǎn | jìn] shì 患[远|近]视
- (*view*)
to catch sight of someone = kànjiàn mǒurén 看见某人
to be out of sight = kàn bú jiàn 看不见

sightseeing *noun*
= guānguāng 观光, yóulǎn 游览

sign
1 *noun*
- (*a mark, symbol*)
a sign = yíge fúhào 一个符号, yíge jìhào 一个记号
the US dollar sign = měiyuán de fúhào 美元的符号
- (*for traffic*)
a sign = yíge biāozhì 一个标志
- (*for shops, advertising*)
a sign = yíge zhāopái 一个招牌
- (*a notice*)
a sign = yíge páizi 一个牌子
- (*evidence, indication*)
a sign = yíge zhèngzhào 一个征兆, yíge jìxiàng 一个迹象

2 *verb*
- (*to put one's signature to*) = zài...shang qiān zì/míng 在…上签字/名
  to sign (one's name on) a cheque = zài zhīpiào shang qiān zì 在支票上签字
  sign on (*British English*) (*to begin a new job*)
  to sign on = kāishǐ yíxiàng xīn gōngzuò 开始一项新工作

signal
1 *noun*
  a signal = yíge xìnhào 一个信号
2 *verb*
- (*using lights, flags, a coding system*) = fā xìnhào 发信号
  to signal to turn left = fāchu xiàng zuǒ guǎi de xìnhào 发出向左拐的信号
- (*using one's hands*) = dǎ shǒushì 打手势
  to signal someone to come = dǎ shǒushì ràng mǒurén lái 打手势让某人来

signature *noun*
  a signature = yíge qiānmíng 一个签名

signpost *noun*
  a signpost = yíge lùbiāo 一个路标

silence *noun*
- (*absence of noise*) = jìjìng 寂静, wúshēng 无声
- (*refraining from speech*) = chénmò 沉默, mò bú zuò shēng 默不作声

silent *adjective*
- (*quiet*) = jìjìng 寂静
- (*not speaking or making any sound*) = chénmò 沉默, mò bú zuò shēng 默不作声

silk *noun*
  = sī 丝, sīchóu 丝绸

silly *adjective*
  = shǎ 傻, yúchǔn 愚蠢, hútu 糊涂

silver
1 *noun*
- (*the metal*) = yín 银, yínzi 银子
- (*silver coins*) = yínbì 银币
2 *adjective*
  = yín 银
  a silver ring = yìzhī yín jièzhi 一只银戒指

SIM card *noun*
  a SIM card = yíge shǒujī zhìnéngkǎ 一个手机智能卡

simple *adjective*
- (*not complicated*) = jiǎndān 简单
- (*plain*) = pǔsù 朴素
- (*unsuspecting*) = dānchún 单纯
- (*ordinary*) = pǔtōng 普通, píngcháng 平常

since
1 *preposition*

> **!** *Note that the phrase or clause beginning with* **since** *appears at the beginning of the sentence in Chinese.*

  = cóng...yǐlái 从…以来, zìcóng 自从
  I haven't been feeling well since Monday = cóng xīngqīyī yǐlái, wǒ yìzhí gǎnjué shēntǐ bù shūfu 从星期一以来，我一直感觉身体不舒服
  she has been living in China since 1988 = zìcóng yījiǔbābā nián, tā yìzhí zhù zài Zhōngguó 自从一九八八年她一直住在中国
  I haven't seen him since last week = wǒ zìcóng shàng xīngqī yìzhí méi jiànguo tā 我自从上星期一直没见过他
2 *conjunction*
- (*from the time when*) = cóng...yǐlái 从… 以来, ...yǐhòu ...以后
  I haven't heard from her since she left = tā líkāi yǐhòu, wǒ hái méi shōudàoguo tāde xìn 她离开以后，我还没收到过她的信
  I've lived here since I was ten = wǒ cóng shí suì yǐlái yìzhí zhù zài zhèr 我从十岁以来一直住在这儿
  it's ten years since she died = tā sǐle shí nián le 她死了十年了
- (*because*) = yīnwèi 因为, jìrán 既然
  since she was ill, she couldn't go = jìrán tā bìng le, suǒyǐ tā bù néng qù 既然她病了，所以她不能去
3 *adverb*
  (*from that time*) = cóng nà yǐhòu 从那以后, hòulái 后来
  I have been living here ever since = cóng nà yǐhòu wǒ yìzhí zhù zài zhèlǐ 从那以后我一直住在这里

sincere *adjective*
  = zhēnchéng 真诚, chéngkěn 诚恳

sincerely *adverb*
  = zhēnchéng de 真诚地, chéngkěn de 诚恳地

Yours sincerely (*British English*), **Sincerely yours** (*US English*) = Nínde zhōngchéng de 您的忠诚的
I sincerely hope that... = wǒ zhōngxīn xīwàng... 我衷心希望...

sing *verb*
= chàng 唱, chànggē 唱歌

singer *noun* ▶ 344
a singer (*one who sings as a profession*) = yìmíng gēshǒu 一名歌手
(*one whose fame for singing is widely recognized*) = yìmíng gēchàngjiā 一名歌唱家

singing *noun*
= chànggē 唱歌, gēchàng 歌唱

single *adjective*
- (*one*) = yī 一
we visited three towns in a single day = wǒmen yì tiān fǎngwènle sānge chéngzhèn 我们一天访问了三个城镇
I didn't see a single person = wǒ méiyǒu kànjiàn yíge rén 我没有看见一个人
- (*without a partner*) = dúshēn 独身
- (*for one person*) = dānrén 单人
a single bed = yìzhāng dānrén chuáng 一张单人床
- (*denoting ticket for transport valid for outward journey only*) (*British English*) = dānchéng 单程
a single ticket = yìzhāng dānchéng piào 一张单程票

sink
1 *noun*
a sink (*in a kitchen*) = yíge shuǐchí 一个水池, yíge xǐdícáo 一个洗涤槽
2 *verb*
- (*to become submerged in water*) = chénmò 沉没, chén 沉
the boat sank in five minutes = nàtiáo chuán bú dào wǔ fēnzhōng biàn chénmò le 那条船不到五分钟便沉没了
- (*subside*) = xiàxiàn 下陷
- (*to cause to sink*)
to sink a ship = shǐ yìsōu chuán chénmò 使一艘船沉没

sister *noun*
a sister (*elder*) = yíge jiějie 一个姐姐
(*younger*) = yíge mèimei 一个妹妹

sister-in-law *noun*
a sister-in-law (*elder brother's wife*) = yíge sǎozi 一个嫂子
(*younger brother's wife*) = yíge dìmèi/dìxí 一个弟妹/弟媳
(*husband's elder sister*) = yíge dàgūzi 一个大姑子
(*husband's younger sister*) = yíge xiǎogūzi 一个小姑子
(*wife's elder sister*) = yíge dàyízi 一个大姨子
(*wife's younger sister*) = yíge xiǎoyízi 一个小姨子

sit *verb*
- (*to take a seat*) = zuò 坐
to be sitting on the floor = zuò zài dì shang 坐在地上
- (*British English*) (*to take*)
to sit an exam = cānjiā kǎoshì 参加考试
sit down = zuòxia 坐下
sit up (*to rise to a sitting position*) = zuòqilai 坐起来

sitting room *noun*
a sitting room = yìjiān qǐjūshì 一间起居室

situated *adjective*
= wèiyú 位于, zuòluòzài 坐落在
situated near the town centre = wèiyú shì zhōngxīn fùjìn 位于市中心附近

situation *noun*
- (*location*) = wèizhi 位置, dìdiǎn 地点
a situation = yíge wèizhi 一个位置
- (*momentary state*) = chǔjìng 处境, jìngkuàng 境况
to be in a dangerous situation = chǔjìng wēixiǎn 处境危险
- (*a set of circumstances*) = xíngshì 形势, júshì 局势
[**international** | **domestic** | **economic**] **situation** = [guójì | guónèi | jīngjì] xíngshì [国际 | 国内 | 经济] 形势

six *number* ▶ 170, ▶ 204
= liù 六

sixteen *number* ▶ 170, ▶ 204
= shíliù 十六

sixteenth *number*
- (*in a series*) = dìshíliù 第十六
- (*in dates*) ▶ 218
the sixteenth of July = qīyuè shíliù rì 七月十六日, qīyuè shíliù hào 七月十六号

S

sixth *number*
- (*in a series*) = dìliù 第六
- (*in dates*) ▶ 218
  the sixth of February = èryuè liù rì 二月六日, èryuè liù hào 二月六号

sixty *number* ▶ 170
= liùshí 六十

size *noun*
- (*when talking about a person*) = shēncái 身材
  she's about your size = tāde shēncái gēn nǐ chàbuduō 她的身材跟你差不多
- (*when talking about hats, socks, shoes*) = hào 号
  a size = yíge hào 一个号
  what size shoes do you wear? = nǐ chuān jǐ hào de xié? 你穿几号的鞋?
- (*when talking about clothes*) = chǐcùn 尺寸
  do you have trousers of this size? = nǐmen yǒu zhège chǐcùn de kùzi ma? 你们有这个尺寸的裤子吗?
- (*when talking about how big something is*)
  what is the size of [**your house** | **England** | **that school** | **the apple**] **?** = [nǐde fángzi | Yīnggélán | nàsuǒ xuéxiào | píngguǒ] yǒu duō dà? [你的房子 | 英格兰 | 那所学校 | 苹果] 有多大?
  I like a garden of this size = wǒ xǐhuan zhème dàxiǎo de huāyuán 我喜欢这么大小的花园
  the size of the window = chuānghu de dàxiǎo 窗户的大小, chuānghu de chǐcùn 窗户的尺寸

skateboard *noun* ▶ 390
a skateboard = yíge (sìlún) huábǎn 一个(四轮)滑板

skating *noun* ▶ 390
ice-skating = huábīng 滑冰
roller-skating = liūbīng 溜冰

skating rink *noun*
a skating rink (*for ice-skating*) = yíge huábīngchǎng 一个滑冰场
(*for roller-skating*) = yíge liūbīngchǎng 一个溜冰场

sketch *noun*
- (*a drawing*) = cǎotú 草图, sùmiáo 素描
  a sketch = yìzhāng cǎotú 一张草图
- (*a funny scene*) = xiǎopǐn 小品
  a sketch = yíge xiǎopǐn 一个小品

ski
1 *noun*
a ski = yìzhī huáxuěbǎn 一只滑雪板
a pair of skis = yífù huáxuěbǎn 一副滑雪板
2 *verb*
to go skiing = qù huáxuě 去滑雪

skiing *noun* ▶ 390
= huáxuě 滑雪

skilful (*British English*), **skillful** (*US English*) *adjective*
= shúliàn 熟练, língqiǎo 灵巧

skill *noun*
- (*the quality*) = jìyì 技艺, jìqiǎo 技巧
- (*a particular ability*) = jìnéng 技能, jìshù 技术

skin *noun*
= pífū 皮肤, pí 皮

skinny *adjective*
(*thin*) = jí shòu 极瘦, píbāogǔ de 皮包骨的

skip *verb*
- (*to give little jumps*) = bèng 蹦
- (*with a rope*) = tiàoshéng 跳绳
- **to skip classes** = táoxué 逃学, táokè 逃课

ski resort *noun*
a ski resort = yíge huáxuě shèngdì 一个滑雪胜地

skirt *noun*
a skirt = yìtiáo qúnzi 一条裙子

sky *noun*
the sky = tiān 天, tiānkōng 天空
a clear sky = qínglǎng de tiānkōng 晴朗的天空

skydiving *noun* ▶ 390
= tiàosǎn yùndòng 跳伞运动

slap *verb*
to slap someone's face = dǎ mǒurén ěrguāng 打某人耳光
to slap someone on the back = zài mǒurén bèi shang pāi yíxià 在某人背上拍一下

sled, sledge (*British English*)
1 *noun*
a sled = yíge xuěqiāo 一个雪橇
2 *verb*
to go sledging (*British English*) = chéng xuěqiāo qù 乘雪橇去

sleep
1 *noun*

= shuìjiào 睡觉, shuìmián 睡眠
to go to sleep = shuìzháo 睡着, rùshuì 入睡
I cannot go to sleep = wǒ shuì bù zháo 我睡不着
to go back to sleep = chóngxīn shuìzháo 重新睡着
to put someone to sleep = shǐ mǒurén rùshuì 使某人入睡

2 *verb*
- (*to be asleep*) = shuì 睡, shuìjiào 睡觉
- **to sleep with someone** = hé mǒurén fāshēng xìng guānxi 和某人发生性关系, hé mǒurén shuìjiào 和某人睡觉

sleep in (*to let oneself sleep longer than usual*) = wǎn qǐchuáng 晚起床, shuìlǎnjiào 睡懒觉

sleeping bag *noun*
a sleeping bag = yíge shuìdài 一个睡袋

sleepy *adjective*
to be sleepy, to feel sleepy = xiǎng shuìjiào 想睡觉, gǎnjué kùn 感觉困

sleet *noun*
= yǔ jiā xuě 雨夹雪

sleeve *noun*
a sleeve = yìzhī xiùzi 一只袖子
to roll up one's sleeves = juǎnqi xiùzi 卷起袖子

slice
1 *noun*
a slice of [**bread** | **meat** | **lemon** | **cucumber**] = yípiàn [miànbāo | ròu | níngméng | huángguā] 一片 [面包 | 肉 | 柠檬 | 黄瓜]
2 *verb*
to slice bread = bǎ miànbāo qiēchéng piàn 把面包切成片

slide
1 *verb*
- (*to slip or slide*) = huá 滑, huádòng 滑动
  to slide on ice = huábīng 滑冰
- (*to slip off*) = huáluò 滑落
  the plates slid off the table = pánzi cóng zhuōzi shang huáluòxiaqu 盘子从桌子上滑落下去

2 *noun*
- (*an image from a photograph*)
  a slide = yìzhāng huàndēngpiàn 一张幻灯片
- (*in a playground*)
  a slide = yíge huátī 一个滑梯

slim
1 *adjective*
= miáotiáo 苗条, xìcháng 细长
2 *verb* (*British English*)
= jiǎn féi 减肥

slip *verb*
- (*to glide or slide*) = huá 滑, huádòng 滑动
- (*to fall down by sliding*) = huádǎo 滑倒
  she slipped when coming down the mountain = tā xià shān de shíhou huádǎo le 她下山的时候滑倒了
- (*to fall off by sliding*) = huáluò 滑落
  the glass slipped out of my hands = bōlìbēi cóng wǒ shǒu zhōng huáluòxiaqu 玻璃杯从我手中滑落下去

slipper *noun*
a slipper = yìzhī tuōxié 一只拖鞋
a pair of slippers = yìshuāng tuōxié 一双拖鞋

slippery *adjective*
= huá 滑

slot machine *noun*
a slot machine = yìtái tóu bì dǔbójī 一台投币赌博机

slow *adjective*
- (*not fast*) = màn 慢, huǎnmàn 缓慢
  to make slow progress = jìnbù hěn màn 进步很慢
- (*not bright*) = chídùn 迟钝, bèn 笨
- (*describing a watch, a clock*) = màn 慢
  the clock is 20 minutes slow = zhège zhōngbiǎo màn èrshí fēn zhōng 这个钟表慢二十分钟

slow down = fàngmàn sùdù 放慢速度, mànxialai 慢下来

slowly *adverb*
= mànmàn de 慢慢地, huǎnmàn de 缓慢地

sly *adjective*
= jiǎohuá 狡猾, jiǎozhà 狡诈

small *adjective*
= xiǎo 小
a small car = yíliàng xiǎo qìchē 一辆小汽车
a small quantity = shǎo liàng 少量

small ad *noun* (*British English*)
a small ad = yíge xiǎo guǎnggào 一个小广告

smart *adjective*
- (*British English*) (*elegant*) = xiāosǎ 潇洒, piàoliang 漂亮
- (*intelligent*) = cōngming 聪明, jīngmíng 精明

smash *verb*
- (*to break*) = dǎsuì 打碎, dǎpò 打破
- (*to get broken*) = pò 破, suì 碎
smash up = dǎohuǐ 捣毁, dǎpò 打破

smell
1 *noun*
- (*an odour*)
a smell = yìzhǒng qìwèi 一种气味
- (*the sense*)
the sense of smell = xiùjué 嗅觉

2 *verb*
- (*to perceive by nose*) = wén 闻
I can smell burning = wǒ néng wéndào húwèir 我能闻到糊味儿
- (*to give off an odour*) = wénqilai 闻起来
this smells nice = zhè wénqilai hěn hǎowén 这闻起来很好闻

smile
1 *verb*
= xiào 笑, wēixiào 微笑
to smile at someone = xiàng mǒurén (wēi)xiào 向某人(微)笑
2 *noun*
a smile = xiào 笑, wēixiào 微笑

smoke
1 *noun*
= yān 烟, yānqì 烟气
2 *verb*
- (*to give off smoke*) = mào yān 冒烟
- (*to inhale and expel tobacco smoke*) = chōu yān 抽烟, xī yān 吸烟
do you smoke? = nǐ xī yān ma? 你吸烟吗?
- (*to inhale and expel smoke from*) = xī 吸, chōu 抽
to smoke a pipe = chōu yāndǒu 抽烟斗

smooth *adjective*
- (*when describing a road, the ground*) = píngtǎn 平坦
a smooth road = yìtiáo píngtǎn de dàolù 一条平坦的道路
- (*when describing the surface of paper, glass, a table, a floor*) = guānghuá 光滑
the floor is very smooth = dìmiàn hěn guānghuá 地面很光滑
- (*when describing an action*) = píngwěn 平稳
the flight was not very smooth = fēixíng bú tài píngwěn 飞行不太平稳
- (*when describing a writing style*) = tōngshùn 通顺, liúchàng 流畅

smother *verb*
(*to suffocate by excluding air*) = shǐ...zhìxī 使... 窒息, shǐ...tòu bú guò qì lai 使... 透不过气来
to smother someone = shǐ mǒurén zhìxī 使某人窒息

snack *noun*
= xiǎochī 小吃, kuàicān 快餐

snail *noun*
a snail = yíge wōniú 一个蜗牛

snake *noun*
a snake = yìtiáo shé 一条蛇

snapshot *noun*
a snapshot = yìzhāng kuàizhào 一张快照

sneaker *noun* (*US English*)
a sneaker (*a shoe*) = yìzhī yùndòngxié 一只运动鞋
a pair of sneakers = yìshuāng yùndòngxié 一双运动鞋

sneeze *verb*
= dǎ pēntì 打喷嚏

snobbish *adjective*
= shìlì 势利, chǎnshàng qīxià 谄上欺下

snooker *noun* ▶ 390
= táiqiú 台球

snore *verb*
= dǎ hān 打鼾, dǎ hūlu 打呼噜

snow
1 *noun*
= xuě 雪
2 *verb*
= xiàxuě 下雪
it's snowing = zhèngzài xiàxuě 正在下雪

snowball *noun*
a snowball = yíge xuěqiú 一个雪球

snowman *noun*
a snowman = yíge xuěrén 一个雪人

so
1 *adverb*

- (*to such an extent*) = zhème 这么, nàme 那么

he's so [happy | stupid | smart...] = tā nàme [gāoxìng | bèn | cōngming...] 他那么[高兴 | 笨 | 聪明...]

they speak so fast = tāmen shuō de zhème kuài 他们说得这么快

I have so much work to do = wǒ yǒu zhème duō gōngzuò yào zuò 我有这么多工作要做

- (*also*) = yě 也

> ! *Note that in this sense, the meaning conveyed by* **so** *in English has to be stated overtly in Chinese.*

I'm fifteen and so is he = wǒ shíwǔ suì, tā yě shíwǔ suì 我十五岁, 他也十五岁

if you go, so will I = rúguǒ nǐ qù, wǒ yě qù 如果你去, 我也去

- (*very*) = fēicháng 非常, hěn 很

I'm so pleased to hear the news = tīngdào zhège xiāoxi, wǒ fēicháng gāoxìng 听到这个消息, 我非常高兴

- (*other uses*)

I think so = wǒ xiǎng shì zhèyàng 我想是这样

I'm afraid so = kǒngpà shì zhèyàng 恐怕是这样

who says so? = shéi shuō de? 谁说的?

so what? = nà yòu zěnmeyàng ne? 那又怎样呢?

and so on = děngděng 等等

2 *conjunction*

- (*therefore*) = suǒyǐ 所以, yīncǐ 因此

she was sick, so I went to see her = tā bìng le, suǒyǐ wǒ qù kàn tā 她病了, 所以我去看她

so (that) = yǐbiàn 以便, wèide shì 为的是

he moved to a house near his mother, so that he could look after her better = tā bāndào lí tā mā hěn jìn de yìsuǒ fángzi, yǐbiàn tā néng gèng hǎo de zhàogù tā 他搬到离他妈很近的一所房子, 以便他能更好地照顾她

- (*then, in that case*) = nàme 那么, zhèyàng kànlai 这样看来

so you are going to study Chinese = nàme nǐ dǎsuàn xué Zhōngwén 那么你打算学中文

3 so as = yǐbiàn 以便, wèide shì 为的是

we left early so as not to miss the train = wǒmen hěn zǎo jiù líkāi le, wèide shì bú wù huǒchē 我们很早就离开了, 为的是不误火车

soap *noun*

- (*for washing*) = féizào 肥皂
- (*on TV*)

a soap = yíbù diànshì liánxùjù 一部电视连续剧

soccer *noun* ▶ 390

= zúqiú 足球

social *adjective*

- (*relating to society*) = shèhuì de 社会的
- (*sociable*) = xǐhuan jiāojì de 喜欢交际的

social studies *noun*

= shèhuì yánjiū 社会研究, shèhuìxué 社会学

social worker *noun* ▶ 344

a social worker = yíge shèhuì gōngzuòzhě 一个社会工作者

sock *noun*

a sock = yìzhī duǎnwà 一只短袜

a pair of socks = yìshuāng duǎnwà 一双短袜

sofa *noun*

a sofa = yíge shāfā 一个沙发

soft *adjective*

- (*not hard or tough*) = ruǎn 软

the ground is soft here = zhèr de dì hěn ruǎn 这儿的地很软

a soft toffee = yíkuài ruǎn nǎitáng 一块软奶糖

- (*when describing colours, lights, voice*) = róuhé 柔和

soft lights = róuhé de dēngguāng 柔和的灯光

- (*when describing a manner, an action*) = wēnhé 温和

a soft answer = yíge wēnhé de dáfù 一个温和的答复

- (*yielding easily to pressure*) = ruǎnruò 软弱, shùncóng 顺从

you are too soft with him = nǐ duì tā tài ruǎnruò 你对他太软弱

- **soft drinks** = ruǎn yǐnliào 软饮料

software *noun*

= ruǎnjiàn 软件

soldier *noun* ▶ 344

a soldier = yíge shìbīng 一个士兵, yíge zhànshì 一个战士

sole *noun*
- the sole (of the foot) = jiǎodǐ 脚底
- (*of a shoe*)
  a sole = yíge xiédǐ 一个鞋底

solicitor *noun* ▶ 344 (*British English*)
  a solicitor = yíge lǜshī 一个律师

solution *noun*
  a solution = yíge jiějué bànfǎ 一个解决办法

solve *verb*
  = jiě 解, jiějué 解决
  to solve a problem = jiějué yíge wèntí 解决一个问题

some
1 *determiner*
- (*an amount or number of*)
  (*when used in mid-sentence*) = yìxiē 一些
  I have to buy some bread = wǒ děi mǎi yìxiē miànbāo 我得买一些面包
  she ate some strawberries = tā chīle yìxiē cǎoméi 她吃了一些草莓
  we visited some beautiful towns = wǒmen fǎngwènle yìxiē měilì de chéngzhèn 我们访问了一些美丽的城镇
  (*when used at the beginning of a sentence*) = yǒuxiē 有些
  some shops don't open on Sunday = yǒuxiē shāngdiàn xīngqītiān bù kāimén 有些商店星期天不开门
- (*certain*) = mǒu(yī) 某(一)
  she is studying at some university in Beijing = tā zài Běijīng de mǒu (yì)suǒ dàxué xuéxí 她在北京的某(一)所大学学习
  some people don't like travelling by plane = mǒu (yì)xiē rén bù xǐhuan zuò fēijī lǚxíng 某(一)些人不喜欢坐飞机旅行

2 *pronoun*
- (*an amount or number of*)
  (*when used in mid-sentence*) = yìxiē 一些
  I know where you can find some = wǒ zhīdào zài nǎr nǐ néng zhǎodào yìxiē 我知道在哪儿你能找到一些
  (*when used at the beginning of a sentence*) = yǒu yìxiē 有一些
  some are useful = yǒu yìxiē hěn yǒuyòng 有一些很有用
- (*certain people*) = yǒu (yì)xiē rén 有(一)些人
  some (of them) are Chinese = (tāmen dāngzhōng) yǒu yìxiē rén shì Zhōngguórén (他们当中)有一些人是中国人
- (*certain things*) = yǒu (yì)xiē dōngxi 有(一)些东西
  some are quite expensive = yǒu yìxiē dōngxi xiāngdāng guì 有一些东西相当贵

someone *pronoun* (*also* **somebody**)
  = mǒurén 某人, mǒu (yí)ge rén 某(一)个人
  someone famous = mǒu yíge yǒumíng de rén 某一个有名的人

something *pronoun*
- (*an undefined thing*) = yíge dōngxi 一个东西, mǒuwù 某物
  I saw something interesting = wǒ kàndào yíge yǒuqù de dōngxi 我看到一个有趣的东西
- (*an undefined matter*) = yíjiàn shì 一件事, mǒushì 某事
  I'd like to discuss something with you = wǒ xiǎng gēn nǐ tǎolùn yíjiàn shì 我想跟你讨论一件事

sometimes *adverb*
  = yǒushíhou 有时候, yǒushí 有时

somewhere *adverb*
- = zài mǒu (yí)ge dìfang 在某(一)个地方, zài shénme dìfang 在什么地方
  they live somewhere in Scotland = tāmen zhù zài Sūgélán de mǒu ge dìfang 他们住在苏格兰的某个地方
- let's go somewhere else = zánmen qù lìngwài yíge dìfang ba 咱们去另外一个地方吧

son *noun*
  a son = yíge érzi 一个儿子

song *noun*
  a song = yìshǒu gē 一首歌, yìzhī gē 一支歌

son-in-law *noun*
  a son-in-law = yíge nǚxu 一个女婿

soon *adverb*
- (*before long, in a short time*) = hěn kuài 很快, bùjiǔ 不久
  he'll go to China soon = tā hěn kuài jiùyào qù Běijīng le 他很快就要去北京了

- (*in a moment*) = yíhuìr 一会儿
  I'll come back soon = wǒ yíhuìr jiù huílai 我一会儿就回来
- (*early*) = zǎo 早
  the sooner the better = yuè zǎo yuè hǎo 越早越好
  as soon as possible = jìn zǎo 尽早
- (*quickly*) = kuài 快
  as soon as possible = jìn kuài 尽快
  come as soon as you can = nǐ jìn kěnéng kuài lái 你尽可能快来

sore *adjective*
to have a sore [**throat** | **leg** | **back...**] = [sǎngzi | tuǐ | hòubèi...] téng [嗓子 | 腿 | 后背] 疼
my arm is very sore = wǒde gēbo hěn téng 我的胳膊很疼

sorry
1 *adjective*
- (*when apologizing*) = duìbuqǐ 对不起, bàoqiàn 抱歉
  sorry! = duìbuqǐ 对不起
  I'm sorry I'm late = duìbuqǐ, wǒ lái wǎn le 对不起, 我来晚了
  to say sorry = shuō duìbuqǐ 说对不起
- (*when expressing regret*) = yíhàn 遗憾
  I'm sorry you can't come = hěn yíhàn nǐ bù néng lái 很遗憾你不能来
- (*when expressing regret for what one did in the past*) = hòuhuǐ 后悔, àohuǐ 懊悔
  I feel very sorry for what I did = wǒ duì wǒ suǒ zuò de shì gǎndào hěn hòuhuǐ 我对我所做的事感到很后悔
- (*when expressing pity or sympathy*) = nánguò 难过, wǎnxī 惋惜
  to feel sorry for someone = wèi mǒurén nánguò 为某人难过

sort
1 *noun*
= zhǒng 种, lèi 类
it's a sort of [**bird** | **computer** | **loan...**] = zhè shì yìzhǒng [niǎo | jìsuànjī | dàikuǎn...] 这是一种 [鸟 | 计算机 | 贷款...]
he's not that sort of person = tā bú shì nàlèi rén 他不是那类人
2 *verb*
- (*to classify*) = bǎ...fēn lèi 把... 分类
  to sort files = bǎ dǎng'àn fēn lèi 把档案分类
- (*to arrange*) = zhěnglǐ 整理
  to sort the books into piles = bǎ shū zhěnglǐchéng yíluò yíluò de 把书整理成一摞一摞的

sort out
- (*to solve*) = jiějué 解决
  to sort out a problem = jiějué yíge wèntí 解决一个问题
- (*to deal with*) = chǔlǐ 处理
  I'll sort it out = wǒ huì chǔlǐ zhèjiàn shì 我会处理这件事
- (*to arrange and organize*) = zhěnglǐ 整理
  to sort out these documents = zhěnglǐ zhèxiē wénjiàn 整理这些文件
- (*to classify*) = bǎ...fēn lèi 把... 分类
  to sort out the photos = bǎ zhàopiàn fēn lèi 把照片分类
  to sort out the old clothes from the new = bǎ yīfu àn xīn jiù fēn lèi 把衣服按新旧分类

sound
1 *noun*
= shēng 声, shēngyīn 声音
a sound = yíge shēngyīn 一个声音
I heard the sound of voices = wǒ tīngjian shuōhuà shēng le 我听见说话声了
to turn up the sound of the television = bǎ diànshìjī de shēngyīn tiáo dà 把电视机的声音调大
the sound of a piano = gāngqín shēng 钢琴声
2 *verb*
- (*to give out a sound*) = xiǎng 响
  the alarm clock sounded at 7 o'clock = nàozhōng qī diǎn xiǎng le 闹钟七点响了
- (*to give an impression on hearing*) = tīngqilai 听起来
  it sounds [**dangerous** | **odd** | **interesting...**] = zhè tīngqilai [hěn wēixiǎn | hěn qíguài | hěn yǒu yìsi...] 这听起来 [很危险 | 很奇怪 | 很有意思...]
  it sounds like a piano = zhè tīngqilai xiàng gāngqín 这听起来像钢琴

soup *noun*
a soup = yíge tāng 一个汤

sour *adjective*
= suān 酸
the milk has gone sour = niúnǎi biàn suān le 牛奶变酸了

south
1 *noun*
the south = nánfāng 南方, nánbù 南部
in the south of China = zài Zhōngguó de nánfāng 在中国的南方
2 *adverb*
to go south = qù nánfāng 去南方
to live south of Beijing = zhù zài Běijīng de nánbù 住在北京的南部
3 *adjective*
= nán 南
to work in south London = zài nán Lúndūn gōngzuò 在南伦敦工作

South Africa *noun*
= Nán Fēi 南非

South America *noun*
= Nán Měi(zhōu) 南美(洲)

southeast *noun*
the southeast = dōngnán 东南

southwest *noun*
the southwest = xīnán 西南

souvenir *noun*
a souvenir = yíge jìniànpǐn 一个纪念品

space *noun*
- (*room*) = kōngjiān 空间
to take up space = zhàn kōngjiān 占空间
- (*an area of land or a place*) = kòng dì 空地, dìfang 地方
an open space = yíkuài kòng dì 一块空地
- (*outer space*) = tàikōng 太空
- (*a gap*) = kòng 空, kòngbái 空白
a space = yíge kòng 一个空
fill the spaces with verbs = yòng dòngcí tián kòng 用动词填空

Spain *noun*
= Xībānyá 西班牙

spam *noun*
= lājī yóujiàn 垃圾邮件

Spanish ▶ 288
1 *adjective*
= Xībānyá de 西班牙的, Xībānyárén de 西班牙人的
2 *noun*
= Xībānyáyǔ 西班牙语, Xībānyáwén 西班牙文

spare *adjective*
- (*extra*) = duōyú 多余
I've got a spare ticket = wǒ yǒu yìzhāng duōyú de piào 我有一张多余的票
- (*not in actual use*) = kòng 空
are there any spare seats? = hái yǒu kòng zuòwèi ma? 还有空座位吗?

spare room *noun*
a spare room = yìjiān kòng fángjiān 一间空房间

spare time *noun*
spare time = kòngyú shíjiān 空余时间

speak *verb*
- (*utter words*) = shuōhuà 说话, jiǎnghuà 讲话
to speak to a friend = gēn yíge péngyou shuōhuà 跟一个朋友说话
who's speaking, please? = qǐng wèn, nín shì nǎ wèi? 请问, 您是哪位?
generally speaking = yìbān shuōlai 一般说来
- (*to utter*) = shuō 说, jiǎng 讲
to speak Japanese = shuō Rìyǔ 说日语
speak up
- (*to speak boldly*) = dàdǎn de shuō 大胆地说
- (*to speak so as to be heard easily*) = qīngchu xiǎngliàng de shuō 清楚响亮地说

special *adjective*
- (*exceptional*) = tèshū 特殊, tèbié 特别
a special purpose = yíge tèshū de mùdì 一个特殊的目的
- (*designed for a particular purpose*) = zhuānmén 专门
a special school = yìsuǒ zhuānmén de xuéxiào 一所专门的学校
- (*intimate*) = tèbié qīnmì 特别亲密
she's a special friend of mine = tā shì wǒ tèbié qīnmì de péngyou 她是我特别亲密的朋友

speciality (*British English*), **specialty** (*US English*) *noun*
a speciality (*an occupation or area of study*) = yìmén zhuānyè 一门专业
(*a skill*) = yíge tècháng 一个特长, yíge zhuāncháng 一个专长
(*a product*) = yíge tèchǎn 一个特产

specially *adverb*
= tèyì 特意, tèdì 特地

spectator *noun*
a spectator = yíge guānzhòng 一个观众

speech *noun*
a speech = yíge jiǎnghuà 一个讲话, yíge fāyán 一个发言

speed
1 *noun*
(*rate of progress*) = sùdù 速度
2 *verb*
- **to speed away** = kuàisù kāizǒu 快速开走, kuàisù shǐqù 快速驶去
- (*to drive too fast*) = chāosù xíngshǐ 超速行驶

speed up = jiā sù 加速, zēng sù 增速

speed camera *noun*
a speed camera = yíge sùchéng xiàngjī 一个速成相机

speed limit *noun*
= sùdù jíxiàn 速度极限

spell *verb*
(*to give letters of a word in order*)
(*when speaking*) = pīn 拼, pīndú 拼读
(*when writing*) = pīn 拼, pīnxiě 拼写
how do you spell this word? = zhège cí (nǐ) zěnme pīn? 这个词(你)怎么拼?

spelling *noun*
= pīnfǎ 拼法

spend *verb*
- (*to pay out*) = huā 花

how much money have you spent? = nǐ huāle duōshǎo qián? 你花了多少钱?
- (*to give or bestow for any purpose*) = huā 花, huāfèi 花费, yòng 用

he spent an hour writing a letter to his girlfriend = tā huāle yíge xiǎoshí gěi tāde nǚpéngyou xiě xìn 他花了一个小时给他的女朋友写信
- (*to pass, as time*) = guò 过, dùguò 度过

I shall spend my Christmas in China = wǒ jiāng zài Zhōngguó guò Shèngdànjié 我将在中国过圣诞节

spider *noun*
a spider = yíge zhīzhū 一个蜘蛛

spill *verb*
- (*to cause to pour or flow over*) = shǐ/bǎ...sǎ 使/把...洒

don't spill the milk = bié bǎ niúnǎi sǎchulai 别把牛奶洒出来
- (*to flow over or fall out*) = yìchū 溢出, jiànchū 溅出

spinach *noun*
= bōcài 菠菜

spit *verb*
- (*to eject from mouth*) = tǔ 吐
- (*to eject saliva*) = tǔ tán 吐痰

spite: in spite of *preposition*
= jǐnguǎn 尽管
we went out in spite of the rain = jǐnguǎn xiàyǔ, wǒmen háishì chūqu le 尽管下雨, 我们还是出去了

> **!** *Note that the phrase introduced by* jǐnguǎn 尽管 *must be at the beginning of the sentence.*

spiteful *adjective*
= yǒu èyì de 有恶意的, yǒu yuànhèn de 有怨恨的

spoil *verb*
- (*to mar*) = huǐle 毁了, nòngzāo 弄糟, gǎozāo 搞糟

the rain spoilt [**the party** | **the football match** | **the picnic**] = yǔ bǎ [jùhuì | zúqiú bǐsài | yěcān] huǐle 雨把[聚会 | 足球比赛 | 野餐] 毁了
- (*to ruin, to damage*) = sǔnhuài 损坏
- (*as a parent*) = jiāoguàn 娇惯, guànhuài 惯坏

to spoil a child = jiāoguàn háizi 娇惯孩子

sponge *noun*
a sponge = yíkuài hǎimián 一块海绵

spoon *noun*
a spoon = yìbǎ sháozi 一把勺子, yìbǎ chízi 一把匙子

sport *noun* ▶ 390
a sport = yìzhǒng yùndòng 一种运动, yìzhǒng tǐyù 一种体育
to be good at sports = shàncháng tǐyù yùndòng 擅长体育运动

sports centre (*British English*), **sports center** (*US English*) *noun*
a sports centre = yíge tǐyù (yùndòng) zhōngxīn 一个体育(运动)中心

sports club *noun*
a sports club = yíge tǐyù jùlèbù 一个体育俱乐部

spot
1 *noun*
- (*on an animal*)

a spot = yíge bāndiǎn 一个斑点

S

Games and sports

In Chinese, the verb *dǎ* 打 is used for ball games played with the hand.

to play tennis	= dǎ wǎngqiú 打网球
to play basketball	= dǎ lánqiú 打篮球
to play volleyball	= dǎ páiqiú 打排球
to play table-tennis	= dǎ pīngpāngqiú 打乒乓球

Chinese uses the verb *tī* 踢 for football, *xià* 下 for chess, *dǎ* 打 for cards and mahjong.

to play football	= tī zúqiú 踢足球
to play chess	= xià qí 下棋
to play cards	= dǎ púkè 打扑克
to play mahjong	= dǎ májiàng 打麻将

Players and events

a tennis player	= yíge wǎngqiú yùndòngyuán 一个网球运动员
a tennis champion	= yíge wǎngqiú guànjūn 一个网球冠军
to win a basketball game	= yíng yìchǎng lánqiú bǐsài 赢一场篮球比赛
to lose a volleyball game	= shū yìchǎng páiqiú bǐsài 输一场排球比赛
to draw in a football game	= zài yìchǎng zúqiú bǐsài zhōng tīpíng 在一场足球比赛中踢平
the Olympic Games	= Àolínpíkè Yùndònghuì 奥林匹克运动会
the World Cup	= Shìjiè Bēi Zúqiúsài 世界杯足球赛
a world champion	= yíge shìjiè guànjūn 一个世界冠军
a national champion	= yíge quánguó guànjūn 一个全国冠军

- (*British English*) (*on the face or body*)
  a spot = yíge bāndiǎn 一个斑点, yíge hēidiǎn 一个黑点
- (*dirt mark or stain*)
  a spot = yíge wūdiǎn 一个污点
- (*a place*)
  a spot = yíge dìdiǎn 一个地点
  on the spot = dāngchǎng 当场, xiànchǎng 现场

2 *verb*
- (*to detect*) = fāxiàn 发现
- (*to see someone you recognize*) = rènchū 认出

sprain *verb*
= niǔshāng 扭伤
to sprain one's wrist = niǔshāng shǒuwàn 扭伤手腕

spring *noun*
= chūntiān 春天, chūnjì 春季
the Spring Festival (*the Chinese New Year*) = Chūnjié 春节

spy *noun*
a spy = yíge jiàndié 一个间谍, yíge mìtàn 一个密探, yíge tèwu 一个特务

square
1 *noun*
- (*the shape*)
  a square = yíge zhèngfāngxíng 一个正方形
- (*in a town*)
  a square = yíge guǎngchǎng 一个广场

2 *adjective*
(*having the geometrical form*) = zhèngfāngxíng de 正方形的, fāng de 方的

squash
1 *noun* ▶ 390
(*the sport*) = bìqiú 壁球

2 *verb*
- (*to crush flat*) = bǎ...yābiǎn 把... 压扁
  be careful not to squash the tomatoes = xiǎoxīn bié bǎ xīhóngshì yābiǎn le 小心别把西红柿压扁了
- (*to crowd*) = jǐ(rù) 挤(入), jǐ(jìn) 挤(进)
  they managed to squash into the lift = tāmen shèfǎ jǐjìnle diàntī 他们设法挤进了电梯

squeak *verb*
= zhīzhī de jiào 吱吱地叫

squeeze *verb*
- (*for the purpose of getting juice*) = zhà 榨
  to squeeze [oranges | lemons | apples...] = zhà [júzi | níngméng | píngguǒ...] zhī 榨[橘子 | 柠檬 | 苹果...] 汁
- (*to injure*) = jǐshāng 挤伤
  to squeeze one's fingers = jǐshāng shǒuzhǐ 挤伤手指
- (*showing affection or friendship*)
  to squeeze someone's hand = jǐnwò mǒurén de shǒu 紧握某人的手
- **to squeeze something into a bag** = wǎng yíge bāo li sāi mǒu jiàn dōngxi 往一个包里塞某件东西
- **all six people were squeezed into a small car** = liùge rén dōu jǐ zài yíliàng xiǎo qìchē li 六个人都挤在一辆小汽车里

squirrel *noun*
a squirrel = yìzhī sōngshǔ 一只松鼠

stable
1 *noun*
a stable = yíge mǎjiù 一个马厩, yíge mǎpéng 一个马棚
2 *adjective*
- (*constant and not ready to change*) = wěndìng 稳定
- (*firmly fixed*) = láogù 牢固, jiāngù 坚固

stadium *noun*
a stadium = yíge tǐyùchǎng 一个体育场, yíge yùndòngchǎng 一个运动场

staff *noun*
the staff (*of a company, a bank*) = quántǐ zhíyuán 全体职员
(*of a school, a college*) = quántǐ jiàozhíyuán 全体教职员

stage *noun*
- (*a step in development*) = jiēduàn 阶段
  a stage = yíge jiēduàn 一个阶段
- **a stage** (*for a performance*) = yíge wǔtái 一个舞台
  (*for a speech*) = yíge jiǎngtái 一个讲台

stain
1 *noun*
a stain = yíge wūdiǎn 一个污点
2 *verb*
- (*to soil or change the colour of*) = zhānwū 沾污
- (*to bring disgrace upon*) = diànwū 玷污

stairs *noun*
= lóutī 楼梯
to fall down the stairs = cóng lóutī shang shuāixialai 从楼梯上摔下来

stamp *noun*
- (*for postage*)
  a stamp = yìzhāng yóupiào 一张邮票
- (*an imprinted mark*)
  a stamp = yíge chuō 一个戳, yíge yìn 一个印
- (*a tool for marking*)
  a stamp = yìméi túzhāng 一枚图章

stamp-collecting *noun*
= jíyóu 集邮

stand *verb*
- = zhàn 站
  he stood by the window = tā zhàn zài chuānghu pángbiān 他站在窗户旁边
  to stay standing, to remain standing = zhànzhe bú dòng 站着不动
- (*to be situated*) = zuòluò 坐落, wèiyú 位于
  the house stands by a river = nàzuò fángzi zuòluò zài yìtiáo hé biān 那座房子坐落在一条河边
- (*to put*)
  to stand a vase on a table = bǎ yíge huāpíng fàng zài zhuōzi shang 把一个花瓶放在桌子上
- (*to step*)
  to stand on a nail = cǎi zài yíge dīngzi shang 踩在一个钉子上
- (*to bear*) = rěnshòu 忍受, shòu de liǎo 受得了
  can you stand the hot weather there? = nǐ néng shòu de liǎo nàr de rè tiānqì ma? 你能受得了那儿的热天气吗?
  he can't stand playing football = tī zúqiú tā shòu bù liǎo 踢足球他受不了
- (*other uses*)
  to stand in someone's way = fáng'ài mǒurén 妨碍某人, dǎng mǒurén de dào 挡某人的道
  to stand for election (*British English*) = cānjiā jìngxuǎn 参加竞选
  to stand trial = shòu shěn 受审

S

stand back = wǎng hòu zhàn 往后站, tuìhòu 退后

stand for

- (*to represent*) = dàibiǎo 代表
- (*to mean*) = yìsi shì 意思是, yìwèizhe 意味着

stand out

- (*to be prominent*) = tūchū 突出, chūsè 出色

stand up

- **to stand up** = zhànqilai 站起来 (*given as an order in the classroom or the army*)

stand up! = qǐlì! 起立!

- **to stand someone up** (*fail to keep an appointment*) = gēn mǒurén shī yuē 跟某人失约

stand up for

- (*to support*) = zhīchí 支持
- (*to defend*) = hànwèi 捍卫

to stand up for one's rights = hànwèi zìjǐ de quánlì 捍卫自己的权利

stand up to

- (*to meet face to face*) = yónggǎn de miànduì 勇敢的面对

to stand up to the hooligans = yónggǎn de miànduì liúmáng 勇敢的面对流氓

- (*to show resistance to*) = dǐkàng 抵抗

star *noun*

- (*in space*)

a star = yìkē xīng 一颗星

- (*a famous person*)

a star = yíge míngxīng 一个明星

stare *verb*

= dīngzhe kàn 盯着看, mù bù zhuǎn jīng de kàn 目不转睛地看

to stare at someone = dīngzhe kàn mǒurén 盯着看某人

start

1 *verb*

- (*to begin*) = kāishǐ 开始

to start [**working** | **writing letters** | **running...**] = kāishǐ [gōngzuò | xiě xìn | pǎo...] 开始[工作 | 写信 | 跑...]

you should start by phoning them = nǐ yīnggāi kāishǐ xiān gěi tāmen dǎ diànhuà 你应该开始先给他们打电话

- (*to begin one's working life*)

to start (out) as a teacher = kāishǐ dāng lǎoshī 开始当老师

- (*to set out*) = chūfā 出发, dòngshēn 动身

when will you start for China? = nǐ shénme shíhou chūfā qù Zhōngguó? 你什么时候出发去中国?

- (*to cause*) = fādòng 发动

to start a war = fādòng yìchǎng zhànzhēng 发动一场战争

- (*to begin working*) = fādòng 发动, qǐdòng 起动

the car won't start = qìchē fādòng bù qǐlai 汽车发动不起来

- (*to put into action*) = kāi(dòng) 开(动)

to start [**a car** | **a machine**] = kāidòng [qìchē | jīqì] 开动[汽车 | 机器]

- (*to set up and run*) = kāibàn 开办, chuàngbàn 创办

they've decided to start a new school in the village = tāmen juédìng zài cūn li kāibàn yìsuǒ xīn xuéxiào 他们决定在村里开办一所新学校

2 *noun*

a start = yíge kāishǐ 一个开始, yíge kāiduān 一个开端

at the start of [**the race** | **the meeting** | **the week**] = [bǐsài | huìyì | zhège xīngqī] kāishǐ de shíhou [比赛 | 会议 | 这个星期] 开始的时候

start off

- (*to set out*) = chūfā 出发, dòngshēn 动身
- (*to begin*) = kāishǐ 开始

start over (*US English*) = chóngxīn kāishǐ 重新开始

starter *noun* (*British English*)

(*of a meal*) = tóupán 头盘

a starter = yíge tóupán 一个头盘

state *noun*

- (*a country*) = guójiā 国家

a state = yíge guójiā 一个国家

- (*a constituent member of a federation*) = zhōu 州

a state = yíge zhōu 一个州

- (*a government*)

the State = zhèngfǔ 政府

- (*a condition*) = zhuàngtài 状态, zhuàngkuàng 状况

the state of her health is worrying = tāde jiànkāng zhuàngkuàng hěn lìng rén dānyōu 她的健康状况很令人担忧

to be in a bad state of repair = xūyào xiūlǐ 需要修理

statement *noun*

a statement (*an account*) = yíge chénshù 一个陈述

(*a formal declaration or account*) = yíxiàng shēngmíng 一项声明

station *noun*
- (*for trains or coaches*) = zhàn 站
  a [train | coach] station = yíge [huǒchē | qìchē] zhàn 一个[火车|汽车]站
- (*on TV or radio*) = tái 台
  a [TV | radio] station = yíge [diànshì | guǎngbō diàn] tái 一个[电视|广播电]台

statue *noun*
a statue = yízuò diāoxiàng 一座雕像, yízuò sùxiàng 一座塑像

stay
1 *verb*
- (*to remain*) = dāi 呆/待, tíngliú 停留
  we stayed there for a week = wǒmen zài nàr dāile yíge xīngqī 我们在那儿呆了一个星期
- (*to have accommodation*) = zhù 住
  to stay with friends = yǔ péngyou zhù zài yìqǐ 与朋友住在一起

2 *noun*
she enjoyed her stay in Shanghai = tā zài Shànghǎi guò de hěn yúkuài 她在上海过得很愉快
to make a short stay here = zài zhèr duǎnqī zhù yíduàn shíjiān 在这儿短期住一段时间
stay away from = bú qù 不去
to stay away from school = bú qù shàngxué 不去上学
stay in = dāi zài jiā li 呆在家里, bù chū mén 不出门
stay out = dāi zài wàimian 呆在外面, bù huí jiā 不回家
to stay out late = dāi zài wàimian hěn wǎn (bù huí jiā) 呆在外面很晚(不回家)
stay up
(*to keep late hours*) = bú shuìjiào 不睡觉

steady *adjective*
- (*constant, stable*) = wěndìng 稳定, bú biàn 不变
  to keep up a steady speed = bǎochí wěndìng de sùdù 保持稳定的速度
- (*not likely to move*) = wěngù 稳固

steak *noun*
a steak (*beef*) = yíkuài niúpái 一块牛排
(*fish*) = yíkuài yú 一块鱼

steal *verb*
- (*to practise theft*) = tōu dōngxi 偷东西
  to steal from someone = cóng mǒurén nàr tōu dōngxi 从某人那儿偷东西
- (*to take by theft*) = tōu 偷
  to steal money from someone = cóng mǒurén nàr tōu qián 从某人那儿偷钱

steam *noun*
= zhēngqì 蒸汽, shuǐzhēngqì 水蒸气

steel *noun*
= gāng 钢, gāngtiě 钢铁

steep *adjective*
- (*when describing a rise or decline in price, living standards*) = jùjù 急剧
- (*when describing a road or a mountain*) = dǒu 陡, dǒuqiào 陡峭

steering wheel *noun*
a steering wheel
(*of a car or lorry*) = yíge fāngxiàngpán 一个方向盘

step
1 *noun*
- (*when walking*) = bù 步
  a step = yí bù 一步
  to take a step = mài/zǒu yí bù 迈/走一步
- (*in a flight of stairs*) = tījí 梯级
  a step = yíge tījí 一个梯级
- (*in front of a door, a doorstep*) = táijiē 台阶
  a step = yíge táijiē 一个台阶
- (*one of a series of actions*) = bùzhòu 步骤
  to take steps = cǎiqǔ bùzhòu 采取步骤

2 *verb*
- (*to walk*) = zǒu 走
  to step into the house = zǒu jìn fángzi 走进房子
- (*to advance by taking a step or steps*) = mài bù 迈步
- **to step on a nail** = cǎi zài dīngzi shang 踩在钉子上
  step aside = zǒu dào pángbiān qu 走到旁边去, kào biān zhàn 靠边站

stepbrother *noun*
a stepbrother (*elder brother by a stepmother*) = yíge yìmǔ gēge 一个异母哥哥
(*younger brother by a stepmother*) = yíge yìmǔ dìdi 一个异母弟弟

S

(*elder brother by a stepfather*) = yíge yìfù gēge 一个异父哥哥
(*younger brother by a stepfather*) = yíge yìfù dìdi 一个异父弟弟

stepfather *noun*
a stepfather = yíge jìfù 一个继父, yíge yìfù 一个异父

stepmother *noun*
a stepmother = yíge jìmǔ 一个继母, yíge yìmǔ 一个异母

stepsister *noun*
a stepsister (*elder sister by a stepfather*) = yíge yìfù jiějie 一个异父姐姐
(*younger sister by a stepfather*) = yíge yìfù mèimei 一个异父妹妹
(*elder sister by a stepmother*) = yíge yìmǔ jiějie 一个异母姐姐
(*younger sister by a stepmother*) = yíge yìmǔ mèimei 一个异母妹妹

stereo *noun*
a stereo = yìtái lìtǐshēng shōulùjī 一台立体声收录机

stewardess *noun* ▶ 344
a stewardess (*on a plane*) = yíge kōng(zhōng xiǎo)jie 一个空(中小)姐
(*on a ship*) = yíge nǚfúwùyuán 一个女服务员

stick
1 *verb*
- (*using glue or tape*) = tiē 贴, zhān 粘
  to stick a stamp on an envelope = zài xìnfēng shang tiē yóupiào 在信封上贴邮票
- (*to attach by a pin or clip*) = bié 别
  she stuck her badge onto her coat = tā bǎ tāde páizi bié zài wàiyī shang 她把她的牌子别在外衣上
- (*when something pointed is pushed into or through something else*) = cì 刺, chā 插
  he stuck the fork into the meat = tā bǎ chāzi chā jìn ròu li 他把叉子插进肉里
- (*to become unmovable*) = kǎzhù 卡住
  the door is stuck = mén kǎzhù le 门卡住了
- (*to reach an obstacle, to be stumped*) = nánzhù 难住
  I'm stuck by this problem = wǒ bèi zhège wèntí nánzhù le 我被这个问题难住了

2 *noun*
- (*a piece of wood*)
  a stick = yìgen zhītiáo 一根枝条
- (*for walking*) = shǒuzhàng 手杖
  a stick = yìgen shǒuzhàng 一根手杖

stick at
to stick at one's work = jiānchí gōngzuò 坚持工作

stick out = shēnchū 伸出, tūchū 凸出
there's a nail sticking out = yǒu yíge dīngzi shēnchulai 有一个钉子伸出来

sticky tape *noun* (*British English*)
= jiāodài 胶带

stiff *adjective*
- (*not soft, not supple*) = jiāngyìng 僵硬, jiāngzhí 僵直
  I had stiff legs = wǒde tuǐ gǎndào jiāngyìng 我的腿感到僵硬
- (*not easy to move*) = bù línghuó 不灵活
- (*rigid and hard*) = yìng 硬
  this pair of shoes is too stiff = zhèshuāng xié tài yìng le 这双鞋太硬了

still[1] *adverb*
- (*when indicating no change*) = hái 还, réngrán 仍然
  does she still play the piano? = tā hái tán gāngqín ma? 她还弹钢琴吗?
  I still don't understand why you left = wǒ réngrán bù míngbai nǐ wèishénme líkāi 我仍然不明白你为什么离开
  she could still win = tā hái néng yíng 她还能赢
- (*used in comparisons*) = gèng(jiā) 更(加), háiyào 还要
  it is hot today, but it'll be still hotter tomorrow = jīntiān hěn rè, dànshì míngtiān huì gèng rè 今天很热, 但是明天会更热

still[2] *adjective*
- (*quiet*) = jìjìng 寂静, ānjìng 安静
- (*motionless*) = jìngzhǐ 静止, bú dòng 不动
  to sit still = zuòzhe búdòng 坐着不动

sting *verb*
- **to sting someone** (*if it's a wasp or an insect*) = zhē mǒurén 蜇某人
  (*if it's a mosquito*) = dīng mǒurén 叮某人, yǎo mǒurén 咬某人

- (*feel sharp pain*) = gǎndào cìtòng 感到刺痛

stir *verb*
- (*to use an implement to mix something*) = jiǎodòng 搅动, jiǎohuo 搅和
  to stir the coffee with a spoon = yòng sháozi jiǎodòng kāfēi 用勺子搅动咖啡
- (*to cause a sensation in*) = hōngdòng 轰动
  the news stirred the whole school = zhètiáo xiāoxi hōngdòngle quán xiào 这条消息轰动了全校
- **stir up hatred** = shāndòng chóuhèn 煽动仇恨, tiǎoqǐ chóuhèn 挑起仇恨
- **stir up patriotism** = jīqǐ àiguózhǔyì 激起爱国主义

stomach *noun* ▶ 189, ▶ 277
the stomach = wèi 胃, dùzi 肚子
to have a pain in one's stomach = wèi téng 胃疼, dùzi téng 肚子疼

stone *noun*
a stone (*a piece of rock*) = yíkuài shítou 一块石头
(*a gem*) = yíkuài bǎoshí 一块宝石, yíkuài zuànshí 一块钻石
- (*the hard seed of a fruit*) = hé 核
  an apricot stone = yíge xìnghé 一个杏核

stop
1 *verb*
- (*to put an end to*) = tíngzhǐ 停止
  to stop [laughing | working | learning Chinese] = tíngzhǐ [xiào | gōngzuò | xué Zhōngwén] 停止[笑 | 工作 | 学中文]
  to stop smoking = jiè yān 戒烟
- (*when giving an order*) = bié 别, búyào 不要

> **!** *Note that when* **bié** 别 *or* **búyào** 不要 *is used to stop what is going on,* **le** 了 *is required at the end of the sentence.*

stop [talking | writing | playing football]! = bié [shuō huà | xiě | tī zúqiú] le! 别[说话 | 写 | 踢足球]了!
- (*to prevent*) = zǔzhǐ 阻止
  to stop someone from [leaving | playing the violin | talking] = zǔzhǐ mǒurén [líkāi | lā xiǎotíqín | jiǎnghuà] 阻止某人[离开 | 拉小提琴 | 讲话]
- (*to come to a halt*) = tíng 停
  the bus didn't stop = qìchē méi tíng 汽车没停
- (*when talking about noise, weather, music*) = tíng 停, tíngzhǐ 停止
  suddenly the noise stopped = tūrán zàoyīn tíng(zhǐ) le 突然噪音停(止)了
  it's stopped raining = yǔ tíng le 雨停了

2 *noun*
a (bus) stop = yíge qìchēzhàn 一个汽车站
to miss one's stop = zuòguòle zhàn 坐过了站

store *noun*
a store (*a shop*) = yíge shāngdiàn 一个商店
(*a place for keeping goods*) = yíge cāngkù 一个仓库

storey (*British English*), **story** (*US English*) *noun*
a storey = yì céng 一层

storm *noun*
a storm = yìchǎng fēngbào 一场风暴
(*with rain*) = yìchǎng bàofēngyǔ 一场暴风雨
(*with snow*) = yìchǎng bàofēngxuě 一场暴风雪

story *noun*
- (*a tale*)
  a story = yíge gùshi 一个故事
- (*a literary genre*)
  a (short) story = yíbù (duǎnpiān) xiǎoshuō 一部(短篇)小说
- (*in a newspaper*)
  a story = yìtiáo bàodào 一条报道
- (*a rumour*)
  a story = yíge yáochuán 一个谣传
- (*US English*) ▶ **storey**

stove *noun* (*US English*)
a stove = yíge lúzi 一个炉子

straight
1 *adjective*
- = zhí 直
  a straight line = yìtiáo zhí xiàn 一条直线
  she had straight hair = tāde tóufa shì zhí de 她的头发是直的
- (*in the right position*) = zhèng 正
  the picture isn't straight = zhèzhāng huà bú zhèng 这张画不正
- (*honest*) = chéngshí 诚实, zhèngzhí 正直

S

2 *adverb*
- = zhí 直
  to stand up straight = zhàn zhí 站直
  to go straight ahead = yìzhí wǎng qián zǒu 一直往前走
- (*without delay*) = lìkè 立刻, mǎshàng 马上
  to go straight home = lìkè huí jiā 立刻回家

strange *adjective*
- (*odd*) = qíguài 奇怪
  it's strange that she didn't come = tā méi lái hěn qíguài 她没来很奇怪
- (*unknown*) = mòshēng 陌生, bù shúxi 不熟悉

stranger *noun*
  a stranger = yíge (mò)shēngrén 一个(陌)生人
  (*someone from another region*) = yíge yìxiāngrén 一个异乡人

straw *noun*
- (*for feeding animals*) = dàocǎo 稻草, màigǎn 麦杆
- (*for drinking*)
  a straw = yìgēn xīguǎn 一根吸管

strawberry *noun*
  a strawberry = yíge cǎoméi 一个草莓

stream *noun*
  a stream = yìtiáo xiǎohé 一条小河, yìtiáo xiǎoxī 一条小溪

street *noun*
  a street = yìtiáo jiē(dào) 一条街(道), yìtiáo mǎlù 一条马路

streetlamp (*British English*), **streetlight** (*US English*) *noun*
  a streetlamp = yíge jiēdēng 一个街灯

strength *noun*
- (*quality of being strong*) = lìliàng 力量, lì(qi) 力(气)
- (*capacity for exertion or endurance*) = qiángdù 强度

stressful *adjective*
  = jǐnzhāng 紧张, yālì dà de 压力大的

stretch *verb*
- (*to extend in space*) = shēnkāi 伸开, shēnchū 伸出
  to stretch one's arms = shēnkāi gēbo 伸开胳膊
- (*to make straight by tension*) = bǎ...lāzhí 把... 拉直
  to stretch the wire = bǎ diànxiàn lāzhí 把电线拉直

strict *adjective*
- (*stern*) = yángé 严格, yánlì 严厉
- (*observing exact rules*) = yánjǐn 严谨

strike *noun*
- (*an attack*)
  a strike = yícì dǎjī 一次打击, yícì gōngjī 一次攻击
- (*a cessation of work*)
  a strike = yícì bàgōng 一次罢工
  to go on strike = jǔxíng bàgōng 举行罢工

string *noun*
  (*thin cord*)
  a piece of string = yìgēn xiànshéng 一根线绳

striped *adjective*
  = yǒu tiáowén de 有条纹的

stroke *verb*
  (*to touch lightly in an affectionate way*) = fǔmó 抚摩, lǚ 捋

stroller *noun* (*US English*)
  (*a push-chair*)
  a stroller = yíge yīng'ér tuīchē 一个婴儿推车

strong *adjective*
- (*having physical strength*) = qiángzhuàng 强壮, qiángjiàn 强健
  she's strong = tā hěn qiángzhuàng 她很强壮
- (*having mental strength*) = jiānqiáng 坚强, jiānjué 坚决
- (*intense*) = qiángliè 强烈
  strong [feeling | contrast | protests] = qiángliè de [gǎnqíng | duìbǐ | kàngyì] 强烈的 [感情 | 对比 | 抗议]
- (*not easily damaged*) = jiēshi 结实, láogù 牢固
- (*when describing one's attitude, standpoint, determination*) = jiāndìng 坚定
- (*having force, power*)
  a strong wind = yìchǎng dà fēng 一场大风
  strong tea = nóng chá 浓茶
  a strong wine = yìzhǒng liè jiǔ 一种烈酒
- (*obvious, noticeable*)
  a strong German accent = yìkǒu hěn zhòng de Déyǔ kǒuyīn 一口很重的德语口音
  a strong smell of garlic = yìzhǒng hěn nóng de dàsuàn wèi 一种很浓的大蒜味

- (*having military power*) = qiángdà 强大

stubborn *adjective*
= wángù 顽固, gùzhí 固执

student *noun* ▶ 344
a student = yíge xuésheng 一个学生

study
1 *verb*
- (*to be engaged in learning*) = xuéxí 学习
  she is studying for an exam = tā zài xuéxí zhǔnbèi kǎoshì 她在学习准备考试
- (*to make study of*) = xuéxí 学习, xué 学
  to study history = xué(xí) lìshǐ 学(习)历史
- (*to scrutinize*) = zǐxì kàn 仔细看

2 *noun*
- (*a room*)
  a study = yìjiān shūfáng 一间书房
- (*act of studying*) = xuéxí 学习

stuff
1 *noun*
- (*things*) = dōngxi 东西
- (*material*) = cáiliào 材料

2 *verb*
- (*to pack, to fill*) = zhuāng 装, sāi 塞
  to stuff a suitcase with clothes = wǎng xiāngzi li zhuāng yīfu 往箱子里装衣服
- (*to feed*)
  to stuff the children with cakes = yòng dàngāo tiánbǎo háizimen de dùzi 用蛋糕填饱孩子们的肚子

stuffing *noun*
= tián(sāi)liào 填(塞)料

stupid *adjective*
= bèn 笨, yúchǔn 愚蠢

style *noun*
- (*a way of dressing, behaviour*)
  her way of dressing always has style = tā chuān de zǒngshì hěn rùshí 她穿得总是很入时
- (*a manner of doing things*)
  a style = yìzhǒng zuòfēng 一种作风, yìzhǒng fēnggé 一种风格
  his working style = tāde gōngzuò zuòfēng 他的工作作风
- (*a way of writing*)
  a style = yìzhǒng wéntǐ 一种文体
- (*a distinctive characteristic*)
  a style (of architecture) = yìzhǒng (jiànzhù) fēnggé 一种(建筑)风格
- (*a design, a type*)
  a style = yìzhǒng shìyàng 一种式样, yìzhǒng yàngshì 一种样式
  the style of a car = qìchē de shìyàng 汽车的式样
- **a hair style** = yìzhǒng fàxíng 一种发型
- (*a way of life*)
  a life style = yìzhǒng shēnghuó fāngshì 一种生活方式
  to live in (grand) style = shēnghuó háohuá 生活豪华
- (*a fashion*)
  a style = yìzhǒng shímáo 一种时髦

stylish *adjective*
= shímáo 时髦, piàoliang 漂亮

subject *noun*
- (*of a conversation*) = huàtí 话题
  a subject = yíge huàtí 一个话题
- (*being studied*) = kēmù 科目, kèchéng 课程
  a subject = yíge kèchéng 一个课程
- (*topic*) = tímù 题目
  a subject = yíge tímù 一个题目

suburb *noun*
the suburbs = jiāoqū 郊区, jiāowài 郊外

subway *noun*
- (*US English*) (*the underground*)
  the subway = dìtiě 地铁
- (*British English*) (*an underground passage*)
  a subway = yìtiáo dìxià tōngdào 一条地下通道

succeed *verb*
- (*to accomplish what is attempted*) = chénggōng 成功
- (*follow, take the place of*) = jìchéng 继承, jiētì 接替

success *noun*
= chénggōng 成功

successful *adjective*
= chénggōng 成功

such
1 *determiner*
= zhèyàng 这样, zhèzhǒng 这种
there's no such thing = méi yǒu zhèyàng de dōngxi 没有这样的东西

2 *adverb*
= nàme 那么
they have such a lot of money = tāmen yǒu nàme duō qián 他们有那么多钱
she's such a strange person = tā shì nàme qíguài de yíge rén 他是那么奇怪的一个人

suddenly *adverb*
= tūrán 突然, hūrán 忽然

suffer *verb* ▶ 277
• (*to be affected by*) = zāoshòu 遭受, zāodào 遭到
to suffer [**heavy casualties** | **enormous economic losses**] = zāoshòu [yánzhòng shāngwáng | jùdà jīngjì sǔnshī] 遭受[严重伤亡 | 巨大经济损失]
• (*to feel pain*) = shòu (tòng)kǔ 受(痛)苦
to suffer from [**TB** | **heart failure** | **a cold**] = déle [fèijiéhé | xīnlì shuāijié | gǎnmào] 得了[肺结核 | 心力衰竭 | 感冒]

sugar *noun*
= táng 糖

suggestion *noun*
a suggestion = yìtiáo jiànyì 一条建议

suicide *noun*
to commit suicide = zìshā 自杀

suit
1 *noun*
a suit (*a man's*) = yítào nánshì xīfú 一套男式西服
(*a woman's*) = yítào nǚshì xīfú 一套女式西服
2 *verb*
• (*to be convenient, to fit*) = héshì 合适, shìhé 适合
to suit someone = duì mǒurén héshì 对某人合适
does Friday suit you? = xīngqīwǔ duì nǐ héshì ma? 星期五对你合适吗?
the hat suits you = zhèdǐng màozi nǐ dài hěn shìhé 这顶帽子你戴很适合

suitable *adjective*
= héshì 合适, shìyí 适宜
a suitable present = yíge héshì de lǐwù 一个合适的礼物
these books are suitable for children = zhèxiē shū shìyí értóng kàn 这些书适宜儿童看

suitcase *noun*
a suitcase = yíge shǒutíxiāng 一个手提箱

sum *noun*
• **a sum of money** = yìbǐ qián 一笔钱
• (*a problem in arithmetic*)
a sum = yídào suànshùtí 一道算术题
to be good at sums = suànshù hěn hǎo 算术很好
sum up = zǒngjié 总结, gàikuò 概括

summer *noun*
= xiàtiān 夏天, xiàjì 夏季

summer holiday (*British English*), **summer vacation** (*US English*) *noun*
= shǔjià 暑假

sun *noun*
• **the sun** = tàiyáng 太阳
• (*sunshine*) = yángguāng 阳光
to sit in the sun = zuò zài yángguāng xia 坐在阳光下

sunbathe *verb*
= jìnxíng rìguāngyù 进行日光浴, shài tàiyáng 晒太阳

sunburn *noun*
= shàishāng 晒伤

sunburned *adjective*
she got sunburned = tā shàishāng le 她晒伤了

Sunday *noun* ▶ 218
= xīngqīrì 星期日, xīngqītiān 星期天, lǐbàitiān 礼拜天

sunglasses *noun*
= tàiyángjìng 太阳镜, mòjìng 墨镜

sunny *adjective*
= qínglǎng 晴朗, yángguāng míngmèi 阳光明媚
a sunny day = yíge qíngtiān 一个晴天

sunset *noun*
= rìluò 日落

sunshade *noun*
a sunshade = yìbǎ yángsǎn 一把阳伞

sunshine *noun*
= yángguāng 阳光

suntan *noun*
= shàihēi 晒黑
you've got a suntan = nǐ shàihēi le 你晒黑了

suntan oil *noun*
a suntan oil = yìzhǒng fángshàiyóu 一种防晒油

supermarket *noun*
a supermarket = yìjiā chāojí shìchǎng 一家超级市场, yìjiā chāoshì 一家超市

supper *noun*
a supper = yídùn wǎnfàn 一顿晚饭, yídùn wǎncān 一顿晚餐

support *verb*
- (*to agree with, to help*) = zhīchí 支持, zhīyuán 支援
  to support the strike = zhīchí bàgōng 支持罢工
- (*to keep*)
  to support a family = yǎng jiā 养家
  to support oneself = yǎnghuó zìjǐ 养活自己
- (*to hold up or bear the weight of*) = zhīchēng 支撑
  what are we going to use to support the roof? = wǒmen yòng shénme lái zhīchēng wūdǐng? 我们用什么来支撑屋顶?

supporter *noun*
a supporter (*of a team, a party*) = yíge zhīchízhě 一个支持者
(*one who supports a view, a policy*) = yíge yōnghùzhě 一个拥护者

suppose *verb*
- (*to posit a hypothetical situation*) = jiǎdìng 假定, jiǎrú 假如
  suppose you can't come, please give us a call = jiǎdìng nǐ bù néng lái, qǐng gěi wǒmen dǎ ge diànhuà 假定你不能来, 请给我们打个电话
- (*to incline to believe, guess*) = xiǎng 想, cāixiǎng 猜想

> **!** *Note that while in English the verb* suppose *is negated in the main clause, the negation is shifted to the subordinate clause in Chinese.*

  I don't suppose you know yet? = wǒ xiǎng nǐ hái bù zhīdào ba? 我想你还不知道吧?
- (*to be meant to*)
  to be supposed to = yīnggāi 应该, yīngdāng 应当
  I'm supposed to arrive there at 10 = wǒ yīnggāi shí diǎn dào nàr 我应该十点到那儿

sure *adjective*
- (*certain*) = gǎn kěndìng 敢肯定, yǒu bǎwò 有把握
  I'm sure he said nine o'clock = wǒ gǎn kěndìng tā shuō de shì jiǔ diǎn 我敢肯定他说的是九点
  are you sure? = nǐ yǒu bǎwò ma? 你有把握吗?
  she is not sure if she can come = tā bù gǎn kěndìng tā néng lái 她不敢肯定她能来
- (*bound*) = yídìng huì 一定会, kěndìng huì 肯定会
  he is sure to win = tā yídìng huì yíng 他一定会赢
- **sure of oneself** = yǒu xìnxīn 有信心
  she's sure of herself = tā hěn yǒu xìnxīn 她很有信心
- **to make sure that...** = yídìng yào... 一定要..., bǎozhèng... 保证...
  to make sure that the door is closed = yídìng yào bǎ mén guānhǎo 一定要把门关好

surf *verb* ▶ 390
to go surfing = qù chōnglàng 去冲浪

surface
1 *noun*
a surface = yíge biǎomiàn 一个表面
2 *verb*
- (*to rise to the surface of the water*) = lùchū shuǐmiàn 露出水面

surfboard *noun*
a surfboard = yíge chōnglàngbǎn 一个冲浪板

surgeon *noun* ▶ 344
a surgeon = yíge wàikē yīshēng 一个外科医生

surgery *noun*
- **to have surgery** = zuò/dòng shǒushù 做/动手术, kāidāo 开刀
- (*British English*) (*the place*)
  a surgery = yíge zhěnsuǒ 一个诊所

surname *noun*
a surname = yíge xìng 一个姓

surprise
1 *noun*
- **a surprise** (*an event*) = yíjiàn yìxiǎng bú dào de shìqing 一件意想不到的事情
  (*a gift*) = yíge yìxiǎng bú dào de lǐwù 一个意想不到的礼物

(*an item of news*) = yìtiáo yìxiǎng bú dào de xiāoxi 一条意想不到的消息

> ! *Note that when* **a surprise** *is translated into Chinese, it is often necessary to categorize the thing that is surprising by using an appropriate noun, and to modify it by* **yìxiǎng bú dào de 意想不到的**, *which means* **unexpected** *or* **surprising**.

- (*the state of being amazed*) = jīngqí 惊奇, jīngyà 惊讶
  to take someone by surprise = shǐ mǒurén hěn jīngqí 使某人很惊奇
  to someone's surprise = shǐ mǒurén jīngyà de shì 使某人惊讶的是
  he looked up in surprise = tā jīngqí de táiqǐ tóu lai 他惊奇地抬起头来

2 *verb*
to surprise someone = shǐ mǒurén jīngqí 使某人惊奇, shǐ mǒurén jīngyà 使某人惊讶

surprised *adjective*
= gǎndào chījīng 感到吃惊, gǎndào yìwài 感到意外
I'm not surprised = wǒ bù gǎndào chījīng 我不感到吃惊
to be surprised at something = duì mǒushì gǎndào chījīng 对某事感到吃惊
I'm surprised that he didn't come = tā méi lái, wǒ gǎndào hěn yìwài 他没来, 我感到很意外

surrender *verb*
- (*to give oneself up to the police, the authorities, etc.*) = zìshǒu 自首
- (*to give up in a fight, battle, or war*) = tóuxiáng 投降
- (*to give something up to an enemy, the police, etc.*) = jiāochū 交出
- (*to give something up as a result of pressure or necessity*) = fàngqì 放弃

surround *verb*
= wéi 围, bāowéi 包围
the police surrounded the house = jǐngchá bāowéile nàzuò fángzi 警察包围了那座房子
the house is surrounded by trees = fángzi zhōuwéi dōu shì shù 房子周围都是树

surroundings *noun*
= zhōuwéi 周围, huánjìng 环境

survey *noun*
a survey = yíxiàng diàochá 一项调查

survive *verb*
= xìngmiǎn yú 幸免于, huóxialai 活下来
to survive an accident = xìngmiǎn yú yìchǎng shìgù 幸免于一场事故
to survive the winter = huóguò dōngtiān 活过冬天

suspect
1 *verb*
- (*to imagine that someone is guilty of*) = huáiyí 怀疑
  she's suspected of stealing money = rénmen huáiyí tā tōu qián 人们怀疑她偷钱
- (*to be inclined to believe*) = cāixiǎng 猜想, rènwéi 认为
  I suspect that this may be true = wǒ cāixiǎng zhè kěnéng shì zhēn de 我猜想这可能是真的

2 *noun*
a suspect = yíge xiányífàn 一个嫌疑犯, yíge kěyí fènzǐ 一个可疑分子

suspicious *adjective*
- (*inclined to suspect*) = huáiyí 怀疑, cāiyí 猜疑
  to be suspicious of someone = huáiyí mǒurén 怀疑某人
- (*giving ground for suspicion*) = kěyí 可疑

swan *noun*
a swan = yìzhī tiān'é 一只天鹅

swap *verb*
= jiāohuàn 交换, jiāoliú 交流

sweat *verb*
= chūhàn 出汗

sweater *noun* (*US English*)
a sweater (*usually woolen*) = yíjiàn máoyī 一件毛衣
(*worn before or after physical exercise*) = yíjiàn yùndòngyī 一件运动衣

sweatshirt *noun*
a sweatshirt = yíjiàn yùndòngshān 一件运动衫, yíjiàn xiūxiánshān 一件休闲衫

Sweden *noun*
= Ruìdiǎn 瑞典

Swedish ▶ **288**
1 *adjective*
= Ruìdiǎn de 瑞典的
2 *noun*
(*the people*) = Ruìdiǎnrén 瑞典人
(*the language*) = Ruìdiǎnyǔ 瑞典语

sweep *verb*
= sǎo 扫, dǎsǎo 打扫

sweet
1 *adjective*
- (*tasting of sugar*) = tián 甜, tiánwèi de 甜味的
  the wine is too sweet = zhè jiǔ tài tián le 这酒太甜了
  to have a sweet tooth = xǐhuan chī tián shí 喜欢吃甜食
- (*fragrant*) = fāngxiāng 芳香
- (*kind, gentle*) = qīnqiè 亲切, hé'ǎi 和蔼
  to be sweet to someone = duì mǒurén qīnqiè 对某人亲切
- (*cute*) = kě'ài 可爱

2 *noun* (*British English*)
a sweet = yíkuài táng 一块糖

swim
1 *verb*
- (*to propel oneself in water*) = yóuyǒng 游泳
- (*to travel by propelling oneself in water*) = yóu 游
  to swim across the lake = yóuguò hú qù 游过湖去

2 *noun*
a swim = yóuyǒng 游泳
to go for a swim = qù yóuyǒng 去游泳

swimming *noun* ▶ **390**
= yóuyǒng 游泳

swimming pool *noun*
a swimming pool = yíge yóuyǒngchí 一个游泳池

swimsuit *noun*
a swimsuit = yíjiàn yóuyǒngyī 一件游泳衣

swing
1 *verb*
- (*to move back and forth*) = bǎidòng 摆动, yáobǎi 摇摆
  to swing on a gate = zài mén shang bǎidòng 在门上摆动
- (*to move something back and forth*) = bǎidòng 摆动, huàngdòng 晃动
  to swing one's legs = huàngdòng tuǐ 晃动腿

2 *noun*
a swing (*for children*) = yíge qiūqiān 一个秋千

Swiss ▶ **288**
1 *adjective*
= Ruìshì de 瑞士的
2 *noun*
the Swiss = Ruìshìrén 瑞士人

switch
1 *noun*
a switch = yíge kāiguān 一个开关
2 *verb*
= (zhuǎn)huàn (转)换, gǎibiàn 改变
to switch seats = huàn zuòwèi 换座位
to switch from English to Chinese = cóng Yīngyǔ huànchéng yòng Hànyǔ 从英语换成用汉语
switch off = guān 关
to switch off the light = guān dēng 关灯
switch on = dǎkāi 打开
to switch the radio on = dǎkāi shōuyīnjī 打开收音机

Switzerland *noun*
= Ruìshì 瑞士

sympathetic *adjective*
(*showing pity*) = tóngqíng 同情
(*showing understanding*) = zànchéng 赞成, yǒu tónggǎn 有同感

syringe *noun*
a syringe = yíge zhùshèqì 一个注射器

system *noun*
- (*a complex whole, an organization*)
  a system = yíge tǐxì 一个体系, yíge xìtǒng 一个系统
- (*of a society or a political organization*)
  a system = yíge zhìdù 一个制度, yíge tǐzhì 一个体制
  a democratic system = yíge mínzhǔ zhìdù 一个民主制度
- (*a method*)
  a system = yítào fāngfǎ 一套方法

Tt

table *noun*
a table = yìzhāng zhuōzi 一张桌子

tablet *noun*
(*when talking about medicine*)
a tablet = yípiàn yào 一片药

table tennis *noun* ▶ 390
table tennis = pīngpāngqiú 乒乓球

tail *noun*
a tail (*of an animal*) = yíge wěiba 一个尾巴
(*of other things*) = yíge wěibù 一个尾部

Taiwan *noun*
= Táiwān 台湾

take *verb*

> **!** *See the usage note on* Talking about time ▶ 412 *for more information and examples.*

- (*to take hold of in the hand*) = ná 拿
  let me take your raincoat = wó gěi nǐ názhe yǔyī 我给你拿着雨衣
- (*to take hold of in one's arms*) = bào 抱
  I took the baby in my arms = wǒ bǎ yīng'ér bào zài huái li 我把婴儿抱在怀里
- (*to take someone by the hand*) = lā 拉
  she took me by the hand = tā lāzhe wǒde shǒu 她拉着我的手
- (*to carry*) = dài 带
  I took my umbrella = wǒ dàizhe yǔsǎn 我带着雨伞
  I'll take the letters to her = wǒ gěi tā dàiqu zhèxiē xìn 我给她带去这些信
- (*to accompany, lead, guide*) = lǐng 领, dài(lǐng) 带(领)
  to take the children for a walk = lǐng háizi qù sànbù 领孩子去散步
  to take someone home = dài mǒurén huí jiā 带某人回家
- (*to cause to go*) = názǒu 拿走
  who's taken my dictionary? = shéi názǒule wǒde cídiǎn? 谁拿走了我的词典?
- (*to remove*)
  to take a book off the shelf = cóng shūjià shang náxia yìběn shū 从书架上拿下一本书
- (*to steal*) = tōu 偷
- (*to cope with, to bear*)
  (*in the negative*) = shòu bù liǎo 受不了
  he can't take the pain = tā shòu bù liǎo téng 他受不了疼
- (*when talking about what is necessary*) = xūyào 需要
  it takes [time | courage | patience...] = xūyào [shíjiān | yǒngqì | nàixīn...] 需要[时间 | 勇气 | 耐心...]
  it takes two hours to get to London = dào Lúndūn xūyào liǎngge xiǎoshí 到伦敦需要两个小时
  to take a long time to do one's homework = zuò zuòyè xūyào hěn cháng shíjiān 做作业需要很长时间
  it won't take long = bú yào hěn cháng shíjiān 不要很长时间
- (*to accept*) = jiēshòu 接受
  to take someone's advice = jiēshòu mǒurén de zhōnggào 接受某人的忠告
- (*to eat, to swallow*) = chī 吃
  to take medicine = chī yào 吃药
  I don't take sugar in my tea = wǒ hē chá bú fàng táng 我喝茶不放糖
- (*when talking about travelling*) = zuò 坐, chéng 乘
  to take [a taxi | the bus | the underground] = zuò [chūzūchē | gōnggòng qìchē | dìtiě] 坐[出租车 | 公共汽车 | 地铁]
- to take exams = kǎoshì 考试
- (*when talking about selecting courses*) = xué 学, xuéxí 学习
  to take [Chinese history | computer studies | driving lessons] = xué [Zhōngguó lìshǐ | jìsuànjī | kāi chē] 学[中国历史 | 计算机 | 开车]
- (*to wear*) = chuān 穿
  to take a size 10 = chuān shí hào de 穿十号的
- (*when used with various nouns*)
  to take [a bath | a rest | a walk | a photograph | a look] = [xǐ ge zǎo | xiūxi yíhuìr | sànbù | zhào zhāng xiàng | kàn yi kàn] [洗个澡 | 休息一会儿 | 散步 | 照张像 | 看一看]

take apart = chāikāi 拆开

take away
to take away the rubbish = bǎ lājī nòngzǒu 把垃圾弄走

the meeting took him away early = yīnwèi kāihuì tā děi zǎo yìdiǎnr líkāi 因为开会他得早一点离开
take back = náhuí 拿回
I had to take the dress back = wǒ bùdébù bǎ yīfu náhuíqu 我不得不把衣服拿回去
take down
- (*to remove*) = náxia 拿下, qǔxia 取下
to take the painting down = bǎ huà náxialai 把画拿下来
- (*to write down*) = jìxia 记下
I took down his address = wǒ jìxia tāde dìzhǐ 我记下他的地址
take hold of = názhe 拿着, zhuāzhe 抓着
take off
- (*from an airport*) = qǐfēi 起飞
- (*to remove*)
to take off one's [coat | shirt | skirt | trousers | shoes...] = tuōxia [wàiyī | chènshān | qúnzi | kùzi | xié...] 脱下[外衣 | 衬衫 | 裙子 | 裤子 | 鞋...]
to take off one's [hat | glasses | gloves | ring | necklace...] = zhāixia [màozi | yǎnjìng | shǒutào | jièzhi | xiàngliàn...] 摘下[帽子 | 眼镜 | 手套 | 戒指 | 项链...]
take out
- (*from a box, a pocket, a bag*) = náchū 拿出
he took a pen out of his pocket = tā cóng kǒudài li náchū yìzhī gāngbǐ 他从口袋里拿出一支钢笔
- (*from a bank account*) = qǔ 取, tí 提
to take money out = qǔ qián 取钱
- (*to release one's anger at*)
to take something out on someone = yīnwèi mǒushì xiàng mǒurén fāxiè 因为某事向某人发泄
take part = cānjiā 参加
to take part in a game = cānjiā yíxiàng bǐsài 参加一项比赛
take place
(*if it's an unexpected incident or accident*) = fāshēng 发生
(*if it's an organized event*) = jǔxíng 举行
take up
- (*as a hobby*) = kāishǐ (cóngshì) 开始(从事)
to take up sailing = kāishǐ fānchuán yùndòng 开始帆船运动
- (*to use up*) = zhàn 占
to take up space = zhàn kōngjiān 占空间

talented *adjective*
= yǒu cáinéng de 有才能的, yǒu cáihuá de 有才华的

talk
1 *verb*
- (*to speak*) = jiǎnghuà 讲话, tánhuà 谈话
to talk in Chinese = yòng Hànyǔ jiǎnghuà 用汉语讲话
to talk to someone = hé mǒurén jiǎnghuà 和某人讲话
I talked to them about the trip = wǒ gēn tāmen tánle zhècì lǚxíng de qíngkuàng 我跟他们谈了这次旅行的情况
they were talking about you = tāmen zài tánlùn nǐ 他们在谈论你
to talk on the phone = dǎ diànhuà 打电话
- (*to speak at a meeting or a conference*) = yǎnjiǎng 演讲, jiǎnghuà 讲话
he is going to talk to the students and teachers at Peking University = tā yào zài Běijīng Dàxué xiàng shīshēngmen yǎnjiǎng 他要在北京大学向师生们演讲
- (*to chat*) = xiánliáo 闲聊

2 *noun*
- (*a conversation*)
a talk = yícì tánhuà 一次谈话, yícì jiāotán 一次交谈
- (*a lecture*)
a talk (*in class*) = yícì jiǎngzuò 一次讲座
(*to a club, a group, a meeting*) = yígè bàogào 一个报告, yícì yǎnjiǎng 一次演讲
- (*discussions*) = huìtán 会谈
the two leaders had friendly talks yesterday = liǎngwèi lǐngdǎorén zuótiān jìnxíngle yǒuhǎo de huìtán 两位领导人昨天进行了友好的会谈

talkative *adjective*
= jiàntán 健谈, xǐhuan jiǎnghuà 喜欢讲话

tall *adjective* ▶ 300 = gāo 高
to be six feet tall = liù yīngchǐ gāo 六英尺高

tan *noun*
a tan = rìshàihòu de fūsè 日晒后的肤色

T

to get a tan = shài de hēihēi de 晒得黑黑的

tanned *adjective*
= shàihēi le 晒黑了

tap
1 *noun* (*British English*)
a tap = yíge shuǐlóng(tóu) 一个水龙(头)
to turn the tap off = bǎ shuǐlóng(tóu) guānshang 把水龙(头)关上
2 *verb*
to tap on the door = qiāo mén 敲门

tape
1 *noun*
• **a tape** (*for a tape recorder*) = yìpán lùyīndài 一盘录音带
(*for a video*) = yìpán lùxiàngdài 一盘录像带
• (*for sticking*)
= jiāodài 胶带
2 *verb*
(*to record*)
= bǎ...lùxiàlai 把 ... 录下来
she's taped that film = tā bǎ nàbù diànyǐng lùxiàlai le 她把那部电影录下来了

tape recorder *noun*
a tape recorder = yìtái lùyīnjī 一台录音机

target *noun*
a target (*in shooting*) = yíge bǎzi 一个靶子
(*what is aimed at*) = yíge mùbiāo 一个目标
(*an object of criticism*) = yíge duìxiàng 一个对象

tart *noun* (*British English*)
a tart = yíge xiànrbǐng 一个馅儿饼
an apple tart = yíge píngguǒ xiànrbǐng 一个苹果馅儿饼

task *noun*
a task = yíge rènwù 一个任务, yíxiàng gōngzuò 一项工作

taste
1 *noun*
• (*when eating, drinking*)
a taste = yìzhǒng wèidào 一种味道, yìzhǒng zīwèi 一种滋味
• (*power of discerning and judging*)
taste = jiànshǎng (néng)lì 鉴赏(能)力
she has good taste = tā jùyǒu liánghǎo de jiànshǎng nénglì 她具有良好的鉴赏能力
2 *verb*
• (*when describing a flavour*) = chángqilai 尝起来, chīqilai 吃起来
to taste good = chángqilai wèidào hěn hǎo 尝起来味道很好
to taste awful = chángqilai wèidào hěn zāogāo 尝起来味道很糟糕
it tastes like cabbage = chīqilai wèidào xiàng juǎnxīncài 吃起来味道像卷心菜
• (*when eating, drinking*) = cháng 尝, pǐncháng 品尝

tax *noun*
= shuì 税

taxi *noun*
a taxi = yíliàng chūzūchē 一辆出租车

taxi rank (*British English*), **taxi stand** (*US English*) *noun*
a taxi rank = yíge chūzū qìchēzhàn 一个出租汽车站

tea *noun*
• (*the product*)
tea = chá 茶
• **a cup of tea** = yì bēi chá 一杯茶
• (*British English*) (*a meal*) = fàn 饭, chádiǎn 茶点

teach *verb*
• (*to train, educate, or impart knowledge*) = jiāo 教
to teach someone [**to read** | **to drive** | **to ride a horse**] = jiāo mǒurén [niàn shū | kāi chē | qí mǎ] 教某人 [念书 | 开车 | 骑马]
to teach Chinese to adults = jiāo chéngrén Zhōngwén 教成人中文
• (*to work as a teacher*) = jiāoshū 教书, jiàoxué 教学
where does she teach? = tā zài nǎr jiāoshū? 她在哪儿教书?

teacher *noun* ▶ 344
a teacher = yìmíng jiàoshī 一名教师, yíwèi lǎoshī 一位老师

team *noun*
a team = yíge duì 一个队
a football team = yìzhī zúqiúduì 一支足球队

teapot *noun*
a teapot = yíge cháhú 一个茶壶

tear[1] *verb*
• (*to pull apart, to rend*) = sī 撕, chě 扯
to tear a page out of a book = cóng shū shang sīxia yíyè zhǐ 从书上撕下一页纸

- (*to become torn*) = sīpò 撕破, chěpò 扯破
  this kind of paper tears easily = zhèzhǒng zhǐ hěn róngyì sīpò 这种纸很容易撕破
  tear off
  (*to remove by tearing*) = chědiào 扯掉
  (*to depart hurriedly*) = xùnsù zǒudiào 迅速走掉, pǎodiào 跑掉
  tear up
  to tear up a letter = bǎ yìfēng xìn sī de fěnsuì 把一封信撕得粉碎
  the wind tore up many houses = dà fēng cuīhuǐle hěn duō fángzi 大风摧毁了很多房子

tear² *noun*
  a tear = yìdī yǎnlèi 一滴眼泪
  to burst into tears = dàkūqilai 大哭起来

tease *verb*
  = dòunòng 逗弄, xìnòng 戏弄

teaspoon *noun*
  a teaspoon = yìbǎ cháchí 一把茶匙

technical *adjective*
  = jìshù de 技术的, zhuānyèxìng de 专业性的

teenager *noun*
  a teenager = yígè shíjǐ suì de háizi 一个十几岁的孩子

telephone *noun*
  a telephone = yíbù diànhuà 一部电话

telephone directory *noun*
  a telephone directory = yìběn diànhuàbù 一本电话簿

telescope *noun*
  a telescope = yíjià wàngyuǎnjìng 一架望远镜

television *noun*
  a television = yìtái diànshìjī 一台电视机
  I saw the film on television = wǒ shì zài diànshì shang kàn de zhèbù diànyǐng 我是在电视上看的这部电影

tell *verb*
- (*to say to*) = gàosu 告诉
  did you tell your parents? = nǐ gàosu nǐ fùmǔ le ma? 你告诉你父母了吗?
  to tell someone about a problem = gàosu mǒurén yíge wèntí 告诉某人一个问题
  don't tell anyone = bié gàosu biéren 别告诉别人
- (*for telling a story, a joke*) = jiǎng 讲
  to tell jokes = jiǎng xiàohua 讲笑话
- (*for telling a lie, a joke*) = shuō 说
  to tell a lie = shuōhuǎng 说谎
- (*when giving orders or instructions*) = ràng 让, jiào 叫, mìnglìng 命令
  to tell someone to leave the classroom = ràng mǒurén líkāi jiàoshì 让某人离开教室
  to tell someone not to smoke = jiào mǒurén búyào chōu yān 叫某人不要抽烟
- (*to work out, to know*) = kànchū 看出, zhīdào 知道, duàndìng 断定
  I can tell (that) she's disappointed = wǒ néng kànchulai tā hěn shīwàng 我能看出来她很失望
  you can tell he's lying = nǐ néng zhīdao tā zài shuōhuǎng 你能知道他在说谎
- (*when making distinctions*) = fēnbiàn 分辨, biànbié 辨别
  to tell him from his twin brother = fēnbiàn tā hé tāde luánshēng xiōngdì 分辨他和他的孪生兄弟
  I can't tell which is which = wǒ biànbié bù chū nǎge shì nǎge 我辨别不出哪个是哪个
  tell off
  to tell someone off = zébèi mǒurén 责备某人

temper *noun*
- (*temperament, disposition*) = píqì 脾气
  she has a rather bad temper = tā píqì hěn huài 她脾气很坏
  to lose one's temper = fā píqì 发脾气
- (*mood*) = xīnqíng 心情
  to be in a good temper = xīnqíng hǎo 心情好

temperature *noun*
- (*of the body*) ▶ 277 = tǐwēn 体温
  to have a temperature = fāshāo 发烧
- (*degree of heat or cold*) = wēndù 温度
- (*about the weather*) = qìwēn 气温

temple *noun*
  a temple = yízuò (sì)miào 一座(寺)庙

temporary *adjective*
  = línshí 临时, zànshí 暂时

T

ten *number* ▶ **170**, ▶ **204**
= shí 十

tennis *noun* ▶ **390**
= wǎngqiú 网球

tense *adjective*
= jǐnzhāng 紧张

tent *noun*
a tent = yìdǐng zhàngpeng 一顶帐篷

tenth *number*
- (*in a series*) = dìshí 第十
- (*in dates*) ▶ **218** = shí rì 十日, shí hào 十号

  the tenth of October = shíyuè shí hào 十月十号

term *noun*
- **a term** (*in schools or universities*) = yíge xuéqī 一个学期

  (*of office or appointment*) = yíge rènqī 一个任期
- (*a word or expression*) = shùyǔ 术语, cíyǔ 词语

  a term = yíge shùyǔ 一个术语
- (*conditions*)

  term = tiáojiàn 条件

terrible *adjective*
- (*expressing shock*) = kěpà 可怕, xiàrén 吓人
- (*used for emphasis*) = jídù 极度, lìhài 厉害
- (*awful,very bad*) = zāogāo 糟糕

terrified *adjective*
= hàipà 害怕, xià de yàomìng 吓得要命

terror *noun*
terror = kǒngbù 恐怖, kǒngjù 恐惧

terrorist *noun*
a terrorist = yìmíng kǒngbù fènzǐ 一名恐怖分子

test

1 *verb*
- (*to put to the proof*) = jiǎnyàn 检验
- (*to try out*) = shìyàn 试验
- (*in exams*) = cèyàn 测验

2 *noun*
- **a test** (*means of trial*) = yícì shìyàn 一次试验

  (*in school, college*) = yícì cèyàn 一次测验

  (*written*) = yícì bǐshì 一次笔试

  (*oral*) = yícì kǒushì 一次口试

  a driving test = yícì jiàshǐ kǎoshì 一次驾驶考试
- **to have an eye test** = zuò yícì yǎnjīng jiǎnchá 做一次眼睛检查

text

1 *noun*
a text (message) = yìtiáo duǎnxìn 一条短信

2 *verb*
= fā duǎnxìn 发短信

than

1 *preposition*
- (*in comparisons*) = bǐ 比

  to be [more intelligent | faster...] **than someone** = bǐ mǒurén [cōngming | kuài...] 比某人[聪明 | 快...]

  I've got more money than you = wǒde qián bǐ nǐde duō 我的钱比你的多
- (*when talking about quantities*) ▶ **349**

  more than = yǐshàng 以上

  more than half of the pupils are absent = yíbàn yǐshàng de xuésheng méi lái 一半以上的学生没来

  less than = bú dào 不到

  it's worth less than £100 = tāde jiàzhí búdào yìbǎi yīngbàng 它的价值不到一百英镑

2 *conjunction*
= bǐ 比

he's older than I am = tā bǐ wǒ dà 他比我大

thank *verb*
= xièxie 谢谢, gǎnxiè 感谢

thanks

1 *adverb*
= gǎnxiè 感谢, gǎnjī 感激

many thanks, thanks a lot = duōxiè 多谢

2 thanks to = xìngkuī 幸亏, yóuyú 由于

thank you *adverb*
= xièxie 谢谢, xièxie nín 谢谢您

thank you for coming = xièxie nín guānglín 谢谢您光临

'more wine?'—'thank you' = 'zài jiā diǎnr jiǔ ma?'—'xièxie, qǐng zài jiā diǎnr' '再加点儿酒吗?'—'谢谢,请再加点儿'

that

> **!** *Note that as a determiner or a pronoun,* **that** *is often translated as* **nàge 那个**, *where* **ge 个** *is a measure word and varies with the noun that follows or with the noun to which it refers.*

1 *determiner* = nà 那, nàge 那个

at that time = nà shíhou 那时候

who is that person? = nàge rén shì shéi? 那个人是谁?

I don't like that novel = wǒ bù xǐhuan nàběn xiǎoshuō 我不喜欢那本小说

2 *pronoun*

• = nà 那, nàge 那个

> ❗ *Note that sometimes* **that** *is specified as a person or as a thing; in the former case,* **that** *is translated as* **nàge rén 那个人**, *and in the latter,* **nàge dōngxi 那个东西**.

what's that? = nà(ge dōngxi) shì shénme? 那(个东西)是什么?

who's that? = nà(ge rén) shì shéi 那(个人)是谁?

who put that on the table? = shéi bǎ nàge fàng zài zhuōzi shang? 谁把那个放在桌子上?

is that Tom? = shì Tāngmǔ ma? 是汤姆吗?

• (*when used as a relative pronoun*)

> ❗ *Note that when used as a relative pronoun,* **that** *is not translated.*

the girl that I met is his sister = wǒ jiàndào de nàge gūniang shì tā mèimei 我见到的那个姑娘是他妹妹

do you know the person that I was talking to just now? = nǐ rènshí wǒ gāngcái gēn tā jiǎnghuà de nàge rén ma? 你认识我刚才跟他讲话的那个人吗?

3 *conjunction*

> ❗ *Note that when used as a conjunction,* **that** *is usually not translated.*

she said that she would come = tā shuō tā huì lái 她说她会来

4 *adverb*

= nàme 那么, nàyàng 那样

the question is not that difficult = zhège wèntí méiyǒu nàme nán 这个问题没有那么难

the *determiner*

• (*when referring to a person or thing mentioned here or previously*) = zhè 这, nà 那

the student you want to meet is not here today = nǐ yào jiàn de nàge xuésheng jīntiān bú zài 你要见的那个学生今天不在

if you like the book, I can lend it to you = yàoshì nǐ xǐhuan zhèběn shū, wǒ kěyǐ jiègěi nǐ 要是你喜欢这本书, 我可以借给你

• (*when referring to something understood, something unique*)

> ❗ *Note that in this sense,* **the** *is not translated.*

please switch off [the radio | the TV | the light...] = qǐng bǎ [shōuyīnjī | diànshìjī | dēng...] guānshang 请把 [收音机 | 电视机 | 灯...] 关上

the sun has come out = tàiyáng chūlai le 太阳出来了

• (*when referring to a particular type, class, or group of people or objects*)

> ❗ *Note that in this sense,* **the** *is not translated.*

the Japanese like to eat raw fish = Rìběnrén xǐhuan chī shēng yú 日本人喜欢吃生鱼

the rich should help the poor = fùrén yīnggāi bāngzhù qióngrén 富人应该帮助穷人

the horse is a useful animal = mǎ shì yǒuyòng de dòngwù 马是有用的动物

• (*when used with the comparative or superlative*)

> ❗ *Note that in this sense,* **the** *is not translated.*

you've made it all the worse = nǐ bǎ tā gǎo de gèng zāole 你把它搞得更糟了

she's the most hardworking student in the class = tā shì bān li zuì nǔlì de xuésheng 她是班里最努力的学生

theatre (*British English*), **theater** (*US English*) *noun*

a theatre (*a place where plays are performed*) = yíge jùyuàn 一个剧院, yíge xìyuàn 一个戏院

(*a surgical operating room*) = yíge shǒushùshì 一个手术室

a lecture theatre = yíge jiētī jiàoshì 一个阶梯教室

their *determiner*

• (*for men, or men and women together*) = tāmende 他们的

T

I don't like their house = wǒ bù xǐhuan tāmende fángzi 我不喜欢他们的房子
- (*for women*) = tāmende 她们的
- (*for non-human and inanimate beings*) = tāmende 它们的

theirs *pronoun*
- (*for men, or men and women together*) = tāmende 他们的

which car is theirs? = nǎliàng chē shì tāmende? 哪辆车是他们的?
- (*for women*) = tāmende 她们的
- (*for non-human and inanimate beings*) = tāmende 它们的

them *pronoun*
- (*for men, or men and women together*) = tāmen 他们

I don't know them = wǒ bú rènshi tāmen 我不认识他们
- (*for women*) = tāmen 她们
- (*for non-human and inanimate beings*) = tāmen 它们

> ! *Note that in this sense,* **them** *is usually not translated if it is an object following a verb.*

please put them on the table = qǐng fàng zài zhuōzi shang 请放在桌子上
when you finish reading these magazines, please remember to return them = nǐ kànwán zhèxiē zázhì, qǐng jìzhù huánhuilai 你看完这些杂志, 请记住还回来
I bought two gifts for my parents and they like them very much = wǒ gěi wǒ fùmǔ mǎile liǎngjiàn lǐwù, tāmen hěn xǐhuan 我给我父母买了两件礼物, 他们很喜欢

themselves *pronoun*
- (*when used as a reflexive pronoun*)

themselves (*for men, or men and women together*) = (tāmen)zìjǐ (他们)自己
they didn't hurt themselves = tāmen méiyǒu shāngzhe zìjǐ 他们没有伤着自己
(*for women*) = (tāmen)zìjǐ (她们)自己
- (*for emphasis*) = zìjǐ 自己, qīnzì 亲自

they said it themselves = tāmen zìjǐ shuōde 他们自己说的
they didn't attend the meeting themselves = tāmen méiyǒu qīnzì cānjiā huì 他们没有亲自参加会

then *adverb*
- (*at that point in time*) = nàshí 那时, dāngshí 当时

I was living in Taiwan then = dāngshí wǒ zhù zài Táiwān 当时我住在台湾
from then on = cóng nàshí qǐ 从那时起
- (*after, next*) = ránhòu 然后, jiēzhe 接着

I went to Beijing and then to Shanghai = wǒ qùle Běijīng, ránhòu yòu qùle Shànghǎi 我去了北京, 然后又去了上海

there
1 *pronoun*
- (*when followed by the verb* **to be**) = yǒu 有

> ! *Note that the negative from of* yǒu 有 *is* méi yǒu 没有.

there is a problem = yǒu yíge wèntí 有一个问题
there aren't any shops = méi yǒu rènhé shāngdiàn 没有任何商店
- (*when used with verbs like* **to exist**, **to appear**, *etc.*)

> ! *Note that in this case,* **there** *is not translated.*

there exist many problems = cúnzài hěn duō wèntí 存在很多问题
there appears some hope = chūxiànle yìxiē xīwàng 出现了一些希望

2 *adverb*
- (*when talking about location*) = nàr 那儿, nàlǐ 那里

who's there? = shéi zài nàr? 谁在那儿?
the train wasn't there = huǒchē bú zài nàlǐ 火车不在那里
when will we get there? = wǒmen shénme shíhou dào nàr? 我们什么时候到那儿?
they don't go there very often = tāmen bù chángcháng qù nàlǐ 他们不常常去那里
- (*when drawing attention*)

there's [the sea | my watch | your mother] = [dàhǎi | wǒde biǎo | nǐ māma] zài nàr [大海 | 我的表 | 你妈妈] 在那儿
there you are, there you go = gěi (nǐ) 给(你)

therefore *adverb*
= yīncǐ 因此, suǒyǐ 所以

these

1 *determiner*

= zhèxiē 这些

these books aren't mine = zhèxiē shū bú shì wǒde 这些书不是我的

2 *pronoun*

= zhèxiē 这些

these are your things = zhèxiē shì nǐde dōngxi 这些是你的东西

these are my friends = zhèxiē shì wǒde péngyou 这些是我的朋友

they *pronoun*

(*for men, or men and women together*) = tāmen 他们

they'll be there too = tāmen yě huì zài nàr 他们也会在那儿

(*for women*) = tāmen 她们

they're intelligent girls = tāmen shì hěn cōngming de gūniang 她们是很聪明的姑娘

(*for non-human and inanimate beings*) = tāmen 它们

thick *adjective*

- (*having a large distance between surfaces*) = hòu 厚
- (*great in diameter*) = cū 粗
- (*dense*) = mì 密, nóngmì 浓密
- (*when describing a liquid*) = chóu 稠, nóng 浓
- (*when describing smoke*) = nóng 浓

thief *noun*

a thief = yíge xiǎotōu 一个小偷

thigh *noun* ▶ 189

the thigh = dàtuǐ 大腿

thin *adjective*

- (*slim, lean*) = shòu 瘦
- (*having little distance between surfaces*) = báo 薄
- (*small in diameter*) = xì 细
- (*of little density*) = xīshǎo 稀少
- (*watery*) = xībó 稀薄

thing *noun*

- (*a material object*) **a thing** = yíge dōngxi 一个东西, yíjiàn dōngxi 一件东西

  what's the thing on the table? = zhuōzi shang de dōngxi shì shénme 桌子上的东西是什么?
- (*a matter, an affair*) **a thing** = yíjiàn shì(qing) 一件事(情)

  I've got things to do = wǒ yǒu shìqing yào zuò 我有事情要做
- (*belongings*) **things** = yòngpǐn 用品, sǒuyǒuwù 所有物

think *verb*

- (*when talking about opinions*) = rènwéi 认为, juéde 觉得

  what do you think of it? = nǐ rènwéi zhège zěnmeyàng? 你认为这个怎么样?

  I think it's unfair = wǒ juéde zhè bù gōngpíng 我觉得这不公平

  'will they come?'—'I don't think so' = 'tāmen huì lái ma?'—'wǒ rènwéi bú huì' '他们会来吗?'—'我认为不会'

  who do you think will win? = nǐ juéde shéi huì yíng? 你觉得谁会赢?
- (*to concentrate on an idea*) = xiǎng 想, kǎolǜ 考虑

  think hard before answering = xiǎnghǎo le zài huídá 想好了再回答
- (*to remember*) = xiǎngqǐ 想起

  I can't think of his name = wǒ xiǎng bù qǐ tāde míngzi 我想不起他的名字

  can you think of where we met him? = nǐ néng xiǎngqǐ wǒmen zài nǎr jiànguo tā ma? 你能想起我们在哪儿见过他吗?
- (*to have in mind*) = xiǎngdào 想到, xiǎngqǐ 想起

  I thought of you when I saw the address = wǒ kàndào zhège dìzhǐ jiù xiǎngdàole nǐ 我看到这个地址就想到了你
- (*to have vague plans to*) = dǎsuàn 打算, jìhuà 计划

  to be thinking of changing jobs = dǎsuàn huàn gōngzuò 打算换工作
- (*to solve by a process of thought*) = xiǎngchū 想出

  to think of a solution = xiǎngchū yíge jiějué bànfǎ 想出一个解决办法

  he couldn't think of a better idea = tā xiǎng bù chū yíge gèng hǎo de zhǔyì 他想不出一个更好的主意

> **!** *Note that when* bù 不 *is used to negate* xiǎngqǐ 想起, xiǎngdào 想到, *or* xiǎngchū 想出, bù 不 *comes between the verb* xiǎng 想 *and its complement as in* xiǎng bù qǐ 想不起, xiǎng bú dào 想不到 *and* xiǎng bù chū 想不出.

third

1 *adjective*

= dìsān 第三

T

2 *noun*
- (*in a series*)
  the third = dìsān 第三
- (*in dates*) ▶ **218**
  = sān hào 三号, sān rì 三日
  the third of June = liùyuè sān hào 六月三号
- (*when talking about quantities*) ▶ **349**
  a third of the population = sānfēn zhī yī de rénkǒu 三分之一的人口

3 *adverb*
= dìsān 第三
to come third in a race = zài bǐsài zhōng dé dìsān 在比赛中得第三

thirsty *adjective*
= kě 渴, kǒukě 口渴
I'm very thirsty = wǒ hěn kě 我很渴

thirteen *number* ▶ **170**, ▶ **204**
thirteen = shísān 十三

thirteenth *number*
- (*in a series*) = dìshísān 第十三
- (*in dates*) ▶ **218** = shísān hào 十三号, shísān rì 十三日
  Friday the thirteenth = shísān hào xīngqīwǔ 十三号星期五

thirty *number* ▶ **170**, ▶ **204**
thirty = sānshí 三十

this

> ! *Note that as a determiner or a pronoun,* **this** *is often translated as* **zhège 这个**, *where* **ge 个** *is a measure word that varies with the noun to which it refers.*

1 *determiner*
- = zhè 这, zhège 这个
  I like [this garden | this book | this shop...] = wǒ xǐhuan [zhège huāyuán | zhèběn shū | zhèjiā shāngdiàn...] 我喜欢[这个花园|这本书|这家商店...]
- (*when referring to today*) = jīntiān 今天
  this [morning | afternoon | evening] = jīntiān [shàngwǔ | xiàwǔ | wǎnshang] 今天[上午|下午|晚上]
  this year = jīnnián 今年

2 *pronoun*
= zhè 这, zhège 这个
what's this? = zhè shì shénme? 这是什么?
who's this? = zhè shì shéi? 这是谁?
this is the kitchen = zhè shì chúfáng 这是厨房

3 *adverb*
= zhème 这么, zhèyàng 这样
he is about this tall = tā chàbuduō yǒu zhème gāo 他差不多有这么高

thorn *noun*
a thorn = yìgēn cì 一根刺

those

1 *determiner*
those = nàxiē 那些
those books are yours = nàxiē shū shì nǐde 那些书是你的

2 *pronoun*
those = nàxiē 那些
what are those? = nàxiē shì shénme? 那些是什么?
those are my friends = nàxiē shì wǒde péngyou 那些是我的朋友

though *conjunction*
= suīrán 虽然, jǐnguǎn 尽管
though he can speak good Chinese, he can't write in Chinese = suīrán tā Hànyǔ shuō de hěn hǎo, dàn(shì) tā bú huì xiě Hànzì 虽然他汉语说得很好, 但(是)他不会写汉字

> ! *Note that in Chinese the use of* **suīrán 虽然** *or* **jǐnguǎn 尽管** *does not exclude the use of* **kěshì 可是** (= but) *or* **dànshì 但是** (= but).

thought *noun*
- **a thought** (*an idea*) = yìzhǒng xiǎngfǎ 一种想法
- (*a school of thought*) = yìzhǒng sīxiǎng 一种思想

thousand *number*
= qiān 千
one thousand, a thousand = yìqiān 一千
four thousand pounds = sìqiān yīngbàng 四千英镑

thread *noun*
a thread = yìgēn xiàn 一根线

threat *noun*
= wēixié 威胁, kǒngxià 恐吓

threaten *verb*
= wēixié 威胁, kǒngxià 恐吓

three *number* ▶ **170**, ▶ **204**
three = sān 三
three schools = sānsuǒ xuéxiào 三所学校

throat *noun* ▶ **189**
the throat = sǎngzi 嗓子, hóulóng 喉咙

through

> **!** *Often* through *occurs in combinations with verbs, for example:* go through, let through, read through, *etc. To find the correct translations for this type of verb, look up the separate dictionary entries at* go, let, read, *etc.*

preposition

- (*from one side to the other*) = chuānguò 穿过, tōngguò 通过
  to drive through the desert = kāi chē chuānguò shāmò 开车穿过沙漠
  to go through the town centre = chuānguò shì zhōngxīn 穿过市中心
  to look out through a window = tōngguò chuānghu xiàng wài kàn 通过窗户向外看
  to go through customs = tōngguò hǎiguān 通过海关
  to go through a red light = chuǎng hóng dēng 闯红灯
- (*from the beginning to the end*) = cóng tóu dào wěi 从头到尾
  he didn't read through all these letters = tā méiyǒu cóng tóu dào wěi kàn suǒyǒu de zhèxiē xìn 他没有从头到尾看所有的这些信
- (*by way of*) = tōngguò 通过
  I came to know her through a friend = wǒ tōngguò yíge péngyou rènshile tā 我通过一个朋友认识了她
  she found a new job through the newspaper = tā tōngguò bàozhǐ zhǎodàole yíge xīn gōngzuò 她通过报纸找到了一个新工作
- (*when talking about time*)
  right through the day = zhěngzhěng yì tiān 整整一天
  from Friday through to Sunday = cóng xīngqīwǔ dào xīngqīrì 从星期五到星期日
  open April through September (*US English*) = cóng sìyuè dào jiǔyuè kāifàng 从四月到九月开放

throw *verb*

- (*to fling, cast*) = rēng 扔
  to throw stones at someone = xiàng mǒurén rēng shítou 向某人扔石头
  throw me the ball = bǎ qiú rēng gěi wǒ 把球扔给我
  to throw a book to the floor = bǎ yìběn shū rēng zài dì shang 把一本书扔在地上
- (*to cause to fall*) = shuāidǎo
  to throw someone to the ground = bǎ mǒurén shuāidǎo zài dì shang 把某人摔倒在地上
  throw away, throw out = rēngdiào 扔掉

thumb *noun* ▶ **189**
  the thumb = dàmǔzhǐ 大拇指

thunder *noun*
  = léi 雷, léishēng 雷声

thunderstorm *noun*
  a thunderstorm = yìchǎng léibàoyǔ 一场雷暴雨

Thursday *noun* ▶ **218**
  Thursday = xīngqīsì 星期四, lǐbàisì 礼拜四

Tibet *noun*
  = Xīzàng 西藏

ticket *noun*
  a ticket = yìzhāng piào 一张票

tickle *verb*

- (*to itch*) = fāyǎng 发痒
- (*to cause to produce laughter*)
  to tickle someone = dòu mǒurén xiào 逗某人笑

tide *noun*
  the tide = cháo 潮, cháoshuǐ 潮水
  the tide is out = tuì cháo le 退潮了
  the tide is coming in = zhǎng cháo le 涨潮了

tidy *adjective*
  = zhěngjié 整洁, zhěngqí 整齐
  tidy up = zhěnglǐ 整理, shōushi 收拾

tie

1 *verb*

- (*to fasten, tether*) = shuān 拴
  to tie a dog to a tree = bǎ yìzhī gǒu shuān zài yìkē shù shang 把一只狗拴在一棵树上
- (*to bind*) = kǔn 捆, zā 扎
  to tie the parcel (up) with string = yòng shéngzi bǎ bāoguǒ kǔnqilai 用绳子把包裹捆起来
- (*to make a knot*) = jì 系
  to tie one's shoelaces = jì xiédài 系鞋带
  to tie one's tie = dǎ lǐngdài 打领带

2 *noun*

- (*worn with a shirt*)
  a tie = yìtiáo lǐngdài 一条领带
- (*in sport*)
  a tie = yíge píngjú 一个平局

Talking about time

For time by the clock ▶ **204**; for days of the week, months, and dates ▶ **218**.

How long?

Note that **for** is not translated when it introduces a phrase indicating a period of time:

***for** a week*	= yíge xīngqī 一个星期
***for** three years*	= sān nián 三年
***for** a long time*	= hěn cháng shíjiān 很长时间

A phrase that expresses a period of time and is introduced by **for** usually appears at the end of the clause in Chinese:

*I worked in a factory **for** a year*	= wǒ zài gōngchǎng gōngzuòle yì nián 我在工厂工作了一年
*she's been here **for** a week*	= tā zài zhèr dāile yíge xīngqī 她在这儿呆了一个星期
how long did you live in China?	= nǐ zài Zhōngguó zhùle duō cháng shíjiān? 你在中国住了多长时间?

Use **xūyào 需要** to express **take** in the present or future tense:

how long does it take?	= zhè xūyào duō cháng shíjiān? 这需要多长时间?
it'll take at least a year	= zhè zhìshǎo xūyào yì nián 这至少需要一年
it'll only take a minute	= zhè zhǐ xūyào yì fēn zhōng de shíjiān 这只需要一分钟的时间

Use **huāle 花了** or **yòngle 用了** for **take** when the event happened in the past, or started in the past and continues in the present:

it took me a week	= zhè huāle wǒ yíge xīngqī de shíjiān 这花了我一个星期的时间
how long has it taken them?	= tāmen huāle duō cháng shíjiān le? 他们花了多长时间了?
it only took him half an hour to finish his homework	= tā zhǐ yòngle bànge xiǎoshí jiù zuòwánle zuòyè 他只用了半个小时就做完了作业

When?

A phrase that indicates a point in time usually appears between the subject and the verb in Chinese:

***when** do you go to bed?*	= nǐ **shénme shíhou** shuìjiào? 你 **什么时候**睡觉?
*I usually go to bed **at 11***	= wǒ yìbān **shíyī diǎn** shuìjiào 我一般 **十一点** 睡觉
*are you going to Beijing **next week**?*	= nǐ **xiàge xīngqī** qù Běijīng ma? 你 **下个星期** 去北京吗?
*I came to know her **in 1991***	= wǒ **yījiǔjiǔyī nián** rènshile tā 我 **一九九一年** 认识了她

It is common to use **guò 过** to translate **in** when something is seen as happening in the future:

*I'll be there **in** an hour*	= wǒ **guò** yíge xiǎoshí dào nàr 我过一个小时到那儿

***in** three weeks' time*	= **guò** sānge xīngqī 过三个星期
when will you see him?	= nǐ shénme shíhou huì kànjiàn tā? 你什么时候会看见他?
***in** a few days*	= **guò** jǐ tiān 过几天
when did it happen?	= zhè shì shénme shíhou fāshēng de? 这是什么时候发生的?
a month ago	= yíge yuè yǐqián 一个月以前
a week ago yesterday	= cóng zuótiān suàn yíge xīngqī yǐqián 从昨天算一个星期以前
a month from tomorrow	= cóng míngtiān suàn zài guò yíge yuè 从明天算再过一个月
when you see him, tell him to call me	= nǐ kànjian tā de shíhou, ràng tā gěi wǒ dǎ ge diànhuà 你看见他的时候，让他给我打个电话

How often?

how often does it happen?	= zhèzhǒng shì duō cháng shíjiān fāshēng yícì? 这种事多长时间发生一次?
(it happens) every year	= (zhèzhǒng shì) měi nián dōu fāshēng (这种事)每年都发生
five times a day	= měi tiān wǔcì 每天五次
once every three months	= měi sānge yuè yícì 每三个月一次

How much an hour (etc.)?

how much do you get an hour?	= yíge xiǎoshí nǐ zhèng duōshǎo qián? 一个小时你挣多少钱?
I earn $20 an hour	= wǒ yíge xiǎoshí zhèng èrshí měiyuán 我一个小时挣二十美元
to pay by the hour	= àn xiǎoshí fù qián 按小时付钱
how much do you get a week?	= nǐ yíge xīngqī zhuàn duōshǎo qián? 你一个星期赚多少钱?
$3000 a month	= yíge yuè sānqiān měiyuán 一个月三千美元

---

tie up
- (*to parcel up*) = kǔnzā 捆扎
- (*to tether*) = shuān 拴

tiger *noun*
a tiger = yìzhī lǎohǔ 一只老虎

tight *adjective*
- (*firmly fixed*) = láogù 牢固, jǐn 紧
- (*taut, tense*) = lājǐn 拉紧, bēngjǐn 绷紧
- (*closely fitting*) = jǐn 紧
  are the shoes too tight for you? = zhèshuāng xié nǐ chuān tài jǐn le ma? 这双鞋你穿太紧了吗?
- (*air-tight, water-tight*) = mìfēng de 密封的

tights *noun*
= jǐnshēnkù 紧身裤

till[1] ▸ until

till[2] *noun*
a till = yíge fàng qián de chōuti 一个放钱的抽屉

timber *noun*
= mùcái 木材, mùliào 木料

time *noun*
- = shíjiān 时间
  I don't have time to go there = wǒ méi yǒu shíjiān qù nàr 我没有时间去那儿
  we haven't seen them for a long time = wǒmen hěn cháng shíjiān méiyǒu kànjian tāmen le 我们很长时间没有看见他们了

there is no time for you to argue = méi yǒu shíjiān ràng nǐmen zhēnglùn 没有时间让你们争论
a long time ago = hěn jiǔ yǐqián 很久以前
- (*when talking about a specific hour or period of time*)

what's the time? what time is it? = jǐ diǎn le? 几点了?
what time does the film start? = diànyǐng jǐ diǎn kāiyǎn? 电影几点开演? diànyǐng shénme shíhou kāiyǎn? 电影什么时候开演?
on time = ànshí 按时, zhǔnshí 准时
to arrive on time = ànshí dàodá 按时到达
in [five days' | a week's | six months'] time = guò [wǔ tiān | yíge xīngqī | liùge yuè] 过[五天 | 一个星期 | 六个月]
this time last year = qùnián zhège shíhou 去年这个时候
by this time next week = xiàge xīngqī zhège shíhou (zhīqián) 下个星期这个时候(之前)
it's time we left = wǒmen gāi zǒu le 我们该走了
- (*a moment*)

at times = yǒushí 有时, bùshí 不时
from time to time = yǒushí 有时, bùshí 不时
at the right time = zài shìdàng de shíhou 在适当的时候
any time now = cóng xiànzài qǐ suíshí 从现在起随时
he may arrive at any time now = cóng xiànzài qǐ tā suíshí dōu huì dàodá 从现在起他随时都会到达
for the time being = zànshí 暂时
- (*a period in the past*)

we didn't know each other at the time = nà shí(hòu), wǒmen hùxiāng bú rènshi 那时(候), 我们互相不认识
- (*an experience*)

to have a good time = guò de hěn yúkuài 过得很愉快
to have a hard time concentrating = wú fǎ jízhōng jīnglì 无法集中精力
- (*an occasion*) = cì 次, huí 回

[this | last | next | first | second | the last] time = [zhè | shàng | xià | dìyī | dì'èr | zuìhòu yí] cì [这 | 上 | 下 | 第一 | 第二 | 最后一] 次
[five | several | many] times = [wǔ | jǐ | xǔduō] cì [五 | 几 | 许多] 次
the first time we met = wǒmen dìyīcì jiànmiàn de shíhou 我们第一次见面的时候
- (*-fold*) = bèi 倍

three times more expensive = guì sānbèi 贵三倍
ten times quicker = kuài shíbèi 快十倍

timetable *noun*
- (*for trains, buses*)

a timetable = yíge shíkèbiǎo 一个时刻表
- (*in school, at work*)

a timetable = yíge shíjiānbiǎo 一个时间表

tin *noun*
- (*the metal*)

tin = xī 锡
- (*British English*) (*a tin can*)

a tin = yìtǒng (guàntou) 一筒(罐头)
a tin of beans = yìtǒng dòuzi guàntou 一筒豆子罐头

tin opener *noun* (*British English*)
a tin opener = yìbǎ guàntou qǐzi 一把罐头起子, yìbǎ kāiguàntoudāo 一把开罐头刀

tiny *adjective*
= jí xiǎo 极小, wēixiǎo 微小

tip *noun*
- (*the point*)

the tip of [a pen | the finger | the nose | the tongue] = [bǐ | shǒuzhǐ | bízi | shétou] jiān [笔 | 手指 | 鼻子 | 舌头] 尖
- (*an extra sum of money given to reward good service*)

a tip = yífèn xiǎofèi 一份小费
- (*a piece of advice*)

a tip = yíge gàojiè 一个告诫
- (*a hint*)

a tip = yíge tíshì 一个提示, yíge ànshì 一个暗示

tire *noun* (*US English*)
a tire = yíge lúntāi 一个轮胎, yíge chētāi 一个车胎

tired *adjective*
- (*needing rest*) = lèi 累, píláo 疲劳, píjuàn 疲倦

he is tired = tā lèi le 他累了
- (*needing a change*)

to be tired of = yànfán 厌烦, yànjuàn 厌倦
I'm tired of being a waitress = wǒ duì dāng nǚfúwùyuán yànfán le 我对当女服务员厌烦了

tiring *adjective*
= lèi rén de 累人的, lìng rén píláo de 令人疲劳的

tissue *noun*
a tissue = yìzhāng wèishēngzhǐ 一张卫生纸, yìzhāng miánzhǐ 一张棉纸

to *preposition* ▶ 204
▶ *See the boxed note on* **to** ▶ **416** *for more information and examples.*

> **!** *There are many adjectives like* **mean, nice, rude,** *etc., and verbs like* **belong, write,** *etc., which involve the use of* **to.** *For translations, look up the adjective entries at* **mean, nice, rude** *or the verb entries at* **belong, write.**

toast *noun*
= kǎomiànbāo 烤面包
a piece of toast = yípiàn kǎomiànbāo 一片烤面包

toaster *noun*
a toaster = yíge kǎomiànbāoqì 一个烤面包器

today *adverb* ▶ 412
= jīntiān 今天, jīnrì 今日

toe *noun* ▶ 189
= jiǎozhǐ 脚趾, jiǎojiān 脚尖

toffee *noun*
= nǎitáng 奶糖, tàifēitáng 太妃糖

together *adverb*
= yìqǐ 一起, yíkuàir 一块儿

toilet *noun*
a toilet = yíge cèsuǒ 一个厕所

toilet paper *noun*
= wèishēngzhǐ 卫生纸

tomato *noun*
a tomato = yíge xīhóngshì 一个西红柿, yíge fānqié 一个番茄

tomorrow *adverb* ▶ 412
= míngtiān 明天, míngrì 明日

tongue *noun* ▶ 189
= shétou 舌头, shé 舌

tonight *adverb* ▶ 412
(*this evening*) = jīntiān wǎnshang 今天晚上, jīnwǎn 今晚
(*during the night*) = jīntiān yè li 今天夜里, jīn yè 今夜

too *adverb*
- (*also*) = yě 也
  I'm going too = wǒ yě qù 我也去
- (*more than is necessary or desirable*) = tài 太
  it's too [big | expensive | far] = tài [dà | guì | yuǎn] le 太[大|贵|远]了
  there were too many people = rén tài duō le 人太多了
  I ate too much = wǒ chī de tài duō le 我吃得太多了

tool *noun*
a tool = yíge gōngjù 一个工具

tooth *noun* ▶ 189
a tooth = yìkē yá 一颗牙

toothache *noun* ▶ 277
he has a toothache = tā yátòng 他牙痛

toothbrush *noun*
a toothbrush = yìbǎ yáshuā 一把牙刷

toothpaste *noun*
= yágāo 牙膏

top
1 *noun*
- (*the highest part*) = dǐng 顶, dǐngbù 顶部
  at the top of [the hill | the tree | the stairs] = (zài) [shān | shù | lóutī] dǐng(shang) (在)[山|树|楼梯]顶(上)
  the fourth line from the top = cóng shàngmian shǔ dìsìháng 从上面数第四行
- (*a cover, a lid*)
  a top (*on a bottle, pot, pan*) = yíge gàir 一个盖儿, yíge gàizi 一个盖子
  (*on a pen*) = yíge bǐmào 一个笔帽
- (*the highest level*)
  to get to the top in the competition = zài bǐsài zhōng huòdé dìyī 在比赛中获得第一
  to be at the top of the class = zài bān li mínglie dìyī 在班里名列第一

2 *adjective*
the top [shelf | drawer | button] = dǐngshang de [jiàzi | chōuti | kòuzi] 顶上的[架子|抽屉|扣子]

top-up card *noun*
a top-up card = yìzhāng chōngzhíkǎ 一张充值卡

torch *noun*
- (*a flashlight*) (*British English*)
  a torch = yíge shǒudiàn(tǒng) 一个手电(筒)

To

See the usage notes on such topics as **The clock** ▶ **204**, **Length and weight measurements** ▶ **300**, **Quantities** ▶ **349**, etc. Many of these show expressions which use the preposition **to**.

As a preposition

- When used with verbs indicating directed movement, it is often unnecessary to translate **to**:

to go to the shops	= qù shāngdiàn 去商店
to return to the office	= huí bàngōngshì 回办公室
please give the book to me	= qǐng bǎ shū gěi wǒ 请把书给我
I've been to China	= wǒ qùguo Zhōngguó 我去过中国

- When it is necessary to translate **to** to indicate the direction of a movement, common translations are **xiàng** 向, **wǎng** 往, **dào** 到.

to turn to the right	= xiàng yòu zhuǎn 向右转
to fly to the south	= wǎng nán fēi 往南飞
to drop to the ground	= diàodao dì shang 掉到地上
to cycle to the hospital	= qí zìxíngchē qù yīyuàn 骑自行车去医院

- When **to** is used with verbs such as **speak, say, talk**, etc., it is usually translated as **hé** 和, **tóng** 同 or **gēn** 跟.

he didn't speak to me	= tā méiyǒu hé wǒ jiǎnghuà 他没有和我讲话
she talked to my father about it	= tā gēn wǒ bàba tánle zhèjiàn shì 她跟我爸爸谈了这件事
did you talk to him?	= nǐ tóng tā tánhuà le ma? 你同他谈话了吗?

- When used to indicate the final point in a length of time or distance, **to** is usually translated as **dào** 到:

from Monday to Saturday	= cóng xīngqīyī dào xīngqīliù 从星期一到星期六
from London to Beijing	= cóng Lúndūn dào Běijīng 从伦敦到北京
to stay to the end of the year	= dāi dào nián dǐ 呆到年底

- When used to indicate comparison or ratio, **to** is usually translated as **bǐ** 比 :

the final score is 4 to 2	= zuìhòu bǐfēn shì sì bǐ èr 最后比分是四比二
the ratio of men and women is 5 to 3	= nán nǚ bǐlì shì wǔ bǐ sān 男女比例是五比三

- When used to mean **in honour of** or **for the purpose of**, **to** is usually translated as **wèile** 为了:

to his health, cheers	= wèile tāde jiànkāng, gānbēi 为了他的健康, 干杯
to that end	= wèile nàge mùdì 为了那个目的

As part of an infinitive

In Chinese, there is no equivalent to the English **to** that forms part of the infinitive. Therefore, this sense of **to** in English is usually not translated into Chinese:

to go = qù 去
he began to study Chinese = tā kāishǐ xuéxí Hànyǔ 他开始学习汉语
it's easy to lose one's way = hěn róngyì mílù 很容易迷路
he came to see me = tā lái kàn wǒ 他来看我

However, when **to** is used at the beginning of a sentence, giving the meaning of **in order to**, it is usually translated as **wèile 为了**:

to improve his Chinese, he's going to spend the whole summer in China = wèile tígāo tāde Hànyǔ shuǐpíng, tā dǎsuàn zhěnggè xiàtiān dōu dāi zài Zhōngguó 为了提高他的汉语水平，他打算整个夏天都呆在中国

In certain expressions:

to tell the truth = lǎoshí de shuō 老实地说
to be frank = tǎnshuài de shuō 坦率地说
to be honest = chéngshí de shuō 诚实地说
to put it differently = huàn jù huà shuō 换句话说

- (*a portable stick of inflammable material for producing a flame*)
  a torch = yíge huǒjù 一个火炬, yíge huǒbǎ 一个火把

torn *adjective*
= sīpòle de 撕破了的, chěpòle de 扯破了的

tortoise *noun*
a tortoise = yízhī (wū)guī 一只(乌)龟

total
1 *noun*
a total = zǒngshù 总数
(*if it's money*) = zǒng'é 总额
2 *adjective*
= zǒng 总, quánbù 全部

touch
1 *verb*
- (*with one's hand*) = mō 摸, chùmō 触摸
- (*come into contact with*) = pèng 碰, jiēchù 接触
- (*affect one's feelings*) = shǐ...gǎndòng 使... 感动
  the story touched us all = zhège gùshi shǐ wǒmen dōu hěn gǎndòng 这个故事使我们都很感动

2 *noun*
to get in touch with someone = yǔ mǒurén liánxì 与某人联系
to keep/stay in touch with someone = yǔ mǒurén bǎochí liánxì 与某人保持联系

tough *adjective*
- (*strong, resilient, not brittle*) = jiānrèn 坚韧, jiēshi 结实
- (*sturdy*) = jiànzhuàng 健壮
- (*unyielding, as a policy, attitude, or view*) = qiángyìng 强硬
  (*when describing a person*) = wánqiáng 顽强, jiānqiáng 坚强
- (*difficult*) = kùnnan 困难, nánbàn 难办
- (*rough*)
  a tough area = yíge hěn luàn de dìqū 一个很乱的地区

tour
1 *noun*
- (*by a singer, a band, a theatre group*)
  a tour = yícì xúnhuí yǎnchū 一次巡回演出
  on tour = zhèngzài xúnhuí yǎnchū 正在巡回演出
- (*by a sports person, a sports team*)
  a tour = yícì xúnhuí bǐsài 一次巡回比赛
- (*by tourists, pupils, visitors*)
  a tour
  (*when travelling from place to place*) = yícì lǚxíng 一次旅行, yícì lǚyóu 一次旅游
  (*visiting a single area*) = yícì yóulǎn 一次游览, yícì cānguān 一次参观
  to go on a tour of the castle = qù yóulǎn chéngbǎo 去游览城堡

T

…ouring = qù lǚxíng 去旅行
to tour the United States = zhōuyóu Měiguó 周游美国

tourism *noun*
= lǚyóuyè 旅游业

tourist *noun*
a tourist = yíwèi yóukè 一位游客, yìmíng lǚxíngzhě 一名旅行者

tourist information office *noun*
a tourist information office = yíge lǚyóu xìnxī fúwùchù 一个旅游信息服务处

toward(s) *preposition*
- (*in the direction of*) = xiàng 向, cháo 朝
  towards the east = xiàng dōngbiān 向东边
- (*shortly before*) = jiāngjìn 将近, jiējìn 接近
  towards evening = jiāngjìn wǎnshang 将近晚上
- (*when talking about attitudes, feelings*) = duì 对, duìyú 对于
  to be friendly towards someone = duì mǒurén hěn yǒuhǎo 对某人很友好

towel *noun*
a towel = yìtiáo máojīn 一条毛巾

tower *noun*
a tower = yízuò tǎ 一座塔

tower block *noun* (*British English*)
a tower block = yízuò gāolóu 一座高楼

town *noun*
a town = yíge chéng(zhèn) 一个城(镇), yíge zhèn 一个镇
to go into town = jìn chéng 进城

town hall *noun*
a town hall = yíge shìzhèngtīng 一个市政厅

toy *noun*
a toy = yíge wánjù 一个玩具

track *noun*
- (*a path*)
  a track = yìtiáo lù 一条路, yìtiáo xiǎodào 一条小道
- (*in sports*)
  a track = yìtiáo pǎodào 一条跑道
- (*rails*)
  the track(s) = tiěguǐ 铁轨, guǐdào 轨道
- (*left by a person, an animal, a car*)
  tracks = xíngzōng 行踪, zōngjì 踪迹

tracksuit *noun*
a tracksuit = yítào yùndòngfú 一套运动服

trade *noun*
- = màoyì 贸易, jiāoyì 交易
- a trade = yìzhǒng zhíyè 一种职业, yìzhǒng hángyè 一种行业

tradition *noun*
a tradition = yíge chuántǒng 一个传统

traffic *noun*
= jiāotōng 交通

traffic jam *noun*
a traffic jam = jiāotōng dǔsè 交通堵塞

traffic lights *noun*
= jiāotōng xìnhàodēng 交通信号灯, hónglǜdēng 红绿灯

train

1 *noun*
a train = yíliè huǒchē 一列火车
the train to Shanghai = qù Shànghǎi de huǒchē 去上海的火车

2 *verb*
- (*to teach, to prepare*) = péixùn 培训, xùnliàn 训练
  to train employees = péixùn gùyuán 培训雇员
  to train athletes = xùnliàn yùndòngyuán 训练运动员
- (*to learn a job*)
  to train as a doctor = jiēshòu zuò yīshēng de xùnliàn 接受做医生的训练
- (*for a sporting event*) = xùnliàn 训练, duànliàn 锻炼
  to train for a better result in the sports meet = wèi zài yùndònghuì shang qǔdé gèng hǎo de chéngjī ér xùnliàn 为在运动会上取得更好的成绩而训练

trainer *noun*
(*a shoe*) (*British English*) = yùndòngxié 运动鞋
a pair of trainers = yìshuāng yùndòngxié 一双运动鞋
(*a person in sports*)
a trainer = yíwèi jiàoliànyuán 一位教练员

training course *noun*
a training course = yíge xùnliànbān 一个训练班

tramp *noun*
a tramp = yíge liúlàngzhě 一个流浪者

translate *verb*
(*to turn from one language into another*) = fānyì 翻译, yì 译
(*to interpret, to explain*) = jiěshì 解释, shuōmíng 说明

translator *noun* ▶ 344
a translator = yìmíng fānyì 一名翻译

transport, transportation (*US English*) *noun*
= yùnshū 运输, jiāotōng交通
a means of transport = yìzhǒng yùnshū gōngjù 一种运输工具, yìzhǒng jiāotōng gōngjù 一种交通工具
public transport = gōnggòng jiāotōng 公共交通, gōnggòng yùnshū 公共运输

trap *noun*
a trap (*a device for catching*) = yíge xiànjǐng 一个陷井
(*a plan to deceive, betray, etc.*) = yíge quāntào 一个圈套
to set a trap for someone = wèi mǒurén shè yíge quāntào 为某人设一个圈套

trash *noun* (*US English*)
= fèiwù 废物, lājī 垃圾

trash can *noun* (*US English*)
a trash can = yíge lājīxiāng 一个垃圾箱

travel *verb*
= lǚxíng 旅行
to travel [**abroad** | **to China** | **by bike**] = [qù guówài | qù Zhōngguó | qí zìxíngchē] lǚxíng [去国外 | 去中国 | 骑自行车] 旅行

travel agency *noun* ▶ 344
a travel agency = yìjiā lǚxíngshè 一家旅行社

traveller (*British English*), **traveler** (*US English*) *noun*
a traveller = yíge lǚxíngzhě 一个旅行者, yíge yóukè 一个游客

traveller's cheque (*British English*), **traveler's check** (*US English*) *noun*
a traveller's cheque = yìzhāng lǚxíng zhīpiào 一张旅行支票

tray *noun*
a tray = yíge pánzi 一个盘子, yíge tuōpán 一个托盘

treat *verb*
- (*to behave towards*) = duìdài 对待
  to treat someone [**badly** | **nicely** | **politely**] = duìdài mǒurén [hěn bù hǎo | hěn hǎo | hěn yǒu lǐmào] 对待某人 [很不好 | 很好 | 很有礼貌]
- (*to deal with, to handle*) = chǔlǐ 处理
  we have to treat this carefully = wǒmen děi xiǎoxīn chǔlǐ zhèjiàn shì 我们得小心处理这件事
- (*to give medical treatment to*) = yīzhì 医治, zhìliáo 治疗
  to treat someone for flu = gěi mǒurén yīzhì liúgǎn 给某人医治流感
- (*to pay for*)
  to treat someone to Peking duck = qǐng mǒurén chī Běijīng kǎoyā 请某人吃北京烤鸭

treatment *noun*
- (*behaviour towards someone*) = dàiyù 待遇, duìdài 对待
  to receive warm and friendly treatment from someone = shòudào mǒurén rèqíng yǒuhǎo de duìdài 受到某人热情友好的对待
- (*by a doctor*) = zhìliáo 治疗
  free treatment = miǎnfèi zhìliáo 免费治疗

tree *noun*
a tree = yìkē shù 一棵树

tremble *verb*
= fādǒu 发抖, duōsuo 哆嗦
they were trembling with fear = tāmen xià de fādǒu 他们吓得发抖

trendy *adjective*
= shímáo 时髦, suí cháoliú 随潮流

trial *noun*
- (*a test or an experiment*)
  a trial = yícì shìyàn 一次试验
- (*in court*)
  a trial = yícì shěnwèn/shěnpàn 一次审问/审判
  to go on trial = shòu shěn(pàn) 受审(判)

triangle *noun*
a triangle = yíge sānjiǎo(xíng) 一个三角(形)

trick
1 *noun*
- (*a joke*)
  a trick = yíge èzuòjù 一个恶作剧

T

to play a trick on someone = zhuōnòng mǒurén 捉弄某人
- (*a means of deceiving*)
a trick = yíge guǐjì 一个诡计, yíge piànjú 一个骗局
- (*to entertain*)
a trick = yíge xìfǎ 一个戏法, yíge bǎxì 一个把戏

2 *verb*
= qīpiàn 欺骗, hǒngpiàn 哄骗

trip
1 *noun*
(*a journey*)
a trip = yícì lǚxíng 一次旅行
to be on a business trip = chūchāi 出差, zuò yícì gōngwù lǚxíng 做一次公务旅行
2 *verb*
(*to stumble*) = bàn(dǎo) 绊(倒)
I tripped over the step at the gate = wǒ ràng ménkǒu de táijiē bànle yíxià 我让门口的台阶绊了一下
to trip someone (up) = bǎ mǒurén bàndǎo 把某人绊倒

trouble *noun*
- (*difficulties*) = kùnnan 困难
he has trouble using this computer = tā yòng zhètái jìsuànjī yǒu kùnnan 他用这台计算机有困难
- (*a scrape*) = kùnjìng 困境
to be in trouble = chǔyú kùnjìng 处于困境
to get someone into trouble = shǐ mǒurén xiànrù kùnjìng 使某人陷入困境
- (*disturbance*) = máfan 麻烦
to make trouble = zhìzào máfan 制造麻烦, nàoshì 闹事
I'm sorry to have given you so much trouble = duìbuqǐ, wǒ gěi nǐmen tiānle zhème duō máfan 对不起, 我给你们添了这么多麻烦
- (*an effort*)
he took the trouble to check every patient = tā bù cí láokǔ wèi měige bìngrén dōu zuòle jiǎnchá 他不辞劳苦为每个病人都做了检查
to go to a lot of trouble helping others = bù cí láokǔ bāngzhù biéren 不辞劳苦帮助别人

trousers *noun*
= kùzi 裤子
a pair of trousers = yìtiáo kùzi 一条裤子

trout *noun*
a trout = yìtiáo zhēnzūn 一条真鳟, yìtiáo guīyú 一条鲑鱼

truck *noun*
a truck = yíliàng kǎchē 一辆卡车

truck driver *noun* ▶ 344
a truck driver = yíwèi kǎchē sījī 一位卡车司机

true *adjective*
- (*genuine*) = zhēn 真
- (*in accordance with facts*) = zhēnshí 真实, zhēn 真
is it true that he's leaving? = zhēn de tā yào zǒu ma? 真的他要走吗?
a true story = yíge zhēnshí de gùshi 一个真实的故事
to come true = shíxiàn 实现
- (*faithful*) = zhōngshí 忠实
a true friend = yíge zhōngshí de péngyou 一个忠实的朋友

trumpet *noun* ▶ 308
a trumpet = yíge (xiǎo)hào 一个(小)号

trunk *noun*
- (*of a tree*)
a trunk = yíge shùgàn 一个树干
- (*of an elephant*)
a trunk = yíge xiàng bízi 一个象鼻子
- (*US English*) (*of a car*)
the trunk = xínglixiāng 行李箱

trust *verb*
- (*believe in*) = xìnrèn 信任, xiāngxìn 相信
I don't trust them = wǒ bú xìnrèn tāmen 我不信任他们
- (*to rely on*) = xìnlài 信赖
you can't trust them = nǐ bù néng xìnlài tāmen 你不能信赖他们

truth *noun*
- (*a proposition that agrees with actuality*)
a truth = yìtiáo zhēnlǐ 一条真理
- (*the actual fact, the real situation*)
the truth = zhēnxiàng 真相, zhēnshí qíngkuàng 真实情况

try
1 *verb*
- (*to endeavour*) = jìnlì 尽力, jìnliàng 尽量, lìtú 力图
to try to [learn Chinese well | come early | forget that matter...] = lìtú [xué hǎo Hànyǔ | zǎo lái | wàngjì nàjiàn shì...] 力图 [学好汉语 | 早来 | 忘记那件事...]

- (*to attempt*) = shì 试, chángshì 尝试
  try phoning him = shìzhe gěi tā dǎ diànhuà 试着给他打电话
  let me try = ràng wǒ shì yíxià 让我试一下
- (*to test*) = shì 试, shìyòng 试用
  to try (out) a new method = shìyòng yìzhǒng xīn de fāngfǎ 试用一种新的方法
  to try (on) a pair of jeans = shì(chuān) yìtiáo niúzǎikù 试(穿)一条牛仔裤
- (*to taste*) = (pǐn)cháng (品)尝
- (*in court*) = shěnxùn 审讯, shěnpàn 审判

2 *noun*
  let me have a try = ràng wǒ shì yíxià 让我试一下

T-shirt *noun*
  a T-shirt = yíjiàn tìxùshān 一件T恤衫

tube *noun*
- **a tube** = yìgēn guǎnzi 一根管子
- (*for a wheel*)
  a tube = yíge nèitāi 一个内胎
- (*British English*) (*the underground*)
  the tube = dìtiě 地铁, dìxià tiědào 地下铁道

Tuesday *noun* ▶ 218
  = xīngqī'èr 星期二, lǐbài'èr 礼拜二

tuna *noun*
  = jīnqiāngyú 金枪鱼

tunnel *noun*
  a tunnel = yìtiáo suìdào 一条隧道

turkey *noun*
  a turkey = yìzhī huǒjī 一只火鸡

turn

1 *verb*
- (*to rotate*) = zhuàn 转, zhuàndòng 转动
  the wheel is turning fast = lúnzi zài hěn kuài de zhuàndòng 轮子在很快地转动
  to turn the handle = zhuàndòng bǎshǒu 转动把手
- (*to move one's body*) = zhuǎn shēn 转身
  she turned and walked away = tā zhuǎn shēn zǒu le 她转身走了
- (*to change direction*) = zhuǎn 转
  to turn right = xiàng yòu zhuǎn 向右转
  she turned her face towards the sun = tā bǎ liǎn zhuǎn xiàng tàiyáng 她把脸转向太阳
- (*when talking about a page*) = fān 翻
  please turn to page 10 = qǐng fāndào dìshíyè 请翻到第十页
- (*to change*) = bǎ...biànchéng 把... 变成
  to turn the bedroom into an office = bǎ wòshì biànchéng yìjiān bàngōngshì 把卧室变成一间办公室
- (*to become*) = biànchéng 变成
  to turn into a butterfly = biànchéng yìzhī húdié 变成一只蝴蝶
  to turn red = biàn(chéng) hóng (de) 变(成)红(的)
- (*on the road, in the corridor*) = guǎi 拐
  don't turn left = bié wǎng zuǒ guǎi 别往左拐

2 *noun*
- (*a bend*)
  a turn = yíge zhuǎnwān 一个转弯, yíge guǎiwān 一个拐弯
  (*when talking about taking turns*)
  whose turn is it? = lúndào shéi le? 轮到谁了?
  it's your turn now = xiànzài lúndào nǐ le 现在轮到你了

turn around, turn round
- (*to face the other way*)
  (*if it's a person*) = zhuǎnguò shēn (qu) 转过身(去)
  (*if it's a car*) = diào tóu 调头
- (*to go round and round*) = zhuàn quān 转圈

turn away
- (*to turn or look in a different direction*) = zhuǎnguò shēn/liǎn qu 转过身/脸去
  she turned away embarrassed = tā bùhǎoyìsi de zhuǎnguò shēn qu 她不好意思地转过身去
- (*to dismiss from service*) = jiěgù 解雇
- (*to cause to leave*) = dǎfā zǒu 打发走, niǎnzǒu 撵走
  the police turned the students away = jǐngchá bǎ nàxiē xuésheng dǎfā zǒu le 警察把那些学生打发走了

turn back
- (*to return*) = zhéhuí 折回, wǎng huí zǒu 往回走
  he found this was the wrong road and then turned back = tā fāxiàn zhètiáo lù bú duì, jiù wǎng huí zǒu le 他发现这条路不对, 就往回走了
- (*when dealing with pages*) = fān huídào 翻回到

please turn back to page 5 = qǐng fānhuídào dìwǔyè 请翻回到第五页

turn down

- (*to lower*) = guānxiǎo 关小, tiáodī 调低
  to turn down the radio = bǎ shōuyīnjī guānxiǎo 把收音机关小
- (*to reject*) = jùjué 拒绝
  to turn someone down = jùjué mǒurén 拒绝某人

turn off = guānshang 关上
to turn off [the oven | the light | the tap...] = bǎ [kǎoxiāng | dēng | shuǐlóngtóu...] guānshang 把 [烤箱 | 灯 | 水龙头...] 关上

turn on = dǎkāi 打开, kāi 开
to turn on [the TV | the radio | the tap...] = bǎ [diànshìjī | shōuyīnjī | shuǐlóngtóu...] dǎkāi 把 [电视机 | 收音机 | 水龙头...] 打开

turn out
to turn out all right (in the end) = (zuìhòu) jiéguǒ búcuò (最后)结果不错
to turn out to be easy = yuánlái hěn róngyì 原来很容易

turn over

- (*to roll over*) = dǎfān 打翻
  he turned the vase over = tā bǎ huāpíng dǎfān le 他把花瓶打翻了
- to turn over the page = fāndào xià yíyè 翻到下一页

turn up

- (*to arrive*) = lái 来, dào 到
- (*to increase*)
  to turn up [the heating | the music | the TV] = bǎ [nuǎnqì | yīnyuè | diànshì] kāidà 把 [暖气 | 音乐 | 电视] 开大

turtle *noun*

- a (sea) turtle = yíge (hǎi)guī 一个(海)龟
- (*US English*) (*a tortoise*)
  a turtle = yíge wūguī 一个乌龟

TV *noun*
a TV = yìtái diànshìjī 一台电视机

twelfth *number*

- (*in a series*) = dìshí'èr 第十二
- (*in dates*) ▶ 218 = shí'èr rì 十二日, shí'èr hào 十二号
  the twelfth of July = qīyuè shí'èr hào 七月十二号

twelve *number* ▶ 170, ▶ 204
twelve = shí'èr 十二

twenty *number* ▶ 170, ▶ 204
twenty = èrshí 二十

twice *adverb*

- (*when talking about the number of times*) = liǎngcì 两次
  I met him twice = wǒ jiànguo tā liǎngcì 我见过他两次
- (*two-fold*) = liǎngbèi 两倍
  twice [as many people | as much time] = liǎngbèi [duō de rén | duō de shíjiān] 两倍 [多的人 | 多的时间]

twin

1 *noun*
a twin = yíge shuāngbāotāi 一个双胞胎

2 *adjective*
= shuāngbāotāi de 双胞胎的, luánshēng de 孪生的
a twin [brother | sister] (*younger*) = yíge shuāngbāotāi de [dìdi | mèimei] 一个双胞胎的 [弟弟 | 妹妹]
(*older*) = yíge shuāngbāotāi de [gēge | jiějie] 一个双胞胎的 [哥哥 | 姐姐]
twin [brothers | sisters] = luánshēng [xiōngdì | jiěmèi] 孪生 [兄弟 | 姐妹]

twist *verb*

- (*to form a spiral*) = níng/nǐng 拧, niǔ 扭
  to twist a rope = níng yìgēn shéngzi 拧一根绳子
- (*to injure*) ▶ 227
  = niǔshāng 扭伤
  he twisted his ankle = tā niǔshāngle jiǎobózi 他扭伤了脚脖子

two *number* ▶ 170, ▶ 204
(*in counting, in numbers, digits*) = èr 二
(the year) 2002 = èrlínglíng'èr nián 2002年
(*when used with a measure word*) = liǎng 两
two brothers = liǎngge xiōngdì 两个兄弟

type

1 *noun*
a type (*a sort, a kind*) = yìzhǒng (lèixíng) 一种(类型)
this type of [person | book | building...] = zhèzhǒng [rén | shū | lóu...] 这种 [人 | 书 | 楼...]
he's not my type = tā bú shì wǒ xǐhuan de nàzhǒng rén 他不是我喜欢的那种人

2 *verb*
= dǎzì 打字

typewriter *noun*
a typewriter = yìtái dǎzìjī 一台打字机

typical *adjective*
= diǎnxíng 典型

typist *noun* ▶ 344
a typist = yìmíng dǎzìyuán 一名打字员

tyre *noun* (*British English*)
a tyre = yíge lúntāi 一个轮胎, yíge chētāi 一个车胎

Uu

ugly *adjective*
(*unpleasant to the sight*) = chǒu(lòu) 丑陋, nánkàn 难看

umbrella *noun*
an umbrella = yìbǎ (yǔ)sǎn 一把雨伞

unbelievable *adjective*
= nán yǐ zhìxìn 难以置信, wúfǎ xiāngxìn 无法相信

uncle *noun*
- **an uncle** (*father's elder brother*) = yíge bófù 一个伯父, yíge bóbo 一个伯伯
  (*father's younger brother*) = yíge shūshu 一个叔叔
  (*mother's younger or elder brother*) = yíge jiùjiu 一个舅舅
  (*husband of father's sister*) = yíge gūfu 一个姑父
  (*husband of mother's sister*) = yíge yífu 一个姨父
- (*not a relation*)
  an uncle (*a man younger than one's father*) = yíge shūshu 一个叔叔
  (*a man older than one's father*) = yíge bóbo 一个伯伯

uncomfortable *adjective*
- (*awkward and uneasy*) = bú zìzài 不自在, bù ān 不安
  to make someone (feel) uncomfortable = shǐ mǒurén (gǎndào) bú zìzài 使某人感到不自在
- (*describing a physical feeling*) = bù shūfu 不舒服
  I felt uncomfortable sitting in that chair = wǒ zuò zài nàbǎ yǐzi shang gǎnjué bù shūfu 我坐在那把椅子上感觉不舒服
  (*describing the physical condition of something*) = bù shūfu 不舒服, bù shūshì 不舒适
  an uncomfortable bed = yìzhāng bù shūfu de chuáng 一张不舒服的床

unconscious *adjective*
- (*not knowing*) = bù zhīdào de 不知道的
  I was unconscious of his presence = wǒ bù zhīdào tā zài chǎng 我不知道他在场
- (*lose consciousness*) = shīqù zhījué de 失去知觉的, bù xǐng rénshì de 不省人事的
  to knock someone unconscious = bǎ mǒurén zhuàng de shīqù zhījué 把某人撞得失去知觉
- (*not aware*) = wú yìshi de 无意识的
  an unconscious act = yíge wú yìshi de dòngzuò 一个无意识的动作

under *preposition*
- **under** = zài...xiàmian 在...下面, zài...dǐxia 在...底下
  to hide under the bed = cáng zài chuáng xiàmian 藏在床下面
  I found the newspaper under the table = wǒ zài zhuōzi dǐxia zhǎodàole bàozhǐ 我在桌子底下找到了报纸
- (*less than*)
  to earn under three pounds an hour = měi xiǎoshí zhèng bú dào sān yīngbàng 每小时挣不到三英镑
  children under five = wǔ suì yǐxià de háizi 五岁以下的孩子, bù mǎn wǔ suì de háizi 不满五岁的孩子

underground *noun* (*British English*)
the underground = dìtiě 地铁

underline *verb*
- (*to put a line under*) = zài...xiàmian huà xiàn 在...下面划线
  to underline all the names = zài suǒyǒu de míngzi xiàmian huà xiàn 在所有的名字下面划线
- (*to emphasise*) = qiángdiào 强调
  to underline the importance of this meeting = qiángdiào zhècì huìyì de zhòngyàoxìng 强调这次会议的重要性

underneath
1 *adverb*
= (zài) xiàmian (在)下面, (zài) dǐxia (在)底下
I want to see what's underneath = wǒ xiǎng kàn yíxià xiàmian yǒu shénme 我想看一下下面有什么
2 *preposition*
= zài...xiàmian 在...下面, zài...xiàbian 在...下边
underneath the building = zài dàlóu xiàmian 在大楼下面

underpants *noun*
= nèikù 内裤

understand *verb*
- (*to comprehend*) = dǒng 懂
I can't understand what they're saying = wǒ bù dǒng tāmen shuō de huà 我不懂他们说的话
do you understand Japanese? = nǐ dǒng Rìyǔ ma? 你懂日语吗?
to make oneself understood = biǎodá qīngchu zìjǐ de yìsi 表达清楚自己的意思
- (*to be able to follow the working, logic, or meaning of*) = lǐjiě 理解
I can understand why he wants to learn Chinese = wǒ kěyǐ lǐjiě tā wèishénme xiǎng xué Zhōngwén 我可以理解他为什么想学中文
- (*to know*) = liǎojiě 了解
he doesn't understand the difficult situation I'm in = tā bù liǎojiě wǒ suǒ chǔ de kùnjìng 他不了解我所处的困境

understanding *adjective*
- (*sympathetic*) = néng liàngjiě rén de 能谅解人的
- (*discerning*)
an understanding smile = huìxīn de wēixiào 会心的微笑
an understanding person = yíge shànjiě rényì de rén 一个善解人意的人

underwater *adverb*
= zài shuǐ xià 在水下

underwear *noun*
= nèiyī 内衣

undo *verb*
- (*for buttons, knots*) = jiěkāi 解开
to undo a button = jiěkāi yíge kòuzi 解开一个扣子
- (*for parcels, boxes*) = dǎkāi 打开
(*to cancel, to annul*) = qǔxiāo 取消

undress *verb*
= gěi...tuōxià yīfu 给...脱下衣服
she undressed her daughter = tā gěi tā nǚ'ér tuōxià yīfu 她给她女儿脱下衣服
I undressed and went to bed = wǒ tuōxià yīfu shàng chuáng shuìjiào 我脱下衣服上床睡觉

uneasy *adjective*
- (*anxious*) = (xīnshén) bù ān (心神)不安, yōulǜ 忧虑
- (*uncomfortable*) = jūshù 拘束, bú zìzài 不自在

unemployed *adjective*
(*out of work*) = shīyè de 失业的
he is unemployed = tā shīyè le 他失业了
unemployed workers = shīyè de gōngrén 失业的工人

unemployment *noun*
= shīyè 失业

unfair *adjective*
= bù gōngpíng 不公平, bù gōngzhèng 不公正

unfortunately *adverb*
= búxìng de shì 不幸的是, yíhàn de shì 遗憾的是

unfriendly *adjective*
= bù yǒuhǎo 不友好, lěngmò 冷漠

ungrateful *adjective*
= wàng'ēn fùyì 忘恩负义, bù lǐng qíng 不领情

unhappy *adjective*
- (*not glad*) = bù gāoxìng 不高兴, bù yúkuài 不愉快
- (*not satisfied*) = bù mǎnyì 不满意
are you unhappy with your new job? = nǐ duì nǐde xīn gōngzuò bù mǎnyì ma? 你对你的新工作不满意吗?
- (*without happiness*) = bú xìngfú 不幸福
he had an unhappy life there = tā zài nàr de shēnghuó hěn bú xìngfú 他在那儿的生活很不幸福

unhealthy *adjective*
- (*describing a person*) = bú jiànkāng de 不健康的, yǒu bìng de 有病的
- (*describing a way of life, food*) = duì jiànkāng yǒu hài de 对健康有害的

- (*not morally or spiritually wholesome*) = bùliáng 不良

uniform *noun*

a uniform = yítào zhìfú 一套制服
a school uniform = yítào xiàofú 一套校服
a police uniform = yítào jǐngfú 一套警服
an army uniform = yítào jūnzhuāng 一套军装

union *noun*

a union
(*a trade union*) = yíge gōnghuì 一个工会
(*a federation*) = yíge liánhéhuì 一个联合会

unique *adjective*

- (*being the only one of its kind*) = wéiyī 唯一, dúyī wú'èr 独一无二
- (*unusual*) = dútè 独特

United Kingdom *noun*

= Liánhé Wángguó 联合王国, Yīngguó 英国

United States (of America) *noun*

= Měilìjiān Hézhòngguó 美利坚合众国, Měiguó 美国

universe *noun*

- (*the whole system of things*) = yǔzhòu 宇宙, tiāndì wànwù 天地万物
- (*the world*) = shìjiè 世界

university *noun*

a university = yìsuǒ dàxué 一所大学

unkind *adjective*

(*when describing a person, an action*) = bù réncí 不仁慈, bù héshàn 不和善
(*when describing a remark*) = kēkè 苛刻, kèbó 刻薄

unknown *adjective*

his telephone number is unknown to me = tāde diànhuà hàomǎ wǒ bù zhīdào 他的电话号码我不知道
an unknown number = yíge wèizhī shù 一个未知数
an unknown hero = yíge wúmíng yīngxióng 一个无名英雄

unless *conjunction*

= rúguǒ (...) bù 如果 (...) 不, chúfēi...fǒuzé 除非... 否则

> **!** *Note that the clause introduced by* **rúguǒ bù** 如果不 *must precede the main clause. Note also that* **rúguǒ** 如果 *and* **bù** 不 *can be separated by the subject or put together after the subject.*

she won't come unless you phone her = rúgǒu nǐ bù gěi tā dǎ diànhuà, tā bú huì lái 如果你不给她打电话, 她不会来
you wouldn't understand this book unless you know Chinese history = nǐ rúguǒ bù liǎojiě Zhōngguó lìshǐ, nǐ jiù huì kàn bù dǒng zhèběn shū 你如果不了解中国历史, 你就会看不懂这本书
I'll cancel the meeting unless he can come = chúfēi tā néng lái, fǒuzé wǒ jiù qǔxiāo zhècì huìyì 除非他能来, 否则我就取消这次会议

unlock *verb*

= bǎ... (de) suǒ dǎkāi 把...(的)锁打开
to unlock the door = bǎ mén suǒ dǎkāi 把门锁打开

unlucky *adjective*

- (*unfortunate*) = bú xìngyùn 不幸运, dǎoméi 倒霉
  you were unlucky = nǐ hěn bú xìngyùn 你很不幸运
- (*ill-omened*) = bù jíxiáng 不吉祥

unpack *verb*

to unpack a suitcase = dǎkāi xiāngzi bǎ dōngxi náchulai 打开箱子把东西拿出来

unsuitable *adjective*

= bù héshì 不合适, bù shìyí 不适宜

untidy *adjective*

(*describing a place*) = bù zhěngqí 不整齐, língluàn 凌乱
(*describing a person*) = lāta 邋遢, bù xiū biānfú 不修边幅

until

1 *preposition*

- = dào 到, (zhí)dào...(wéizhǐ) (直)到...(为止)
  I'm staying until Thursday = wǒ dāi dào xīngqīsì 我呆到星期四
  until now = zhídào xiànzài 直到现在
  I'm going to wait until after Christmas = wǒ dǎsuàn děng dào Shèngdànjié yǐhòu 我打算等到圣诞节以后
- (*when used in a negative sentence*)

U

> ! *Note that when* **until** *is used in a negative sentence, the pattern* **not...until** *is often translated as* (zhí)dào...cái... (直)到...才... *or* (zài)...yǐqián...bù/méi... (在)... 以前...不/没....

she won't get an answer until next week = xiàge xīngqī yǐqián tā bú huì dédào dáfù 下个星期以前她不会得到答复
not until yesterday did I meet him = wǒ zhídào zuótiān cái jiàndào tā 我直到昨天才见到他

2 *conjunction*

- = (zhí)dào (直)到
I'll wait until he gets back home = wǒ yào děng dào tā huí jiā 我要等到他回家
we'll stay here until they come back = wǒmen yào zài zhèr dāi dào tāmen huílai 我们要在这儿呆到他们回来
- (*when used with a negative main clause*)

> ! *Note that when* **until** *is used with a negative main clause, the pattern* **not...until** *is often translated as* (zhí)dào...cái... (直)到...才... *or* (zài)..yǐqián...bù/méi... (在)... 以前.... 不/没....

she didn't go to see the doctor until she was very ill = tā zhídào bìng de hěn lìhài cái qù kàn yīshēng 她直到病得很厉害才去看医生
she won't go to Taiwan until her friend has found her a language school there = zài tāde péngyou gěi tā zhǎodào yǔyán xuéxiào yǐqián, tā bú huì qù Táiwān 在她的朋友给她找到语言学校以前, 她不会去台湾

unusual *adjective*

- (*rare*) = hǎnjiàn 罕见, shǎoyǒu 少有
such a strong wind is quite unusual in this area = zhème dà de fēng zài zhège dìqū shì shǎoyǒu de 这么大的风在这个地区是少有的
- (*not ordinary*) = bù xúncháng 不寻常, bù píngcháng 不平常
it's an unusual day for her today = duì tā láishuō, jīntiān shì ge bù xúncháng de rìzi 对她来说, 今天是个不寻常的日子

up

> ! *Often* **up** *occurs in combinations with verbs, for example:* **blow up, give up, own up**, *etc. To find the correct translations for this type of verb, look up the separate dictionary entries at* **blow, give, own**, *etc.*

1 *preposition*

the cat's up the tree = māo zài shù shang 猫在树上
to go up the street = yánzhe mǎlù wǎng qián zǒu 沿着马路往前走
she ran up the stairs = tā pǎoshang lóutī 她跑上楼梯
the library is up those stairs = túshūguǎn zài nàge lóutī shàngmian 图书馆在那个楼梯上面

2 *adverb*

up in the sky = zài tiān shang 在天上
up on (top of) the wardrobe = zài yīguì shàngmian 在衣柜上面
to go up = shàngqu 上去
to go up to Scotland = shàng Sūgélán 上苏格兰
up there = zài nàr 在那儿
put the painting a bit further up = bǎ huà zài wǎng shàng fàng yìdiǎnr 把画再往上放一点儿
to climb up [a hill | a ladder | a tree] = pá [shān | tīzi | shù] 爬[山 | 梯子 | 树]

3 *adjective*

- (*out of bed*)
is he up yet? = tā qǐchuáng le ma? 他起床了吗?
he was up all night = tā yí yè méi shuì 他一夜没睡
- (*higher in amount, level*)
the price of fish is up by 20% = yú jià shàngzhǎngle bǎifēn zhī èrshí 鱼价上涨了百分之二十

4 up to

- (*well enough*)
he is not up to going out yet = tā hái bù néng chūqu 他还不能出去
- (*capable of*)
is she up to this translation work? = tā néng shèngrèn zhège fānyì gōngzuò ma? 她能胜任这个翻译工作吗?
- (*when talking about who is responsible*)

it's up to [me | you | them] to decide = yóu [wǒ | nǐ | tāmen] (lái) juédìng 由[我|你|他们](来)决定
- (*until*) = zhídào 直到
up to [now | 1996 | yesterday] = zhídào [xiànzài | yījiǔjiǔliù nián | zuótiān] 直到[现在|一九九六年|昨天]

upset
1 *adjective*
to be/get upset
(*annoyed*) = fánnǎo 烦恼, nǎohuǒ 恼火
he got very upset when his car broke down on the way = tāde chē zài lù shang huàile de shíhou, tā fēicháng nǎohuǒ 他的车在路上坏了的时候, 他非常恼火
(*distressed*) = kǔnǎo 苦恼, yōushāng 忧伤
she was very upset to hear the news of the accident = tīngdào zhège shìgù de xiāoxi, tā fēicháng yōushāng 听到这个事故的消息, 她非常忧伤
2 *verb*
- (*to make someone unhappy*) = shǐ...yōushāng/kǔnǎo 使…忧伤/苦恼
to upset someone = shǐ mǒurén yōushāng/kǔnǎo 使某人忧伤/苦恼
- (*to annoy*) = shǐ...fánnǎo/nǎohuǒ 使…烦恼/恼火
to upset someone = shǐ mǒurén fánnǎo/nǎohuǒ 使某人烦恼/恼火

upside down *adverb*
- (*turned over completely*) = dào 倒, diāndǎo 颠倒
you're holding the book upside down = nǐ bǎ shū ná dào le 你把书拿倒了
- (*in disorder or chaos*) = luànqībāzāo 乱七八糟
they turned everything in the room upside down = tāmen bǎ wū li de dōngxi nòng de luànqībāzāo 他们把屋里的东西弄得乱七八糟

upstairs *adverb*
= lóushàng 楼上
to go upstairs = shàng lóu 上楼
to bring the cases upstairs = bǎ xiāngzi nádào lóushàng lái 把箱子拿到楼上来

urgent *adjective*
= jǐnjí 紧急, jíqiè 急切

us *pronoun*
= wǒmen 我们
they don't know us = tāmen bú rènshi wǒmen 他们不认识我们

USA *noun*
= Měiguó 美国

use
1 *verb*
- (*to make use of*) = yòng 用, shǐyòng 使用
I use this car to go to work = wǒ yòng zhèliàng chē shàng bān 我用这辆车上班
he uses this room as an office = tā bǎ zhège fángjiān yòngzuò bàngōngshì 他把这个房间用做办公室
what is it used for? = zhè shì yòng lái zuò shénme de? 这是用来做什么的?
to use [water | petrol | electricity] = (shǐ) yòng [shuǐ | qìyóu | diàn] (使)用[水|汽油|电]
- (*to take advantage of*) = lìyòng 利用
to use [someone | this opportunity] = lìyòng [mǒurén | zhège jīhuì] 利用[某人|这个机会]
2 *noun*
- **to make use of a room** = lìyòng yíge fángjiān 利用一个房间
he has the use of a car = yǒu qìchē gòng tā shǐyòng 有汽车供他使用
she's lost the use of her legs = tāde liǎngtiáo tuǐ bù néng zǒulù le 她的两条腿不能走路了
- (*when talking about what is useful*)
to be of use to someone = duì mǒurén yǒuyòng 对某人有用
to be (of) no use = méi yòng 没用
this bike is no use any more = zhèliàng zìxíngchē méi yòng le 这辆自行车没用了
what's the use of complaining? = bàoyuàn yǒu shénme yòng? 抱怨有什么用?
use up
he's used up all the money = tā bǎ qián dōu huāwán le 他把钱都花完了
have you used up the milk? = nǐ bǎ niúnǎi yòngwán le ma? 你把牛奶用完了吗?

used
1 *verb*
- (*did so frequently or regularly*) = guòqù chángcháng 过去常常

I used to go there by bike = wǒ guòqù chángcháng qí zìxíngchē qù nàr 我过去常常骑自行车去那儿
• (*did so formerly*) = guòqù 过去
I used not to smoke = wǒ guòqù bù chōuyān 我过去不抽烟
there used to be a castle here = zhèr guòqù yǒu ge chéngbǎo 这儿过去有个城堡
2 *adjective*
• **to be/get used to** = xíguàn 习惯
he's not used to living on his own = tā bù xíguàn yíge rén shēnghuó 他不习惯一个人生活
to get used to a new job = xíguàn xīn de gōngzuò 习惯新的工作
• (*not new*) = shǐyòngguo de 使用过的, jiù 旧
used cars = shǐyòngguo de qìchē 使用过的汽车
used furniture = jiù jiājù 旧家具

useful *adjective*
(*of use*) = yǒuyòng 有用
(*helpful*) = yǒu bāngzhù 有帮助

useless *adjective*
• (*having no use, point, or purpose*) = méi(yǒu) yòng 没(有)用, wú yòng 无用
it's useless complaining = bàoyuàn méiyǒu yòng 抱怨没有用
• (*describing a person*) = wúnéng 无能
I'm useless at chemistry = wǒ duì gǎo huàxué hěn wúnéng 我对搞化学很无能

usually *adverb*
= tōngcháng 通常, yìbān 一般

Vv

vacant *adjective*
• (*unoccupied*) = kòng 空, kòngxiánzhe 空闲着
is there a vacant room in the house? = fángzi li yǒu kòng fángjiān ma? 房子里有空房间吗?
• (*when describing a post or a position*) = kòngquē de 空缺的
a vacant post = yíge kòngquē de zhíwèi 一个空缺的职位

vacation *noun* (*US English*)
a vacation = yíge jiàqī 一个假期
to take a vacation = xiū jià 休假
the [summer | winter | Christmas] vacation = [shǔ | hán | Shèngdàn] jià [暑 | 寒 | 圣诞] 假

vacuum *verb*
to vacuum a room = yòng xīchénqì dǎsǎo fángjiān 用吸尘器打扫房间

vacuum cleaner *noun*
a vacuum cleaner = yíge xīchénqì 一个吸尘器

vague *adjective*
• (*indefinite, uncertain*) = hánhu 含糊, bù quèqiè 不确切
a vague answer = yíge hánhu de huídá 一个含糊的回答
• (*indistinct*) = móhu 模糊, bù qīngxī 不清晰
• (*not clearly expressed*) = biǎodá (de) bù qīngchu 表达(得)不清楚

vain *adjective*
• (*pettily self-complacent*) = zìfù 自负
he is vain about his learning = tā duì zìjǐ de xuéwèn hěn zìfù 他对自己的学问很自负
• (*valuing oneself inordinately on some trivial personal distinction*) = ài xūróng 爱虚荣
is he a vain person? = tā shì yíge ài xūróng de rén ma? 他是一个爱虚荣的人吗?
• (*futile*) = túláo 徒劳, báifèi 白费
in vain = túláo 徒劳, báifèi 白费
all my efforts were in vain = wǒde suǒyǒu nǔlì dōu báifèi le 我的所有努力都白费了

valid *adjective*
• (*legally adequate*) = yǒuxiào 有效
is this ticket still valid? = zhèzhāng piào hái yǒuxiào ma? 这张票还有效吗?
• (*capable of being justified*) = zhèngdàng 正当
a valid reason = yíge zhèngdàng de lǐyóu 一个正当的理由
• (*well based*) = quèzuò 确凿, yǒu gēnjù 有根据
valid evidence = quèzuò de zhèngjù 确凿的证据

valley *noun*
a valley (*a low area between hills*) = yíge shāngǔ 一个山谷

(*the basin in which a river flows*) = yíge liúyù 一个流域

valuable *adjective*
- (*very useful*) = bǎoguì 宝贵, yǒujiàzhí 有价值
- (*worth a lot of money*) = zhíqián 值钱, guìzhòng 贵重

this watch is rather valuable = zhèkuài biǎo xiāngdāng zhíqián 这块表相当值钱

van *noun*
a van = yíliàng yùnhuòchē 一辆运货车

vandalize *verb*
= pòhuài 破坏, huǐhuài 毁坏

vanilla *noun*
= xiāngzǐlán 香子兰, xiāngcǎo 香草

various *adjective*
- (*diverse*) = gè zhǒng gè yàng 各种各样, bù tóng 不同

there are various ways of saying it = yǒu gè zhǒng gè yàng de shuōfǎ 有各种各样的说法
- (*several*) = jǐge 几个

they visited several schools = tāmen fǎngwènle jǐge xuéxiào 他们访问了几个学校

vary *verb*
- (*to differ, be different*) = bù tóng 不同, bù yíyàng 不一样

food prices vary from town to town = shípǐn de jiàgé měi gè chéngzhèn dōu bù tóng 食品的价格每个城镇都不同
- (*to change intentionally*) = gǎibiàn 改变, gēnggǎi 更改

to vary one's working style = gǎibiàn gōngzuò fāngshì 改变工作方式

vase *noun*
a vase = yíge huāpíng 一个花瓶

veal *noun*
= xiǎoniúròu 小牛肉

vegetable *noun*
= (shū)cài (蔬)菜
a vegetable = yìkē cài 一棵菜

vegetarian *noun*
a vegetarian = yíge chī sù de rén 一个吃素的人

vein *noun* ▶ 189
a vein (*for carrying blood in the body*) = yìgēn xuěguǎn 一根血管

velvet *noun*
= tiān'éróng 天鹅绒, sīróng 丝绒

versus *preposition*
= duì 对

very

1 *adverb*
- **very** = hěn 很, fēicháng 非常

I don't know him very well = wǒ bù hěn liǎojiě tā 我不很了解他
we like them very much = wǒmen fēicháng xǐhuan tāmen 我们非常喜欢他们
- **not (...) very** = bù hěn 不很, bú tài 不太

it is not very hot today = jīntiān bú tài rè 今天不太热
- (*for emphasis*)

> **!** *Note that in this case,* **very** *is usually not translated.*

for the very first time = dìyīcì 第一次
they called me the very next day = tāmen dì'èr tiān jiù gěi wǒ dǎ diànhuà le 他们第二天就给我打电话了

2 *adjective*

> **!** *Note that when* **very** *is used as an adjective, it is often translated as* **jiù 就** *or* **zhèng 正**.

she studied in that very school = tā jiù zài nàsuǒ xuéxiào xuéxí 她就在那所学校学习
you are the very person I need = nǐ zhèng shì wǒ suǒ xūyào de rén 你正是我所需要的人
at the very beginning = gāng kāishǐ de shíhou 刚开始的时候
to stay to the very end = dāi dào zuìhou 待到最后

vest *noun*
- (*British English*) (*a piece of underwear*)

a vest = yíjiàn hànshān 一件汗衫, yíjiàn bèixīn 一件背心
- (*US English*) (*a waistcoat*)

a vest = yíjiàn bèixīn 一件背心, yíjiàn mǎjiǎ 一件马甲

vet *noun* ▶ 344
a vet = yíge shòuyī 一个兽医

via *preposition*
- (*when talking about a route*) = jīngyóu 经由, jīngguò 经过, lùjīng 路经

to go to Japan via Beijing = jīngyóu Běijīng qù Rìběn 经由北京去日本

- (*when talking about a means*) = tōngguò 通过, lìyòng 利用
  I returned the book to him via a student of his = wǒ tōngguò tāde yíge xuésheng bǎ shū huángěile tā 我通过他的一个学生把书还给了他

vicious *adjective*
- (*ferocious*) = xiōng'è 凶恶 xiōngcán 凶残
- (*nasty, meant to hurt*) = èyì 恶意, èdú 恶毒
- (*addicted to vice or bad habits*) = duòluò 堕落

victory *noun*
a victory = yícì shènglì 一次胜利
to win a victory = yíngdé shènglì 赢得胜利

video
1 *noun*
- (*a recorded film, programme, event*)
  a video = yìpán lùxiàngdài 一盘录像带
- ▶ **video cassette**, **video recorder**

2 *verb*
- (*to record*) = lù 录
- (*to film*)
  to video a wedding = gěi yíge hūnlǐ shèxiàng 给一个婚礼摄像

video camera *noun*
a video camera = yìtái shèxiàngjī 一台摄像机

video cassette *noun*
a video cassette = yìpán lùxiàngdài 一盘录像带

video game *noun*
a video game = yìpán diànzǐ yóuxì 一盘电子游戏

video recorder *noun*
a video recorder = yìtái lùxiàngjī 一台录像机

view *noun*
- (*a scene viewed by the eyes*) = kàn 看, guānkàn 观看
  if you want to get a better view, you'd better come here = yàoshì nǐ xiǎng kàn de qīngchu, zuìhǎo dào zhèr lái 要是你想看得清楚, 最好到这儿来
- (*a line of vision*) = shìxiàn 视线
  you're blocking my view = nǐ dǎngzhùle wǒde shìxiàn 你挡住了我的视线
- (*an opinion*)
  a view = yíge guāndiǎn 一个观点, yíge yìjiàn 一个意见
  a point of view = yíge guāndiǎn 一个观点
  I'd like to know your views on this matter = wǒ xiǎng zhīdào nǐ duì zhèjiàn shì de yìjiàn 我想知道你对这件事的意见

village *noun*
a village = yíge cūnzhuāng 一个村庄

vinegar *noun*
= cù 醋

vineyard *noun*
a vineyard = yíge pútaoyuán 一个葡萄园

violent *adjective*
- (*of great force*) = měngliè 猛烈, qiánglie 强烈, jīliè 激烈
- (*vicious*) = xiōngcán 凶残, cánbào 残暴
- (*marked by extreme force or fierceness*) = bàolì de 暴力的

violin *noun* ▶ 308
a violin = yìbǎ xiǎotíqín 一把小提琴

visit
1 *verb*
- (*to pay an official call upon*) = fǎngwèn 访问
  the British delegation is visiting China = Yīngguó dàibiǎotuán zhèngzài fǎngwèn Zhōngguó 英国代表团正在访问中国
- (*to come or go to see formally*) = cānguān 参观, fǎngwèn 访问
  they visited some hospitals and schools = tāmen cānguānle yìxiē yīyuàn hé xuéxiào 他们参观了一些医院和学校
- (*for sightseeing and pleasure*) = cānguān 参观, yóulǎn 游览
  are you going to visit the Great Wall? = nǐmen yào qù yóulǎn Chángchéng ma? 你们要去游览长城吗?
- (*out of affection*) = kàn 看, kànwàng 看望
  to go to visit [a patient | my grandmother | my old friend...] = qù kàn [yíge bìngrén | wǒde nǎinai | wǒde lǎo péngyou...] 去看[一个病人 | 我的奶奶 | 我的老朋友...]
- (*to stay with*)

we visited my parents for a week = wǒmen zài wǒ fùmǔ nàr zhùle yíge xīngqī 我们在我父母那儿住了一个星期

2 *noun*

a visit (*an official call*) = yícì fǎngwèn 一次访问

(*when talking about visits to institutions, museums, exhibitions, etc.*) = yícì cānguān 一次参观

(*a sightseeing excursion*) = yícì yóulǎn 一次游览

(*a call at someone's home*) = yícì bàifǎng 一次拜访, yícì tànwàng 一次探望

(*a stay*)

I paid my elder brother a visit for two days = wǒ zài wǒ gēge nàr dāile liǎngtiān 我在我哥哥那儿呆了两天

visitor *noun*

- (*a guest*)

a visitor = yíge kèrén 一个客人

to have visitors = yǒu kèrén 有客人

- (*a tourist*)

a visitor = yíge yóukè 一个游客

vocabulary *noun*

= cíhuì 词汇

voice *noun*

- (*the sound of a person speaking, singing, etc.*)

a voice = yíge shuōhuà shēngyīn 一个说话声音

to speak [**in a low voice** | **in a loud voice**] = [xiǎo shēng de | dà shèng de] shuōhuà [小声地 | 大声地] 说话

- (*the quality of the sound one makes while singing or speaking*) = sǎngzi 嗓子, sǎngyīn 嗓音

she has a good voice = tāde sǎngzi hěn hǎo 他的嗓子很好

voicemail *noun*

= yǔyīn liúyán 语音留言

volleyball *noun* ▶ 390

= páiqiú 排球

vomit *verb*

= ǒutù 呕吐, tù 吐

vote *verb*

- (*to express one's choice by vote*) = tóupiào 投票

to vote [**for** | **against**] **someone** = tóupiào [xuǎn | bù xuǎn] mǒurén 投票[选 | 不选] 某人

to vote [**for** | **against**] **a plan** = tóupiào [zànchéng | fǎnduì] yíge jìhuà 投票[赞成 | 反对] 一个计划

- (*to determine by vote*) = tóupiào juédìng 投票决定

to vote in a new policy = tóupiào juédìng yíxiàng xīn zhèngcè 投票决定一项新政策

wages *noun*

= gōngzī 工资

waist *noun* ▶ 189

the waist = yāo 腰, yāobù 腰部

waistcoat *noun* (*British English*)

a waistcoat = yíjiàn bèixīn 一件背心, yíjiàn mǎjiǎ 一件马甲

wait *verb*

- **to wait** = děng(hòu) 等(候)

to wait for someone = děng mǒurén 等某人

I'm waiting to use the phone = wǒ zài děngzhe yòng diànhuà 我在等着用电话

I can't wait to see them = wǒ jíqiè de xiǎng jiàndào tāmen 我急切地想见到他们

- (*in a restaurant*)

to wait on tables, to wait tables (*US English*) = fúshì kèrén chī fàn 服侍客人吃饭

wait up

wait up = děng(hòu)zhe bú shuìjiào 等(候)着不睡觉

waiter *noun* ▶ 344

a waiter = yíge fúwùyuán 一个服务员

waiting room *noun*

a waiting room

(*at a train or a bus station*) = yíge hòuchēshì 一个候车室

(*at an airport*) = yíge hòujīshì 一个候机室

(*at a port*) = yíge hòuchuánshì 一个候船室

(*in a hospital*) = yíge hòuzhěnshì 一个候诊室

waitress *noun* ▶ 344
a waitress = yíge nǚzhāodài 一个女招待

wake *verb*
- (*to be roused from sleep*) = xǐng 醒, xǐnglai 醒来
  has she woken (up)? = tā xǐng le ma? 她醒了吗?
- (*to rouse from sleep*) = jiàoxǐng 叫醒, nòngxǐng 弄醒
  to wake someone (up) = bǎ mǒurén jiàoxǐng 把某人叫醒

Wales *noun*
= Wēi'ěrshì 威尔士

walk
1 *verb*
- (*to go on foot*) = zǒu 走, zǒulù 走路
  are you walking to the station? = nǐ yào zǒulù qù chēzhàn ma? 你要走路去车站吗?
- (*for pleasure*) = sànbù 散步
  to walk in the park = zài gōngyuán sànbù 在公园散步
- (*to take an animal out on a leash, etc.*) = liù 遛
  to walk the dog = liù gǒu 遛狗
- (*to escort by walking*) = péi(zhe)...zǒu 陪(着)... 走, sòng 送
  I'll walk you to the bus stop = wǒ péi(zhe) nǐ zǒu dào chēzhàn 我陪(着)你走到车站

2 *noun*
- **a walk** = sànbù 散步
  to go for a walk = qù sànbù 去散步
- (*act of walking*) = zǒu 走, zǒulù 走路
  my school is five minutes' walk from here = wǒde xuéxiào lí zhèr zǒulù yào wǔ fēnzhōng 我的学校离这儿走路要五分钟

walk around = sànbù 散步
to walk around town = zài chéng li sànbù 在城里散步
to walk around the lake = zài hú zhōuwéi sànbù 在湖周围散步
walk away = zǒukāi 走开
walk back = zǒu huí 走回
to walk back home = zǒu huí jiā 走回家
walk by = zǒuguò 走过
walk in(to) = zǒujìn 走进
walk out = zǒuchū 走出
to walk out of the room = zǒuchū fángjiān 走出房间
walk up to = zǒujìn 走进, zǒuxiàng 走向

walkman® *noun*
a walkman = yìtái biànxiéshì lùfàngjī 一台便携式录放机

wall *noun*
a wall = yìdǔ qiáng 一堵墙
the Great Wall = Chángchéng 长城

wallet *noun*
a wallet = yíge qiánbāo 一个钱包, yíge píjiāzi 一个皮夹子

wallpaper *noun*
= qiángzhǐ 墙纸

walnut *noun*
a walnut = yíge hétao 一个核桃

wander *verb*
(*to ramble, to roam*) = xiánguàng 闲逛, mànbù 漫步
to wander around town = zài chéng li xiánguàng 在城里闲逛
wander away, wander off = mànmàn de zǒukāi 慢慢地走开

want *verb*
- (*to desire something or someone*) = (xiǎng)yào (想)要
  do you want another coffee? = nǐ hái (xiǎng)yào yìbēi kāfēi ma? 你还(想)要一杯咖啡吗?
  do you want me to go with you? = nǐ (xiǎng)yào wǒ hé nǐ yìqǐ qù ma? 你(想)要我和你一起去吗?
- (*to desire to do something*) = xiǎng(yào) 想(要), yào 要
  he wants [**to go out** | **to go home** | **to play basketball ...**] = tā xiǎng [chūqu | huí jiā | dǎ lánqiú...] 他想 [出去 | 回家 | 打篮球...]
  she didn't want to stay there = tā bù xiǎng dāi zài nàr 她不想呆在那儿
- (*to need*) = xūyào 需要
  the house wants repairs = zhèdòng fángzi xūyào xiūlǐ le 这栋房子需要修理了

war *noun*
a war = yìchǎng zhànzhēng 一场战争

wardrobe *noun*
a wardrobe = yíge yīguì 一个衣柜, yíge yīchú 一个衣橱

warm
1 *adjective*
- (*moderately hot*) = nuǎnhuo 暖和, wēnnuǎn 温暖

I'm very warm = wǒ hěn nuǎnhuo 我很暖和
he doesn't feel warm = tā gǎnjué bù nuǎnhuo 他感觉不暖和
the weather is getting warm = tiānqì nuǎnhuoqǐlai le 天气暖和起来了
- (*ardent, enthusiastic*) = rèqíng 热情, rèliè 热烈
they gave us a warm reception = tāmen rèqíng de jiēdàile wǒmen 他们热情地接待了我们
a warm welcome = rèliè de huānyíng 热烈地欢迎
- (*hearty*) = rèxīn 热心, rèqíng 热情
a warm person = yíge rèxīn de rén 一个热心的人

2 *verb*
to warm the plates = bǎ pánzi rè yíxià 把盘子热一下
to warm one's hands = bǎ shǒu nuǎnhuo yíxià 把手暖和一下
warm up
- (*to get warm*) = nuǎnhuoqǐlai 暖和起来
the room is warming up = fángjiān nuǎnhuoqǐlai le 房间暖和起来了
- (*for a sport event*) = zuò zhǔnbèi huódòng 做准备活动
- (*to make warm*) = rè 热, jiārè 加热
to warm up the food = bǎ fàn rè yíxià 把饭热一下

warn *verb*
= jǐnggào 警告, gàojiè 告诫
to warn someone about the risks = jǐnggào mǒurén yǒu wēixiǎn 警告某人有危险
to warn someone to be careful = gàojiè mǒurén yào xiǎoxīn 告诫某人要小心

wash *verb*
- (*to clean*) = xǐ 洗
to wash one's clothes = xǐ yīfu 洗衣服
to wash one's face = xǐ liǎn 洗脸
- (*to get clean*) = xǐ 洗
this sheet doesn't wash easily = zhètiáo chuángdān bù hǎo xǐ 这条床单不好洗
wash out (*to remove by washing*) = xǐdiào 洗掉, xǐqù 洗去
to wash a stain out = bǎ wūdiǎn xǐdiào 把污点洗掉
wash up
- (*British English*) (*to do the dishes*) = xǐ wǎn 洗碗, xǐ cānjù 洗餐具
- (*US English*)
(*to clean one's hands*) = xǐ shǒu 洗手
(*to clean one's face*) = xǐ liǎn 洗脸

washbasin (*British English*) *noun*
a washbasin = yíge xǐliǎnpén 一个洗脸盆, yíge xǐshǒupén 一个洗手盆

washing *noun*
the washing (*to be washed*) = yào xǐ de yīfu 要洗的衣服
(*being washed*) = zhèngzài xǐ de yīfu 正在洗的衣服
(*washed*) = xǐhǎole de yīfu 洗好了的衣服
to do the washing = xǐ yīfu 洗衣服

washing machine *noun*
a washing machine = yìtái xǐyījī 一台洗衣机

washing-up *noun* (*British English*)
the washing-up (*to be washed*) = yào xǐ de cānjù 要洗的餐具
(*being washed*) = zhèngzài xǐ de cānjù 正在洗的餐具
(*washed*) = xǐhǎole de cānjù 洗好了的餐具
to do the washing-up = xǐ wǎn 洗碗, xǐ cānjù 洗餐具

wasp *noun*
a wasp = yìzhī huángfēng 一只黄蜂, yìzhī mǎfēng 一只马蜂

waste
1 *verb*
= làngfèi 浪费
to waste [**money** | **time** | **energy...**] = làngfèi [qián | shíjiān | jīnglì...] 浪费[钱 | 时间 | 精力...]
2 *noun*
- = làngfèi 浪费
it's a waste of [**money** | **time** | **energy...**] = zhè shì làngfèi [qián | shíjiān | jīnglì...] 这是浪费[钱 | 时间 | 精力...]
it's a waste of time going there = qù nàr shì làngfèi shíjiān 去那儿是浪费时间
- (*an uncultivated region*) = huāngdì 荒地, huāngyě 荒野
a waste = yípiàn huāngdì 一片荒地
- (*refuse or rejected material*) = lājī 垃圾, fèiwù 废物

watch
1 *verb*
- (*to look at*) = kàn 看

to watch [television | a football match | a Peking opera] = kàn [diànshì | zúqiú sài | jīngjù] 看 [电视 | 足球赛 | 京剧]
she watched me making the meal = tā kàn wǒ zuò fàn 她看我做饭
• (*to observe, to follow*) = jiānshì 监视
I feel I'm being watched = wǒ juéde yǒu rén zài jiānshì wǒ 我觉得有人在监视我
• (*to pay attention to*) = zhùyì 注意
please watch your spelling = qǐng zhùyì nǐde pīnxiě 请注意你的拼写
• (*to tend*) = zhàokàn 照看, zhàoliào 照料
2 *noun*
a watch (*a timepiece*) = yíkuài shǒubiǎo 一块手表
watch out = zhùyì 注意, dāngxīn 当心

water
1 *noun*
= shuǐ 水
drinking water = yǐnyòng shuǐ 饮用水
2 *verb*
• to water [the flowers | the tree | the garden] = gěi [huā | shù | huāyuán] jiāo shuǐ 给 [花 | 树 | 花园] 浇水
• (*to irrigate with water*) = guàngài 灌溉
• (*to salivate*) = liú kǒushuǐ 流口水

waterfall *noun*
a waterfall = yíge pùbù 一个瀑布

water-skiing *noun* ▶ 390
= huáshuǐ 滑水

wave
1 *verb*
• (*to greet or call someone*) = zhāoshǒu 招手
to wave to someone = xiàng mǒurén zhāoshǒu 向某人招手
• (*to say farewell or send signals*) = huīshǒu 挥手
to wave goodbye = huīshǒu gàobié 挥手告别
• to wave red flags = huīwǔ/huīdòng hóngqí 挥舞/挥动红旗
2 *noun*
a wave (*on the surface of the sea, river, etc.*) = yíge (bō)làng 一个(波)浪
(*in physics*) = yíge bō 一个波

way
1 *noun*
• (*a means, a method*)
a way = yìzhǒng fāngfǎ 一种方法
it's a way of earning money = zhè shì yìzhǒng zhuàn qián de fāngfǎ 这是一种赚钱的方法
it's a good way to make friends = zhè shì yìzhǒng jiāo péngyou de hǎo fāngfǎ 这是一种交朋友的好方法
he does it the wrong way = tā zuò de fāngfǎ bú duì 他做的方法不对
• (*when referring to the manner of doing something*)
a way = yìzhǒng fāngshì 一种方式
I like their way of life = wǒ xǐhuan tāmende shēnghuó fāngshì 我喜欢他们的生活方式
I don't like this way of educating children = wǒ bù xǐhuan zhèzhǒng jiàoyù háizi de fāngshì 我不喜欢这种教育孩子的方式
• (*a route, a road*) = lù 路, dàolù 道路
a way = yìtiáo lù 一条路
I can't remember the way to the station = wǒ bú jìde qù chēzhàn de lù le 我不记得去车站的路了
we can buy something to eat along the way = wǒmen kěyǐ mǎi yìdiǎn dōngxi zài lù shang chī 我们可以买一点东西在路上吃
on the way back (*going back*) = zài huíqu de lù shang 在回去的路上
(*coming back*) = zài huílai de lù shang 在回来的路上
I met them on the way back from town = wǒ zài cóng chéng li huílai de lù shang yùjiànle tāmen 我在从城里回来的路上遇见了他们
on the way to Shanghai = zài qù Shànghǎi de lù shang 在去上海的路上
where's the way out? = cóng nǎr kěyǐ chūqu 从哪儿可以出去
can you tell me the way to the underground = qǐng wèn qù dìtiě zěnme zǒu? 请问去地铁怎么走?
to lose one's way = mílù 迷路
• (*a direction*) = fāngxiàng 方向
which way are you going? = nǐ qù nǎge fāngxiàng 你去哪个方向
they went that way = tāmen qùle nàge fāngxiàng 他们去了那个方向
come this way = zhè biān lái 这边来
• (*someone's route*)
to be in someone's way = dǎng mǒurén de dào/lù 挡某人的道/路

to be in the way = dǎngdào 挡道, àishì 碍事

Get out of the way! = Gǔnkāi! 滚开!✖

- (*when talking about distances*)

the airport is a long way from here = fēijīchǎng lí zhèr hěn yuǎn 飞机场离这儿很远

to come all the way from Tibet = cóng Xīzàng yuǎndào ér lái 从西藏远道而来

- (*what one wants*)

she always wants her own way = tā zǒngshì wǒ xíng wǒ sù 她总是我行我素

if I had my own way, I'd go alone = jiǎrú wǒ néng shuōle suàn, wǒ jiù yíge rén qù 假如我能说了算, 我就一个人去

2 by the way

- (*when used with a question*) = shùnbiàn wèn yíxià 顺便问一下

what's his name, by the way? = shùnbiàn wèn yíxià, tā jiào shénme míngzi? 顺便问一下, 他叫什么名字?

- (*when used with a statement*) = shùnbiàn shuō yíxià 顺便说一下

by the way, I've bought the train tickets = shùnbiàn shuō yíxià, wǒ yǐjīng mǎile huǒchēpiào le 顺便说一下, 我已经买了火车票了

we *pronoun*

we = wǒmen 我们

we didn't agree = wǒmen méi tóngyì 我们没同意

weak *adjective*

- (*having very little power*) = ruǎnruò 软弱, wúlì 无力

a weak government = yíge ruǎnruò (wúlì) de zhèngfǔ 一个软弱(无力)的政府

- (*not healthy*) = ruò 弱, xūruò 虚弱

she has a weak heart = tāde xīnzàng hěn xūruò 她的心脏很虚弱

- (*not good or able*) = chà 差, bóruò 薄弱

I'm weak at foreign languages = wǒde wàiyǔ hěn chà 我的外语很差

- (*describing tea or coffee*) = dàn 淡

✖an offensive word

wealthy *adjective*

= fù(yǒu) 富(有), yǒuqián 有钱

wear *verb*

- (*when talking about wearing coats, shirts, dresses, trousers, socks, shoes*) = chuān 穿

she's wearing jeans = tā chuānzhe niúzǎikù 她穿着牛仔裤

to wear black = chuān hēisè de yīfu 穿黑色的衣服

- (*when talking about wearing hats, scarves, glasses, or accessories such as rings, necklaces, etc.*) = dài 戴

he's wearing a red tie today = jīntiān tā dàizhe yìtiáo hóngsè de lǐngdài 今天他戴着一条红色的领带

- (*to damage, as clothes*) = mópò 磨破, chuānpò 穿破

the trousers are all worn = kùzi dōu chuānpò le 裤子都穿破了

wear out

- (*to damage by wearing*) = chuānpò 穿破

to wear one's shoes out = bǎ xié chuānpò 把鞋穿破

- (*to damage through use*) = yònghuài 用坏

the toothbrush is worn out = yáshuā yǐjīng yònghuài le 牙刷已经用坏了

- (*to make tired and exhausted*)

the work has worn everyone out = zhège gōngzuò bǎ měi ge rén dōu lèi de jīngpí lìjìn 这个工作把每个人都累得精疲力尽

I feel worn out = wǒ gǎndào hěn pífá 我感到很疲乏

weather *noun*

the weather = tiānqì 天气

what's the weather like? = tiānqì zěnmeyàng? 天气怎么样?

[**fine** | **cloudy** | **wet**] **weather** = [qíng | yīn | yǔ] tiān [晴 | 阴 | 雨] 天

weather forecast *noun*

the weather forecast = tiānqì yùbào 天气预报

webpage *noun*

a webpage = yìzhāng wǎngyè 一张网页

website *noun*

a website = yíge wǎngzhǐ 一个网址

wedding *noun*

a wedding = yíge hūnlǐ 一个婚礼

to attend a wedding = cānjiā yíge hūnlǐ 参加一个婚礼

Wednesday *noun* ▶ 218
= xīngqīsān 星期三, lǐbàisān 礼拜三

week *noun* ▶ 218, ▶ 412
a week = yíge xīngqī 一个星期, yì zhōu 一周
[this | last | next] week = [zhège | shàng(ge) | xià(ge)] xīngqī [这个 | 上(个) | 下(个)] 星期

weekend *noun* ▶ 218, ▶ 412
a weekend = yíge zhōumò 一个周末

weigh *verb* ▶ 300
• (*to find the weight of*) = chēng 称
to weigh the luggage = chēng xíngli 称行李
to weigh oneself = chēng zìjǐ de tǐzhòng 称自己的体重
• (*to have the weight of*) = zhòng 重, zhòngliàng shì 重量是
how much do you weigh = nǐ yǒu duō zhòng? 你有多重?
my luggage weighs 20 kilos = wǒde xíngli zhòng èrshí gōngjīn 我的行李重二十公斤

weight *noun* ▶ 300
• (*the heaviness of a thing*) = zhòngliàng 重量
• (*the heaviness of one's body*) = tǐzhòng 体重
[to lose | to gain] weight = [jiǎnqīng | zēngjiā] tǐzhòng [减轻 | 增加] 体重

weird *adjective*
(*strange, bizarre*) = qíguài 奇怪, bùkěsīyì 不可思议

welcome
1 *verb* ▶ 238
= huānyíng 欢迎
to welcome someone = huānyíng mǒurén 欢迎某人
2 *adjective*
• (*when receiving people*)
= huānyíng 欢迎
welcome to the United States = huānyíng (nǐmen) dào Měiguó lái 欢迎(你们)到美国来
suggestions are welcome = huānyíng dàjiā tíchū jiànyì 欢迎大家提出建议
a welcome guest = yíwèi shòu huānyíng de kèrén 一位受欢迎的客人
• (*when acknowledging thanks*)
'thanks'—'you're welcome' = 'xièxie'—'bú yòng kèqì' '谢谢'—'不用客气'
3 *noun*
a welcome = huānyíng 欢迎

well
1 *adverb* ▶ 238
• (*in good manner or degree*)

> **!** *Note that in this sense* **well** *is often translated as* **hǎo 好**. *However, it can also be expressed as* **búcuò 不错**, **shùnlì 顺利**, *etc.*

well = hǎo 好
she speaks Chinese well = tā Hànyǔ shuō de hěn hǎo 她汉语说得很好
well done = gàn de hǎo 干得好
he's not eating well (*because of a poor appetite*) = tā chī fàn bú tài hǎo 他吃饭不太好, ta shíyù bú zhèn 他食欲不振
did everything go well? = yíqiè shùnlì ma? 一切顺利吗?
he treated us well = tā duì wǒmen búcuò 他对我们不错
she was dressed well = tā chuān de hěn piàoliang 她穿得很漂亮
• (*fully, thoroughly*)
I understand her feeling well = wǒ wánquán lǐjiě tāde xīnqíng 我完全理解她的心情
please clean the room well before you leave = qǐng nǐ líkāi qián bǎ fángjiān chèdǐ dǎsǎo yíxià 请你离开前把房间彻底打扫一下
• (*very possibly*) = hěn kěnéng 很可能
you may well be right = nǐ hěn kěnéng shì duì de 你很可能是对的
he may well come to see you = tā hěn kěnéng lái kàn nǐ 他很可能来看你
• (*to a considerable degree*)
this is well beyond her ability = zhè dàdà chāochūle tāde nénglì 这大大超出了她的能力
it's well worth considering = zhè hěn zhíde kǎolǜ 这很值得考虑
his exam result is well above the average = tāde kǎoshì chéngjī gāochū píngjūn fēn hěn duō 他的考试成绩高出平均分很多
2 *adjective*
he's not feeling well = tā juéde bù shūfu 他觉得不舒服
everyone is well = dàjiā dōu hěn hǎo 大家都很好

I'm very well = wǒ hěn hǎo 我很好
you don't look very well = nǐ (kànshangqu) liǎnsè bú tài hǎo 你(看上去)脸色不太好
I hope you'll get well soon = wǒ xīwàng nǐ zǎorì huīfù jiànkāng 我希望你早日恢复健康
3 as well = yě 也
he speaks Japanese as well = tā yě huì shuō Rìyǔ 他也会说日语
4 as well as = bùjǐn...érqiě... 不仅... 而且..., jì...yòu... 既... 又...
he bought a Japanese dictionary as well as a Chinese dictionary = tā bùjǐn mǎile yìběn Zhōngwén cídiǎn, érqiě hái mǎile yìběn Rìwén cídiǎn 他不仅买了一本中文词典, 而且还买了一本日文词典

well-known *adjective*
• (*celebrated*) = zhùmíng 著名, chūmíng 出名
• (*fully and widely known*) = zhòng suǒ zhōu zhī 众所周知

Welsh ▶ 288
1 *adjective*
= Wēi'ěrshì de 威尔士的
2 *noun*
• (*the people*)
the Welsh = Wēi'ěrshìrén 威尔士人
• (*the language*)
Welsh = Wēi'ěrshìyǔ 威尔士语

west
1 *noun*
= xībù 西部, xībian 西边
in the west of China = zài Zhōngguó de xībù 在中国的西部
the West = Xīfāng 西方
2 *adverb*
to go west = wǎng xī(bian) qù 往西(边)去
to live west of Beijing = zhù zài Běijīng xībù 住在北京西部
3 *adjective*
= xī 西
to work in west London = zài xī Lúndūn gōngzuò 在西伦敦工作

wet
1 *adjective*
• (*saturated with water*) = shī 湿
your hair is wet = nǐde tóufa shīle 你的头发湿了
• (*damp*) = cháo 潮, cháoshī 潮湿
• (*rainy*)
wet weather = duōyǔ de tiānqì 多雨的天气
a wet day = yíge yǔ tiān 一个雨天
• (*not yet dry*) = bù gān 不干
the paint is still wet = yóuqī hái méi gān 油漆还没干
2 *verb*
(*to make wet*) = nòng shī 弄湿

what
1 *pronoun*
• (*used in questions*) = shénme 什么
what's that box? = nàge hézi shì shénme? 那个盒子是什么?
what does he look like? = tā zhǎng de shénme yàng? 他长得什么样?
I don't know what he's doing = wǒ bù zhīdào tā zài zuò shénme 我不知道他在做什么
what's your name? = nǐ jiào shénme míngzi? 你叫什么名字?
what's the time? = jǐ diǎn le? 几点了?
what's the Chinese for 'boring'? = Zhōngwén 'boring' zěnme shuō? 中文 'boring' 怎么说?
what's her phone number? = tāde diànhuà hàomǎ shì duōshǎo? 她的电话号码是多少?
• (*used as a relative pronoun*)
what he [bought | sold | asked for...] was a computer = tā(suǒ) [mǎi | mài | yào...] de shì yìtái jìsuànjī 他(所) [买 | 卖 | 要...] 的是一台计算机
is this what he [said | needed | wrote...]? = zhè shì tā (suǒ) [shuō | xūyào | xiě...] de ma? 这是他(所)[说 | 需要 | 写...] 的吗?
do what you want = nǐ xiǎng zuò shénme jiù zuò shénme 你想做什么就做什么
2 *determiner*
• = shénme 什么
what [books | colours | food...] do you like? = nǐ xǐhuan shénme [shū | yánsè | fàn...]? 你喜欢什么 [书 | 颜色 | 饭...]?
what time is it? = jǐ diǎn le? 几点了?
• (*in exclamations*) = duōme 多么
what [a good idea | cold weather | a pretty girl]! = duōme [hǎo de zhǔyì | lěng de tiānqì | měilì de gūniang] a! 多么[好的主意 | 冷的天气 | 美丽的姑娘] 啊!
3 *adverb*
what do you think of him? = nǐ juéde tā zěnmeyàng? 你觉得他怎么样?
what does it matter to him? = zhè gēn tā yǒu shénme guānxì? 这跟他有什么关系?

4 what if

- (*what would happen if*) = rúguǒ...zěnme bàn 如果... 怎么办
  what if I can't get there on time? = rúguǒ wǒ bù néng ànshí dàodá nàr, zěnme bàn ne? 如果我不能按时到达那儿, 怎么办呢?
- (*what would it matter if*) = jíshǐ...yòu yǒu shénme guānxì 即使... 又有什么关系
  what if I don't get there on time? = jíshǐ wǒ bú ànshí dàodá nàr, yòu yǒu shénme guānxì ne? 即使我不按时到达那儿, 又有什么关系呢?

whatever *pronoun*

- (*when anything is possible*)
  take whatever you want = nǐ yào shénme jiù ná shénme ba 你要什么就拿什么吧
  whatever you think is useful = fánshì nǐ xiǎng de dōu hěn yǒuyòng 凡是你想的都很有用
- (*when it doesn't matter*)
  whatever [happens | they do | you say...], I won't change my mind = bùguǎn [fāshēng | tāmen zuò | nǐ shuō...] shénme, wǒ dōu bú huì gǎibiàn zhǔyì 不管 [发生 | 他们做 | 你说...] 什么, 我都不会改变主意

wheat *noun*

= xiǎomài 小麦, màizi 麦子

wheel *noun*

a wheel = yíge lúnzi 一个轮子

wheelchair *noun*

a wheelchair = yíge lúnyǐ 一个轮椅

when

1 *adverb* ▶ 204

= shénme shíhou 什么时候
when did she leave? = tā shì shénme shíhou líkāi de? 她是什么时候离开的?
when is your birthday? = nǐ shénme shíhou guò shēngri? 你什么时候过生日?
I don't know when the film starts = wǒ bù zhīdào diànyǐng shénme shíhou kāiyǎn 我不知道电影什么时候开演

> **!** *See the usage note on* Talking about time ▶ 412 *for further information on time expressions.*

2 *conjunction*

- = (dāng/zài)...deshíhou (当/在) ... 的时候
  he didn't study any Chinese when he was at school = tā zài zhōngxué de shíhou méi xué Zhōngwén 他在中学的时候没学中文
  when I'm 18, I'll have my own car = wǒ shíbā suì de shíhou, wǒ yào yǒu yíliàng zìjǐ de qìchē 我十八岁的时候, 我要有一辆自己的汽车
- (*when talking about something unexpected happening in the midst of another action*)
  I was asleep when the phone rang = wǒ zhèngzài shuìjiào, tūrán diànhuàlíng xiǎng le 我正在睡觉, 突然电话铃响了
  we were playing basketball when it started to rain = wǒmen zhèngzài dǎ lánqiú, tūrán tiān xiàqi yǔ lai 我们正在打篮球, 突然天下起雨来

3 *pronoun*

- (*used as a relative pronoun*)

> **!** *Note that in this case,* when *is usually not translated.*

  in the days when there was no TV = zài méi yǒu diànshì de rìzi li 在没有电视的日子里
- (*used in questions*) = shénme shíhou 什么时候
  until when did you work last night = zuótiān yè li nǐ yìzhí gōngzuò dào shénme shíhou? 昨天夜里你一直工作到什么时候?

where

1 *adverb*

= nǎlǐ 哪里, nǎr 哪儿
where are you going? = nǐ shàng nǎr? 你上哪儿
where do they work? = tāmen zài nǎlǐ gōngzuò? 他们在哪里工作?
do you know where [he is | Tom is | we're...] going? = nǐ zhīdào [tā yào | Tāngmǔ yào | wǒmen yào...] qù nǎr ma? 你知道 [他要 | 汤姆要 | 我们要...] 去哪儿吗?
I wonder where he lives = wǒ xiǎng zhīdào tā zhù zài nǎlǐ 我想知道他住在哪里

2 *conjunction*

= ...de dìfang ... 的地方
that's where she fell = nà jiù shì tā diēdǎo de dìfang 那就是她跌倒的地方

I'll leave the key where you can see it = wǒ huì bǎ yàoshi fàng zài nǐ néng kànjian de dìfang 我会把钥匙放在你能看见的地方

3 *pronoun*

- (*used as a relative pronoun in a defining relative clause*)

> **!** *Note that in this case,* **where** *is usually not translated.*

the village where we live = wǒmen zhù de cūnzi 我们住的村子

- (*used as a relative pronoun in a non-defining relative clause*)

= zài nàlǐ 在那里, zài nàr 在那儿

I went to Shanghai last year, where I visited some Chinese families = qùnián wǒ qùle Shànghǎi, zài nàlǐ wǒ fǎngwènle yìxiē Zhōngguó jiātíng 去年我去了上海, 在那里我访问了一些中国家庭

- (*used in questions*) = nǎlǐ 哪里, nǎr 哪儿

where do you come from? = nǐ cóng nǎlǐ lái? 你从哪里来?

whether *conjunction*

- (*if*) = shìfǒu 是否, shì bú shì 是不是

I don't know whether or not to accept her invitation = wǒ bù zhīdào shìfǒu yīnggāi jiēshòu tāde yāoqǐng 我不知道是否应该接受她的邀请

- **whether... or...**

(*when introducing two alternatives*) = ...háishì... ...还是...

I wonder whether I should go to Beijing or Shanghai = wǒ bù zhīdào (wǒ) yīnggāi qù Běijīng háishì qù Shànghǎi 我不知道(我)应该去北京还是去上海

(*in any case, in any event*) = bùguǎn/búlùn...háishì... 不管/不论... 还是...

whether you come to me or I go to you, we must find time to discuss this problem this week = bùguǎn nǐ lái wǒ zhèr háishì wǒ qù nǐ nàr, zhège xīngqī wǒmen bìxū zhǎo shíjiān tǎolùn zhège wèntí 不管你来我这儿还是我去你那儿, 这个星期我们必须找时间讨论这个问题

which

1 *pronoun*

- (*used as a relative pronoun in a defining relative clause*)

> **!** *Note that in this case,* **which** *is usually not translated.*

the house which I told you about = wǒ gàosu nǐ de nàzuò fángzi 我告诉你的那座房子

the book which is on the table = (zài) zhuōzi shang de shū (在)桌子上的书

- (*used as a relative pronoun in a non-defining relative clause*)

> **!** *Note that in this case,* **which** *is often translated as the noun it refers to, or as the pronouns,* **zhè 这** *or* **nà 那**.

he was teaching at Peking University, which was very far from the city centre = tā zài Běijīng Dàxué jiāoshū, Běijīng Dàxué lí shì zhōngxīn hěn yuǎn 他在北京大学教书, 北京大学离市中心很远

he has given up smoking, which makes his wife very pleased = tā jiè yān le, zhè shǐ tā tàitai fēicháng gāoxìng 他戒烟了, 这使他太太非常高兴

- (*in questions*)

which...?

> **!** *Note that in questions,* **which** *as a pronoun is usually translated as* **nǎxiē 哪些** *if it refers to a plural noun, and as* **nǎ (yí)ge 哪(一)个** *if it refers to a singular noun. In* **nǎ (yí)ge 哪(一)个**, *the measure word* **ge 个** *may be replaced with a different measure word depending on the noun being referred to.*

(*when the noun is plural*) = nǎxiē 哪些

which of these books are yours? = zhèxiē shū zhōng nǎxiē shì nǐde? 这些书中哪些是你的?

(*when the noun is singular*) = nǎ (yí)ge 哪(一)个

of these parks, which is the largest? = zhèxiē gōngyuán nǎ yíge zuì dà? 这些公园哪一个最大?

of these books, which is most useful? = zhèxiē shū nǎ yìběn zuì yǒuyòng? 这些书哪一本最有用?

there are three computers; which do you want to buy? = yǒu sāntái jìsuànjī, nǐ xiǎng mǎi nǎ yìtái? 有三台计算机, 你想买哪一台?

2 *determiner*

- (*when the noun that follows is plural*) = nǎxiē 哪些

which books did he borrow? = tā jièle nǎxiē shū? 他借了哪些书?

- (*when the noun that follows is singular*) = nǎ (yí)ge 哪(一)个

> ! *Note that in* nǎ (yí)ge 哪(一)个, *the measure word* ge 个 *may be replaced by a different measure word depending on the noun being referred to.*

which one of the nurses speaks Chinese? = nǎ yíge hùshì huì shuō Hànyǔ? 哪一个护士会说汉语?

which car is yours? = nǎ yíliàng chē shì nǐde? 哪一辆车是你的?

he asked me which shirt I liked = tā wèn wǒ xǐhuan nǎ yíjiàn chènshān 他问我喜欢哪一件衬衫

while *conjunction*

(*in the time that*) = (dāng)...de shíhou (当)... 的时候

I was ill while I was on holiday in Japan = wǒ zài Rìběn dùjià de shíhou bìng le 我在日本度假的时候病了

she fell asleep while watching TV = tā kàn diànshì de shíhou shuìzháo le 她看电视的时候睡着了, tā kànzhe diànshì shuìzháo le 她看着电视睡着了

whisper *verb*

(*to say in soft, hushed tones*) = xiǎoshēng de shuō 小声地说, dīshēng de shuō 低声地说

whistle

1 *verb*

- (*with the mouth*) = chuī kǒushào 吹口哨
- (*with a whistle*) = chuī shàozi 吹哨子
- (*when referring to a train*) = míng dí 鸣笛

2 *noun*

a whistle (*blown with the mouth*) = yíge shàozi 一个哨子

(*sounded by escaping steam*) = yíge qìdí 一个汽笛

white *adjective*

= bái 白, báisè de 白色的

who *pronoun*

- (*used in questions*) = shéi/shuí 谁

who told you? = shéi gàosu nǐ de? 谁告诉你的?

who did you invite? = nǐ qǐngle shéi? 你请了谁?

who did he buy the book for? = tā gěi shéi mǎi de shū? 他给谁买的书?

- (*used as a relative pronoun in a defining relative clause*)

> ! *Note that in this case,* who *is usually not translated.*

those who can't come by bike = nàxiē bù néng qí zìxíngchē lái de rén 那些不能骑自行车来的人

the man who you want to see = nǐ xiǎng jiàn de nàge rén 你想见的那个人

- (*used as a relative pronoun in a non-defining relative clause*) = tā 他, tā 她, tāmen 他们

> ! *Note that in this case,* who *is translated as* tā 他 *if it refers to a man, as* tā 她 *if it refers to a woman, and as* tāmen 他们 *if it refers to a plural noun.*

I went to see my mother, who had just come back from China = wǒ qù kàn wǒ māma, tā gāng cóng Zhōngguó huílai 我去看我妈妈, 她刚从中国回来

he is waiting for his friends, who are coming to celebrate his birthday = tā zài děng tāde péngyou, tāmen yào lái gěi tā guò shēngri 他在等他的朋友, 他们要来给他过生日

whole

1 *noun*

the whole of [**the country** | **London** | **August...**] = zhěnggè [guójiā | Lúndūn | bāyuè...] 整个 [国家 | 伦敦 | 八月...]

2 *adjective*

a whole day = yì zhěng tiān 一整天

three whole weeks = zhěngzhěng sānge xīngqī 整整三个星期

the whole world = quán shìjiè 全世界

I don't want to spend my whole life here = wǒ bù xiǎng zài zhèlǐ dùguò wǒde zhěnggè yìshēng 我不想在这里度过我的整个一生

whom *pronoun*

- (*used in questions*) = shéi/shuí 谁

whom did you meet? = nǐ yùjiànle shéi? 你遇见了谁?

- (*used as a relative pronoun in a defining clause*)

> ! *Note that in this case,* whom *is usually not translated.*

the person whom you met yesterday = zuótiān nǐ jiàn de nàge rén 昨天你见的那个人

• (*used as a relative pronoun in a non-defining clause*) = tā 他, tā 她, tāmen 他们

> ! *Note that in this case,* whom *is translated as* tā 他 *if it refers to a man, as* tā 她 *if it refers to a woman, and as* tāmen 他们 *if it refers to a plural noun.*

my younger brother, whom you met in my house, is going to Taiwan to study Chinese = wǒ dìdi yào qù Táiwān xuéxí Hànyǔ, nǐ zài wǒ jiā jiànguo tā 我弟弟要去台湾学习汉语, 你在我家见过他

these students, for whom I have to arrange accommodation, came from China = zhèxiē xuésheng lái zì Zhōngguó, wǒ děi gěi tāmen ānpái zhùsù 这些学生来自中国, 我得给他们安排住宿

whose

1 *pronoun*

• (*used in questions*) = shéi de/shuí de 谁的

whose is this nice hat? = zhèdǐng piàoliang de màozi shì shéi de? 这顶漂亮的帽子是谁的?

• (*used as a relative pronoun*)

> ! *Note that in this case,* whose *is often translated as* tāde 他的 *if it refers to a masculine singular noun, as* tāde 她的 *if it refers to a feminine singular noun, as* tāde 它的 *if it refers to a non-human singular noun, as* tāmende 他们的 *if it refers to a human plural noun, and as* tāmende 它们的 *if it refers to a non-human plural noun. Sometimes,* whose *is not translated at all in a defining relative clause.*

the boy whose bike was stolen = (tāde) zìxíngchē bèi rén tōuzǒule de nàge nánháir (他的)自行车被人偷走了的那个男孩儿

the woman whose house I'm buying = wǒ yào mǎi tāde fángzi de nàge nǚde 我要买她的房子的那个女的

they are Mr. and Mrs. Brown, whose son used to be a student of mine = tāmen shì Bùlǎng xiānsheng hé Bùlǎng tàitai, tāmende érzi yǐqián shì wǒde xuésheng 他们是布朗先生和布朗太太, 他们的儿子以前是我的学生

the chair whose leg is broken = duànle tuǐ de nàbǎ yǐzi 断了腿的那把椅子

2 *determiner*

= shéi de/shuí de 谁的

whose car is that? = nà shì shéi de chē? 那是谁的车?

whose pen did you borrow? = nǐ jiè shéi de bǐ? 你借谁的笔?

why

1 *adverb*

= wèishénme 为什么

why did you tell him? = nǐ wèishénme gàosu tā? 你为什么告诉他?

why aren't they coming? = tāmen wèishénme bù lái? 他们为什么不来?

why not? = wèishénme bù? 为什么不?

why don't we eat out tonight? = jīntiān wǎnshang wǒmen wèishénme bù chūqu chī ne? 今天晚上我们为什么不出去吃呢?

2 *conjunction*

= ...de yuányīn ...的原因

that's (the reason) why I can't stand him = zhè jiù shì wǒ bù néng rěnshòu tā de yuányīn 这就是我不能忍受他的原因

please tell me why you want to learn Chinese = qǐng nǐ gàosu wǒ nǐ yào xué Zhōngwén de yuányīn 请你告诉我你要学中文的原因, qǐng nǐ gàosu wǒ nǐ wèishénme yào xué Zhōngwén 请你告诉我你为什么要学中文

W

wide *adjective* ▶ 300

• (*in size*) = kuān 宽

a wide garden = yíge hěn kuān de huāyuán 一个很宽的花园

the room is ten metres wide = zhège fángjiān shí mǐ kuān 这个房间十米宽

• (*in range*)

a wide range of choices = guǎngfàn de xuǎnzé fànwéi 广泛的选择范围

a person with wide interests = yíge xìngqù guǎngfàn de rén 一个兴趣广泛的人

a wide range of games = zhǒnglèi fánduō de yóuxì 种类繁多的游戏

width *noun* ▶ 300

- (*the distance between*) = kuāndù 宽度
- (*being wide*) = kuānkuò 宽阔

  a road of great width = yìtiáo kuānkuò de mǎlù 一条宽阔的马路

wife *noun*

- (*less formal*) = qīzi 妻子, àirén 爱人
- (*more formal*) = fūrén 夫人, tàitai 太太

  a wife = yíwèi fūrén 一位夫人

wild *adjective*

- (*describing animals, plants*) = yěshēng 野生

  wild plants = yěshēng zhíwù 野生植物

  wild animals = yěshēng dòngwù 野生动物
- (*noisy, out of control*) = fāfēng 发疯, fākuáng 发狂

  he's gone wild = tā fāfēng le 他发疯了
- (*not cultivated*) = huāngwú 荒芜, huāngliáng 荒凉

wildlife *noun*

= yěshēng dòngwù 野生动物

will *verb*

- (*when talking about the future*)

  (*in positive statements and questions*) = huì 会, jiāng(yào) 将(要)

  will she agree? = tā huì tóngyì ma? 她会同意吗?

  it will rain tomorrow = míngtiān jiāngyào xiàyǔ 明天将要下雨

  we will discuss this problem = wǒmen jiāng tǎolùn zhège wèntí 我们将讨论这个问题

  (*in negative sentences*)

  will not = (jiāng) bú huì (将)不会

  she won't agree = tā bú huì tóngyì 她不会同意

  I won't forget = wǒ bú huì wàngjì 我不会忘记
- (*when talking about willingness*) = yuànyì 愿意

  I will do my best to help this child = wǒ yuànyì jìn zuì dà nǔlì bāngzhù zhège háizi 我愿意尽最大努力帮助这个孩子

  she won't come = tā bú yuànyì lái 她不愿意来
- (*when talking about intentions*) = xiǎng 想, yào 要

  will you visit the Great Wall? = nǐ yào qù cānguān Chángchéng ma? 你要去参观长城吗?

  we won't stay too long = wǒmen bù huì dāi hěn cháng shíjiān 我们不会呆很长时间
- (*in invitations and requests*) = (qǐng)...hǎo ma? (请)... 好吗?

  will you have some coffee? = nín hē diǎnr kāfēi, hǎo ma? 您喝点儿咖啡, 好吗?

  will you pass me the salt, please? = qǐng nǐ bǎ yán dìgěi wǒ, hǎo ma? 请你把盐递给我, 好吗?
- (*when making an assumption about the future*) = huì 会

  they won't know what's happened = tāmen bú huì zhīdào fāshēngle shénme shì 他们不会知道发生了什么事

win *verb*

- (*be victorious*) = yíng 赢, huòshèng 获胜
- (*to gain in a battle, match, contest*) = yíngdé 赢得, huòdé 获得

  to win a gold medal = huòdé yìméi jīnpái 获得一枚金牌

wind *noun*

a wind = fēng 风

window *noun*

a window (*in a house, a car, a plane*) = yìge chuānghu 一个窗户

(*in a shop*) = yíge chúchuāng 一个橱窗

windsurfing *noun* ▶ 390

= fānbǎn yùndòng 帆板运动

windy *adjective*

= guā (dà) fēng 刮(大)风, fēng dà 风大

it's very windy outside = wàimian guā dà fēng 外面刮大风

wine *noun*

= pútaojiǔ 葡萄酒

wing *noun*

a wing (*of a bird*) = yìzhī chìbǎng 一只翅膀

(*for a plane*) = yíge jīyì 一个机翼

winter *noun*
= dōngtiān 冬天, dōngjì 冬季

wipe *verb*
= cā 擦
to wipe [one's nose | one's tears | the table...] = cā [bízi | yǎnlèi | zhuōzi...] 擦 [鼻子 | 眼泪 | 桌子...]

wise *adjective*
(*when describing a person*) = cōngming 聪明
(*when describing a decision, a choice, or a leader*) = yīngmíng 英明, míngzhì 明智

wish
1 *noun*
- (*a hope*)
a wish = yíge yuànwàng 一个愿望
- **best wishes** (*in greetings*) = zuì liánghǎo de zhùyuàn 最良好的祝愿
to give one's best wishes to someone = xiàng mǒurén zhìyì 向某人致意
(*in a letter*)
with best wishes = zhù hǎo 祝好

2 *verb*
- (*to want, to be inclined*) = xiǎng 想, yào 要
how long do they wish to stay here for? = tāmen xiǎng zài zhèr dāi duō jiǔ? 他们想在这儿呆多久?
- (*to long, to hope*) = kěwàng 渴望
I wish to visit Hong Kong = wǒ kěwàng qù Xiānggǎng fǎngwèn 我渴望去香港访问
- (*expressing what one would like to happen or to have happened*) = yàoshì...jiù hǎo le 要是... 就好了
I wish they could come = yàoshì tāmen néng lái jiù hǎo le 要是他们能来就好了
she wished she hadn't lied = tā xiǎng yàoshì tā méi sāhuǎng jiù hǎo le 她想要是她没撒谎就好了
- (*in greetings*) = zhù 祝, zhùyuàn 祝愿
to wish someone a happy birthday = zhù mǒurén shēngri kuàilè 祝某人生日快乐

with *preposition*
- (*in the company of*) = hé...(yìqǐ) 和...(一起), gēn...(yìqǐ) 跟... (一起)
he went away with his friends = tā hé tāde péngyou (yìqǐ) zǒu le 他和他的朋友(一起)走了
I'm living with my parents = wǒ gēn wǒ fùmǔ zhù zài yìqǐ 我跟我父母住在一起
- (*by means of*) = yòng 用
she is wiping her tears with her hands = tā zài yòng shǒu cā yǎnlèi 她在用手擦眼泪
- (*in the possession of*)

> ! *Note that in this case,* with *is often not translated.*

a girl with black hair = yíge hēi tóufa de nǚháir 一个黑头发的女孩儿
the boy with the broken leg = nàge duànle tuǐ de nánháir 那个断了腿的男孩儿
a man with a great sense of humour = yíge hěn yōumò de rén 一个很幽默的人
he left with a smile = tā xiàozhe zǒu le 他笑着走了
she's married with two children = tā jiéhūn le, yóu liǎngge háizi 她结婚了, 有两个孩子
- (*denoting support*) = zàntóng 赞同, zhīchí 支持
most people are with this proposal = dàduōshù rén dōu zàntóng zhège tíyì 大多数人都赞同这个提议
- (*denoting understanding*) = dǒng 懂, míngbai 明白, lǐjiě 理解
I'm with you = wǒ dǒng nǐde yìsi 我懂你的意思
- (*because of*)

> ! *Note that in this case,* with *is often not translated.*

she jumped with joy = tā gāoxìng de tiàole qǐlai 她高兴地跳了起来
she shivered with fear = tā xià de fādǒu 她吓得发抖
- (*at hand*)
I haven't got any money with me = wǒ (shēn shang) méi dài qián 我(身上)没带钱
you'd better take a dictionary with you = nǐ zuìhǎo suíshēn dài yìběn cídiǎn 你最好随身带一本词典
- (*at the same time as*) = suízhe 随着
the living standard improves with the increase in the people's income = shēnghuó shuǐpíng suízhe rénmen shōurù de zēngjiā ér gǎishàn 生活水平随着人们收入的增加而改善

without *preposition*
= méiyǒu 没有
we got in without paying = wǒmen méiyǒu fù qián jiù jìnqu le 我们没有付钱就进去了

wolf *noun*
a wolf = yìtiáo láng 一条狼

woman *noun*
a woman = yíwèi fùnǚ 一位妇女
a single woman = yíge dānshēn fùnǚ 一个单身妇女

wonder *verb*
- (*to ask oneself*) = xiǎng zhīdào 想知道
I wonder [how he came | why he came | who came...] = wǒ xiǎng zhīdào [tā shi zěnme lái de | tā wèishénme lái | shéi lái le...] 我想知道 [他是怎么来的 | 他为什么来 | 谁来了...]
I was wondering when you'd arrive = wǒ xiǎng zhīdào nín shénme shíhou dào 我想知道您什么时候到
- (*in polite requests*)
I wonder if you could help me? = bù zhī nǐ néng bù néng bāng wǒ ge máng? 不知你能不能帮我个忙?

wonderful *adjective*
- (*when describing a performance, a match*) = jīngcǎi 精彩
- (*when describing someone's courage, memory*) = jīngrén 惊人
- (*when describing the weather, an idea, a plan, etc.*) = jí hǎo 极好, jí miào 极妙
the weather is wonderful = tiānqì hǎo jí le 天气好极了
what a wonderful idea! = zhège zhǔyì miào jí le! 这个主意妙极了!
wonderful! = tài hǎo le! 太好了!

wood *noun*
- (*timber*) = mùtou 木头
the table is made of wood = zhèzhāng zhuōzi shì mùtou zuò de 这张桌子是木头做的
- (*a small forest*)
a wood = yípiàn shùlín 一片树林

wool *noun*
- (*soft hair of a sheep, goat, etc.*) = yángmáo 羊毛, máo 毛
- (*yarn spun from sheep or goat hair*) = máoxiàn 毛线, róngxiàn 绒线

word *noun*
- (*the smallest meaningful unit in a language*)
a word = yíge (dān)cí 一个(单)词
what's the Chinese word for 'break'? = 'break' de Zhōngwén dāncí shì shénme? 'break' 的中文单词是什么?
- (*utterance*) = huà 话
I didn't say a word = wǒ yíjù huà yě méi shuō 我一句话也没说
in other words = huàn jù huà shuō 换句话说
- (*a brief conversation*)
can I have a word with you? = wǒ kěyǐ gēn nǐ tán yíxià ma? 我可以跟你谈一下吗?

work
1 *verb*
- (*to do a job*) = gōngzuò 工作
to work at home = zài jiā li gōngzuò 在家里工作
- (*to have a job*)
to work as [a doctor | a teacher | an actor...] = dāng [yīshēng | lǎoshī | yǎnyuán...] 当 [医生 | 老师 | 演员...]
- (*to operate properly*) = gōngzuò 工作
the TV isn't working = diànshìjī bù gōngzuò le 电视机不工作了
- (*to be successful*)
(*if it's an idea, a plan, a trick*) = xíng de tōng 行得通

> **!** *Note that the negative form is* xíng bù tōng 行不通.

the plan doesn't work = zhège jìhuà xíng bù tōng 这个计划行不通
(*if it's a medicine, a treatment*) = qǐ zuòyòng 起作用
- (*to use, to operate*) = shǐyòng 使用, cāozuò 操作
do you know how to work the computer? = nǐ zhīdào zěnme shǐyòng zhètái jìsuànjī ma? 你知道怎么使用这台计算机吗?

2 *noun*
- **work** = gōngzuò 工作, huór 活儿
I've got a lot of work to do = wǒ yǒu hěn duō gōngzuò yào zuò 我有很多工作要做
- (*employment*)
have you found work yet? = nǐ zhǎodào gōngzuò le ma? 你找到工作了吗?
she is out of work = tā shīyè le 她失业了
- (*students' work*) = zuòyè 作业

- (*for building, for repairs*) = gōngchéng 工程
  there are road works outside at the moment = wàimian zhèngzài jìnxíng xiū lù gōngchéng 外面正在进行修路工程
- (*by a writer, an artist, a musician*)
  a work = yíge zuòpǐn 一个作品
- (*a book*)
  works = zhùzuò 著作

work out
- (*to find*) = zhǎochū 找出
  to work out the answer = zhǎochū dá'àn 找出答案
- (*to understand*) = nòng míngbai 弄明白, nòng qīngchu 弄清楚
- (*with figures*) = suànchū 算出
- (*to take exercise*) = duànliàn 锻炼
- (*to devise*) = shèjìchū 设计出
- (*to formulate, to make*) = zhìdìngchū 制订出
  to work out a plan = zhìdìngchū yíxiàng jìhuà 制订出一项计划

work up
- (*when talking about getting excited*)
  to get worked up = jīdòngqilai 激动起来
- (*to rouse*) = huànqǐ 唤起, jīqǐ 激起
  to work up enthusiasm for learning Chinese = huànqǐ xuéxí Zhōngwén de rèqíng 唤起学习中文的热情

worker *noun*
a worker (*in a factory*) = yíge gōngrén 一个工人
(*in an office, a bank*) = yíge gōngzuò rényuán 一个工作人员

world *noun*
the world = shìjiè 世界
all over the world = quán shìjiè 全世界
the biggest city in the world = shìjiè shang zuì dà de chéngshì 世界上最大的城市

World Cup *noun*
the World Cup = Shìjiè Bēi 世界杯

World Wide Web, WWW *noun*
the World Wide Web = Wàn Wéi Wǎng 万维网

worm *noun*
a worm = yìtiáo chóngzi 一条虫子

worried *adjective*
= dānxīn 担心, bú fàngxīn 不放心
to be worried about someone = dānxīn mǒurén 担心某人

worry *verb*
- (*to be worried*) = dānxīn 担心, bú fàngxīn 不放心
  there's nothing to worry about = méi yǒu shénme kě dānxīn de 没有什么可担心的
- (*to make someone worried*) = shǐ...dānxīn 使... 担心, shǐ...bù ān 使... 不安
  it's worrying me = zhè shǐ wǒ hěn dānxīn 这使我很担心

worse *adjective*
- (*evil in a higher degree*) = gèng huài 更坏
  this idea is worse than that one = zhège zhǔyì bǐ nàge gèng huài 这个主意比那个更坏
- (*when describing a standard, the weather, a condition*) = gèng chà 更差, gèng zāo 更糟
  she's worse than me at sports = zài tǐyù fāngmiàn tā bǐ wǒ gèng chà 在体育方面她比我更差
  the weather is going to get worse = tiānqì huì biànde gèng zāo 天气会变得更糟
- (*when describing an illness*) = gèng zhòng 更重
  he is getting worse= tāde bìng gèng zhòng le 他的病更重了

worst
1 *noun*
the worst (*when talking about a wicked person*) = zuì huài de rén 最坏的人
(*when talking about an ability, a condition, a standard, the weather*) = zuì chà de 最差的, zuì zāo(gāo) de 最糟(糕)的
I'm the worst at Chinese = zài xuéxí Zhōngwén fāngmiàn, wǒ shì zuì chà de 在学习中文方面，我是最差的
2 *adjective*
- (*most wicked or evil*) = zuì huài 最坏
- (*when talking about an ability, a condition, a standard, the weather*) = zuì chà 最差, zuì zāo(gāo) 最糟(糕)
  the worst hotel in town = chéng li zuì chà de lǚguǎn 城里最差的旅馆
  the worst film I've ever seen = wǒ suǒ kànguo de zuì zāo(gāo) de diànyǐng 我所看过的最糟(糕)的电影

- **his worst enemy** = tā zuì xiōng'è de dírén 他最凶恶的敌人
- (*the most severe or serious*) = zuì yánzhòng 最严重
  the worst accident = zuì yánzhòng de shìgù 最严重的事故

worth *adjective*
- (*equal in value to*) = zhí 值
  to be worth £100 = zhí yìbǎi yīngbàng 值一百英镑
- (*deserving of*) = zhídé 值得
  the exhibition is not worth visiting = zhège zhǎnlǎnhuì bù zhíde cānguān 这个展览会不值得参观

would *verb*
- (*when talking about hypothetical rather than real situations*) = huì 会, jiù huì 就会
  if I had more money, I would buy a car = wǒ yàoshì yǒu gèng duō de qián, wǒ huì mǎi yíliàng qìchē 我要是有更多的钱, 我会买一辆汽车
  we would have missed the train if we'd left later = rúguǒ wǒmén zài wǎn diǎnr zǒu, wǒmen jiù huì wùle huǒchē le 如果我们再晚点儿走, 我们就会误了火车了
- (*when used as the past tense of* **will**) = jiāng 将, (jiāng)huì (将)会

> **!** *Note that in this sense, the negative form is* **(jiāng) bú huì (将)不会.**

  I thought you'd forget to come = wǒ yǐwéi nǐ huì wàngle lái 我以为你会忘了来
  we knew she wouldn't like it = wǒmen zhīdào tā bú huì xǐhuan 我们知道她不会喜欢
- (*when talking about probability or likelihood*) = dàgài 大概, yěxǔ 也许
  she'd be 30 now = tā xiànzài dàgài sānshí suì le 她现在大概三十岁了
  he would be in the library now = xiànzài tā yěxǔ zài túshūguǎn 现在他也许在图书馆
- (*to be willing to*) = yuànyì 愿意, yào 要
  he wouldn't listen to me = tā bú yuànyì tīng wǒde huà 他不愿意听我的话
- (*when talking about one's wishes*) = xiǎng 想
  I'd like a beer = wǒ xiǎng yào yìbēi píjiǔ 我想要一杯啤酒
  we would like to stay another night = wǒmen xiǎng zài dāi yíge wǎnshang 我们想再呆一个晚上
- (*when making a polite request*) = qǐng...hǎo ma 请... 好吗, qǐng...kěyǐ ma 请... 可以吗
  would you turn the TV off, please? = qǐng bǎ diànshì guānshang, hǎo ma? 请把电视关上, 好吗?
  would you pass the book to me, please? = qǐng bǎ nàběn shū dìgěi wǒ, kěyǐ ma? 请把那本书递给我, 可以吗?
- (*when talking about a habitual action in the past*) = zǒngshì 总是, zǒnghuì 总会
  she would sit beside me = tā zǒngshì zuò zài wǒde pángbiān 她总是坐在我的旁边

wrap *verb*
- (*to cover by putting something all over*) = bāo 包
  to wrap (up) a present = bāo yíge lǐwù 包一个礼物
- (*to cover by putting something round the middle*) = guǒ 裹, bāo 包
  to wrap the child in a blanket = yòng tǎnzi bǎ háizi guǒqilai 用毯子把孩子裹起来

wreck
1 *verb*
- (*to destroy, to ruin*) = pòhuài 破坏, sǔnhài 损害
- **be wrecked**
  (*if it's a ship, a train, or a plane*) = shīshì 失事
  the ship was wrecked = nàsōu chuán shīshì le 那艘船失事了

2 *noun*
- (*if it's damaged but might be fixed*)
  a wreck (*of a ship*) = yìsōu shīshì de chuán 一艘失事的船
  (*of a car*) = yíliàng shīshì de qìchē 一辆失事的汽车
- (*if it's completely in ruins*) = cánhái 残骸
  the wreck of [**a ship** | **a car** | **a plane**] = yì [sōu chuán | liàng qìchē | jià fēijī] de cánhái 一[艘船 | 辆汽车 | 架飞机]的残骸

wrestling *noun* ▶ 390
= shuāijiāo yùndòng 摔跤运动

wrist *noun* ▶ 189
the wrist = shǒuwàn 手腕, wànzi 腕子

write *verb*
- **write** = xiě 写
  to write [**an essay** | **a cheque** | **a letter...**] = xiě [yìpiān wénzhāng | yìzhāng zhīpiào | yìfēng xìn...] = 写 [一篇文章 | 一张支票 | 一封信...]
- (*to write a letter*) = xiě xìn 写信
  to write (to) someone (*US English*) = gěi mǒurén xiě xìn 给某人写信
  write back = huí xìn 回信
  write down = jìxia 记下, xiěxia 写下
  write out
- (*to transcribe*) = xiěchu 写出
- (*to write in full*) = quánbù xiěchu 全部写出

writing *noun*
- (*the act of one who writes*) = xiě 写
- (*a literary production or composition*) = xiězuò 写作
- (*handwriting*) = bǐjì 笔迹, zìjì 字迹

writing pad *noun*
a writing pad = yìběn biànjiānběn 一本便笺本

wrong *adjective*
- (*not as it should be*)
  there's something wrong with the TV = diànshìjī yǒu diǎnr bú zhèngcháng 电视机有点儿不正常
  what's wrong (with you)? = (nǐ) zěnme le? (你)怎么了?
  what's wrong with that? = nà yǒu shénme bú duì? 那有什么不对?
  there isn't anything wrong with him = tā méi yǒu shénme wèntí 他没有什么问题
- (*not proper or suitable*) = bù héshì 不合适
  I'm sorry I've said the wrong thing = duìbuqǐ, wǒ shuōle bù héshì de huà 对不起, 我说了不合适的话
  that's the wrong thing to do = nà yàng zuò bù héshì 那样做不合适
- (*not correct*) = cuò 错, bú duì 不对
  that's wrong = nà shì bú duì de 那是不对的
  to dial the wrong number = bōcuò hàomǎ 拨错号码
  it's the wrong answer = zhège dá'àn shì cuò de 这个答案是错的
  you are wrong = nǐ cuò le 你错了
  I took the wrong key = wǒ nácuòle yàoshi 我拿错了钥匙
  they went the wrong way = tāmen zǒucuòle lù 他们走错了路
- (*immoral*) = bú dàodé 不道德, bú duì 不对
  it's wrong to steal = tōu dōngxi shì bú dàodé de 偷东西是不道德的
  she hasn't done anything wrong = tā méiyǒu zuò shénme bú duì de shì 她没有做什么不对的事

xerox
1 *noun*
= fùyìn 复印
2 *verb*
= fùyìn 复印

X-ray
1 *noun*
an X-ray = yìzhāng àikesi guāng piàn 一张X光片
to have an X-ray = jìnxíng àikesi-guāng jiǎnchá 进行X光检查
2 *verb*
= yòng àikesi guāng jiǎnchá 用X光检查

yacht *noun*
a yacht
(*for pleasure*) (*US English*) = yìsōu yóutǐng 一艘游艇
(*for racing*) = yìsōu sàitǐng 一艘赛艇
(*for sailing*) = yìsōu fānchuán 一艘帆船

yard *noun*
- (*a measurement of length*) ▶ 300
  a yard = yì mǎ 一码
- (*area around a building*)
  a yard = yíge yuànzi 一个院子

- (*US English*) (*a garden*)
  a yard = yíge huāyuán 一个花园

yawn *verb*
= dǎ hāqian 打哈欠

year *noun*

- (*when talking about time*) ▶ 412
  a year = yì nián 一年
  [last | this | next] year = [qù | jīn | míng] nián [去 | 今 | 明] 年
  the year [before last | after next] = [qián | hòu] nián [前 | 后] 年
  two years ago = liǎng nián (yǐ)qián 两年(以)前
  to work all year round = quán nián gōngzuò 全年工作
  he's lived there for years = tā zài nàlǐ zhùle hěn duō nián le 他在那里住了很多年了
- (*when talking about age*) ▶ 170
  a year = yí suì 一岁
  he is 15 years old, he is 15 years of age = tā shíwǔ suì (le) 他十五岁(了)
  a four-year old = yíge sì suì de háizi 一个四岁的孩子
- (*in a school system*) = niánjí 年级
  first year, year one = yī niánjí 一年级
  she is in second year, she is in year two = tā zài èr niánjí 她在二年级

yell
1 *verb*
= (jiào)hǎn (叫)喊
to yell at someone = chòngzhe mǒurén hǎn 冲着某人喊
2 *noun*
a yell = yìshēng dàhǎn 一声大喊

yellow *adjective*
= huáng 黄, huángsè de 黄色的
the leaves have gone yellow = yèzi biàn huáng le 叶子变黄了

yes *adverb*

- = shì (de) 是(的), duì 对
  'are you going with us?'—'yes, I am' = 'nǐ gēn wǒmen yìqǐ qù ma?'—'shìde, wǒ gēn nǐmen yìqǐ qù' '你跟我们一起去吗?'—'是的, 我跟你们一起去'
- (*when providing a positive response to a negative statement or question*) = bù 不
  'they don't know each other'—'yes, they do' = 'tāmen hùxiāng bú rènshi'—'bù, tāmen hùxiāng rènshi' '他们互相不认识'—'不, 他们互相认识'
  'didn't he tell you?'—'yes, he did' = 'tā méi gàosu nǐ ma?'—'bù, tā gàosu wǒ le' '他没告诉你吗?'—'不, 他告诉我了'

yesterday *adverb*
= zuótiān 昨天
the day before yesterday = qiántiān 前天

yet
1 *adverb*

- (*in a negative sentence*) = hái 还
  not yet = hái méiyǒu 还没(有)
  it's not ready yet = hái méi zhǔnbèihǎo 还没准备好
  I haven't told him yet = wǒ hái méiyǒu gàosu tā 我还没有告诉他
- (*in a question*) = yǐjīng 已经

> **!** *Note that in this case,* **yet** *is often not translated.*

  have they arrived yet? = tāmen (yǐjīng) dào le ma? 他们(已经)到了吗?
  has she met them yet? = tā (yǐjīng) jiàndào tāmen le ma? 她(已经)见到他们了吗?

2 *conjunction*
= rán'ér 然而, dànshì 但是

yogurt *noun*
= suānnǎi 酸奶

you *pronoun*

- (*singular*) = nǐ 你
  do you speak Chinese = nǐ huì shuō Hànyǔ ma? 你会说汉语吗?
  he will help you = tā huì bāngzhù nǐ 他会帮助你
- (*plural*) = nǐmen 你们
  are you students? = nǐmen shì xuésheng ma? 你们是学生吗?
- (*the polite form, singular*) = nín 您
  may I ask you a question? = wǒ kěyǐ wèn nín yíge wèntí ma? 我可以问您一个问题吗?
- (*when used impersonally*) = nǐ 你, rénmen 人们
  you can buy anything here = zài zhèlǐ shénme nǐ dōu néng mǎi de dào 在这里什么你都能买得到
  you never know what will happen = shéi yě bù zhīdào huì fāshēng shénme shì 谁也不知道会发生什么事

these mushrooms can make you ill = zhèxiē mógu néng shǐ rén dé bìng 这些蘑菇能使人得病

young
1 *adjective*
- = niánqīng 年轻, niánqīng 年青
  a young lady = yíwèi niánqīng de nǚshì 一位年轻的女士
  young people = niánqīng rén 年青人, niánqīng rén 年轻人, qīngnián 青年
  she is a year younger than I = tā bǐ wǒ xiǎo yí suì 她比我小一岁
  to look young = xiǎnde niánqīng 显得年轻
  a younger brother = yíge dìdi 一个弟弟
  a younger sister = yíge mèimei 一个妹妹
- (*when describing children, babies, animals*) = yòuxiǎo 幼小
  a young [**baby** | **animal**] = yíge yòuxiǎo de [yīng'ér | dòngwù] 一个幼小的[婴儿 | 动物]
  a young child = yíge yòutóng 一个幼童

2 *noun*
the young (*of people*) = qīngnián 青年, niánqīng rén 年轻人
(*of animals*) = yòuzǎi 幼崽
(*of birds*) = yòuniǎo 幼鸟, chúniǎo 雏鸟

your *determiner*
▶ *See the usage note on* The human body ▶ 189
- (*singular*) = nǐde 你的
  is this your book? = zhè shì nǐde shū ma? 这是你的书吗?
- (*plural*) = nǐmende 你们的
- (*the polite form, singular*) = nínde 您的
  here is your room = zhè shì nínde fángjiān 这是您的房间
- (*when used impersonally*)

> **!** *Note that in this case,* your *is usually not translated.*

smoking is bad for your health = xīyān duì shēntǐ yǒu hài 吸烟对身体有害

yours *pronoun*
- (*singular*) = nǐde 你的
  the red car is yours = nàliàng hóng chē shì nǐde 那辆红车是你的
- (*plural*) = nǐmende 你们的
  our garden is bigger than yours = wǒmende huāyuán bǐ nǐmende dà 我们的花园比你们的大
- (*polite form, singular*) = nínde 您的
  is this suitcase yours? = zhège xiāngzi shì nínde ma? 这个箱子是您的吗?

yourself *pronoun*
- (*when used as a reflexive pronoun*)
  yourself = (nǐ) zìjǐ (你)自己
  you should trust yourself = nǐ yīnggāi xiāngxìn (nǐ) zìjǐ 你应该相信(你)自己
  (*polite form*) = (nín) zìjǐ (您)自己
  you haven't poured any wine for yourself = nín hái méiyǒu gěi (nín) zìjǐ dào jiǔ ne 您还没有给(您)自己倒酒呢
- (*when used for emphasis*) = qīnzì 亲自, běnrén 本人, zìjǐ 自己
  you don't have to go yourself = nǐ bú bì qīnzì qù 你不必亲自去

yourselves *pronoun*
- (*when used as a reflexive pronoun*) = (nǐmen) zìjǐ (你们)自己
  what have you bought for yourselves? = nǐmen gěi (nǐmen) zìjǐ mǎile xiē shénme? 你们给(你们)自己买了些什么?
- (*when used for emphasis*) = qīnzì 亲自, zìjǐ 自己
  are you going to organize it yourselves? = nǐmen dǎsuàn zìjǐ zǔzhī ma? 你们打算自己组织吗?

youth *noun*
- (*a young man*)
  a youth = yíge nán qīngnián 一个男青年, yíge xiǎohuǒzi 一个小伙子
- (*young people*)
  the youth = niánqīng rén 年轻人, niánqīng rén 年青人

youth club *noun*
a youth club = yíge qīngnián jùlèbù 一个青年俱乐部

youth hostel *noun*
a youth hostel = yíge qīngnián lǚguǎn 一个青年旅馆

youth worker *noun*
a youth worker = yíwèi qīngshàonián gōngzuòzhě 一位青少年工作者

Zz

zap *verb*
- (*to destroy*) = huǐdiào 毁掉, cuīhuǐ 摧毁
- (*British English*) (*to switch channels*) = (zhuǎn)huàn píndào (转)换频道
  to zap from channel to channel = bù tíng de (zhuǎn)huàn píndào 不停地(转)换频道

zapper *noun* (*British English*)
a zapper (*a remote control*) = yíge yáokòngqì 一个遥控器

zebra *noun*
a zebra = yìpí bānmǎ 一匹斑马

zebra crossing *noun* (*British English*)
a zebra crossing = yìtiáo rénxíng héngdào 一条人行横道

zero *number*
= líng 零

zip (*British English*), **zipper** (*US English*)
1 *noun*
a zip = yìtiáo lāliàn 一条拉链, yìtiáo lāsuǒ 一条拉锁
to undo a zip = lākāi lāliàn 拉开拉链
2 *verb*
= lāshang...de lāliàn 拉上 ... 的拉链
to zip up [**one's trousers** | **one's jacket** | **the bag...**] = bǎ [kùzi | jiákè | bāo...] de lāliàn lāshang 把[裤子 | 夹克 | 包...]的拉链拉上

zip code *noun* (*US English*)
a zip code = yíge yóuzhèng biānmǎ 一个邮政编码

zone *noun*
a zone = yíge dìdài 一个地带, yíge dìqū 一个地区

zoo *noun*
a zoo = yíge dòngwùyuán 一个动物园

Learning and lifestyle kit

Dictionary know-how

This section contains a number of short exercises that will help you to use your dictionary more effectively. You will find answers to all of these exercises at the end of the section from p. 460.

1 Understanding Chinese radicals

Here are twelve Chinese characters for looking up on the Chinese-English side of the dictionary. The first step is to identify which element of each character is the radical and to find this in the radical index on p. xiv. (The radicals are restricted to those for 'water', 'grass' and 'mouth'.) Then go on to find the pronunciation of the character in the character index on pp. xv–xxix, and finally its meaning in the body of the dictionary. Can you see a pattern of meaning linking radicals and characters? The first one has been completed for you as an example.

character	radical number	radical meaning ('water', 'grass' or 'mouth')	character pronunciation	character meaning
泪	32	water	lèi	tear, tears, teardrop
吃				
海				
花				
唱				
草				
洗				
喝				
湖				
叫				
茶				
汽				

2 **How Chinese characters make up words**

Look up the following English words on the English-Chinese side of the dictionary, and find their Chinese translations. Then examine the individual characters that make up the Chinese words. Do these contribute to the meaning of the word, or have they been chosen for how they are pronounced (most common in words of foreign origin, such as Australia *Àodàlìyà* 澳大利亚)?

English	Pinyin	characters	meaning or pronunciation elements (or mixture)?
train			
internet			
e-mail			
television			
Aids			
telephone			
computer			
Scotland			
America			
mobile			

3 Recognizing measure words

On the English-Chinese side of the dictionary, nouns that take measure words are shown with measure-word phrases. As a reminder, examples of measure words include zhāng 张 (for flat things), běn 本 (for volumes), zhī 支 (for stick-like things), tiáo 条 (for long narrow things), wèi 位 (for respected people) and gè 个 (generic measure word). Identify the measure words in the following phrases, and translate the phrases into English.

Pinyin	characters	measure word: Pinyin	measure word: character	English translation
yìzhāng chuáng	一张床			
sānběn shū	三本书			
zhèwèi lǎoshī	这位老师			
jǐzhī bǐ	几支笔			
wǔge rén	五个人			
nàzhāng zhǐ	那张纸			
yìtiáo gǒu	一条狗			
yìtiáo kùzi	一条裤子			
shí'èrběn zázhì	十二本杂志			
jǐge wèntí	几个问题			

4 Translating the Chinese particle de 的

The Chinese particle de 的 is very common – it occurs frequently in the example sentences in this dictionary, for example. It may be used to indicate a modifying word or phrase, or to turn an adjective into a noun. Translate these phrases/sentences containing de 的, to reinforce how the particle works.

Pinyin	characters	English translation
lánsè de qìqiú	蓝色的气球	
háizimen de shùxué lǎoshī	孩子们的数学老师	
yízuò hěn gāo de lóu	一座很高的楼	
Xiǎode hěn piàoliang.	小的很漂亮。	
Yòubiande shì nǐde.	右边的是你的。	
yíge dài màozi de gūniang	一个戴帽子的姑娘	
wǒde gēge	我的哥哥	
yǐjīng mǎi hǎo piào de rén	已经买好票的人	
zuì piányi de píngguǒ	最便宜的苹果	
tā xīngqīyī fā de nàge diànzǐ yóujiàn	他星期一发的那个电子邮件	

5 **Identifying Chinese adjectives and their role**

In the following passage about tea, locate the Chinese adjectives, translate them into English (by looking them up on the Chinese-English side of the dictionary), and identify their role. Are they functioning as modifiers – as noted in exercise 4 often, but not always, followed by de 的, or are they functioning as stative verbs – often, but not always preceded by hěn 很 (literally 'very'), fēicháng 非常 ('extremely'), or similar?

中国的茶种很多。有红茶、绿茶以及各种各样的特殊茶。最香的茶可能是茉莉花茶。有的茶浓，有的茶淡。茶对身体有很大的好处。历史上，欧洲人开始喝茶很晚。不过，现在中国茶在西方非常普遍。

Chinese adjective: characters	Chinese adjective: Pinyin	English translation	modifier or stative verb?

6 **Questions in Chinese**

Test your questioning skills by trying to construct the following questions in Chinese. If in doubt, look up key words on the English-Chinese side of the dictionary. Bear in mind different questioning structures in Chinese – use of the question particle ma 吗, other question words such as jǐ 几 'how many', or shénme 什么 'what', or the 'verb'/bù 不 'not'/ 'verb' pattern.

English	Chinese Pinyin	Chinese characters
What time is it now?		
How old is your daughter?		
What did he say?		
Is that book interesting?		
Are there many students?		
How much is this skirt?		
Where is the library?		
May I smoke?		
Is the computer expensive?		
How far is it to the park?		

7 Chinese prepositions

Choose the right Chinese preposition to fill the blanks in the following sentences. These are the prepositions to pick from: gěi 给, cóng 从, dào 到, lí 离, wǎng 往 and zài 在. You might want to check their meanings on the Chinese-English side of the dictionary.

Chinese Pinyin	Chinese characters	preposition: Pinyin	preposition: character	English translation
Wǒ ... cháguǎn hé tā jiànmiàn le.	我 ... 茶馆和他见面了。			
Kāfēi guǎn ... xuéxiào hěn jìn.	咖啡馆 ... 学校很近。			
Wǒmen ... Shànghǎi chūfā.	我们 ... 上海出发。			
Qǐngwèn, ... yínháng zěnme zǒu.	请问, ... 银行怎么走。			
Tā nánpéngyǒu ... tā zuòfàn le.	她男朋友 ... 她做饭了。			
Wáng Dōngyuè bǎ shū sòng ... wǒ le.	王冬月把书送 ... 我了。			
Nǐ ... běi zǒu.	你 ... 北走。			
Tā ... fēijī shàng kànwán le bàogào.	他 ... 飞机上看完了报告。			

8 **Tense, aspect and mood in Chinese**

Since Chinese is not an inflected language, tense, aspect and mood are indicated by other means, notably through particles le 了, guo 过, ne 呢, zhe 着, etc, and auxiliary verbs/adverbs xiǎng 想, huì 会, zhēngzài 正在, etc. Look up these words on the Chinese-English side of the dictionary for more information. Then test your grasp of tense, aspect and mood in Chinese by translating the following sentences.

Chinese Pinyin	Chinese characters	English translation
Nǐ qùguo Měiguó ma?	你去过美国吗?	
Tā yídìng huì lái.	她一定会来。	
Wǒ bǎ huār yǐjīng mǎi hǎo le.	我把花儿已经买好了。	
Tāmen zhèngzài xiū zìxíngchē.	他们正在修自行车。	
Chīwán fàn le, tā jiù zǒu.	吃完饭了，他就走。	
Ānnà zài nàr zhànzhe, bù shuōhuà.	安娜在那儿站着，不说话。	
Yǒu rén zhǎo nǐ ne.	有人找你呢。	
Nǐ xiǎng qù kàn diànyǐng ma?	你想去看电影吗?	

Answers

1

character	radical number	radical meaning ('water', 'grass' or 'mouth')	character pronunciation	character meaning
泪	32	water	lèi	tear, tears, teardrop
吃	50	mouth	chī	eat
海	32	water	hǎi	sea, ocean
花	42	grass	huā	flower, blossom, bloom
唱	50	mouth	chàng	sing
草	42	grass	cǎo	grass, straw
洗	32	water	xǐ	wash, clean
喝	50	mouth	hē	drink
湖	32	water	hú	lake
叫	50	mouth	jiào	call out, cry out, shout
茶	42	grass	chá	tea
汽	32	water	qì	steam, vapour

2

English	Pinyin	characters	meaning or pronunciation elements (or mixture)?
train	huǒchē	火车	meaning
internet	hùliánwǎng	互联网	meaning
	yīntèwǎng	因特网	mixture
e-mail	diànzǐ yóujiàn	电子邮件	meaning
television	diànshì	电视	meaning
Aids	àizībìng	艾滋病	mixture
telephone	diànhuà	电话	meaning
computer	jìsuànjī	计算机	meaning
	diànnǎo	电脑	meaning
Scotland	Sūgélán	苏格兰	pronunciation
America	Měiguó	美国	mixture
mobile	shǒujī	手机	meaning

3

Pinyin	characters	measure word: Pinyin	measure word: character	English translation
yìzhāng chuáng	一张床	zhāng	张	a bed
sānběn shū	三本书	běn	本	three books
zhèwèi lǎoshī	这位老师	wèi	位	this teacher
jǐzhī bǐ	几支笔	zhī	支	several pens
wǔge rén	五个人	gè	个	five people
nàzhāng zhǐ	那张纸	zhāng	张	that piece of paper
yìtiáo gǒu	一条狗	tiáo	条	a dog
yìtiáo kùzi	一条裤子	tiáo	条	a pair of trousers
shí'èrběn zázhì	十二本杂志	běn	本	twelve magazines
jǐge wèntí	几个问题	gè	个	several questions

4

Pinyin	characters	English translation
lánsè de qìqiú	蓝色的气球	the blue balloon
háizimen de shùxué lǎoshī	孩子们的数学老师	the children's mathematics teacher
yízuò hěn gāo de lóu	一座很高的楼	a tall building
Xiǎode hěn piàoliang.	小的很漂亮。	The small one is pretty.
Yòubiande shì nǐde.	右边的是你的。	The one on the right is yours.
yíge dài màozi de gūniang	一个戴帽子的姑娘	a girl wearing a hat
wǒde gēge	我的哥哥	my elder brother
yǐjīng mǎi hǎo piào de rén	已经买好票的人	people who have already bought tickets
zuì piányi de píngguǒ	最便宜的苹果	the cheapest apples
tā xīngqīyī fā de nàge diànzǐ yóujiàn	他星期一发的那个电子邮件	that e-mail he sent on Monday

5

Chinese adjective: characters	**Chinese adjective: Pinyin**	**English translation**	**modifier or stative verb?**
多	duō	many (different part of speech in English)	stative verb
红	hóng	red (or in the context of tea, 'black')	modifier
绿	lǜ	green	modifier
特殊	tèshū	special	modifier
香	xiāng	fragrant	modifier
浓	nóng	strong	stative verb
淡	dàn	weak	stative verb
大	dà	big (or 'great')	modifier
晚	wǎn	late	stative verb
普遍	pǔbiàn	common	stative verb

Translation of text: There are many different kinds of Chinese tea (literally 'The kinds of Chinese tea are many'). Black tea, green tea, and all sorts of special teas. The most fragrant tea is perhaps jasmine tea. Some teas are strong, others weak. Tea is of great benefit to health. Historically, Europeans started to drink tea quite late. However, Chinese tea is now very common in the West.

6

English	**Chinese Pinyin**	**Chinese characters**
What time is it now?	Xiànzài jǐ diǎn le?	现在几点了?
How old is your daughter?	Nǐ nǚ'ér jǐ suì le?	你女儿几岁了?
What did he say?	Tā shuō shénme?	他说什么?
Is that book interesting?	Nà běn shū yǒu yìsi ma?	那本书有意思吗?
Are there many students?	Xuéshēng duō bu duō?	学生多不多?
	Xuéshēng duō ma?	学生多吗?
How much is this skirt?	Zhè tiáo qúnzi duōshǎo qián?	这条裙子多少钱?
Where is the library?	Túshūguǎn zài nǎr?	图书馆在哪儿?
May I smoke?	Wǒ kěyǐ chōuyān ma?	我可以抽烟吗?
Is the computer expensive?	Diànnǎo guì bu guì?	电脑贵不贵?
	Diànnǎo guì ma?	电脑贵吗?
How far is it to the park?	Dào gōngyuán yǒu duō yuǎn?	到公园有多远?

7

Chinese Pinyin	Chinese characters	preposition: Pinyin	preposition: character	English translation
Wǒ ... cháguǎn hé tā jiànmiàn le.	我 ... 茶馆和他见面了。	zài	在	I met him at the teahouse.
Kāfēi guǎn ... xuéxiào hěn jìn.	咖啡馆 ... 学校很近。	lí	离	The café is close to school.
Wǒmen ... Shànghǎi chūfā.	我们 ... 上海出发。	cóng	从	We are leaving from Shanghai.
Qǐngwèn, ... yínháng zěnme zǒu.	请问, ... 银行怎么走。	dào	到	Which way is it to the bank, please.
Tā nánpéngyǒu ... tā zuòfàn le.	她男朋友 ... 她做饭了。	gěi	给	Her boyfriend cooked for her.
Wáng Dōngyuè bǎ shū sòng ... wǒ le.	王冬月把书送 ... 我了。	gěi	给	Wang Dongyue gave me the book.
Nǐ ... běi zǒu.	你 ... 北走。	wǎng	往	Go north.
Tā ... fēijī shàng kànwán le bàogào.	他 ... 飞机上看完了报告。	zài	在	He finished reading the report on the plane.

8

Chinese Pinyin	Chinese characters	English translation
Nǐ qùguo Měiguó ma?	你去过美国吗?	Have you ever been to America?
Tā yídìng huì lái.	她一定会来。	She'll certainly come.
Wǒ bǎ huār yǐjīng mǎi hǎo le.	我把花儿已经买好了。	I've already bought the flowers.
Tāmen zhèngzài xiū zìxíngchē.	他们正在修自行车。	They are mending the bike.
Chīwán fàn le, tā jiù zǒu.	吃完饭了，他就走。	Having eaten, he left.
Ānnà zài nàr zhànzhe, bù shuōhuà.	安娜在那儿站着，不说话。	Anna just stood there, without speaking.
Yǒu rén zhǎo nǐ ne.	有人找你呢。	Someone is looking for you.
Nǐ xiǎng qù kàn diànyǐng ma?	你想去看电影吗?	Would you like to go to the cinema?

The Chinese words and phrases you must know

A

ǎi 矮
Ài'ěrlán 爱尔兰
ānquán 安全
Àodàlìyà 澳大利亚

B

bàba 爸爸
bēi 背
běi 北
Běijīng 北京
bí 鼻
bǐ 比
bǐsài 比赛
bìyè 毕业
biǎoyǎn 表演
bìng 病
bówùguǎn 博物馆
bù 不

C

cài 菜
càidān 菜单
cǎo 草
cèsuǒ 厕所
chá 茶
Chángchéng 长城
chànggē 唱歌
chàngpiàn 唱片
chāojí shìchǎng 超级市场
chǎo 炒
chēzhàn 车站
chéngrén 成人
chéngshì 城市
chī 吃
chōuyān 抽烟
chūqu 出去
chūshēng 出生
chúfáng 厨房
chuāng 窗
chuáng 床
chūn 春
Chūnjié 春节
cuòwù 错误

D

dàxué 大学
dàn 蛋
dào 到
dàodá 到达
de 的
Déguó 德国
Déyǔ 德语
dēng 灯
dìdiǎn 地点
dìfang 地方
dìlǐ 地理
dìqiú 地球
dìqū 地区
dìtiě 地铁
dìzhǐ 地址
dìdi 弟弟
diǎnxīn 点心
diànhuà 电话
diànnǎo 电脑
diànshì 电视
diànyǐng 电影
diànzǐ yóujiàn 电子邮件
dìng 订
dōng 东
dōng 冬
dòngwùyuán 动物园
dōu 都
Duānwǔjié 端午节
duì 队
duì 对
duìmiàn 对面
duōshǎo 多少

E

è 饿
ěrduo 耳朵

F

fāshāo 发烧
Fǎguó 法国
Fǎyǔ 法语
fàndiàn 饭店
fànguǎn 饭馆
fàntīng 饭厅
fángjiān 房间
fángzi 房子
fǎngwèn 访问
Fēizhōu 非洲
fēng 风
fēngjǐng 风景
fēngsú 风俗
fúwùyuán 服务员
fùmǔ 父母

G

gǎnmào 感冒
gāo 高

gāoxìng 高兴
gēge 哥哥
gēn 跟
gèng 更
gōngchǎng 工厂
gōngchéngshī 工程师
gōngrén 工人
gōngzī 工资
gōngzuò 工作
gōnggòng qìchē zhàn 公共汽车站
gōnglù 公路
gōngyuán 公园
gǒu 狗
gòuwù 购物
guǎnggào 广告
guójí 国籍
guójì 国际
guò nián 过年

H

háizi 孩子
hǎi 海
Hànyǔ 汉语
hǎochī 好吃
hē 喝
hēzuì 喝醉
hé 河
hěn 很
hòu 后
hùliánwǎng 互联网
hùshi 护士
hùzhào 护照
huā 花
huāyuán 花园
huà 画
huānyíng 欢迎
huídá 回答
huì 会
huódòng 活动
huǒchēzhàn 火车站

J

jī 鸡
jǐ 几
jìsuànjī 计算机
jìniànpǐn 纪念品
jiājù 家具
jiāng 江
jiāoqū 郊区
jiǎo 脚
jiàoshī 教师
jiàoshì 教室
jiàoyù 教育
jiē 街
jiémù 节目
jiéhūn 结婚
jiějie 姐姐
jìn 近
jiǔ 酒
jiù 就

K

kāfēi 咖啡
kāi chē 开车
kànbìng 看病
kǎoshì 考试
kējì 科技
kēxué 科学
kēxuéjiā 科学家
késou 咳嗽
kě'ài 可爱
kě 渴
kètīng 客厅
kèběn 课本
kōngtiáo 空调
kùzi 裤子
kuàilè 快乐
kùnnan 困难

L

lái 来
lánqiú 篮球
lǎo 老
lǎoshī 老师
léi 雷
lěng 冷
líkāi 离开
lǐtáng 礼堂
lìshǐ 历史
liànxí 练习
lùyīnjī 录音机
lǚguǎn 旅馆
lǚxíng 旅行
lǚxíngshè 旅行社

M

māma 妈妈
mǎlù 马路
māo 猫
méiyǒu 没有
Měiguó 美国
mèimei 妹妹
mén 门
mǐfàn 米饭
miànbāo 面包
miàntiáo 面条
miào 庙
míngzi 名字

N

nǎ 哪
nǎli 哪里
nǎr 哪儿
nà 那
nán 南

nán 男
nèi 内
niúnǎi 牛奶
niúròu 牛肉
nǚ 女
nǚshì 女士

O
Ōuzhōu 欧洲

P
páng (biān) 旁(边)
pàng 胖
pǎobù 跑步
péngyou 朋友
piào 票

Q
qīzi 妻子
qí 骑
qìwēn 气温
qìchē 汽车
qìshuǐ 汽水
qián 前
qiáo 桥
qīngnián 青年
qiū 秋
qù 去
qúnzi 裙子

R
rè 热
Rìběn 日本
Rìyǔ 日语
rìqī 日期

S
sànbù 散步
sēnlín 森林
shān 山
shāngchǎng 商场
shāngdiàn 商店
shàng 上
Shànghǎi 上海
shǎo 少
shéi 谁
shēntǐ 身体
shénme 什么
shēngqì 生气
shēngri 生日
Shèngdànjié 圣诞节
shīyè 失业
shízì lùkǒu 十字路口
shíjiānbiǎo 时间表
shìchǎng 市场
shì 是
shōuyīnjī 收音机
shǒu 手
shǒubiǎo 手表
shǒujī 手机
shòuhuòyuán 售货员
shòu 瘦
shūdiàn 书店
shūfǎ 书法
shūjià 书架
shǔjià 暑假
shù 树
shùxué 数学
shuǐguǒ 水果
shuìjiào 睡觉
sījī 司机
sòng 送
Sūgélán 苏格兰
suīrán 虽然
sūnnǚ 孙女
sūnzi 孙子
suǒyǐ 所以

T
Táiwān 台湾
tàitai 太太
tàiyáng 太阳
tǐyù 体育
tǐyùguǎn 体育馆
Tiān'ānmén 天安门
tiānkōng 天空
tiānqì 天气
tiělù 铁路
tòng 痛
tóu 头
túshūguǎn 图书馆
tǔdì 土地

W
wài 外
wàiwén 外文
wàiyǔ 外语
wǎnfàn 晚饭
wǎngqiú 网球
Wēi'ěrshì 威尔士
wèishénme 为什么
wòshì 卧室
wūrǎn 污染
wǔfàn 午饭
wù 雾

X
xī 西
xǐyījī 洗衣机
xǐhuan 喜欢
xìjù 戏剧
xià 下
xiàtiān 夏天
xiānsheng 先生
Xiānggǎng 香港
xiǎng 想

xiǎochī 小吃
xiǎojiě 小姐
xiǎoxué 小学
xiàozhǎng 校长
xié 鞋
xiě 写
xīnnián 新年
xīnwén 新闻
xīngxing 星星
xíngli 行李
xìngbié 性别
xìngmíng 姓名
xióngmāo 熊猫
xiūxi 休息
xuéqī 学期
xuésheng 学生
xuéxí 学习
xuě 雪
xùnliàn 训练

Y

yā 鸭
yá 牙
Yàzhōu 亚洲
yǎnjing 眼睛
yǎnyuán 演员
yángròu 羊肉
yào 药
yě 也
yìzhí 一直
yīfu 衣服
yīyuàn 医院
yǐzi 椅子
yìshù 艺术
yìwài 意外
yīnwei 因为
yīnyuè 音乐
yīnyuèhuì 音乐会
yínháng 银行
Yīnggélán 英格兰
Yīngguó 英国
Yīngyǔ 英语
yóujú 邮局
yóuyǒng 游泳
yǒu 有
yòu 右
yú 鱼
yǔmáoqiú 羽毛球
yǔ 雨
yùshì 浴室
yuǎn 远
yuèdú 阅读
yuèliang 月亮
yún 云
yùndòng 运动
yùndòngchǎng 运动场

Z

zài 在
zǎofàn 早饭
zěnme 怎么
zhǎnlǎn 展览
zhàngfu 丈夫
zhàoxiàngjī 照相机
zhè 这
zhèngzài 正在
zhíwù 植物
zhíyè 职业
Zhōngguó 中国
Zhōngqiūjié 中秋节
Zhōngwén 中文
Zhōngyào 中药
zhōngxīn 中心
zhōngxué 中学
zhōng 钟
zhūròu 猪肉
zhǔ 煮
zhǔnbèi 准备
zhuōzi 桌子
zìxíngchē 自行车
zúqiú 足球
zǔfù 祖父
zǔmǔ 祖母
zuǒ 左
zuòjiā 作家
zuòyè 作业
zuò shēngyi 做生意

Numbers

Cardinal numbers in Chinese

0 líng 零
1 yī 一
2 èr 二
3 sān 三
4 sì 四
5 wǔ 五
6 liù 六
7 qī 七
8 bā 八
9 jiǔ 九
10 shí 十[a]
11 shíyī 十一[a]
12 shí'èr 十二[a]
13 shísān 十三[a]
14 shísì 十四[a]
15 shíwǔ 十五[a]
16 shíliù 十六[a]
17 shíqī 十七[a]
18 shíbā 十八[a]
19 shíjiǔ 十九[a]
20 èrshí 二十
21 èrshíyī 二十一
22 èrshí'èr 二十二
30 sānshí 三十
40 sìshí 四十
50 wǔshí 五十
60 liùshí 六十
70 qīshí 七十
80 bāshí 八十
90 jiǔshí 九十
100 yìbǎi 一百[b]
101 yìbǎilíngyī 一百零一[b, c]
102 yìbǎilíng'èr 一百零二[b, c]
110 yìbǎiyìshí 一百一十[a, b]
111 yìbǎiyìshíyī 一百一十一[a, b]
200 èrbǎi 二百 *or* liǎngbǎi 两百[d]
250 èrbǎiwǔshí 二百五十
or liǎngbǎiwǔshí 两百五十[d]
1000 yìqiān 一千[b]
1001 yìqiānlíngyī 一千零一[b, c]
1020 yìqiānlíng'èrshí 一千零二十[b, c]
1300 yìqiānsānbǎi 一千三百[b]
2000 liǎngqiān 两千 *or* èrqiān 二千[d]
10 000 yíwàn 一万[b, e]
13 000 yíwànsānqiān 一万三千[b, e]
100 000 shíwàn 十万[e]
103 000 shíwànsānqiān 十万三千[e]
1 000 000 yìbǎiwàn 一百万[b, e]
1 234 567 yìbǎi'èrshísānwànsìqiānwǔbǎiliùshíqī
一百二十三万四千五百六十七[b, e]
10 000 000 yìqiānwàn 一千万[b, e]
100 000 000 yíyì 一亿[b, e]
1 000 000 000 shíyì 十亿[e]

[a] For numbers shí 十 (ten) to shíjiǔ 十九 (nineteen), the 'teens', there is no need for an yī 一 (one) before the shí 十 (ten). After yìbǎi 一百 (a hundred), however, any numbers with a final 'teen' element have to have yìshí 一十 (one 'ten') made explicit.

[b] Bear in mind that pronunciation of the tone on yī 一 (one) varies, depending on the tone of the syllable that follows: it is pronounced fourth tone yì if the following syllable is first, second or third tone, but it is pronounced second tone yí if the following syllable is fourth tone.

[c] Between yìbǎi 一百 (100) and yíwàn 一万 (ten thousand), any zeros that separate other digits in a number have to be made explicit by using líng 零.

[d] Èrbǎi 二百 (two hundred), èrqiān 二千 (two thousand), èrwàn 二万 (twenty thousand), etc., may alternatively be written using liǎng 两 (another character for 'two'): liǎngbǎi 两百, liǎngqiān 两千, liǎngwàn 两万, etc.

[e] Whereas English uses the denominations 'million' and 'billion' for large numbers, Chinese uses wàn 万 (ten thousand) and yì 亿 (a hundred million). This can lead to confusion when converting large numbers.

Ordinal numbers in Chinese

In Chinese, ordinal numbers are created simply by adding dì 第 before the number: dìyī 第一 (first), dì'èr 第二 (second), dìsān 第三 (third), dìsì 第四 (fourth), dìwǔ 第五 (fifth), dìliù 第六 (sixth), dìshí 第十 (tenth), dìshíwǔ 第十五 (fifteenth), dìyìbǎi 第一百 (hundredth), etc.

Phrasefinder

Contents / Mùlù 目录

❶ Useful phrases — Chángyòng duǎnyǔ 常用短语 ❶

yes/no	shì/bù 是/不
thank you	xièxie 谢谢
sorry	duìbuqǐ 对不起
excuse me	láojià 劳驾
I'm sorry, I don't understand	duìbuqǐ, wǒ tīng bù dǒng 对不起，我听不懂

Meeting people	**Yǔ rén huìmiàn 与人会面**
hello/goodbye	nǐ hǎo/zàijiàn 你好/再见
how are you?	nǐ hǎo ma? 你好吗？
nice to meet you	rènshi nǐ zhēn hǎo 认识你真好

Asking questions	**Wèn wèntí 问问题**
do you speak English/Chinese?	nǐ jiǎng Yīngwén/Zhōngwén ma? 你讲英文/中文吗？
what's your name?	nǐ jiào shénme míngzi? 你叫什么名字？
where are you from?	nǐ cóng nǎli lái? 你从哪里来？
how much is it?	zhè yào duōshǎo qián? 这要多少钱？
where is ...?	... zài shénme dìfang? ...在什么地方？
can I ...?	wǒ néng bù néng ...? 我能不能 ...？
would you like ...?	nǐ xiǎng bù xiǎng ...? 你想不想 ...？

Statements about yourself	**Jièshào zìjǐ 介绍自己**
my name is ...	wǒ jiào ... 我叫 ...
I'm English/I'm American	wǒ shì Yīngguórén/Měiguórén 我是英国人/美国人
I don't speak Chinese	wǒ bù jiǎng Zhōngwén 我不讲中文
I live near Beijing/Chester	wǒ zhù Běijīng/Qièsītè fùjìn 我住北京/切斯特附近
I'm a student	wǒ shì yíge xuéshēng 我是一个学生
I work in an office	wǒ zaì bàngōngshì gōngzuò 我在办公室工作

Emergencies	**Jǐnjí qíngkuàng 紧急情况**
can you help me, please?	nǐ néng bāng wǒ yíxià ma? 你能帮我一下吗?
I'm lost	wǒ mílù le 我迷路了
I'm ill	wǒ shēngbìng le 我生病了
call an ambulance	jiào jiùhùchē 叫救护车

Reading signs	**Rènshi zhǐshìpái 认识指示牌**
no entry	jìnzhǐ rùnèi 禁止入内
no smoking	jìnzhǐ chōuyān 禁止抽烟
fire exit	fánghuǒmén 防火门
for sale	dàishòu 待售

❷ Going places

Chūyóu 出游 ❷

By rail	Zuò huǒchē 坐火车
where can I buy a ticket?	wǒ zài nǎli mǎi piào? 我在哪里买票?
what time is the next train to Beijing?	dào Běijīng de xià yìbān huǒchē shì shénme shíjiān? 到北京的下一班火车是什么时间?
do I have to change?	wǒ xūyào zhuǎnchē ma? 我需要转车吗?
can I take my bike on the train?	wǒ néng bù néng bǎ zìxíngchē dàishàng huǒchē? 我能不能把自行车带上火车?
which platform for the train to Beijing?	dào Běijīng de huǒchē zaì nǎge zhàntái? 到北京的火车在哪个站台?
there's a train to Beijing at 10 o'clock	yǒu yítàng shídiǎn fā wǎng Běijīng de huǒchē 有一趟十点发往北京的火车
a single/return to Shanghai, please	qǐng mǎi yìzhāng dào Shànghǎi de dānchéngpiào/wǎngfǎnpiào 请买一张到上海的单程票/往返票
I'd like to reserve a seat	wǒ xiǎng yùdìng yíge zuòwèi 我想预定一个座位

At the airport	Zài jīchǎng 在机场
when's the next flight to Shanghai?	dào Shànghǎi de xià yícì hángbān shì shénme shíjiān? 到上海的下一次航班是什么时间?
where do I check in?	wǒ zài shénme dìfang jiǎnpiào? 我在什么地方检票?
I'd like to confirm my flight	wǒ xiǎng quèrèn yíxià hángbān 我想确认一下航班
I'd like a window seat/an aisle seat	wǒ xiǎngyào yíge kào chuāng de zuòwèi/kào zǒudào de zuòwèi 我想要一个靠窗的座位/靠走道的座位
I want to change/cancel my reservation	wǒ xiǎng gēnggǎi/qǔxiāo yùdìng de piào 我想更改/取消预定的票

On the road	Zài lùshang 在路上
where's the nearest petrol station, (*US*) gas station?	qǐngwèn zuìjìn de qìchē jiāyóuzhàn zài shénme dìfang? 请问最近的汽车加油站在什么地方?
what's the best way to get there?	dào nàli zěnme zǒu zuì jìn? 到那里怎么走最近?
I've got a puncture	wǒde lúntāi zhāpò le 我的轮胎扎破了
I'd like to hire a bike/car	wǒ xiǎng zū yíliàng zìxíngchē/qìchē 我想租一辆自行车/汽车
there's been an accident	chū le yìchǎng chēhuò 出了一场车祸
my car's broken down	wǒde chē pāomáo le 我的车抛锚了
the car won't start	chē fādòng bù liǎo 车发动不了

Finding the way	Zhǎolù 找路
could you tell me the way to the railway station?	qǐngwèn qù huǒchēzhàn zěnme zǒu? 请问去火车站怎么走?
how long will it take to get there?	dào nàli xūyào duō cháng shíjiān? 到那里需要多长时间?
how far is it from here?	nàr lí zhèr yǒu duō yuǎn? 那儿离这儿有多远?
which bus do I take for the temple?	dào sìmiào zuò nǎ lù chē? 到寺庙坐哪路车?
can you tell me where to get off?	nǐ néng gàosu wǒ zài nǎli xiàchē ma? 你能告诉我在哪里下车吗?
what time is the last bus?	zuìhòu yícì bānchē shì shénme shíjiān? 最后一次班车是什么时间?
how do I get to the airport?	wǒ zěnme qù jīchǎng? 我怎么去机场?
where's the nearest underground station, (*US*) subway station?	zuìjìn de dìtiě zhànkǒu zài shénme dìfang? 最近的地铁站口在什么地方?
can you call me a taxi?	nǐ néng wèi wǒ jiào liàng chūzūchē ma? 你能为我叫辆出租车吗?
take the first turning on the right	yòushǒubiān dìyíge lùkǒu zhuǎnwān 右手边第一个路口转弯
turn left at the traffic lights	guò le jiāotōngdēng xiàng zuǒ zhuǎn 过了交通灯向左转
I'll take a taxi	wǒ zuò chūzūchē qù 我坐出租车去

❸ Keeping in touch — Bǎochí liánxì 保持联系 ❸

On the phone	Dǎ diànhuà 打电话
hello	wèi 喂
where can I buy a phone card?	wǒ zài nǎli néng mǎidào diànhuàkǎ? 我在哪儿能买到电话卡？
may I use your phone?	wǒ kěyǐ yòng yíxià nǐde diànhuà ma? 我可以用一下你的电话吗？
do you have a mobile phone, (*US*) cell phone?	nǐ yǒu shǒujī ma? 你有手机吗？
what is the code for Beijing?	Běijīng de qūhào shì shénme? 北京的区号是什么？
I want to make a phone call	wǒ xiǎng dǎ yígè diànhuà 我想打一个电话
the line's busy/engaged	diànhuà zhànxiàn 电话占线
there's no answer	méi yǒu rén jiē diànhuà 没有人接电话
hello, this is John	nǐ hǎo, wǒ shì Yuēhàn 你好，我是约翰
is Li Hong there, please?	qǐngwèn Lǐ Hóng zài ma? 请问李红在吗？
who's calling?	shì nǎwèi? 是哪位？
sorry, wrong number	duìbuqǐ, dǎcuò diànhuà le 对不起，打错电话了
just a moment, please	qǐng shāo děng 请稍等
would you like to hold?	qǐng děng yíxià, hǎoma? 请等一下好吗？
please tell him/her I called	qǐng gàosu tā wǒ gěi tā dǎ diànhuà le 请告诉他/她我给他打电话了
I'd like to leave a message for him/her	wǒ xiǎng gěi tā liú gè kǒuxìn 我想给他/她留个口信
... I'll try again later	... wǒ yǐhòu zài dǎ ba 我以后再打吧
please tell him/her that Sarah called	qǐng gàosu tā Shālà dǎ diànhuà le 请告诉他/她莎拉打电话了
can he/she ring me back?	tā néng gěi wǒ huí diànhuà ma? 他/她能给我回电话吗？
my home number is ...	wǒ jiā de diànhuà hàomǎ shì ... 我家的电话号码是 ...
my business number is ...	wǒde bàngōng diànhuà shì ... 我的办公电话是 ...
my fax number is ...	wǒde chuánzhēn hàomǎ shì ... 我的传真号码是 ...
we were cut off	wǒmen de diànhuà bèi guàduàn le 我们的电话被挂断了

Writing	Xiěxìn 写信
what's your address?	nǐde dìzhǐ shì shénme? 你的地址是什么?
where is the nearest post office?	zuìjìn de yóujú zài nǎli? 最近的邮局在哪里?
could I have a stamp for England, please?	qǐng gěi wǒ yìzhāng dào Yīngguó de yóupiào, hǎoma? 请给我一张到英国的邮票好吗?
I'd like to send a parcel/a telegram	wǒ xiǎng jì yíge bāoguǒ/fā yìfēng diànbào 我想寄一个包裹/发一封电报

On line	Shàngwǎng 上网
are you on the Internet?	nǐ zài shàngwǎng ma? 你在上网吗?
what's your e-mail address?	nǐde diànzǐ yóujiàn dìzhǐ shì shénme? 你的电子邮件地址是什么?
we could send it by e-mail	wǒmen kěyǐ yòng diànzǐ yóujiàn fāchūqù 我们可以用电子邮件发出去
I'll e-mail it to you on Tuesday	wǒ xīngqī'èr yòng diànzǐ yóujiàn fā gěi nǐ 我星期二用电子邮件发给你
I looked it up on the Internet	wǒ zài hùliánwǎng shàng cházhǎo guo 我在互联网上查找过
the information is on their website	xìnxī zài wǎngzhàn shàng 信息在网站上

Meeting up	Huìmiàn 会面
what shall we do this evening?	wǒmen jīntiān wǎnshang gàn shénme? 我们今天晚上干什么?
where shall we meet?	wǒmen zài shénme dìfang jiànmiàn? 我们在什么地方见面?
I'll see you outside the café at 6 o'clock	wǒ liùdiǎnzhōng zài kāfēiguǎn wàimian jiàn nǐ 我六点钟在咖啡馆外面见你
see you later	huítóu jiàn 回头见
I can't today, I'm busy	wǒ jīntiān bù xíng, wǒ hěn máng 我今天不行，我很忙

❹ Food and drink / Shíwù hé yǐnliào 食物和饮料 ❹

Booking a restaurant / Yùdìng fàndiàn 预订饭店

can you recommend a good restaurant?
nǐ néng tuījiàn yìjiā hǎo fàndiàn ma? 你能推荐一家好饭店吗?

I'd like to reserve a table for four
wǒ xiǎng dìng yìzhāng sìge rén de cāntái 我想订一张四个人的餐台

make a reservation for tomorrow evening at eight o'clock
yùdìng míngtiān wǎnshang bā diǎnzhōng 预订明天晚上八点钟

Ordering / Diǎncài 点菜

could we see the menu, please?
wǒmen néng kàn yíxià càidān ma? 我们能看一下菜单吗?

do you have a vegetarian menu/children's menu?
nǐmen yǒu sùshí càidān/értóng càidān ma? 你们有素食菜单/儿童菜单吗?

could we have some more rice?
wǒmen néng duō yào yìxiē mǐfàn ma? 我们能多要一些米饭吗?

what would you recommend?
nǐ néng tuījiàn xiē shénme? 你能推荐些什么?

we'd like
wǒmen xiǎngyào xiē 我们想要些

... tea
... chá 茶

... beer
... píjiǔ 啤酒

... wine
... pútáojiǔ 葡萄酒

... coffee
... kāfēi 咖啡

the bill, (*US*) check, please
jiézhàng ba 结账吧

You will hear	Nǐ huì tīngdào 你会听到
can I take your order?	nǐ yào diǎncài ma? 你要点菜吗?
what would you like to drink?	nǐ xiǎng hē xiē shénme? 你想喝些什么?
what dishes will you have?	nǐ yào shénme cài? 你要什么菜?
what would you like for dessert?	nǐ xiǎng chī shénme tiándiǎn? 你想吃什么甜点?
would you like tea/beer?	nǐ yào hē chá/píjiǔ ma? 你要喝茶/啤酒吗?
anything else?	hái yào biéde shénme ma? 还要别的什么吗?
enjoy your meal!	nín chīhǎo 您吃好
service is not included	fúwùfèi wèi bāokuò zàinèi 服务费未包括在内

The menu	Càidān 菜单
fish	**yú 鱼**
bass	lúyú 鲈鱼
carp	lǐyú 鲤鱼
eel	shàn 鳝, mán 鳗
mussels	yíbèi 贻贝, kécài 壳菜
oyster	háo 蚝, mǔlì 牡蛎
prawns	duìxiā 对虾, míngxiā 明虾
salmon	dàmǎhāyú 大马哈鱼
sardines	shādīngyú 沙丁鱼
shrimps	xiǎoxiā 小虾
squid	yóuyú 鱿鱼
trout	zūnyú 鳟鱼
tuna	jīnqiāngyú 金枪鱼

Càidān 菜单	The menu
yú 鱼	**fish**
dàmǎhāyú 大马哈鱼	salmon
duìxiā 对虾	prawns
háo 蚝	oyster
jīnqiāngyú 金枪鱼	tuna
kécài 壳菜	mussels
lǐyú 鲤鱼	carp
lúyú 鲈鱼	bass
mán 鳗	eel
míngxiā 明虾	prawns
mǔlì 牡蛎	oyster
shādīngyú 沙丁鱼	sardines
shàn 鳝	eel
xiǎoxiā 小虾	shrimps
yíbèi 贻贝	mussels
yóuyú 鱿鱼	squid
zūnyú 鳟鱼	trout

meat	**ròu 肉**
beef	niúròu 牛肉
chicken	jīròu 鸡肉
chicken feet	fèngzhǎo 凤爪
duck	yā 鸭
ham	huǒtuǐ 火腿
lamb	yángròu 羊肉
pork	zhūròu 猪肉
steak	niúpái 牛排

vegetables	**shūcài 蔬菜**
aubergine	qiézi 茄子
beans	dòu 豆
black fungus	mù'ěr 木耳
carrots	húluóbo 胡萝卜
Chinese cabbage	báicài 白菜
chives	xìxiāngcōng 细香葱
celery	qíncài 芹菜
lettuce	wōjù 莴苣, shēngcài 生菜
mushrooms	mógu 蘑菇
peas	wāndòu 豌豆
pepper	làjiāo 辣椒
potato	tǔdòu 土豆, mǎlíngshǔ 马铃薯
spring onions	yángcōng 洋葱
tomato	xīhóngshì 西红柿

ròu 肉	**meat**
fèngzhǎo 凤爪	chicken feet
huǒtuǐ 火腿	ham
jīròu 鸡肉	chicken
niúpái 牛排	steak
niúròu 牛肉	beef
yā 鸭	duck
yángròu 羊肉	lamb
zhūròu 猪肉	pork

shūcài 蔬菜	**vegetables**
báicài 白菜	Chinese cabbage
dòu 豆	beans
húluóbo 胡萝卜	carrots
làjiāo 辣椒	pepper
mǎlíngshǔ 马铃薯	potato
mógu 蘑菇	mushrooms
mù'ěr 木耳	black fungus
qiézi 茄子	aubergine
qíncài 芹菜	celery
shēngcài 生菜	lettuce
tǔdòu 土豆	potato
wāndòu 豌豆	peas
wōjù 莴苣	lettuce
yángcōng 洋葱	spring onions
xīhóngshì 西红柿	tomato
xìxiāngcōng 细香葱	chives

the way it's cooked	**pēngtiáo fāngfǎ 烹调方法**
boiled	zhǔ 煮
braised	dùn 炖
deep-fried	zhá 炸
grilled	zhì 炙, kǎo 烤
roast	kǎo 烤, hōng 烘
shallow-fried	jiān 煎
steamed	zhēng 蒸
stewed	dùn 炖, mèn 焖
stir-fried	chǎo 炒

pēngtiáo fāngfǎ 烹调方法	**the way it's cooked**
chǎo 炒	stir-fried
dùn 炖	stewed, braised
hōng 烘	roast
jiān 煎	shallow-fried
kǎo 烤	roast, grilled
mèn 焖	stewed
zhá 炸	deep-fried
zhēng 蒸	steamed
zhì 炙	grilled
zhǔ 煮	boiled

traditional dishes	**chuántǒng cài 传统菜**
braised fish	hóngshāo yú 红烧鱼
Gongbao diced chicken	Gōngbǎo jīdīng 宫保鸡丁
hundred-year-old egg	cháyèdàn 茶叶蛋
Mongolian hotpot	shuàn yángròu 涮羊肉
Peking roast duck	Běijīng kǎoyā 北京烤鸭
spicy beancurd	mápó dòufu 麻婆豆腐
sweet-and-sour pork	gūlǎo ròu 咕老肉

chuántǒng cài 传统菜	**traditional dishes**
cháyèdàn 茶叶蛋	hundred-year-old egg
Běijīng kǎoyā 北京烤鸭	Peking roast duck
Gōngbǎo jīdīng 宫保鸡丁	Gongbao diced chicken
gūlǎo ròu 咕老肉	sweet-and-sour pork
hóngshāo yú 红烧鱼	braised fish
mápó dòufu 麻婆豆腐	spicy beancurd
shuàn yángròu 涮羊肉	Mongolian hotpot

dim sum	**diǎnxīn 点心**
boiled dumplings	shuǐjiǎo 水饺
spring rolls	chūnjuǎn 春卷
steamed dumplings	zhēngbāo 蒸包
wonton	húntun 馄饨

desserts	**tiándiǎn 甜点**
ice cream	bīngqílín 冰淇淋
fritters	jiānbǐng 煎饼
pie	xiànbǐng 馅饼

other	**qítā 其他**
beancurd	dòufu 豆腐
fish-flavoured sauce	yúwèi jiàng 鱼味酱
ginger	jiāng 姜
noodles	miàntiáo 面条
oyster sauce	háoyóu 蚝油
rice	mǐfàn 米饭
sesame oil	zhīmayóu 芝麻油
sesame sauce	zhīmajiàng 芝麻酱
soy sauce	jiàngyóu 酱油
sweet-and-sour sauce	tiánsuān jiàng 甜酸酱
vinegar	cù 醋

diǎnxīn 点心	**dim sum**
chūnjuǎn 春卷	spring rolls
húntun 馄饨	wonton
shuǐjiǎo 水饺	boiled dumplings
zhēngbāo 蒸包	steamed dumplings

tiándiǎn 甜点	**desserts**
bīngqílín 冰淇淋	ice cream
jiānbǐng 煎饼	fritters
xiànbǐng 馅饼	pie

qítā 其他	**other**
cù 醋	vinegar
dòufu 豆腐	beancurd
háoyóu 蚝油	oyster sauce
jiāng 姜	ginger
jiàngyóu 酱油	soy sauce
mǐfàn 米饭	rice
miàntiáo 面条	noodles
tiánsuān jiàng 甜酸酱	sweet-and-sour sauce
yúwèi jiàng 鱼味酱	fish-flavoured sauce
zhīmajiàng 芝麻酱	sesame sauce
zhīmayóu 芝麻油	sesame oil

drinks	**yǐnliào 饮料**
beer	píjiǔ 啤酒
green tea	lǜchá 绿茶
jasmine tea	mòlìhuā chá 茉莉花茶
Maotai	Máotái 茅台
mineral water	kuàngquán shuǐ 矿泉水
rice wine	mǐjiǔ 米酒
soft drink	ruǎn yǐnliào 软饮料
tea	chá 茶
wine	pútáojiǔ 葡萄酒

yǐnliào 饮料	**drinks**
chá 茶	tea
kuàngquán shuǐ 矿泉水	mineral water
lǜchá 绿茶	green tea
Máotái 茅台	Maotai
mǐjiǔ 米酒	rice wine
mòlìhuā chá 茉莉花茶	jasmine tea
píjiǔ 啤酒	beer
pútáojiǔ 葡萄酒	wine
ruǎnyǐnliào 软饮料	soft drink

❺ Places to stay

Zhùchù 住处 ❺

☆☆☆

At the hotel

Zài jiǔdiàn 在酒店

I'd like a double/single room with bath	wǒ xiǎngyào yìge dài yùgāng de shuāngrénjiān/dānrénjiān 我想要一个带浴缸的双人间/单人间
we have a reservation in the name of Morris	wǒmen yòng Mòlǐsī de míngzi dìng de fáng 我们用莫里斯的名字订的房
we'll be staying three nights, from Friday to Sunday	wǒmen zhǔnbèi cóng xīngqīwǔ dào xīngqītiān zhù sānge wǎnshang 我们准备从星期五到星期天住三个晚上
how much does the room cost?	zhège fángjiān yào duōshǎo qián? 这个房间要多少钱?
I'd like to see the room	wǒ xiǎng kàn yíxià fángjiān 我想看一下房间
what time is breakfast?	shénme shíjiān chī zǎocān? 什么时间吃早餐?
can I leave this in your safe?	wǒ néng bǎ zhège fàng zài nǐmen de bǎoxiǎnguì ma? 我能把这个放在你们的保险柜吗?
bed and breakfast	zhùsù jiā zǎocān 住宿加早餐
we'd like to stay another night	wǒmen xiǎng duō zhù yíge wǎnshang 我们想多住一个晚上
please call me at 7:30	qǐng qī diǎn bàn jiàoxǐng wǒ 请七点半叫醒我
are there any messages for me?	yǒu méiyǒu wǒde xìn? 有没有我的信?

Hostels	**Zhāodàisuǒ 招待所**
could you tell me where the youth hostel is?	nǐ néng gàosu wǒ qīngnián zhāodàisuǒ zài shénme dìfang ma? 你能告诉我青年招待所在什么地方吗?
what time does the hostel close?	zhāodàisuǒ shénme shíjiān guānmén? 招待所什么时间关门?
I'll be staying in a hostel	wǒ yào zhù zhāodàisuǒ 我要住招待所
the hostel we're staying in is great value	wǒmen zhù de zhāodàisuǒ hěn hésuàn 我们住的招待所很合算
I know a really good hostel in Guangzhou	wǒ zhīdao Guǎngzhōu yìjiā hěn hǎo de zhāodàisuǒ 我知道广州一家很好的招待所
I'd like to go backpacking in Australia	wǒ xiǎng qù Àodàlìyà bēibāo lǚxíng 我想去澳大利亚背包旅行

Rooms to rent	**Zū fángjiān 租房间**
I'm looking for a room with a reasonable rent	wǒ zài zhǎo yìjiān jiàgé hélǐ de fángjiān 我在找一间价格合理的房间
I'd like to rent an apartment for a few weeks	wǒ xiǎng zū jǐge xīngqī de tàofáng 我想租几个星期的套房
where do I find out about rooms to rent?	wǒ zài nǎli kěyǐ zhǎodào chūzū de fángjiān? 我在哪里可以找到出租的房间
I'm staying with friends at the moment	wǒ xiànzài hé péngyou zhù yìqǐ 我现在和朋友住一起
I rent an apartment on the outskirts of town	wǒ zài chéngwài zū le yítào fáng 我在城外租了一套房
the room's fine – I'll take it	fángjiān búcuò, wǒ yào le 房间不错，我要了

❻ Shopping and money | Gòuwù hé huòbì 购物和货币 ❻

At the bank | Zài yínháng 在银行

I'd like to change some money — wǒ xiǎng huàn yìxiē qián 我想换一些钱

I want to change some dollars into Renminbi — wǒ xiǎng bǎ yìxiē měijīn duìhuàn chéng Rénmínbì 我想把一些美金兑换成人民币

what's the exchange rate today? — jīntiān de duìhuànlǜ shì duōshǎo? 今天的兑换率是多少?

I prefer traveller's cheques, (*US*) traveler's checks to cash — wǒ xǐhuan lǚxíng zhīpiào, bù xǐhuan xiànjīn 我喜欢旅行支票, 不喜欢现金

I'd like to transfer some money from my account — wǒ xiǎng cóng wǒde zhànghàoshang huàzhuǎn yìxiē qián 我想从我的账号上划转一些钱

I'll get some money from the cash machine — wǒ yào cóng qǔkuǎnjī qǔ yìxiē qián 我要从取款机取一些钱

I'm with another bank — wǒde qián cún zài lìng yìjiā yínháng 我的钱存在另一家银行

Finding the right shop | Zhǎo shāngdiàn 找商店

where's the main shopping district? — zhǔyào de shāngyèqū zài nǎli? 主要的商业区在哪里?

where can I buy batteries/postcards? — wǒ zài shénme dìfang nénggòu mǎidào diànchí/míngxìnpiàn? 我在什么地方能够买到电池/明信片?

where's the nearest pharmacy/bookshop? — zuìjìn de yàodiàn/shūdiàn zài nǎr? 最近的药店/书店在哪儿?

is there a good food shop around here? — fùjìn yǒu hǎo de shípǐndiàn ma? 附近有好的食品店吗?

what time do the shops open/close? — shāngdiàn shénme shíjiān kāimén/guānmén? 商店什么时间开门/关门?

where did you get those? — nǐ zài nǎli mǎidào de nàxiē dōngxi? 你在哪里买到的那些东西?

I'm looking for presents for my family — wǒ zài zhǎo kěyǐ gěi jiārén mǎi de lǐwù 我在找可以给家人买的礼物

we'll do our shopping on Saturday — wǒmen xīngqīliù qù mǎi dōngxi 我们星期六去买东西

I love shopping — wǒ xǐhuan gòuwù 我喜欢购物

Are you being served?	**Yǒu rén wèi nín fúwù ma?** 有人为您服务吗?
how much does that cost?	nà yào duōshǎo qián? 那要多少钱?
can I try it on?	wǒ néng shì chuān yíxià ma? 我能试穿一下吗?
could you wrap it for me, please?	nǐ néng bāng wǒ bāoqǐlái ma? 你能帮我包起来吗?
can I pay by credit card?	wǒ néng yòng xìnyòngkǎ fùzhàng ma? 我能用信用卡付账吗?
do you have this in another color, (*GB*) colour?	zhèzhǒng dōngxi nǐmen yǒu qítā yánsè ma? 这种东西你们有其他颜色吗?
I'm just looking	wǒ zhǐ shì kànkàn 我只是看看
I'll think about it	wǒ kǎolǜ yíxiàzi 我考虑一下子
I'd like a receipt, please	wǒ xiǎngyào zhāng shōujù 我想要张收据
I need a bigger/smaller size	wǒ xūyào yíge dà/xiǎo diǎn de 我需要一个大/小点的
I take a medium	wǒ yào zhōnghào de 我要中号的
it doesn't suit me	zhè bú shìhé wǒ 这不适合我
I'm sorry, I don't have any change/anything smaller	duìbuqǐ, wǒ méiyǒu língqián/xiǎoqián 对不起, 我没有零钱/小钱
that's all, thank you	jiù zhèxiē, xièxie 就这些, 谢谢

Changing things	**Huàn dōngxi** 换东西
can I have a refund?	wǒ néng tuìdiào ma? 我能退掉吗?
can you mend it for me?	nǐ néng bāng wǒ xiū yíxià ma? 你能帮我修一下吗?
can I speak to the manager?	wǒ néng hé jīnglǐ tántán ma? 我能和经理谈谈吗?
it doesn't work	zhège huài le 这个坏了
I'd like to change it, please	wǒ xiǎng huàn yíge 我想换一个
I bought this here yesterday	wǒ zuótiān zài zhèr mǎide 我昨天在这儿买的

❼ Sport and leisure — Yùndòng yǔ xiūxián 运动与休闲 ❼

Keeping fit — Duànliàn shēntǐ 锻炼身体

where can we play football/squash?	wǒmen zài nǎli kěyǐ tī zúqiú/dǎ bìqiú? 我们在哪里可以踢足球/打壁球
where is the local sports centre, (*US*) center?	dāngdì de yùndòng zhōngxīn zài shénme dìfang? 当地的运动中心在什么地方?
what's the charge per day?	měitiān xū fù duōshǎo qián? 每天需付多少钱?
is there a reduction for children/a student discount?	xiǎohái/xuésheng kěyǐ dǎzhé ma? 小孩/学生可以打折吗?
I'm looking for a swimming pool/tennis court	wǒ zài zhǎo yóuyǒngchí/wǎngqiúchǎng 我在找游泳池/网球场
you have to be a member	nǐ bìxū shì huìyuán 你必须是会员
I play tennis on Mondays	wǒ měige xīngqīyī dǎ wǎngqiú 我每个星期一打网球
I would like to go fishing/riding	wǒ xiǎng qù diàoyú/qímǎ 我想去钓鱼/骑马
I want to do aerobics	wǒ xiǎng zuò zēngyǎng jiànshēncāo 我想做增氧健身操
I love swimming/rollerblading	wǒ ài yóuyǒng/liūbīng 我爱游泳/溜冰
we want to hire skis	wǒmen xiǎng zū huáxuěbǎn 我们想租滑雪板

Watching sport — Guānkàn bǐsài 观看比赛

is there a football match on Saturday?	xīngqīliù yǒu zúqiúsài ma? 星期六有足球赛吗?
which teams are playing?	nǎxiē duì zài bǐsài? 哪些队在比赛?
where can I get tickets?	wǒ zài nǎli kěyǐ mǎidào piào? 我在哪里可以买到票?
I'd like to see a football match	wǒ xiǎng kàn yìchǎng zúqiúsài 我想看一场足球赛
my favourite, (*US*) favorite team is ...	wǒ zuì xǐhuan de qiúduì shì ... 我最喜欢的球队是 ...
let's watch the match on TV	wǒmen zài diànshì shàng kàn bǐsài ba 我们在电视上看比赛吧

Going to the cinema/to the theatre/clubbing	Qù kàn diànyǐng/kànxì/jùlèbù 去看电影/看戏/俱乐部
what film is showing?	fàng shénme diànyǐng? 放什么电影?
when does the box office open/close?	shòupiàochù shénme shíjiān kāimén/guānmén? 售票处什么时间开门/关门?
what time does the concert/performance start?	yīnyuèhuì/biǎoyǎn shénme shíjiān kāishǐ? 音乐会/表演什么时间开始?
when does it finish?	shénme shíjiān jiéshù? 什么时间结束?
are there any seats left for tonight?	jīntiān wǎnshang hái yǒu zuòwèi ma? 今天晚上还有座位吗?
how much are the tickets?	zhèxiē piào yào duōshǎo qián? 这些票要多少钱?
where can I get a programme, (*US*) program?	wǒ zài shénme dìfang kěyǐ nádào jiémùdān? 我在什么地方可以拿到节目单?
I want to book tickets for tonight's performance	wǒ xiǎng dìng jīntiān wǎnshang de piào 我想订今天晚上的票
somewhere in the middle, but not too far back	zhōngjiān shénme dìfang, bú yào tài yuǎn 中间什么地方，不要太远
four, please	sìzhāng 四张
for Saturday	xīngqīliù de 星期六的
we'd like to go to a club	wǒmen xiǎng qù jùlèbù 我们想去俱乐部
I go clubbing every weekend	wǒ měige zhōumò dōu qù jùlèbù 我每个周末都去俱乐部

Hobbies	Yèyú àihào 业余爱好
what do you do at the weekend?	nǐ zhōumò zuò shénme? 你周末做什么?
I like yoga/listening to music	wǒ xǐhuan yújiā/tīng yīnyuè 我喜欢瑜伽/听音乐
I spend a lot of time surfing the Net	wǒ huā hěn duō shíjiān shàngwǎng 我花很多时间上网
I read a lot	wǒ dú hěn duō shū 我读很多书
I collect musical instruments	wǒ shōují yuèqì 我收集乐器

❽ Weights and measures　Dùliànghéng 度量衡 ❽

Length/Chángdù 长度

inches / yīngcùn 英寸	1.30	13	26	39	52	65	130
cm / límǐ 厘米, gōngfēn 公分	3.33	33.3	66.7	100	133.3	166.7	333.3
cun / cùn 寸	1	10	20	30	40	50	100

Distance/Jùlí 距离

miles / yīnglǐ 英里	0.31	3.1	6.2	9.3	12.4	15.5	31
km / qiānmǐ 千米, gōnglǐ 公里	0.5	5	10	15	20	25	50
li / lǐ 里	1	10	20	30	40	50	100

Weight/Zhòngliàng 重量

pounds / bàng 磅	1.1	11	22	33	44	55	110
kg / qiānkè 千克, gōngjīn 公斤	0.5	5	10	15	20	25	50
jin / jīn 斤	1	10	20	30	40	50	100

Capacity/Róngliàng 容量

gallons / jiālún 加仑	0.22	2.2	4.4	6.6	8.8	11	22
litres / shēng 升	1	10	20	30	40	50	100

Temperature/Wēndù 温度

°C	0	5	10	15	20	25	30	37	38	40
°F	32	41	50	59	68	77	86	98.4	100	104

Women's clothing sizes

UK	10	12	14	16	18
US	8	10	12	14	16
China/Europe	38	40	42	44	

Men's waist sizes

UK/US	24	26	28	30	32	34	36	38
China/Europe	61	66	71	76	80	87	91	97

Shoe sizes

UK women	4	5	6	7	7.5	8			
UK men				6	7	8	9	10	11
US	6.5	7.5	8.5	9.5	10.5	11.5	12.5	13.5	14.5
China/Europe	37	38	39	40	41	42	43	44	45

⑨ Street signs and information notices

Jiēdào zhǐshìpái hé xìnxī gōnggào 街道指示牌和资讯公告 ⑨

open	kāifàng	开放
closed	guānbì	关闭
entrance	rùkǒu	入口
exit	chūkǒu	出口

push	tuī	推
pull	lā	拉
arrivals	dàodá	到达
departures	dēngjīkǒu	登机口
floor	lóucéng	楼层

for sale	dàishòu	待售
cash desk	fùkuǎnchù	付款处
ticket office	shòupiàochù	售票处
admission free	miǎnfèi	免费

motorway	gāosù gōnglù	高速公路
car park	tíngchēchǎng	停车场
halt	tíngzhǐ	停止
stop (bus etc.)	chēzhàn	车站
room for rent	fángwū chūzū	房屋出租
24-hour access	24 xiǎoshí fúwù	24小时服务
danger	wēixiǎn	危险
police	jǐngchá	警察

Dates for your diary

January

①	8	15	22	29
2	9	16	23	30
3	10	17	24	31
4	11	18	25	
5	12	19	26	
6	13	20	27	
7	14	21	28	

February

1	8	15	22
2	9	16	23
3	10	17	24
4	11	18	25
5	12	19	26
6	13	20	27
7	14	21	28

March

1	⑧	15	22	29
2	9	16	23	30
3	10	17	24	31
4	11	18	25	
5	⑫	19	26	
6	13	20	27	
7	14	21	28	

April

1	8	15	22	29
2	9	16	23	30
3	10	17	24	
4	11	18	25	
5	12	19	26	
6	13	20	27	
7	14	21	28	

May

①	8	15	22	29
2	9	16	23	30
3	10	17	24	31
④	11	18	25	
5	12	19	26	
6	13	20	27	
7	14	21	28	

June

①	8	15	22	29
2	9	16	23	30
3	10	17	24	
4	11	18	25	
5	12	19	26	
6	13	20	27	
7	14	21	28	

July

①	8	15	22	29
2	9	16	23	30
3	10	17	24	31
4	11	18	25	
5	12	19	26	
6	13	20	27	
7	14	21	28	

August

①	8	15	22	29
2	9	16	23	30
3	10	17	24	31
4	11	18	25	
5	12	19	26	
6	13	20	27	
7	14	21	28	

September

1	8	15	22	29
2	9	16	23	30
3	⑩	17	24	
4	11	18	25	
5	12	19	26	
6	13	20	27	
7	14	21	㉘	

October

①	8	15	22	29
2	9	16	23	30
3	10	17	24	31
4	11	18	25	
5	12	19	26	
6	13	20	27	
7	14	21	28	

November

1	8	15	22	29
2	9	16	23	30
3	10	17	24	
4	11	18	25	
5	12	19	26	
6	13	20	27	
7	14	21	28	

December

1	8	15	22	29
2	9	16	23	30
3	10	17	24	31
4	11	18	㉕	
5	12	19	26	
6	13	20	27	
7	14	21	28	

○ Celebrated in China

1st of the first lunar month

Chūnjié 春节 (Spring Festival)

The most important festival in the Chinese calendar, Spring Festival, or Chinese New Year, occurs on the first day of the traditional Chinese lunar year (falling between the end of January and the end of February in the Gregorian calendar). People return home to be with their families. Traditions include cleaning the home; wearing new clothes; presenting gifts; pasting up auspicious couplets (duìlián 对联) on either side of the front door; giving children small amounts of money in red envelopes (hóngbāo 红包); in the North, making and eating boiled dumplings (jiǎozi 饺子) together; and letting off firecrackers and fireworks. In business, all debts should be cleared at New Year. Celebrations can start late in the preceding month, and go on till the following Lantern Festival. Official holiday, however, is just three days, sometimes extended to a week.

15th of the first lunar month

Yuánxiāojié 元宵节 (Lantern Festival)

The Lantern Festival falls on the first full moon of the lunar year. The main activity is watching lanterns, and guessing the 'lantern riddles' written on them. The traditional food is round glutinous rice dumplings (yuánxiāo 元宵). The Lantern Festival marks the end of the New Year period.

8 March

Sānbā fùnǚ jié 三八妇女节

(Women's Day)

Introduced under Communism, this celebratory day gives women a half or whole day's holiday.

12 March

Zhíshù jié 植树节 (Tree-planting Day)

Begun in 1979, this is a day for addressing concerns about soil erosion.

early (between 4th and 6th) April

Qīngmíngjié 清明节 (Qingming Festival)

Linked to the early Chinese solar calendar, the traditional Qingming Festival marked an important transition to warmer weather in the agricultural year. The main activity is 'sweeping the tombs' of the ancestors. At gravesides people conduct a symbolic sweeping with new willow fronds; offer food, gifts and flowers; and burn incense and paper money. It is also a festival for spring outings and kite flying.

1 May

Wǔyī guójì láodòng jié 五一国际劳动节

(International Labour, (*US*) Labor Day)

As in other parts of the world, May Day has been denoted a day for workers. There is an official three-day holiday, sometimes extended to a week, at this time of year.

4 May

Wǔsì qīngnián jié 五四青年节

(Youth Day)

This day commemorates the May 4th Movement of 1919, when students in Beijing and across China demonstrated for nationalism and modernization.

8th of the fourth lunar month

Fódànjié 佛诞节 (Buddha's Birthday)

Although more popular in Hong Kong, and long suppressed in mainland China, Buddha's Birthday is making a comeback. It is especially celebrated in Buddhist temples.

1 June

Liùyī értóng jié 六一儿童节

(Children's Day)

On this day children are presented with gifts, and get free entrance to various kinds of entertainment.

5th of the fifth lunar month

Duānwǔjié 端午节 (Dragon Boat Festival)

A traditional festival, ostensibly commemorating the poet Qu Yuan (340–278 BC) of the state of Chu. Qu Yuan wrote long, mystical, seemingly patriotic poems – on hearing the news of the defeat of Chu by Qin, he is said to have committed suicide by jumping into the Miluo River. The traditions of dragon-boat racing and eating glutinous rice pyramids (zòngzi 粽子) are meant to mark Qu Yuan's death – since supposedly at the time local people threw rice into the river to divert the fish from eating his body.

1 July

Qīyī jiàndǎngjié 七一建党节 (Founding of the Chinese Communist Party)

The CCP was founded in Shanghai in 1921. This is a day for political newspaper editorials.

1 August

Bāyī jiànjūn jié 八一建军节 (Army Day)

A ceremonial day, it emphasizes collaboration between the People's Liberation Army and the people.

7th of the seventh lunar month

Qīxījié 七夕节 (Double Seventh Festival)

This festival is associated with the traditional love story of the mortal Cowherd and celestial Weaving Girl. According to the story, the couple fell in love and she came down to earth to marry him. However, they were discovered by the Queen of Heaven, who separated them by creating the Milky Way and took the Weaving Girl back to heaven. Subsequently, magpies took pity on the pair and once a year form themselves into a bridge between heaven and earth so that the Cowherd and Weaving Girl can be reunited. In contemporary China the festival is a day for lovers.

15th of the seventh lunar month

Zhōngyuánjié 中元节 (Hungry Ghost Festival)

Traditionally, the whole of the seventh month is Ghost Month, when spirits wander the earth. At the Hungry Ghost Festival, ritual food offerings are made and paper money burnt to appease these spirits. Under Communism this festival has been downplayed as negative and superstitious – it is more popular in Hong Kong.

10 September

Jiàoshī jié 教师节 (Teachers' Day)

The new official day for honouring teachers – a far cry from how intellectuals were reviled during the Cultural Revolution.

15th of the eighth lunar month

Zhōngqiūjié 中秋节 (Mid-Autumn Festival)

Another traditional festival when the moon is full. On this day people enjoy the moon, set out food, and in particular eat moon cakes (yuèbing 月饼). It is timed to celebrate the harvest.

28 September

Kǒngzǐ dànshēng rì 孔子诞生日 (Confucius' Birthday)

For much of the Commmunist era Confucius was reviled, but he is now increasingly popular as a national figure. His birthday is particularly celebrated at the Confucian temple in the city of Qufu, but also at other Confucian temples around the country.

1 October

Shíyī guóqìngjié 十一国庆节 (National Day)

This was the day that Chairman Mao proclaimed the founding of the People's Republic of China in 1949. Today, it is celebrated with grand processions of school children, workers, minority representatives and troops, and displays of military hardware. There are three days' official holiday, sometimes extended to a week.

9th of the ninth lunar month

Chóngyángjié 重阳节 (Double Ninth Festival)

The number nine symbolizes Yang (yáng 阳), the positive principle in nature. So, on the 9th day of the 9th month, this principle is at its strongest. Traditionally, people climb mountains on this day. The chrysanthemum is also symbolic of the festival.

mid-Winter (22nd or 23rd December)

Dōngzhì 冬至 (Winter Solstice)

Another festival determined by the Chinese solar calendar. As the turning point away from winter, it marks the time in the year when the Yang (yáng 阳) principle is at its lowest. Various kinds of dumplings are eaten, to build up strength.

25 December

Shèngdànjié 圣诞节 (Christmas Day)

A foreign import, but increasingly celebrated in a small way. It is particularly important in Hong Kong.

1 January

Yuándàn 元旦 (New Year's Day)

Though it does not have traditional significance, this day is an official holiday in China.

Quick reference guide to life and culture

Bālùjūn 八路军 or the **Eighth Route Army** was one of the Communist armies active in resisting the Japanese invaders before Liberation in 1949. The army gained a reputation for looking after the interests of the common people.

Běijīng dàxué 北京大学 **Peking University** was first founded in 1898. Throughout the 20th century, it was closely associated with China's political and cultural upheavals. Students there were key to the May Fourth Movement of 1919, calling for national unity and modernization.

Chángchéng 长城 The **Great Wall** was joined together from pre-existing walls after the unification of China by Qin Shi Huang (*reg* 221–210 BC). Its function was to protect the newly established Qin dynasty from marauding northern barbarians. The current brick-faced edifice was built under the Ming dynasty (1368–1644).

Chángzhēng 长征 Of the 100,000 men (and some women) who began the **Long March** (1934–35), only about 20,000 survived. Fleeing from the Nationalists, the Communists started on the march in Jiangxi in the southeast. They then took a roundabout route of 10,000 kilometres through some of China's most rugged terrain, and ended in bleak Shaanxi in the northwest, where they established the base of Yan'an.

chūguó 出国 Since the 1980s, **studying abroad** has become increasingly highly prized among China's educated elite. Fluency in English and experience of Western business offer greater opportunities in the home job market.

dānwèi 单位 The **work unit** has been standard for social planning under Communism, responsible for not only work, but also health, marriage, family planning, housing, travel and political control.

dìwǔ dài diànyǐng 第五代电影 So-called **'fifth generation' films** started to be made in the 1980s. These included *Yellow Earth* (1984) directed by Chen Kaige and *Red Sorghum* (1987) directed by Zhang Yimou. Like other art forms at the time, the films reflected a new openness in their mood of moral uncertainty.

Dōngběi 东北 The **Northeast** comprises the Chinese provinces of Liaoning, Jilin and Heilongjiang. The area is often known in English as Manchuria.

gànbù 干部 **Cadres** are Communist Party officials, crucial to the workings of government bureaucracy.

gāokǎo 高考 **College entrance exams** are taken at the end of secondary school, (*US*) high school. Owing to the large population of China, there is huge competition for entry to the prestigious universities.

Gōng'ānjú 公安局 or the **Public Security Bureau** (PSB) has a regular policing function, but also oversees public order, residence permits, foreigners' travel and other control issues.

Gòngchǎndǎng 共产党 The **Chinese Communist Party** (CCP) was founded in 1921 and came to power under Chairman Mao in 1949, with the establishment of the People's Republic of China (PRC). In the early years, the party worked to improve the lot of the Chinese peasants and workers. Especially during the Cultural Revolution, however, it was responsible for severe repression and persecution. Today, despite significant economic reform, China remains a one-party state.

guānxì 关系 Personal **connections** are vital to getting things done in China. To achieve good business relations it is important to sustain networking efforts over the long-term. When blocked by bureaucracy, it is often easier to use a personal contact or 'go through the back door' (zǒu hòumén 走后门).

Guómíndǎng 国民党 The **Nationalist Party**, or Kuomintang (KMT), was active and formed governments in mainland China between 1912 and 1949. The first party leader, Sun Yat-sen (Sun Zhongshan), was later succeeded by Chiang Kai-shek (Jiang Jieshi). During the 1920s and 1930s the KMT became locked in military struggles with the Communists, ignoring the Japanese threat. With the establishment of the PRC, the KMT fled to Taiwan, taking with them the name Republic of China (ROC). Since 1949, however, the PRC has consistently asserted that Taiwan is simply a province of China.

hézuò 合作 A **joint venture** (JV) with a Chinese company is more or less the only way a foreign company can currently conduct business in China. The term in Chinese sounds slightly less entrepreneurial, however – it simply means 'collaboration'.

Hónglóu mèng 红楼梦 Written in the Qing period (1644–1911), ***Dream of Red Mansions*** is one of the greatest Chinese classic novels. It tells the story of a privileged, aristocratic household, focusing on the young scholar Baoyu and twelve young female characters. With apparently uncanny prescience, the book seems to suggest a time of poverty and suffering ahead.

hùkǒu 户口 **Residency** is controlled by the residence permit. It has been particularly difficult to get permission to live in Beijing, Shanghai and other big cities. However, according to a new ruling, if you are able to buy a home in the area, in principle residency is automatic.

huáqiáo 华侨 This term means **'overseas Chinese'**. In some contexts, foreigners of Chinese origin are perceived as having a special connection with mainland China.

huángdì 皇帝 The **emperor** was a consistent feature of Chinese government from the Qin dynasty (221–206 BC) through to the Qing (1644–1911). The notion of an autocratic and aloof ruler is consequently vivid in the Chinese imagination. Children born during the one-child policy era are sometimes known as 'little emperors'. A common Chinese saying is 'Heaven is high, and the Emperor is far away' (Tiān gāo, Huángdì yuǎn 天高，皇帝远) – alluding to the possibility of unobtrusive independence of thought.

Huánghé 黄河 The **Yellow River** is important as a national symbol. Chinese civilization is thought to have originated in the Xi'an and Luoyang area along the Yellow River. The second-longest river in the country, in its majestic course from the inland mountains to the sea, it is often seen to represent the huge strength of China. In history, the Yellow River has flooded extensively many times causing much death and destruction.

huángjīn zhōu 黄金周 **'Golden weeks'** were established in 1999 to promote domestic tourism. They are weeklong vacations taken around the Spring Festival, International Labour Day, (*US*) Labor Day, and National Day official three-day holidays. They reflect the increased affluence of some sections of the population.

jiěfàng 解放 **Liberation** is the official Chinese name for the Communist revolution of 1949, which established the People's Republic of China (PRC).

Jiěfàngjūn 解放军 The **People's Liberation Army** (PLA) was founded in 1927 as the military wing of the Chinese Communist Party (CCP), and was active in campaigns before the establishment of the People's Republic of China (PRC). It was originally called the Red Army. Today, it is China's national military force. In terms of manpower, it is the largest army in the world.

jīngjù 京剧 **Peking opera** is the 'total theatre' of the Beijing region – comprising acting, singing, music, acrobatics, dance and stylized movement, as well as elaborately symbolic costume, makeup and props. The traditional plays take historic tales and set stories as their theme. In other parts of the country, there are hundreds of similar local operas (dìfang xì 地方戏).

jīngjì tèqū 经济特区 The first **special economic zones** (SEZs) were set up in the 1980s. They included Shenzhen, Zhuhai and Shantou in Guangdong Province, Xiamen in Fujian Province, and the whole province of Hainan island. Then, further coastal cities were opened to foreign investment. Pudong, the business district of Shanghai, was given special status in 1990. Originally, SEZs offered foreign companies the incentive of tax breaks, but this is changing since China's accession to the WTO in 2001. However, special zones still offer foreign business the benefits of good infrastructure and economic specialization.

kāifàng 开放 **'Opening up'** is the term used to describe the economic and cultural liberalization that gradually came about after the end of the Cultural Revolution, essentially from the 1980s onwards. This period of reform was largely presided over by Deng Xiaoping.

Kàng Rì zhànzhēng 抗日战争 The **War of Resistance Against Japan** (1937–1945) involved both the Communists and the Nationalists – and on occasion united them. Among atrocities committed by the Japanese invaders, the Nanjing Massacre (1937–1938) stands out: it is estimated that between 250,000 and 300,000 people, the vast majority civilians, were killed in this massacre.

lóng 龙 The **Chinese dragon** is traditionally the symbol of the emperor. It also represents Yang (yáng 阳), the positive principle in nature.

Máo zhǔxí 毛主席 Mao Zedong (1893–1976), or **Chairman Mao**, remains a controversial figure. Although he succeeded in uniting China (establishing the PRC in 1949) and bringing about huge changes in society, he was also responsible for great suffering, especially during the Cultural Revolution. While championing the cause of the Chinese peasant, he is alleged to have had a strikingly extravagant lifestyle himself. He is known for establishing the school of Communist thought known as Maoism, and also for the quotations from his writings collected in his Little Red Book. Today, Mao is still respected in some Chinese quarters – but the days of his 'personality cult' are long gone, with deliberately kitsch Mao 'memorabilia' readily available in many tourist outlets.

Míng Qīng xiǎoshūo 明清小说 Novels of the Ming (1368–1644) **and Qing** (1644–1911) periods represent the high point of the genre. The rise of fiction in China coincided broadly with that in Europe. Outstanding examples include *Dream of Red Mansions* (Hónglóu mèng 红楼梦); *Journey to the West* (Xīyóu jì 西游记), also known in English *as Monkey*; and *The Water Margin* (Shuǐhǔ zhuàn 水浒传).

nóngcūn 农村 The **countryside** and poor Chinese farmers or peasants (nóngmín 农民) played a special role in the Chinese Communist revolution, according to Mao. It remains the case that most of the Chinese population live in the countryside. Today, many Chinese farmers have become quite wealthy. But there are still concerns about an economic imbalance between the cities and the countryside, and between the coastal business areas and the undeveloped hinterland in the West of the country.

Pǔtōnghuà 普通话 Mandarin Chinese is China's *lingua franca*. It is based on the local dialect of the North, notably Beijing. Apart from Mandarin, there are hundreds of local Chinese dialects. These fall into broad families, including Cantonese, Shanghainese, Fujian dialect and Hakka.

qìgōng 气功 Qigong is a health technique based on deep breathing exercises. Qi or Ch'i (qì 气) literally means 'breath', but is also an important Chinese philosophic concept – the cosmic energy that runs through all things.

Qín shǐ huáng 秦始皇, the **first emperor of the Qin** dynasty (reg 221–210 BC), is important as the original unifier of China. His despotic rule ended the period known as the Warring States. He linked the Great Wall, and was buried in his mausoleum near Xi'an with thousands of life-size terracotta warriors.

Rénmín rìbaò 人民日报 or the ***People's Daily*** is the main Chinese newspaper and takes a conventional party line. New political developments are often first signalled by editorials in this paper.

Sānge dàibiǎo 三个代表 The **'Three Represents'** of Jiang Zemin, initially put forward in 2000, is an opaque piece of political theory. Its main thrust seems to be to legitimize the inclusion of capitalists and business people within the Communist Party.

Sānxiá 三峡 The **Three Gorges** are three spectacular narrow and steep-sided sections of the Yangzi River, downstream from the city of Chongqing. The environmentally controversial construction of the Three Gorges Dam, due for completion in 2009, has changed the face of the surrounding countryside, causing the uprooting of well over a million people, and impacting on a scale as yet unknown on the wildlife and ecosystems of the region.

Shǎoshù mínzú 少数民族 or **'Minority Peoples'** is the official name given to non-Han Chinese peoples who live in the PRC. These include Tibetans, Uygurs (Muslims native to Xinjiang in the West), the Hui (Chinese Muslims descended from Arab immigrants), the Dai (in Xishuangbanna), and the Miao and Dong (in Guizhou and Guangxi).

sìhéyuàn 四合院 or traditional **courtyard houses**, located on the alleyways of old Beijing, were originally the residences of single, wealthy families. Under Communism, they were requisitioned and split up among several families. Today, the upwardly mobile, and foreigners, are restoring them to their former grandeur as single-family establishments. Courtyard houses are laid out with single-storey buildings around a central open courtyard.

Sū Háng 苏杭 or **Suzhou and Hangzhou**, cities in the southeast, are traditionally considered the most beautiful places in China. The saying goes 'Above there is heaven, below Suzhou and Hangzhou' (Shàng yǒu tiāntáng, xià yǒu Sū Háng 上有天堂，下有苏杭).

tàijíquán 太极拳 Taijiquan is a gentle form of martial art, largely practised by older people in China. Outdoor classes are often held in the early morning, before breakfast.

Táng shī 唐诗 Tang poetry is considered the acme of classical Chinese poetry. Tang dynasty (618–907) poets include the socially committed Confucianist Du Fu and the free-spirited Daoist Li Bai.

Tiān'ānmén 天安门 The **Gate of Heavenly Peace** is the entrance at the south side of the Forbidden City, and the symbolic centre of Beijing. It has been the site of momentous events in the history of the nation. On 1 October 1949, for example,

Chairman Mao stood here to declare the founding of the People's Republic of China (PRC). In front of the gate lies Tian'anmen Square (Tiān'ānmén guǎngchǎng 天安门广场), where the student-led demonstrations of 1989 occurred, and were brutally suppressed. (This view, however, is not commonly expressed in China, where the events are a taboo topic.)

Wénhuà dà gémìng 文化大革命 The **Cultural Revolution** (1966–69) reflected a struggle in the Communist Party between Maoists and other factions. To enhance his standing, Mao advocated radical social revolution and upheaval. Prominently, educated city dwellers were sent to the countryside to learn first hand the work of the peasants. So-called 'rightists', often intellectuals and artists whose work was not considered appropriately revolutionary, were persecuted and killed. Mao recruited youthful Red Guards (Hóngweìbīng 红卫兵) to harass them, often with tragic consequences. In the resulting extreme emotional atmosphere, people were persuaded to denounce their neighbours, and children their parents. The result was chaos: families were separated, and, with the closure of schools and colleges, a generation lost out on education. The effects of the Cultural Revolution played out well beyond its official end. In 1976, Mao died and the so-called Gang of Four (Sìrén bāng 四人帮), blamed for many of the excesses of the Cultural Revolution, were removed from power. Only then did a new, more open era start to be ushered in.

Yuánmíng yuán 圆明园 The **Old Summer Palace**, outside Beijing, was built by the Qianlong emperor (*reg* 1736–1795) of the Qing dynasty. Fascinated by European culture, on the advice of Jesuit scholars, he constructed European-style buildings, likened at the time to Versailles; there were also Chinese-style halls. Unfortunately, much of the palace was burnt down by British and French troops, motivated it seems by revenge, during the second Opium War of 1860.

zhēnjiǔ 针灸 **Acupuncture and moxibustion** are two techniques used in traditional Chinese medicine. Acupuncture needles are inserted just below the skin at defined points thought to affect the flow of Qi or Ch'i (qì 气) through the body. Acupuncture has been used effectively as an anaesthetic. Moxibustion, a heat therapy, involves burning mugwort close to the skin.

Zhōngguó tèsè 中国特色 The phrase **'Chinese characteristics'** was coined by the leader Deng Xiaoping, as in the slogan 'Socialism with Chinese characteristics' (yǒu Zhōngguó tèsè de Shéhuìzhǔyì 有中国特色的社会主义). It is a cipher for the possibility of limited capitalistic enterprise, within the existing system.

Zhōngguó zhōngyāng diànshì tái 中国中央电视台 **China Central Television** (CCTV) started to broadcast in 1958 as Beijing Television, changing its name in 1978. Firmly controlled by the government, it is China's foremost news, information and entertainment medium. CCTV has fifteen channels, including international broadcasts in English.

Zhōngnánhǎi 中南海 **Zhongnanhai**, or China's Kremlin, is located to the west of the Forbidden City in Beijing. Inaccessible to the public, it is the headquarters of the Communist Party and the Chinese government. Successive leaders of the PRC have resided there.

zìzhìqū 自治区 **Autonomous Regions** were established in China by the Communists for regions dominated by ethnic groups other than Han Chinese. Inner Mongolia Autonomous Region was created within Communist-held territory in 1947, Xinjiang was converted to an autonomous region in 1955, Guangxi and Ningxia followed in 1957, and and Tibet Autonomous Region was established in 1965. Separatist movements in the autonomous regions are not tolerated by the Chinese government. Hong Kong, in contrast, is defined as Special Administrative Region (tèbié xíngzhèng qū 特别行政区).

Social survival guide

Greeting and meeting

The standard Chinese greeting is nǐ hǎo 你好 or 'hello', to which the appropriate response is nǐ hǎo 你好. The plural form is nǐmen hǎo 你们好, and the polite form nín hǎo 您好. A polite way of saying 'good morning' is nín zǎo 您早.

Generally, Chinese people are not tactile on greeting (kissing is not the norm), although in a business context, or as a mark of respect, a handshake is appropriate.

In a business context, exchange of business cards is popular. Business cards should be received with both hands and studied carefully to express respect.

The standard farewell is zàijiàn 再见, 'goodbye' – less formally, you might say míngtiān jiàn 明天见, 'see you tomorrow' or hǎo zǒu 好走, 'take care'.

Host–guest relationship

Crucial to understanding Chinese etiquette is recognizing the importance of the host–guest relationship. As a family-based and hierarchical society, traditional China depended on elaborate host–guest rituals to cement social bonds and create social structures. Despite a modern emphasis on the nuclear family and work unit/company, the importance of hospitality and courtesy hold good.

Visitors to China are often overwhelmed by the generosity and welcome offered them by ordinary Chinese people (and feel trepidation at the thought of how Chinese might feel received in some of the more individualistic societies of the English-speaking world). There are cultural reasons for this – as a foreigner, you are a 'guest' within the 'host' country, so deserve to be treated with the utmost hospitality. In the large cities, there is more understanding that foreigners may not grasp this point – and consequently you are more likely to be left to your own devices.

Gifts

Part of the role of a guest, either in someone's home, or as a visitor to a company with which you have a business relationship, is to bring gifts. In the business context, you should try to offer a gift to every person with whom you have significant contact. As a foreigner, giving craft items from your home country would be appropriate – alternatives might include chocolates or wine/spirits.

Do not be offended if your host does not open a wrapped gift in your presence. It is the norm to open gifts after the guest has departed.

Meals and entertaining

Part of the role of the host is to keep the guest amply supplied with food and entertainment.

When eating out in China, it is unknown to split the bill. As a foreign guest, rest assured that when eating out your Chinese host will not allow you to reciprocate in equal measure. Even if you succeed in paying for one meal, your host will undoubtedly respond with another more lavish one. This can be embarrassing – especially if your host has modest means. It is simply unthinkable for the guest to outdo the host in entertainment – it would constitute severe loss of face (see *Face* below).

In people's homes too, you will find yourself treated with the greatest honour. It is important for the host to stint at nothing in offering food and comfort to the guest. As a guest, it is polite to accept and indeed rude not to – but there is also a protocol of initially declining and only accepting on being pressed a number of times. If you really do not want something, you will have to be firm.

In China, unlike in Europe or America, it is the host who gives the signal to begin eating, rather than the guest who takes the initiative.

It is polite to keep your neighbour's teacup filled. To express your thanks at having your own cup filled, especially in the South, tap your first two fingers on the table.

Do not polish off everything in your bowl – this implies that the host has not provided enough food.

At the end of the meal, you will be politely asked whether you have had enough – nǐ chī bǎo le ma? 你吃饱了吗？ The appropriate response is chī bǎo le 吃饱了 or 'yes'.

Please and thank you

It is important to be polite when making requests – láojià 劳驾 ('excuse me' and qǐngwèn 请问 ('may I ask') are common phrases. It is also appropriate to say thank you (xièxie 谢谢) and sorry (duìbuqǐ 对不起) within reason.

However, some Chinese admit to finding the tendency of some English speakers to apologize profusely for small things, for example squeezing past someone on a bus, rather strange. To thank or to apologize too much starts to sound like loss of face (see *Face* below).

Directness

Do not be perturbed if you are asked direct personal questions, such as nǐ jiéhūn le ma? 你结婚了吗? ('Are you married?') or quizzed about your salary. To Chinese ears, especially outside the large cities, such questions are not an indication of prying, but a mark of friendly interest.

Face (miànzi 面子)

'Face' really amounts to a sense of pride, self-respect and a desire not to be humiliated. Being seen to fulfil one's role as a host or guest (see *Host-guest relationship* above) is important in maintaining face. It is not unusual to see Chinese acquaintances in a heated but respectful argument over who should treat the other – this is all about the balance of the host-guest relationship, and the retention of face on both sides.

Incidents that might cause 'loss of face', diū miànzi 丢面子, might include being shown to have made a serious mistake, losing one's temper, or being seen to be ungenerous. For this reason, where at all possible, it is important to try to avoid showing up other people's errors, making a scene in public, or revealing someone's lack of ability to play the host.